ENGLISH-ALBANIAN DICTIONARY OF IDIOMS

ILO STEFANLLARI

HIPPOCRENE BOOKS, INC.
New York

For information, address:
HIPPOCRENE BOOKS, INC.
171 Madison Avenue
New York, NY 10016

Library of Congress Cataloging-in-Publication Data

Stefanllari, Ilo.
    English-Albanian dictionary of idioms / Ilo Stefanllari.
        p.   cm.
    ISBN 0-7818-0783-2
        1. English language--Dictionaries--Albanian. 2. English
    language--idioms. I. Title

PG9591 .S737 1999
423'.91991--dc21   99-046942

Printed in the United States of America.

PARATHENIE

Fjalori Idiomatik Anglisht-Shqip është fryt i një pune hulumtuese shumëvjeçare të autorit. Në fjalor përfshihen idiomat e gjuhës angleze e amerikane me denduri të lartë përdorim—bashkimet e qëndrueshme që janë formuar historikisht e janë kristalizuar si njësi të pandashme. Në fjalor përfshihen idiomat me strukturë togfjalëshi e strukturë fjalie, idiomat me vlerë emërore, mbiemërore, foljore e ndajfoljore.

Idiomat jepen me gërma të theksuara sipas rendit alfabetik. Në krah të idiomës jepet barazvlerësi në shqip. Kur idiomat kanë më shumë se një kuptim, ndarja e kuptimeve bëhet me numra.

Idiomat ilustrohen me fjali të plota të shkëputura nga vepra artistike të autorëve anglezë e amerikanë, fjalorë njëgjuhësh e dygjuhësh, fjalorë idiomatikë, manuale etj. Para çdo shembulli ilustrues është vendosur nje simbol □ per te dalluar fillimin e tij.

Vëmendje e veçantë i është kushtuar shqipërimit të idiomave. Në shqipërimin e idiomave nga gjuha angleze në gjuhën shqipe kemi zbatuar këto lloj përkthimesh:

a) Përkthimin e idiomave me barazvlerës të plotë të gjuhës shqipe. Barazvlerësit e plotë janë ata monoekivalentë të gjuhës shqipe që përputhen me njësitë përgjegjëse të gjuhës angleze nga kuptimi, përbërja leksikore, figuracioni, vlerat stilistikore dhe struktura gramatikore, si p.sh., **an apple of discord—mollë sherri, Achilles' heel—thembra e Akilit, break the ice—thyej akullin, build castles in the air—ndërtoj kështjella në erë, buy a pig in a poke -ble derr në thes, a drop in the ocean—një pikë ijë në oqean, fish in troubled waters—peshkoj në ujëra të turbullta, play with fire—luaj me zjarrin etj.**

b) Përkthimin e idiomave me barazvlerës të pjesshëm. Përkthimi me barazvlerës frazeologjikë të pjesshëm transmeton plotësisht kuptimin e njësisë, por ruan dallime leksikore, gramatikore ose leksiko-gramatikore, si p.sh., **a wolf in sheep's clothing—ujk me lëkurë qengji, one swallow does not make a summer—me një dallëndyshe s'vjen pranvera, cudgel (beat) one's brains—vras mendjen, eat one's words—ha fjalën etj.** Shpesh në përkthimin e idiomave të gjuhës angleze na është dashur të zgjedhim variantin më të saktë për kontekstin e dhënë.

c) Përkthimin me anë të togfjalëshave të ndryshueshëm e të qëndrueshëm. Përkthimi i idiomave me anë të togfjalëshave të lirë e të qëndrueshëm është bërë në disa forma. Së pari, nëpërmjet përkthimit me perifrazë, d.m.th., përkthimit përshkrues. Ky lloj përkthimi është veçanërisht i përshtatshëm për idiomat që lidhen me ngjarje konkrete historike ose episodike si she idiomat me karakter terminologjik. Njëkohësisht, përkthimi i idiomave është bërë edhe me ndihmën e frazeologjizmave kalke, si p.sh., **take part—marr pjesë, take measures—marr masa, break the ice—thyej akullin etj.**

iii

d) Përkthimin e idiomave me anë të ekuivalentit me një fjalë, si p.sh., **hook, line and sinker—tërësisht, plotësisht.**

e) Përkthimin e kombinuar. Hera herës, kemi pëdorur forma të kombinuara të përkthimit të idiomave, pra përkthimin e kemi dhënë me paralele frazeologjike, me perifrazë dhe me një fjalë të vetme, si p.sh., **keep a quiet (still) tongue in one's head—hesht, kyç gojën, mbaj gjuhën e mbledhur, talk nineteen to the dozen—llomotis, flas pa pushim, flas si çatalle mulliri.**

Për lehtësi përdorimi, fjalori është pajisur edhe me tregues alfabetik.

Për përmirësimin e mëtejshëm të fjalorit, autori mirëpret të gjitha vërejtjet e mundshme.

I. S.

FOREWORD

The **English-Albanian Dictionary of Idioms** is the product of an investigating work by the author for years on end. The dictionary includes English and American idioms of the highest frequency value—stable word-combinations formed and crystallised historically as indivisible units. The Dictionary includes clause and phrase idioms.

Idioms are printed in bold type and are arranged alphabetically according to the first word that forms an integral part of them. This makes the location of individual entries as easy as possible. On the right side of the idiom the Albanian equivalent is given. In the event of polysemantic idioms, the various meanings are marked with numbers.

Idioms are illustrated by complete sentences taken from works of fiction of English and American authors, from monolingual and bilingual dictionaries, specialised English and American dictionaries, handbooks of idioms etc. The illustrations are preceded by a box □. They are printed in *italic*.

Special attention is paid to the adequate translation in the target language of every idiom in the source language. In rendering the idioms from English into Albanian, the following types of translations are used:

a) Translation with full Albanian equivalents which have the same meaning, composition, stylistic value and grammatical structure, as for instance: **an apple of discord—mollë sherri, Achilles' heel—thembra e Akilit, break the ice—thyej akullin, build castles in the air—ndërtoj kështjella në erë, buy a pig in a poke—ble derr në thes, a drop in the ocean—një pikë uji në oqean, fish in troubled waters—peshkoj në ujëra të turbullta, play with fire—luaj me zjarrin** etc.

b) Translation with partial equivalents which convey completely the meaning of the unit but preserve the lexico-grammatical distinctions, as for instance: **a wolf in sheep's clothing—ujk me lëkurë qengji, one swallow does not make a summer—me një dallëndyshe s'vjen pranvera, cudgel (beat) one's brains—vras mendjen, eat one's words—ha fjalën** etc.

c) Translation with free and stable word-groups.

The bilingual **English-Albanian Dictionary of Idioms** is useful for various kinds of people, to specialists reading English and American literature, to translators, to travellers and to all Albanian learners of English far and wide.

To help the readers with the location of the idiom, an Index has been provided at the back of the Dictionary.

I. S.

A

A1 (A number one, A NO. 1) i mrekullueshëm, i shkëlqyeshëm; shkëlqyeshëm
□ *'He must be a first-rater,' said Sam. 'A1-, replied Mr. Roker.'* □ *It was an A1 dinner.*

abandon oneself to bie, e lëshoj veten; jepem pas
□ *He abandoned himself to despair.*

abide by respektoj; pranoj; i përmbahem; mbaj fjalën, premtimin etj.
□ *The two persons agreed to abide by the referee's decision.* □ *Both parties must agree to abide by the court's decision.* □ *Unless they abide by the rules of the club, they will have to leave.*

abound in/with ka me bollëk; mizëron; gëlon; është plot e përplot me
□ *Modern industry abounds in opportunities for young men with imagination.* □ *The countryside abounds in wild life of any kind.* □ *This language abounds in difficulties for the foreign learner.*

above all (else) mbi të gjitha, mbi gjithçka
□ *He longs above all else to see his family.* □ *In choosing the curtains for a room you should consider the material from the point of view of texture, its weight, its pattern—but its color above all.*

above board i ndershëm, i hapur; hapur, me letra (karta) të hapura
□ *The deal was completely above board.* □ *They say that he accepts bribes but I have always found him to be honest and above board.* □ *I know that you know that there is something between Aileen Butler and me, and we might as well have it open and above board.*

absent oneself (from) mungoj
□ *The Chairperson of the housing committee deliberately absented oneself from the meeting, realizing that he could not face up to the criticism of his opponents.*

abstain (from) përmbahem, jam i përkorë; abstenoj
□ *His doctor told him to abstain from beer and wine.* □ *Several MPs abstained from voting at the end of the debate.*

accord with përkon, përputhet, pajtohet
□ *My information does not accord with what this report states.* □ *What you say does not accord with the previous evidence.*

according to sb (sth) sipas
□ *According to documents discovered, the Albanian language began to be written from the 16th century.* □ *Every thing went according to plan.* □ *According to John you were in London last week.*

according to/by one's lights sipas mendimit, mundësive, aftësive etj. të dikujt
□ *Nothing that you have done requires forgiveness.* □ *One acts according to one's lights, and more than that one cannot do.* □ *He did his best; he worked according to his lights.*

1

account for shpjegoj, sqaroj
- *He was always ready to account for his actions.* □ *Science can now account for many things that were thought to be mysterious by the ancients.*

account to përgjigjem, jap llogari
- *You have to account to me if anything happens to this girl while she is in your care.*

accustom oneself to mësohem, më bëhet shprehi
- *You'll have to accustom yourself to the new conditions, and stop complaining.* □ *The old man slowly accustomed himself to life without companionship.*

Achilles' heel thembra e Akilit, pikë e dobët
- *Tom started off as a prosperous businessman but was soon heavily in debt; a love of gambling was his Achilles' heel.* □ *Spelling is my Achilles' heel.*

acquaint with njoh; njihem
- *Did he acquaint you with the facts?* □ *When I was a teacher I always made a point of acquainting myself with the home background of all my pupils.*

across the board në tërësi, pa përjashtim
- *The wages of everyone in the factory were raised by ten per cent across the board.* □ *This firm needs radical changes across the board.*

act on (upon) 1. veproj sipas
- *Acting on your recommendation, I have decided to emigrate to Canada.* □ *The border guards, acting upon the information they had received, caught the spy.*
2. vepron, ndikon, ka efekt
- *These pills act on liver.* □ *Heat acts on bodies and causes them to expand.*

act the part/role of shtirem, hiqem si, luaj rolin e
- *I don't think that John is ill at all; he is just acting a part.* □ *He found it hard to act the role of the genial host that night.*

add in 1. hedh, derdh, shtoj
- *Should you add in the lemon juice before or after mixing the flour and sugar?*
2. përfshij
- *If you add in his gains of last year he'd made no less than $20,000.*

add to rrit, shtoj
- *The recent excavations have added greatly to our knowledge of life in our country.*

add together 1. mbledh
- *If you add these two numbers together what do you get?*
2. përziej, bashkoj
- *She got one pail of boiling water and one of cold water and added them together in a tub.*

add up mbledh
- *Every time I add these figures up I get a different answer.*

add up to 1. arrin, kap shumën
- *The figures add up to 12,345.*
2. rezulton
- *Most of the evidence adds up to the clear conclusion that human beings are able to control their feelings.* □ *Your evidence, then really adds up to this—that you were nowhere near the scene of the crime?*

adhere to i përmbahem, i qëndroj besnik
- *He resolutely adhered to what he had said at the meeting; he had not changed his mind in any way.*

after a fashion deri diku, njëfarësoj
- *He plays violin after a fashion, but nobody in their right mind would pay to listen to him.* □ *'Has the new*

2

secretary typed the report?'—'*Well, **after a fashion**. I'll have to have some parts typed again.'* □ *Kent McKibenn was thirty-three years old, tall, athletic and, **after a fashion**, handsome.*

after all në fund të fundit, në analizë të fundit

□ *What could he do? Talk it over with Soames? That would only make matters worse. And, **after all**, there was nothing in it, he felt sure.* □ *After all, he is your husband.*

after hours pas pune, jashtë orarit të punës

□ *Staff must stay behind **after hours** to catch up on their work.* □ *Look, you know as well as I do that I'd loose my license if I served you drink **after hours**.*

after one's/its fashion në mënyrën e vet; në stilin e vet

□ *Braxman was really interesting **after his fashion**.* □ *It was an imposing building **after its fashion**, but neither old enough nor beautiful enough to attract the tourists.*

after one's own heart siç më pëlqen, si ma do zemra

□ *My new neighbour is a man **after my own heart**. He also likes walking and fishing, so we often go away at the weekend together.* □ *Cheer up, we are going to have a day **after your heart**.*

again and again vazhdimisht, parreshtur

□ *I've told you **again and again** not to do that.* □ *Now the holiday was over, and he still repeated **again and again**: 'Tomorrow, tomorrow."*

against the/one's grain kundër dëshirës, natyrës, prirjeve të

□ *I'm afraid I'll have to speak firmly to Miss Jones for coming in late,* although it **goes against the grain**. □ *Everything in fact, was driving him towards the simple solution of Irene's return. If it were still **against the grain** with her, had he no feeling to subdue, injury to forgive, pain to forget?*

against the tide kundër rrymës

□ *He knew he would be unlikely to succeed in swimming **against the tide** in the controversial issue.*

against one's/sb's will kundër vullnetit të

□ *Students should never be forced to study a subject **against their will**.*

ahead of time/schedule para afatit, para kohe

□ *The new section of the motorway was completed two months **ahead of schedule**.* □ *He must have arrived **ahead of time**. He was not expected until this evening.*

aim at 1. marr shenjë, marr nishan

□ *The hunter **aimed at** a rabbit, but hit a bird.* □ *The marksman **aimed at** the center of the target.*

2. synoj, kam si qëllim, e kam syrin te

□ *I don't understand that girl's behaviour. What's she **aiming at**?* □ *They **aimed at** a higher production level.*

air a/one's grievance(s) shpreh, paraqit (një) ankesë (ankesat)

□ *The factory manager called a meeting of all the workers, so that they would have a chance to **air their grievances**.*

air one's views shpreh, shfaq mendimet

□ *He finished by saying that the purpose of the meeting was to **air our views**, and to give him ideas which he could think over.*

airs and graces naze, spitullim

□ *I don't think much of her son—he is so conceited, and as full of **airs and graces** as a young lord.*

alight on gjej rastësisht

□ *Sir Alexander Fleming alighted on the antibiotic properties of penicillin when he was engaged on research of a quite different nature.*

alive and kicking/well shëndoshë e mirë

□ *I was glad to hear that your grandmother is still alive and kicking.* □ *Well, you see I'm alive and kicking.*

alive to i vetëdijshëm

□ *He is fully alive to the dangers of the situation.* □ *I'm fully alive to that possibility, but I have decided to take the risk.*

alive with plot e përplot me

□ *When the winning team returned to their hotel, they discovered that it was alive with reporters.* □ *The lake was alive with fish.*

all agog mezi duroj, mezi pres, s'më durohet sa

□ *The children were all agog for the show to begin.*

all along gjatë gjithë kohës, ngahera

□ *You've been very nice to me all along, Mr. Cowperwood, and I appreciate it.* □ *We thought he was our friend, but he was betraying us all along.*

all along the line në të gjitha drejtimet

□ *The speaker defended the government's policies all along the line.* □ *These newer family magazines are making the older ones fight for existence all along the line because they are their direct competitors and successors.*

all and sundry të gjithë pa përjashtim

□ *He spared no pains in trying to see all and sundry who might be of use to him.* □ *The Smiths invite all and sundry to their parties.*

all at once befas, papritur

□ *Confused sounds came from behind the door of Annixter's room. All at once and before Harron had a chance to knock on the door, Annixter flung it open.* □ *I found myself all at once on the brink of panic.*

all the best gjitha të mirat

□ *Goodbye then, and all the best till next Christmas.* □ *He lifted his whisky. 'All the best, boys.'*

all but thuajse, gati, për pak sa

□ *I thought he was lying, and I all but told him so.*

all ears/eyes gjithë, tërë sy e veshë

□ *He was all ears when he heard his name being mentioned by the woman at the next table.* □ *Now children, I want you to be all eyes and ears for the first part of the lesson and then we'll have questions afterwards.*

all in i lodhur, i këputur, i rraskapitur

□ *He was all in at the end of the race.* □ *After a day's teaching, I go home feeling all in.*

all in all 1. në tërësi

□ *Some people don't like Jim as a boss but, all in all, I think he does a good job.*

2. gjithçka

□ *The daughter who had been her all in all had left home.* □ *They were all in all to each other.*

all is not gold that glitters çdo gjë që ndrit nuk është ar (flori)

□ *We should not deter our younger scientists from going overseas. They will gain experience, and perhaps learn that all is not gold that glitters.*

all is well with sb gjithçka është (shkon) mirë me

□ *It has taken a little time to recover from the accident but I am glad to say that all is now well and I'll be back at work next week.*

all manner of lloj-lloj

□ *And the foundations of the wall of*

the city were garnished with **all manner of** *precious stones.* □ *He will give you* **all manner of** *excuses for his absence.*

all of a sudden befas, papritur
□ *But finally it occurred to me* **all of a sudden** *that these animals didn't reason.* □ **All of a sudden** *the door swung open and the girls screamed with fright.*

all one njësoj, njëlloj
□ *It is* **all one** *to me whether he stays or goes.*

all over 1. gjithandej, kudo
□ *They were delighted to see the little child, for they'd been looking* **all over** *for her.* □ *Sand had been blown* **all over** *everything in the tent.*
2. (ka) kaluar, përfunduar, marrë fund
□ *The pain is* **all over***; the patient is all right.* □ *The firemen tried to fight the blaze, but by midnight it was* **all over***. The house was completely burnt down.*
3. krejt, tamam si
□ *She is not a bit like me. She's your mother* **all over.**

all right 1. mirë, në rregull
□ *'But you were wrong, weren't you?' '***All right, all right***, so I was wrong! Can't you change the subject?'* □ *'Stand firm, Sam', said Mr. Pickwick, looking down. '***All right***, sir', replied Mr. Weller.*
2. natyrisht; pa dyshim
□ *She pretended to be very busy looking at the shopwindows, but she saw me* **all right.**
3. i përshtatshëm, i pranueshëm
□ *That sort of bike may be* **all right** *for little kids, but now I am twelve I want a proper racing model.*

all roads lead to Rome të gjitha rrugët të çojnë në Romë

□ *In other words, the starting point is quite irrelevant; as* **all roads lead to Rome***, so a person's thoughts and associations tend to lead towards his personal troubles, desires and wishes of the present moment.*

all the better aq më mirë
□ *'Bill says he can't come.'—'***All the better***, it will give more room in the car.'*

all the go/rage në modë, të modës
□ *Rubber-soled shoes are* **all the go** *these days.* □ *It was that time in the sixties when mini-skirts were* **all the go***.* □ *She had already had her heart fixed upon the peculiar little tan jacket which was* **all the rage** *that fall.*

all there normal, me mendjen në vend
□ *But they were of the real Lancashire type, and were, as the phrase goes* **all there***.* □ *That old man is behaving strangely—do you think he is* **all there?**

all/just the same 1. njëlloj
□ *Do what you like—it's* **all the same** *to me.* □ *As long as there's a golf course nearby, it's* **all the same** *to Tony where we go for our holiday.*
2. megjithatë
□ *I know he's very strict but,* **all the same***, he is very efficient.* □ *Although we met with some unexpected difficulties at the beginning, we fulfilled our task* **all the same.**

all square with sb barabar, fit e fit
□ *At half-time the teams were* **all square** *with three goals each.* □ *I've just returned his loan, so I am* **all square with** *him at last.*

all the time 1. gjatë gjithë kohës, vazhdimisht
□ *That letter I was searching for was in my pocket* **all the time***.* □ *He said*

he loved her and *all the time* he was going out with someone else.
2. gjithmonë, gjithnjë, kurdoherë
□ *He's a business man all the time.*

all the world and his wife djalli me të birin, të gjithë pa përjashtim
□ *'All the world and his wife', as the saying goes, were trying to trample upon me.*

all things considered duke marrë gjithçka parasysh
□ *All things considered, he is not to be blamed.*

all thumbs s'më bëjnë duart
□ *'Could you fix this brooch for me? I seem to be all thumbs today.'* □ *I'm sorry, I am all thumbs this morning. I don't seem able to type one short letter correctly.*

all together/told gjithë e gjithë
□ *There were twenty people in the boat, all told.* □ *All the real work was done with the horses; all together we had about eighty on the place.*

all the year round gjatë gjithë vitit
□ *Buy a deep freezer and enjoy fresh fruits and other garden produce all the year round, in season and out of season.*

allow for marr parasysh, marr në konsideratë
□ *Don't forget to allow for a little shrinkage when you are making that material up.* □ *The journey usually takes six weeks but you should allow for delays caused by bad weather.*

allow of lejon, pranon, toleron
□ *His responsible position allowed of no unseemly behavior in public.* □ *The situation allows of no delay.*

allude to aludoj, bëj aluzion, përmend tërthorazi
□ *They very soon learned not to allude to the subject in the presence*

of their father. □ *This is rarely alluded to in even indirect terms.*

ally oneself with lidhem me
□ *Great Britain was allied with United States in both World Wars.*

alpha and omega alfa dhe omega, fillimi dhe mbarimi
□ *I am Alpha and Omega, the beginning and the ending, saith the Lord, which is, and which was, and which is to come, the Almighty.* □ *... the alpha and omega of my heart's wishes broke involuntarily from my lips in the words Jane! Jane! Jane!*

amount to 1. arrin, kap shumën
□ *His debts amount to $5,000.*
2. është njësoj si, është baraz; do të thotë
□ *Whether I pay or whether my wife pays amounts to the same thing, because we share our money.* □ *Riding on a bus without paying the fare amounts to cheating the bus company.* □ *What it amounts to is simply that he is not willing to give us his support.*

ancient/past history histori e vjetër, histori e shkuar
□ *Well, that's ancient history. I was using it for an example.* □ *I was quite a good singer when I was younger, but that's all ancient history now.* □ *I know my name's not Larsen, because I changed it after I quarrelled with my old man. But that's past history; never mind that now.*

and all si dhe, përfshirë dhe
□ *The dog ate the whole rabbit, head, bones and all.* □ *The wind blew everything off the table, tablecloth and all.*

and all that e të tjera e të tjera
□ *The shop sells fruits, vegetables and all that.*

and so on/forth e të tjera

□ *He went on about the need to work harder, moderate wage demands, invest more **and so on and so forth**.*

another cup of tea gjë tjetër, çështje tjetër

□ *I don't object to giving you a helping hand now and then, as I have said before; but being made use of like this is **another cup of tea**.*

answer back kthej fjalë

□ *When we were young, we never dared to **answer back** to our parents.* □ *He is not really an ill-mannered boy, but he has a bad habit of **answering back**.*

answer for përgjigjem për

□ *You will have to **answer for** your wrongdoing one day.* □ *My opinion is that you are the best man for the job, but I can't **answer for** the other members of the committee, of course.* □ *If you drive that car without a licence, you'll have to **answer for** the consequences!*

answer the door/the bell hap derën (kur troket apo bie zilja)

□ *Rat tat. 'I am afraid that's not a London knock', thought Tom. 'It didn't sound bold. Perhaps that's the reason why nobody **answers the door**.*

answer to the description përkon, i përgjigjet përshkrimit të

□ *He doesn't **answer to the description** of the missing man that appeared in the newspapers.* □ *The car exactly **answers to the description** of the stolen vehicle.*

answer to the name quhet, ka emrin

□ *The dog **answers to the name** of Spot.* □ *There's no one here **answering to that name**.*

apart from përveç, me përjashtim të, veç, përpos

□ *This composition is pretty well written, **apart from** a few grammatical mistakes.* □ ***Apart from** a few scratches, he was unhurt.*

an/the apple of discord mollë sherri

□ *The girls had got on well together until **the apple of discord** in the person of a handsome young apprentice arrived in their midst.*

apple of one's eye drita e syve

□ *'Dick', said the dwarf, thrusting his head in at the door, my pet, my pupil, the **apple of my eye**, hey, hey!' □ Her youngest son was **the apple of her eye**. □ I sacrificed everything to make you happy and safe. I won't talk about your father, but you were **the apple of my eye**.*

apply oneself/one's energies to sth jepem i tëri pas, derdh (shkrij) të gjitha energjitë për

□ *If you **apply yourself to** the job in hand, you'll soon finish it.* □ *We must **apply our energies to** finding a solution.*

apply to/for kërkoj, bëj kërkesë

□ *Mary has just **applied to** the company for a job.*

argue down i mbyll gojën me argumenta

□ *Jack delights in **arguing** his opposers **down**.* □ *When we're discussing art, I can always **argue** him **down**.*

argue sb into/out of doing sth i mbush mendjen dikujt të bëjë/të mos bëjë diçka

□ *They tried to **argue him into joining** them.*

argue out rrah, diskutoj (një çështje)

□ *They've been **arguing** the matter **out** since it was brought up at the meeting this morning.* □ *Can't the problem be **argued out** tomorrow evening?*

armed to the teeth armatosur deri në dhëmbë

□ *The police force was armed to the teeth.*

arm in arm krah për krah

□ *Of our going, arm in arm, and Dora stopping and looking back, and saying, 'If I have ever been cross or ungrateful to anybody, don't remember it!' and bursting into tears.* □ *'John and Mary had quite a quarrel this evening.' 'Well they must have made it up, because I've just seen them going down the road arm in arm.'*

around/round the clock pa pushim, njëzet e katër orë, ditë e natë

□ *They worked around the clock and over the entire weekend to get the export order ready for dispatch on the Monday.* □ *Doctors attended the sick man around the clock.*

arrive at arrij

□ *We arrived at the station just as the train was leaving.* □ *The two scientists arrived at the same conclusion quite independently.*

(as) a/one's last resort si mjet të fundit

□ *I discovered that all grassland squirrels made straight for the trees when pursued, and only chose holes in the ground, or hollow logs, as a last resort.*

as a matter of fact në fakt, në të vërtetë

□ *I don't think we shall be able to show him to you, as a matter of fact.* □ *As a matter of fact, I know nothing about the matter.* □ *As a matter of fact there was just a little uncertainty as to whether there was a single house left.*

as a rule si rregull

□ *As a rule, he was always home by seven p.m.* □ *We don't as a rule give*

credit to customers, but are willing to make an exception in your case.

as a whole në tërësi; si e tërë

□ *The population as a whole is in favor of reform.* □ *Is the collection going to be divided up or sold as a whole?*

(as) black as coal i zi si qymyr, i zi sterrë

□ *Look at your hands, boy, they're as black as coal—you can't come to the table like that.*

(as) broad as it's long njëlloj, aty-aty; një okë e dhjetë, një okë pa dhjetë

□ *The plane fare is much dearer of course, but then you save on overnight accommodation and meals. Financially it's as broad as it's long; it really comes down to which way you prefer to travel.*

(as) busy as a bee si bletë punëtore

□ *The children are busy as bees, helping their mother in the garden.* □ *My wife never has time to get bored. She is as busy as a bee from morning to night.*

(as) clean as a new pin i pastër dritë

□ *Jim's mother was a big woman, who kept her house as clean as a new pin.*

(as) clear as crystal i pastër, i qartë, i tejdukshëm si kristal

□ *The river ran as clear as crystal and if you watched closely you could now and then catch a glimpse of a trout hovering over the pebbles on the bottom.*

(as) clear as day/daylight si drita e diellit

□ *The matter was as clear as daylight and would be disposed of in half an hour or so.*

(as) cold as ice akull i ftohtë

□ *The central heating had been switched off and the room was as cold as ice.*

(as) cunning as a fox dinak si dhelpër
□ *There is a good deal of crooked dealing in the property business but the people involved in it are **as cunning as foxes** and know how to keep just on the right side of the law.*

(as) deep as well i thellë pus
□ *'I never knew Harold could handle a boat!' 'There's a lot we don't know about Harold. He's **as deep as a well**.*

(as) different as chalk from/and cheese janë, ndryshojnë si nata me ditën
□ *The two brothers resembled each other physically, but were **as different** in their natures **as chalk from cheese**.*

(as) easy/simple as ABC fare kollaj, fare lehtë, si bukë e djathë
□ *You will quickly learn how to use this machine; it's **as simple as ABC**.*
□ *First lessons in any subject are usually designed to make you think that the whole course is going to be **as easy as ABC**.*

as far as 1. deri
□ *I've read **as far as** the third chapter.*
□ *I'll walk with you **as far as** the post office.*
2. me sa
□ *His parents supported him **as far as** they could.* □ ***As far as** I know he hasn't come yet.*

as far as one can see me sa shoh, me sa kuptoj
□ *We don't know of course what the cost of living may be in five years' time, but **as far as I can see**, we'll be able to live comfortably enough on our pensions.*

as far as sb/sth is concerned sa i takon, lidhur me
□ *Don't bring me into the argument. **As far as I'm concerned**, the boy can go to London if he likes.*

(as) fit as a fiddle si kokërr molle
□ *'How are you feeling, Tom?' '**Fit as a fiddle**...'* □ *I'll tell your parents that you're **as fit as a fiddle** and having the time of your life.*

as follows si më poshtë
□ *The main events were **as follows**: first the president's speech, secondly the secretary's reply and thirdly, the chairman's summing-up.*

as for sb/sth sa për, sa i takon, sa i përket
□ ***As for me** I know nothing about it.*
□ ***As for** the cost, that will be very little.*

as good as thuajse, gati
□ *A cool breeze began to blow, and that was **as good as** saying the night was about done.* □ *When the search-party found him, he was **as good as** dead from hunger and exposure.*

as good as one's word besnik i fjalës së dhënë
□ *He said he would be there by midnight, and he was **as good as his word**.* □ *If he said he would lend you the deposit for a house, he will. Uncle Fred has always been **as good as his word**.*

(as) hard as steel i fortë si çeliku
□ *General discipline and academic achievements improved greatly under the headmastership of Mr. Gray, a man **as hard as steel**, but very just.*

(as) hard as (a) stone i fortë si shkëmb
□ *I can't do any digging today, the ground's **as hard as stone** after last night's frost.*

(as) heavy as lead i rëndë plumb
□ *When he woke the following morning his throat felt sore and swollen and his limbs **heavy as lead**.*

as if/though sikur
□ *He moves toward Stephen **as if** to shake hands with him.* □ *He made as*

if to leave the room but, thinking better of it, returned to comfort the weeping girl.

as it were si të thuash
- □ *Everyone loved the President: he was, as it were, a father to his people.*
- □ *He is not equal to the task, as it were.*

ask after pyes, interesohem
- □ *She asked after my father.* □ *Don't forget to ask after your uncle when you see Mary this afternoon.*

ask for kërkoj
- □ *If you get into difficulties, don't hesitate to ask for advice.*

ask for it/trouble e kërkoj vetë, e kërkoj vetë belanë
- □ *You're really asking for it if you come in late again.* □ *All right, you asked for it.*

(as) light as a feather i lehtë pendë
- □ *'Can you manage to carry her?' 'Oh, she's as light as a feather.'*

(as) like as two peas/peas in a pod si dy pika uji
- □ *We haven't met before, but I am sure you must be Alec Brown's brother; you're as like as two peas.*

as like sb as if he (she) had been spit out of his (her) mouth sikur e ka nxjerrë (qitur) nga hunda
- □ *Well, comparisons are odious; but she's as like her husband as if she were spit out of his mouth.*

as/so long as sa kohë që, përderisa
- □ *He's satisfied as long as you let him talk.* □ *I don't mind where we go so long as there's sun, sand and sea.*

as (good/ill) luck would have it për fat (të mirë/të keq); fatmirësisht; fatkeqësisht
- □ *He had just all the qualifications we wanted, and as luck would have it we happened to have a vacancy.* □ *As ill luck would have it he was on holiday at that time.*

(as) meek as a lamb i urtë, i butë si qengj
- □ *If he'd thought I would sit there meek as lamb while he abused my family, he must have got a real surprise.*

(as) obstinate/stubborn as a mule kokëfortë si mushka
- □ *But this is the old thing, though he is impulsive he's as obstinate as a mule.*

as one man si një trup i vetëm
- □ *There were some differences of opinion about hours of work, but on the need of a rise in pay they were as one man.*

(as) quick as lighting si rrufe
- □ *I didn't mean to let the dog out, but he shot past me, as quick as lighting, when I opened the door to the postman.*

(as) quiet/silent/still as the grave/tomb i heshtur si varri
- □ *I do miss the children. The house seems as silent as the grave without them.* □ *There's no use peering through the mailbox. The place is as still as the grave. They must have forgotten we were coming.*

(as) red as a rooster i kuq si lafsha e gjelit, flakë i kuq
- □ *I felt myself turning as red as a rooster when the teacher praised my essay and read it to the class.* □ *When I told her that she was vain, she went as red as a rooster.*

(as) regular as a clockwork i përpiktë si sahat
- □ *He is as regular as a clockwork.* □ *She came in here every morning, regular as clockwork.*

(as) sharp as a needle i mprehtë nga mendja, e ka mendjen (gjykimin) brisk
- □ *Young though he was, the child was*

as sharp as a needle and sensed the disharmony between his parents in spite of the fact that they never quarrelled in front of him.

as soon as sapo, porsa, menjëherë sa
□ *He left **as soon as** he heard the news.* □ *I'll tell him **as soon as** I see him.*

(as) sour as vinegar/crab i thartë uthull
□ *Don't eat those oranges yet—they're not ripe and **as sour as vinegar**.*

(as) strong as a horse/an ox i fortë si kalë
□ *Physically he had always been broad-shouldered and athletic. He's **as strong as a horse**.*

as such si i tillë
□ *He is a brilliant scholar and everywhere is known **as such**.*

(as) sure as eggs is eggs si një e një që bëjnë dy
□ *If he goes on driving like that, **as sure as eggs is eggs** he'll end up in hospital.*

(as) sweet as honey i ëmbël mjaltë
□ *I can't drink this tea. It's **as sweet as honey**.*
□ *She's the kind of woman who'll be **sweet as honey** in your face and as malicious as hell behind your back.*

as the case may/might be sipas rastit, sipas rrethanave
□ *The manner of his meal was this: Mr. Swiveller, holding the slice of toast or cup of tea in his left hand, and taking a bite of drink, **as the case might be**, constantly kept in his right hand.* □ *You will be given back the money you paid for a hotel or for lodging, **as the case may be**.*

as the crow flies në vijë të drejtë, në vijë ajrore

□ *We cut over the fields—straight **as the crow flies**—through hedge and ditch.* □ *'Just how far are you from your nearest neighbour out there?' 'About a mile **as the crow flies**, but three miles up-river by boat and seven miles round by road.'*

(as) thick as thieves miq për kokë
□ *Jack and Jim were always quarrelling until recently, but now they are **as thick as thieves**.*

as things stand/stood në kushtet e krijuara, në kushte të tilla, në gjendjen e krijuar
□ *As things stand with me at the moment, I simply can't find time for voluntary work.*

as though sikur
□ *He rubbed his eyes and yawned **as though** waking up after a long sleep.* □ *Arthur went back to his lodging feeling **as though** he had wings.*

as to sth sa i takon
□ *As to correcting our homework, the teacher always makes us do it ourselves.*

as usual si zakonisht
□ *Despite the cold weather that morning he got up very early, **as usual**.* □ *You're late **as usual**.* □ *As usual, there weren't many people at the meeting.*

as well (as sb/sth) edhe, gjithashtu, si dhe
□ *He had to carry a light sleeping-bag and ground sheet **as well as** a blanket.* □ *'I thought you said you wanted fruit-juice?' 'So I do, but I want soup **as well**.'*

(as) white as chalk/snow/a sheet e bardhë si bora, i bardhë qumësht
□ *The sheets were rough but **as white as snow**.* □ *It was dreadful to see him lying there **white as a sheet** and in such pain.* □ *His face was **as white as***

chalk when he arrived home from work this evening.

as yet tani për tani, hë për hë, deri më tani

☐ *We are waiting patiently, but we have not received any news from him as yet.* ☐ *As yet he had consumed but a pint and a half and was still rational.*

at a blow me një goditje

☐ *He felled his three attackers at a single blow.*

at a distance nga larg

☐ *The picture looks better at a distance.*

at a glance me një shikim, me një vështrim

☐ *He could tell at a glance what was wrong with the car.* ☐ *He sized up the situation at a glance.*

at all 1. krejt, krejtësisht

☐ *They were not careless at all, they thought all things were cocksure.*

2. aspak, fare

☐ *I don't know him at all.* ☐ *That won't help things at all.*

3. përgjithësisht, në përgjithësi

☐ *You must know it if you know anything at all.*

4. paksa, në një farë mënyre

☐ *Were you at all surprised to hear that Sarah had decided to become a nun?*

at all costs me çdo kusht, me çdo çmim

☐ *You must at all costs get a visa; otherwise you will not be allowed to land in the country.* ☐ *The right and the left wings of the party are now united to avoid a split at all costs.*

at all events sido që të ndodhë, për çdo rast, sido që të vijë puna

☐ *'I won't press you go back there, at all events, just now,' he said in his most caressing tone.* ☐ *At all events, I will come with you immediately.* ☐ *'It was my duty to stop her misconduct;*

she is thankful to me for it now.' 'She ought to be at all events.'

at all times gjithmonë, në çdo kohë, orë e çast

☐ *He was the best kind of teacher, firm yet relaxed, exacting yet ready with encouragement and all times strictly impartial with his favors.* ☐ *You can find me there at all times.*

at any moment në çdo çast

☐ *I'll see if I can find him for you, but he's out a lot and it's difficult to know where he is at any given moment.*

at any price me çdo kusht

☐ *The people wanted peace at any price.* ☐ *I'm enjoying myself here, but we'll go now if that's what you want. Peace at any price, I always say.*

at any rate sidoqoftë, për çdo rast, sido që të jetë puna

☐ *I know he failed. But, at any rate, he did his best.* ☐ *I'll do nothing until I hear from you, at any rate.* ☐ *We made merry about Dora's wanting to be liked..., and she didn't like me at any rate.*

at a pinch në rast nevoje

☐ *At a pinch we could manage without any extra provision.* ☐ *We can get six people at the table at a pinch.* ☐ *At a pinch, you can always try to make a fire by rubbing two sticks together.*

at a run me vrap

☐ *She started off at a run up the path.* ☐ *He started off at a run but soon tired and began to walk.*

at a snail's pace (gallop) me hap breshke, shumë ngadalë

☐ *Two mules strained leisurely in the traces, moving at a snail's pace.* ☐ *Granny prefers to drive herself. She knows it irritates young people to have to go at a snail's pace.* ☐ *They were under a great shadowy shed,* *where the lamps were beginning to shine out, with passenger cars all about the train moving **at a snail's pace**.*

at a stretch pa pushim, pa u ndalur
□ *Jim had marvellous powers of concentration: he could study for six hours **at a stretch**.* □ *They walked five miles **at a stretch**.* □ *She can sit and watch the fire for an hour **at a stretch**.*

at a stroke me veprim të menjëher-shëm, menjëherë; me një goditje
□ *The politician promised that prices would be reduced **at a stroke** if he were returned to power.* □ *They threatened to cancel the whole project **at a stroke**. This caused the other side to change the initial decision.*

at a time në të njëjtën kohë, njëherazi
□ *Michael went up the stairs two **at a time**.*

at a venture kuturu, kot e më kot, në erë, në tym
□ *He answered all the questions **at a venture**.* □ *As I no longer knew where I was, I continued to roam **at a venture**.*

at bay në gjendje të pashprese, në gjendje pa rrugëdalje, me shpatulla pas muri
□ *The criminals were **at bay**, and willing to take any risk.* □ *He had an aspect of a man found out and held **at bay**.*

at best në rastin më të mirë
□ *I think that I might sell my old car for around $500—perhaps $550, **at best**.* □ *When she wanted to talk about her work, he would change the subject, or **at best** listen condescendingly.* □ *At best, we can only hope to be there by three o'clock. We cannot arrive before.*

at bottom në thellësi të shpirtit, thellë në shpirt (në karakter)

□ *He's a good fellow **at bottom**.* □ *She never seemed to resent her sister's popularity, but I dare say that she was sometimes a little jealous **at bottom**.*

at close quarters nga afër, në distancë të afërt
□ *This was the first chance he had of seeing him **at close quarters**.* □ *Seen **at close quarters** she looked even more formidable.* □ *I've never seen a lion **at close quarters** before.*

at death's door në buzë të varrit, duke vdekur
□ *When I heard that Jim was **at death's door**, I immediately rushed to see him.* □ *And his father—**at death's door**, waiting for the news.* □ *Stop groaning! You are not **at death's door**!*

at every turn kudo, në çdo hap
□ *When I started my career I met difficulties **at every turn**.* □ *I've been coming across old friends **at every turn** during this reunion.*

at first në fillim, fillimisht
□ *Diabetes is symptomless **at first**.* □ *At first I thought he was shy, but then I discovered he was just not interested in other people.* □ *At first we thought he was joking, but then we realised that he really meant what he said.*

at first blush/glance/sight në pamje të parë, në shikimin e parë
□ *At first blush the cliff seemed unscalable, though we have heard the islanders used to climb it in search of sea-birds' eggs.* □ *At first glance the offer seemed most attractive, but we later found some draw-backs.* □ *At first sight I thought the picture uninteresting.*

at first hand drejtpërdrejt, nga burime të drejtpërdrejta
□ *It must be a great comfort to you to*

*have all the news **at first hand**.* □ *We secured the information **at first hand**.*

at full length sa gjatë gjerë
□ *The snake lay **at full length** on the rock, sunning itself.*

at full speed me tërë shpejtësinë
□ *Though I was running **at full speed**, I could not overtake him.* □ *They were away **at full speed** down the river in a couple of minutes.*

at hand 1. afër, pranë
□ *They reside in various boarding-houses near **at hand**.* □ *One of my friends live close **at hand**, the other lives at a distance.* □ *We turned into a room near **at hand**.*
2. në prag
□ *I saw that a crisis was **at hand**, and it came.* □ *The winter was near **at hand**, she had no clothes, and now she was out of work.*

at heart në zemër, në shpirt; në thelb
□ *He may appear a bit rude, but **at heart** he is a very kind man.* □ *Your father is strict with you, but he has your best interests **at heart**.* □ *They are a little stiff, but they are all right **at heart**.*

at home 1. në shtëpi
□ *His children are married and he stays **at home** all the time.* □ *I have left my books **at home**.*
2. në fushën vendase
□ *Is our next match **at home** or away?*
3. në vend, brenda vendit
□ *Sales since October, both **at home** and abroad, show a marked increase.*

at intervals me intervale, kohë më kohë, herë pas here
□ *The runners started **at 5-minute intervals**.* □ *At intervals she would stop for a rest.* □ *The trees were planted **at 20 ft intervals**.* □ *Trains*

*and buses were leaving **at short intervals**.*

at issue në diskutim, në shqyrtim
□ *The conference took up the most urgent questions **at issue**.* □ *That is not the point **at issue**.*

at large 1. i lirë
□ *They say there's a wild animal **at large**.* □ *I'll hand him over; he's not fit to be **at large**.*
2. i lirë, i pazënë me punë
□ *'Yes, sir, please. I have a note from Mr. Mont. 'Are you **at large**?... or have you any other occupation?' 'Not at present, sir.'* □ *Down upon the river that was black and thick with dye, some Coketown boys who were **at large**—a rare sight there—rowed a boat.*
3. në përgjithësi; në tërësi
□ *He talked **at large** on the problems of mankind.* □ *Shelton did not answer because he could not tell whether Berryman was addressing him or society **at large**.* □ *He had been out of touch with the Forsyte **at large** for twenty-six years.*

at last në fund, më në fund
□ *She looked for her purse in her handbag, then in her basket and all her pockets, and finally in the car, where **at last** she found it.* □ *At last we reached London.* □ *At last it seemed that all our troubles were at an end.*

at least së paku, të paktën
□ *She may be slow but **at least** she is reliable.* □ *You might **at least** have written to me.* □ *This trip will take three days **at least**.*

at leisure 1. me nge
□ *I'll take the report home and read it **at leisure**.*
2. me nge, i lirë, i pazënë
□ *I should like to have a few words*

*with you when you are **at leisure**.*
□ *They're seldom **at leisure**.*
at length 1. më në fund
□ *I tried for years to find a sponsor
for my invention but **at length** I
became discouraged and abandoned
the thing.* □ *We waited for hours, but
at length they arrived.* □ *At length,
my restlessness attained to such a
pitch that I hurried on my clothes and
went down-stairs.*
2. gjerë e gjatë, hollësisht, nga të
gjitha anët
□ *We discussed the problem **at great
length** before making a decision.* □
*The fourteen chapter of the Hand-
book deals **at some length** with the
special conditions and problems of
motorway driving.*
at liberty i lirë
□ *You are **at liberty** to come or go, as
you please.* □ *You are **at liberty** to say
what you like.* □ *I shall be **at liberty**
after midday, so come round to see
me then.* □ *He is very busy now, but he
will be **at liberty** presently.*
at long last më së fundi
□ *At long last they were buying a
home, they had been able to move
away from the factories of East End.*
at (the) most shumë-shumë, të shumtën
□ *I should say there were about 1,500
people present, or 2,000 **at the most**.*
□ *I'll only be away for a week **at the
most**—probably only four or five
days.* □ *We haven't much farther to
go—three miles **at most**.*
at once 1. menjëherë, në çast, aty për
aty
□ *June, her mind free from care, fell
asleep **at once**.* □ *I am leaving for
Rome almost **at once**.* □ *Soames
refused a drink and came **at once** to
the point.* □ *We began to search **at
once**, Mrs. Jarkis unlocking the*

*drawers and desks, and we all taking
out the papers.*
2. njëkohësisht, në të njëjtën kohë
□ *But it wasn't so much a cry as an
order; an order delivered in a voice
that was **at once** indulgent but firm.*
□ *The film is **at once** humorous and
moving.* □ *Don't all speak **at once**!*
at one's best në kulmin e vet, në formë
të shkëlqyer
□ *Chaplin was **at his best** playing the
little tramp.* □ *Daisy, if anything
should ever separate us, you must
think of me **at my best**.* □ *He was **at
his best** yesterday evening and kept
us all amused.*
at one's command nën urdhërat e
□ *I am here **at King's command**.*
at one's earliest convenience në
mundësinë më të parë, sa më shpejt
që të jetë e mundur
□ *Please deliver the goods **at your
earliest convenience**.* □ *Please send
the books **at your earliest convenience**.*
at one's ease rehat, qetë-qetë, lirshëm,
shpenguar, pa druajtje
□ *We'll leave you free this afternoon,
so you can explore the village **at your
ease**.* □ *'Why should I do all the
fetching and carrying, while you sit
there **at your ease**?' she complained.*
□ *Mr. Jack Maldon tried to be very
talkative, but was not **at his ease** and
made matters worse.*
at one's elbow afër, pranë, në krah
□ *Magnus, with Harran **at his elbow**,
prepared to depart.* □ *Didn't you
know him? He was **at your elbow**
during the entire performance.*
at one/a sitting në një herë të vetme,
pa ndërprerje; pa u ngritur nga vendi
□ *All members of the Committee
agreed that they would prefer to
stay on a little longer and finish their*

business **at one sitting.**
2. sakaq, aty për aty
□ *She asked me to knit her a sweater,
quite casually, as if it was something
I could do* **at one sitting.**
at one's last gasp 1. në grahmat e
fundit, në frymën e fundit
□ *The old man was virtually* **at his
last gasp.**
2. s'ka më frymë
□ *When the runner reached the tape
he was* **at his last gasp.**
at one's leisure në kohën e lirë
□ *When she had finished her breakfast, my aunt very deliberately leaned
back in her chair, knitted her brow,
folded her arms, and contemplated
me* **at her leisure** *with such a tired-
ness of attention that I was quite
overpowered by embarrassment.*
□ *She would have preferred the children to go ahead and leave her to
follow on* **at her leisure.**
at one's own risk me përgjegjësinë e
vet, duke vënë veten në rrezik
□ *Persons swimming beyond this
point do so* **at their own risk.** □ *Inexperienced climbers who attempt these
mountains should remember that they
are not doing so* **at their own risk**
*only, but at the risk of those who will
be called out to rescue them.* □ *These
regulations are made for your safety,
if you disobey them, you do so* **at your
risk.**
at one's peril duke vënë veten në
rrezik, duke rrezikuar veten
□ *The bicycle has no brakes—you
ride it* **at your own peril.** □ *'You'll go
on smoking* **at your peril,'** *the doctor
told my husband, but he was wasting
his time.*
at one's wits' end s'di nga t'ia mbajë,
s'di si t'ia bëjë, as në qiell as në tokë
□ *I shall have to find some money to*

pay my rent on Friday: I'm almost **at
my wits' end.** □ *Jurgis was* **at his wits'
end** *and he was in need of some
friends.* □ *Indeed, she seemed almost*
at her wit's end, *and as I set out
beside her half running, towards
Ward B, she kept on repeating, like a
lesson she had learned, while she
scurried along: 'I didn't do it. I didn't
do it.'*
at one time or another në një rast apo
në një tjetër
□ *The irrational guilt which they felt
for her distress could in some degree
be expiated by the panic that,* **at one
time or another,** *they all experienced
from her erratic driving.*
at present tani, në këtë çast
□ *'I would like to employ you if I
could,' the manager said,' 'but we
have no vacancies* **at present.** □ *I'm
afraid I can't help you just* **at present—I'm too busy.**
at random kuturu, në erë, në tym
□ *They chose the committee members
by picking some names* **at random**
from a list. □ *The terrorists fired into
the crowd* **at random.** □ *He spoke* **at
random.** □ *I wrote a long letter to
Peggotty, and asked her incidentally,
if she remembered, pretending that I
had heard of such a lady living at a
certain place I named* **at random**
*and was curious to know if it were
the same.*
at rest 1. në qetësi, në pushim; në
gjendje të palëvizur
□ *The sails of the windmill are now* **at
rest.** □ *He sat in his chair, still, but not*
at rest: *expectant evidently.*
2. në prehje, në paqe
□ *He lies* **at rest** *in a country churchyard.*
at second hand tërthorazi, nga burime
të tërthorta

□ *With regard to the world of female fashion and its customs, the present writer, of course, can only speak at second hand.* □ *Tell your wife you got into a fight last night. She'll probably get it at second hand from somebody else anyway, and she'll be all the more angry.*

at short notice pa paralajmërim; për një kohë të shkurtër

□ *The students had to prepare for the examination at very short notice.*

at sight me të parë; në shikimin e parë

□ *The sentry has orders to shoot at sight.* □ *If one of those renegades came prowling round my house, I'd shoot him at sight.* □ *We don't need a concert musician for this job, but we do need somebody who can play accompaniments at sight.*

at sb's bidding me urdhër të

□ *Remember, I only invited the boy on holiday at your bidding. I expect you to devote some of your time to entertaining him, not to leave it all to me.*

at somebody's discretion sipas gjykimit të, në bazë të gjykimit të

□ *A supplementary grant may be awarded at the discretion of the committee.* □ *I have made out a program of events for Sports Day, but do feel free to make any alterations at your discretion.*

at sb's disposal në dispozicion të

□ *Students have a well-stocked library at their disposal.* □ *The firm put a secretary at my disposal.*

at somebody's expense 1. në kurriz të, në dëm të

□ *They had a good laugh at Tom's expense.*

2. me shpenzimet e, me harxhet e

□ *We were entertained at the editor's expense.*

at somebody's hands në duart e

□ *Imagine a child suffering such cruelties at the hands of his own parents!* □ *But I am no beggar; I look for no favor at your hands.*

at (on) somebody's heels në gjurmët e, pas gjurmëve të

□ *The little man took up a candle and went to open the door. When he came back, Kit was at his heels.* □ *Between the brother and sister he remained in this posture, quite unresisting and passive, until Mr. Swiveller returned with a policeman at his heels.* □ *There is little use to describe these monotonous and perpetual westerly gales. One is very like another, and they follow so fast on one another's heels that the sea never has a chance to grow calm.*

at somebody's service në shërbim të

□ *If you need advice, I am at your service.*

at stake në rrezik

□ *His reputation was at stake.* □ *This decision puts our lives at stake.*

attach oneself to i ngjitem pas, i qepem pas

□ *A young man attached himself to me at the party and I couldn't get rid of him.* □ *A stray dog attached itself to me while I was walking and would not leave me.*

at that madje, bile, për më tepër

□ *He is not a manager; he is only a trainee, and a very poor one at that.* □ *This seems to me to be full of fallacies, and dangerous fallacies at that.*

at that (this) rate atëhere, po qe kështu, në rast të tillë, në kushte të tilla

□ *At this rate, we shall soon be bankrupt.* □ *'I did say to the babysitter that we'd be home in time to put the children in bed.' 'We should have left half an hour ago at that rate. Why didn't you say so earlier?'*

at the back of beyond në fund të botës
□ *They live somewhere at the back of beyond.* □ *I just can't understand this craze for buying up derelict cottages at the back of beyond, and cutting oneself off from everything and everyone.*

at the back of one's mind në mendje, në kokë
□ *At the back of his mind was the vague idea that he had met her before.*

at the best of times në momentet më të mira
□ *Life on a river barge was, at the best of times, uncomfortable and monotonous.*

at the drop of a hat menjëherë, aty për aty, sakaq, pa vonesë, në rastin më të parë
□ *You can't expect me to move my home at the drop of a hat.* □ *You ask him to sing, he'll do it at the drop of a hat.*

at the eleventh hour në çastin e fundit, në minutën e fundit
□ *The president's visit was called off at the eleventh hour.* □ *The condemned man was pardoned at the eleventh hour, just as he was about to be executed.* □ *The newspaper at the eleventh hour inserted an imported news item in its front page.*

at the end of në fund të
□ *I'm at the end of my patience.*

at the end of one's tether në fund të durimit, fuqisë etj.
□ *I've been looking after four young children all day and I really am at the end of my tether.* □ *Sir Patric Cullen is more than twenty years older, not yet quite at the end of his tether, but near it and resigned to it.*

□ *The children misbehaved all day, so that by dinner time she was at the end of her tether.*

at the latest jo më vonë se
□ *Passengers should check in one hour before their flight time at the latest.* □ *Be here on Monday at the latest.*

at the moment tani, në këtë moment
□ *The number is engaged at the moment.* □ *He's unemployed at the moment and has been for six months.*

at the outside shumë-shumë, të shumtën, jo më shumë se
□ *With tips I can earn $ 150 a week, at the very outside.* □ *There were only twenty people there at the outside.*

at the risk of duke rrezikuar
□ *The men may grumble about their conditions of work, but are they prepared to make an open protest at the risk of losing their jobs altogether?*
□ *Even when dislodged, he still kept the letter in his mouth and on my endeavouring to take it from him, at the imminent risk of being bitten, he kept it between his teeth.*

at the same time 1. në të njëjtën kohë, njëkohësisht
□ *You can't watch television and do your homework at the same time.* □ *She was laughing and crying at the same time.*

2. megjithatë; në të njëjtën kohë
□ *I was deeply moved. Yet at the same time I took the thing with a grain of salt.* □ *I'll forgive you, at the same time you must never do it again.*

at the top of one's voice në kupë të qiellit, me sa ka në kokë, me sa fuqi që ka
□ *It was left to Jakob and me to go to the rescue of the Beagle who was lashing about in the undergrowth, screaming at the top of his voice.*

18

□ *Here you are talking **at the top of
your voice**, scandalizing the whole
neighbourhood.*

at (the) worst në rastin më të keq

□ *It's not a serious offence; he'll
probably get a warning or, **at worst**, a
light fine.* □ *I don't think this cake will
be as good as the last one I baked for
you, but it'll be eatable **at worst**.*

at times nganjëherë, në ndonjë rast

□ *Robert and I got on each other's
nerves **at times**.* □ *She felt **at times** as
if she could cry out and make such
a row that someone could come to
her aid.*

at variance with në kundërshtim me

□ *The information you have given is
at variance with what I have been
told by other people.* □ *The shock of
such an event happening so suddenly,
and happening to one **with** whom I
had been in any aspect **at variance** ...
this is easily intelligible to any one.*

at war with në luftë me

□ *The country has been **at war with**
its neighbour for two years.*

at will sipas dëshirës, sipas qejfit

□ *The animals are allowed to wander
at will in the park.* □ *The sergeant
gave the command for the soldiers to
fire **at will**.* □ *Discipline was non-
existent. Students roamed about the
campus **at will**, as if there had never
been such a thing as a timetable.*

attempt the impossible orvatem të bëj
të pamundurën

□ *'You're **attempting the impossible**
if you think you're going to reform a
hardened character like him.'*

augur ill/well for ka shenja të këqia/të
mira; ka shenja ogurzeza/ogurbardha

□ *The quality of your work **augurs
well for** the examinations next month.*
□ *John and Mary have started quarrelling already. That doesn't **augur***

well for their future happiness. □ *The
arrival of our crack troops in the
battle area **augurs ill for** the enemy.*

avail oneself of shfrytëzoj, përfitoj

□ *You must **avail yourself of** every
opportunity to speak English.* □ *I
went down, with a book in my hand,
to **avail myself**, for half an hour, of
his permission.* □ *The means of which
he **availed himself** to achieve his
ends were not beyond criticism.*

avenge oneself on (for) hakmerrem,
marr hakun

□ *He swore to **avenge himself on** his
enemy **for** the insult that had been
offered to his name and reputation.*
□ *She **avenged herself on** her father's
killers.* □ *The young king **avenged** his
father's murder **on** the conspirators.*

average out (at) është, rezulton,
përllogaritet mesatarisht

□ *The rainfall for the period under
review **averaged out at** about three
inches a month.* □ *Our speed averaged out at 40 miles an hour.*

avoid sb/sth like the plague ruhet,
shmanget si djalli nga temjani, i
shmanget me çdo kusht dikujt a
diçkaje

□ *He's been **avoiding me like the
plague** since our quarrel.* □ *I don't
know whether I've unintentionally
offended her or whether somebody
has turned her against me, but she
has certainly been **avoiding me like
the plague** for the last six months.*

awake(n) to sth kuptoj, jam i
ndërgjegjshëm, i vetëdijshëm për
diçka

□ *Are you fully **awake to** the danger
you're in?* □ *It's time you **awoke to**
the realities of the situation.*

awaken sb to sth ndërgjegjësoj

□ *We must try to **awaken** society **to**
the dangers of drugs.*

B

babe in arms, a foshnjë në pelena (në shpërgënj), foshnjë e pamëkëmbur; njeri i pafajshëm, i pambrojtur
□ *I am not a babe in arms. I am entitled to go out for a walk by myself if I want to.*

back and forth para e prapa, poshtë e lartë
□ *He travels back and forth to the United States at least once a week.* □ *Pulleys slide back and forth on the construction site.* □ *The pendulum swung back and forth.*

back away from sth tërhiqem, zmbrapsem, zbythem
□ *As the men at the bar reached for their guns, the onlookers backed away.* □ *The child backed away from the big dog.*

back down tërhiqem, heq dorë, lëshoj pe
□ *After being confronted with our evidence, the other side had to back down.* □ *Even those who seemed to have good reason to criticize have backed down.* □ *I see he has backed down from the position he took last week.*

back out/out of tërhiqem, heq dorë, nuk i përmbahem më
□ *Once you have given your word, don't try to back out.* □ *You can't back out now. A deal is a deal.* □ *Arthur said he would help me, but soon he backed out.*

back up 1. mbështes, përkrah
□ *Andy backed me up wholeheartedly as he always did.* □ *Bill is expecting us to back him up at the meeting tomorrow.*

backward(s) and forward(s) lart e poshtë, poshtë e përpjetë, tutje-tëhu, para mbrapa
□ *He began to pace backward and forward on the bridge.* □ *The last of the old Forsytes was on his feet, moving with the most impressive slowness, backward and forward between the foot of his bed and the window.* □ *He began to sway backwards and forwards in his chair, feverishly flicking his short fingers.*

bad blood between A and B armiqësi, ndjenja armiqësore mes
□ *There has been bad blood between those two families for generations.* □ *There had been bad blood between them for so long that neither was willing to make the first friendly approaches.* □ *The unfair distribution of their father's wealth made for bad blood between the brothers.*

bad egg, a njeri i poshtër, njeri i keq, maskara; njeri i pabesë
□ *Their nephew, who was a real bad egg, got his hands on nearly all the old couple's savings on the pretext that he would buy them a little place in the country.* □ *I would never trust Brown: he's a bad egg.*

bad/good form sjellje e pahijshme/e hijshme; është keq/mirë
□ *He should not have kept his guests waiting: it's very bad form.* □ *In some parts of the world it is considered quite good form to belch after food-it shows proper appreciation.*

bad/poor hand at sth dorëngathët, s'i vjen ndoresh

□ *'Well, Mr. Cherrell, what would you do?' 'I am a **poor hand** at advice.'* □ *I know I don't express myself properly; I'm a **bad hand** at sentimentality.* □ *'Your father is such a **poor hand at** business', she went on, 'and gets so worried at times.'*

bad luck on sb fat i keq për

□ *'I didn't get that job after all.' 'What **bad luck**! But I suppose you'll be looking around again.'* □ *If her husband couldn't get away at that time of year, she thought, well, **bad luck on** him, but she wasn't going to lose the opportunity of a trip abroad.*

badly off në gjendje të vështirë financiare, jam ngushtë (financiarisht)

□ *We shouldn't complain about being poor—many families are much **worse off** than we are.*

bad news travels fast lajmi i keq merr dheun

□ ***Bad news**, it is said, **travels fast**.* □ *The accident happened at five o'clock. By half past five everyone in the village knew about it. **Bad news travels fast**!*

bag and baggage me laçkë e me plaçkë, me tesha e kotesha

□ *His landlady couldn't tell the police where he might be. All she knew was that he'd left, **bag and baggage**, without paying the rent.* □ *I can't understand why Ted puts up with a drunken brother-in-law in his house. Most people would have turned him out, **bag and baggage**, long ago.*

bag of bones, a kockë e lëkurë, i numërohen brinjët

□ *The cat had not been fed for weeks and was just **a bag of bones**.* □ *I'm glad to see you putting on weight again. You were just **a bag of bones** when you came back from hospital.*

baker's dozen, a trembëdhjetë

□ *Mrs. Joe has been out a dozen times, looking for you, Pip. And she's out now, making it **a baker's dozen**.*

bandy sth about qarkulloj, kaloj gojë më gojë

□ *The stories being **banded about** are completely false.* □ *They are **bandying** his name **about** a good deal.*

bandy words with bëj, shkëmbej fjalë me

□ *I don't propose to waste my time **bandying words with** you!* □ *I am not going to **bandy words**, I require you to give up this friendship.*

bang into sb/sth përplasem me

□ *He ran round the corner and **banged** straight **into** a lamp-post.*

bang one's head against a brick wall i bie murit me kokë

□ *Don't try to persuade him—you'll just be **banging your head against a brick wall**: he'll never change.* □ *'Can't you see that he has no intention of paying you back? You're **banging your head against a brick wall**.'*

bank on sb/sth mbështetem, shpresoj, var shpresat

□ *Bill is **banking on** Bob to lend him the money he needs.* □ *Don't **bank on** fine weather for the weekend—it's going to rain!* □ *Those brakes can't be **banked on** if we have to pull up suddenly.*

bar the door to i mbyll derën, nuk pranoj

□ *The club decided to **bar the door** to anyone who did not live locally.*

bargain away shes; sakrifikoj; braktis

□ *They've **bargained away** in a few*

21

minutes privileges which took us many years to secure. □ *The leaders* **bargained away** *the freedom of their people.*

bargain for sth pres, parashikoj, shpresoj
□ *When Mary offered to look after her neighbour's four children, she got more than she* **bargained for!** □ *We didn't exactly* **bargain for** *him turning up like that, out of the blue.*

barge in/into hyj, ndërhyj në mënyrë të pahijshme
□ *I tried to stop him coming through the door but he just* **barged** *his way* **in.** □ *'Why must you always come* **barging into** *the conversation.*

bark up the wrong tree gaboj adresë, i bie më qafë, i ngarkoj një faj padrejtësisht
□ *If the police think I was mixed up in the train robbery, they're* **barking up the wrong tree.**

□ *And what you call the black-market... it's now an integral part of our national life. But if you infer from what I have said that Swintons is tangled up in a network of trifling illegal transactions, you're* **barking up the wrong tree.**

base on/upon bazoj, mbështet
□ *His success in business is* **based on** *a shrewd assessment of what the customer want.* □ *This novel is* **based on** *historical facts.* □ *I* **base** *my hopes* **on** *the good news I had yesterday.*

be afraid for sb/sth kam frikë, kam shqetësim për
□ *Parents are* **afraid for** *the safety of their children.*

be afraid of sb/sth kam frikë nga
□ *There's nothing to* **be afraid of.**
□ *He's* **afraid of** *nothing and nobody.*

be afraid of doing sth kam frikë të
□ *I didn't mention it because I was*

afraid of upsetting him. □ *She* **was** *afraid of falling ill and having to go to the hospital again.*

be afraid of one's own shadow ka frikë nga hija e vet
□ *The government may have only a slim majority of votes, but that does not explain why it* **is** *so ineffectual and so* **afraid of its own self.**

be afraid (that) më vjen keq
□ *I'm* **afraid** *we can't come.* □ *I'm* **afraid** *you're wrong. The quotation is from Milton not from Shakespeare.*

be all at sea jam tym, e kam kokën (mendjen) tym (lëmsh), jam fare i hutuar
□ *'But what are you up to generally? What are you doing with your life?' 'I'm at sea', she said at last.'* □ *I'm* **all at sea.** *I've no idea how to repair cars.*

bear a grudge against sb e kam inat dikë
□ *I once beat him in a competition and he's* **borne a grudge against** *me ever since.* □ *Ever since the terrible illness of his daughter, he had* **borne** *Renwick* **a** *bitter* **grudge** *for the aspersions made during that memorable interview when he had refused to assist his daughter in the crisis of her pneumonia.*

bear/stand comparison with krahasohet, ka krahasim
□ *That's a good dictionary, but it does not* **bear comparison with** *this one.*

bear fruit jep fryt, ka (jep) rezultat
□ *I've tried dozens of ways to make him change his mind, but none of them have* **borne fruit** *so far.* □ *Our improved methods and modern machines are already* **bearing fruit** *in the shape of increased output and better staff relations.*

bear/keep sb/sth in mind kam parasysh

□ *We have no vacancies now, but we'll* **bear** *your application in* **mind**. □ *Please* **bear in mind** *that we don't know any Mr. Hawthorne.* □ *Three factors must be* **borne in** **mind**.

bear resemblance ngjan, shëmbëllen, ka ngjashmëri

□ *Your story* **bears resemblance** *to the facts.* □ *He* **bore** *no* **resemblance** *to the smart coachman of a successful doctor.* □ *Tennessee Williams' own character* **bears no resemblance to** *the people depicted in his plays.*

bear the brunt of sth mbaj peshën kryesore

□ *Winifred—a plucky woman who had* **borne the brunt of** *him for exactly twenty-one years, had never really believed that he would do what he now did.* □ *They* **bore the brunt of** *the attack.*

bear witness to dëshmoj

□ *The village* **bore** *silent* **witness to** *the passage of the cyclone.* □ *I did my best for him, and you can* **bear witness to** *that.*

beat about the bush ia sjell (ia bie, ia hedh) fjalën rrotull (larg e larg)

□ *Stop* **beating about the bush**: *tell me directly why you have come to see me.* □ *'I won't* **beat about the bush**,' *said the general suddenly. 'You seem to have got my daughter into a mess.'*

be at a loose hand/be at loose ends jam i lirë, kam kohë të lirë, s'jam i zënë me punë

□ *Come and see us if you're* **at a loose end**.

be at a loss jam i hutuar, humb toruan (fillin), s'di nga t'ia mbaj, s'di ç'të bëj (ç'të them)

□ *I'm* **at a loss** *what to do next.* □ *The*

question *was so unexpected that, for a moment, Arthur was* **at a loss** *how to reply.* □ *Mr. Jonas was evidently disconcerted, and* **at a loss** *how to proceed.*

beat a retreat largohem, tërhiqem, prapsem

□ *When he saw that his former girlfriend was at the party, he* **beat a swift retreat**. □ *The poacher* **beat a hasty retreat** *when he saw the police coming.*

be at home in sth ndihem lirshëm, ndihem i familjarizuar me, njoh mirë

□ *That kind of acting had been rendered familiar to him by long practice and he was quite* **at home** *it.* □ *He is* **at home** *in many foreign languages, which he speaks fluently.* □ *She was at* **home** *with everybody in the place.* □ *In less than a fortnight I was quite* **at home** *and happy among my new companions.*

be at loggerheads with sb grindem, kam mosmarrëveshje me

□ *He and his wife are always* **at loggerheads**. □ *They* **are at loggerheads** *on the problem of where the students' cars should be parked.*

be at odds with sb kam grindje, kam mosmarrëveshje me

□ *The two lectures were* **at odds** *over the best way of teaching the students.* □ *They're constantly* **at odds** *with each other.*

beat one's brains vras mendjen

□ *I've been* **beating my brains** *all evening, trying to think of an excuse for not going to Martin's wedding.*

beat one's breast rrah gjoksin, i bie gjoksit me grushte

□ *She wanted to* **beat her breast** *and scream but fought down the rising wave of hysteria.*

be at sixes and sevens jam rrëmujë, lesh e li

□ *There's a regular shindy in the house; and everything **at sixes and sevens**.* □ *I'm doing my level best, but everything **is at sixes and sevens**.*

beat sb black and blue zhdëp në dru, rrah paq, ia bëri kurrizin më të butë se barku, ia zbuti kurrizin

□ *His father lost his temper and **beat him black e blue**.*

beat sb hollow mund thellë, mund në të gjitha drejtimet

□ *We thought it would be a close match, but, in fact, the challenger was **beaten hollow**.* □ *I played Tony at chess last night and **beat him hollow**.*

be at sb's beck and call jam gati për çdo gjë, jam lepe peqe, i rri qiri më këmbë dikujt, i rri më këmbë

□ *He seems to think that all I have to do is **be at his beck and call** all day.* □ *He had many influential newspapers, corporations, banks and the like **at his beck and call**.*

beat the air rrah ujë në havan

□ *Aren't you **beating the air**, Blythe? Is it any good telling a man who's lost a lung, that which he wants is a new one?* □ *These men labor harder than other men—result nil. This is literally **beating the air**.*

beat the drum i bie daulles së, bëhem tellall i, shkoj pas avazit të, trumbetoj (reklamoj) me të madhe

□ *It has been noticed that when a newspaper of a certain type lights on an incident which enables it at once to exhibit virtue and **beat the drum** of its own policy, it will exploit that incident without regard to the susceptibility of individuals.*

beat time to sth ruaj, mbaj tempin (ritmin)

□ *He **beat time** to the music with his fingers.* □ *The teacher played the tune, while the children **beat time** with their pencils on the desks.*

be badly off for sth ka nevojë për, është ngushtë për

□ *The refugees **are badly off for** blankets, and even worse off for food.*

be better off doing sth bën mirë

□ *He'd **be better off** going to the police about it.*

be better off without sb/sth do të ishim më mirë pa

□ *We'd **be better off without** them as neighbours.*

be beyond sb është e pakuptueshme, e paimagjinueshme

□ *It's **beyond me** why she wants to marry Tom.* □ *How people design computer games **is beyond me**.*

bed of roses, a fushë me lule, kopsht (bahçe) me lule.

□ *We had a terrible struggle to survive when we were young: life certainly wasn't **a bed of roses**.* □ *A parochial life is not **a bed of roses**.*

be down on one's luck jam fatkeq, jam në mjerim (në fatkeqësi)

□ *They say that, Mrs. Crawley **was** particularly **down on her luck**, she gave concerts and lessons in music here and there.* □ *When I see a mangy cat or a dog that's lost, or a fellow-creature **down on his luck**, I always try to put myself in his place.*

before one can say Jack Robinson sa hap e mbyll sytë, në çast

□ *The equipage dashed forward and **before you could say Jack Robinson**, with a rattle and flourish drew up at Soames's door.* □ *I mentioned to the boys that there was a bag of sweets on the table, and, **before you could say Jack Robinson**, they were all eaten.*

□ *Let me fetch your newspaper for you. It's no trouble to run down to the shop—I'll be there and back again before you can say Jack Robinson.*

before one's very eyes para syve të
□ *'Ladies and gentlemen! Before your very eyes I will cut this man in half,' said the magician.*

before one knows where he is aty për aty, në çast, sa hap e mbyll sytë
□ *'Hurry, doctor. We'll have this roof down before we know where we are.'*

before one's time para kohës së vet, tepër i avancuar për kohën
□ *Although he lived a long time ago, it is only recently that many of Robert Owens's ideas have been accepted; he was really before his time.*

beggar description është vështirë të përshkruhet, është i papërshkrueshëm, s'përshkruhet dot me fjalë
□ *The scene at the reception was so impressive that it completely beggars description.* □ *I was accustomed to scenes of misery and squalor but the conditions in which the refugees were forced to live beggared all description.* □ *The spectacle was so dazzlingly beautiful that it beggared description.*

beggars can't be choosers kalit të dhuruar nuk i shihen dhëmbët, lypsari s'mund të zgjedhë
□ *The people made homeless by the floods will have to take whatever accommodation is offered to them; beggars can't be choosers.*

behind bars në burg
□ *The murderer is now safely behind bars.* □ *The criminal spent twenty years behind bars.*

behind closed doors me dyer të mbyllura
□ *We don't know what they are planning, all the meetings have taken place behind closed doors.* □ *But while the rows over oil are headline news, the fights over coffee tend to take place behind closed doors.*

behind sb's back prapa shpinës së dikujt, prapa krahëve të dikujt
□ *'Don't trust him, he will be pleasant to you face-to-face, and then criticise you behind your back.* □ *They enjoyed talking about him behind his back.* □ *It will be a bit of a job arranging it all behind her back, but we should manage.*

behind the scenes në prapaskenë; nën rrogoz
□ *On the first night there was a great deal of frantic activity and improvisation behind the scenes when it was realised that the costumes had been mislaid.* □ *Those were political deals done behind the scenes.*

behind the times prapa botës, prapa dynjasë
□ *We shall have to introduce some new methods: we are very much behind the times.*

behind time vonë, me vonesë
□ *The plane was an hour behind time.* □ *He's always behind time with the rent.*

be in love with sb dua, dashuroj
□ *They're very much in love with each other.* □ *I'm madly in love with her.*

be in love with sth pëlqej, dashurohem me
□ *He's in love with the sound of his own voice.*

be in the dark s'kam dijeni për, s'jam në dijeni të
□ *And so the news was out. Mrs. Tremaine threw up her hands and forgot her fears in her annoyance at being left in the dark.* □ *...Trench and I were putting our heads together*

over the letter just now; and there certainly were one or two points on which we **were** *a little* **in the dark**.

be in the same boat (box) në kushte të njëjta, në pozitë të njëjtë

□ *She and I* **are in the same boat**: *we both failed the exam.* □ *It's no less than natural he should keep dark: so would you and me* **be in the same box**.

believe in sb/sth besoj në

□ *Prissie gave an excited laugh. 'Oh! One doesn't really* **believe in** *ghosts, does one?'* □ *You can* **believe in** *him; he'll never let you down.* □ *He* **believes** *very strongly* **in** *female emancipation.*

believe it or not daç besoje, daç mos e beso

□ **Believe it or not**, *we were left waiting in the rain for two hours.* □ *You know,* **believe it or not** *you've got a funny kind of resemblance to a bloke I once knew in London.*

believe (you) me më beso

□ **Believe you me**, *the government won't meddle with the tax system.* □ *You think too little of that boy, you know.* **Believe you me**, *he won't do too badly.*

(not) believe one's ears/eyes nuk u besoj veshëve (syve)

□ *I could hardly* **believe my ears** *when I heard that Davis had married again.*

(not) believe a word of sth s'besoj asnjë fjalë nga

□ *I've had no trouble myself from any phone calls. Between ourselves, I think it's all made up. I don't* **believe a word of** *what they say.*

belong to i takon, i përket

□ *He has never* **belonged to** *a trade union.* □ *This land does not* **belong to** *university.*

below/under one's breath nën zë, me zë të ulët

□ *What are you muttering there* **below your breath**, *Simpson? If you don't agree with what I've been suggesting, kindly speak up and give us all the benefit of your opinion.* □ *When the workman was told the small amount that he was to be paid, he muttered something* **below his breath**.

below par jo aq mirë, nën gjendjen mesatare

□ *I'm feeling a bit* **below par** *today.* □ *What with his anxiety about Fleur and his misgivings about the public eye, he was sleeping badly, eating little, and feeling* **below par**.

below standard nën standartin e kërkuar

□ *Their work is* **below standard**.

beneath one's dignity s'është në dinjitetin e

□ *Some husbands still think it is* **beneath their dignity** *to do the shopping.* □ *It should be* **beneath your dignity** *to reply to such a remark.*

beneath one's notice jashtë vëmendjes së, s'meriton vëmendjen e

□ *He regarded all these administrative details as* **beneath his notice**. □ *Donald was such a conceited man that he considered much of what others accomplished quite* **beneath his notice**.

be of the opinion that kam mendimin se

□ *I'm* **of the opinion that** *he is right.*

be of use hyn në punë

□ *These maps might* **be of use** *to you on your trip.*

be on tenter-hooks rri varur, jam (rri) si mbi gjemba

□ *We were kept* **on tenter-hooks** *for hours while the judges were deciding the winners.*

be on the go jam në lëvizje
□ *I've been on the go all week.* □ *He's been on the go ever since daybreak.* □ *Her real faith—what was it? Not to let a friend down; to do things differently from other people; to be always on the go; not to be stuffy.*

be on the look-out for sb/sth jam (rri) syhapët, rri, (qëndroj) në përgjim, ruaj, survejoj, përgjoj, hap sytë
□ *Police will be on the look-out for trouble-makers at today's match.* □ *Here's the Sewer! Here's the wide awake Sewer, always on the look-out, the leading journal of the United States.*

be quits with sb jam fit e fit me, lahem me
□ *Are we quits or do you still owe me a pound?* □ *He caused me to lose my job; if I can make him lose his job, then I'll be quits with him.*

beside oneself with sth çmendem, tërbohem
□ *When Jack discovered that his new car had been damaged, he was beside himself with rage.* □ *He was beside himself with rage when he saw the mess.* □ *He was beside himself with joy.*

beside the point jashtë teme
□ *His comments were quite beside the point; the discussion was about wages, but he kept talking about prices.* □ *What you say may be true enough, but it is beside the point.*

bet sb anything/what he likes that vë bast me se të duash se
□ *I bet you anything you like we won't get an invitation to the wedding.* □ *Bet you what you like he won't come.*

bet one's bottom dollar on sth that vë bast me gjithçka

□ *'I bet you that the day after tomorrow by this time Mummy will be back.' 'What will you bet?' 'I'll bet my bottom dollar.'* □ *'I don't think the shopkeeper meant to cheat us.' 'I'll bet my bottom dollar he did—probably thought we were in too much of a hurry to count our change.'*

better late than never më mirë vonë se kurrë
□ *Come along in. I'm sorry you had such a journey, but better late than never.* □ *The manager was not pleased when John turned up late, but all he said was, 'Better late than never.'*

between ourselves/between you and me/between you, me and the bed/gate/lamp-post mes nesh
□ *Between you and me, I think this matter has been very badly handled.* □ *And between you and me and the post sir, it will be a very nice portrait too.*

between the devil and the deep blue sea mes dy zjarreve, keq andej e keq këtej
□ *His enemy was close behind him, and the bridge over the ravine was rotten and swaying. Caught between the devil and the deep blue sea, he hesitated.* □ *If the explores went forward, they faced new dangers; if they went back, their mission had failed: they were between the devil and the deep blue sea.*

between two fires mes dy zjarreve
□ *The enemy troops were encircled in a tight ring. Finding themselves between two fires they had to surrender.*

betwixt and between diçka ndërmjet
□ *'Are you glad or sorry your husband hasn't been posted abroad?' 'Sort of betwixt and between, really.'*

□ *The color of the ribbon was* **betwixt and between** *neither blue nor green, but something of both.* □ *'And you should be a Whig?' '***Betwixt and between,***' said I, not to annoy him.*

be up to sb 1. kërkohet, është detyra e
□ *It's* **up to** *us to help those in need.*
□ *It's not* **up to** *you to tell me how to do my job.*
2. varet nga, është në dorën e
□ *An Indian or a Chinese meal? It's* **up to** *you.*

beyond (all) measure pa masë, jashtë mase
□ *He fascinates me* **beyond measure.**
□ *My friends and I are grateful to you* **beyond measure** *for your kindness.*
□ *It's natural for parents to love their children, and Richard's nice enough, but his father dotes on him* **beyond all measure.**

beyond (all) question pa dyshim
□ *The result of this additional inspection was to convince Mr. Swiveller that the objects by which he was surrounded were real, and that he saw them* **beyond all question** *with his waking eyes.*

beyond belief i pabesueshëm
□ *His behavior is outrageous: some of the things he has done are* **beyond belief.** □ *Imagine these Pyramids being built by physical labor alone! It's almost* **beyond belief.**

beyond compare i pakrahasueshëm, i pakundshoq, s'krahasohet, s'ka të krahasuar
□ *She's lovely* **beyond compare.**

beyond dispute jashtë çdo diskutimi, jashtë çdo dyshimi, pa diskutim
□ *Her courage is* **beyond all dispute.**
□ *This is* **beyond dispute** *the best book on the subject.* □ *It is* **beyond dispute** *that she is correct in her conclusion.*

beyond doubt pa asnjë dyshim, pa pikë dyshimi
□ *She was* **beyond** *all* **doubt** *the finest ballerina of her day.* □ *What he said is absolutely true; it is* **beyond doubt.**
□ *The truth of the story is* **beyond doubt.**

beyond one's ken jashtë sferës së njohurive të
□ *The workings of the Stock Exchange are* **beyond** *most people's ken.*

beyond one's reach 1. nuk ia arrin dora
□ *The shelf is so high it is well* **beyond my reach.**
2. që s'e kupton, që s'e merr vesh, që s'ia kap mendja
□ *She sat very still, her face hard above the baby's. And the young man, aware of thoughts* **beyond his reach,** *got up.*

beyond the pale jashtë caqeve (kufijve) të pranuar nga pikëpamja shoqërore
□ *Those remark he made were quite* **beyond the pale.** □ *Harry's rude behaviour at dinner last night was* **beyond the pale.** □ *Without one overt act of hostility, one upbraiding word, he contrived to impress me momently with the conviction that I was put* **beyond the pale** *of his favor.*

bid fair to do sth duket, ka sy, ka të ngjarë, i ka të gjitha ngjasat
□ *It* **bids fair to** *be a nice day.* □ *Our scheme for building a new community center* **bids fair to** *succeed.* □ *This year's meeting* **bids fair to** *be the largest we've ever had.*

bid sb goodbye përshëndetem
□ *We have just called in to* **bid** *you* **goodbye** *and to thank you for all you have done to make our holiday so pleasant.* □ *Have you* **bidden** *the children* **goodbye?**

bide one's time pres çastin, kohën e përshtatshme
□ *We have decided not to start the expedition yet; we shall **bide our time** until the weather conditions are right.* □ *'I don't think you should let the house go for that price,' the agent said. 'If you are prepared to **bide your time** I'm sure I could get a higher price.'*

big cheese/shot/wheel/wig njeri me peshë, njeri me zë, njeri me shumë rëndësi
□ *Here comes **the big cheese** himself. Have you got the red carpet out?* □ *Make sure you keep friendly with that chap: he's a **big shot** in the Civil Service.*

big head mendjemadh, mburravec
□ *I get tired listening to that **big head** talking: he is always boasting about the wonderful things he has done.*

big talk/words mburrje, lëvdata, fjalë të mëdha
□ *I've heard a lot of **big talk** from her about other members of her family than never came to anything.*

bind sb hand and foot lidh këmbë e duar
□ *A trader who becomes an authorized distributor of a product may soon find that he has agreed to the conditions of sale that **bind** him **hand and foot**.* □ *They **bound** him **hand and foot** and placed a gag in his mouth.*

bird's-eye view, a pamje fluturimthi; vë-shtrim i shpejtë, pamje e përgjithshme
□ *I had not realized how very indented the coastline was until I had a **bird's-eye view** of it in my first trip in a glider.* □ *In my opening lecture I propose to give you a **bird's-eye view** of 19th Century American literature.*

birds of a feather buka e një mielli, nga një brumë, të një kallëpi
□ *He has conspired against me like the rest, and they are but **birds of one feather**.* □ *His expenses were two pence a day for food and four pence for his bed in a café full of other **birds of his feather**.* □ *It's only natural that Martin, being lazy, should mix with other lazy students: **birds of a feather flock together**.*

bit by bit 1. pak e nga pak, ca nga ca, dalëngadalë
□ *If I had nothing else to do I could get this garden in order in a couple of weeks. As it is, doing it **bit by bit**, it may take me the whole summer.* □ *Bit by bit, feeling cautiously for holds and trying not to panic, he hauled himself out of the crevasse.*
2. pjesë-pjesë
□ *The only way to tackle one of these plastic model kits is to assemble it **bit by bit**, following the instructions carefully.* □ *Bit by bit a complete picture was built up of the murderer's movements up to the moment of crime.*

bite off more than one can chew shtrij këmbët më shumë se kam jorganin, e bëj vrapin jo sa e kam hapin
□ *'You've **bitten off more than you can chew**,' said my brother, when he saw the trouble I was having with my business.* □ *I'm trying to study for a degree while doing my normal work, and I'm afraid I may have **bitten more than I can chew**.*

bite one's lip kafshoj buzën, ha buzën me dhëmbë
□ *'You watch your language, or I'll have you in the office.' Joe **bit his lip** and said no more for a while.* □ *She walked up and down, **biting her lip** and thinking desperately hard.* □ *At the thought of Fergus hurrying home*

to an invalid wife, Brigit bit her lip and turned her head on the pillow.

bite one's tongue kafshoj gjuhën
□ *I had no sooner made the remark than I could have **bitten my tongue**.* □ *It was a stupid thing to say, I could **bite my tongue** whenever I think of it.*

bite/kiss the dust 1. bie i vdekur, ha dhe
□ *There was some shooting and two men **bit the dust**. □ Squire and Gray fired again. Two had **bit the dust**, one had fled.*
2. dështon, hidhet poshtë
□ *It looks as if the plan to build a new school library has **bitten the dust**.*

bite the hand that feeds one shkel bukën me këmbë, tregohem mosmirënjohës, ia kthej të mirën me të keqe
□ *I started Jones off on his career and now that he is successful, he won't even speak to me—talk about **biting the hand that feeds you**! □ And we are astonished that Mr. Mackay, who in the past enjoyed our hospitality, should turn around and **bite the hands that fed him** by lending himself to the exploitation of a chimera.*

bits and bobs/bits and pieces çikërrima
□ *And he felt in his pocket and pulled our all that was inside, throwing the handful of **bits and bobs** on the table.* □ *I started to collect wood for my shed and all those **bits and pieces** that I thought might come in handy for the flat.*

bitter pill (for sb) to swallow, a kafshatë (pilulë) e hidhur të kapërdihet, gjë e papëlqyer të pranohet
□ *Defeat in the election was a **bitter pill for him to swallow**. □ Poor old Morgan: he has been dismissed to*

*make room for a younger man—it's a **bitter pill for him to swallow**.*

black day for sb, a ditë e zezë për
□ *The **blackest day** I can remember was in the great storm of '52 when three of our boats went down together. □ If your superiors take the same hopeless attitude as you do, Eliot, it will be a **black day** for this country.*

blacken sb's name/character nxij (njollos) emrin, figurën morale të
□ *Some of the press reports amount to **blacken the character** of someone who is still a highly respected public figure. □ Then **their names** were **blackened** in sensational media coverage.*

black out 1. errësoj
□ *The room has been completely **blacked out**.*
2. humb vetëdijen
□ *The plane dived suddenly, causing the pilot to **black out**. □ I had a fight with the man, and after it I **blacked out**.*

blacken the picture nxij, njollos realitetin; shtrembëroj të vërtetën
□ *Sometimes Wormold felt a tinge of jealousy towards Paul and he tried to **blacken the picture**! 'He gets through a bottle of whisky a day,' he said.*

blame the other fellow ia hedh fajin një tjetri
□ *Unfortunately it is a common human failing to **blame the other fellow** when something is not done that everyone agrees ought to be done. □ Face up to the fact that you simply aren't capable of handling the business, will you, and stop **blaming the other fellow**.*

blank check çek i bardhë
□ *When the millionaire was building*

*the new house, he practically gave the architect a **blank check.***

blast sth away/down/in shpërthej me lëndë plasëse

□ *The explosion **blasted** the door **in.***

blaze a trail çaj rrugë (udhë, shtigje) të reja (të pashkelura)

□ *By using revolutionary new methods, the young engineer **blazed a trail** which others could follow.* □ *Antiseptic treatments have been greatly refined and improved since Lister's day, but it was he who **blazed the trail** with his use of carbolic acid spray during surgical operations.*

blaze away qëlloj parreshtur (me artileri)

□ *Our gunners kept **blazing away** at the enemy.* □ *The boys **blazed away** with their airguns until the tin can was full of holes.*

blaze up 1. shpërthen në flakë

□ *The fire **blazed up** when he added paraffin.*

2. inatoset, merr flakë shpejt

□ *He **blazed up** without warning.*

bleed sb white i piu (i thithi) gjakun, e shfrytëzon pa mëshirë

□ *He **bled** them **white** with his demands for more and still more money.* □ *For thirty years on end he had **bled** his men **white**. He was an old scoundrel.*

blind alley, a qorrsokak, rrugë (udhë) qorre

□ *He took the next turning to the left as had been told, but found himself in a **blind alley**.* □ *Thinking that the motive was robbery led the police up a **blind alley**; the crime had really been committed as an act of revenge.*

blind drunk i pirë tapë

□ *His one idea of a good night out is to get **blind drunk**.*

blend in (with) harmonizoj, kombinoj harmonishëm me

□ *The curtains **blend in** perfectly **with** the carpet.* □ *There has been no attempt to **blend in** the new office blocks **with** the Victorian surrounding.*

blind to sth më errësohen sytë para, nuk jam në gjendje të shoh (të dalloj)

□ *Mothers are sometimes **blind to** the faults of their children.* □ *I am not **blind to** the drawbacks of the method.*

blink the fact (that) mbyll sytë para faktit se, mohoj të vërtetën se

□ *You can't **blink the fact that** the country's economy is suffering.* □ *Our business is on the decline and we can't **blink the fact** any longer.*

blink away/back (one's) tears mbaj lotët

□ *Although in pain, she bravely **blinked back her tears**.* □ *Her voice rose higher and higher. She **blinked away the tears**.*

block sth in/out skicoj, bëj në dorë të parë

□ *He **blocked in** the plan of the house.*

block sth off bllokoj

□ *Police **blocked off** the street after the explosion.* □ *A landslide has **blocked off** traffic moving south towards the motorway.*

block sth up bllokoj

□ *Never **block up** ventilators.* □ *Drains must be left clear, so don't let leaves **block** them **up**.*

blood is thicker than water s'bëhet gjaku ujë

□ *'Are you sure he's your boy? Why didn't you recognize him before?' 'I wasn't too proud of him—wanted to forget him—but **blood is thicker than water**.* □ *I appointed my brother Jack to the post: after all, **blood is thicker than water**.*

blot one's copy book njollos (përlyej) emrin e, njollos veten

□ *She blotted her copybook by being an hour late for work.* □ *One of the security branches had some evidence that there might have been a leakage. 'We don't want to blot our copybook,' said captain Smith.* □ *Jim has blotted his copybook by making that blunder: It may prevent him from being promoted.*

blot on sb's/the escutcheon njollë në emrin e mirë, në nderin e

□ *Her family were less concerned about the human problem of Leila's illegitimate baby than about having to acknowledge a blot on their escutcheon.* □ *'You have not only disgraced yourselves and your families,' the headmaster said in his usual pompous style, 'but your conduct is a blot on the escutcheon of this ancient and honorable school.*

blot sth out 1. zë, pengoj, mbuloj

□ *The resulting dust cloud could have blotted out the sun.* □ *The mist came down and blotted out the view.*

2. heq, largoj

□ *You should never blot it out of your memory.*

blow hot and cold lëkundem, jam i paqëndrueshëm, ndryshoj mendje, ndryshoj si era

□ *You're a fool, Dick. While you blow hot and cold about whether you want to get married or not, the girl will be off with somebody else.* □ *I don't know whether Joe is coming with us on the trip; he keeps blowing hot and cold about it.* □ *He blows hot one minute and cold the next; I never know where I am with him.* □ *So, you see, it comes to the same thing as saying yes or no or do and don't, blowing hot and cold out of the same mouth.*

blow off steam shfrej, nxjerr dufin; derdh (shfryj) ndjenjat, energjinë

□ *The children were out in the playground letting off steam.* □ *He was by nature secretive and had been repressed too much and too early to be capable of railing and blowing off steam where his father was concerned.* □ *Don't discuss that touchy matter with him now; after he blows off a little steam he will be more reasonable.* □ *Dancing started on New Year's Day. This is a traditional time to blow off steam.*

blow one's nose shfryj hundët

□ *Give the child a handkerchief to blow his nose.*

blow one's own trumpet/horn mburrem, mburr veten, reklamoj veten, lëvdohem

□ *That chap is very boring: he's always blowing his own horn.* □ *I don't like to blow my own trumpet, but I must say the sales conference would have been utter chaos if I hadn't been there to organize it.* □ *But you don't do the usual thing. Put blames on others. Pass the buck. Blow your horn loud enough to drown out your occasional failures.* □ *'Not that I ever did a thing like that! No! I was respectable and could scrub the house without that kind of cleanser!' 'That's right! Blow your own trumpet,' he sneered.*

blow one's top/one's stack nxehem, zemërohem, humbas gjakftohtësinë

□ *Dad fairly blew his top. He told me not to be so silly.* □ *Shortly after he settled in a chair, the phone rang. 'Yes?' 'Now, don't blow your top, Annie. It's me again.* □ *Having blown his top, he became apologetic.*

blow down rrëzoj, rrëzohem

□ *Several chimneys blew down*

during the storm. □ *The gale raged all night and* ***blew down*** *a TV aerial from the roof.*

blow out shuaj, fik

□ *Someone opened the door and the lamp* ***blew out.*** □ *He* ***blew out*** *the candle before he went to bed.* □ *Every time he tried to light his pipe the wind* ***blew*** *the match* ***out.***

blow one's brains out hedh trutë në erë, vras veten (me plumb në kokë)

□ *The unlucky gambler left the casino and* ***blew his brains out.*** □ *When finally his wife left him, Peter thought there was nothing left for him to do but to* ***blow his brains out.***

blow sb/sth sky-high hedh në erë

□ *That boy's left a full can of petrol in the kitchen again! We'll all be* ***blown sky-high*** *one of these days.*

blow the gaff nxjerr të fshehtën në shesh

□ *We were trying to keep the party for Jim as a surprise, but someone* ***blew the gaff,*** *and now Jim knows about it.* □ *'Well,' said Martin, turning to the grandparents, 'since young Tommy has* ***blown the gaff*** *I might as well admit we'll be emigrating to America in February.*

blow up 1. qortoj rëndë

□ *She got* ***blown up*** *by her boss for being late.*

2. humb durimin, nxehem, marr zjarr

□ *It takes considerable character not to* ***blow up.***

3. shpërthej, hedh në erë

□ *The bomb* ***blew up*** *with an ear-splitting crash.* □ *'There's only one way to make them build a new sewer.' 'How?' 'Blow up the old one.'*

4. fryj

□ *Could you lend me a pump to* ***blow up*** *my bicycle tires?* □ *You should see that the tires are* ***blown up*** *the correct pressure.*

5. zmadhoj

□ *'Those photographs look promising. Why not get an expert to* ***blow*** *them* ***up*** *a bit bigger?'* □ *Once the photos had been* ***blown up,*** *the gun in his hand was clearly visible.*

blue blood gjak fisnik, derë (pre-jardhje) fisnike

□ *The wealthy businessman was looking for a wife with* ***blue blood*** *in her vein.*

bluff into mashtroj, ia hedh

□ *He wanted to try to* ***bluff*** *them* ***into*** *thinking that he was being stern.* □ *There were* ***bluffed into*** *believing we were not ready for the attack.*

bluff it out/bluff one's way out/out of dal (shpëtoj) nga situata (duke mashtruar të tjerët)

□ *When he was caught in the bank strong-room after hours, the cashier could tell the truth, and risk imprisonment, or try to* ***bluff it out.*** □ *She turned to the officers. 'The man is trying to* ***bluff his way out of*** *the whole thing,' she said.*

blunder about/around lëviz, eci, sillem rrotull (me ngathtësi, në mënyrë të pasigurt)

□ *He* ***blundered about*** *in the room, feeling for the light switch.* □ *She was* ***blundering around*** *the kitchen.*

blurt sth out llomotit; flas pa menduar (pa takt)

□ *He* ***blurted out*** *the bad news before I could stop him.* □ *James was tongue-tied with embarrassment; then he* ***blurted out*** *to his guest, 'You needn't bother to come to this house again!'*

board and lodging ushqim e fjetje

□ *He got Andrew a job in the paper-mills and arranged* ***board and lodging*** *for him in the hostel.*

board out ha jashtë

□ *Shall we* ***board out*** *tonight?*

board sb out i siguroj ushqim e fjetje (jashtë shkollës, vendit të punës etj.)
□ *Most students can still be accommodated in College, but increasing numbers are having to be **boarded out** in the town.*

Bob's your uncle dhe gjithçka është gati, dhe gjithçka shkon për mrekulli
□ *It's very easy to operate this machine: you simply push this button, and **Bob's your uncle**. It's quite simple, really. Turn this knob to the right then this other knob to the right, press the red button, switch on—and **Bob's your uncle**.*

bob up del shpejt në sipërfaqe; shfaqet, rishfaqet papritur
□ *She dived below the surface, then **bobbed up** like a cork again a few seconds later.* □ *He keeps **bobbing up** in the most unlikely places.*

body blow, a zhgënjim i rëndë, goditje e rëndë, humbje e rëndë
□ *He has had a good many ups and downs in his life but his wife's leaving him was **a body blow**.* □ *Failing the examination was **a body blow** to his hopes of a successful academic career.*

body and soul tërësisht, me gjithçka, me gjithë shpirt, me gjithë hovin e zemrës, me të gjitha fuqitë
□ *He had flung himself into the project **body and soul**.* □ *He fought for his country **body and soul**.*

bog down ngec
□ *Our discussions got **bogged down** in irrelevant detail.* □ *The tank got **bogged down** in the mud.*

boil down përmbledh
□ *The good advice we gave him **boiled down** to this: that after tea he should stroll to the window.* □ *The plot of the play, which is very slight can be **boiled down** to the following simple facts.* □ *Read through this passage of prose and then **boil it down** to about a hundred words.*

boil over, to 1. derdhet
□ *'You'd better turn the gas down or else the vegetables will **boil over**.* □ *The kettle has **boiled over**.*
2. nxehem, inatosem, ziej përbrenda
□ *John was **boiling over** and it was soon clear why; nobody had told him of our plans to move house.* □ *When Uriah Heep found himself ignored, he **boiled down**.*
3. shpërthen, pëlcet
□ *The crisis is in danger of **boiling over** into civil war.* □ *The simmering quarrel between the opposing parties **boiled over**.*

boil up 1. ziej, valoj
□ *I kept a stockpot last winter and **boiled** it **up** every day.* □ *When the juice is **boiled up** with sugar it forms jelly.*
2. lind, zien, vlon, zhvillohet, shfaqet
□ *A dispute is **boiling up** over who should be the first to greet our royal visitors.* □ *The feelings of fury **boils up** in them.*

bolster up mbështes, përkrah; forcoj, përforcoj
□ *The government borrowed money to **bolster up** the economy.* □ *Micky, trying to **bolster up** his own status, assumed an assurance that he did not feel.*

bolt down gëlltit, kapërdij shpejt
□ *You'll have violent indigestion if you **bolt down** your food like that.* □ *The surgeon on casualty duty just had time to **bolt down** a sandwich before the first case was wheeled in.*

bolt from/out of the blue, a si vetëtimë, si bubullimë në qiell të kthjellët (të kaltër)
□ *When Frank suddenly came home from Australia, it was a **bolt from the***

blue. □ *Well, your resignation has certainly come as* **a bolt from the blue**, *Watkins. I was counting on you staying with the firm for at least another three years.*

bone of contention, a mollë sherri

□ *The boundary line between their farms has been* **a bone of contention** *between the two families for years.* □ *I don't think it's a good idea at all to give the boys a motor-bike between them. If they've got to share it'll be just* **a bone of contention**.

book in regjistrohem, regjistroj në hotel

□ *'Carry these cases upstairs while I* **book** *the guests* **in**. □ *It was too late to go shopping, so he* **booked in** *at the Ritz Hotel.*

book up rezervoj

□ *I'd like to* **book (up)** *three seats for tonight's concert.* □ *If you like to go to the Continent for your holiday, you ought to* **book up** *now.*

born and bred lindur e rritur

□ *He's London* **born and bred**. □ *She's a Londoner* **born and bred**.

born before one's time lindur para kohe

□ *Some artists are* **born before their time**: *their genius is not recognized until long after death.*

born in the gutter lindur fukara, lindur nga prindër të panjohur (lypësa), lindur në rrugë

□ ***Born in the gutter*** *and surviving first by good luck and then by his own cunning, Emilio at sixteen was a ripe recruit for any of the gangster mob then prevalent in the city.*

born in/to the purple lindur në familje mbretërore (aristokrate)

□ *From a very early age the Prince was aware that he was* **born in the purple** *and was very conscious of his*

elevated state. □ *From the way he talks and behaves you'd think he was* **born to the purple** *or something. Whereas the truth is his parents are ordinary middle class.*

born under a lucky star ka lindur me këmishë, është njeri fatlum

□ *That's how it goes, son; if you haven't been* **born under a lucky star** *you just have to work all the harder to get what you want.* □ *'Did the driver survive?' 'Survive! He was hardly scratched. He must have been* **born under a lucky star** *when you see what happened to the lorry cab.*

born with a silver spoon in one's mouth është në gjendje shumë të mirë, ha me lugë të florinjtë

□ *The son of a Texas millionaire, young Elmer was certainly* **born with a silver spoon in his mouth**. □ *He has never had to work in his life: he was* **born with a silver spoon in his mouth**.

bosom friend/pal, a mik (shok) i ngushtë

□ *Jan and Tom were* **bosom friends** *and are still very fond of each other.* □ *He's not the sort I would choose for a* **bosom pal**, *but he's so witty you can't help enjoying his company.* □ *'You astonish me!' 'Not know the Clickits! Why, you are the very people of all others who ought to be their* **bosom friends**.'

bother one's head about vret (lodh) mendjen

□ *Why* **bother your head about** *what's happening on the other side of the world?* □ *This is something worth* **bothering one's head about**. □ *They* **bother their heads about** *how Miss Page is running things!*

bottle up mposht, përmbaj, ndrydh

□ *Instead of discussing their problems,*

they **bottle up** all their anger and resentment. □ *It's better to express your anger now and then, rather than* **bottle** *it* **up** *and have an almighty explosion.* □ *All the rage that had been* **bottled up** *in him for so long flooded out in a torrent of abuse.*

bottoms up! me fund
□ *She sipped her wine. 'Drink it all down.* **Bottoms up!** *Like this, see?'*

bound up in sth i zënë me, i dhënë pas
□ *He seems very* **bound up in** *his work.*

bound up with sth i lidhur me
□ *The welfare of the individual is* **bound up with** *the welfare of the community.* □ *She had her own existence now, even if that existence was* **bound up with** *an unfaithful husband.*

bow and scrape sillem me përunjësi (servilizëm)
□ *I'm not going to go* **bowing and scraping** *to the new manager for special favors.* □ *A waiter approached us and, with much* **bowing and scraping**, *led us to a table in the dining-room.* □ *The Old Man jumped up from his chair and roared. 'Shut up! Omit* **bowing and scraping**! *Omit your eternal yessing!'*

bow down/to/before sb/sth përkul trupin/kokën (në shenjë nderimi e respekti)
□ *The servants were commanded to* **bow down**.

bow to sth përkulem, jepem, thyhem para
□ *They are inclined to* **bow to** *all their wishes.*

box sb's ears qëlloj, i bie me shpullë (grusht)
□ *She* **boxed** *the impolite boy's* **ears**. □ *I was rescued at last by a gracious lady who* **boxed** *a few* **ears** *and dried my face.*

branch out (into sth) shtrihem, zgjerohem
□ *The company began by specializing in radios but has now decided to* **branch out into** *computers.* □ *Hitherto we have only been concerned with heavy metal castings; now we are* **branching out into** *light alloys and plastics.*

brass farthing, a kacidhe
□ *'Haven't you any money at all?' 'Not* **a brass farthing**.' □ *She had already pawned the few articles of any value that she possessed. Nothing she had left was worth* **a brass farthing**.

brave it out përballoj me shpërfillje
□ *I don't want to see him, because I know he suspects me of disloyalty. But I suppose I'll just have to* **brave it out**. □ *He tried to* **brave it out** *when the police questioned him.*

brazen it out sillem me paturpësi, s'më skuqet faqja
□ *Everybody ignored his remark for what it was, the lowest form of wit, and contemptible into the bargain—but Miller just sat there and* **brazened it out**. □ *Of course he'll* **brazen it out**; *he's got no scruples at all.*

bread and butter mënyrë për sigurimin e bukës së e gojës (mjetet elementare të jetesës)
□ *As a photographer, taking wedding photographs is my* **bread and butter**; *I do other kinds of photography only when I have time.* □ *Acting is his* **bread and butter**.

bread and water bukë e ujë
□ *We couldn't possibly afford a holiday like that! Why, we'd have to live on* **bread and water** *the rest of the year.*

break away from 1. shkëputem, ndahem

□ *He's broken away from his family and gone to live in Australia.* □ *He decided to break away from the Party and seek re-election as an Independent.*

2. iki, shpëtoj

□ *The prisoner broke away from his guard while being taken to another goal.*

3. shkëputet, fiton pavarësinë, mëvetësinë

□ *One part of a federal state may attempt to break away to form an independent entity.*

4. lë, heq dorë

□ *Can't you break away from your old habit?*

break an appointment s'vete në takim

□ *I broke the appointment with my friend today.*

break cover del nga strofka

□ *Once the fire has been lit and piled with green leaves, it generally takes about three minutes before the smoke percolates to every part and the animals start to break cover.* □ *'Halloo!' he shouts as he sees the fox break cover at that moment.*

break down 1. prishet, nuk punon, del jashtë përdorimit, pëson defekt

□ *The telephone system has broken down.* □ *We are sorry to arrive late but the car broke down.*

2. thyej, copëtoj

□ *We tried in vain to break down the rock into smaller pieces with sledge hammers.*

3. zhduk, flak, hedh tej

□ *Wouldn't it be wonderful, dear, if we could form a little front line unit, scientifically and—yes—let me say it, spiritually, a kind of pioneer force to try and break down prejudices, knock out the old fetishes, may be start a*

complete revolution in our whole medical system.

4. ndaloj

□ *He broke down in the middle of his speech.*

5. dëmtohet, keqësohet shumë (shëndeti), bie nga shëndeti

□ *His health had been affected, and might break down altogether if the strain continued.* □ *The old man broke down on account of illness.* □ *Her health broke down under the pressure of work.*

6. mposht, kapërcej

□ *We encountered a good deal of resistance to our pensions scheme, but by patient negotiation we broke it down.*

7. dështoj

□ *The pupil broke down in his answers in mathematics today.*

8. humb kontrollin, s'përmbahem dot, lë ndjenjat të shfaqen lirisht

□ *She appeared to be pretty calm, but at times she would break down and start weeping.* □ *Jurgis stood by and saw another man put into his place, and then picked up his coat and walked off, doing all that he could to keep from breaking down and crying like a boy.*

break even dal fit e fit

□ *We had to invest a lot of money in the factory, but the profits were high, so that we broke even within a year.* □ *It will be a year before the firm makes a profit, but at least it's breaking even.*

break fresh/new ground çaj shtigje (udhë) të reja, hedh hapat e para

□ *The professor's work broke new ground in the treatment of cancer.* □ *Could I thus, as it were, not exhaust my subject, but so much as break ground upon it.* □ *But as he only liked*

Hardy more, he very soon made up his mind to **break ground** *himself, and to make a dash for something more than a mere speaking acquaintance.*

break in 1. shpërthej, hyj me forcë

□ *The police* **broke in** *and arrested all the brothers.* □ *Tell them that those inside need protection against desperate characters who are trying to* **break in** *from outside.*

2. ndërpres (bisedën etj.), ndërhyj

□ *'But what's going to happen to us?' one of the miners* **broke in.** □ *I could tell this story better if so many people didn't* **break in.**

3. shtroj

□ *I've spent nearly six months* **breaking in** *the pony.*

break into 1. hyj me forcë, shpërthej dyert

□ *His house was* **broken into** *last week.*

2. nis, ia jap, shpërthej

□ *The man* **broke into** *a run when he saw the police.* □ *They* **broke into** *a loud laugh.* □ *Suddenly they* **broke into** *a song.* □ *The little girl* **broke into** *tears.*

3. zë, merr (kohën)

□ *All this extra work I am doing is* **breaking into** *my leisure time.* □ *He is not right when he says that sports activities* **break into** *his leisure time.*

break loose zgjidhet, lirohet

□ *A wounded steer had* **broken loose** *and smashed him against a pillar.* □ *The dog has* **broken loose.**

break off 1. ndërpres menjëherë

□ *Our trading connection has been* **broken off** *owing to a disagreement over prices.* □ *No settlement of the dispute is in sight. The talks were* **broken off** *an hour ago and will not be resumed today.*

2. këpus, thyej

□ *He* **broke off** *a piece of chocolate and offered it to me.* □ *He* **broke off** *a branch from the tree and threw it into the river.*

3. pushoj, bëj pushim

□ *The whole cast* **broke off** *for coffee in the middle of rehearsals.*

break one's faith shkel (thyej) fjalën, pres në fjalë

□ *If you* **break faith** *once, you won't be believed the next time.*

break one's fast prish agjërimin

□ *To say the truth I had promised myself to* **break my fast** *in the pavilion, and hunger began to prick me sharply.* □ *Does the prisoner understand that if he cannot be persuaded to* **break his fast,** *he will be forcibly fed?*

break one's heart ia thyej zemrën dikujt, ia copëtoj zemrën, ia bëj zemrën copë

□ *I don't know what's wrong with Mary and she won't tell me. But she's been upstairs crying fit to* **break her heart** *all afternoon.* □ *You see, my father was made bankrupt. It nearly* **broke his heart.** □ *Aniele, who was a widow and had three children, and did washing for the tradespeople at prices it would* **break your heart** *to hear named.* □ *Don't think ill of me, because I use her help. She gives it cheerfully as you see, and it would* **break her heart** *if she knew that I suffered anybody else to do for me what her little hands could undertake.*

break one's journey ndaloj (gjatë udhëtimit)

□ *On his way from Paris to Moscow, he* **broke his journey** *at Berlin.* □ *He would have caught an express, but had discovered that if he travelled by a slower train he could change trains* *at Stotwell, and* **break his journey** *for long enough to visit the Oak Lounge.*

break one's neck thyej qafën; veproj me ngut, me rrëmbim

□ *I'm not going to* **break my neck** *to finish my essay today—my teacher doesn't want it until next week.* □ *You're not exactly* **breaking your neck** *to get me that book from the library, are you?*

break one's spirit thyej, vras shpirtërisht

□ *The life of convicts in nineteenth-century Australia was one of hard labor, heat, disease, and poor food, with the threat of the lash or the gallows if they showed rebellion— enough to* **break** *even the proudest man's* **spirit.** □ *I'm not surprised Featherstone's a widower; any woman's* **spirit** *would be* **broken** *by life with that old miser!*

break one's word shkel fjalën, thyej fjalën

□ *If you say you are going to do something, do it; never* **break your word.** □ *I have promised you and I'll not* **break my word.**

break out 1. shpërthen

□ *A fire* **broke out** *on the third floor.* □ *The plague* **broke out** *that Summer, and hundreds died.* □ *Rioting* **broke out** *between rival groups of fans.*
2. shpërthej

□ *The smiles broaden, laughter* **breaks out.** □ *He* **broke out** *into a fury of language.*

break out in shpërthej në

□ *The soft music of the jazz quartet was like people who had been locked up,* **breaking out in** *tears and laughter.* □ *He suddenly* **broke out in** *a rage of sobs and curses.*

break out in a cold sweat më shkojnë (më dalin, më mbulojnë) djersë të ftohta

□ *He* **broke out in cold sweat.** □ *He began to imagine he had strange noises, and* **broke out in cold sweat.**

break ranks braktis, dal nga radhët

□ *When they were threatened with being dismissed, some of the strikers* **broke ranks** *and returned to work.*

break the back of bëj (kryej) pjesën më të madhe, më të vështirë

□ *Moving the stones from the garden was hard work, but we had* **broken the back of it** *by lunch time.*

break the ice thyej akullin

□ *Playing party-games sometimes helps to* **break the ice** *at a party, especially if the guests have never met before.* □ *On the instant he was thinking how natural and unaffected her manner was now that* **the ice** *between them* **had been broken.** □ *They nodded to each other by way of* **breaking the ice** *of unacquaintance.*

break the silence thyej (prish) heshtjen

□ *We were comfortably dozing off in our deck-chairs when a piercing shriek* **broke** *the afternoon* **silence.** □ *I left him to* **break the silence.** *Our steps remained the only noise, until he remarked, as though casually: 'Walter Luke didn't say much tonight, did he?'* □ *Suddenly Teto Elzbieta* **broke the silence** *with a wail, and Maria began to wring her hands and sob.* □ *At last he* **broke silence.** *'That's very strange way of thinking,' he said, 'I don't agree with you at all.'*

break the news to sb about sth njoftoj, jap lajmin (e keq, të pakëndshëm)

□ *I had a letter this morning telling me I've failed my exam. That's bad enough, but I don't know how I'll* **break the news to** *Dad.* □ *I had a wonderful surprise this morning. Ann* and David rang up from New Zealand to **break the news** that they are having a baby. □ I had to **break the news** of his father's death to him.

break the peace prish rendin
□ He was very noisy and abusive, and alarmed the other customers. The proprietor was very forbearing in not sending for the police and having him charged with **breaking the peace**. □ 'If you **break the peace** in this way again, you'll go to prison,' said the magistrate.

break the spell prish magjinë
□ I wish something could **break the spell** that binds her to that worthless fellow. □ I had seen photographs of women that streamlined their shapes and made them look so alluring that you knew it was all a trick, that once **the spell** was **broken**, and they moved, you would see that they were just ordinary, if pretty, women.

break the thread ndërpres, prish fillin e
□ The fact that the students came late **broke the thread** of the professor's argument, so he had to start again.

break through 1. depërtoj
□ Thieves **broke through** a wall and a steel partition to get at the safe. □ Some of the crowd attempted to **break through** police cordons.
2. del, shfaqet
□ At half past eleven the sun **broke through**, beginning to dry at last the heavy dew on the grass.
3. kapërcej, mund, mposht
□ She could not **break through** such a barrier of indifference. □ No matter how hard one tries to bring him out, it's almost impossible to **break through** his reserve.
4. bëj zbulime të reja e të rëndë-sishme
□ Scientists say they are beginning to

break through in the fight against cancer. □ Chemists working on animal dye-stuffs have **broken through** in a number of directions.

break up 1. thyej, copëtoj, shkatërroj
□ John **broke up** the old box for fuel to cook the dinner. □ The boat was caught in a south-easterly gale. She went aground and started to **break up** on the rocks.
2. mbyll, mbyllet, mbaron
□ The meeting **broke up**. □ The school has **broken up** for the summer holidays. □ When do you **break up** for the Easter holiday?
3. rrënohem, shkatërrohem, thyhem, marr fund (mendërisht ose fizikisht)
□ I looked at his face again. If I ever saw a man on the point of **breaking up**, I saw one then. □ I know what he has to endure, but there is no sign of him **breaking up** under the strain yet.
4. ndaj, shpërndaj
□ The fat policeman, whose duty was to **break up** the fights drew up a chair to the foot of the table and joined the conversation. □ The meeting was threatening to get out of hand and the police were forced to **break** it **up**.
5. prishet, merr fund
□ Their marriage has virtually **broken up**—they are hardly ever in each other's company.
6. ndërron, ndryshon, hapet (koha, moti etj.)
□ The weather is **breaking up**.

break with 1. prishem (me dikë)
□ John has **broken with** his family; they can't agree over the choice of his wife. □ He was your friend a month ago, but you now seem to have **broken with** him altogether.
2. shkëputem, heq dorë

□ *We have **broken** irretrievably from the past. Several painters in the exhibition have **broken with** tradition.*

breathe a sigh of relief marr frymë i çliruar

□ *Brigit **breathed a sigh of** deep **relief** as she heard Nicky shrilly making some explanation, and then the rapid patter of feet approaching the door.*

breathe easily/freely marr frymë lirisht

□ *It was a dangerous journey, but after we had crossed the river we were able to **breathe** more easily.* □ *Only after we received the news that they had arrived safety did we begin to **breathe freely**.* □ *I was in the tunnel when the train came up before I was aware, but I squeezed myself close to the wall and escaped. Not till the last coach passed did I **breathe freely**.*

breathe in/out marr/nxjerr frymë

□ *We lifted our heads to **breathe in** fresh air.* □ *The doctor told me to **breathe in** and then **breathe out** slowly.*

breathe one's last jap shpirt, jap frymën e fundit

□ *Her condition worsened during the night and toward midday the following day she **breathed her last**.* □ *When you come to **breathe your last**, you may be sorry to have this cruelty on your conscience.*

breathe sth into sb mbush, i jap

□ *The new manager has **breathed** fresh life **into** the company.*

brew up përgatis (çajin)

□ *A group of men were **brewing up** in a sheltered corner of the building-site.*

bribe sb with sth/into doing sth mitos, i jap mitë (rryshfet) dikujt për të bërë diçka

□ *There were attempts to **bribe** the jury **with** offers of money.* □ *One of the witnesses was **bribed into** giving false testimony.*

bridge a/the gap zhduk dallimet

□ *How can we **bridge the gap** between rich and poor?*

bridle one's tongue i vë fre gjuhës (gojës)

□ *His language is appallingly coarse sometimes.* □ *He might at least try to **bridle his tongue** in front of the children.*

bright and early herët në mëngjes, që pa gdhirë

□ *You're **bright and early** today!* □ *'Yes, it's true. I heard it on the 7 o'clock news.' 'Goodness, you must have been up **bright and early** this morning.*

bright lights, the vezullimi, jeta joshëse e qytetit

□ *'Well, a week tonight and it'll be back to **the bright lights**.' 'Don't talk of it,' he groaned. 'I wish I could stay here for ever.' □ I've never really been lured by **the** proverbial **bright lights**.*

bright spark, a shpuzë, zjarr, shumë i shkathët nga mendja

□ *'She's **a bright spark**, that littlest one of George's, isn't she?' 'Yes, she's a lively child.'*

brim over derdhet

□ *The boys had loaded on too much sand; the wheelbarrow was **brimming over**.*

bring about shkaktoj, realizoj, krijoj, sjell

□ *The administration helped **bring about** a peaceful settlement.* □ *The politicians don't seem to have **brought** any miraculous changes **about**.*

bring a charge of sth against sb akuzoj, padit, ngre akuzë (padi) kundër dikujt

41

bring along | **bring home to**

□ *If you found someone loitering at the back of your house after dark, you might feel justified in bringing charges against him.* □ *'Of course, you could bring a charge of dangerous driving against him, but you might have some difficulty proving it in court.*

bring along 1. sjell me vete

□ *'I'm having a short staff meeting in my office at eleven. Oh, and would you bring your friend along, too?'* □ *You can bring a friend along to the party.*

2. ndihmoj, inkurajoj

□ *We're trying to bring along one or two promising swimmers.*

bring around/round 1. sjell

□ *'Do bring your wife around one evening. We're longing to meet her.'* □ *'If you don't find room for these people, you're welcome to bring them around to our place.*

2. i kthej mendjen

□ *Father wasn't keen to let us have the flat for our party, but we managed to bring him round.*

bring a lump to one's throat iu lidh (iu bë, iu mblodh) një nyjë në grykë (në fyt)

□ *Waving goodbye to him brought a lump to my throat.*

bring back 1. kthej, sjell

□ *He's gone away from home and nothing will bring him back again.* □ *'If you borrow my electric drill don't forget to bring it back.'*

2. kujtoj, sjell ndërmend

□ *The sight of that photograph brings back the happy days we spent in Paris.* □ *I know it happened, but I cannot bring it back to mind.*

3. rivendos

□ *He's very much in favor of bringing back capital punishment.* □ *He feels*

that compulsory attendance at school should be **brought back**.

4. përtërij, ia përmirësoj shëndetin

□ *Her stay among the mountains brought her back to health.*

bring back to life kthej në jetë

□ *And anyway he was dead. I couldn't bring him back to life.*

bring down 1. përmbys

□ *A general strike would bring the government down.*

2. rrëzoj

□ *Several aircraft were intercepted and brought down.* □ *A rifleman actually managed to bring down an enemy airplane.*

3. ul

□ *The promise measures included steps to bring down prices.*

4. rrëzoj (lojtarin)

□ *Our center-forward was tripped and brought down inside their penalty area.*

bring forth sjell, nxjerr, jap, lind

□ *I suppose Smith is unlikely to bring forth any sparkling new suggestions for improving our product.* □ *In time, this policy will bring forth new results.*

bring forward 1. ngre, parashtroj, paraqes

□ *At our next Council meeting, he is proposing to bring forward the question of developing the city center.* □ *The proposal he brought forward seemed a constructive one.*

2. afroj, avancoj

□ *The meeting has been brought forward from May 10 to May 3.*

bring home to sb sqaroj, kthelloj, e bëj të qartë

□ *My cousin's death from cancer brought home to me the dangers of being a heavy smoker.*

□ *Nothing that she could have done, nothing that she had done,* **brought home to him** *like this the inner significance of her act.* □ *It was* **brought home** *to me that every day I had much to learn.*

bring in 1. korr, mbledh
□ *They could be sure of a few more days of fine weather in which to* **bring in** *the harvest.*
2. sjell, siguroj
□ *Tourism is a big industry,* **bringing in** *$7 billion a year.* □ *He does odd jobs that* **bring** *him* **in** *$300 a week.*
3. shpall, jap një vendim
□ *The jury* **brought in** *a verdict that Christine had died from falling off a cliff, but there was no evidence to show how she had come to fall off the cliff.*
4. fut, introduktoj, përhap
□ *We intend to* **bring in** *legislation to control their activities.*

bring into action vë në veprim
□ *Because of the state of the ground, the artillery could not be* **brought into action** *at once.*

bring into being/existence lind, krijoj, themeloj, sjell në jetë
□ *The new government* **brought into being** *a completely new system of education.* □ *An information bureau was* **brought into existence** *to deal with the inquiries.*

bring into blossom/flower bën të lulëzojë, të çelë lule
□ *The mildness of the early Spring weather will have helped to* **bring** *the fruit trees* **into blossom.**

bring into contact with vë në lidhje me
□ *These visits* **brought me into contact with** *a large public outside the army.* □ *They were* **brought into contact** *through an interest in music.*

bring into disrepute diskreditoj, bëj që të humbasë emrin e mirë
□ *Unofficial strikes are so common, and shop stewards so often involved, that trade unionism is* **brought into disrepute.** □ *The inefficiency of one department can* **bring** *a whole industry* **into disrepute.**

bring into fashion sjell, fut në modë
□ *The growing prestige of British designers did a lot to* **bring** *the miniskirt* **into fashion.**

bring into focus sjell, vë në qendër të vëmendjes
□ *Advances in space exploration have* **brought into focus** *one of the most dramatic questions in human history.*

bring into force sjell në fuqi
□ *If the present regulations are not effective, then others may have to be* **brought into force.**

bring into line with pajtoj, përputh, sjell (fus) në një vijë (kurs, hulli) me
□ *Why not have done with this superstition of monarchy, and* **bring** *the British commonwealth* **into line with** *all the other great Powers today as a republic?* □ *He managed to* **bring** *the whole committee* **into line.** □ *It seems that nothing can* **bring** *him* **into line with** *his fellows.*

bring into play vë në veprim
□ *Old enmities have once more been* **brought into play** *in the struggle for the leadership.*

bring into service/use vë në përdorim
□ *The Victoria Line was* **brought into service,** *as part of the London Underground, to link important parts of the city.* □ *These canals were* **brought back into use** *for pleasure traffic.*

bring into sight/view zbuloj, nxjerr në dukje
□ *A sudden movement of the clouds* **brought** *the airfield* **into view.**

bring into the open nxjerr në dritë (në shesh), bëj të njohur

□ *If you had not allowed him to make the speech, this matter need never have been brought into open.*

bring into the world lind, sjell në jetë

□ *'And now, Heaven forgive me, I'm bringing another child into the world.*

bring off 1. shpëtoj

□ *The lifeboat brought off the crew of the stricken tanker.* □ *The passengers and crew were brought off by the lifeboat.*

2. kryej, bëj, realizoj me sukses

□ *It was a difficult task but we have brought it off.* □ *You've brought it off at last. I'm proud you passed the test.*

bring on shkaktoj, sjell

□ *He was out all day in the rain and this brought on a bad cold.* □ *You have brought shame and disgrace on yourself and your family.* □ *The child has brought all that trouble on himself.*

bring out 1. nxjerr në grevë

□ *He has brought the engineering apprentices out on the strike.* □ *The shop-stewards brought out the miners.*

2. nxjerr në treg, prodhoj; botoj

□ *The company is bringing out a new sports car.* □ *This local newspaper was brought out some years ago.* □ *The publishing house is going to bring out a new edition of that book.*

3. sqaroj, bëj të qartë

□ *The meaning of the poem was admirably brought out.*

4. bëj të çelë, të hapë

□ *The hot weather has brought out all the blossom on the fruit trees.*

5. nxjerr në shesh, zbuloj

□ *The excavations brought out some interesting results.*

6. heq turpin, ndrojtjen

□ *She's a retiring sort of girl, but he's doing his best to bring her out.*

bring out into the open zbuloj, nxjerr në shesh

□ *The scandal was brought out into the open. The President had a lot of questions to answer.*

bring out/out of nxjerr

□ *He rummaged about in the attic and brought out a pile of old documents.* □ *They gathered up the few belongings that they'd managed to bring out of the burning house.*

bring out of his shell nxjerr nga guaska

□ *It will take all of your patience and tact to bring Tom out of his shell.* □ *What brought him out of his shell was the invitation to talk about his only interest—astronomy.*

bring over bëj të ndërrojë mendje, bëj me vete

□ *What she said brought him over to our opinion.* □ *You cannot bring the child over by such an argument.*

bring round 1. sjell në vete

□ *The cool air outside soon brought her round.*

□ *We threw water over him to bring him round.*

2. sjell, vërtis (fjalën, bisedën, etj.)

□ *By talking about Scotland, Brown managed to bring the discussion round to salmon fishing—his favorite pastime.* □ *He brought the conversation round to his favorite subject.*

3. e bëj për vete, e bëj të ndërrojë mendje

□ *He wasn't keen on the plan, but we managed to bring him round.*

bring sb back down to earth e zbres në tokë, e bëj të njohë jetën e vërtetë

□ *He is not at all a practical person:*

perhaps having to earn his living will
bring him down to earth.
bring sb good/bad luck i sjell dikujt
fat të mirë (të keq)
□ *The house has* **brought** *us nothing*
but **bad luck** *ever since we worked we*
moved into it. □ *The stalls were full of*
charms and bracelets that if you lis-
tened to the salesman would **bring**
***good luck** to everybody.*
bring sb down a peg or two i ul hundën
□ *Now Jim Cardegee, with the sailor's*
love for a sailor's joke, had deter-
mined, when he pulled into the
cabin, to **bring** *its inmate* ***down a***
peg or two.
bring sb to book for sth i kërkoj
llogari (hesap) për
□ *I want a little more control over the*
money. You may have all the honor;
I'll never **bring** *you* **to book** *for that.*
bring sb to his knees gjunjëzoj,
përgjunj, përul
□ *The country was almost* **brought to**
***its knees** by the long strike.*
bring sb to his senses sjell në të, sjell
në vete, i sjell mendjen në vend
□ *All hope is that this recent accident*
will have **brought** *him* **to his senses.**
□ *Nothing but a strong letter from his*
bank manager will **bring** *him* **to his**
senses.
bring sb to reason sjell në vete, i sjell
mendtë në vend
□ *'Captain Tommasi,' he went on,*
turning to one of them, 'ring for the
guard, if you please, and have this
young gentleman put in the punish-
ment cell for a few days. He wants a
lesson, I see, to **bring** *him* **to reason.'**
□ *The punishment cell was a dark,*
damp, filthy hole under ground.
Instead of **bringing** *Arthur* **'to**
***reason,'** it thoroughly exasperated*
him.

bring sth to sb's notice ia bëj të
njohur, vë në dijeni
□ *It has been* **brought to my notice**
that some senior boys are in the habit
of visiting public houses in the town.
□ *It was Susan who* **brought** *the*
problem **to our notice.** □ *He promised*
to **bring** *the matter to his parents'*
***notice** at the earliest opportunity.*
bring the house down ngre sallën më
këmbë, duartrokitet nxehtësisht
□ *The young singer's performance*
***brought the house down;** the ap-*
plause lasted for about twenty min-
utes.
bring to a close mbyll, përfundoj, i jap
fund
□ *The ceremony was* **brought to a**
***close** by the singing of the national*
anthem. □ *The service was* **brought to**
***a close** with a hymn.*
bring to a dead end fus në rrugë pa
krye (në rrugë qorre)
□ *The reluctance of the local people*
to talk had **brought** *his investigation*
to a dead end.
bring to a head acaroj në kulm
□ *The atmosphere in the office had*
been tense for some time but the latest
dismissal **brought** *matters* **to a head.**
□ *Matters were* **brought to a head**
when the boss tried to force more
work onto him. He resigned. □ *'Well I*
shall moot it at the next Board,' he
said. 'Quite!' said the manager.
'Nothing like **bringing to a head,** *is*
there?'
bring to an end mbyll, i jap fund
□ *I hope we have* **brought** *our argu-*
ments on fundamentals **to an end.** □
Leaders were anxious to **bring to an**
***end** the dissensions of the last two*
months.
bring to a stand, to ndaloj, qëndroj
□ *We were* **brought to a stand** *on this*

very plain by a heavy rain. □ *He brought the car to a stand.*

bring to a standstill ndaloj, ndërpres, pezulloj

□ *A movement in the crowd brought him to a standstill at the window, his nose touching the pane and whitening from the chill of it.* □ *A strike in the paint-shop brought production to a standstill.*

bring to a stop ndaloj

□ *Upon seeing the signal the driver brought his car to a stop.*

bring to attention jap komandën gatitu

□ *The sergeant brought the guard smartly to attention and saluted the inspecting officer.*

bring to bay ia pres, ia mbyll të gjitha rrugët (shtigjet), fus në udhë pa krye (gjendje pa rrugëdalje)

□ *After a long chase the dogs brought the stag to bay at the edge of a cliff.* □ *The police brought the robbers to bay in a deserted house.* □ *Though Jude had hitherto taken the medicines of that skilful practitioner with the greatest indifference, he was now so brought to bay by events that he vented his opinion of Vilbert in the physician's face, and so forcibly that Vilbert soon scurried downstairs again.*

bring to fruition realizoj

□ *Years of patient work had at last brought all his plans to fruition.* □ *The scheme was locally conceived, and brought to fruition with help from overseas.*

bring to grief shkaktoj mjerim, fatke-qësi

□ *Dinny hated driving, and not without reason, for her peculiar way of seeing the humors of what she was passing had often nearly brought her to grief.*

bring to heel mposht, nënshtroj, bëj zap

□ *It is no simple matter to bring a break-away region of several millions to heel.*

bring to justice nxjerr para gjyqit

□ *This base design is revealed, and two of its plotters must be brought to justice.*

bring to life i jap jetë (vitalitet, gjallëri)

□ *Let's invite Ted—he knows how to bring a party to life.* □ *She couldn't act very well, but for me she brought the whole play to life.*

bring to light nxjerr në dritë

□ *One newspaper claims to have brought to light some important new evidence.* □ *Some little-known details of his early life have been brought to life.*

bring to mind kujtoj, sjell ndër mend

□ *Seeing the child reading brought to my mind the books I read when I was a boy.* □ *I am the head boy now, and look down on the line of boys below me, with a condescending interest in such of them as bring to my mind the boy I was myself, when I first came here.*

bring to naught (nought) shkon kot, përfundon në hiç

□ *Let's exert our efforts a little more to complete the task so that our previous efforts will not be brought to nought.*

bring to one's feet ngre më këmbë

□ *It was finally a remark of Edith's that brought him to his feet in a rush of anger.* □ *A jolt nearly threw me from the bed, and a second jolt brought me to my feet.*

bring to pass kryej, realizoj, plotësoj, për-mbush

□ *After several unsuccessful experiments he finally brought it to pass.* □ *He was determined to bring to pass the task appointed to him.*

bring to sb's aid/assistance sjell në ndihmë të

□ *A broadcast appeal **brought** rescue teams hurrying **to the aid** of the flood victims.* □ *Skilled mechanics can quickly be **brought to the assistance** of motorists.*

bring to the fore shquaj, nxjerr në pah

□ *The conditions of the post-war years **brought** many enterprising men **to the fore.***

bring under nënshtroj

□ *After some incidents that the police could not prevent, the rioters were **brought under**.* □ *The horse was soon **brought under**.*

bring under control vë nën kontroll

□ *Five fire engines **brought** the blaze **under control** in just over an hour.* □ *Such bodies may sabotage the trade union movement if they are not **brought under control**.*

bring up 1. edukoj, rrit

□ *The fact of being **brought up** in a shabby and dirty town was another thing that helped us to be competitive.* □ *The child was **brought up** by his aunts.* □ *All children should be **brought up** to respect the elders.*

2. ngre, parashtroj (një çështje, etj.)

□ *'I think we're agreed on the main points. Does anyone want to **bring up** anything further?'* □ *They decided to **bring up** the matter at their next meeting.*

3. nxjerr, vjell (ushqimin)

□ *'I don't seem to take my meals well,' he said.* □ *'I **bring up** most of what I've taken, if you'll pardon the phrase.* □ *The sick **brought up** his dinner.* □ *The greedy child **brought up** all he had eaten.*

bring sb/sth up to sth ngre në nivelin (standartin) e kërkuar

□ *His work in maths needs to be*

brought up to the standard of the others.

bring sb up against sth bëj të përballlojë

□ *Working in a multi-racial community had **brought** him **up against** the realities of intolerance.* □ *Working in the slums **brought** her **up against** the realities of poverty.*

bring up to date përditësoj, aktualizoj

□ *I have only a few additional facts to add to **bring** the report **up to date**.*

bring up the rear mbyll praparojën (procesionin, garën, marshimin etj.)

□ *The mounted soldiers went at the front, and the foot-soldiers **brought up the rear**.* □ *A short distance behind came a Peugeot, and the **rear** was **brought up** by a powerful dark-green Mercedes.*

bring word sjell lajm

□ *A man **brought word** that Perdemis had returned to the hotel and was waiting to see his nephew.*

broken/fractured English anglishte e thyer

□ *'Who are you?' they asked in French. 'Ah, English,' they murmured and changed gear into **broken English**.*

broken reed, a njeri i pasigurt, njeri (send) ku nuk mund të mbështetesh

□ *After the scandal he continued to hold office, but even the most naturally sycophantic of his colleagues avoided close involvement, regarding him as **a broken reed**.*

brood on/over/upon sth mendoj, bluaj me mend, sjell e përsjell nëpër mend, zhytem në mendime të trishtuara

□ *The problem won't improve for being **brooded over**.* □ *It's no use **brooding** too much **over** one's past mistakes. The thing to do is to correct them.*

brush aside 1. largoj, spostoj mënjanë
□ *The enemy column **brushed aside** our defence and advanced south.*
2. shpërfill
□ *He **brushed aside** my objections to his plan.*
brush off heq, fshi me furçë
□ *I can't **brush** the dirt **off**.*
brush up freskoj, ripërtërij
□ *I must **brush up** my Italian before I go to Rome.* □ *You'll have to **brush up** your history of art if you want a job in the museum.*
buckle down i përvishem punës
□ *You can't play around with this assignment: it's something that needs to be **buckled down** to seriously.* □ *She's really **buckling down** to her new job.*
buckle to shtrëngohem, bëj përpjekje të veçanta
□ *When their mother died, the children simply had to **buckle to** and run the house themselves.*
build castles in Spain/in the air ndërtoj kështjella në erë (në ajër), shoh ëndrra me sy hapur
□ *You should give yourself aims that you know you can achieve; there is no point **building castles in the air**.* □ *Poor Martin! Forever **building castles in the air**. Forever, in his very selfishness, forgetful of all but his own teeming hopes and sanguine plans.*
build one's hopes on mbështet shpresat te
□ *It was **on** Mr. Maudling that this group within the Conservative Party now **built its hope**.*
build up 1. krijoj, siguroj
□ *He has **built up** a good reputation.*
2. forcohem
□ *You need more protein to **build you up**.*

3. rritet, shtohet
□ *Traffic is **building up** on roads into the city.*
□ *Tension **built up** as the crises approached.*
4. zhvilloj
□ *Japan successfully **built up** a modern capitalist economy.* □ *His organizational knowledge and personal reputation has **built** the business **up**.*
bull in a china shop, a njeri i ngathët
□ *'You have strength ... it's untutored strength.' 'Like a **bull in china shop**' he suggested and won a smile.* □ *Yes, a clumsy and timid horseman did not look to advantage in the saddle. 'Look at him, Amelia dear... such a **bull in china shop** I never saw.*
burn away 1. vazhdon të digjet
□ *The fire was still **burning away** cheerfully in the grate.*
2. digjet, konsumohet
□ *Half the oil in the lamp had **burnt away**.*
burn down shkrumbohet, bëhet shkrumb e hi
□ *The woodshed **burned down** in half an hour.*
burning question, the çështje therëse (e mprehtë, e ngutshme, e rëndësishme)
□ *Entry or non-entry into the European Common Market was one of **the burning questions** in British politics in the early 1970s.* □ *It's not whether we can get a good meal or not, but whether we could pay for it if we did-that's **the burning question**.*
burn one's boats/bridges (behind one) këput (pres) të gjitha urat
□ *I was cut off from the kind of people I'd always known, my family, my friends, everybody. And I'd **burnt my boats**. After all those weeks of*

brawling with Mummy and Daddy about Jimmy. I knew I couldn't appeal to them without looking foolish and cheap. □ *'You've sold your house before you've got your emigration clearance to go to Australia?' 'Yes, it's the only way I'll have the courage actually to go—I just had to* **burn my boats behind me.**
□ *Think carefully before you resign— if you do that you will have* **burnt your boats.**

burn oneself out rrënoj (shkatërroj) shëndetin
□ *If you don't give up this evening work, you'll* **burn yourself out.** □ *If he doesn't stop working so hard, he'll* **burn himself out.**

burn one's fingers digjem, e pësoj
□ *If you have never played the stock-market this is not the time to start. You're liable to* **get your fingers burnt.** □ *I'm not going to interfere with people's private lives any more, even in the most well-meaning way.* **My fingers** *have been* **burnt** *once too often.*

burn out 1. shuhet, fiket
□ *When we got back from the theatre we found that the fire had* **burned itself out.**
2. digjet
□ *The hotel was completely* **burned out.**

burnt child dreads/fears the fire u dogj nga qulli, e i fryn edhe kosit
□ *He would be better off getting married again, but I suppose it's a case of the* **burnt child fearing the fire.** *His first marriage was a disaster.* □ *The boy's had a fright, but it'll do him no harm.* **The burnt child dreads the fire,** *so he is not likely to make the same mistake.*

burn the candle at both ends derdh (shkrij) të gjitha energjitë; shter forcat

□ *Jack has got a difficult job and yet he also goes to parties almost every night: I wonder how long he can go on* **burning the candle at both ends.**
□ *He had, in fact,* **burned the candle at both ends,** *but he had never been un-ready to do his fellows* **a** *good turn.*

burn the midnight oil punoj (studioj) në orët e vona, natën vonë
□ *I've got three exams next month: I'm afraid I shall have to start* **burning the midnight oil.** □ *I expect you'll be* **burning the midnight oil** *for the next week or two, getting ready for your exams.*

burn up 1. djeg, asgjësoj me zjarr
□ *Throw the scraps in the incinerator and* **burn** *them* **up.**
2. përflaket, merr flakë
□ *He threw a log on the fire, and it* **burned up** *with a crackle*

burst in/into hyj papritur
□ *Suddenly Mr. Tony* **burst in,** *in his shirtsleeves, and rushed across the living room into his bedroom.*

burst in/on/upon ndërpres
□ *A staff officer* **burst in upon** *their discussion with the news that the enemy was only five miles away.* □ *How dare you* **burst in on** *us without knocking!*

burst into sth shpërthej
□ *The aircraft crashed and* **burst into flames.** □ *The orchards seemed to have* **burst into** *blossom overnight.*
□ *Mrs. Gummadge had been in a low state all day, and had* **burst into** *tears in the forenoon, when the fire smoked.*

burst into/upon sight/view duket, shfaqet befas
□ *The cavalry escort went by; then the royal coach with its outriders* **burst into view.** □ *She raised her eyes*

to the bright stars, looking down so mildly from the wide world of air and, gazing on them, found new stars burst upon her view.

burst out shpërthej, flas me zjarr
□ *He angrily **burst out**, 'Why don't you stop pretending you know all the answers!'*

burst out crying/laughing shpërthej në vaj/në gaz
□ *He looked about ready to **burst out crying**. □ I mentioned the incident later to a tailor friend and he **burst out laughing**.*

bury oneself in 1. mbyllem, izolohem
□ *What made him go and **bury himself in** the country?*
2. kridhem, zhytem, jepem i tëri pas
□ *Right after dinner, he would go into the study and **bury himself in** his paperwork.*

bury one's face/head in mbuloj fytyrën (kokën) me
□ *Suddenly the truth struck me, and I wanted to sit down and **bury my face in** my hands. □ Guy sat down and **buried his head in** the bedclothes. He began to sob.*

bury the hatchet i jap fund armiqësisë
□ *Jack and Jim are quite friends now; they've decided to **bury the hatchet**. □ Those two are the best of friends now. **The hatchet was buried** years ago.*

bury the past harroj të shkuarën, të shkuara të harruara
□ *Well, let's admit there were mistakes on both sides; we'll **bury the past** and try to make a fresh start. □ With the marriage of their children, the two families could finally look on **the past** as being **buried**, and their reconciliation was complete.*

busy oneself with merrem
□ *She always manages to find something to **busy herself with**. □ He **busied himself with** all sorts of little tasks.*

but then nga ana tjetër
□ *He speaks very good French—**but then** he did live in Paris for three years.*

butt in ndërhyj, ndërpres
□ *I wish you wouldn't keep **butting in** when we are in the middle of a conversation. □ It's better that his affairs should be handled by one man. It makes confusion if someone else **butts in**.*

button sth up përfundoj
□ *The deal should be **buttoned up** by tomorrow. □ I haven't said a word about it yet and I shan't till it's all **buttoned up**.*

buy a pig in a poke ble derr në thes
□ *In the case of his new house, he really **bought a pig in a poke**, because he paid for it before it was finished. □ 'Well I'll take it now.' 'You mustn't **buy a pig in a poke**,' he said. 'You mightn't like it.' □ Buying land by mail is **buying a pig in a poke**: sometimes the land turns out to be under water.*

by accident rastësisht, pa dashur
□ *You might cut yourself **by accident**; you wouldn't cut yourself on purpose. □ Completely **by accident** my uncle happened to be booked into the same hotel as I was.*

by a hair/a hair's breadth për një qime, për një fije floku, për pak
□ *He just missed hitting the target **by a hair**. □ Woe betide you if you fail to do it, or disobey me **by a hair's breadth**. □ Valentine... If I swerve **by a hair's breadth** from the straight*

*line of the most rigid respectability,
I'm done for.*

by/from all accounts në bazë të gjithë
të dhënave, në bazë të informacionit
të dhënë; siç thonë të gjithë
□ *I've never been there but it is, by all
accounts, a lovely place.* □ *I had never
met him; he was clearly a fine soldier.
But from all accounts he was completely worn out and needed a rest.*

by all means natyrisht, sigurisht; patjetër, doemos, me domosdo
□ *He sat down again. 'Look, Norah,'
he said, 'I'll come straight to the
point if I may.' 'By all means.'* □ *'You
were wishing to speak to Christopher,
sir?' 'Yes, I was. Have I your permission?' 'By all means.'* □ *'The point is,
Mr. Elderson, a young man in the
office came to me yesterday with a
very queer story. Mont and I think
you should hear it.' 'By all means.'*
□ *'May I go first?' 'By all means.'*

by and by shpejt, së shpejti, brenda një
kohe të shkurtër
□ *You'll be getting married and having
a family by and by, and then you'll
understand why parents want to protect their children.* □ *He said that he
would me at the pub by and by.*

by and large përgjithësisht, në
përgjithësi, në tërësi
□ *The students are well-behaved, by
and large, although there are some
exceptions.* □ *This is quite a full program, and by and large surely a sensible one.* □ *'Taking it by and large' ...
we had a pleasant ten day's run from
New York to the Azores Islands.*

by any chance ndoshta
□ *Would you by any chance have
change for $5?* □ *I was wondering if
by any chance you could lend me $50
until the end of next week?*

by chance rastësisht
□ *Last Sunday I met him on the street
by chance.* □ *'I didn't try to get off
with your girlfriend,' he protested. 'I
just ran into her by chance on the
way home from library.'*

by common consent me miratim
(pëlqim) unanim
□ *By common consent the ladies
remained in the room after dessert.*
□ *She was chosen as a leader by
common consent.*

by day ditën
□ *The fugitives travelled by night and
rested by day.*

by degrees pak e nga pak, shkallë-
shkallë, dalëngadalë
□ *Mr. Micawber considered it necessary to prepare either my aunt or his
wife, by degrees, and said, sooner
than he had expected yesterday.* □ *By
degrees their friendship grew into love.*

by design me qëllim, qëllimisht
□ *Three times Wilson had been on the
spot to thwart his plans. Whether or
not this was by design, further interference could not be tolerated.*

by dint of something nëpërmjet, me
anë të
□ *The police had now, by dint of persistent enquiry over several weeks,
obtained enough evidence to con-
vict.* □ *He succeeded by dint of hard
work.*

by fair means or foul me rrugë të
ndershme e të pandershme, me të
gjitha mjetet
□ *It was a thing to be avoided, by any
means, fair or foul, that I could contrive.* □ *And if you want a salmon, or
a couple of rabbits to take home with
you, just say so, and I'll get them—by
fair means or foul.* □ *I want that site
and I've offered him a reasonable*

price for it. *I've tried **fair means**, but
I won't hesitate to use **foul**.*

by far më

□ *John is **by far** the cleverest boy in
the class.* □ *Of the two poems the
young man submitted for the competition, the shorter was **by far** the
better.*

by/in fits and starts me hope; herë-
herë

□ *Not withstanding these protections,
she could get none but broken sleep
by fits and starts.* □ *If you work **by fits
and starts** you will never achieve
much.* □ *He's been trying to learn
Spanish for three years, but I tell him
it's no use studying **by fits and** starts.*
□ *I can only work at the project in my
spare time, so it is being done **by fits
and starts**.* □ *The other unsolved
problem which I had upon my hands
was the problem of the dog, and
about this I worried **in fits and starts**.*

by force of circumstances i detyruar
nga rrethanat

□ *He had gambled away all his
money so, **by force of circumstances**,
he had to start work again.*

by hand me dorë

□ *If you're sending that account to
old Johnson, you'd better get it delivered **by hand**. He's too fond of
claiming that our bills get lost in the
post!* □ *We're trying to preserve the
old ways on this farm. We use horses
to pull the plough, and milk our cows
by hand.*

by heart përmendsh

□ *Learn the poem **by heart**.*

by hook or by crook me të gjitha
mjetet, me çdo mënyrë

□ *As soon as he heard there was to be
an evening party for the impresario,
he determined that **by hook or by
crook** he would be present too and*

get himself introduced. □ *Mr. Withers
having learned **by some hook or
crook** where she resided, bowed himself politely in.*

by inches 1. pak e nga pak, ca e nga ca

□ *But that he had seen her come to
this **by inches**, he never could have
believed her to be the same.* □ *The
small town grew **by inches**.*

2. për një qime, për një fije floku

□ *The car missed me **by inches**.*

by itself/oneself 1. vetiu, automatik-
isht; vetë, vetëm

□ *My room is in the old part of the
house. The door opens **by itself** if you
don't latch it.* □ *The trouble with these
automatic washing machines is that
they work happily **by themselves** for
some time but then suddenly break
down.* □ *Baby walked **by himself** this
morning—all the way from that mat
to the bookcase.* □ *'My wife hasn't
come back with the car yet. I'm
beginning to get worried.' 'Did she
go **by herself**?'*

2. më vete, veçan, i mëvetësishëm, i
veçuar

□ *The statue stands **by itself** in the
square.* □ *The house stands **by itself**.*

by/in leaps and bounds me shpejtësi,
me hapa të shpejtë, me hapa vigane

□ *I thought Johnny was never going
to learn to read, but since he got this
new teacher he's getting on **by leaps
and bounds**.* □ *And under the control
of a few persons, our trusts wax and
exploitation grows **by leaps and
bounds**.* □ *You will be pleased to
know that your son's English is
improving **by leaps and bounds**.*

by little and little dalëngadalë, pak e
nga pak

□ *The old man had come **by little and
little** into the room, until he now
touched my guardian with his elbow.*

by means of me ndihmën e, me anë të, nëpërmjet

□ *The general idea is to link up the islands as far as possible with the national road system by means of a short sea crossing.* □ *Two similar sets are used simultaneously, and communication between the operators are maintained by means of a built-in telephone.* □ *They got rid of the stones by means of a truck.* □ *We lifted the load by means of a crane.*

by mistake gabimisht

□ *You can't go on taking tablet after tablet till you've taken twenty by mistake.* □ *I took your bag instead of mine by mistake.*

by mouth/by word of mouth me gojë, gojarisht

□ *Jones got his invitation to join the company by word of mouth, but he said he couldn't reach a decision unless he had it in writing too.* □ *I'm so pleased you've been able to come this evening, and I hope you didn't mind getting your invitation by word of mouth, but I didn't know how to contact you.* □ *After attempting several letters, and failing in them all, he resolved to do it by word of mouth.*

by name me emër

□ *A strange man, Fred by name, came to see me.* □ *The teacher knows all his students by name.*

by nature nga natyra

□ *He was by nature so exceedingly compassionate who seemed to be ill at ease.* □ *She is proud by nature.*

by night natën

□ *We attacked the enemy camp by night*

by night and day ditë e natë, pa pushim

□ *We travelled by night and day for a week.*

by no (manner of) means/not by any (manner of) means 1. kurrsesi, në asnjë mënyrë, në asnjë rast

□ *And by no means, Tom-pray bear this in mind, for I am very serious, by no means lend him money any more.* □ *'No. I say No. I advise you not. I say by no means.'* □ *Poor old Benjy—he was not her equal by no manner of means but what he would do alone one couldn't think.*

2. aspak

□ *It is by no means clear.*

by reason of për shkak të

□ *Judge Lorne Stewart said that by reason of their refusal to authorise a transfusion the parents in the legal sense neglecting their child.* □ *He was excused by reason of his age.*

by right/as of right me të drejtë

□ *The property belongs to her as of right.*

by right(s) me drejtësi, me të drejtë

□ *Well, whether the gentlemen really do deprive us of any little matters which ought to be ours by rights I cannot say for certain, but the opinion of the old ones is they do.* □ *They say he's like a mummy. Where are you going to put him? He ought to have a pyramid by rights.* □ *He took all the credit for making a success of the hotel when, by rights, it should have gone to his wife.*

by/through the agency of sth/sb falë, me ndihmën e, në sajë të

□ *He obtained his position by the agency of friends.* □ *Rocks worn smooth through the agency of water.*

by the by meqë ra fjala

□ *By the by, here is the pen you lent me.*

by then atëhere, në atë kohë

□ *We didn't manage to get to the shops until the second day of the* *sales. **By then**, of course, all the best bargains had been sold.* □ *Phone the family a bit later on. Your father will be home **by then** and I know he wants to have a few words with you.* □ *I shall come back five years from now, you'll be a big boy **by then**.*

by/from the look of sb/sth nga pamja, në dukje, në të parë; me sa duket

□ ***By the look of** the sky, it's going to rain before the day is over.* □ *David can't be arriving tonight, **by the look of** it. We'll wait another half hour, and then go to bed.*

by the skin of one's teeth për një qime, për një fije floku

□ *We had a breakdown on the way and expected to miss the last ferry service, but we caught it **by the skin of our teeth**.* □ *I didn't do well in the exam: in fact, I just got through **by the skin of my teeth**.*

by the sweat of one's brow me djersën e ballit

□ *Jurgis was denied the chance to earn his living **by the sweat of his brow**.* □ *The poor farmer earned his living **by the sweat of his brow**.*

by the way meqë ra fjala

□ *I had a long talk with Jack Smith tonight—**by the way**, do you happen to know his address?* □ *'**By the way**,' she said, 'how did you know I wanted a caretaker?'* □ ***By the way**, dad, Mrs. Baines has come to march with us*

to our big meeting this afternoon. □ *'There's rather a good thing about that in his new book, where is it?' 'Do you know him, **by the way**?' she asked.*

by turns me radhë

□ *Traddles stared **by turns** at the ground and at Mr. Micawber, without so much as attempting to put in a word.* □ *She was laughing and crying **by turns** for the best part of half an hour.* □ *He unfolded the note, reading it and looking at Andrea **by turns**.* □ *My wife and I take it **by turns** to make the breakfast.*

by virtue of sth për arsye se, në bazë të, për hir të, falë

□ *He is entitled to free drinks **by virtue of** the fact that he is President of the club.* □ *He was exempt from charges **by virtue of** his youth.*

by way of 1. nga, nëpërmjet

□ *They are travelling to France **by way of** London.* □ *I can easily come home **by way of** the Post Office and get you stamps.*

2. si, si mjet (mënyrë), në formën e

□ *I think his offer to drive you home was **by way of** an apology for his behavior last night.* □ *It looked quite a cosy domestic picture, but, **by way of** greeting, he started straight away to grumble about having to have a fire at all.* □ *What are you thinking of doing **by way of** a holiday this year?*

C

call a halt ndaloj, ndërpres, i them ndal
□ *Let's* ***call a halt*** *to the meeting and continue tomorrow.* □ *After we had walked eight miles, we decided to* ***call a halt.*** □ *He has been allowed to play fast and loose long enough. It's time someone* ***called a halt*** *on him.*

call a spade a spade i quaj gjërat me emrin e vet, flas shkoqur, e them të vërtetën në sy, i them gjërat hapur
□ *I wouldn't live anywhere except London. But I like the Scots. They* ***call a spade a spade****, they say what they mean and they have a sense of humor.* □ *If you think the design is ridiculous, say so: don't be afraid to* ***call a spade a spade.*** □ *They were a little frightened at this young fellow, and the swing and smash of his words, and his trait of* ***calling a spade a spade****.*

call attention to tërheq vëmendjen për
□ *We shall have to* ***call*** *the local authority's* ***attention to*** *the poor state of the roads.* □ *I* ***called*** *his* ***attention to*** *what had happened.*

call away thërres
'I'm afraid the doctor isn't in. He was ***called away*** *a few minutes ago.'*
□ *He's been* ***called away*** *on business.*
□ *'Well, have you seen anything?'*
'I'm sorry I was ***called away.****'*

call back 1. i bëj zë, i thërras (të kthehet)
□ *He moved away as inconspicuously as he could, but Binta* ***called*** *him* ***back****, probably to reprimand him.*
□ *She walked away heavily and slowly, as if waiting to be* ***called back.***

2. ritelefonoj, marr sërish në telefon
□ *I told him I would* ***call*** *him* ***back*** *when I had some news.* □ *I shall make some enquires and* ***call*** *you* ***back.***

call by kaloj nga
□ *'Will you be in at five o'clock this evening? If so, I'll* ***call by*** *and pick up my saw and other tools, if you don't mind.'*

call for 1. shkoj, kaloj të marr (dikë)
□ *I'll* ***call for*** *you at six o'clock and we'll go to the theatre together.* □ *I'll* ***call for*** *you about eight.*

2. kërkoj
□ *Democrats are* ***calling for*** *a two-year tax cut.* □ *This question* ***calls for*** *prompt settlement.* □ *The rapid development of industry and agriculture* ***calls for*** *modern technical skills.*

call forth shkaktoj, nxit
□ *His speech* ***called forth*** *an angry response.*
□ *The proposal* ***called forth*** *a good deal of discussion.* □ *This is a task that will* ***call forth*** *his energies.*

call in 1. kërkoj kthimin
□ *The university* ***called in*** *all the library books for stocktaking.* □ *The army is* ***calling in*** *all the unwanted ammunition.* □ *He had to* ***call in*** *the loans he had made.*

2. thërres
□ *If the child does not improve, it will be necessary to* ***call in*** *a doctor.*
□ *Before you* ***call in*** *the water board, check that the pipes are not frozen.*

call (in) (at) kaloj, ndaloj
□ *We* ***called (in) at*** *Joe's Bar on the way home.*

call in/into question/doubt vë në dyshim

□ *From the sixteenth century onwards, learned men began to **call into doubt** the idea that the Earth was the center of the Universe.* □ *Have you the impertinence to **call** my truthfulness **into question**.*

call into play vë në lëvizje

□ *Chess is a game that **calls into play** all one's powers of concentration.* □ *The case **called** every faculty of the doctor **into play**.*

call it quits e lë, e mbyll barazim (barabar, fit e fit) ndeshjen etj.

□ *The chess-players drew every game until they finally decided to **call it quits**.*

call it a day e mbyll, i jap fund me kaq

□ *We'll have one more drink and **call it a day**.*

□ *After more than eight hours of fruitful labor they decided to **call it a day**.* □ *'Tell them we've **called it a day**,' said Luke with fatigue.* □ *After forty years in politics he thinks it's time to **call it a day**.* □ *We searched for the ring everywhere, but eventually we had to **call it a day**.*

call off 1. anuloj

□ *'I don't see any point in going on with our idea of a picnic, in weather like this. Let's **call it off**.'* □ *The basketball match was **called off** because of bad weather.*

2. urdhëroj ndalimin e

□ *The pursuit was **called off** when it was clear that we had won the day.*

call on (upon) 1. vizitoj, i bëj dikujt një vizitë

□ *Our representative will **call on** you in the course of next week.* □ *Why does Traddles look so important when he **calls upon** me this afternoon.*

2. ftoj, kërkoj

□ *'I will now **call on** Mr. White to propose a vote of thanks to the committee.'* □ *I now **call upon** the chairman to address the meeting.*

3. i bëj thirrje

□ *We are **calling upon** you to help us.* □ *We shall have to **call upon** our friends to help us.*

call sb's bluff zbuloj blofin (mashtrimin) e

□ *Cheek is one of his professions, and here he was exercising it even before opening his mouth. When his **bluff** was finally **called**, he carried off his resignation with dashing style.* □ *They thought of me as having definitely chosen a life of cosy provincial mediocrity and, outwardly, I had. I should have gone mad if my **bluff** had been **called** and I'd been asked to settle into that position for good.* □ *The landlord said he would throw us out if we didn't pay our rent: we decided to **call his bluff** and refused to pay.*

call sb names shaj, s'i lë gjë pa thënë

□ *He flew into a tremendous passion, **called him** all manner of **names**.* □ *'Is it true, what Billy says, that you punched his nose so hard that it bled?' 'Yes, sir. But he was **calling** me **names**.'*

call out 1. thërras, bërtas

□ *'If you want anything from the larder, just **call out** and I'll bring it.* □ *If you know the answer, put your hand up; don't **call out**.* □ *'Please keep quiet while I **call out** the names of the successful competitors.*

2. thërras (për ndihmë etj)

□ *The ambulance had been **called out**.* □ *The fire brigade was **called out** last night.*

3. urdhëroj, këshilloj daljen në grevë

☐ *Bus-drivers may be **called out** on strike in support of their recent wage-claim.*

call to account kërkoj llogari, vë para përgjegjësisë

☐ *His boss **called him to account** for falling to meet the deadline.* ☐ *Jim was in charge when the accident happened, so he will have to be **called to account**.* ☐ *We should not overlook his mistakes. It is about time we **call** him **to account**.* ☐ *He may think that all this petty pilfering goes unnoticed, but one day he'll be **called to account**.*

call to memory kujtoj, sjell ndër mend

☐ *What you have just said **calls to** my memory a story I heard long ago.*

call to mind sjell ndër mend

☐ *I'm sure I've met the girl you're referring to, but I can't **call** her **to mind**.* ☐ *The accused said that he could not **call to mind** making any of the statements quoted by the police.* ☐ *We will forget them or if we ever **call** them **to mind**, it shall be only as some uneasy dream that has passed away.* ☐ *Again, I wonder whether any of the neighbours **call to mind**, as I do, how, we used to walk home together, she and I.*

call to order kërkoj që të vendoset rregulli (qetësia)

☐ *At two o'clock, the chairman **called** us **to order** and the afternoon session began.* ☐ *Despite attempts to **call** them **to order**, the audience continued to stamp.*

call up 1. marr në telefon, telefonoj

☐ *The radio station had an open line on which listeners could **call up** to discuss various issues.* ☐ *What time shall I **call** you **up**?* ☐ *The doctor was **called up** three times during one night to attend urgent cases.*

2. kujtoj, sjell ndër mend

☐ *The sound of seagulls **called up** happy memories of his childhood holidays.* ☐ *The museum **called up** memories of my childhood.* ☐ *His poems **call up** those pleasant days when we worked together with the farmers in the countryside.*

3. thërres (në shërbim ushtarak)

☐ *He was **called up** right at the beginning of the war.* ☐ *I was extremely lucky not to be **called up** at that time.*

4. thërres në ndihmë

☐ *He saw that he would have to **call** his reserves **up** if defeat was to be avoided.*

calm down qetësoj; qetësohem

☐ *The sea **calmed down** as soon as the wind fell.* ☐ *He ran his hand lightly over his forehead, surprised by the accumulation of sweat and the coolness of his skin. He began to **calm down**.* ☐ *It was a real lesson in the power of a woman to **calm** a man **down**.* ☐ ***Calming** him **down** took longer than I had expected.*

camp out fushoj

☐ *They **camped out** in the woods for a week.*

cannot help (but) nuk mund të mos

☐ *You may not like him, but you **can't help but** admire his courage.*

cannot hold a candle as që mund të krahasohet, s'i vjen (s'i afrohet) as te thoi (gishti) i këmbës

☐ *She writes quite amusing stories but she **can't hold a candle** to the more serious novelists.*

cancle out eliminoj; balancoj

☐ *A large inflow of investments has **cancelled out** their indebtedness.* ☐ *Her kindness and generosity **cancel out** her occasional flashes of temper.*

can't say bo (boh, boo) to a goose s'e nxjerr dot qimen nga qulli

□ *Grandpa was quite surprised, and said, 'That fellow! Why, I didn't think he could say boo to a goose!'—but I know he could, couldn't he, mama?*

cap in hand me nderim, plot respekt (përulje, përunjësi)

□ *The taxi driver, cap in hand, withdrew, and Alec who, as usual, was bareheaded, asked if he might take off his overcoat.* □ *All pensions should be at or above subsistence level. Retired workers should not have to go cap in hand to ask for supplementary allowances.*

care about shqetësohem, bëhem merak

□ *All she cares about is her social life.* □ *The Murdstones cared about nobody but themselves.*

care for 1. kujdesem

□ *'Who is to care for me when I am old.'* □ *Who would care for the farm when they were away?*

2. pëlqej, kam qejf

□ *I don't care for her curtains.* □ *He may be a very nice man, but I don't care for him.*

carry all/everything before one kam sukses të plotë; arrij gjithë pikësynimet

□ *Tom carried all before him at the athletics, winning every event he entered for.* □ *With the overwhelming forces that he had managed to build, Montgomery finally carried everything before him in Africa.*

carry away rrëmben, pushton, çon peshë

□ *Isabel was carried away by the thought that almost for the first time she was having a serious conversation with her husband about books.* □ *Don't be carried away by success.*

carry (send) coals to Newcastle çoj ujë në det, bëj një punë të kotë

□ *Building another restaurant in this district would be carrying coals to Newcastle: the place is full of restaurants already.* □ *It would be sending coals to Newcastle.... not to mention salt to Dysart.*

carry conviction ta mbush mendjen, është bindës

□ *Don't get so fiery. Truths don't have to be shouted at people in order to carry conviction.* □ *Mr. Jack Jones is fond of fulminating against the supposed iniquities of the Industrial Relations Act, but he would carry more conviction if he showed that he was capable of looking after his own cabbage patch.* □ *His story does not carry much conviction.*

carry into effect realizoj, zbatoj, vë në jetë

□ *He will surely carry his promise into effect.* □ *It was a constructive idea and we shouldn't be altogether surprised if he had carried it into effect.*

carry into execution vë në zbatim, vë në jetë

□ *He would find it difficult to carry it into execution.* □ *When these arrangements had been well considered and were fully understood by all, it was time to begin to carry them into execution.*

carry it off kaloj, përballoj me sukses

□ *If Mary's former husband had come in a little earlier, the guests would have been able to carry it off all right, but he had caught them off balance.* □ *My remark had obviously annoyed him. I tried feebly to carry it off.* □ *Although she had only rehearsed the part a few times, she carried it off beyond all expectation.*

carry it too far teproj, kaloj masën, kapërcej kufijtë, çoj në ekstrem, nuk ruaj masën e duhur

58

□ *Come on, Bob, give me a serious answer. You've **carried** your teasing too far.* □ *It's very rude to reject well-meant offers of help.* □ *You can **carry** independence too far.*

carry off marr, fitoj

□ *The visiting team of athletes **carried off** most of the medals.* □ *This factory **carried off** a prize medal at the late Exhibition.*

carry one's point arrij synimin (qëllimin); sqaroj qartë, përçoj mendimin (pikëpamjen etj.)

□ *Having **carried the point** about not overloading the boat, he got them to settle among themselves what should be left behind.* □ *Look, Margaret, we've all agreed now that it's hopeless to think of going away next weekend. You've **carried your point**, and there's no need to be thinking up fresh arguments every half hour.* □ *That's the surest way of **carrying** his **point**.*

carry on 1. bëj, zhvilloj

□ *You shouldn't **carry on** long conversations with your friends when somebody else is waiting to use the telephone.* □ *It is difficult to **carry on** a conversation with all this noise around us.*

2. vazhdoj

□ *'Please **carry on** as usual when I listen to the class.'* □ *It was the worst possible place to **carry on** his research.* □ *They **carried on** their work even under the most difficult conditions.*

3. zihem, grindem, nervozohem, qahem

□ *Old Tom was **carrying on** about his pen; he made such a fuss you'd think it was his head.*

4. drejtoj, bëj, kryej

□ *A great many shady business are **carried on** through the small-ad*

columns *of respectable newspapers.*

carry one's head high jam krenar, mbaj kokën lart

□ *Mrs. Cowperwood could never understand how a girl could **carry** her head so high.*

carry on its face e ka të shkruar në ballë, duket qartë

□ *This sentence **carries** its meaning on its face.*

carry out 1. përmbush, plotësoj

□ *He explained that he was simply **carrying out** instructions.*

2. kryej, zbatoj, vë në jetë

□ *Before testing this method on patients, Dr. Baronofsky **carried out** tests for two years on three hundred dogs.* □ *These orders must be **carried out** at once.*

carry over shtyj

□ *'I propose that some minor matters on the agenda should be **carried over** for consideration at the next meeting.'* □ *The group agreed to **carry over** its discussion to the next meeting.*

carry (sweep) somebody off his feet ngre peshë, entuziazmoj pa masë

□ *He was **swept off his feet** by the other's work, and astonished that no attempt had been made to publish it.* □ *The audience was **carried off their feet** by his performance.*

carry the ball veproj me gjallëri, veproj aktivisht

□ *'He was a dolt he thought. How he had sat through the dinner without once opening his trap, letting Yates **carry the ball** for something which he himself, somehow, felt was right!'*

carry the can mbaj përgjegjësinë, fajin

□ *I think we should do what Bob says: he is in charge and he is the one who has to **carry the can** if anything goes wrong.*

carry/win the day fitoj, dal fitimtar, korr fitore

□ *The committee had a long discussion about the new regulations, but finally the people who supported them* **carried the day**. □ *The conceders* **carried the day**, *but only by majority of one.* □ *His arguments* **carried the day**, *his choice was approved by the committee.* □ *Our basketball team made a most spectacular performance and* **carried the day**.

carry through kryej, përmbush, plotësoj, çoj deri në fund

□ *We are united on these policies and determined to* **carry** *them* **through**. □ *These aims will be* **carried through** *to the end.*

carry/have/bear two faces under one hood jam njeri me dy fytyra, jam si mësalla me dy faqe

□ *You are a specious fellow... and* **carry two faces under your hood**.

carry weight ka rëndësi, ka peshë, i shkon fjala, ka influencë

□ *If such representations are to* **carry weight** *they will have to avoid bias and be of high intellectual standard.* □ *People have a great deal of respect for that man, therefore what he says* **carries weight**. □ *That argument doesn't* **carry** *much* **weight**.

carve sth out for oneself krijoj për vete

□ *He managed to* **carve out** *a career* **for oneself** *as an actor, though at first he hardly earned enough to keep body and soul together.* □ *She* **carved out** *a name* **for herself** *as a reporter.*

case in point, a rast në fjalë, rast (shembull) tipik

□ *There are too many lazy people in this office, and Jim is* **a case in point**: *he hardly ever does any work.* □ *I tell*

you he has a real sense of discipline. His readiness to take up that work is **a case in point**.

cash down me para në dorë

□ *'You won't get a better used car for the price anywhere,' the salesman assured him,' and don't forget you get 9 percent discount for* **cash down**.' □ *He took his note from his dress coat pocket. Four hundred pounds in fives and tens—the remainder of the proceeds of his half of sleeve—links, sold last night,* **cash down**, *to George Forsyte.*

cash (down) on the nail me para në dorë

□ *He sold... it every year for* **cash on the nail**.

cast a damp (damper) on shkurajoj, ftoh, ul (fashit) vrullin (entuziazmin etj.)

□ *Here there was another pause. Mr. Pickwick was a stranger, and his coming had evidently* **cast a damp upon** *the party.*

cast a glance hedh një sy, një vështrim

□ *He* **cast a** *keen* **glance** *of surprise at the group before him.* □ *Diana* **cast a** *pitying* **glance** *at her, and her voice was less sharp.*

cast a gloom on brengos, trishtoj

□ *The death of the child* **cast a gloom** *on the family.*

cast a look hedh një vështrim

□ *She* **cast a** *hurried* **look** *back.*

cast an eye/one's eye(s) over sb/sth hedh një sy

□ *Would you* **cast your eye over** *these calculations to check that they are correct?* □ *'Why?' I cried, as I* **cast my eye over** *it.* □ *Perry, ...* **cast an** *envious* **eye upon** *it.*

cast a shadow zymtoj, errësoj, zbeh, hedh hije mbi

□ *These recollections being of a kind*

calculated to **cast a shadow** *on the brightness of the holiday. Kit diverted the conversation to general topics.*

cast a slur on njollos, hedh baltë mbi
□ *Roger's attempts to* **cast an intolerable slur** *on his reputation were in vain.*

cast a spell over magjeps, mahnit
□ *The fiery young politician* **cast a spell over** *his audience.*

cast aspersions on sb/sth shpif
□ *How dare you* **cast aspersions on** *my wife's character?* □ *You oughtn't* **cast aspersions** *like that. I am surprised at you Donald.*

cast/draw/throw a veil mbuloj, ruaj (mbaj) të fshehtë
□ *I must* **throw a veil** *over some mortifying circumstances.* □ *The headmaster was very angry, but I think I had better* **draw a veil** *over what he actually said.*

cast about for kërkoj
□ *He* **cast about** *in his mind for some plausible excuse for not turning up at the meeting.* □ *The suspect* **cast about for** *some way of escaping from the police car.*

cast aside heq, largoj, flak tej
□ *As soon as he inherited his father's fortune, he* **cast** *his old friends* **aside.**
□ *He* **cast aside** *all his inhibitions.*

cast away lë, braktis
□ *'If you were* **cast away** *on a desert island, would you be able to fend for yourself?'*

cast dirt at sb hedh baltë, shpif (për dikë)
□ *It's not in his nature to* **cast dirt at** *the others.*

cast in a different mould është nga tjetër brumë
□ *But I don't mean to flatter you: if you are* **cast in a different mould** *to the majority, it is not merit of yours.*

cast (in) one's lot with lidh fatin me
□ *She felt thoroughly bound to him as a wife, and that* **her lot was cast** *with his, whatever it might be.*
□ *After much hesitation, he decided to* **cast in his lot** *with the rebels.*
□ *'If you* **cast your lot in with** *that crowd of layabouts, you'll soon be in trouble.'*

cast in the same mould është nga një brumë, bukë e një mielli, janë prerë me një gërshërë
□ *They are all* **cast in the same mould.** □ *The old and the new opportunists are* **cast in the same mould.**

castles in Spain/in the air kështjella në erë (ajër), ëndrra me sy hapur
□ *I am not less hopeful now ... my Highland mansion may prove to be a* **castle in Spain** *after all.* □ *... her mind as she always said, was on something not so practical-* **castles in the air** *really.*

cast light on (upon) sth hedh dritë mbi
□ *I should like to* **cast some light** *on the matter.* □ *The fresh evidence* **cast a new light** *on the matter.*

cast lots hedh short
□ *They* **cast lots** *as to who should begin.*

cast off 1. heq
□ *He* **cast off** *his clothes and dived in to the cool water of the lake.* □ *Now that the warmer weather has come we can* **cast off** *winter clothes.*
2. braktis, flak tej
□ *When he grows tired of a woman, he just* **casts** *her* **off** *like an old coat.*
□ *Organizations must* **cast off** *those bureaucratic practices.*

cast one's mind back kujtoj, sjell ndër mend
□ *Cast your mind back* *to the last time you saw Bill Jones: did he seem worried or depressed at all?*

cast pearls before swine ku di dhia ç'është tagjia, ku di derri këmborë

□ *I gave a series of lessons on Shakespeare to the sixth form, but it was really a case of* **casting pears before swine**: *they were too lazy or too stupid to appreciate them.* □ *Tom took his friends to the Art Gallery, but it was* **casting pears before the swine.** □ *Oh, I do a thankless thing, and* **cast pearls before swine.**

cast something in somebody's face (teeth) ia përplas në fytyrë

□ *You wouldn't* **cast** *what you have done for me* **in my face.**

cast the first stone sulmoj, akuzoj i pari

□ *The case against Mr. Brown had to be dropped because none of his neighbours wanted to be the one to* **cast the first stone.**

cat's paw vegël, mashë

□ *The ambitious young politician did not realize that he was being used as a* **cat's paw** *by the president.* □ *Pothinus. ...You are to be her* **catspaw;** *you are to tear the crown from her brother's head and set it on her own.*

catch a cold ftohem, marr të ftohtë

□ *'Go back to bed, Prissie,' said Fergus with a note of protectiveness in his voice. 'You'll* **catch cold.'** □ *But she wore flimsy shoes in all that snow! No wonder she wrote to us once that she had* **caught an** *awful* **cold** *and been under the care of two doctors.* □ *Felix* **caught a cold** *that kept him at home for a month.*

catch a crab dal bosh, bëj një lëvizje bosh (të rremave)

□ *Fleur sped on. She was late, and wanted all her wits about her when she got in ... Mont* **caught a little crab.** *'Please row.'*

catch a glimpse of sb/sth shoh kalimthi, fluturimthi

□ *Again, I* **catch** *rare* **glimpses of** *my mother moving her lips timidly between the two, with one of them muttering at each ear like low thunder.* □ *I* **caught a glimpse of** *my native village at the foot of the mountain from the window of the train.* □ *He* **caught a glimpse of** *her before she vanished into the crowd.*

catch at a straw kapem pas fijes së kashtës

□ *A drowning man will* **catch at a straw.** □ *Our close questioning had him floundering about,* **catching at straws.** □ *He acted like a drowning man trying to* **catch at a straw.**

catch fire merr zjarr, ndizet

□ *Don't leave your coat too near the heater: it may* **catch fire.** □ *We collected sticks to boil our kettle, but they were damp and would not* **catch fire.** □ *She was standing far too near the open hearth and her nightdress* **caught fire.**

catch hold of kap, kapem

□ *I threw the rope and he* **caught hold of** *it.* □ *... One of the clerks* **caught hold of** *me.*

catch in the act zë me presh në dorë, zë në akt e sipër

□ *The police* **caught** *the thieves* **in the act**: *they were just opening the factory safe.* □ *He was* **caught in the act** *of embezzling money.*

□ *Having been* **caught in the act,** *the culprit had no way of denying the crime.*

catch it ndëshkohem, e pësoj, e ha keq

□ *Look at your shirt—all torn! You'll* **catch it** *from your mum, when she sees it!* □ *You'll* **catch it** *if the headmaster discovers you've been coming in late.* □ *It is I who* **catch it** *every time* *anything goes wrong.* □ *You will* **catch it** *when your father finds you have been trampling over the flower beds.* □ *When the child spilled the milk, he was afraid he would* **catch it** *from his mother.*

catch on 1. përhapet shumë, hyn në modë, bëhet e njohur, bëhet popullor, gëzon popullaritet

□ *Mini-skirts first* **caught on** *in the 1960s.* □ *That's a song that has* **caught on.**

2. kuptoj, i bie në të, marr vesh

□ *He followed the conversation rather blankly for a while, then his expression changed. He was* **catching on.** □ *She has an alert mind so it will not take her long to* **catch on.**

catch one's breath 1. shtang, mbaj frymën (nga habia, etj.)

□ *The people in the crowd* **caught their breath** *when the man fell from the window.* □ *He paused. Looking fixedly out of the window at the beautiful skyline, halting not so much to find the right words, but to* **catch his breath.** □ *He* **caught his breath** *for a second and felt a slight pain round the heart as he heard Eric's voice.*

2. mbushem me frymë

□ *I'm not used to climbing hills: let's stop for a few minutes while I* **catch my breath.**

catch one's death of cold plevitosem, marr të ftohur të rëndë, marr plevit

□ *What on earth are doing? Sam, get back into bed at once, do you want to* **catch your death of cold?** □ *Don't go out without your coat on: otherwise, you'll* **catch your death of cold.**

catch out kap, zë ngushtë

□ *The little girl saw she had been* **caught out.** *She looked as if she were going to cry; but then her face bright-*

ened again. □ *His explanation of the circumstances seemed rather convincing, until someone* **caught him out** *by putting a question which caused him to contradict himself.*

catch sight of shoh, vërej, më zë syri

□ *I was just passing by when I* **caught sight of** *my brother in the crowd.* □ *She* **caught sight of** *what was going forward.* □ *Hilary stepped out of the witness—box and in doing so* **caught sight of** *his niece and waved a finger.*

catch sb napping zë gafil (në befasi), zë të papërgatitur, zë në gjumë

□ *In the football match, the striker* **caught** *the whole defence* **napping** *and scored a goal.* □ *Stevenson would have loved to find an excuse to get me fired, but I was wise to him and wasn't going to be* **caught napping.** □ *He feared financial storms ... and where so much was at stake he did not propose to be* **caught napping.**

catch sb off (one's) guard zë (kap) në befasi, zë të papërgatitur

□ *When dawn came and the waiting seemed at an end, he fell asleep and was vexed to have been* **caught off his guard,** *to have been aroused by Verona's entrance and her agitated 'Oh, what is it, Dad?'*

catch sb red-handed kap me presh në dorë

□ *The thieves had no defence in the trial. They had been* **caught red-handed** *in the bank they were robbing.* □ *Virginia* **caught** *Helen* **red-handed,** *shut the door and leaned against it. 'Reading my letters again, Helen?'* □ *She flushed... looking as guilty as though she had been* **caught red-handed.**

catch sb's eye 1. shihem sy më sy, kryqëzoj shikimin (vështrimin) me, kap vështrimin e

□ *'I think perhaps one oughtn't to,' said Huga, and he was deadly serious. Then I caught his eye and we both laughed enormously.* □ *He looked for a moment at Elizabeth, till catching her eye.*

2. më zë syri, më bie në sy

□ *I was just looking at the shop-window when this very nice watch caught my eye, and I bought it.* □ *As I turned something caught my eye in the wall behind the bookcase.* □ *I did not catch his eye, else I should have greeted him.*

catch sb's fancy pëlqej, më duket i mirë (i bukur, i këndshëm etj.)

□ *The only thing in the auction sale that caught my fancy was a little French clock.* □ *She saw a dress in the shop window and it caught her fancy immediately.*

catch sb with his/her pants/trousers down zë me brekë nëpër këmbë (shalë, zvarrë)

□ *The reporting of the scandal caught the committee with their pants down: they had not expected that it would be public soon.*

catch up on sth arrij, kompensoj

□ *The secretary had to work in the lunch hour to catch up on her neglected filing.*

catch up with sb/catch sb up kap, arrij

□ *He's working hard to catch up with the others.* □ *Go on in front. I'll soon catch you up.*

cater for kënaq, përmbush, plotësoj nevojat (kërkesat)

□ *This play center caters for children of all ages.* □ *In a consumer society*

no effort is made to **cater for** the needs of the elderly.

caught up in 1. i angazhuar

□ *She was caught up in the anti-nuclear movement.* □ *For a time my father, with a young wife, was caught up in a circle which included many famous names.*

2. i zhytur, i përhumbur

□ *When one is adolescent, one often gets caught up in one's thoughts and dreams.*

cause a stir shkaktoj pështjellim, sensacion

□ *The news caused quite a stir in the village.* □ *Such revelations of corruption in high places were bound to cause a considerable stir.*

cave in 1. shembet, bie përbrenda

□ *The roof of the tunnel caved in on the workmen.* □ *The roof of the mine caved in as a result of the explosion.*

2. thyhem, epem, lëshoj pe

□ *I more or less caved in, though I still defended my explanation.* □ *Under close questioning, the wretched man caved in abjectly and confessed all his misdemeanours.*

center in/on/upon/round përqëndroj

□ *Her research is centered on the social effects of unemployment.* □ *For some time all my interests have centered in the people's me-thod of agri-culture.*

chain up lidh me zinxhir

□ *That dog ought to be chained up; it's dangerous.*

chalk out vizatoj, skicoj (me shkumës)

□ *To explain his design to the visitors, the architect chalked out a simple plan on the blackboard.* □ *Goalposts were roughly chalked out on the playground wall.*

chalk up 1. regjistroj

□ *The team has chalked up its fifth win in a row.* □ *As a result of technical innovation the melting steel mill chalked up new records in its average daily output.*
2. shënoj

□ *'I see your name is chalked up on the messages board.' 'Oh, is it? Thanks very much for telling me.'* □ *Chalk this round up to me, please, barman.*

chance acquaintance/companion, a i njohur (shok) i rastit

□ *I don't know what made me start confiding in him. He was a chance acquaintance, after all, someone I'd met on a train journey.* □ *The boy had been climbing on the rocks with a couple of chance companions, young holiday-makers like himself, when the accident occurred.*

chances are (that), the ngjasat janë që, ka mundësi (të ngjarë) që

□ *I'm not going to let you go off on that long drive as you are, with all that drink in you. The chances are you'd fall asleep on the wheel.* □ *The chances are that she'll be coming.* □ *You could try phoning him, but the chances that he won't be home yet.*

chance one's arm/luck provoj fatin

□ *I know that the concert has been very popular, and I don't have a ticket, but I'll just go along to the theatre anyway and chance my arm.* □ *He considered the pros and cons of making the investment for a full week and then decided to chance his arm and hope to get a return for his capital.*

change color ndërroj fytyrë

□ *The thief changed color when he saw that the policeman was pointing a gun at him.* □ *If this young man means nothing to her, as she claims, why did she change color at the mention of his name?* □ *Look at him! See how he changes color. Which of us looks the guilty person—he or I?* □ *As I looked steadily at him, I saw him change color.*

change for the better ndryshim për mirë

□ *The situation is now so bad that any change is likely to be a change for the better.*

change for the worse ndryshim për keq

□ *The weather had been bad enough, but from the looks of the sky we expect a change for the worse.*

change hands ndërron duar, ndryshon pronar, kalon nga dora në dorë

□ *This house has changed hands twice in the last ten years.* □ *The hotel has changed hands, I believe, since I stayed there. It may be better managed now.* □ *All over the world a great demand for diamonds and other precious stones has risen. They change hands a dozen more times until finally they disappear and cannot be traced.*

change/swap horses in midstream (while crossing a stream) bëj ndryshime në moment të papërshtatshëm (të rrezikshëm); bëj punë pa mend

□ *When the 'New Mathematic' syllabus was adopted most schools introduced it at the lower end of the curriculum only, and pupils who had completed two or more years' instruction under the old system were not required to change horses in midstream.*

change of air/climate, a ndryshim klime (havaje)

□ *'But I'll tell you what, I believe I can get you Arty Nares: you've seen Arty; he's a first-rate navigator.' And he proceeded to explain to me that Mr. Nares would be pleased to have **a change of air**.* □ *A **change of air** will do you good.*

change course ndryshoj kursin (drejtimin)

□ *The river had **changed its course**.* □ *It's a winding river that **changes course** twenty times in as many miles.* □ *This information made me **change my course**.*

change of heart, a ndryshim në qëndrim, në gjendjen shpirtërore

□ *Seeing the iron manner in which he had managed to wrest victory out of defeat after the first seriously contested election, these gentlemen had experienced **a change of heart** and announced that they would gladly help finance any enterprise which Cowperwood might undertake.* □ *When recently he had announced his intention of 'turning Catholic', his wife was delighted at Ted's **change of heart**, little suspecting his real motives.*

change one's coat kthej (ndërroj) fletën (pllakën)

□ *He managed to survive by **changing his coat** with every swing of political opinion.*

change one's mind ndërroj mendje (mendim)

□ *He had not a seat, and he intended not to take any at first, but now he **changed his mind** and bought one.* □ *I began to cherish hopes I had no right to conceive; that the match was broken off, that rumor had been mistaken; that one or both parties had **changed their minds**.*

change one's tune ndryshoj qëndrim; ndërroj (ndryshoj) tonin; kthej (ndërroj) pllakën (fletën)

□ *Hawkins smiled secretively as if he knew something that would **change their tune** if they knew it.* □ *The boss said we would have to accept a cut in our salaries, but when he saw how angry we were, he quickly **changed his tune**.*

change one's ways ndryshoj mënyrën e jetesës (për t'ju përshtatur kushteve të reja); ndryshoj metodë (udhë)

□ *I'm not against modern methods of teaching at all. It's just that I'm too old to **change my ways**.* □ *She has her own idea of how a house should be run and you'd never get her to **change her ways**.*

change over from in (to) kaloj, ndryshoj nga ... në

□ *The country has **changed over from** military **to** democratic rule.* □ *He suddenly **changed from** a well-behaved child **into** a loutish adolescent.* □ *My wife wants to **change over from** gas **to** electricity for her cooking; she says it's cleaner.*

change places with sb ndryshoj vend me

□ *Let's **change places** so you can be nearer the fire—I can see you're very cold.* □ *'I wouldn't **change places with** Joe for all the tea in China: working on a sewage farm must be hellish!'*

change the face of sth ndryshoj faqen (pamjen) e

□ *They worked under good leadership, and they **changed the face of** their country.* □ *These new inventions will **change the face of** offices and factories over the next thirty years.*

change the record ndryshoj pllakën

□ *'When I was a boy I didn't do this, I didn't have that!'*—I *wish Grandpa would change the record occasionally.* □ *'Change the record, will you?'* shouted Ann from the kitchen. *'Do you realize you've been whistling the same tune over and over, all the time you have been fixing that window.*

change sides hidhem (kaloj) në anën tjetër

□ *He... had changed sides at the very nick of time.*

change the subject ndërroj temë

□ *The two teachers had been criticising the headmaster but, when they saw him coming, they quickly changed the subject.* □ *When she wanted to talk about her work, he would change the subject, or at best listen condescendingly, as if she was a child telling of school excitement.*

chapter and verse referenca të sakta; të dhëna (hollësi) të plota

□ *He was able to give the lawyer chapter and verse for everything that had happened since the beginning of the dispute.* □ *I can't quote chapter and verse but I can give you the main points the author was making.* □ *I haven't got one of those memories that can quote chapter and verse, but I think I can give you the gist of the passage you are asking about.*

chapter of accidents, a një varg ndodhish (aksidentesh, incidentesh) të papritura

□ *The result of this incredible chapter of accidents was that Jim's car was in the garage for a week, being repaired.* □ *We've had a proper chapter of accidents this morning,' the school Matron told the headmistress. 'I've just about emptied the First Aid box.*

charge at sb/sth sulmoj

□ *The troops charged at the enemy lines.* □ *He charged at me with his head down and both fists flying.*

charge for kërkoj (si pagesë)

□ *'How much do they charge for washing a car?'*

charge up to debitoj, ngarkoj, vë (shënoj) në llogari të

□ *'Please charge these goods to my husband's account.'*

charge with 1. akuzoj

□ *The offence with which he is charged carries a heavy penalty.* □ *The policeman charged him with driving a car while under the influence of alcohol.*

2. rëndoj, ngarkoj

□ *The atmosphere was tense and charged with fear.*

3. ngarkoj (me një detyrë)

□ *The young officer was charged with the task of taking 200 prisoners to the rear.* □ *She was charged with an important mission.*

charity begins at home bamirësia fillon në shtëpi

□ *Before you busy yourself with telling us how to put the rest of the world right, just remember that charity begins at home.*

chatter away/on flet si çakalle mulliri, flet pa pushim, grin sallatë

□ *Despite the horrors and anxieties of the previous two months, she chattered away as if it had been a gay adventure.* □ *Do stop chattering on about the weather when I'm trying to read.*

chatter like a magpie si pushon goja, nuk i rri gjuha rehat, grin si çakalle mulliri

□ *And as school children started to get everything ready, chattering like* *a lot of **magpies**, she turned back to Miss Elliot.* □ *I was looking forward to exchange news with Morton after all these years, but I could hardly get a word in, because of **his chattering magpie** of a wife.*

cheat out of mashtroj, ia hedh me dredhi

□ *The poor child was **cheated out of** his inheritance by a dishonest lawyer.* □ *'Be careful! He'll **cheat** you **out of** your entitlement if he possibly can.*

check in (at) regjistrohem (në hotel), zë hotel

□ *They had an accident on the road and did not **check in at** their hotel until after midnight.* □ *They **checked in at** the hotel in less than an hour after their arrival at the station.*

check off spuntoj, verifikoj

□ *Please **check off** these parcels before they are dispatched.* □ *They **checked off** all the items in their inventory one by one.*

check out of paguaj dhe largohem nga hoteli

□ *'Has Mr. Jones left yet?' 'Yes, he **checked out** five minutes ago.'* □ *He had **checked out** just before I came in.*

check sth out kontrolloj

□ *When all the instruments had been **checked out** according to the established routine, the pilot signalled that he was ready for take-off.*

□ *We'd better **check** the whole place **out** in case it's been bugged.*

check through verifikoj, kontrolloj; korrigjoj

□ *'Have you **checked** these proofs **through** ?'*

□ *'This account is full of mistakes! Wasn't it ever **checked through**?'*

check up (on) hetoj; kontrolloj, verifikoj

□ *The police are **checking up on** him.*

□ *An experiment was carried out to **check up on** the reliability of certain criteria.*

cheek by jowl pranë e pranë, afër e afër, gju më gju

□ *It is a city of contrasts: luxury hotels stand **cheek by jowl** with terrible slums.* □ *The other two took no notice of him at all, though they were standing **cheek by jowl**.* □ *All sorts and conditions of men and women and he **cheek by jowl** with them—like sardines in a box and he didn't mind.*

cheer on inkurajoj, i jap zemër

□ *The crowd **cheered** the runners **on** as they started on the last lap of the race.* □ *There was no one there to **cheer** him **on** or applaud.*

cheer up gëzohem, gjallërohem, më shndrit fytyra

□ *When she heard that her mother was safe she immediately **cheered up**.* □ *'You must **cheer up**, Mrs. June. You'll soon be walking again.'* □ *She was **cheered up** by the news that she was likely to be out of hospital in a day or two.*

chew over mendoj, peshoj mirë

□ *'You've had long enough to **chew** the matter **over**; I want my answer now.'* □ *Just **chew** those facts **over** and let us know your opinion.* □ *That matter has been **chewed over** again and again.*

chew the cud reflektoj, përbluaj, rrah me mend, shoshit me vete, bluaj në mendje

□ *During the evening, moodily **chewing the cud** of these reflections, he gradually convinced himself of Alec's bona-fides.* □ *Whenever you two get together you do nothing but **chew the cud** of schoolboy memories.* □ *He sat there polishing the nail of one forefinger against the back of the*

other, and **chewing the cud** *of life.*
□ *Don't decide hastily.* **Chew the cud**
on it for a time.

chew the fat/rag bisedoj gjerë e gjatë;
flas duke u ankuar; hahem, zihem,
grindem

□ *I met my old friend Bill in town yes-*
terday; we **chewed the fat** *for about*
an hour. □ *'The other typist won't like*
you appointing the new girl to be
your private secretary.' 'Oh, it'll give
them something to **chew the rag**
about in their coffee breaks.'

chicken out/out of heq dorë nga frika
□ *He had an appointment to see the*
dentist but he **chickened out of** *it at*
the last moment. □ *They feared that*
their allies would **chicken out** *at the*
last moment.

child's play gjë e thjeshtë, gjë e lehtë,
punë (lodër) kalamajsh

□ *He has electric shears that make*
cutting a hedge **child's play.** □ *'Isn't it*
awfully difficult to work those
machines?' 'Child's play, my dear
girl. Let me show you.' □ *The books of*
Mrs. Waterman and Co., fairly com-
plicated as they were, **child's play** *to*
Frank. □ *It's not a difficult climb—it*
should be **child's play** *for an experi-*
enced mountaineer.

chill sb to the bone/marrow/spine;
chill sb's spine/marrow bëj t'i
shkojnë mornica në trup (nga të ftohtit, nga frika etj.); bëj t'i hyjë frika
(të ftohtit) në palcë

□ *Come by the fire—you must be*
chilled to the marrow! □ *'A collec-*
tion of horror stories,' *the blurb went*
on, 'guaranteed to **chill the spines of**
the most sceptical readers.'

chill sb's blood i ngrij gjakun
□ *'Are you ready, Matt dear?' in a*
tone of such forced cheerfulness that
it **chilled** *Matthew's very* **blood.**

chime in (with) 1. futem (ndërhyj) në
bisedë

□ *'Can you think of some ready way*
of stopping him from **chiming in?'**
□ *The rest of us* **chimed in with** *short*
accounts of various ways we had
developed of annoying the poor old
chap. □ *'Of course,' he* **chimed in.**
2. përputhet me, pajtohet me

□ *This* **chimed in with** *Mr. Dombey's*
own hope and... belief. □ *What he had*
said **chimed in** *perfectly with Isabel's*
own immediate reaction; she ex-
claimed: 'Well, I am glad.'

chip in (with) 1. ndërhyj, ndërpres
(fjalën); futem në bisedë

□ *'Do you know,' said Mrs. Oliver,*
chipping in *again, 'whether Celia*
was there or not?' □ *You shouldn't*
chip in *that way, when your elders*
are holding a conversation. □ *I wish*
you wouldn't keep **chipping in** *with*
frivolous remarks.
2. kontribuoj, ofroj të holla

□ *As usual, George was broke, so he*
couldn't **chip in** *towards Mr. Goatly's*
retirement present. □ *'When Dad*
offered to **chip in with** *$1000 toward*
our holiday, we realized that it might
be possible to buy an old car and do
a tour of Europe.'

chip of/off the old block gjallë i ati, i
ati në vend, sikur e ka nxjerrë i ati nga
hundët

□ *If you knew Jim's father, then you*
will find Jim very like him: Jim's a
real **chip off his old block.** □ *Mrs.*
Warren. Get out! I'm begging to think
your're **a chip of the old block.**
□ *'That daughter of hers,' observed*
the Colonel 'is **a chip of the old**
block, *unless I miss my guess.'* □ *Ed-*
mund Burke said of the Younger Pitt
that he was 'not merely **a chip of the**
old block, *but the old block itself.'*

chivy sb into/along urdhëroj, shtyj dikë të bëjë diçka (në mënyrë irrituese)
□ *The men were getting tired of being* **chivied along** *by the corporal, and though they made a show of busy activity, progress in fact became slower and slower.*

choke back (down) mbaj, përmbaj (lotët, inatin etj.)
□ *When he saw the pitiful condition of the children, she could barely* **choke back** *her tears.* □ *He hardly* **choked back** *the sobs.*

choke off (for) 1. ndërpres (befas e në mënyrë të vrazhdë)
□ *Gerald felt a revulsion from the whole subject and hoped he would hear no more about it; he decided that if Vin phoned he would* **choke** *him* **off.**
2. qortoj rëndë
□ *He got a terrible* **choking off** *from his father* **for** *borrowing the car without permission.*

choke the life out of mbyt; i marr frymën
□ *He grasped her by the throat and started to* **choke the life out of** *her.*
□ *The government has nearly* **choked the life out of** *privately-run schools.*

choke up zë, bllokoj
□ *The drains are all* **choked up** *with leaves.*

chop and change ndërroj, ndryshoj vazhdimisht (mendim, punë etj)
□ *You never know what sort of clothes to put on in the morning, when the weather keeps* **chopping and changing** *like this.* □ *He was never content with anything he had written until he had* **chopped and changed** *it about twenty times.*
□ *You'll never make any headway at anything, if you keep* **chopping and changing** *jobs like this.* □ *When a person is constantly* **chopping and changing** *his job, we may suspect that the fault is in him, not in the job.*

chop down pres
□ *I'm going to* **chop down** *some of the old apple trees; they've almost stopped producing fruit.*

chop off pres (me sëpatë)
□ *These branches are overhanging the road; we'd better* **chop** *them* **off.**

chop up pres, çaj copa-copa, pres në copa të vogla
□ *Fruit tastes delicious when* **chopped up** *and sprinkled with wine.* □ *This furniture is so old and useless that you might as well* **chop** *it* **up** *for firewood.*

chuck away 1. shkapërderdh, prish të hollat andej-këndej
□ *There were plenty of people ready to help Paul* **chuck** *his money* **away,** *but few to stand by him when he ended up bankrupt.*
2. hedh, flak
□ *'What are you going to do with those old clothes?'—'Oh, just* **chuck** *them* **away** *I think.'*
3. nuk e shfrytëzoj, nuk e përdor si duhet
□ *He* **chucked away** *his opportunity of making a career for himself.*

chuck out of detyroj të largohet, përzë, nxjerr jashtë, përjashtoj
□ *He didn't leave of his own free will; he was* **chucked out.** □ *I met him shortly after he'd been* **chucked out** *of University for persistent idleness.*

chuck sb under the chin cek, lëmoj gushën e (në shenjë përkëdheljeje, dashurie etj.)
□ *The father* **chucked** *his little daughter* **under the chin** *and said 'Have you been a good girl today?'*

chuck up lë, braktis

☐ *John just chucked up his job at the factory and said he intended never to work again.* ☐ *The job at the sewage farm was so unpleasant that it was chucked up by everyone who tried it.*

churn out nxjerr, prodhoj në sasi të madhe (me cilësi të dobët)

☐ *Some pulp writers churn out two or three thousand words a day.* ☐ *They've got factories working round the clock churning out cheap cloth for the mass market.*

claim sth back kërkoj kthimin e diçkaje

☐ *You can claim the money back if the goods are damaged.* ☐ *A lot of people do not understand why they cannot claim back the income tax that has been paid by the Building Societies.*

clam up nuk bëzaj, nuk bëj gëk, nuk nxjerr fjalë nga goja, i vë kyçin gojës

☐ *He always clammed up when we asked him about his family.* ☐ *When inspector Smart began to question the arrested man's girlfriend about his whereabouts at eight o'clock the previous evening, she immediately clammed up and refused to say anything.*

clamp down marr masa shtrënguese kundër; përdor forcën të ndaloj (të pengoj); ia mbledh (ia shtrëngoj) rripat (frerin)

☐ *There has been much tax evasion through expense accounts, but the Government is going to clamp down.* ☐ *The government intends to clamp down on soccer hooliganism.*

clarion call, a kushtrim

☐ *He sounds no clarion call, and points no direction; it would be entirely out of his family's character if he did.* ☐ *Mary Wollstonecroft sounded a new clarion call to battle in 1792 with her vigorous work 'A Vindication of the Rights of Woman.'*

clap sb in/into jail, prison fus në burg (pa gjykuar)

☐ *The prisoners were clapped in prison and kept there for several months without trial.*

clap eyes on sb shoh, më zë syri

☐ *I haven't clapped eyes on Bill for months. What's happened to him?* ☐ *How can I describe her? I'd never clapped eyes on her till five minutes ago.*

clean down fshij, pastroj, bëj një pastrim të përgjithshëm

☐ *My mother always insists on cleaning the whole house down at least once a month.* ☐ *She cleaned down the walls.*

clean oneself up lahem

☐ *'Just give me five minutes to clean myself up. I'm covered in oil.'* ☐ *My hands are filthy; I'd better go and clean myself up.*

clean out pastroj

☐ *The stables are in a filthy condition. When were they last cleaned out?*

clean out of lë trok, lë pa një lek në xhep; lë pa gjë

☐ *I haven't a penny left; buying all those books has completely cleaned me out.* ☐ *The tobacconist was cleaned out of cigarettes by people who expected the price to go up.*

clean sheet/slate, a 1. një faqe të re

☐ *I suggest that we ignore everything that has happened until now and start with a clean slate.*

2. emër i pastër, i papërlyer, i panjollë

☐ *'I don't know anything about the man's past history,' he told the Inspector, 'but I can give him a clean sheet for the five years he's been working here.'*

clean up 1. pastroj, fshij

□ *I wish you'd* **clean up** *your mess after you have been repairing your bicycle.* □ *They would stay behind to help me* **clean up** *the classroom.*
2. pastroj, spastroj (nga kriminelët etj.)

□ *It's time that the police took some effective action to* **clean up** *this town.*
3. bëj, fitoj para

□ *His invention was immediately successful, and in less than a year he* **cleaned up** *ten thousand dollars.*

clear away heq, pastroj

□ *After dinner, when we had* **cleared away** *and washed up, we went for a walk.* □ *'I'll* **clear** *these dishes* **away;** *then we'll be able to work at the table.* □ *Will you please* **clear away** *the tea-things?*

clear of çlirohem; shfajësohem, shkarkohem

□ *The signalman was* **cleared of** *all responsibility for the railway accident.* □ *The accusations you are making relate to charges of which my client has been* **cleared.**

clear off 1. iki, largohem, zhdukem

□ *Now you* **clear off** *at once and leave me alone.* □ *He* **cleared off** *as soon as he saw the policeman coming.* □ *I told the boys to* **clear off** *immediately.*
2. laj, shlyej, paguaj

□ *The first thing I would do if I won a big prize in the football pools would be to* **clear off** *all my hire purchase payment.*

clear one's/sb's character provoj pafajësinë (ndershmërinë); dal i larë (me faqe të larë), dal i pafajshëm (i papërlyer)

□ *You don't need to try to* **clear your character** *with me, my dear. I know you too well to believe malicious gossip of that sort.*

clear one's/sb's head kthjelloj mendjen

□ *I'm not making much progress with this essay. I think I'll take a little walk to* **clear my mind.** □ *It's your own fault if you have got a hangover. Still, I'll make you some coffee. It might* **clear your head** *a bit before you go to work.*

clear one's mind of heq, largoj nga mendja

□ *The jury were told that in considering their verdict they must* **clear their minds of** *all the feelings of repugnance for the behavior of the accused during the trial.*

clear one's throat kruaj (pastroj) zërin (gurmazin)

□ *He* **cleared his throat** *and took a swift but profound sniff at the inhalant to do the same for his nasal passages.* □ *He paused,* **cleared his throat** *and then went on.* □ *He* **cleared his throat** *and then went on reading the story.*

clear out (of) 1. zbraz, boshatis, pastroj

□ *The workmen are* **clearing out** *the tank.* □ *There will be plenty of room in that cupboard when it is* **cleared out.**
2. iki, largohem

□ *'I'm fed up with being told what I can do and what I can't do; I'm* **clearing out.** *Goodbye!'* □ *Go and* **clear** *those children* **out of** *the garden.* □ *Now then,* **clear out of** *here quickly.*

clear the air 1. freskoj ajrin

□ *Do you mind if I open the windows, just for five minutes, to* **clear the air?** □ *In the sultry thunder weather of that week I longed for a real storm to break and* **clear the air.** □ *It's too stuffy in the room! Please open the window to* **clear the air.**

2. sqaroj situatën; heq (eliminoj) keqkuptimet

□ *This talk did a great deal to clear the air. It was the beginning of a friendship between Grigg and myself.* □ *You may have to write a difficult letter to an acquaintance but it should clear the air quite a bit.* □ *His remarks did a great deal to clear the air.*

clear the decks (for action) bëhem gati, përgatitem për (një veprim të caktuar)

□ *We are going to have our rehearsals for the play in this room: so we had better clear the decks for action by moving the furniture out.* □ *When the decks are cleared for action we go below and wait.* □ *If we're going to dance, some of you can give me a hand to clear the decks. Carry the small stuff into the hall, and shove the rest out of the centere of the room.*

clear the way for hap rrugën

□ *Let's find out what our members want now, and that will clear the way for immediate action later on.* □ *Clear the way, please.*

clear up 1. pastroj, rregulloj, vë në rregull

□ *'Aren't we going to clear up before we go out?'* □ *I spent nearly an hour clearing up the room.* □ *Clear up the litter before you go away.*

2. zgjidh; sqaroj

□ *I decided to go and see him and get the point cleared up quickly, before trouble arose.* □ *I went to clear the matter up with him.* □ *This book has cleared up many difficulties for me.* □ *I am trying to clear up any misunderstanding.*

3. hapet, kthjellohet (koha)

□ *The weather was bad early this morning but it cleared up before ten*

o'clock. □ *It looks as though the rain will continue into the night, but it may clear up by morning.*

clench one's teeth/fists etc. shtrëngoj dhëmbët (grushtat) etj.

□ *I can't get anything out of the child about who he is or where he came from. He just stands there with his teeth clenched and refuses to answer.* □ *From the tone of his voice you would have thought him calm enough, but I observed he had his fists clenched till the knuckles shone white.*

click one's heels përpjek (përplas) takat

□ *The chief of police rose to his feet, bowed to us, and then clicked his heels together with such vigor that one of the constables dropped his rifle.* □ *Introductions were accompanied by a considerable amount of clicking of heels and kissing of hands, formalities she was unused to in an English drawing-room.*

climb down 1. zbres

□ *Cats often find it easier to climb up a tree than to climb down it.*

2. tërhiqem, pranoj gabimin

□ *When he was proved wrong by the new evidence he was forced to climb down and accept that he was mistaken.* □ *As new facts became known, the government was forced to climb down over its handling of the spy scandal.*

clinch a deal arrij, përfundoj një marrëveshje

□ *I'm not saying that Robert didn't find Jenny attractive, but he didn't marry her for love. I'm sure it was her having the capital to set him up in business that clinched the deal.*

cling to 1. kapem pas

□ *Some of the victims of the fire*

*climbed out of the building, **clung to** the window ledges for a minute or two and then dropped to their death a hundred feet below.*

2. përmbahem, nuk luaj, nuk heq dorë

□ *The refugees **clung to** the hope that one day they would all be able to return to their native land.*

clip sb's wings i pres krahët; i lidh duart (krahët)

□ *She'll find that having a new baby to look after will **clip her wings** more than she thinks.* □ *David wanted to run the whole thing himself, but the committee **clipped his wings**: he has to report to them.* □ *Whatever happens we have to go on... If it **clips our wings** we have to hop along with clipped wings.*

closed/sealed book, a çështje e mbyllur

□ *As far as I am concerned, our quarrel last night is **a closed book**: I don't want to discuss it.*

close call, a shpëtim për një qime

□ *In those cold valley cottages, a child could sicken and die in a year, and it was usually the strongest who went. I was not strong; I was simply tough, self-inoculated by all the plagues. But sometimes, when I stop to think about it, I feel it must have been **a very close call**.*

close down mbyll (shkollën, uzinën etj.); ndërpres (prodhimin, transmetimin etj.)

□ *Many businesses have **closed down** because of the recession.* □ *The factory had to **close down** through lack of orders.* □ *If the firms failed to make enough money, they would **close down**.* □ *The television **closes down** for the night just after eleven o'clock.*

close in (on/upon) 1. shkurtohet, zvogëlohet (dita)

□ *Days are **closing in**.*

2. rrethoj, pështjell, mbështjell

□ *The mist **closed in** on us.* □ *When he realized that he was being **closed in** upon, the fugitive shot himself.*

3. afrohem

□ *I can feel the danger **closing in**.* □ *The sound of mortar fire seemed to be **closing in**.*

close one's ear to bëj veshin e shurdhër, nuk ia vë veshin

□ *You should never **close your ear to** your friend's advice.*

close one's eyes to mbyll sytë para

□ *There is a certain amount of stealing from the shop going on, but the shopkeeper just **closed his eyes to** it.* □ *That progressive author never **closed his eyes to** the poverty, injustice and exploitation of the system.*

close/narrow shave/squeak, a shpëtim për një qime (për një fije)

□ *I had **a very close shave** while driving to work yesterday: I was almost involved in a serious accident.* □ *You have had **a close squeak**, like William Pitt before you. The next man may not be so lucky.*

close the/one's ranks ngjesh, shtrëngoj radhët; bashkohem edhe më fort rreth

□ *When one of the doctors was criticised, his colleagues in the hospital **closed ranks** behind him.* □ *'You mean we should **close the ranks**?' 'Something like that, she said.'*

close (shut) the door to i mbyll rrugën

□ *The government has **closed the door to** any more wage increases for the time being.* □ *For, you see, we have adroitly **shut the door upon** the meeting between Jos and the old father, and the poor little gentle sister inside.*

close with 1. kapem me, hyj në ndeshje, në luftë me

□ *After a long period of shelling, the infantry surged forward and closed with the enemy in hand-to-hand fighting.* □ *The wrestler closed with his opponent, and for some minutes he brought him down.*

2. bie në ujdi

□ *After a good deal of discussion over the value of the picture I finally closed with him at a reasonable figure.* □ *Manson thought the price a very reasonable one, so he closed with him.*

cloud one's brain/judgement turbulloj mendjen (gjykimin etj.)

□ *In general, I consider that excessive smoking and drinking tend to cloud the brain.* □ *It is not easy sometimes to prevent one's moral judgement from being clouded by self-interest.*

cloud over 1. mbulohet me re

□ *Just as we were beginning to enjoy the sunshine, the sky clouded over and a cold wind began to blow.*

2. vrenjtet (fytyra)

□ *When he heard the news of his friend accident, his face clouded over.*

club together kontribuoj, vë para

□ *All the members of the orchestra clubbed together to present a silver baton to their conductor on his sixtieth birthday.* □ *They clubbed together to buy the chairman a present.*

cluster around/round mblidhem, grumbullohen rreth

□ *Reporters clustered around the distinguished guest.*

clutch at straws/a straw kapem pas fijes së kashtës

□ *Every time Peter heard a noise he thought it was someone coming to rescue him: he was clutching at straws.*

cock-and-bull story/tale, a përrallë me mbret, dokrra

□ *As an excuse for being late, he told some cock-and-bull story about being involved in an accident.* □ *He's been telling some cock-and-bull story about seeing the footprints of this imaginary monster.* □ *Connor invented a cock-and-bull story, which I am sure I never told him.*

cock a snook at sb tregoj përçmim, mos-përfillje

□ *The students took every opportunity to cock a snook at authority.*

cock of the walk i kapardisur (i krekosur) si gjeli majë plehut; i pari i fshatit

□ *He wouldn't want to take a job in New York, where he'd be nobody in particular. He's cock of the walk here and that's what he likes.* □ *After winning the competition, Fred was cock of the walk.*

cock an/one's ear(s) ngre veshët

□ *The horse cocked up its ears when it heard the noise.*

cock up pështjelloj, bëj lesh e li, bëj çorbë

□ *Don't let him organize your trip; he completely cocked up ours.*

coin money bëj para, fitoj para me grushta

□ *With a big house like that full of bed-and breakfasters every night, the woman must be absolutely coining money.* □ *His garage is a small one, but he is still coining money.*

cold fish, a njeri i ftohtë

□ *I find Frank's company boring: he's a bit of a cold fish.*

collect one's faculties mbledh veten, e marr veten në dorë

□ *He collected his faculties very soon.*

collect one's thoughts përqëndroj
mendimet
□ *Before you begin to deliver a lecture, you should* **collect your thoughts.**
collect/gather one's wits mbledh
mendjen, vij në vete, mbledh veten
□ *I like an early morning cup of tea in bed. It gives me time to* **gather my wits** *again.* □ *I needed time to* **collect my wits** *before seeing him again.*
color up skuqem
□ *She* **colored up** *at the mention of the young man's name.* □ *She* **colored up** *with embarrassment at his remarks.*
come about 1. ndodh, ngjan
□ *Can you tell me how the accident* **came about?** □ *How did it* **come about** *that he knew where we were?*
2. ndryshoj kursin (drejtimin e anijes etj.)
□ *We* **came about** *and went off on a new tack.*
come across 1. takoj, has (rastësisht)
□ *Have you ever* **come across** *this expression?* □ *While searching amongst some papers in an old trunk, she* **came across** *a diary which had apparently been kept by her grandfather.*
2. kuptohet, merret vesh
□ *The preacher spoke for a long time but I'm afraid his meaning did not* **come across.**
come after 1. ndjek
□ *As soon as we started across the field the farmer* **came after** *us waving a big stick.*
2. pason, vjen pas
□ *Learning should* **come after** *play.*
come along 1. del, vjen
□ *He went to London whenever the chance* **came along.**
2. eci, shkoj (gjatë rrugës, etj.)
□ *I saw him* **coming along** *the road.*

□ *The children* **came along** *the beach.*
3. eci, përparoj
□ *My son has begun to* **come along** *very well in English.*
4. ec, luaj, hajde, jepi
□ **Come along** *Tony; we can't wait all day!*
5. zhvillohet
□ *'Those seedlings are* **coming along** *well in the greenhouse; I'll plant them outside when the weather gets a little warmer.'*
come and go shkon e vjen
□ *But there are sadnesses of growth, moods that* **come and go** *with the awakening consciousness of passing time.* □ *She was chained to her place. But other people could* **come and go** *as they pleased.*
come at 1. gjej, zbuloj
□ *The purpose of the official inquiry is to* **come at** *the true facts leading up to the loss of the ship at sea.*
2. sulmoj
□ *The bull* **came at** *me with his head down.* □ *The crazed man* **came at** *me with a meat-axe.*
come away 1. iki, largohem
□ *We* **came away** *with the uneasy feeling that all was not well with their marriage.*
2. del, shkëputet, shqitet
□ *I pulled the rotten wood and it* **came away** *without difficulty.* □ *The door handle* **came away** *in my hand.*
come back 1. kthehem
□ *I'm going away and I may never* **come back.** □ *At what time will he* **come back?**
2. sjell ndër mend, kujtoj
□ *At first I could not remember why everything seemed so familiar; then it all* **came back.** □ *Their names are all* **coming back** *to me now.*
3. rivendoset

□ *There are some people who would be glad to see corporal punishment* **come back** *for certain offences.*
4. rikthehet në modë
□ *Long skirts have been out of fashion for a long time, but they are* **coming back.**

come before 1. paraqitet para
□ *The case* **comes before** *the court next week.* □ *My claim* **comes before** *the court tomorrow morning.*
2. është, vjen para
□ *Fighting poverty and unemployment should* **come before** *all other political considerations.*

come between sb and sb/sth 1. pengoj
□ *I'm not going to let a small matter like that* **comes between** *me and my sleep.* □ *He never lets anything* **come between** *him and his pint of beer.*
2. ndërhyj në punët e
□ *It's not a good idea to* **come between** *a man and his wife.*

come by 1. shkoj, kaloj
□ *I moved my car out of the way so that the heavy truck could* **come by.** □ *At that moment a number of people came by.* □ *Did you see anyone* **come by**?
2. siguroj, gjej
□ *Jobs were not so easy to* **come by** *when I was a boy as they are now.* □ *How did you* **come by** *this rare specimen of ancient art?*
3. përftoj
□ *How did you* **come by** *that scratch on your cheek?*

come clean pranoj me sinqeritet, them të drejtën (të vërtetën)
□ *After being questioned for three hours, the criminal finally* **came clean** *and admitted his part in the robbery.* □ *Now* **come clean,** *Myra. What's really eating you up? You've*

been talking around and around it.
□ *Why not* **come clean** *here and now as to those, facts, anyhow before it's too late to take advantage of any mitigating circumstances?*

come down 1. bie, shëmbet, rrëzohet
□ *Two enemy intruders* **came down** *inside our lines.* □ *The ceiling* **came down.**
2. bie (shi, dëborë etj.)
□ *The rain* **came down** in torrents.
3. kalon, transmetohet brez pas brezi
□ *These stories* **come down** *to us from our forefathers.* □ *The religious doctrines which have* **come down** *to us.*
4. ulet
□ *The price of petrol is* **coming down.**
□ *Prices could* **come down** *only if wages* **came down.**

come down hard on qortoj, kritikoj ashpër
□ *The headmaster is going to* **come down hard on** *students who leave litter lying about.*

come down in the world bie nga dynjallëku
□ *Mr. Jones has really* **come down in the world**: *he only works in a shop now, but at one time he owned many shops himself.* □ *Poor old George has* **come down in the world** *since his business failed.*

come down on sb 1. qortoj, kritikoj rëndë, e bëj për ujë të ftohtë; ndëshkoj
□ *The new traffic laws* **come down** *heavily* **on** *drunken drivers.* □ *The boss will* **come down on** *you like a ton of bricks when he finds out what you've done.* □ *If any man was slow in obeying orders, the sergeant would* **come down on** *him like a ton of bricks.* □ *His teammates* **came down on** *Gordon quite hard for fumbling the ball.* □ *The courts are* **coming down** *heavily* **on** *young offenders.*

2. kërkoj (të holla, dëmshpërblim etj.)
□ *All his creditors* **came down on** *him for prompt payment of his bills when they heard of his financial difficulties.*
□ *He* **came down on** *the driver of the car for heavy damages.*

come down to sth 1. përmblidhet; është fjala për
□ *It* **comes down to** *two choices: you either improve your work, or you leave.* □ *The whole dispute* **comes down to** *a power struggle between management and trade unions.*
2. arrin, përfundon deri në
□ *I never thought she would* **come down to** *asking my advice about her affairs.*

come down to bedrock hyj në thelb të çështjes, të problemit
□ *'Well,' he said, 'we're like any other people when it* **comes down to bedrock.'**

come down to brass tacks hyj në thelb të çështjes
□ *It was like his brother to* **come down to 'brass tacks'.** *If Lester were only as cautious as he was straightforward and direct, what a man he would be!*

come down to earth zbres në tokë, njoh (kuptoj) jetën e vërtetë
□ *Mary has all sorts of ideas at the moment about becoming a film star: sooner or later she will have to* **come down to earth.** □ *The lovers are living in a kind of dream world; but one day they'll* **come down to earth.**

come forth dal
□ *A witness* **came forth** *to testify that the young man had been present.* □ *I had very great hopes of Jenkins' speech last night, but nothing very new* **came forth.**

come forward 1. ofrohem, dal vullnetar

□ *All of them* **came forward** *to help.*
□ *He* **came forward** *to lend us a hand.*
2. paraqitem
□ *The police want any witness of the incident to* **come forward** *and help them with their inquiries.*
3. paraqitet për diskutim
□ *The matter was deferred at last evening's meeting, but will* **come forward** *at our next session.*

come hell or high water sido që të ndodhë; të bëhet ç'të bëhet
□ *I promised to visit Jim in Paris and,* **come hell or high water,** *I intend to keep my promise.* □ *She was right of course. I was fuddled. On the third day I just had to sleep,* **come hell or water.**

come home to sb bëhet e qartë, kuptohet
□ *It eventually* **came home to** *the people that the war would be long and bloody.* □ *It was enough before, but now it* **came home** *with peculiar force.* □ *For the first time it* **came home** *sharply to Aileen how much his affairs meant to him.*

come in 1. hyj, futem brenda
□ *There was a knock on the door. 'Come in.'* □ *He opened the door and is seen in the light which* **comes in** *from the hall.*
2. vjen, arrin, mbrrin (treni, anija, etj)
□ *She waited near the bus terminus until the last bus* **came in.** □ *What time does the train* **come in?** □ *The mail has* **come in** *early this morning.*
3. hyn në përdorim të gjerë, hyn në modë
□ *'Do you know exactly when wigs first* **came in,** *in this country?'*
□ *When did the plastics* **come in?**
4. disponohen, vihen në treg
□ *'Fresh salmon doesn't* **come in**

before February, does it?' □ *'We haven't any nylon net curtains in stock just at present; but they should* **come in** *any moment now.* □ *These apples won't* **come in** *till September.*

5. shërben, hyn në punë

□ *Don't throw that string away; it may* **come in** *useful some day.* □ *Good suggestions always* **come in** *handy.*

6. fitoj, marr të ardhura

□ *There is practically no money* **coming in** *to buy food, furniture or clothing.*

7. vij në pushtet

□ *When the present government* **came in** *the country was in a difficult financial situation.*

come in (into) contact with takoj, hyj në kontakt (lidhje) me

□ *When this piece of metal* **comes into contact with** *the wires the circuit is complete.* □ *His hand* **came into contact with** *a hot surface.* □ *There they* **came into** *close* **contact with** *the people.*

come in for tërheq; bëhem objekt i; marr

□ *The government's economic policies have* **come in for** *much criticism in the newspapers.* □ *The young artist's pictures* **came in for** *a great deal of attention.* □ *If Oliver carries on his pranks much longer, he will* **come in for** *a beating.*

come in handy është i dobishëm, hyn në punë

□ *You should always carry a flashlight in the boot of your car; it sometimes* **comes in handy.** □ *Don't throw that cardboard box away—it may* **come in handy.**

come in/into sight dal, dukem, shfaqem

□ *As the plane came down through the clouds, green fields and white*

houses **came into sight.** □ *By-and-by a small boat* **came in sight.** □ *The ship* **came in sight** *out of the fog.*

come in sight of shoh

□ *They* **came in sight of** *the village.*

come into 1. hyj, futem

□ *Boylan* **came** *silently* **into** *the room.* □ *They* **came into** *the bookstore.*

2. trashëgoj

□ *She* **came into** *a fortune when her uncle died.* □ *She* **came into** *some money on her mother's death.*

come into action futet në veprim

□ *There was a lull of a few seconds before the oiled machinery of pursuit* **came into action.**

come into being lind, krijohet, vjen në jetë

□ *Later, two more armies* **came into being.** □ *When did the world* **come into being?** □ *In our country a good number of new customs and traditions have* **come into being.**

come into blossom/flower lulëzon, çel lule

□ *The trees are late* **coming into blossom** *this year.*

come into collision with përplaset

□ *His car* **came into collision with** *a bus at the crossroads.* □ *The two vehicles* **came into collision** *at great speed.*

come into disuse del nga përdorimi

□ *This old machine has* **come into disuse.**

come into effect hyn në fuqi

□ *The new seat belt regulations* **came into effect** *last week.* □ *The new cuts in income tax will not* **come into effect** *until the beginning of August.* □ *The revised work schedule* **comes into effect** *next week.*

come into existence lind, krijohet, vjen në jetë

□ *Do you know when Parliament first*

came into existence? □ *When did the world come into existence?*

come into fashion hyn në modë, hyn në përdorim të gjerë

□ *Long skirts have come into fashion again.* □ *Short hair and short skirts came into fashion at about the same time during the 1920's.* □ *When did that style of dress come into fashion?*

come into focus vihet në fokus; duket (kuptohet) qartë

□ *Draw the eyepiece towards you and the object will come into sharp focus.* □ *Now that you've explained the important issues, everything comes into much clearer focus.*

come into force hyn në fuqi, vihet në zbatim

□ *New regulations will soon come into force for the drivers of heavy vehicles.* □ *The new law comes into force beginning from January 1st. The new regulations come into force from next September.*

come into leaf/bud bulon, bulëzon, mugullon; gjethon (pema)

□ *The rose bushes have come into bud much later than usual.* □ *The trees come into leaf in Spring.*

come into line with pajtohem me

□ *He is not the sort of man to come easily into line with the rest of his colleagues.* □ *He will soon be convinced of the correctness of the proposal and come into line with us.*

come into one's head i vjen (i bie) ndër mend

□ *He gave the first name that came into his head.* □ *I don't know why it came into my head.*

come into one's own arrij suksesin (nderimin, reputacionin etj.) që meritoj; arrij pjekurinë e personalitetit (aftësive etj.); gjej veten, shfaq në shkallën më të lartë aftësitë e veta

□ *It was when the primitive vigor of his carving united with the human sensuality of his life drawing, at the end of twenties, that Henry Moore came into his own as a sculptor.* □ *George was quiet for most of the evening, but when the conversation switched to sport, he came into his own: he is a great sportsman.*

come into operation hyn në veprim, vihet në jetë, në zbatim

□ *When does the plan come into operation?* □ *The new regulations will come into operation next Tuesday.*

come into play hyn në veprim, nis të veprojë, vihet në lëvizje

□ *Personal feelings should not come into play when one has to make business decisions.* □ *All kind of forces come into play when a nation's vital interests are threatened.* □ *If we want to sell abroad, a new set of factors— different tastes, local competition, and so on—come into play.* □ *His first effort was to get an upper clerkship in one of the departments where his Oxford education could come into play and do him service.*

come into power vij në fuqi (në pushtet)

□ *This government came in(to) power at the last election.*

come into prominence bëhet i njohur

□ *He suddenly came into prominence as a result of his refusal to obey the party line on the nationalization of steel.*

come into question shtrohet për shqyrtim, diskutim

□ *When will the plan come into question?*

come into season piqet (pema), ka kohën (sezonin)
□ *Tomatoes come into season much earlier in Italy than in Northern Europe.*

come into service/use vihet në funksionim (përdorim)
□ *The new type of bus comes into service later this month.* □ *This stretch of motorway will not come back into use until extensive tests have been made.*

come into sb's possession vihet në zotërim të
□ *The police asked the arrested man how he had come into the possession of the revolver.* □ *On that date the accused was said to have come into the possession of a stolen car.*

come into the open dal hapur
□ *Why don't you come into the open and say exactly what's on your mind?* □ *His hatred of his brother would have come into the open long before if he had not left home at such an early age.*

come into the world lind, vij në jetë
□ *One of the arguments in favor of birth control is that only those children come into the world who are genuinely wanted.* □ *He died six months before I came into the world.*

come into view duket, shfaqet, del para sysh
□ *The church spire came into view as we rounded the next bend.* □ *Two people came into view and passed out of sight down the road.*

come of del, vjen, rrjedh nga
□ *He promised to help, but I don't think anything will come of it.* □ *No harm can come of trying.* □ *That's what comes of being overconfident.*

come of age 1. arrij moshën madhore, moshën e pjekurisë
□ *When she comes of age, she will be able to do what she likes with the money her father left her.*
2. arrij një fazë zhvillimi
□ *We might say that space travel came of age in 1969, when Man first landed on the surface of the moon.*

come off 1. bie, rrëzohem
□ *The horse refused at the first fence, and that's when I came off.* □ *He came off his horse when it refused to take a fence.*
2. këputet, shqitet; del, hiqet
□ *He tugged at the metal handle and it came off in his hand.* □ *'Do these knobs come off?' 'No, they're fixed on permanently.'* □ *A button has come off my coat.* □ *The whitewash has come off.*
3. dal me sukses
□ *It was a good scheme and it nearly came off.* □ *Their attempt to rob the mail-train didn't come off.* □ *Did everything come off all right?*
4. zhvillohet, mbahet, bëhet
□ *My friend's marriage didn't come off; his fiancèe broke off the engagement at the last minute.* □ *When does the concert come off?* □ *When does the football match come off?*
5. përfundoj
□ *The journalist has just come off an assignment which had taken him half way round the world.* □ *'I want you to come off that fraud case,' said the inspector. 'I've some more urgent work for you to do.'*

come off scot-free (scot free) shpëtoj paq, dal pa lagur
□ *It seems Gary is coming off scot-free again.*

come off second best nuk arrij të fitoj, pësoj humbje
□ *He has had a number of fights with*

the champion, but he has always come off second best.

come off/through with flying colors
dal fitimtar, dal me sukses

□ *She came through her exams with flying colors.* □ *With his persistence and keen mind he is sure to come off with flying colors in this research task.* □ *It will be a stern struggle, but we are sure we'll come off with flying colors.*

come off with honor dal me nder

□ *She has always come off with honor in carrying out any task assigned to her.*

come off your high horse ul hundën

□ *Please come off your high horse; let's discuss it as man to man.*

come off your perch ul hundën, ul bishtin

□ *After having been criticized by his classmates, he began to come off his perch.*

come on 1. dal, futem (në skenë, në lojë etj.)

□ *When Lawrence Oliver came on for the first time, the audience applauded.* □ *Marsh came on as a substitute for Cooper only ten minutes before the end of the game.* □ *Oliver dominated the play from the moment he came on stage.*

2. zhvillohet, rritet, përmirësohet

□ *His French has come on a lot since he joined the conversation class.* □ *The crops are coming on nicely.* □ *The baby is coming on well.*

3. fillon

□ *'My throat's dry and a bit sore; perhaps I've got a cold coming on.* □ *Just as we were beginning to enjoy ourselves, the rain came on and spoiled everything.*

4. bie, vjen, afrohet (nata, etj)

□ *The travellers wanted to reach the*

inn before the night came on. □ *Winter is coming on: You can feel it in the air.*

5. shfaqet

□ *'The big film doesn't come on until nine o'clock, so there's plenty of time for us to get to the cinema.'* □ *There is a very good play coming on at The Lyric next week.*

6. shqyrtohet në gjyq

□ *They have been waiting a long time for their case to come on.* □ *When does the case come on for trial?*

7. hajde! jepi! ec! forca! hë! hë de!

□ *I'll help you back to the hotel. Come on, Mike, say you'll do it.* □ *Come on, let me hear the whole story.* □ *Come on! Let's race to the end of the road.*

8. hapet, ndizet

□ *At nine the streets lights came on.*

come on the scene arrij në vendngjarje

□ *By the time I came on the scene, it was all over.* □ *I came on the scene long after the treasure had been largely plundered, but I am still enchanted by the glimpses I get, from time to time, of the riches that remain.*

come on/upon sb/sth has, ndesh, takoj rastësisht

□ *As we turned the corner we came on a group of men who were waiting for the shop to open.* □ *I came upon a group of children playing in the street.*

come out 1. dal

□ *The rain has stopped and the sun came out.* □ *The child loved to watch the stars come out at night.* □ *During the morning the sky was overcast, but in the afternoon the sun came out.*

2. del në shitje; del (nga shtypi)

□ *'Have you found a little for the book?' 'No, not yet.' 'When will it come out?'* □ *Several new books have* **come out** *this month.*

3. zbulohet, del në shesh, bëhet i njohur

□ *The full story* **came out** *at the trial.* □ *The news has just* **come out** *that the Princess is going to have a baby next March.*

4. çel, lulëzon

□ *The crocuses have* **come out** *early this year because of the mild winter.* □ *Owing to the long and cold winter, most spring flowers* **came out** *later than usual this year.*

5. bëj grevë, dal në grevë

□ *The dockers have* **come out** *to a man.* □ *The whole of London transport* **came out** *in protest when a conductor got the sack.*

6. dal (nga burgu)

□ *Jones got a three-year sentence, but he may* **come out** *early for good conduct.*

7. spikat, del në pah, shquhet

□ *The detail of the carving* **comes out** *very sharply in this oblique light.* □ *Everyone* **came out** *well in the wedding photograph except the bride, unfortunately.*

8. dal (në provim)

□ *They were very disappointed when their son* **came out** *bottom in the examination.*

come out against dal kundër

□ *In her speech, the Minister* **came out against** *any change to the existing law.*

come out at arrin (kap) koston (shumën)

□ *What is the cost of putting your car back on the road going to* **come out at?** □ *The total cost* **comes out at** *$5550.*

come out for/to dal

□ *Would you like to go* **out for** *a drive in the country?*

come out in mbulohem me

□ *Shortly after I had eaten the lobster I* **came out in** *spots.* □ *Hot weather makes her* **come out in** *a rash.*

come out in favor of dal në favor (mbrojtje) të

□ *The Liberals, who held the balance of power in Parliament,* **came out in favor of** *the Government.*

come out/out of 1. dal

□ *Police went into the house to try to persuade the man to* **come out.** □ *The little girl's front tooth* **came out** *when she bit the apple.* □ *We were caught in a rush of people* **coming out of** *the football ground.*

2. del, hiqet

□ *Do you think these ink marks will* **come out of** *my dress if I boil it?* □ *Will the color* **come out** *if the material is washed?*

come out in one's true colors tregoj (zbuloj) fytyrën e vërtetë

□ *Then the young woman* **came out in her true colors.** *A more outrageous person I never did see.*

come out in the open dal hapur

□ *The rapacious plans of that country have already* **come out in the open.**

come out of action dal jashtë luftimit

□ *As a result of our attack a great number of enemy vehicles* **came out of action.**

come out of one's shell hapem, dal nga guaska e vet

□ *I think she was rather pleased with me and the way I was* **coming out of my shell.** □ *He has to know you for a long time before he really begins to* **come out of his shell.** □ *He is rather sociable when he* **comes out of his shell.**

come out of the blue vjen papritur

□ *His resignation came right* **out of the blue.**

□ *Those remarks of his tend to come right out of the blue, and anyone not knowing him is invariably shocked.* □ *She had come out of the blue just when she was wanted but, like so many others involved in the case, she was out to make money.*

come out on top dal në krye (në ballë, në pararojë)

□ *He had a long struggle in his early days as a manufacturer, but he came out on top in the end.* □ *There is no doubt our team will come out on top in the basketball finals.*

come out with clean hands dal i papërlyer, dal i larë

□ *You came out of court with clean hands.*

come out with shprehem, them, flas, nxjerr (lëshoj) nga goja

□ *Occasionally they come out with fascinating snippets of gossip.* □ *He came out with a string of four-letter words that brought blushes to quite a few of the elderly ladies present.*

come over 1. vij (nga një vend te tjetri)

□ *Why don't you come over to New York for a holiday?*

2. bëj një vizitë, vizitoj

□ *If you can get leave, please come over this weekend.* □ *Come over and see us next week.*

3. marr anën e, kaloj në anën e

□ *At a crucial point in the war, one of the enemy's most powerful allies came over to our side.* □ *How would you like to come over to us? You could double your salary within a year.* □ *He will surely come over to our side.*

4. më zë, më kap, më gjen

□ *A fit of stubbornness came over him and he refused to have anything further to do with the scheme.* □ *'I've never seen him looking so cheerful! What has come over him?*

come round 1. bëj një vizitë (të shkurtër)

□ *Come round this evening, we shall welcome you.* □ *Won't you come round and see me some time?*

2. vij në vete, përmendem

□ *'Thank goodness, dear, you're coming round. You fainted you know.* □ *This man has had a severe accident but he is coming round again.*

3. i bie qark

□ *The road was blocked, so we had to come round by the fields.*

4. vij sërish në humor

□ *He's sulking because his parents wouldn't let him go to the pictures; but he'll soon come round.*

5. ndërroj qëndrim (pikëpamje)

□ *He knew I would have to come round to his way of thinking in the end.*

come short nuk përligj shpresat e, nuk arrij

□ *He did not come short of the expectations of his colleagues.* □ *He tries much but his efforts come short of what is required.*

come sb's way has, takoj, takohem, ndesh në jetë

□ *Of all the impudent suggestions that had ever come his way, none had astounded him more.* □ *You seem to be afraid that life might pass you by without giving you the time to enjoy it to the full and so you are always ready to take advantage of any chances that come your way.* □ *... a warrant empowering them to take all Portuguese vessels which should come in their way.*

come through 1. kaloj, kapërcej; mbijetoj

□ *I knew there was something that I ought to say, something that would reassure my doctor that I had come*

through, *only I did not know what it was.* □ *He considered himself fortunate to have* **come through** *two world wars unscathed.* □ *With such a weak heart she was lucky to* **come through** *the operation.*
2. arrin
□ *A message was* **coming through** *from USA when the signal went completely.*

come to 1. vij në vete, përmendem
□ *When he* **came to,** *he could not, for a moment, recognize his surroundings.* □ *She fainted, but has now* **come to.** □ *It was quite ten minutes after the accident before the man* **came to** *his senses.*
2. arrin
The bill **came to** *fifty dollars, fifty cents.* □ *I didn't expect those few items to* **come to** *so much.*
3. lind, vjen një mendim
□ *The idea* **came to** *him in his bath.* □ *It suddenly* **came to** *her that she had been wrong all along.*
4. ndalon (anija)
□ *The boat* **came to** *with a few feet of clear water to port.* □ *A police patrol boat hailed to us to* **come to.**

come to a climax arrin kulmin, arrin pikën kulmore
□ *Their discussions* **came to a noisy climax** *late in the evening.* □ *Their argument* **came to a climax** *when she threw a plate at him.*

come to a conclusion arrij në përfundim
□ *Talks aimed at settling the fisheries dispute have at last* **come to a successful conclusion.**
□ *I came to the conclusion that he'd been lying.*

come to a dead end hyj në rrugë pa krye
□ *It was puzzling; we seemed to have*

come to a dead end. *'Have you any idea why she did it?' 'None at all,' he replied.*

come to a decision marr një vendim
□ *He had already* **come to a decision.**
□ *You should* **come to a decision** *quickly.*

come to a halt ndalet, ndalon
□ *Don't open the door until the car* **comes to a complete halt.** □ *Work* **came to a halt** *when the machine broke down.*

come to a handsome (pretty) pass arrin një gjendje të keqe, një gjendje kritike
□ *Things have* **come to a pretty pass** *when she says she can't live on $30 a week.* □ *Things have* **come to a pretty pass** *when the children have to prepare their own meals.* □ *Things have* **come to a handsome pass** *when men sworn and elected to perform given services turn on their backers and betray them in this way!*

come to a head mahiset, malcohet
□ *The pimple* **came to a head** *before bursting.* □ *The medication should be applied before the infection* **comes to a head.**
2. arrin kulmin, arrin pikën kritike
□ *The trouble* **came to a head** *with the murder of an Opposition journalist.* □ *In recent years the monetary crises in our country has* **come to a head.**

come to an agreement arrij marrëveshje
□ *You know very well that you won't be able to* **come to** *any kind of* **agreement** *without having had a meeting on it first.*

come to an arrangement rregulloj, arrij në marrëveshje
□ *We can* **come to some arrangement** *over the price.*

come to an end merr fund, përfundon
□ *We are all relieved that the month-old strike seems to be **coming to an end**.* □ *The good relationship which existed between managers and men has **come to an end**.* □ *We enjoyed our stay in the countryside so much that we regretted it **came to an end** so soon.*

come to an understanding gjej mirëkuptim, gjuhë të përbashkët
□ *My wife and I have **come to an understanding** about the use of the car: I shall use it for going to work and she can have it at the weekends.* □ *You and I must **come to an understanding** as to how to proceed with this work.*

come to a standstill ndalon, bie në gjendje amullie
□ *Production has **come to a standstill** owing to the lack of raw materials.* □ *If the steam is shut off the machine soon **comes to a standstill**.* □ *He came to a standstill in the hall and there he lit a cigarette.* □ *'How odd to find that even this industry has its financial panics and at times sees it assignats and greenbacks languish to zero, and everything **come to a standstill**.'*

come to a stop ndalet, qëndron
□ *Production at the factory has **come to a complete full stop**.* □ *The train **came to a sudden stop**.*

come to blows over sth zihem, rrihem me grushta
□ *We almost **came to blows over** what color our new carpet should be.* □ *We didn't actually **come to blows**, but we spent the rest of the day staring out of opposite windows.* □ *The quarrel between Fred and Bill was very serious: they almost **came to blows**.*

come to fruition realizohet, përm-bushet, jep fryt

□ *Their hopes of a happy life together never **came to fruition**.* □ *After years of work, he had the pleasure of seeing all his plans **come to fruition**.*

come to grief 1. dështoj, përfundoj keq
□ *The cocktail party nearly **came to grief** for the chief guest did not arrive until it was well under way.* □ *You are all alike; you won't be satisfied till you've got what you want. If you must **come to grief**, you must, I wash my hands of it.* □ *'I made certain he'd **come to grief** over that betting,' he said.*

2. përplaset, pëson avari (aksident), shkatërrohet
□ *The ship **came to grief** on a hidden rock.*

come/get to grips (with) 1. përleshem, përfytem, kacafytem, ndeshem trup me trup
□ *She was unable to **get to grips with** her assailant.*

2. merrem, trajtoj
□ *Man was really **coming to grips with** the question of how his newly acquired skills could help in the process of economic and social development.* □ *This was a problem with which he never quite **came to grips**.* □ *We have at last managed to **come to grips with** the problem of things being stolen from the school.*

come to hand vjen, bie në dorë
□ *For stuffing the cushion, you can use anything that **comes to hand**.* □ *It was not often that a letter demanding decision or involving responsibility **came to her hands**.* □ *His letter **came to hand** yesterday.* □ *She has been reading anything that **came to her hand**.*

come to harm dëmtohet, prishet, pëson dëm
□ *I shall really have to accompany*

you, if only in order to see that you **come to no harm.** □ *Most parents think that their children will* **come to** *no great* **harm** *if they go to a discotheque now and then.*

come to heel ndjek pas, ndjek këmbakëmbës, hap pas hapi (për qenin)
□ *I'm training my dog to* **come to heel.**

come to life gjallërohem, përtërihem, marr përsëri jetë e forcë, bëhem më i gjallë
□ *You're very cool with your brother, but with your friends you really* **come to life.** □ *The class suddenly* **came to life** *when the professor said that what they were doing would be tested the next day.* □ *Spring is the season when all nature* **comes to life** *again.* □ *Everybody thought that the tree was dead but after the rain, it* **came to life** *again.*

come to light zbulohet, del në shesh, del në dritë, bëhet e qartë (e njohur)
□ *So far no case has* **come to light** *where false confession have been produced because of psychological effect of the instrument.* □ *His crimes did not* **come to light** *until many years after his death.* □ *The accountant's part in the fraud* **came to light** *when a customer asked for an up-to-date statement of payments and withdrawals.* □ *But the most suspicious of all the evidence that has* **come to light** *so far, Orville, is the testimony of two men and a boy.* □ *Following a frank discussion, every side of the problem* **came to light.**

come to loggerheads grindem, zihem
□ *A stupid thing this wretched man Rivarez sent in to yesterday's committee. I knew we should* **come to loggerheads** *with him before long.*

come to naught (nothing) dështon, përfundon në hiç

□ *No one had mentioned the security inquiries, which I assumed had* **come to nothing.** □ *All his schemes have* **come to nothing.** □ *All his years of hard work on the house* **came to nothing** *when it was destroyed by fire.* □ *The dog's attempts to climb the tree after the cat* **came to nothing.**

come to one's feet ngrihem, çohem më këmbë
□ *Several members* **came to their feet** *to answer the accusation.* □ *The audience* **came to their feet** *as the National Anthem was played.*

come to one's knowledge mësoj, marr vesh, marr njoftim
□ *It has* **come to our knowledge** *that you have been cheating the company.* □ *It has* **come to my knowledge** *that you have been unwell.*

come to one's senses (reason) 1. vij në vete, përmendem, fitoj vetëdijen
□ *After his heavy fall, it was fully thirty minutes before he* **came to his senses.** □ *The patient* **came to his senses** *three hours after the operation.*
2. vij ndër mend, i bie mendjes pas, mbledh mendjen, i vë gishtin kokës, vij në rrugë të mbarë
□ *Don't worry about John's obstinate refusal to collaborate; he'll* **come to his senses** *before long.* □ *A boy threw a snowball at me and before I could* **come to my senses** *he ran away.* □ *I hope he will* **come to his senses** *and behave more wisely.*

come to pass ndodh, ngjan
□ *I don't know how it* **came to pass** *that John was late.* □ *Many people would like the electoral system to be reformed but I don't believe this will ever* **come to pass.** □ *It* **came to pass** *some years ago.*

come to pieces thyhet copë-copë, bëhet copë e thërrime

□ *The vase came to pieces in his hand.*

come to rest ndalon

□ *The car skidded off the road and came to rest a foot or two from somebody's front door.*

come to sb's aid/assistance/help vij në ndihmë të

□ *Firemen came to the aid of a man trapped on the top floor of a burning house.* □ *The motorist was asked to give his position, so that the breakdown truck could come to his assistance.*

come to sb's attention/notice vë re, më bie në sy

□ *It came to his attention that his wife was often seen in the company of another man.* □ *It has come to my notice that you have not been working as well as you used to.* □ *It has come to my notice that he is doing quite well lately.*

come to sb's ear(s) dëgjoj, më kap (më zë veshi)

□ *This news came to my ear but yesterday.*

come to sb's rescue vij në shpëtim të

□ *Let's now wait for somebody to come to our rescue—let's build a raft.* □ *When he became seriously ill as a result of heart attack, the doctors came to his rescue.*

come to terms (with) 1. bie në ujdi (me), arrij marrëveshje me

□ *Management and labor came to terms about a new wage agrement and a strike was averted.* □ *After many hours of discussion the two sides finally came to terms.* □ *I'm afraid then, we can't come to terms.* □ *We came to terms and struck the bargain.*

2. pranoj, pajtohem, arrij një modus vivendi me

□ *'Every great artist has come to terms with life—think of Beethoven—how tortured he was in middle-age, and how serene at the end.* □ *The famous footballer finally came to terms with his injury and gave up playing.* □ *Man will have to come to terms with his environment.*

come to the fore shquhet, dallohet, del në pah.

□ *After the election several new members of the parliament came to the fore.* □ *In the field of technical innovation, the firm has made outstanding contributions and many researches have come to the fore.*

come to the ground bie, rrëzohet për tokë

□ *The chimney came crashing to the ground.*

come to the point hyj në temë

□ *The speaker was both brusque and tactfully subtle at the same time. He came to the point straight away.* □ *A good newspaper story must come right to the point and save the details for later.* □ *Tom was giving a lot of history and explanation, but his mother asked him to come to the point.* □ *'Come to the point,' said Miss Sally, 'and don't talk so much.'*

come true bëhet realitet, realizohet, vihet në jetë

□ *'You've got to make it come true,' he says gently.* □ *'You've just got to work and be so determined that it's got to come true, because you believe in it.'* □ *It took years of planning and saving, but the dream of their seagoing vacation came true at last.* □ *His hope of living to 99 did not come true.*

come unstuck dështon, nuk ka sukses

□ *His plan to escape came badly unstuck.* □ *He had not felt like somebody for a long time, not since the pub-lisher had written so encouragingly about the book, which had somehow* **come unstuck** *since then, and had lain untouched in its drawer for weeks.*

come under somebody's notice (observation) bie në sy të, vihet re nga

□ *If such behavior as you have described* **comes under our notice,** *we will deal with it severely.*

come up 1. del mbi tokë (fara)

□ *The snowdrops are just beginning to* **come up.** □ *I sowed some runner beans three weeks ago, but they haven't* **come up** *yet.* □ *The seeds haven't* **come up** *yet.*

2. ngrihet, shtrohet

□ *The question of wage increases* **came up** *at the board meeting.* □ *The question of drug taking is bound to* **come up** *at the next conference.*

3. përmendet, zihet në gojë

□ *His name* **came up** *whenever the matter of nuclear energy was dis-cussed.*

4. lëviz, sjell, transportoj

□ *Roads and bridges were destroyed to prevent the enemy's reserves from* **coming up.** □ *All our supplies have to* **come up** *by this single railway.*

5. nxjerr, vjell

□ *The child doesn't seem to be able to keep anything down. Everything he eats* **comes up** *again.*

6. afrohem

□ *We saw a big black bear* **coming up** *on us from woods.* □ *While we were talking, David* **came up.** □ *He came* **up** *to her and threw his arms around her.*

7. ngjitem, shkoj në qytet

□ *She* **came up** *to me one evening, when I was very low.* □ *Tony will*

come up *in the middle of the week, and shall go down on the weekend.*

8. vjen, arrin deri

□ *The water* **came up** *to my waist.* □ *My younger sister hardly* **comes up** *to my shoulder.*

9. ndodh, ngjan

□ *I'm afraid something urgent has* **come up;** *I won't be able to see you tonight.*

10. dal nga uji

□ *He breathed like a diver* **coming up** *for air.* □ *An instant later he* **came up** *splut-tering.*

11. jap

□ *The teacher asked a difficult ques-tion, but finally Ben* **came up** *with a good answer.*

come up against përballem, ndeshem ballë për ballë

□ *We expect to* **come up against** *a lot of opposition to the scheme.* □ *Not for the first time her will* **came up against** *her husband's.*

come up for konsiderohet si kandidat për

□ *She* **comes up for** *re-election next year.* □ *Members of the faculty* **come up for** *election to the Board of Studies every two years.*

come up for auction/sale vihet në ankand (shitje)

□ *An unusual collection of firearms dating from 16th century* **comes up for auction** *next week.* □ *Is this house likely to* **come up for sale** *in the fore-seeable future?*

come up to (one's) expectations justi-fikoj shpresat

□ *Your work has not* **come up to our expectations.** □ *His film performance didn't* **come up to expectations.** □ *For one reason or another their holiday in Italy didn't* **come up to expectations.**

come up with 1. gjej, jap, dal
□ *Scientists will have to come up with new methods of increasing the world's food supply.* □ *Some people apparently have an almost uncanny ability to come up with the right answer.*
2. arrij, kap
□ *The horseman came up with a group of people who were making the pilgrimage on foot.* □ *Let's go slowly so that the others may come up with us.*

come upon has, ndesh
□ *Searching through a drawer, I came upon just the thing I had been looking for.*

come what may/might të bëhet ç'të bëhet, të dalë ku të dalë, le të ndodhë çfarë të dojë
□ *Come what might, he would never leave Jane.* □ *That's agreed then: we play on Saturday, come what may.* □ *My mother taught us to speak the truth, come what may.* □ *He determined, come what may, to return the visit he had just received.*

coming(s) and going(s) 1. hyrje-dalje(t), vajtje-ardhje(t), ecejake(t)
□ *There's been a tremendous amount of coming and going in the apartment upstairs all morning. I'm dying to know what's going on up there.* □ *With all the comings and goings I haven't been able to do any work.*
2. aktivitet (biznes etj.) i dendur
□ *June knows all the comings and goings in the neighbourhood.*

command esteem/respect gëzon respektin e
□ *Great men command our respect.*

common ground gjë e përbashkët, pikë takimi
□ *Tony and Tom don't like each other because they have no common ground.* □ *The judge tried to solve the dispute by looking for some common ground between the two sides.* □ *Although we think differently and serve different masters, we do have sufficient common ground to be able to talk together.*

common knowledge gjë e njohur, gjë e ditur nga të gjithë
□ *It's pointless trying to keep your friendship secret—it's common knowledge already.*

common sense gjykim i shëndoshë
□ *I stood there silenced. Of course there were lots of common sense arguments I could have brought up, but common sense itself told me that it would be a waste of time.*

commit an offence shkel rregullin (ligjin etj.); kryej (bëj) shkelje
□ *He was sued for committing an offence against the law.*

commit an error (mistake) gaboj, bëj gabim
□ *He committed an unforgivable error.*

commit oneself 1. angazhohem, marr përsipër; jap fjalën
□ *He has committed himself to support his brother's children.* □ *I have committed myself and must keep my promise.*
2. jap mendim; mbaj (anësi)
□ *I asked her what she thought, but she refused to commit herself.* □ *When asked by a press representative whether he thought intervention was justified he managed to talk for a full ten minutes without committing himself one way or another*

commit to memory mësoj përmendsh
□ *She has got a very strong memory, as a result she committed to memory the poem in two days.*

commit to paper shkruaj, hedh në letër

□ *Andy is such a brilliant talker; I wish he would **commit** some of his ideas **to paper**.*

compare notes këmbej përvojën, këmbej mendime

□ *I was interested to hear that you are going to Germany; I was there last year—when you come back, we can **compare notes**. □ We saw the play separately and **compared notes** afterwards. □ The matter is not as simple as it seems. Suppose you come to my room and then we can **compare notes**.*

compare to krahasoj me

□ *Poets have **compared** sleep **to** death. □ The sculpture of Rodin has been **compared** by some critics **to** that of Michelangelo.*

compare with krahasohem

□ *The north of Albania is certainly beautiful, but it can't be **compared with** the south for sunshine.*

compensate for kompensoj për

□ *Nothing will ever **compensate** him **for** the injuries he received in the accident. □ She was **compensated** by the insurance company **for** her injuries.*

compete against/with sb konkurroj me, hyj në garë (konkurrencë) me

□ *Several companies are **competing against/with** each other for the contract. □ Small suburban shops can't **compete with** the chain-stores in price. □ The young golfer has often **competed against** famous players, but so far he has always been beaten.*

complain of ankohem nga; qahem

□ *Several patients were admitted **complaining of** acute stomach pains. □ You don't often hear a woman with two or three children **complaining of** not having enough to do.*

comply with respektoj, zbatoj, përmbush, veproj në përputhje me

□ *When you become a member of a club you generally agree to **comply with** the rules. □ The rules must be **complied with**.*

concentrate on/upon përqëndrohem në

□ *'I can't **concentrate on** what I'm doing while that noise is going on.'*

□ *If all one's efforts are **concentrated upon** reducing disharmony, there must be some improvement.*

concern oneself about/over/with interesohem; shqetësohem

□ *There is no need for you to **concern yourself about** where I was last night.*

□ *You would do better to **concern yourself with** your own business and not mine!*

confide in kam besim te, rrëfehem, i tregoj dikujt një të fshehtë

□ *Modern girls seldom **confide in** their mothers. □ He is not the sort of man in whom I would readily **confide**.*

confine to kufizohem, përmbahem

□ *I wish you would **confine** yourself **to** the matter under discussion.*

congratulate on/upon uroj

□ *I am writing to **congratulate** you most sincerely **on** your appointment as Headmaster of the Grammar School.*

congratulate oneself on/upon përgëzohem; e quaj veten me fat

□ *You can **congratulate yourself on** a very narrow escape; It's a miracle you weren't all burnt alive. □ The bank robbers were just **congratulating themselves on** the success of their raid when the police burst in on them.*

console oneself with ngushëlloj veten me

□ *You may have failed the examination, but you can at least console yourself with the thought that you did the best.*

consult with sb konsultohem me; diskutoj me

□ *You'd better consult with your doctor before you take on a job in such an extremely hot climate.*

contain oneself përmbahem, e mbaj veten

□ *I was so furious I couldn't contain myself.* □ *But at that point Nicky couldn't contain himself any longer. He began banging on the door and screaming.*

content oneself with kënaqem me

□ *We can't go abroad this year, so we'll have to content ourselves with a family holiday in Durrës.*

cook sb's goose rrënoj dikë në mënyrë të pashpresë, rrënoj shpresat (mundësitë, planet e), siguroj dështimin (humbjen e), i bëj gropën dikujt, e marr dikë në qafë

□ *The bank treasurer cooked his own goose when he stole the bank's funds.* □ *The dishonest official knew that his goose was cooked when the newspapers printed the story about him.* □ *Had Fleur cooked her own goose by trying to make too sure?* □ *Do you know that I was in the room when the ceiling fell in—it just about cooked my goose.*

cook the books falsifikoj (shtrembëroj) shifrat (llogarinë, faktet)

□ *Our last accountant is in jail now: the police discovered that he was cooking the books.* □ *'Joe's practically accused me of cooking the books.'*

cook up sajoj, shpik, thur, trilloj, fabrikoj

□ *Tony cooked up an excuse to* explain his absence from school. □ *He cooked up an excuse for being late.*

cool down/off 1. qetësoj; qetësohem

□ *She's very angry; don't speak to her until she's cooled down.* □ *'Keep these two men apart until they've cooled down a bit.'* □ *I had the greatest difficulty in cooling him down.*

2. ftohet, freskohet

□ *'I'm going into the wood to cool off!'* □ *We cooled off from the heat with a refreshing swim.* □ *As the weather cooled off he exchanged the robe for a blanket.* □ *These metal attachments normally take longer than that to cool off.*

cool it qetësohem

□ *Cool it! Don't get so excited!* □ *The crowd started to get angry and the police captain told them to cool it.*

cool one's heels pres gjatë, lë dikë të presë gjatë

□ *The headmaster decided to let the two mischievous boys cool their heels outside his study for ten minutes.* □ *Indeed his annoyance had time to augment a great deal; for he was allowed to cool his heels a full half hour in the anteroom before those gentlemen emerged and he was ushered into the presence.* □ *So you may imagine how unhappy it makes me to have to cool my heels at Newhaven, waiting for the trains to run again.*

coop up/in mbaj, mbyll brenda

□ *I've been cooped up indoors all day.* □ *She would implore me to come outside for a 'breather' when I felt like it, and not to stay all day 'cooped up in that furnace.'*

cork sth up ndrydh, përmbaj ndjenjat (emocionet etj.)

□ *Don't cork it all up: if you feel angry, show it.* □ *It is very bad for you* *to **cork** your emotions **up** like that: you'd feel much better if you could 'let yourself go.'*

cost a pretty penny kushton shumë, kushton shtrenjt, kushton një djall (një dreq) e gjysmë

□ *Renovating that house will **cost you a pretty penny**.* □ *And he heard that the house was **costing** Soames **a pretty penny** beyond what he had reckoned on spending.*

cost money kushton, do para

□ *Even to sleep on the pavement there can **cost money**.* □ *All I'm saying is that you can't just come up to me and say 'I'm pregnant. Now it's your move' as coolly as that. These things **cost money**, and I just haven't enough.*

cost sb dearly i kushton shtrenjt

□ *That mistake **cost** him **dear**: he lost the game because of it.* □ *Mr. Gamble's first fight on behalf of his students and their parents has **cost** him **dear**. 'But I hope,' he told me,' that our experience has a lesson to teach.'*

cost sb a fortune i kushton shtrenjt, kushton një djall e gjysmë

□ *See, Janet, this huge yellow rose wreath here from Mrs Pettigrew has **cost** her **a fortune**.* □ *The party was very good and we didn't leave until very late, so it was a jolly good thing we did take Sally with us or the babysitter would have **cost a fortune**.*

cost sb his life i kushtoi jetën

□ *But remember that one false move could **cost** Sally **her life**.* □ *He made his way apprehensively along the ledge, well aware that one false step would **cost** him **his life**.*

cost sth out llogaris, nxjerr koston

□ *I thought I could afford it, then I* **cost it out** *properly and I found it was too expensive.*

cotton on to sth 1. kuptoj

□ *At last she's **cottoned on to** what they mean.* □ *The man-in-the-street seems to be very slow in **cottoning on to** the significance of the new tax law.*

could go sth do të pëlqeja

□ *The kettle's nearly boiling—**could** you **go** a cup of tea?* □ *'I hope I won't snore so much tonight.' 'I hope so too. I **could go** a night's peace.'*

count against sb llogaritet (kon-siderohet) kundër (në disfavor të)

□ *Your criminal record could **count against** you in finding a job.* □ *His inability to arrive at work on time **counted against** him when he asked for promotion.*

count among llogarit, konsideroj (llogaritet, konsiderohet) si

□ *She **counts among** the most gifted of the current generation of composers.* □ *Mr. Heffer no longer **counts among** my friends since he refused to lend me his lawnmower.*

count for nothing s'bën (s'vlen) asnjë grosh, s'ka asnjë vlerë

□ *I am surprised to find that all the deportment and good conduct I have been taught seem to **count for nothing** when I am with you.*

count one's chickens before they are hatched peshku në det, tigani në zjarr; bëj hesapet pa hanxhinë

□ *'If I get the new job, the first thing I shall buy is a car.' 'Don't **count your chickens before they are hatched**: you haven't even been interviewed yet.'* □ *She's been boasting all over the village about her son going to Oxford and now he hasn't been given a place. It shows you that you shouldn't **count your chickens before they are hatched**.*

count on/upon mbështetem, var shpresën

□ He **counted on** his sister for everything—the care of his children, the nursing of his sick wife, and even for a little pleasant company in the evenings. □ I'll do it; you know you can **count on** me. □ You can always **count on** Bill for a pound or two when you're in difficulties.

count sb/sth in përfshij, përllogaris

□ If the cost of the trip is no more than five pounds, you can **count me in**. □ See how many plates we have, but don't **count in** the cracked ones.

count sb/sth out 1. heq nga llogaria, nuk llogaris

□ 'Will this party cost anything? If it does, **count me out**, because I'm broke. □ If it's going to be a rowdy party, you can **count me out**.

2. llogarit një për një

□ The old lady laboriously **counted out** fifteen pence, snapped her purse shut and said, 'There! Is that right?' □ June **counted out** the number of pennies she had.

count up to sth arrin, kap shumën

□ These small contributions soon **count up** to a sizable amount.

course of action, a mënyrë veprimi

□ What is the best **course of action** we can take?

course of events rrjedhë, ecuri e ngjarjeve

□ In the normal **course of events**, someone so young would not be admitted into the university.

cover oneself with glory mbulohem me lavdi

□ The regiment **covered itself with glory** in the invasion battle.

cover (the) ground 1. përshkoj, mbuloj (një distancë)

□ We **covered** a lot of **ground** on our tour of Spain. □ Mr. Tony likes to travel in planes, because they **cover** a lot of **ground** so quickly.

2. mbuloj një fushë

□ Asked if the course could be shortened to two years, the professor replied that the majority of students would not be able to **cover the ground** in less than three years. □ Their talks, although less formal than the others, **covered** largely the same **ground**.

cover up mbuloj, fsheh

□ The government is trying to **cover up** the scandal. □ There are too many people in this office trying to **cover up** the mistakes of the past few years.

cover (up) one's tracks mbuloj gjurmët

□ The police are still searching for the murderer; he has been very clever at **covering up his tracks**. □ Nobody ever knew what Johnson might be up to. It was second nature to him to **cover his tracks**.

crack a joke tregoj, bëj një shaka

□ The men sat around the fire, smoking and **cracking jokes**. □ Stout men with shapeless hats on, looked out of windows, and **cracked jokes** with friends in the street. □ John's great fun at the party—he's forever **cracking jokes**.

crack down on marr masa të rrepta kundër, trajtoj ashpër; sulmoj, shtyp

□ The police **cracked down** and hauled away cars that were double-parked. □ If the revenue officers had time they would **crack down on** tax evaders more quickly. □ The police are always being urged to **crack down on** drug addicts.

crack the whip fshikulloj kamzhikun; përdor kërcënimin për ndëshkim

□ If the children won't behave when I

reason with them, I have to **crack the whip.**

crack up 1. rrënohem (shkatërrohem) fizikisht (mendërisht)

□ *If Tom goes on working and worrying as he has been doing he's bound to* **crack up** *sooner or later.* □ *It seemed to be family problems that made him* **crack up.**

2. përplas(et)

□ *When the driver skidded off the road he* **cracked up** *his car against a tree.* □ *The airplane* **cracked up** *as it landed.*

3. shkrihem gazit; bëj të shkrihet gazit

□ *That comedian* **cracks** *me* **up.** □ *And then Fred shouts: 'I'm the great pumpkin!' The whole room* **cracks up.**

cramp sb's style pengoj dikë të veprojë lirisht, pengoj dikë të shfaqë aftësitë (dhurëtitë etj.)

□ *He hates playing golf in rainy weather: it* **cramps his style.** □ *The presence of curious onlookers watching him paint* **cramped his style.** □ *It* **cramps my style** *to have you watching over me all the time.*

create a sensation krijoj sensacion

□ *The play* **created a sensation** *when it was first produced.* □ *The outrageous book* **created a sensation.**

crop up dalin, shfaqen, ndodhin papritur

□ *Problems* **cropped up** *almost every day when Tom was building his new house.* □ *'Why don't you stay at home tomorrow? I can call you if anything* **crops up** *in the office.'*

cross a bridge/one's bridges before one comes to it/them bëj hop pa kapërcyer (hedhur) gardhin, shqetësohem, orvatem të zgjidh një problem përpara kohe

□ *I suggest that we make our decision*

later: let's not **cross that bridge before we come to it.** □ *'Can I be a pilot when I grow up, mother?' asked Tony. 'Don't* **cross that bridge until you come to it.**

cross a bridge/one's bridges when one comes to it/them orvatem të zgjidh një problem në kohën e duhur

□ *'How could you keep up those enormous mortgage payments, though, if you fell ill or lost your job? 'How, indeed. But I don't believe in* **crossing my bridges before I come to them.'** □ *We'll* **cross that bridge when we come to it.**

cross one's mind më bie (shkon) ndër mend

□ *I'm afraid I only bought tickets for two: it never* **crossed my mind** *that your wife might want to come too.* □ *The thought* **crossed his mind,** *among other thoughts, that Jean's brain might be undergoing a softening process.* □ *It has just* **crossed my mind** *that he might be away from home.*

cross sb's path has, ndesh në rrugë (udhës)

□ *I know you can't get on with Clark, but you shouldn't let that worry you. You'll be working in such very different departments, there'll be no need for you to* **cross his path** *unless you want to.* □ *I had heard a lot about Barker, and he of me, but up till then* **our path** *had never been* **crossed.** □ *I should fear even to* **cross his path** *now: my view must be hateful to him.*

cross sth off/out i vë kryq (vizë)

□ *We can* **cross** *his name* **off** *the list, as he's not coming.* □ *Two words have been* **crossed out.**

cross swords with hahem, grindem, kapem me fjalë

□ *Brown and I are not on friendly*

*terms: we've **crossed swords** twice this week already.* □ *Don't argue with the teacher. You're not old enough to **cross swords** with him.* □ *The chairman and I have **crossed swords** before over this issue.*

cross the t's and dot the i's vë pikat mbi i

□ *The sales manager went over the whole program **crossing the t's and dotting the i's**, so that every salesman knew exactly what was to be done.* □ *The first speaker has explained it so ably that all that remains for me to do is **to cross the t's and dot the i's**.*

crouch one's back before sb kërrus (ul, përkul) shpinën (kurrizin) para

□ *Historically the Albanian people have never **crouched their back before** foreign invaders.*

crowd in on/upon vërshojnë në mendjen e

□ *Memories **crowded in on** me.* □ *Scenes of his past life came **crowding in upon** the drowning man.*

crown everything i vë kapak

□ *He arrived late, accidentally knocked over a lamp, and then to **crown everything**, he broke a valuable crystal vase.*

crown it all i vë kapak, e mbyll, e përfundoj

□ *They gave us a delicious meal and, to **crown it all**, a very old brandy which must have cost a fortune.* □ *'I've a good mind to throw you out of the house,' his father said. 'You're lazy, dirty, and impudent and now, to **crown it all**, I find you're dishonest as well.'*

crush in the bud shtyp, mbys që në embrion

□ *... he knew it had been poor Merry's mission to **crush him in the bud**.*

cry down zhvlerësoj, ul vlerën (rëndësinë), i jap pak rëndësi

□ *'Don't **cry down** the very real progress these people have made.'* □ *Don't **cry down** her real achievements.*

cry for the moon kërkoj të pamundurën, kërkoj qiqra në hell

□ *'They're always wishing they could afford a cottage in Sardinia, or take a cruise round the world, or something equally impossible. Just **crying for the moon**.* □ *He was a mere child in the world, but he didn't **cry for the moon**.*

cry off heq dorë, ndërroj mendje, nuk i përmbahem (premtimit etj.)

□ *It was the only foggy night in November and Gerald was sorely tempted to **cry off** going to dinner but Leonie got him there somehow.* □ *'I don't think I'll go swimming after all.' 'Oh, you're not going to **cry off** now are you, when I've persuaded everyone to join us.'*

cry one's eyes out shkrihem së qari, shkrihem në lot

□ *When the woman finally came down from the bedroom she looked as if she'd been **crying her eyes out**.* □ *Where have you been wretch? Here is Emmy **crying her eyes out** for you.* □ *The sister... **cried her eyes out** at the loss of the necklace.*

cry one's heart out qaj me ngashërim, me dënesë

□ *Amelia... got out and went upstairs to her room and **cried her** little **heart out**.* □ *The poor little girl **cried her heart out** when her father came home and told her that her dog had been run over.*

cry out for sth 1. fton, bën thirrje

□ *The coastline is full of possibilities, industrial, commercial, and residential: it's just* **crying out for** *development.*

2. kërkon

□ *People are* **crying out for** *free elections.* □ *This system is* **crying out for** *reform.*

cry over split milk u bë ç'u bë, buka që thyhet s'ngjitet më

□ *'Look! The sooner you realize that your money has gone, the better it will be for you. It's no use* **crying over spilt milk.** □ *What's done can't be helped; there is no use* **crying over spilt milk.**

cry wolf bërtas 'ujku, ujku'; jap alarm të panevojshëm

□ *The employer had* **cried wolf** *so many times about the danger of high wage increases, that the workmen began to ignore his warnings.* □ *The newspaper placards that had* **cried** *'wolf' so often,* **cried** *'wolf' now in vain.* □ *When the voices, especially those of the Press, really have something important to speak to the common man about, he gives them the old smile and continues to read the comics. The have* **cried** *'wolf' too often.*

cuddle up/to/against tulatem pas

□ *The twins* **cuddled up** *close together and fell asleep.* □ *The child* **cuddled up** *to her mother.*

cudgel one's brains vras mendjen

□ *Hard as I* **cudgelled my brains,** *I couldn't remember her name.* □ *You don't know the answer? Well,* **cudgel your brains** *to find it.*

cup of tea gjëja që pëlqej, që më tërheq; ajo që më pëlqen

□ *I've never been to the opera; it's not my* **cup of tea.** □ *'You may find this sort of job rather difficult. But it's just my* **cup of tea.'** □ *Certainly Frank was doing well for himself. Import-export*

was booming, but it wasn't his **cup of tea.**

curl one's lips ngërdheshem, përdredh buzët

□ *He was a very narrow-minded pedant, academic rather than scholarly, and far too ready to* **curl the lip** *when such subjects as 'modern studies' or 'student rights' came up for discussion.*

curry favor (with) i bëj lajka, i kreh bishtin (për të fituar simpatinë e dikujt)

□ *Most students disliked him because he tried to* **curry favor with** *the teacher.* □ *John tried to* **curry favor with** *the new girl by telling her she was the prettiest girl in the class.* □ *She had called being three doors away, to leave her card; and Aileen, willing to* **curry favor** *here and there, had responded.*

cut across 1. i bie shkurt, pres shkurt, i bie përmes

□ *Whenever the grass was dry the children would* **cut across** *the fields instead of keeping to the road.* □ *I usually* **cut across** *the park on my way home.*

2. shpërfill, jam (dal, veproj) kundër

□ *When he voted he* **cut across** *party lines.*

cut and dried/cut-and-dried i gatshëm, i parapërgatitur, i përfunduar

□ *There are no more arrangements to be made for the ceremony; the whole thing is* **cut-and-dried.** □ *'You have to spread things out a bit here,' he said in earnest appeal to Essex. 'You can't have everything* **cut and dried.**

cut at pres, çaj, plagos

□ *He* **cut** *desperately* **at** *the rope in an attempt to free his foot.* □ *His attacker* **cut at** *him with a knife.*

cut away pres, heq (me prerje)

□ *The surgeon* **cut away** *the tumor*

with expert skill. □ *We cut away all the dead wood from the tree.*

cut and run iki me të katra, ua mbath këmbëve

□ *Grady would cut and run like a scared rabbit.* □ *... I'll let go your arm and then cut and run.*

cut and thrust debat i gjallë i ndërsjellë, sulme e kundërsulme

□ *The new MP was not used to the cut and thrust of parliamentary debates.*

cut back 1. pres, krasit

□ *Some gardeners believe in cutting rose bushes back very hard indeed— almost down to the ground.*

2. ul, shkurtoj

□ *Owing to the unfavorable economic climate, the motor-car industry has cut back production by fifteen per cent.*

cut both/two ways është thikë me dy presa, ka efekt (ndikim) të dyanshëm

□ *The speaker argued that the imposing of sanctions could cut both ways.*

cut corners i bie për shkurt, pres shkurt; gjej rrugën më të shkurtër

□ *He cut corners going home in a hurry.* □ *If you want the job done quickly, then we shall have to cut some corners while we are doing it.*

cut down 1. pres

□ *When I returned to my childhood home I was distressed to find that all the apple trees had been cut down.*

2. ul, shkurtoj, pakësoj (shpenzimet etj.)

□ *'We must cut our expenses down somehow. I'll stop smoking and you had better spend less on beer.'* □ *'The doctor told me to cut down my consumption of carbohydrates.'* □ *If you can cut your article down to about 1,000 words, we will publish it in our next issue.*

cut each other's (one another's) throat i hanë kokën njëri-tjetrit

□ *Ah! And here came Counsel Foskisson and Bullfry together... They would soon be calling each other 'my friend' now and cutting each other's throats!* □ *The essence of business is to combine. Suppose I had started on my own? There'd just been two of us cutting each other's throat, and neither of us able to expand at all.*

cut it/things fine llogaris kohën me përpikmëri të madhe

□ *'Will it be OK if we get to the station ten minutes before the train leaves?'* *'I think that would be cutting things rather fine. We have to buy our tickets and look for the right platform, you know.'* □ *If we only allow five minutes for catching our train, we'll be cutting it too fine.* □ *Well, you've caught the train, but you cut it fine.*

cut from (out of) the same cloth njerëz të një brumi, bukë e një mielli

□ *There is not the slightest difference between them. They are cut from the same cloth.*

cut in 1. ndërpres, ndërhyj

□ *Edith's mouth had opened to yelp out the prepared condemnation, when Robert unexpectedly cut in.* □ *I wish you would not keep cutting in with your remarks.* □ *'The facts, Robert, the facts!' Ned cut in.*

2. përfshij

□ *Next time you form a syndicate, don't forget to cut me in.* □ *The gang decided they would have to cut the Weasel in if only to keep his mouth shut about their plans.* □ *We haven't got to cut Sam in, have we? He didn't help much.* □ *I think we should cut in all those who helped us organize the auction in the first place.*

3. i pres udhën një makinë (në të njëjtën korsi)

□ *Impatient drivers who habitually cut in are bound to cause an accident sooner or later.* □ *After passing several cars, David cut in too soon and nearly caused an accident.*

cut into 1. pakësoj, ul

□ *The union made the company pay higher wages, which cut into the profits.*

2. ndërpres, futem në bisedë etj.

□ *John's unwelcome voice cut gratingly into their quiet discussion.* □ *She heard the other women talking and cut into the conversation.* □ *She kept cutting into out conversation.*

3. pres, ndaj

□ *As the little girl cut into her birthday cake, everyone cheered and clapped their hands.* □ *I cut into meat and I felt a sudden twinge of nausea.*

cut loose 1. shkëputem

□ *'Do you remember Dollie at all?' he asked. 'Dollie Stoksey?' Robin blushed involuntarily. 'Yes, of course,' he remarked with what he hoped was a casual air. 'I was fourteen or fifteen when you cut loose from her.'*

2. çlirohem

□ *I will cut loose from every entanglement.*

3. veproj (flas) lirshëm

□ *He really cut loose and told me what he thought of me.*

cut no ice s'ka efekt (ndikim); s'është bindës; s'bën fajde

□ *His excuses cut no ice with me.* □ *If you are late there is no use giving excuses to Mr. Brown; they cut no ice with him.* □ *Boanereges. O, sit down, man, sit down. You're in your own house; ceremony cuts no ice with me.*

cut off 1. pres, këpus

□ *From the carcass roasting over the fire, the man cut off a succulent piece and handed it to me on a knife.* □ *The workman had a finger cut off by the machine he was operating—a moment of inattention, and it was too late.* □ *He cut off a hard cloth from the roll.*

2. izoloj

□ *The village was cut off by the snow for more than a month.* □ *Although the platoon was cut off by the enemy, they managed to hide until nightfall and regain their own lines under cover of darkness.* □ *The children were cut off by the tide and had to be carried up the cliff to safety.*

3. ndërpres

□ *Final notice: Unless your outstanding account is paid within seven days of the date on this notice, we regret that we shall be obliged to cut off your supply of electricity.* □ *The television show was cut off by a special news report.* □ *The telephone operator cut us off before we had finished our conversation.* □ *The oil producing countries threatened to cut off all the supplies of oil to Europe unless their terms were met.*

cut off one's nose to spite one's face në vend që t'i vinte vetulla, i nxori sytë

□ *He showed his displeasure with his boss by resigning: but he was really cutting off his nose to spite his face, because he had no other job to go.* □ *If the Trades Unions refuse to register under the Industrial Relations Act they will be cutting off their noses to spite their faces.* □ *Still, if he refused to make any advantageous deals with Mr. George W. Stener, or*

*any other man..., he was **cutting off
his nose to spite his face.***

cut one's cables pres, shkëpus lidhjet
me; pres (këpus) urat me
□ *There was still time to draw back,
he reflected, before he **cut his cables.***
□ *'I've got to make a success of this
job I've taken on,' he said, 'because
I've **cut my cables** as far as getting
back into the Civil Service is concerned.'*

**cut one's (the) coat according to
one's (the) cloth** shtrij këmbët sa
kam jorganin
□ *Now that he is earning less than he
used to, he will have to take a shorter
holiday; he must **cut his coat
according to his cloth.** □ Fleur—so
far as he knew—**cut her coat
according to her cloth.***

cut one's losses ndal, ndërpres një
aktivitet (biznes) jofitimprurës; ndërpres humbjet
□ *It's tempting to hang on to shares
you once paid a lot of money for, in
the hope that they'll appreciate. But if
I were you, I'd sell out now and **cut
my losses.***

cut one's own throat ha kokën e vet
□ *We'll take over your business and
put you in as manager at a fair salary.
We can't stop you from trying to go it
alone, but if you do you'll be **cutting
your own throat.***

cut short ndërpres, i jap fund
□ *The chairman **cut short** the final
speech by announcing that there was
no time left.* □ *'Not at all,' he said.
'Delighted. Well, I'm afraid we must
cut our conversation short. □ Young
Jolyon felt a desire to **cut** their enjoy-
ment **short.***

cut sb dead bëj sikur nuk e njoh (sikur
nuk e shikoj), injoroj
□ *Oh yes, he did take offense, and*

*very much so. I've run into him sev-
eral times since then and he has
simply **cut me dead.** □ Dora... I've
met Babby walking with his mother,
and of course he **cut me dead.***

cut sb off with a shilling i heq të
drejtën e trashëgimisë, përjashtoj nga
trashëgimia
□ *The old man's patience was finally
exhausted and, in disgust at his eldest
son's behavior, he **cut him off with a
shilling.***

cut sb to the heart plagos (prek,
lëndoj) zemrën e
□ *His ingratitude **cut her to the heart.***
□ *And I say it again, you've been
acting the part of a selfish, light-
minded man, though it **cuts me to the
heart** to say so.*

cut sb to the quick lëndoj (prek, fyej)
thellë
□ *The student was **cut to the quick**
by the lecturer's sarcastic remark.*
□ *Helen's sarcastic remarks about
my efforts to help her and her family
cut me to the quick. □ He was **cut
to the quick** by such a display of
callousness.*

cut the cackle lë llafet (muhabetin)
□ *The job was several days behind
schedule, so the foreman told his men
to **cut the cackle** and get on with it.*

cut the (Gordian) knot zgjidh (pres)
nyjën gordiane
□ *At one stroke he had **cut the knot,**
by passing all the preliminaries—
the manoeuvring for position, the
attacking at one point and giving way
at another.*

**cut the ground from under sb (sb's
feet)** bëj t'i dridhet (shkasë, lëvizë)
toka nën këmbë
□ *We must be doing something, you
know; we mustn't allow these people
to **cut the ground from under us***

while we sit looking on. □ *The thief denied that he had ever been in the shop, but the police inspector **cut the ground from under him** by showing him a photograph as proof.*

cut to bits/pieces/ribbons/shreds dërrmoj, shpartalloj

□ *The retreat turned into a rout and the would-be-attackers were **cut to ribbons** by the enemy, who gave them no respite.* □ *The heavy cavalry caught the foot soldiers in line before they could form a square, and **cut them to pieces**.* □ *Becky ... could **cut her rival to pieces** with her wit.* □ *Our group tried to persuade the meeting that the most effective course of action would be to strike, but we were utterly **cut to shreds** by Cavendish and his supporters.*

cut to the heart /to the soul e lëndoj në shpirt, plagos zemrën e

□ *'It **cuts me to the soul**,' said Mr. Pecksniff, 'but I cannot quarrel you, Mary.'* □ *Gregory. Seraphita, you **cut me to the soul**. [He weeps].* □ *Mrs. Lung. Serve you right! You'd think it quite proper if it **cut me to the heart**.*

cut up 1. dëshpërohem, pikëllohem

□ *Eve was very **cut up** when she heard that her friend had been sacked.* □ *The parents were naturally **cut up** at the news of their son's arrest on a charge of fraud.* □ *Tom was badly **cut up** when June gave him back his ring.*

2. plagos

□ *All the occupants of the two cars were badly **cut up** in the smash.* □ *Those fellows weren't too gentle with him. They **cut him up** very badly.*

3. pres copa-copa

□ *The vegetables should be **cut up** into small pieces and dropped into boiling water.*

cut up rough zemërohem, nxehem, tërbohem, marr zjarr

□ *I am afraid that some of the customers might **cut up rough** when they find out that they are not getting their money back. It may be very dangerous if this happens.* □ *The potential clients were lining up, tumbling over themselves, only waiting for a word from Alec. Would that word be given, if Harold started to **cut up rough**.*

D

dab off heq, thith, pi
 □ *If you apply this cleaning fluid, you'll find you can simply **dab** the dirt off.*

dab on/onto vë, vendos lehtë (ëmbël)
 □ *The furniture cream should be **dabbed on** with a soft cloth.* □ *The painter slowly built up his landscape, **dabbing on** small areas of green and yellow.*

dally with sth 1. luaj, qesëndis, tallem me
 □ *He **dallied with** her affections for a bit, but quickly moved on when she showed signs of wanting a more permanent relationship.*
 2. mendoj joseriozisht
 □ *We discussed a proposal **with** which he had been **dallying** for some time, but about which little had been done.*

damn all asgjë, hiçgjë, kurrgjë, hiç
 □ *If that's what they do with money they collect, they'll get **damn all** from me the next time they come round for subscriptions.*

dam up mbaj, përmbaj
 □ *She tried hard to **dam up** her feelings which will burst out at some stage in a more violent form than if they had been expressed in the first place.*

damp down fashit
 □ *We **damped** the fire **down** before we went to bed.*

dance after (to) sb's pipe/piping/ whistle shkoj (i hedh hapat) sipas avazit të, hedh vallen sipas avazit të
 □ *I thought I had the prettiest girl in the Castle **dancing after my whistle**.*

dance attendance (up) on i rri qiri më këmbë, i rri më këmbë, me lepe e me peqe
 □ *John must be hoping for some favours from his new boss: he is always **dancing attendance on** him.*
 □ *A swarm of would-be suitors **danced attendance on** the best-looking girls.* □ *She loves to have servants **dance attendance upon** her.*

dance to sb's tune shkoj sipas avazit të
 □ *He has lost control of Congress as completely as he had it **dancing to his tune** three years ago.*

dark horse, a person (kandidat) pak i njohur; njeri i pashfaqur
 □ *He's a bit of **a dark horse**: He was earning a fortune, but nobody knew.* □ *Whatever the outcome of the election, Mr. Michael Foot—**the dark horse**—emerges more and more as a figure of moderation and sound sense.*

darken sb's door(s) (again) shkel pragun e shtëpisë të, shkel në derë
 □ *If anybody had spoken to me like that when I was a guest in their house, it would be a long time before I would **darken their door again**.*
 □ *'Go! Now!' shouted his indignant, but slightly inebriated father, adding with a touch of melodrama. 'And never **darken my doors again**!'* □ *I am afraid he would resent it so as never to **darken my door again**.*

dart a glance/look at hedh një shikim (vë-shtrim) të shpejtë
 □ *She **darted an** interested **glance at** the handsome newcomer from under*

lowered eyelids. □ **Darting** *a resentful* **glance** *at Lucy he muttered: 'The whole thing's new to me.'* □ *'Well!'* exclaimed Mr. Bumble, stopping short, and **darting at** *his little charge* *a* **look** *of intense malignity.*

dash/shatter sb's hopes shuaj shpresat e
□ *Well, I'm sorry to* **shatter your** **hopes**, *but I don't believe your furniture will fetch anything like the price you mention.* □ *The first runner's poor performance* **dashed our hopes** *of winning the relay.* □ *Dunstant's* **hopes** *were again* **dashed** *by the news of Edward's death.*

dash something off shkruaj (vizatoj, pikturoj, hedh në letër) shpejt e shpejt
□ *The thing had obviously been* **dashed off** *but it consisted of just the right number of lines.* □ *I must* **dash** **off** *a few letters before I go out.* □ *The impressions of the moment...* **dashed** **off** *with a careless but graceful pen.*

dash sb's brains out ia hedh trutë në erë
□ *One of the bodyguard* **dashed his** **brains out** *with a single blow from his club.*

date from/back to daton
□ *From* *what period do the ceremonies* **date***?*
□ *This castle* **dates from** *the 14th century.* □ *My interest in stamp collecting* **dates from** *my school days.*

dawn on/upon kthjellohet, bëhet i qartë e i kuptueshëm; më vjen (shkon) ndërmend
□ *The idea that they had either feelings or rights had never* **dawned** **upon** *her.* □ *It has just* **dawned upon** *me that he might be away.* □ *It* **dawned on** *David that he would fail if he did not study harder.*

day after day ditë për ditë, për ditë
□ **Day after day** *she waited in vain for*

him to telephone her. □ **Day after day** *he kept at it and, as a result, his progress this term has been considerable.* □ *We waited* **day after day** *but Dick never arrived.*

day and night ditë e natë
□ *Some filling stations on highways are open* **day and night.** □ *There was a ten feet high electrified double wire fence all round, and dogs and guards patrolling between the fences* **day** **and night.** □ *He is now working* **day** **and night** *to finish the experiment.*

day by day çdo ditë, nga dita në ditë
□ **Day by day** *she learned more about her job.*
□ *At the steel plant production is increasing* **day by day.**

day in (and) day out ditë për ditë
□ **Day in, day out**, *no matter what the weather is like, she walks ten miles.*
□ *The postman is busy delivering letters* **day in and day out.**

daylight/highway robbery vjedhje (hajdutëri) në mes të ditës
□ *Even allowing for wages and other overheads it's* **daylight robbery** *to charge 60 pence for a cup of tea.*
□ *I'm not going to the show: at the prices they are charging it's* **daylight** **robbery.**

day off ditë pushimi
□ *'How nice of you all to come,' she told the nurses, 'especially on your* **day off.'** □ *I've a good mind to take a* **day off** *and go down to Brighton with you. The office could get on without me, for once.*

dead ahead përpara, ballë për ballë
□ *The car skidded to a halt a few inches from the curb with a lamppost* **dead ahead** *of it.* □ *Father was driving in a fog, and suddenly he saw another car* **dead ahead** *of him.*

dead beat i rraskapitur, i dërrmuar

☐ *You look* **dead beat**, *and no wonder. There was no need to dig the whole potato patch in one go.* ☐ *'Help me to carry this case, will you?—I'm* **dead beat**.'

dead certain/sure of/about sth plotësisht i sigurt

☐ *We locked all the doors when we left. I'm* **dead certain of** *that.* ☐ *I'm* **dead certain** *he has a lot of money stashed away that he never lets on about.*

dead drunk tapë, i dehur keq

☐ *There was a bloke lying on the road* **dead drunk**, *so we pulled him over on the verge and left him propped up against the hedge.*

dead duck, a 1. njeri i mbaruar

☐ *Anyone who is caught up in those mountains in bad weather is a* **dead duck**.

2. plan (projekt etj.) i braktisur (i dështuar)

☐ *The plan is a* **dead duck**: *there is no money.*

dead easy/simple fare lehtë, fare kollaj

☐ *It would have been* **dead easy** *to burgle his house, except that there wasn't anything much worth pinching.* ☐ *'It's* **dead easy**,' *David assured him.*

dead end, a qorrsokak, rrugë pa krye

☐ *With the failure of the experiment, we had reached* **a dead end**.

dead from the neck up trutharë, trudalë, kokëtrashë

☐ *And there were, two old ladies,* **dead from the neck up**. ☐ *He's very correct, very courteous—and* **dead from the neck up**.

dead letter, a letër e vdekur

☐ *In fact, the rule has become a* **dead letter**.

dead silence qetësi e plotë, heshtje varri

☐ *He heard me through in* **dead silence**, *giving no sign of approval or disapproval until I had finished.* ☐ *The darkness and* **dead silence** *of the cave began to oppress him.*

dead still i ngrirë në vend

☐ *I stood* **dead still** *on the floor of the store room. There was a silence into which it seemed to me I had just let loose a vast quantity of sound.*

dead tired i rraskapitur, i lodhur për vdekje

☐ *Jurgis came home* **dead tired**.

deal a blow i jap një goditje, i jap një grusht

☐ *She* **dealt** *him a tremendous* **blow** *with the poker.* ☐ *He was just beginning to take heart again after the death of his wife when fate* **dealt** *him another* **blow**. *His younger son was drowned in a yachting accident.* ☐ *Her death* **dealt** *us a terrible* **blow**.

deal in trajtoj, tregtoj

☐ *The small post office on the corner* **deals in** *a lot else besides stamps and postal orders.* ☐ *We* **deal in** *hardware but not software.*

deal out 1. jap

☐ *And the same punishment would be* **dealt out** *to any boy who was ever late for his class.*

☐ *The judge* **dealt out** *harsh sentences to the rioters.*

2. shpërndaj

☐ *The profits will be* **dealt out** *among the investors.*

deal with 1. tregtoj, bëj tregti

☐ *We've* **dealt with** *the same firm for years and can thoroughly recommend them to you.*

☐ *I hate* **dealing with** *large impersonal companies.*

2. merrem

☐ *'I'll* **deal with** *you when I get home from the office.'* ☐ *The problem of*

*unemployment is the most serious of those **with** which the government has to **deal**.*
3. trajtoj
□ *The subject isn't very well **dealt** with in his latest book.* □ *This book **deals with** the problem of agricultural chemistry.*

declare war against/on shpall luftë kundër
□ *Hostilities were opened without **war** being **declared**.*

deep in thought i zhytur, i kredhur në mendime
□ *She answered nothing, partly because it was not necessary to speak in order to sustain a conversation with little Ann, and partly because she was **deep in thought**.* □ *Some students scribbled away furiously, others sat **deep in thought**, and others glanced in all directions as if seeking inspiration from any source.*

deliver the goods kryej (përmbush) detyrën sipas parashikimeve; mbaj fjalën (premtimin) e dhënë
□ *Under the terms of the agreement the union undertook to get the men back to work, but it was unable to **deliver the goods**.* □ *Don't worry about Jack: If he says he will help you, then you can be sure he will **deliver the goods**.*

depart from shkëputem, ndahem, heq dorë, braktis
□ *The chairman **departed from** normal procedure by allowing reporters to be present during Council business.* □ *These were hallowed traditions **from** which he had no intention of **departing**.* □ *He is a man of honour; he never **departs from** his word.*

depend on/upon 1. mbështetem
□ *The town **depends** almost solely on*

the tourist trade. □ *They could **depend on** John to support them.*
2. besoj, jam i sigurt, i zë besë
□ *One could never **depend on** his arriving on time.* □ *He'll be there when he is needed; on that you can **depend**.*

depend on/upon it me siguri; pa dyshim
□ *He may **depend upon it** that we shall never surrender.* □ *'You can **depend upon it**. I shall be there.'* □ *And she will copy the list before she gives it back to Blueloo, you may **depend on it**—all is lost.*

descend on/upon sb/sth sulmoj befas, papritur
□ *The police **descended on** their hide-out.*

die a natural death vdes në mënyrë të natyrshme
□ *There was no reason to suppose that he had not **died a natural death**.*

die away humbet, shuhet, zhduket
□ *The thunder and lightning **died away** in heavy rain and her mind too faded away in vague confusion.* □ *The snow had covered our late footprints; my new track was the only one to be seen; and even that began to **die away**.* □ *Ona's voice **died away**—then he heard her sobbing again.*

die down shuhet, fashitet, bie, zhduket
□ *She waited until the laughter had **died down**.* □ *In the afternoon the wind **died down**.* □ *Twenty minutes later, the sun peeped out again from behind the clouds, the thunder-claps **died down**, the rain turned into a drizzle, then stopped.*

die hard ndryshojnë, zhduken me zor
□ *Customs **die hard**; and I'm glad of it for there are many Gaelic customs which I would hate to see die, and with them our individuality as a people.* □ *Old habits **die hard**.*

die in harness vdes në punë e sipër
□ *I am as fit as a fiddle. Mixing with youngsters keeps me youthful. No, I'll never retire. Actors die in harness.*

die in one's bed vdes i mbërthyer në shtrat
□ *I'd rather die in my boots than die in my bed.*

die in one's boots/with one's boots on vdes në punë e sipër, vdes më këmbë, vdes në krye të detyrës
□ *I don't want to think up things to do when I retire. I'd rather die in my boots. □ Most of the private captains in the old days died with their boots on.*

die is cast zaret u hodhën
□ *Now it was done; the die was cast: she hadn't realized that a doubt still lingered, but there must have been one, to judge by her relief. □ Since I have entered for the exam, the die is cast: I shall have to sit in.*

die like flies vdesin si mizat
□ *'We have given up cremating them because the refugees are dying like flies, and we do not have enough fuel, so we bury them.'*

die off thahet, vyshket; vdes; ngordh
□ *A water shortage had struck the area and the wild life was dying off alarmingly in the intense heat. □ They had to watch their young family die off through lack of food and proper medical attention. □ The leaves of this plant are dying off. □ Those trees will die off for sure if they are not watered in time.*

die out shuhet, zhduket
□ *Only those species sufficiently adaptable to cope with changing conditions survived. The others died out.*
□ *With the development of transport and the building of new factories many of the traditional crafts have died out.*

□ *Following a period of babel, the noise gradually died out.*

die laughing vdes së qeshuri
□ *It was so funny, I nearly died laughing. □ Yes, he told us the whole story. Laugh? I nearly died.*

dig in/into 1. mbjell, përziej duke punuar tokën
□ *You'll need to dig those young trees in a bit deeper, unless you want the wind to blow them over. □ Manure should be well dug into the soil.*
2. ngul
□ *The dog dug its teeth in.*
3. i futem, i hyj
□ *An enormous first course of turkey did not prevent them from digging into the Christmas pudding.*

dig oneself in 1. vetëgroposem
□ *As soon as they had seized the enemy position, the infantry dug themselves in. □ During a lull in the fighting the commander ordered the soldiers to dig themselves in.*
2. ngulem, zë vend, hedh rrënjë
□ *'Do you work here or something? We all thought you would dig yourself in at Oxford.'*

dig one's heels/toes in ngul këmbë si mushkë
□ *But when it came to separation, his wife dug her heels in firmly. □ I have stood a great deal from you without complaint, but after your last ridiculous and offensive letter I am going to dig my toes in.*

dig out/out of 1. nxjerr nga toka (duke gërmuar)
□ *It was buried by the avalanche and had to be dug out. □ A whole family was dug out from underneath a tangle of fallen beams and masonry.*
2. gërmoj, rrëmoj
□ *'Where did he get hold of that*

information?' 'He managed to dig it out of some private library.

dig up 1. nxjerr nga toka

□ *We must dig up those bushes; they're blocking the view.* □ *An old statue dating back to the 5th century was dug up in Durrës.* □ *Police have dug up the body of his first wife.*

2. zbuloj

□ *Journalists had dug up some hair-raising facts about the company.*

3. lëroj, punoj tokën

□ *They were using machinery to dig up the front garden.*

4. shkul

□ *We dug up the tree by the roots.*

dig up the hatchet/tomahawk armiqësohem, futem në grindje (armiqësi) me

□ *I have come too late, I fear they must have dug up the hatchet.*

din in sb's ears gumëzhin, buçet, oshëtin në veshët e

□ *The noise of the traffic was still dinning in his ears after he had shut the doors and windows.* □ *They drove away from the city center, the roar of the traffic still dinning in their ears.*

din sth into sb i them, ia përsëris dikujt me zë të lartë

□ *I dinned it into him that he had to manage things differently.*

dine out darkohem, ha darkë jashtë

□ *'Don't prepare anything for me tonight, I shall be dining out.* □ *By seven he was showering in his own apartment before dining out in the West End.*

dip into 1. prish, harxhoj, prek, vë dorë

□ *The bank had to dip into its investments overseas to meet a financial crises at home.* □ *He would be compelled to dip into capital to maintain his standard of living.*

2. studioj shpejt e shpejt; hedh një sy,

lexoj përciptazi

□ *I can't say that I know a great deal about modern painting—I've just dipped into one or two books on the subject.* □ *I have only been able to dip into your book; I hope soon to be able to read it seriously.*

dip one's finger in sth ndërhyj, përzihem, fus hundët

□ *When should you learn not to dip your finger in my affairs.*

direct one's/sb's attention to drejtoj vëmendjen; tërheq vëmendjen e

□ *The shortage has been ignored for some months, but I am glad to say that the new minister is directing his attention to it.* □ *The policeman directed the driver's attention to a notice which read 'No entry'.* □ *Please direct your attention to what I am demonstrating.*

dirty/soil one's hands njollos veten

□ *The teacher warned the children not to dirty their hands by cheating in the examination.* □ *I would not soil my hands by going with bad people and doing bad things.*

disagree with nuk më përshtatet, nuk më bën mirë

□ *He's not feeling well; something he ate must have disagreed with him.* □ *Hot climates disagree with her.*

disappear/melt/vanish into thin air avullon, zhduket pa lënë gjurmë

□ *My notebook was on the table a few minutes ago, but now it seems to have vanished into thin air.* □ *I couldn't find him anywhere. He seemed to have disappeared into thin air.*

disburden one's mind (of) zmbrapsem, ia them të gjitha

□ *The boy disburdened his mind to his mother by confessing that he had broken the expensive lamp accidentally.* □ *I waited now his return; eager*

to **disburden my mind**, *and to seek of him the solution of enigma that perplexed me.*
dish out shpërndaj
□ *There were students **dishing out** leaflets to passers-by.* □ *New overalls and hamlets were **dished out** before the party went underground.*
dish up 1. shërbej, vendos në pjatë
□ *Mother **dished** the food **up** straight out of the saucepan.*
2. ofron, paraqet
□ *They're **dishing up** the usual arguments in a new form.* □ *In his latest article Smith **dishes up** a familiar mixture of irrational opinions and thinly-disguised personal abuse.*
dismiss from one's mind/thoughts heq nga mendja
□ *In spite of the reassuring nature of her thought she sighed unable to **dismiss from her mind** the sudden outburst which had recently occurred.* □ *These suspicions weren't easily **dismissed from his thoughts**. After all, Janet had been seen out with Carter on two occasions.*
dispense with sb/sth 1. bëj pa, s'kam nevojën e
□ *You may dislike having to depend upon him, but it will be some time before you can **dispense with** his support altogether.* □ *He is not yet well enough to **dispense with** the doctor's services.*
2. lë mënjanë
□ *I suggest we **dispose with** formality and proceed with our discussion on an informal basis.*
dispose of sb/sth 1. shes
□ *When the crash came, the family was forced to **dispose of** all possessions.* □ *The silver was **disposed of** to an antique dealer.*
2. zgjidh

□ *The problem of who to select as his successor was quickly **disposed of**.*
3. eliminoj, zhduk, heq qafe
□ *Most of the opposition had been **disposed of**; only a few remained alive and out of prison.*
dissociate oneself from sb/sth ndahem, shkëputem, distancohem
□ *The chairman **dissociated himself** and his colleagues **from** the views expressed in the report.* □ *I wish to **dissociate myself from** those views.*
divide and rule përça e sundo
□ *We are all struggling to overcome the vestiges of the feudal order which was encouraged by the policy of 'divide and rule'.*
do a bunk largohem menjëherë, ua mbath këmbëve, iki me të katra
□ *The cashier has **done a bunk** with the day's takings.* □ *These boys have more cheek than courage. If a policeman appeared they'd soon **do a bunk**.*
do as you would be done by sillu si do të të sillen
□ *Do as you would be done by is the surest method I know of pleasing.*
do all in one's power bëj ç'është e mundur, bëj gjithçka që kam në dorë
□ *I'll **do all in my power** to help you.*
do away with 1. eliminoj, zhduk
□ *The death penalty has been **done away with** in many European countries.* □ *She thinks it's time we **did away with** the monarchy.*
2. vras, asgjësoj, heq qafe
□ *Who on earth would want to **do away with** a harmless boy like Antonio?* □ *They were prepared to **do away with** John, and anyone else who stood in the way.*
do by trajtoj, sillem
□ *His father **did well by** him, sending him to the best schools.* □ *A humane*

*society always **does** well **by** its old people.* □ *Do as you would be **done by.***

do as I say, not as I do bëj si them unë, mos bëj si bëj unë

□ *But despite his mother's well-meaning efforts, Simon comes to the inevitable conclusion that parental guidance is really a case of 'Don't do as I do—Do as I say'.*

do better to do sth bën mirë të

□ *'I am revolted by men who don't work,' continued Fiorella. 'You'd **do better to** work instead of nattering.'*

□ *If it's clothes you want, Jimmy, Spencer will let you buy anything you want, although you would **do better to** wait until we get to the States.*

do duty for 1. kryej detyrën e, zëvendësoj

□ *In the absence of the chairman of the council one of his assistants **does duty for** him.* □ *In the absence of the director she **does duty for** him.*

2. përdoret, shërben

□ *This saucer will have to **do duty for** an ashtray until I get around to buying one.*

dog eat dog ha njeriu njerinë

□ *He left his job because he couldn't stand the **dog eat dog** conditions in which he had to work.* □ *Bluff Court was far too large to live in. You needed to keep twenty servants to wait on you and another twenty to wait on them. It was very **dog eat dog**.*

do for 1. bëj punët e shtëpisë, mbaj shtëpinë

□ *Old Mrs. Green has **done for** us for over 20 years.* □ *They can't afford domestic help, so they have to **do for** themselves.*

2. rrënohet, zhduket, asgjësohet, merr fund

□ *Unless the Government provides*

*more money, the steel industry is **done for**.* □ *There were heavy casualties on the first day. The general nearly **did for** the lot of us with his plan of attack.*

3. bëj për, siguroj

□ *How will the crews **do for** drinking water when they're afloat in an open raft?* □ *How did you **do for** coal during the miners' strike?*

dog in the manger, a egoist

□ *Because Jim was not invited to the party, he tried to prevent it being held at all: he's **a real dog in the manger**.*

dog one's/sb's (foot)steps ndjek hap pas hapi (këmba-këmbës)

□ *He worked hard enough in his farm, God knows, but drought and pestilence **dogged his footsteps** season after season.* □ *That tiresome old bore, Perkings, seems to be **dogging my footsteps** these days. I swear I can't go anywhere but he turns up too.*

do homage to nderoj, sillem me nderim (respekt); bëj homazh

□ *The Romans **did homage to** the talents of Virgil by always rising when he entered the theatre.* □ *Many came to **do** the dead man **homage**.*

do honor to sb/do sb an/the honor nderoj, i bëj nder

□ *They **did** me **the honor of** asking me to chair the Commission.* □ *He is a very great man and his compatriots don't **do** him enough **honor** in my opinion.* □ *Captain Hopkins had washed himself to **do honor to** so solemn an occasion.*

do in 1. vras; vritem

□ *These were professional killers who **'did in'** John Regan, and they knew more about fingerprints and ballistics than I did.*

2. rrënoj, shkatërroj

□ *Mr. Smith's business was **done in** by fire that burned down his store.*
3. këputem, rraskapitem
□ *The boys were **done in** after their long hike.*
4. mashtroj
□ *Mr. James was **done in** by two men who claimed to be collecting money for orphans and widows.*

do justice to sb/sth çmoj, vlerësoj si duhet, i jap hakun që meriton
□ *'Why Dousy, here's a good supper', he exclaimed, starting out of his silence with a burst, and taking his seat at the table. 'I shall **do it justice**, for I have come from Yarmouth.'*
□ *Some unkind things have been said about my work, but nothing has yet been written which would have **done justice to** those three paragraphs.* □ *'I only entreat you to believe, my favorite child, that I have meant to do right.' He said it earnestly, and to **do him justice** he had.*

done to a turn pjekur tamam sa duhet
□ *This meat is delicious: it's been **done to a turn**.*

don't mention it 1. ju lutem
□ *'Thank you very much indeed for your kindness.' '**Don't mention it**.'*
2. s'ka gjë, s'ka përse; ju lutem
□ *'I apologize for what I have said.' '**Don't mention it**.'* □ *'You are so kind!' '**Don't mention it**.'*

do miracles/wonders bëj çudira (mrekullira)
□ *Some patients expect their doctors to **do miracles** in the way of instant relief.* □ *'There Mr. Dick too', said Traddles, 'has been **doing wonders**!'*
□ *'But help me. **Do the miracle**.'*

do more harm than good bën më shumë keq se mirë
□ *What is needed is a new drug which will relieve and console our suffering*

species without **doing more harm** in the long run **than** it does good in the short.

do/try one's level/very best bëj ç'është e mundur, bëj çmos
□ *I **did my best to** stop her, but she was in such a state of mind, there was simply nothing I could do.* □ *Ona understood now that the real reason that Miss Henderson hated her was that she was a decent, married girl and she knew that the Toadies hated her for the same reason, and were **doing their best** to make her life miserable.*

do one's bit bëj timen, bëj (kryej) detyrën, jap kontributin tim
□ *I thought I ought to **do my bit**. I wasn't much use for anything, but they were glad to have anyone then.*
□ *'Yes, we're going all out for pigs at Condaford. Is Uncle Lawrence doing anything at Lipping hall?' 'No. He invented the plan, so he thinks he's **done his bit**....'*

do one's duty bën (kryen) detyrën e vet
□ *Milly: Do come and **do your duty**.*
□ *Myra: I can't cope with all these people any longer by myself.* □ *'In short, you are provided for', observed his sister, 'and will please **do your duty**'.* □ *Our dad wasn't a particularly loving father but he **did his duty** by us.*

do one's part bën (kryen) detyrën e vet
□ *This work assigned to our group is to be completed by Monday; we must all **do our part**.*

do one's share bëj detyrën time, jap kontributin tim
□ *The delegate explained to him how it depended upon their being able to get every man to join and stand by the organization, and so Jurgis signified that he was willing to **do his share**.*

do one's stuff bëj detyrën; tregoj se ç'mund të bëj, tregoj veten
□ *Some day a war might come again and I would have to leave my peace and go to* **do my stuff** *as my father had before me.* □ *It's your turn to sing now, so* **do your stuff.**

do one's utmost bëj ç'është e mundur
□ *I* **did my utmost** *to stop them.* □ *We* **did our utmost** *to fulfil the plan ahead of schedule.*

do out fshij, pastroj, rregulloj
□ *'You must* **do out** *your desk drawer: it's full of waste paper and unanswered letters.'* □ *It's time the children's toy cupboard was* **done out.** *It looks a mess and they can never find anything they want.*

do over pastroj; ripunoj, përpunoj, rizbukuroj
□ *'The kitchen's always so messy after we've had guests. Give me a hand to* **do it over.'**

do sb a service i bëj dikujt një shërbim
□ *Since he doesn't realize that his arrogance is antagonizing people I think you would be* **doing** *him* **a service** *if you told him so.* □ *'I've got you in a hole, in a way, and I'd like to get you out of it.' 'Oh! no; you* **did me a service.** *I don't want to put you about telling falsehoods for me.'*

do sb a bad turn i bëj keq dikujt, i bëj dikujt një të keqe, i prish punë, i bëj dikujt një shërbim të keq
□ *I'm afraid I* **did you** *all* **a bad turn** *when I introduced you to the Barkers.* □ *Don't trust that man; he will* **do you a bad turn,** *if he can.* □ *I think you've* **done me a bad turn.**

do sb a favor i bëj një favor (një nder) dikujt
□ *I thought I was* **doing you a favor** *by coming to warn you.* □ *'Do me a favor,* *Baxter,' said Robert, jigging*

the cup up and down in his hand. □ *'Mr. Brass,' said Kit, '***do me a favor.** *Take me to Mr. Witherden's first.'* □ *... if Mr. Copperfield would* **do them the favor** *to call upon a certain day they would be happy to hold some conversation on the subject.*

do sb a good turn i bëj dikujt një shërbim të mirë (një të mirë, një nder)
□ *He'll go a long way out of his way, a long way to* **do you a good turn.** □ *If you want to* **do me a good turn** *on your trip abroad, could you bring me back some duty-free whisky?* □ *... but as I know you'll* **do me a good turn** *another time.*

do sb a mischief dëmtoj, i bëj dëm
It will be as well to stop that young screamer though in case I should be tempted to **do him a mischief.** □ *You could* **do yourself a mischief** *on that barbed-wire fence!* □ *'My orders are to bring him in,' went on the corporal. 'Take his sword, Fred, he might* **do himself a mischief.**

do sb an injustice 1. gjykoj padrejtësisht
□ *In saying this you* **do her an injustice.**
2. i bëj dikujt një padrejtësi
□ *'Charity, my dear,' said Mr. Pecksniff, 'when I take my chamber candlestick tonight, remind me to be more than usually particular in praying for Mr. Anthony Chuzzlewit, who has* **done me an injustice.'**

do sb credit nderon, i jep emër të mirë
□ *But his wide-ranging sympathy, though it no doubt* **did me credit,** *didn't do anything to make me less uncomfortable.* □ *This exhibition from which many of his best paintings are absent, doesn't* **do the artist credit.** □ *Traddles and I both expressed, by a feeling of murmur,*

*that this great discovery was no doubt true of Mr. Micawber and that it **did** him much **credit**.*

do sb/sth good i bën mirë

□ *Jo: Will you get me a drink of water, Helen? Helen: No, have a dose of this. It'll **do** you more **good**.* □ *Harry's been getting much too cocky lately, and it'll **do** him **good** to be taken down a peg or two.* □ *Why don't you go to the country? It would **do** you a lot of **good**.* □ *'Oh, dear me, dear me, do you think it (the tea) will **do** me any **good**?' cried my mother in a helpless manner.* □ *Mrs. Cedarquist and her two daughters declared that the air of Los Muertos must certainly have **done** him a world of **good**. He was stronger.*

do sb harm i bën keq, i bën dëm

□ *A few late nights never **did** anyone any **harm**.* □ *The books kept alive my fancy, and my hope of something beyond that place and time, they and the Arabian Nights and the Tales of Genti—and **did** me no **harm**.* □ *You'd better give up smoking. It's **doing** you a lot of **harm**.*

do sb in the eye 1. mashtroj, ia hedh sy për sy

□ *They were fellows never happy unless they were **doing** someone **in the eye**.*

2. fyej, poshtëroj

□ *He certainly **did** his colleagues **in the eye** when he got the boss's approval.*

do sb proud nderoj, trajtoj me nderim të madh; bëj të ndjehet krenar

□ *The college **did** us **proud** at the centenary dinner.* □ *'May I take my soda-water at your table?' 'Sir, you **do** me **proud**,' said Mr. Foker with much courtesy.* □ *I saw your son's*

*performance in the play last night: I thought he **did** you **proud**.*

do sb's bidding zbatoj urdhërin e

□ *The solder **did** the captain's **bidding** without question.* □ *She was always gentle with children. The wildest would **do** her **bidding**-she had a tender way with them, indeed she had!* □ *No anaesthesia, no theatre, no row of nurses to run to **do** his **bidding**.*

do sb wrong ia bëj me të padrejtë

□ *'I **do** him no **wrong**,' she returned.* □ *What business had his father to come and upset his wife like this?... but when did a Forsyte ever imagine that his conduct could upset anybody? □ And in his thought he **did** old Jolyon **wrong**.*

do sth by halves bëj diçka përgjysmë, lë diçka përgjysmë (në mes)

□ *Now gentlemen, I am not a man who **does** things **by halves**. Being in for a penny, I am ready, as the saying is for a pound.* □ *George was not the man to **do** things **by halves**. He would either refuse to support the venture at all or send us a very handsome cheque.*

do the dirty on sb mashtroj; tradhtoj

□ *I know who **did the dirty on** me and he needn't think he'll get away with it.*

do the honors bëj nderet

□ *How very kind of you to bring me a bottle of my favorite brandy. But, first let me **do the honors** of the house and offer you a drink.* □ *'If I am called away this evening before our dinner party,' he told his eldest son, 'I shall rely on you to **do the honors** of the table for me.'*

do the right thing bëj atë që duhet; veproj me maturi (mençuri)

□ *I never regretted joining up. I felt I **did the right thing**.* □ *If she took sides* *in their disputes, as she sometimes did, she never knew if she was **doing the right thing.***

do the spadework bëj punën e vështirë paraprake (përgatitore)

□ *She got the praise for the job but he did all **the spadework**.* □ *Theory and exercises are very boring, I know, but you can't be a real musician without **doing the spadework**.*

do the trick 1. arrij (realizoj) qëllimin, arrij rezultat (sukses)

□ *Broadbent. ... I think I've **done the trick** this time. I just gave them a bit of straight talk and it went home.* □ *Tom was not passing in English, he studied harder and that **did the trick**.* 2. bën (kryen) punë

□ *After you have put the glue on the broken toy, you will need to put a weight on it until the glue sets: a heavy book would **do the trick**.*

do time bëj burg

□ *George is a well-known drug smuggler. He was **doing time** for illegal possession of drugs.*

do to death vras

□ *The few guards soon lost their nerve and simply **did** their charges **to death** in some wood or quarry.*

do up 1. fshij, pastroj, rregulloj, vë në rregull

□ *The room was **done up** for the visitors. Working together the children did up the kitchen.* □ *The house needs to be **done up**.* 2. rinovoj, modernizoj, riparoj, ndreq

□ *We're getting a professional decorator to **do** the boys' bed room **up**.* □ *If we decide to buy the cottage we'll have to **do it up**.* 3. mbledh, paketoj, mbështjell

□ *Will you **do up** this parcel for me?* □ *Please **do up** these books and post them to him.*

4. mbërthej; mbërthehet

□ *The skirt does up **at the back**.* □ *He never bothers to **do** his jacket **up**.*

double back 1. kthehem mbrapsht (prapa)

□ *Half-way through the wood we lost the fox; it must have **doubled back** on its tracks.* □ *The road ahead was flooded so we had to **double back**.* 2. bëj dysh, përthyej

□ *When making a bed you **double** the top edge of the seat **back** over the blankets.*

double up 1. bëhem dyshe, formoj dyshe

□ *'We haven't any single rooms left. Do you mind **doubling up**?* 2. palosem, mblidhem kruspull

□ *The pain caught me and **doubled me up** in agony.* □ *Someone struck him hard in the stomach; the pain **doubled** him **up**.*

do violence to sth dhunoj, veproj në kundërshtim me

□ *It would **do violence to** her principles to eat meat.* □ *It would **do violence to** her principles to work on Sunday.*

do well 1. bën mirë

□ *You will **do well** to comply with our request.* 2. dal (paraqitem) mirë, kam sukses

□ *Our Folk and Dance Ensemble has **done well** at the Festival.* □ *Andy is **doing** very **well** at school this term.* 3. e marr veten, shërohem shpejt

□ *... she had been brought to herself, and was expected to **do well**.* □ *He has had a very hard time of it, ever since he began to recover; but, as you see, he is now **doing well**.* □ *'Well, nurse, how is she.' Bessie answered that I was **doing** very **well**.*

do well (badly) by sb trajtoj (sillem) mirë (keq) me dikë

□ *He does **well by** his friends.*

do with 1. ka lidhje me, ka të bëjë me
□ *Mind your own business; it's got nothing to do with you.* □ *Also, there was an invention of Duane's; Jurgis could not understand it clearly, but it had to do with telegraphing.*
2. duroj
□ *I can't do with his insolence.* □ *If there's one thing I can't do with, it's untidiness.* □ *I can't do with selfishness.*
3. bëj, më mjafton, kënaqem me, dua, kam nevojë
□ *You look as if you could do with a good night's sleep.* □ *'I could do with two weeks away from the children and the washing-up.'*

do without bëj pa
□ *'Do you need an umbrella?' '- No, I can do without.'* □ *'You cannot do without me, and I can do without you.'* □ *'I can do without that kind of advice, thank you.'*

down and out i rrënuar (fizikisht, financiarisht etj.); i braktisur
□ *The tramp was down and out without any place to turn for help.* □ *And you're just as badly licked now. You're beaten to a pulp. You're down and out.* □ *'You've never been down and out, I imagine, Mr. Forsyte?'* □ *As long as you're up and around and have money everybody's your friend. But once you're down and out no one wants to see you any more—see?*

down at (the) heel (s) veshur si mos më keq
□ *After some months without a job, he began to look a bit down-at-heel.* □ *Some three or four years later I began to use for cleaning purposes an impoverished and down at heels yet rather intelligent and interesting character—Johnny Marton by name.*

down in the dumps/mouth i trishtuar, i brengosur, i dëshpëruar
□ *My son has been down in the dumps ever since his team was knocked out of the cup.* □ *Young Burkitt, the architect, had seen him coming out of a third-rate restaurant, looking terribly down in the mouth.* □ *He's one of those people who can't stand his own company. As soon as he finds himself alone he gets down in the dumps.*

down one's alley/street ajo që pëlqen; ajo që i vjen ndoresh
□ *Baseball is right down Tony's alley.* □ *If your television needs to be fixed, ask Joe to do it: that sort of thing is right down his alley.*

down on one's luck i pafat, fatkeq, fatzi
□ *I visit Mary regularly these days: she has been down on her luck recently and need cheering up.* □ *... He's down on his luck, and I am sorry for him.* □ *They say that, when Mrs. Grawley was particularly down on her luck, she gave concerts and lessons in music here and there.*

down the drain në erë, kot
□ *I don't know why Jack gambles so much on horses; it's just money down the drain.* □ *Do you mean to say you're going to sit there twiddling your thumbs and watch him throwing all the money down the drain?*

down tools ndërpres (lë) punën; bëj grevë
□ *As soon as the clock strikes five, they down tools and off they go.* □ *He had realized that he could not carry on without taking some decisive step to help himself. It was then he had 'downed tools' and retreated here, he explained.* □ *The workmen downed tools to demand a rise in wages.*

down with! poshtë!

□ *Myra: Are you pleased about it or are you not? Tony: Of course I'm pleased.* **Down with** *poverty.*

drag in/into ngre një çështje, e sjell muhabetin rreth, nis e flet për

□ *No matter what we talk about, John* **drags in** *politics.* □ *There are some people about with only one thought in their heads: they must* **drag** *sex* **into** *every conversation.*

drag one's feet/heels eci (veproj) duke u matur shumë; veproj ngadalë, pa u nxituar; bëj diçka pa qejf

□ *The manager is* **dragging his heels** *over making these improvements we suggested: I think we shall have to speak to him again.* □ *The children wanted to watch television, and* **dragged their feet** *when their mother told them to go to bed.*

drag sb/sb's name through the mire/ mud njollos dikë, njollos emrin e mirë të

□ *He would put an end to that sort of thing once and for all; he would not have her* **drag his name in the mud.** □ *... Grawley* **has dragged his name through the mud,** *Miss Briggs.* □ *The wretched boy was solemnly accused of* **dragging the** *honored* **name of the school** *through the mud.*

drag out zgjat, stërzgjat, bëj tërkuzë

□ *'Do you think we might end the discussion there? I see no point in* **dragging** *it* **out** *any further.'* □ *Let's not* **drag out** *this discussion, we've got to reach a decision.* □ *They tried to* **drag out** *the inquiry as long as possible in the hope of new evidence.*

drain away ulet, shuhet, fashitet, zhduket

□ *Robert yawned. His tension seemed to have* **drained away,** *leaving him, if*

anything, rather bored with the discussion.

draw a (complete) blank orvatem më kot, dështoj, s'kam sukses

□ *He rang up... his own father's clubs in case they might have gone there together after the meeting. He* **drew a blank** *everywhere.* □ *The detectives checked at every house to ask if anyone had seen anything suspicious, but they* **drew a complete blank.** □ *I came upon various interesting objects, but not the typescript. There was no sign of the thing. Finn had* **drawn a blank** *too.*

draw a comparison (parallel) between krahasoj, bëj krahasim

□ *The history teacher* **drew a parallel between** *the French and Russian revolution.* □ *... your case and mine are diametrically different and it is nonsense attempting to* **draw a parallel.** □ *Punish or reward a child as he deserves, but don't* **draw comparisons** *with his brothers or sisters.*

draw a conclusion arrij në përfundim

□ *What* **conclusion** *do you* **draw** *from the evidence you've heard?*

draw a (the) line 1. vë kufi

□ *I insist that all my children have to be home before midnight: you've got to* **draw the line** *somewhere.* □ *We would like to invite everybody to our party, but we have to* **draw the line** *somewhere.*

2. refuzoj të

□ *I'll do what I can to help, but I* **draw the line** *at working on Sundays.* □ *I don't mind helping, but I* **draw the line** *at doing everything myself.*

draw a distinction between bëj dallim midis

□ *It is difficult to* **draw a distinction between** *the meanings of these two words.*

draw aside heq mënjanë

□ *An inquisitive neighbour **drew** the lace curtain **aside** to see what was going on.* □ *The room was full of people so I had to **draw** him **aside** and tell the bad news.*

draw/cast/throw a veil/curtain over mbuloj, mbaj të fshehur, lë në heshtje, nuk zë në gojë, nuk përmend

□ *I propose to **draw a veil over** the appalling events that followed.* □ *The headmaster was very angry, but I think I had better **draw a veil over** what he actually said.* □ *It **throws a veil over** grossness of its error.* □ *She **drew a veil over** what the child said.* □ *Let us **draw the curtain over** the rest of the scene.*

draw back tërhiqem, largohem

□ *It seemed that he **drew back** for a moment, alarmed, as if the scrappy, grubby piece of paper frightened him.* □ *Seeing a snake in the grass, the little boy **drew back** in alarm.* □ *He will not **draw back** from what he has promised.*

draw/take breath marr frymë

□ *'Good evening, MacGregor,' Essex said—too lazily. MacGregor **drew a breath**. 'I didn't expect to see you standing there,' he said.* □ *Sarah **drew** a deep **breath** before replying.*

□ *'**Take** two or three deep **breaths** before you jump in,' said the swimming instructor.* □ *He kept on with his restless walk not speaking any more, but **drawing** a deep **breath** from time to time as if endeavouring to throw off some annoying thought.*

draw blood gjakos; lëndoj, nxeh dikë

□ *Jane looks furious. I think that the last remark of Mary's about her **drew blood**.* □ *If you want to **draw blood**, ask him about his last money-making scheme.* □ *Her sarcastic comments **drew blood**.*

draw in 1. vjen, arrin (treni etj)

□ *As I reached the ticket barrier the London train was just **drawing in**.* □ *The train **drew in** at 8—two minutes late.*

2. shkurtohen (ditët)

□ *The days were **drawing in**, for it was early September.*

draw in one's horns përmbahem; tërhiqem; tregohem i përmbajtur; ul pendët

□ *The fellow **drew in his horns** and acknowledged he might have been mistaken.* □ *If Malouel was going to **draw in his horns** he would need every penny he could lay his hands on.*

draw lots hedh short

□ *We **drew lots** and it fell to Oliver.* □ *They **drew lots** as to who should begin.*

draw one's last/dying breath jap frymën e fundit, jap shpirt, vdes

□ *My grandmother **drew her last breath** last year.*

draw out 1. zgjat

□ *She **drew** the interview **out** to over an hour.*

□ *He heated the metal and **drew** it **out** into a long wire.*

2. zgjaten (ditët)

□ *Thank goodness the days are **drawing out** again, though. I'm so sick of the winter.* □ *With the approach of Spring the days begin to **draw out** quite noticeably.*

3. tërheq në bisedë, bëj të flasë

□ *From his mother, Eric had learned the wonderful gift of **drawing** people **out**.* □ *He had chattered away to her in German; he had **drawn** her **out**, had made her laugh.* □ *Jack Duane **drew** Jurgis **out**, and heard all about his life and then he told stories about his own life.* □ *Carrie was at first shy* *in her new surroundings and would say very little but after a while some of the other girls managed to draw her out.*

draw sb's attention to tërheq vëmendjen
□ *A headline on the front page draws attention to the fuller story inside.* □ *She drew my attention to an error in the report.* □ *I'm embarrassed about my mistake; please don't draw attention to it.*

draw sb's fire tërheq zjarrin e; tërheq sulmin (kritikën etj.) e
□ *There was no shortage of police volunteers to draw the killer's fire by attacking the front of the building while an attempt was made to rescue his hostages from the rear.* □ *It's hardly likely that any of the Springfield politicians will want to draw the fire of the newspapers again.* □ *Elsie feared that tempers were rising and, brave girl, she drew her father's fire upon herself.*

draw sth to a conclusion përfundoj, i jap fund
□ *He drew the interview to a conclusion.*

draw to a close mbyll, i jap fund
□ *My stay in Bafut eventually drew to a close.* □ *The long day of work which had been their lives was driving to a close.* □ *The meeting drew to a close around seven o'clock.* □ *There was a gentle bustle at the Quaker house as the afternoon drew to a close.*

draw to an end mbyll, mbaroj, i jap fund
□ *She felt her period of parsimonious endurance drawing swiftly towards its end.*

draw up 1. përpiloj, hartoj
□ *They were to come on the morrow and he would have the papers all drawn up.* □ *The plan drawn up by*

the Committee has been adopted at the meeting.
2. ndaloj, qëndroj, frenoj
□ *The bus drew up at the stop by the pavement.* □ *A taxi drew up in front of the house.*
3. rreshtoj
□ *The cars had to be drawn up close together in a dead straight line to facilitate loading.*
4. afroj
□ *Draw up a chair, and we'll go through these notes of yours.*

drenched to the bone/skin jam bërë qull, jam lagur deri në palcë, jam bërë për t'u shtrydhur
□ *We were caught in the storm and got drenched to the skin.* □ *A brisk shower was falling at the time and she must have been drenched to the skin.*

dress sb down qortoj rëndë
□ *The force of his personality was so blasting that for a moment he had me feeling that I was in for a dressing-down myself.* □ *His roommates dressed him down severely for his carelessness which almost caused a fire.*

dress up vishem si për festë; vishem me veshje ceremoniale
□ *It's quite an informal gathering; you needn't dress up for it.* □ *She was dressed up for the occasion.*

drink like a fish pi shumë, pi me opingë
□ *He claims that it was the loss of his wife that drove him to drink, but believe me, he was drinking like a fish long before that.* □ *It stands to reason, doesn't it, that you can't have money for clothes, or anything else, if you drink like a fish.*

drink sth in përpij
□ *A packed audience drank in every*

word he said. □ *The boy **drank in** every word of the grandmother's story.*
2. sodis me kënaqësi
□ *They sat outside on the terrace, **drinking in** the beauty of the landscape.*

drink sb's health/drink a health to sb pi për shëndetin e
□ *Allow me to **drink to your health**.*

drink up pi me fund, pi deri në fund
□ *'I brought them to heel,' said Robert gaily, tapping his inside pocket. 'I extracted some money out of them, so **drink up**, lads.'* □ *'**Drink** your milk **up**, Johnie, or you won't go out and play!'*

drive a bargain arrij një marrëveshje tregtare
□ *Tony's colie is a champion; it should be easy for Tony to **drive a bargain** when he sells her puppies.*
□ *I'll **drive a bargain** with you: if you let me stay here rent-free, I'll look after the house for you.*

drive a hard bargain arrij një marrëveshje me kushte favorizuese
□ *Father **drove a hard bargain** with the real estate agent when we bought our new house. 'Whether we buy the furnishings along with the house depends on what you're asking for them.'* □ *'Look, I'm not trying to **drive a hard bargain**. If you are to get any reputable valuer in to look at the stuff, I'll let you have them at his valuation.'*

drive at dal, bëj aluzion, hedh fjalën
□ *'What on earth are you **driving at**? Can't you come to the point?' 'You can see what I am **driving at**, can't you?'* □ *'Oh, well, come Miss Vivie; you needn't pretend you don't see what I'm **driving at**?'* □ *'Just what are you **driving at**? Come on, tell me!'*

drive a wedge between fus pyka
□ *Differences of outlook may **drive a wedge between** the various national groups which make up the team.*
□ *June's intention was to **drive a wedge** of suspicion **between** friends.*

drive back zmbraps, zbyth
□ *The attacking force was **driven back** to its starting point.* □ *The police **drove** the spectators **back** behind the crash barriers.*

drive home to sb ia bëj të qartë, ia ngulit në mendje (në kujtesë)
□ *I **drove home** to him that he must be here by ten.* □ *I spoke to him plainly of his duty and I think I **drove** the point **home**.* □ *It is no use mentioning the fact in passing, it needs to be **driven home** by emphasis and repetition.*

drive sb into a corner e vë dikë me shpatulla pas murit
□ *Quoting facts and figures quickly **drove** him **into a corner**.* □ *When he is **driven into a corner** he invariably loses his temper.* □ *'I'm through with you entirely.' 'It's a lie,' he said, **driven to a corner** and knowing no other excuse.*

drive sb mad/crazy çmend, prish nga mendtë
□ *'Don't talk of lending money, Mrs. Nickleby,' said Miss Knag, 'or you'll **drive me crazy**, perfectly crazy.'*
□ *'Oh Jurgis! Think what you are doing! You must not do it! It'll **drive me mad** ... !'*

drive sb out of his mind/wits/senses çmend, luaj mendsh, prish nga mendtë
□ *'You did so!' returned Nessie agitatedly. 'Everybody thinks the same thing. They think it's that easy for me because I'm so clever. They don't know the work and the toil that I've been forced to put in. It's been enough*

to *drive me out of my mind.'* □ *She was driven almost out of her mind with anxiety.* □ *How can it be, if Sir Leicester is driven out of his wits, or laid upon a death bed?*

drive (force) sb to the wall vë me shpatulla në mur

□ *The one thing that seemed eventually to have saved him was the fact that quite all of his creditors were fully aware that should he be broken and driven to the wall, there would be no cash for anyone.* □ *... She would be a marvellous person—Dinny thought—in a crisis, or if driven to the wall, would be loyal to her own side.* □ *... What has become of the owners of the small drugstores that you forced to the wall?*

drop a brick/clanger këpus një mufkë, lëshoj (më shpëton) një fjalë pa vend, veproj (ndërhyj) pa takt

□ *Mary did not realize what a clanger she had dropped when she asked her hostess if the soup came out of a tin.* □ *'Whatever happens,' Michael thought, 'I've got to keep my head shut, or I shall be dropping a brick.* □ *'I wouldn't know how to behave at a grand function like that,' the old man said. 'I'd be dropping bricks the whole time and upsetting you by doing everything wrong.'*

drop a curtsey përkulem me nderim, bëj temena

□ *Nell dropped a curtsey, and told him they were poor travellers who sought a shelter for the night.*

drop a hint aludoj, bëj aluzion, ia hedh fjalën larg e larg, përmend tërthorazi

□ *I always go to Professor Brown's lectures; he often drops a hint about what topics will come up in the exam.* □ *I dropped him a hint that his work*

was too satisfactory, but he failed to take it.

drop a line/note dërgoj dy gisht letër, dërgoj një pusullë (një shënim)

□ *Drop me a line to let me know that you have arrived safely.* □ *I must drop a line to my old friend to thank him for the book he sent me.* □ *Relax with an ice cold drink. Day dream about Marlon Brando or some celebrity you admire, then drop him a note to say so.*

drop a remark bëj vërejtje

□ *His spirits were low. The remark which Miss Aldclyffe had dropped in relation to Cytherea still occupied his mind.* □ *He dropped several remarks.*

drop an allusion bëj aluzion, lë të nënkuptohet

□ *Did he drop any allusion?*

drop back/behind mbetem mbrapa

□ *We found that one of the three escort trucks had dropped back in the dust with a mechanical defect.* □ *John and Mary had dropped behind in order to be alone.* □ *The two old men dropped behind the rest of the party.*

drop dead bie i vdekur

□ *I've got enough money in my pocket to last me the rest of my life—provided I drop dead this afternoon.* □ *He dropped dead from a heart attack.*

drop in/by/around kaloj, bëj një vizitë të shkurtër (të rastit)

□ *She should say to the parents, 'Come to tea on Friday,' rather than ask them just to drop in any time.* □ *Drop by any time you are in town.* □ *My sister dropped around last night. He sometimes drops in to see me in the evenings.*

drop in a good word for them një fjalë të mirë për

□ *Vic wanted Mr. Michael Mont to drop in a good word for her husband.*

drop in the bucket/ocean, a një pikë ujë në oqean (në det)

□ *They are a big company with very big outlays of money. The amount they pay for your salary is only a drop in the ocean.* □ *In fact, the total resources of the hospital services would furnish no more than a drop in the bucket by comparison with the needs of the community.*

drop off 1. bie, zvogëlohet, paksohet

□ *Our sales of ice-cream and soft drinks start to drop off at the beginning of September.* □ *The attendance in the class never drops off.*

2. kotem, dremis, më merr (gjumi)

□ *Just as he was dropping off, there was a loud bang from downstairs.* □ *Completing his resemblance to a man who was sitting for his portrait Mr. Larry dropped off to sleep.* □ *As I sat before the fire I became more and more drowsy, until I was on the point of dropping off.*

3. vdes

□ *The patient dropped off in his sleep.*

drop out/out of 1. lë (braktis) shkollën

□ *He had dropped out of college in the first term.*

2. largohem, tërhiqem

□ *On account of his illness, he had to drop out of the race.* □ *He has dropped out of politics.*

drop the matter (subject) ndërroj bisedë, kaloj në një temë tjetër, lë (një çështje, muhabet etj.)

□ *I have heard enough about that matter, so let us drop the subject.* □ *'Your father wouldn't have told you anything about the wounded man either, but what could he do, you were here,' said Kristina. 'Can we drop the subject now,' said Alma and stood up.*

drown one's sorrows/troubles (in drink) mbyt hidhërimin (hallet) duke pirë

□ *If his team loses, he usually goes to the pub to drown his sorrows.*

drown out mbys me zhurmë

□ *I started shouting, but Mike drowned me out.* □ *A gang of rowdies tried to drown out any speaker who tried to present a quietly reasoned case.*

Dutch treat, a pagesë secili për vete

□ *'I thought Gerald had invited you all for this game of golf and dinner at his clubhouse.' 'Oh no, he has organized it because he's a member, but it's to be a Dutch treat.*

due to falë, në sajë të

□ *The team's success was largely due to her efforts.* □ *His success is due to hard work.*

dust sb's eyes i hedh hi syve

□ *We are well informed and you cannot simply dust our eyes.*

dwell on/upon flas (shkruaj) me hollësi, trajtoj gjerë e gjatë

□ *It doesn't do to dwell over much on one's shortcomings.* □ *People are reluctant to dwell on the subject of death.*

E

each other njëri-tjetri
□ *We write to **each other** regularly.*
□ *They saw **each other** every day.*

each and every secili, çdonjëri
□ *There is not one of you men and women who is not a volunteer. In the hands of **each and every** one of you lies a civilization.* □ *The astonishing thing was that **each and every** one of the patients thus treated made a better and quicker recovery than any patient in the control group.*

early bird, an zog nate, njeri që ngrihet qëmenatë (pa gdhirë, pa zbardhur drita)
□ *You're are a bit of **an early bird**, aren't you? I didn't expect to see you down for breakfast after that party last night.* □ *'Shall I leave the door open?' 'If you don't mind,' she said. 'I expect several little **early birds** will be in soon.'*

early bird catches/gets the worm, the kush mëngoi, bloi; kush mëngoi, gëzoi
□ *If you want to be sure of a ticket for next week's performance, buy it now: **the early bird catches the worm**.* □ *When Tony's father woke him up for school he said, '**The early bird catches the worm**.'*

early days (yet) akoma herët
□ *'I'm beginning to think I shall never be a grandmother.' 'For goodness' sake It's **early days** to be talking like that!'* □ *I'm not sure if our book will be a success—it's **early days yet**.*

earn/turn an honest penny fitoj dy lek me djersën e ballit

□ *The notion of **earning an honest penny** is all my eye. A man can work a whole lifetime and when he is 65 he considers himself rich if he has saved a thousand pounds. Rich!* □ *... Lewis was gradually making it possible to **earn an honest penny** by his hard work.*

earn one's/its keep fitoj (nxjerr) bukën (shpenzimet) e veta
□ *Jill more than **earns her keep** with the help she gives me about the house and looking after the children and so on.* □ *I don't keep hens any more. What with the high price of feeding-stuff and the little I got for eggs, they weren't **earning their keep**.* □ *Though it's quite expensive to hire and maintain, the new copying machine is **earning its keep** as we've been able to reduce the number of office staff.*

earn a/one's living siguroj jetesën
□ *He had always gathered that manual workers belonged to Unions and that anyone who tried to **earn a living** with his hands without the blessing of the Unions was in a very dangerous position.* □ *It's high time you were **earning your** own **living** my boy. You can't expect me to support you for ever.*

earth up mbuloj me dhe
□ *The gardener conscientiously **earthed up** the young plants.* □ *He **earthed up** the celery.*

ease sb/sth across/along/away etc. lëviz lehtë, me kujdes
□ *The man skillfully eased the pillar **down** until it stood exactly where it*

was required. □ *He* **eased** *himself* **along** *the ledge to reach the terrified boy.*

ease down ul shpejtësinë

□ *There's a narrow bridge ahead, so you had better* **ease down**. □ ***Ease down**: there's a sharp bend ahead.*

ease off/up bie, ulet, qetësohet

□ *The tension between the two countries has* **eased off**.

ease sb's conscience/mind qetësohem, lehtësohem, qetësoj ndërgjegjen (shpirtin, mendjen), heq shqetësimin (frikën etj.) nga mendja

□ *It would* **ease my mind** *to know where he was.* □ *'It would* **ease my mind**,' *said Martin, 'if I could explain a little what I mean.'* □ *Doctors must use their own judgment of course, but in many cases the patient's* **mind** *is greatly* **eased** *if his treatment is explained to him.* □ *I'm sure my husband wasn't offended by anything you said last night. Still, if it'll* **ease your mind**, *I can ask and make sure.*

easier said than done është më kollaj të thuash se të bësh

□ *The essence of all reducing diets is to eat less—often* **easier said than done**. □ *Forcing a child to eat is* **easier said than done**.

East or West, home is best bukë e hi e në shtëpi, s'ka si shtëpia

□ *'I was born there. Yes. It is a very small town, some old walls, a castle in ruins -'* **'East or West,'** *Beatrice said,* **'home's best.'**

easy come, easy go shpejt fitove, shpejt harxhove

□ *Within a year she had spent the fortune she had won by gambling: as they say,* **easy come, easy go**. □ *Grandpa thought Tony should have to work for the money Dad gave him, saying* **'Easy come, easy go.'**

easy/gently does it punët e mira bëhen avash—avash; kush ecën ngadalë soset më tej

□ *We'll slip the edge of the blanket under you and use it to slide you on to the stretcher. There you are, you see,* **easy does it!** □ *'Easy does it,'* *said the boss, as they moved the piano through the narrow doorway.*

easy in one's mind me mendje të qetë (të mbledhur)

□ *Phone us in the morning, Lilian. Your mother won't be* **easy in her mind** *till she knows you got back safely.* □ *I know he's said he doesn't need the money just now, but I'd be* **easier in my mind** *if we got out of debt now while we have the chance.*

eat away (at) gërryen

□ *The sea has been* **eating away at** *the cost for years, and now the houses on the cliff-top are in danger.* □ *You can see from here how the river bank is slowly being* **eaten away**.

eat humble pie e ha turpin me bukë, ul kokën, poshtëroj veten, shfajësohem përulësisht

□ *He boasted about what he was going to do when he won, but after his defeat he had to* **eat humble pie**. □ *He tolerated Mrs. Morse, wondering the while how it felt* **to eat such humble pie**. □ *Soames sat silently, chewing the injustice of it all. Fifteen hundred! Monstrous! Still he would pay to keep Fleur out of Court. But* **humble pie!** *She wouldn't* **eat it**.

eat into 1. ha, gërryen, dekompozon

□ *Acids* **eat into** *metals.* □ *The sulphuric acid* **eats into** *those parts of the metal that remain exposed after the wax coating has been applied.*

2. ha, konsumon

□ *Paying for that new carpet has* **eaten into** *my savings.* □ *The costs of* *the legal action **ate** deep **into** my savings.*

eat like a bird ha shumë pak

□ *Mrs. June is on a diet and she **eats like a bird**.*

eat like a horse ha si i babëzitur

□ *Jack has a very good appetite; he **eats like a horse**.* □ *It doesn't seem fair that I should have a constant struggle to keep my weight down while you can **eat like a horse** and always stay the same.*

eat one's head off ha si i babëzitur

□ *The children came in an hour ago from their long walk, and now they're in the dining room **eating their heads off**.*

eat one's heart out ligështohem, ha veten përbrenda, vuaj përbrenda

□ *Ever since her boyfriend walked out, the poor girl has been **eating her heart out**.* □ *He was one of the temperament that, in idleness, **eats his heart out**.* □ *'Don't let her **eat her heart out** like this!'* □ *Since he left, she's been sitting at home **eating her heart out**.*

eat one's words i marr mbrapsht fjalët

□ *My brother said that I would never pass the exam, but he has had to **eat his words**.* □ *Tony has called Andy a coward, but the boys made him **eat his words** after Andy bravely fought a big bully.* □ *You will have to **eat your words**, I am afraid.*

eat out ha jashtë

□ *It's a good idea to **eat out** once in a while; a change of scene and cooking is good for you.*

□ *I'm too tired to cook tonight; shall we **eat out**?*

eat somebody out of house and home e faroj me shtëpi e katandi

□ *I used to own two large dogs, but they were **eating me out of house and**

home, so I had to give them away.*

□ *I hope your brother won't stay much longer, he's **eating us out of house and home**!* □ *These friends of yours are **eating us out of house and home**! When are they going to leave?*

□ *Hostess. I am a poor widow of East—cheap, and he arrested at my suit. Chief Justice. For which sum? Hostess. It's more than for some, my lord; it is for all, all I have. He hath **eaten me out of house and home**: he hath put all my substance into that fat belly of his.*

eat/drink (sth) till/until it comes out of one's ears ha si i del për hundësh (nga hundët)

□ *Her cooking is disappointingly received by her two children. 'I think they'd **eat** beefburgers and chips and sausages and mash **until it came out of their ear**.*

eat up 1. ha me kënaqësi; mbaroj së ngrëni

□ *'There's plenty for everyone, so **eat up**!* □ *'You're not going out to play until you've **eaten** all your carrots **up**.'*

2. ha, bren; shqetëson

□ *She was simply **eaten up** with curiosity—she had to know who had given me such an expensive present.* □ *It's what we all do, shamelessly, when we're **eaten up** by suspicion.*

ebb and flow, the uljen dhe ngritjen; rritjen dhe rënien

□ *The cameraman and his sound-recordist had to catch **the ebb and flow** of conversation and the peaking of tension between one member of the family and another.*

edge (one's way) across/along/back/away etc eci (lëviz) brinjas; lëviz me ngadalë e me kujdes

□ *The climber **edged** carefully **along**

the narrow rock ledge. □ *The policeman **edged his way forward**, towards the distraught woman who was threatening to throw herself and her child from the roof to the street below.*

edit out/out of heq

□ *The four-letter words were always **edited out of** radio scripts until quite recently.* □ *They must have **edited** bits of his interview **out**.*

egg on shtyj, cys, nxis

□ *The older children were **egging** the younger ones **on** to steal money from their parents.* □ *I didn't want to do it but Peter kept **egging** me **on**.*

eke out nxjerr, siguroj me mundim

□ *In some countries thousands of graduates are forced to **eke out** a living by doing work of a menial nature.* □ *He failed to **eke out** an existence by usury.*

elbow sb out of the way/aside nxjerr (shtyj) mënjanë me bërryla

□ *He **elbowed me out of the way**.*

elbow one's way across/along/back/into etc. çaj rrugën me bërryla

□ *The ambulance men had to **elbow their way through** the huge crowd standing round the crashed car.* □ *By slow degrees he **elbowed his way** to the front.* □ *Mr. Guppy **elbowed** his own **way through** the confused little crowd of people coming in and going out.*

end in 1. ka në fund

□ *The tube **ended in** a large bulb, where the gas condensed into a color-less liquid.* □ *Not all English words that **end in** -ly are adverbs.*

2. mbyllet, mbaron, përfundon

□ *It was obvious to everyone that the marriage would sooner or later **end in** separation if not divorce.* □ *The debate **ended in** an uproar.*

end in itself, an qëllim në vetvete

□ *For the old lady buying the daily newspaper soon became **an end in itself**, since she really just wanted to chat with the shopkeeper.* □ *We almost came to look upon a meeting at the summit as **an end in itself**, as though what we were seeking to achieve was a meeting for its own sake.*

end in smoke përfundon në zero (hiç), përfundon kot, përfundon pa rezultat

□ *I take it for granted, this whole affair will **end in smoke**.* □ *You must take practical measures to carry out the plan: otherwise it will **end in smoke**.*

end it all/end one's life i jap fund jetës, vras veten

□ *He was so miserable that he seri-ously thought about **ending it all**.*

end justifies the means, the qëllimi justifikon mjetin

□ *The hazard is now that they will think that **the end justifies the means**. It is that they will allow the means to dictate the end.*

end one's days ngrys ditët, kaloj ditët e fundit të jetës

□ *I am reminded of this by a letter from an old friend who writes to me that he has decided to **end his days** in Hollywood.*

end up përfundon

□ *If you continue to steal you'll **end up** in prison.* □ *If he carries on dri-ving like that, he'll **end up** dead.*

end up with mbyll

□ *We **ended** the dinner **up with** fruit and coffee.*

engage sb in sth merrem, angazho-hem, marr pjesë

□ *John and his brother are **engaged in** some plan for acquiring land and starting in business as market gardeners.* □ *If you **engage in** local* *politics, you cannot expect to have much time for your family.*

enough is enough boll më, boll me kaq
□ *The teacher said 'Sit down all of you and be quiet; enough is enough.'*

enough and to spare del dhe tepron
□ *We have enough fruit and to spare.*

enter into 1. hyj, futem
□ *Susan could see that the man in the opposite seat was dying to enter into conversation with her.* □ *He and Cutter at once entered into an excited conversation.* □ *'There's no need to enter into a lot of unnecessary detail: just tell the court the main facts of the case.'* □ *You will excuse my entering into any further detail at present.*
2. hedh, fus, shkruaj
□ *When the last item had been duly entered in the ledger, the clerk closed it and put it in its usual place before locking up and going home.*

enter on/upon nis, filloj
□ *When the President entered upon his second term of office, everyone hoped that he should show more wisdom than in his first.*

enter up hedh, regjistroj
□ *All expenditure must be entered up in the account book.*

enter sb's head/mind më bie, më shkon ndërmend
□ *This was something which had never for a moment entered her head.*
□ *Any other thought regarding her had never entered his mind.*
□ *Economy was important to him but on this occasion the matter of money never entered his head.*

escape sb's lips më shpëton nga goja
□ *Even I didn't know how it escaped my lips.*

escape sb's memory më del nga mendja (nga kujtesa)
□ *His name has escaped my memory.*

escape sb's attention/notice i shpëton vëmendjes së dikujt
□ *It won't have escaped your notice that I've been unusually busy recently.* □ *It surely cannot have escaped Tony's attention.*

even as ndërsa, teksa, në kohën kur
□ *'We're going to have a storm, I think,' Andrew said, and even as he spoke the first flash of lightning shot across the sky.* □ *Even as he shouted the warning the car skidded.*

even if/though edhe sikur
□ *I don't regret lending her the money, even if I never see it again.*
□ *Even if I have to walk all the way I'll get there.*

even now/then 1. as tani (as atëhere)
□ *I could never do sums at school—in fact I have difficulty in adding up a column of figures correctly, even now.* □ *Even then he would not accept his mistake.*
2. edhe tani (edhe atëhere)
□ *While we are talking and debating, the opposition is even now forming an alliance with the dissidents to overthrow the established government.* □ *The troops are even now preparing to march into the city.*

even so megjithatë
□ *There are many spelling mistakes; even so it's a good essay.*

ever and anon kohë pas kohe, nga koha në kohë
□ *The dog was restless too, ever and anon rising to lay his head on his master's knee.*

ever more akoma më shumë, edhe më
□ *She became ever more nervous as the interview continued.* □ *Encouraged by each small, but positive piece of new evidence, he pursued his enquiries ever more persistently.*

ever since qysh kur, që nga koha kur
□ *I have known him **ever since** he was a boy.* □ *He went to the countryside in 1997 and has been living there **ever since**.*

ever so shumë, tepër
□ *Jenny went back to her perch on the stool. 'Can I have another of these chocolates? They're **ever so** good.'* □ *I am **ever so** happy to see you again.*

every cloud has a silver lining çdo e keqe e ka një të mirë
□ *John was most upset at his uncle's death, but **every cloud has a silver lining**: his uncle had left him all his money.* □ *Oh well, **every cloud has a silver lining**. I may not be so well off now, but I'll have more time to enjoy my family.*

every dog has his/its day çdo njeri ka ditën e tij
□ *After years of neglect, the old artist's work was recognised and honored: **every dog has his day**.* □ *Never mind, his time will come. **Every dog has its day**, and we are all mortal.*

every inch 1. krejt, nga çdo pikëpamje, kokë e këmbë
□ *Those who remembered the captain his father declared Master George was his pa **every inch** of him.* □ *Now, there's Professor Caldwell—he's different. He's a man, **every inch** of him.* 2. gjithkund, cep më cep, pëllëmbë për pëllëmbë
□ *The police examined **every inch** of the house for clues.*

every last/single one etc çdo njëri
□ *The other four shook their heads as though butter wouldn't melt in their mouths, **every last one of them** lying in actual sin.*

every man jack (of sb) të gjithë pa përjashtim

□ *He did it defying the farmer and the farmer's wife and the farmer's lad, and **every man Jack** among them.* □ *There's only one way to describe the people who run this country, incompetent. I'd sack the ruddy lot— **every man jack of** them.*

every now and then/again herë pas here, kohë pas kohe
□ *I wouldn't read the newspapers if it wasn't for this ridiculous idea about being well informed. Conscience stirs me **every now and again**.* □ *Every now* and then she would glance up at the clock. □ *Every now and then*, his mother went to John's room to check that he was still sleeping.

every so often kohë pas kohe, herë pas here, nga koha në kohë
□ *Every so often*, the manager comes along to check that everyone is working.

exception proves the rule, the përjashtimi provon rregullin
□ *Jim was on time today, but it's just a case of **the exception proving the rule**, I'm afraid.* □ *All his family have red hair except John. He is **the exception** which **proves the rule**.*

exchange words bëj fjalë
□ *They **exchanged** angry **words** before the meeting but were finally persuaded to agree.* □ *'Come on home, George! It's ridiculous to waste your time **exchanging words with** such an ignorant hypocrite!'*

exercise due/proper care (and attention) tregoj kujdesin (dhe vëmendjen) e duhur
□ *Residents claimed that the city Engineer's Department had failed to **exercise due care and attention**, by leaving a manhole uncovered during the hours of darkness.* □ *Provided you **exercise proper care** there is no*

reason why you shouldn't live to a great age.

explain sth away shfajësohem, gjej sqarim justifikues

□ *You will find it difficult to explain away your use of such offensive language.* □ *He explained away his late arrival by blaming it on the crowded roads.*

explore every avenue përdor të gjitha format (mjetet, mënyrat), përdor të gjithë gurët

□ *'Let the public be assured,' the speaker continued, 'that we'll explore every avenue in our efforts to keep down the cost of living.'* □ *'It's*

my business to explore every avenue,' the Inspector answered.

extol to the skies ngre në qiell

□ *The teacher was extolling her work to the skies.*

eye for an eye and tooth for a tooth dhëmb për dhëmb; kokë për kokë

□ *Anyone who commits a murder should be executed; you know the old saying: an eye foe an eye, and a tooth for a tooth.* □ *In ancient times if a man's eye was put out by his enemy, he might get revenge but putting his enemy's eye out. This was the rule of an eye for an eye and a tooth for a tooth.*

F

face about kthehem prapa

□ *The troops were ordered to **face about**.* □ *At first I did not recognize him, as he had his back towards me but as soon as he **faced about** I knew I had seen him somewhere before.*

face (the) facts e shikoj të vërtetën në sy, i vlerësoj gjërat ashtu siç janë, i shikoj gjërat drejt

□ *I must **face the facts** and take what might be coming to me.*

face the music pranoj, vuaj pasojat (kritikën, vështirësitë etj.), përballoj një situatë të vështirë (me pasoja të pakëndshme)

□ *He has been caught stealing, and he will have to **face the music** today in court.* □ *The boy was caught cheating in the examination and he had to **face the music**.* □ *There is no need for you to worry, if anything goes wrong it is I who will have to **face the music**.*

face to face ballë për ballë

□ *The burglar turned the corner and found himself **face to face** with a policeman.* □ *The two rival politicians came **face to face** in a TV interview.* □ *I stood **face to face** with Mr. Peggotty!* □ *... And now for just ten years Jurgis had been travelling up and down the country, standing **face to face** with the people, and pleading with them for justice.*

face value vlera nominale

□ *The treasury bond had a **face value** of $ 10,000.*

face up to pranoj; përballoj ndershmërisht e burrërisht

□ *He just can't **face up to** the fact that he's too old to work any more.* □ *She's finding it difficult to **face up** the possibility of an early death.*

facts of the matter is that, the e vërteta (fakti) është se, puna është se

□ *You keep on saying that a camping holiday will be no real rest for me but **the fact of the matter is**, you don't want to go yourself.*

facts and figures të dhëna të sakta, informacion të saktë

□ *Before we make detailed plans, we need some more **facts and figures**.*

fact remains that, the e vërteta është se

□ *I agree that he tried hard but **the fact remains that** he has not finished the job in time.*

facts speak for themselves, the faktet flasin vetë

□ *'I am suggesting nothing. But do not **the facts speak for themselves?'***

fade away 1. shuhet, fashitet, venitet

□ *The clip-clop of the horse's hooves **faded away** into the distance.*

2. shpërndahen (njerëzit)

□ *The crowd just **faded away**.*

3. vdes

□ *She's **fading away**.*

fair and square/fairly and squarely

1. i drejtë, i ndershëm

□ *As a businessman, he was **fair and square**.*

2. ndershmërisht, në mënyrë të ndershme

□ *We won't have a local referee for the re-play, and then if we beat them again everybody will know it's been fairly and squarely* done. □ *She won the game* **fair and square.**

3. tamam në shenjë

□ *At length the awaited sign flashed to us from the beach; the commander signalled 'full speed ahead' and we struck the beach* **fairly and squarely.**

4. pa diskutim, pa dyshim

□ *The blame rests* **fair and square** *on my shoulders.* □ *No, the blame rests* **fairly and squarely** *on the shoulders of the motorist.*

fair game objekt sulmi (talljeje, fyerje, shfrytëzimi, abuzimi etj.)

□ *In fact, now that she had cut loose from the poor threads of occupation, he couldn't imagine she would go on—so beautiful a creature, hopeless, and* **fair game** *for only one!* □ *Politicians are* **fair game** *for the cartoonists.*

fair play ndershmëri, drejtësi; lojë e ndershme; kushte të barabarta për të gjithë

□ *True, the newspapers, obedient to this larger financial influence, began to talk of* **'fair play** *to the old companies' and the uselessness of two large rival companies in the field.* □ *The judges decided against Tom, but he said that he had gotten* **fair play.** □ *Whenever we had a game with a team from another class, one of the teachers would be there to see* **fair play.**

fair to middling çka, njëfarësoj, as mirë as keq

□ *'Have you had a good day?' '***Fair to middling,** *you know.'*

fair-weather friend shok për ditë të mirë

□ *'Since then, long experience had convinced him that this clumsy human bear was no* **fair-weather friend.'** □ *I discovered that Alan was*

a **fair-weather friend:** *when I lost my money, he refused to have anything to do with me.*

fall about (laughing/with laughter) shkrihem gazit, vdes së qeshuri

□ *Nick is a born clown. Just the sight of him is enough to make you* **fall about laughing.** □ *We all* **fell about with laughter** *when he did his imitation of the tea-lady.*

fall all one's length shtrihem sa gjerë gjatë

□ *I followed him at once, and instantly I* **fell all my length,** *so weak was I and so giddy with that long exposure.*

fall apart prishet, shkatërrohet, shpërbëhet, merr fund

□ *I don't know how Mick managed to keep the car on the road for so long. At the end, it was practically* **falling apart.** □ *Ann did what she could to keep the marriage from* **falling apart.** *If she and Robert broke up, she decided, it wouldn't be her fault.*

fall prey to bie pre (viktimë) e

□ *When Carrie reached her own room she had already* **fallen prey to** *those doubts and misgivings which are ever the result of a lack of decision.*

fall away 1. ndahem; braktis, lë në baltë

□ *Jackson suffered a severe accident and some of his former supporters began to* **fall away.**

□ *We* **fell away** *from one another without a word.*

2. zhduket

□ *In a crisis, all prejudices* **fall away** *and everyone works together.*

3. priret

□ *Beyond the garden, an area of woodland* **fell** *sharply* **away** *to the river bank.*

fall back sprapsem, tërhiqem

□ *You find me* **fallen back,** *for a*

spring, and I have every reason to believe that a vigorous leap will shortly be the result. □ *Our attack was so vigorous that the enemy had to* ***fall back***.

fall back on (upon) i drejtohem për ndihmë

□ *She's completely homeless—at least I have my parents to* ***fall back on***. □ *If the men didn't respond to a reasoned approach there were other methods we could* ***fall back on***.

fall behind mbetem prapa

□ *This country has* ***fallen behind*** *several of its competitors in the manufacture of cheap cotton goods.* □ *He always* ***falls behind*** *when we are going uphill.*

fall behind with sth mbetem (rri, ngelem) pa paguar etj.

□ *Don't* ***fall behind with*** *the rent, or you will be evicted.* □ *He'd stopped deliveries, because I* ***fell behind with*** *the bill.*

fall down 1. bie për tokë

□ *The steel scaffolding* ***fell down*** *and narrowly missed a couple of bystanders.*

2. bie, rrëzohet

□ *The Council's answer to the population expansion is to build high blocks of flats, but that's where the plan* ***falls down***—*who wants to live in them?*

fall flat dështon, nuk ka sukses, nuk bën përshtypjen e duhur

□ *Tastes and habits of humor vary not only from country to country but from region to region within them. A story that makes a West Highlander laugh may* ***fall*** *very* ***flat*** *in Edinburgh.* □ *The speaker tried to liven up his speech with a joke, but it* ***fell flat***. □ *... She had a curious clouding over*

her cheerfulness, the feeling that her entry had ***fallen*** *strangely* ***flat***.

fall for 1. pëlqej, shtie dashuri

□ *They met,* ***fell for*** *each other and got married six weeks later.* □ *I* ***fell for*** *the picture as soon as I saw it.*

2. bie brenda, gënjehem

□ *'And do you mean to tell me you* ***fell for*** *an old trick like that?'*

fall foul of përplasem, grindem, hyj në konfrontim (mosmarrëveshje) me

□ *The police never caught him in any criminal activity but he eventually* ***fell foul of*** *the tax authorities.* □ *... I really don't want to* ***fall foul of*** *him again.* □ *He instantly* ***fell foul of*** *the commissary in very high terms.*

fall from grace dal nga hiri, humb simpatinë e; dal udhe

□ *Your son behaved very well for a week, but I'm afraid he's* ***fallen from grace***. □ *... he had assisted in extricating from the consequences of their folly several young girls of good family who had* ***fallen from grace*** *and could not otherwise be rescued.*

fall/be taken ill/sick sëmurem, bie i sëmurë, më zë një sëmundje

□ *I must expect to* ***fall sick***. *I cannot expose the body to this hardship and expect the poor beast to behave as if it were in clover.* □ *... while I was on the road this time I* ***fell ill*** *of a fever.* □ *I am afraid he might have* ***fallen ill***.

fall in 1. rrëzohet, shëmbet, rrënohet

□ *The roof of the new tunnel hasn't been properly supported: it shows signs of* ***falling in***. □ *The sides of the pit* ***fell in***.

2. rreshtohem, vihem në rresht

□ *The company* ***fell in*** *and took up their dressing from the right.* □ *Platoon sergeants* ***fell*** *their men* ***in*** *on the barrack square.*

fall in action bie në fushën e betejës

□ *There were altogether twenty men who had **fallen in action** in that battle.*

fall in love with bie në dashuri me

□ *But if Guy were **falling in love with** her, was she genuinely returning Guy's affection?* □ *You're still crazy about Fergus. What are you going to do if he **falls in love with** another woman?*

fall in with 1. takoj rastësisht

□ *At the place where we stopped for lunch, we **fell in with** two or three students.* □ *He **fell in with** bad company.* 2. tregoj mbështetje

□ *He believed he had been looking forward to **falling in with** Alec's request.*

fall into 1. përftoj, kultivoj

□ *It was to be expected that a young man with easy going parents and considerable private means should keep bad company and **fall into** undesirable habits.* 2. ndahet

□ *The present talk **falls into** three parts.* □ *The subject **falls into** four divisions.*

fall into abeyance shfuqizohet, del jashtë përdorimit

□ *This law **falls into abeyance** when the country's security is threatened.* □ *The law **fell into abeyance**.*

fall into decline pëson rënie

□ *The intense competition from overseas has caused the cotton industry to **fall into decline**.* □ *Without government help, these local theatres will not recover from the serious **decline into** which they have **fallen**.*

fall into a (deep) depression bie në depresion të thellë

□ *After the loss of her second child,*

*she **fell into a depression** from which it was difficult to rouse her.*

fall into a flutter nervozohem, bëhem nervoz

□ *He... immediately **fell into a great flutter**.*

fall into a snare/trap bie në kurth (në grackë)

□ *You **fell** right **into my trap**.* □ *It was one of these melees that Jurgis **fell into** his **trap**.*

fall into decay rrënohet, shembet, zhduket, shkatërrohet; kalbëzohet

□ *During the long period of the Depression, the sheds and warehouses were allowed to **fall into decay**.* □ *The laws and institutions of the republic had long **fallen into decay**.*

fall into despair bie në dëshpërim

□ *You should always be optimistic and never **fall into despair**.*

fall into disfavor/disgrace dal nga hiri, shikohem me sy të keq

□ *A little indiscreet gossip isn't enough to make you **fall into disgrace** with all your friends.* □ *From a level of easy success I suppose it's a simple matter to **fall into disgrace**.* □ *With that he disappeared into his inner room, and Polly had the satisfaction of feeling that he had thoroughly misunderstood her object and that she had **fallen into disgrace** without the least advancement of her purpose.*

fall into disrepute merr emër (nam) të keq

□ *The company has **fallen into disrepute** in recent years.* □ *Since the scandal, the school has rather **fallen in disrepute**.*

fall into disuse del jashtë përdorimit

□ *Words which **fall into disuse** may sometimes be revived with a new* meaning. □ *The practice of wearing gowns to attend lectures has now **fallen into disuse**.*

fall into line with pajtohem, pranoj, jam i një mendje me

□ *It was lucky she and Bosinney got on, she seemed to be **falling into line with** the idea of the new house.* □ *When the Chairman proposed a tightening-up of a credit facilities, most of the Board **fell into line**.* □ *He'll have to **fall into line with** the others.*

fall into oblivion bie, lihet në harresë

□ *His work **fell into oblivion** after his death.*

□ *I won't let it **fall into oblivion**.*

fall into sb's clutches bie në kthetrat e

□ *He is ever better understanding the danger coming from them and will not let itself **fall into their clutches**.*

fall into sb's hands bie në duart e

□ *Old Mother Curry's always there to help. It's a good thing you've **fallen into** the right **hands**.* □ *An interesting novel has **fallen into my hands**.* □ *If their plan **falls into the hands of** the enemy, they will suffer heavy losses.*

fall into step filloj të eci me një hap me

□ *Charles followed him into the street, and **fell into step** as they trudged along.* □ *The militants on the executive are unlikely to **fall into step with** leaders they regard as over-conciliatory.*

fall into talk hyj në bisedë

□ *... but now he **fell into** an interesting **talk** and soon modified his original intentions.*

fall into the habit of doing sth më bëhet zakon, më bëhet shprehi

□ *... how easily they had **fallen into the habit of** using the word 'home' about a place where they'd be for only a few days!*

fall into want bie në varfëri

□ *The old man **fell into** perpetual want.*

fall off 1. bie, pakësohet

□ *Attendances at our matinees have **fallen off** this season.* □ *When the measles broke out the school attendance **fell off**.* □ *The quantity of defective goods has **fallen off** very rapidly.*

2. keqësohet

□ *It used to be my favorite restaurant but the standard of cooking has **fallen off** recently.*

fall on/upon sb/sth 1. sulmoj, hidhem mbi

□ *Bandits **fell on** the village and robbed many inhabitants.* □ *The 2nd Cavalry roamed the marshy length of the river Teberev, **falling upon** isolated units of German infantry.*

2. bie

□ *His birthday **falls on** a Sunday this year.* □ *When anything goes wrong, the blame usually **falls on** his younger brother.*

fall on deaf ears bie në vesh të shurdhër

□ *Claims for a twenty percent salary increase are likely to **fall on deaf ears**.*

fall on evil days/hard times kaloj ditë të zeza (kohë të vështira)

□ *During the reign of Henry VI the country **fell on evil days**.*

fall on one's feet bie në këmbë, shpëtoj shëndoshë e mirë, dal pa lagur, s'më hyn gjemb në këmbë

□ *'He came back from war penniless and landed a good job right away.' 'Yes, he has the knack of **falling on his feet**, hasn't he?'* □ *Some people always seem to **fall on their feet**.* □ *He's a fortunate fellow, he always seems to **fall on his feet**.*

fall on/upon sb's ears dëgjoj, ma zë (kap) veshi
□ *As we entered the temple, a curious chanting **fell upon our ears**.* □ *The sound of a closing door **fell upon my ear**.* □ *Upon their ears **fell** a low, humming sound.*

fall on/to one's knees bie në gjunjë
□ *The prisoners **fell on their knees** to beg for clemency.*

fall out 1. shpërndahem
□ *At the end of the drill parade, the battalion **fell out**.* □ *The officer gave the order to fall in and then almost at once shouted 'Fall out'.*
2. grindem, zihem
□ *I have sent him a letter that I'll trouble him to attend to, or he and I will **fall out** I can tell you.* □ *'There, Peggotty,' said my mother, changing her tone, 'don't let us **fall out** with one another, for I couldn't bear it.'*
3. ndodh, ngjan
□ *I was pleased with the way things had **fallen out**.* □ *Everything **fell out** as we had hoped.* □ *It so **fell out** that we were in Durrës on that very day.*

fall out of love (with) nuk e dua më, më del nga zemra
□ *Sarah's not particularly fickle. She's just of an age when girls **fall in and out of love** all the time.* □ *Possibly he might **fall out of love** again some day, but not so long as she kept him on her tenter-hooks.*

fall/jump out of pan in the fire bie nga shiu në breshër
□ *If they thought they could get away from the State by disestablishment, they would find that they were **jumping out of the frying pan into the fire**.*

fall out of use del nga përdorimi
□ *As a language grows new words are introduced and a number of words **fall out of use**.*

fall over sb/sth bie, rrëzohem
□ *Johnny slipped on a banana skin and **fell over**.* □ *Mrs. Jenkins missed her footing and **fell over**.*

fall over oneself to do sth bie copë, bëj çmos, përpiqem me mish e me shpirt, bëj ç'është e mundur
□ *The oil firms were **falling over themselves** to obtain concessions from the Government.* □ *People were **falling over themselves** to be introduced to the visiting film guest.* □ *They almost **fell over themselves** in their anxiousness to act there quickly.*

fall short of 1. mungon, nuk mjafton
□ *They **fell short of** water.*
2. nuk arrin
□ *The money collected **fell short of** the amount required.* □ *Unfortunately the supply of spare parts has **fallen short of** our requirements.*
3. nuk justifikon shpresat, nuk del siç pritet
□ *His achievements had **fallen short of** his hopes.* □ *What right have you to say that, Sir? In what way have I **fallen short**?* □ *His work **fell short of** our expectations.*

fall through dështon, nuk ka sukses
□ *Our holiday plans **fell through** because of transport strikes.* □ *The scheme **fell through** because of some big business deal Ned had to stay and attend to.* □ *The experiment **has fallen through**.*

fall to nis, filloj
□ *She **fell to** eating with great gusto.* □ *And she **fell to** wondering again who her enemy might be.*

fall to pieces rrënohet, shkatërrohet
□ *No wander the car's **falling to pieces**. Have you seen how he drives*

it? □ *The old building was **falling to pieces**.*

fall to sb's lot to do sth është detyra (përgjegjësia) e, i takon

□ *It **fell to my lot to** form an administration.* □ *It **fell to my lot to** open the discussion.*

fall to the ground bie, rrëzohet, hidhet poshtë

□ *This hypothesis **falls to the ground** because intelligence correlates only to a slight extent with 'good taste'.* □ *Hazel's whole argument, based on a false premise, **fell to the ground** and became null and void.*

fall under hyn, përfshihet, ndahet, klasifikohet

□ *What heading do these items **fall under**?* □ ***Under** what class does this **fall**?* □ *These goods **fall under** the class marked.*

fall under sb's eye/notice/observation bie në sy të

□ *Has it ever **fallen under your notice**?*

fall upon sulmoj

□ *They could tell the whole hateful story of it, set forth the inner soul of a city in which justice and honor... were for sale in the marketplace, and human beings writhed and fought and **fell upon** each other like wolves in a pit...*

fall victim to bie viktimë e

□ *He soon **fell victim to** her charms.*

false alarm, a alarm i rremë

□ *People were saying that the river had flooded its banks, but it turned out to be **a false alarm**.* □ *Even though a warning system may give some **false alarm**, it is probably worthwhile since quite minor precautions should be able to reduce the number of casualties.*

false step, a një hap i gabuar

□ *A **false step** could have cost the climbers their lives.*

fan out hapen, shpërndahen (trupat)

□ *The troops **fanned out** as they advanced.* □ *Police with tracker dogs were **fanning out** over the moor.*

fan the flames of i fryj zjarrit, nxis (ndez) pasionet

□ *Such jokes do not promote 'integration'- they merely **fan the flames of** strife and discontent.* □ *Her wild behavior merely **fanned the flames of** his jealousy*

far/out and away tejet; pa krahasim

□ *She's **far and away** the best actress I've seen.* □ *The railway building was the most significant of all, and railroad stocks were **far and away** the most valuable and important on every exchange.*

far and near/wide gjithkund, gjithandej, në të katër anët

□ *They searched **far and wide** for the missing child.* □ *The news of our victory spread **far and wide**.* □ *Off went the mail at a canter down the dark road; the lamps gleaming brightly and the horn awakening all the echoes **far and wide**.*

far be it from me to është larg mendsh, as që mund të mendohet, as që më shkon ndër mend

□ ***Far be it from me to** interfere in your affairs but I would like to give you just one piece of advice.* □ *I am acquainted with my faults. **Far be it from me to** deny them.* □ ***Far be it for me to** suggest any change in your admirable program.*

far cry from, a s'krahasohet me, si nata me ditën me

□ *The room is chilly, but full of light—*

a far cry from his Oxford digs. □ *His last statement was a far cry from his first story.* □ *The first automobile could run, but it was a far cry from a modern one.* □ *... What a far cry from this man to this woman, I thought.*

far from doing sth në vend që të

□ *Far from enjoying dancing, he loathes it.* □ *I stuck it in a pot and forgot about it, but the plant, far from dying, seemed to thrive on neglect.*

far from it aspak, kurrsesi, në asnjë mënyrë, në të kundërt

□ *'Are you happy here?' 'No, far from it; I've never been so miserable in my life.'* □ *'Is he generous with his money?' 'Far from it. He doesn't even like to spend it on himself.'*

far from sth aspak; në asnjë mënyrë, natyrisht që jo

□ *The problem is far from easy.* □ *Your account is far from the truth.*

far gone i vajtur

□ *The victim of the attack was already far gone when the ambulance brought him in.* □ *The roof is far gone but the rest of the house is in fair condition.*

fast and furious i gjallë, i zjarrtë, i ndezur, plot gjallëri

□ *Father swore he was right and mother swore he was wrong, and various members of the family siding with one or the other of them, the argument raged fast and furious for an hour and more.* □ *The shelter had to be completed before darkness fell and as the sun slid down to the horizon the pace of work grew ever more fast and furious.*

fasten one's eyes on ngul sytë, mbërthej shikimin në

□ *She fastened her eyes on the picture.* □ *He fastened his eyes on me.*

fasten on sb/sth kapem pas

□ *He was looking for someone to blame and fastened on me.*

fat chance, a mundësi e vogël, shumë pak mundësi (ngjasë)

□ *A fat chance he has of winning a prize in the music contest: he hardly knows one note from another.*

feast one's eyes on kullot sytë, kënaqet duke parë

□ *The visitors feasted their eyes on the beautiful display of paintings.* □ *Foreign visitors feasted their eyes on the beautiful scenery.* □ *He feasted his eyes on the beauty of the valley.*

feather in one's cap, a nder; shenjë (arritje) nderi (krenarie)

□ *The young salesman knew that, if he could get the valuable contract, it would be quite a feather in his cap.* □ *Obviously it would be a feather in their cap if they could get this scheme off the ground without a public inquiry.* □ *It was a feather in his cap to win first prize.* □ *Louis. ... they think it will be a feather in their cap to cure a rising artist.*

feather one's (own) nest mbush xhepin e vet

□ *The former finance minister was accused for using state funds to feather his nest.* □ *His spouse was disposed to feather her own nest at the expense of him and his heirs.* □ *I'm sure she feathered her nest well after they got too old and confused to be bothered with housekeeping accounts.* □ *The district attorney was supposed to return the money to the robbery victims, but instead he feathered his nest with it.*

feed on sth ushqehet

□ *Hatred feeds on envy.* □ *Creativity*

*and curiosity are part of the same thing, they **feed on** each other.*

feel at home ndjehem si në shtëpinë time
☐ *They always make us **feel** very much **at home**.*

feel cheap më vjen turp, ndjehem i turpëruar
☐ *His treatment of her made her **feel cheap**.* ☐ *You must be **feeling cheap**, I suppose.*

feel good ndjehem mirë
☐ *'Why have you got these crazy ideas?' 'I **feel good** when I'm singing.'* ☐ *I might not have left her off with remark on another occasion, but I had just downed a couple of whiskies and I was **feeling good**.*

feel in one's bones that e ndiej thellë në shpirt
☐ *I **felt in my bones that** Archer didn't do him justice.* ☐ *I knew that something of the sort would happen. I **felt** it **in my bones**.*

feel like kam dëshirë të, më pëlqen të, jam gati të
☐ *'Does anybody **feel like** a game of poker?' he asked hopefully, but nobody did.* ☐ *Those who **felt like** hearing the story again came over and added themselves to the audience.* ☐ *He didn't **feel like** anything to eat.*

feel like a fish out of water ndjehem si peshku pa ujë
☐ *With my working class background I **feel like a fish out of water** among these high-society people.* ☐ *I **felt like a fish out of water** amongst all those elegantly dressed people.*

feel/look like a million dollars ndjehem (dukem) për bukuri
☐ *He has completely recovered from his operation; he says he **feels like a million dollars**.* ☐ *I'm on holiday, it's a beautiful morning, and I **feel like a**

million dollars.* ☐ *It's good to see you both again. Jake, you **look like a million dollars**.*

feel oneself ndjehem mirë
☐ *I don't quite **feel myself** today.*

feel on top of the world ndjehem me krahë
☐ *'You look depressed, Peter.' 'I'm not depressed. I'm **feeling on top of the world**.'*

feel one's age ndiej peshën e viteve
☐ *I know I'm not exactly young any more but, really, I never **felt my age** till this last winter.* ☐ *Yes, thank you, grandfather is pretty well **feeling his age** of course, but that's only to be expected.*

feel one's way eci, gjej rrugën (me të prekur)
☐ *The child was cautiously **feeling his way** in the dark.*
2. veproj me kujdes
☐ *It was the first training scheme of its kind and we would have to **feel our way** carefully to avoid unforeseen difficulties.* ☐ *We should **feel our way** carefully in doing the work and not make any hasty decision.*

feel small ndjehem keq; ndjehem i fyer, i poshtëruar
☐ *Harold had been left at the end of the interview **feeling** very **small**.* ☐ *A good teacher does not indulge in sarcasm. Children can be guided or reproved or, for that matter, punished, without being made to **feel or look** small.*

feel sb's pulse i mat (i shoh) pulsin dikujt
☐ *As I did not know whether he would agree to my proposal, I had to **feel his pulse** on the subject.*

feel the ground sliding/slipping from under one's feet ndien t'i shkasë toka nën këmbë

□ *Inch by inch the ground beneath him was **sliding from his feet**; faster and faster the encircling ruin contracted and contracted toward himself, its wicked center; until should close in and crush.*

feel the pinch ndiej mungesën e parave, ndjehem ngushtë për para

□ *The high rate of unemployment is making many families **feel the pinch**.* □ *Lisa's money will make a great difference to a man of Guy's tastes. He has been **feeling the pinch**.*

fence in 1. gardhoj, rrethoj me gardh

□ *Thousands of acres of open range were **fenced in** to prevent cattlemen trespassing on what have become private property.*

2. kufizoj, mbyll

□ *He felt **fenced in** by domesticity, by his nine-to-five routine.*

fence off (from) ndaj me gardh

□ *The children can't play in the front garden until it's been **fenced off from** the main road.*

fend for oneself ia del vetë, mban veten, siguron jetesën, ecën me këmbët e veta

□ *The old couple have no one to do the washing and heavy cleaning: they have to **fend for themselves**.* □ *The rations issued to the patrols would last for two days; after that they would **fend for themselves**.* □ *When his father died, Tom had to **fend for himself**.* □ *Most animals let their young **fend for themselves** at an early age.*

few and far between i rrallë, i pakët në numër

□ *While we were touring, we tried to stay only at good hotels; but we discovered that they were **few and far between**.* □ *The buses to our village are **few and far between**.* □ *Places*

where you can get water are **few and far between** in the desert.

fiddle while Rome is burning tjetrit i digjet mjekra, ai kërkon të ndezë cigaren; fshati digjet, kurva krihet

□ *Meanwhile, plans are going forward for a new opera house and an enormous sports stadium and swimming pool in a city where over half the population are inadequately or insanitarily housed. This is **fiddling while Rome burns**.* □ *It was time he got back to Elderson, and what was to be done now, and left this **fiddling while Rome burned**.*

fifty-fifty barabar, në mënyrë të barabartë

□ *We went **fifty-fifty** on the dinner.* □ *When Tony and Andy bought an old car, they divided the cost **fifty-fifty**.*

fight back/down mposht, ndrydh, mbaj nën kontroll

□ *He told me what the trouble was. He **fought** it **down** and as the minutes passed I thought he was going to win out.*

fight like a tiger luftoj me trimëri (trimërisht, si luan)

□ *Except as regards its natural prey the weasel is a timid animal but will **fight like a tiger** in defence of its young.*

fight like Kilkenny cats zihen (hahen) si qentë në garroq, hanë kokat njëri me tjetrin

□ *They **fought like Kilkenny cats** and the only result of their quarrel was that they both lost the respect of those who had supported them.*

fight off largoj, zmpraps

□ *The police had a difficult job **fighting off** the reporters.* □ *The fans had to be **fought off** before the film star could safely get into the car.*

fight sth out zgjidh një mosmarrëveshje, një grindje etj.

□ *I can't help them to resolve their quarrel—they must **fight it out** between themselves.* □ *Don't interfere in a matrimonial squabble—let husband and wife **fight it out** among themselves.*

fight shy of druhem, tutem

□ *He was unhappy in his job for years but always **fought shy of** telling his boss.* □ *Some people **fight shy of** a visit to the dentist.* □ *She was a very reserved person who always **fought shy of** strangers.*

fight to the finish luftoj deri në fund

□ *The liberation of the country cannot be achieved without **fighting to the finish**.*

fight to the last ditch luftoj deri në fund, luftoj deri në pikën e fundit të gjakut

□ *Britain **would fight to the last ditch** to maintain the level of the pound.*

fight tooth and nail luftoj dhëmb për dhëmb, majë më majë

□ *The government will find it difficult to get the new airport built in that area: the local people will **fight** it **tooth and nail**. Industry has been pressing hard for the abolition of fuel-oil duty, which adds to industrial costs; and the local Board has been **fighting tooth-and-nail** on the other side.*

fight with one's own shadow lufton me hijen e vet, hahet me rrobat e trupit

□ *By so acting you are **fighting with your own shadow**.*

figure in përfshij, fus në llogari

□ *Have you **figured in** the cost of food for our holiday?*

figure out 1. arrij të kuptoj, marr me mend

□ *We can't **figure out** why he's been behaving so oddly.*

2. llogaris, përllogaris

□ *Have you **figured out** how much the holiday will cost?* □ *The cost of the operation will need to be **figured out** very precisely.*

3. zgjidh

□ *Tony couldn't **figure out** the last problem on the arithmetic test.*

fill in for sb zëvendësoj, zë vendin e

□ *My partner is on holiday this week so I'm **filling in for** him.*

fill in 1. mbush, plotësoj

□ *You must **fill in** your name, age, and address on the application form.* □ *This form has been **filled in** wrongly.* □ *They drove downtown and stopped before an imposing granite building in which they interviewed an official who had the papers all ready, with only the names to be **filled in**.*

2. mbush, mbyll (një gropë etj.)

□ *The hole has been **filled in**.* □ *If we **fill in** that old fireplace, we'll have a wall free for bookshelves.*

3. mbush, zë kohën

□ *He **filled in** the time of waiting by reading a magazine.* □ *He **filled in** the rest of the day watching television.*

fill one's shoes zëvendësoj, zë vendin e

□ *Bill was a wonderful head of department; it will be very difficult for them to find someone to **fill his shoes**.* □ *The old doctor was worshipped round here. The son's a nice enough young man, but he'll never **fill** his father's **shoes**.*

fill out mbush

□ *A man might work full fifty minutes, but if there was no work to **fill out** the hour, there was no pay for him.* □ *What's a doctor for? Not to sit all* day *filling out forms for the National Health.*

fill/fit the bill mbush, plotëson kërkesat
□ *We are looking for someone to be in charge of the office; we thought that Miss Jones might fit the bill.* □ *I thought I would need a special tool, but this wrench fill the bill.*

fill the gap mbush boshllëkun
□ *We hope to fill the gap in our missile program very soon.* □ *He worked hard to fill up the gaps in his studies.*

fill up mbush
□ *Following the heavy rains, the storage tanks were filling up again.* □ *I've filled up all the buckets I can lay hands on.*

find a solution gjej zgjidhje
□ *A solution has not yet been found to the fundamental problems of industrial relations.*

find fault with gjej, nxjerr kleçka (bishta); gjej të meta
□ *No matter how carefully I prepare work for Professor Smith, he always finds fault with me.* □ *I have one great fault to find with Tom, however, which I cannot forgive, and for which I take him heavily to account.* □ *...he is prone to find fault with others when he should be blaming himself.*

find favor in sb's eye gjej përkrahjen, simpatinë e
□ *He found favor in the eyes of Miss Sally Brass.*

find it in one's heart/oneself to do sth më bën zemra, jam në gjendje
□ *I cannot find it in myself to condemn a mother who steals food for a hungry child.* □ *He cannot find it in his heart to tell her the news.* □ *He had worked so hard that I couldn't find it in my heart to tell him that he had failed.* □ *But as I went on my way*

to the city I felt so lost and lonesome that I could have *found it in my heart to* sit down by the dyke and cry and weep like a baby.

find one's bearings orientohem
□ *Though I had lived in New York as a child, the city had altered so much it took me some time to find my bearings again.*

find one's feet 1. mëkëmbem, ngrihem më këmbë, e marr veten
□ *After a six-week illness it took me some time to find my feet again.* □ *How old was the baby when it began to find its feet?*
2. eci me këmbët e mia, veproj në mënyrë të pavarur
□ *It was good experience for her, for it enabled her to find her feet in the new country and to learn a little of its ways.* □ *... Perhaps you can do something for him, till he finds his feet.*

find one's tongue/voice më vjen goja (zëri)
□ *Peter was rather shy and did not say anything at first; but eventually he found his tongue and spoke up.* □ *After a long stretch of silence he found his voice.* □ *She made a slight movement, as if she were trying to speak, but could not find voice...*

find one's way gjen udhën, arrin në destinacion, depërton
□ *Don't bother to meet me at the station. I'm sure I'll be able to find my way to your house by myself.* □ *But, tears were not the things to find their way to Mr. Bumble's soul; his heart was waterproof.*

find out gjej, zbuloj
□ *He had been cheating the taxman but it was years before he was found out.* □ *One day someone will start asking questions and find out*

precisely why we've been losing so much money.

find sb/sth wanting e gjej të mangët
□ *Shaw applauded Neitzche for laying low false ideals, but found him wanting politically.* □ *Fashions in education are constantly changing as various methods are tried and all, in some degrees, found wanting.*

fine feathers do not make fine birds njerinë nuk e bën rrobja
□ *Do not be influenced too much by his smart appearance: remember that fine feathers don't make fine birds.*

finish off 1. mbaroj, përfundoj
□ *Old Smith came round for a chat and finished off the remains of my whisky.*
2. vras, asgjësoj, shkatërroj
□ *That last climb nearly finished me off.*

finish with mbaroj me
□ *'Have you finished with our lawn-mower yet?'*

finish up përfundoj
□ *He could finish up dead or badly injured.*

fire away jepi
□ *'I've got a couple of questions I'd like to ask you.' 'Right, fire away.'*
□ *'I want to ask you something.' 'Ask on', Pop said. 'Fire away'.*

firm hand, a një dorë të fortë
□ *It was obvious to Irene within two days of taking up her appointment that a very firm hand would be needed.* □ *That boy needs a firm hand to help him grow up.*

first and foremost para së gjithash, pikë së pari, në radhë të parë, së pari
□ *You've been soaked through by the rain: first and foremost, we'll get these wet clothes off, and then we'll give you something to eat.* □ *Will we now let cars eat men and our cities?*

First and foremost people want space to live in at a price they can afford. □ *He does a bit of writing, but first and foremost he's a teacher.*

first and last 1. gjithë e gjithë
□ *It took four years to build the Towers and cost about four hundred thousand pounds first and last.*
2. kokë e këmbë, në të gjitha drejtimet
□ *'His father wouldn't have done business that way.' 'No, he was a gentleman, first and last.'*

first catch your hare (then cook him) bëj hesapet pa hanxhinë, peshku në det tigani në zjarr
□ *You should be more modest. First catch your hare and then cook him.*

first come, first served kush mëngoi, bloi; kush mëngoi (shpejtoi), gëzoi
□ *In the dining hall, it's a case of first come, first served; so if you're late there may not be much left.* □ *Get in line for your ice cream, boys. First come, first served.*

first of all e para, së pari, para së gjithash
□ *First of all she just smiled, then she started to laugh.* □ *Well, first of all we can't spare the time.* □ *If you want to speak English well, you must first of all learn to pronounce all the words correctly.*

fish for peshkoj, gjuaj, kërkoj tërthor
□ *Don't be taken in by his charm: he's fishing for an invitation to the big party.* □ *By his manner of speaking we could see that he was fishing for compliments.*

fish in the air rrah ujë në havan, bëj një punë të kotë
□ *He must be orientated in his work for up to now he has been fishing in the air.*

fish in troubled waters peshkoj në ujëra të turbullta
□ *The Mafia has at all times delighted*

*in **fishing in troubled waters**.* □ *When a civil war breaks out within a small country, the danger is that one of the bigger powers will try to **fish in** these troubled **waters**.*

fit in (with) harmonizohet, përshtatet, përputhet

□ *He's never done this type of work before; I'm not sure how he'll **fit in with** the other employees.* □ *The answer disappoints you or doesn't appear to **fit in with** your temperament.* □ *Our holidays must be timed to **fit in with** yours.*

fit out pajis

□ *The ship is being **fitted out** for a new expedition to the Arctic.* □ *I went to a large clothes shop where they could **fit** you **out** for anything.*

fit sb like a glove 1. i bie për shtat, i rri mirë (pas trupit)

□ *Mary and Jane are almost exactly the same size: when Mary wears one of Jane's dresses it usually **fits** her **like a glove**.* □ *Aren't I lucky? The only dress in the shop that I fancied and it **fitted** me **like a glove**.*

2. i shkon për shtat, i përshtatet

□ *'Cautious' is a description that certainly **fits** the new president **like a glove**.*

fit up (with) 1. montoj, instaloj

□ *There's room at the end of the garage to **fit up** a work-bench.* □ *The most up-to-date appliances have been **fitted up** in the new flats.*

□ *It took us about half an hour to **fit up** the apparatus.*

2. pajis

□ *If you speak to your oculist he'll see that you're **fitted up with** new spectacles.* □ *He's had the new place **fitted up with** every labor-saving device.*

fix it/things up (with) rregulloj

□ *'You won't go to goal. I've **fixed it***

up.' □ *They can leave school early to play football. John's **fixed it up with** the Headmaster.*

fix on sb/sth zgjedh, caktoj

□ *They've **fixed on** Ashby as the new chairman.* □ *Have you **fixed on** a date for the wedding?*

fix one's eyes on mbërthej shikimin, ngul sytë

□ *He **fixed his eyes** on me.*

fix up 1. ngre, ndërtoj, riparoj, rregulloj, përshtat

□ *He **fixed up** the cottage before they moved in.* □ *They **fixed up** a temporary platform at one end of the square.*

2. rregulloj, organizoj, siguroj

□ *'Try to **fix** me **up** an appointment for eleven tomorrow morning.'* □ *He's **fixed** himself **up with** a very smart flat on the sea-front.* □ *I've **fixed up** a visit to the theatre for next week.*

3. furnizoj

□ *I think we can **fix** you **up** with what you want.*

fix with mbërthej

□ *Small boys should not burst into a master's study unannounced. The housemaster **fixed** Jenkins **with** a decidedly hostile look.*

fizzle out shuhet, fashitet, bëhet tym; humbet si pluhuri në erë, shkrin si kripa në ujë

□ *After a promising start, the project soon **fizzled out**.* □ *The fuse **fizzled out** before exploding the fire-cracker.*

flake out këputem, bie në gjumë (nga lodhja)

□ *When I got home from the airport, I **flaked out** in the near armchair.* □ *After the guests had gone and the dishes were cleared away, we simply **flaked out** in a couple of armchairs.*

flare up 1. nxehem, inatosem, marr zjarr

□ *Robert looked as if he were about to*
flare up *and tell me to mind my own
business.* □ *It was only intended as a
jocular remark, but he **flared up** and
turned angrily upon him.*
2. ndizet, merr flakë
□ *The fire **flared up** again and then
died.* □ *The fire **flared up** as I put
more logs on it.*
3. rishfaqet, ringjallet
□ *Gray's arthritis **flared up** sometimes.* □ *My back trouble has **flared
up** again.*

flash along/by/past/across/through
kalon vetëtimthi si shkrepëtimë
□ *The train **flashed by** at high speed.*
□ *A flight of aircraft **flashed** low
across the field.*

flash across/into one's mind i shkrep,
i vjen papritur një mendim (një ide)
në mendje
□ *An idea **flashed into my mind**.*

flash a glance/a look at hedh një
vështrim të shpejtë
□ *Dinny saw the girl **flash a look**
at her aunt.* □ *Leonie responded
promptly. He **flashed** him **a glance**
out of the corner of her eyes.*

flash in the pan, a flakë (zjarr)
kashte
□ *Jack is really not a very good
runner: his victory in the trials was
probably just **a flash in the pan**.* □ *It
soon became clear that he would
have to follow his success with a new
play, but Sherrif decided that
'Journey's End' was **a flash in the
pan** and that he should carry out
another ambition.*

flat out 1. me sa fuqi kam, me gjithë
fuqinë; me gjithë shpejtësinë
□ *The ambitious senator went **flat
out** to become president.* □ *He was
working **flat out**.*
2. i këputur, i rraskapitur

□ *After running in the marathon, she
was **flat out** for a week.*

flay/skin sb alive ia marr shpirtin; e
kritikoj ashpër
□ *'If it's one of my boys that did this,'
said the woman, surveying the
damage, 'I'll **skin** him **alive**.'*

flesh and blood 1. njeri i gjallë; trupi i
njeriut; natyra njerëzore
□ *I can't stay here and listen to such
nonsense: it is more than **flesh and
blood** can stand.* □ *Clare... I'm not
wax.—I'm **flesh and blood**. Something snapped inside Monsieur Bon-
neval.* □ ***Flesh and blood** could
endure no more.*
2. njeri i një gjaku, njeri i afërm
□ *He ran away and left his family:
how could he treat his own **flesh and
blood** so badly?* □ *Such an answer
from her -and she's my own **flesh and
blood**.*

flight of fancy, a fluturim i fantazisë
□ *Her latest **flight of fancy** is to go
camping in the Sahara desert!* □ *In
my opinion this poem—so homely
and spontaneous and apt and accurate—is worth a hundred **flights of
fancy**.*

fling dirt/mud at sb hedh baltë mbi, i
nxjerr nam të keq, marr nëpër gojë
□ *During the electioneering campaign, the politicians are wont to
fling dirt at each other.*

fling on vesh shpejt e shpejt
□ *She **flung on** her coat and ran to
the bus-stop.*

fling oneself into/upon i hyj, i futem, i
përvishem punës
□ *... He honestly **flings himself upon**
his task.* □ *She **flung herself into** her
new job.*

fling sth in sb's face ia përplas në
fytyrë
□ *I **fling** the words **in your face**, my*

lord! □ I have got courage enough to throw it in his face.
flip one's lead 1. humb kontrollin
□ *When that pushy salesman came back, Mom really flipped her lead.* 2. luaj mendsh, humb fiqirin
□ *When he offered me three times the pay I was getting, I thought he had flipped his lead.*
flog a dead horse rrah ujë në havan, fshikulloj një kalë të ngordhur, merrem me një punë të kotë
□ *You may have amazed people by your advanced views on education forty years ago but now you're just flogging a dead horse.* □ *Why a man should waste his time, flogging dead horses.* □ *Jim is still trying to arrange a picnic on Saturday, but he is flogging a dead horse: no one is interested.*
flood the market mbyt tregun
□ *Japanese cars have flooded the American market.* □ *In Western economies if the market shows signs of being flooded by a commodity, be it wheat, coffee or butter, production will be cut back.*
flood in/into vijnë lumë
□ *Donations have been flooding in since the appeal made for help over the radio.* □ *The applications flooded into the office.*
fly a kite mas (hetoj) pulsin e opinionit publik
□ *The group decided to fly a kite at the conference: they put forward their ideas for discussion.*
fly high vras (synoj) lart, kam plane (synime etj.) të mëdha
□ *In his youth he saw himself flying high.* □ *She'd say he was flying too high.*
fly in the face of sth shpërfill me qëllim; kundërshtoj, veproj kundër; është në kundërshtim me

□ *He was obviously guilty, but the jury decided to fly in the face of evidence, and acquitted him.* □ *'But I would have you know, Miss Edwards,' resumed the governess in a tone of increased severity, 'that you shall not be permitted to fly in the face of your superiors in this exceedingly gross manner.'* □ *What pride he had in his boy!... And this, was the end of all!—to marry a bankrupt and to fly in the face of duty and fortune.*
fly in the ointment, a njeriu (gjëja) që prish bukurinë e gjithçkaje, një lugë katran në një fuçi mjalti
□ *I quite like my new job; the only fly in the ointment is my boss, Miss Pringle: she is always finding new things for me to do.* □ *We had a lot of fun at the beach; the only fly in the ointment was Tony's cutting his foot on a piece of glass.* □ *We were having a picnic, when suddenly there came a downpour, which was rather a fly in the ointment.*
fly into a passion/rage/temper nxehem, marr zjarr, më nxehet gjaku
□ *The child flew into a rage and began scattering its toys about.* □ *He'll fly into a temper and tell me the contract for the murals is off.* □ *Little Stanislovas spent most of the day dancing about in horrible agony, till Jurgis flew into a passion of nervous rage and swore like a madman.*
fly off the handle zemërohem, nxehem, marr zjarr
□ *Every time I ask him for permission to leave early, he flies off the handle.* □ *Tony flew off the handle whenever Andy made a mistake.* □ *Don't fly off the handle for nothing every time you run up against a small problem.* □ *I was surprised when he flew off the handle.*

foam at the mouth shkumëzoj, nxjerr shkumë nga goja (nga inati)
□ *Don't go near Brown: he's **foaming at the mouth** because you did not turn up for work yesterday.* □ *After having to wait an hour the customer was **foaming at the mouth** with rage.* □ *By the time Uncle Tom had the third flat tire, he was really **foaming at the mouth**.*

fold in/into përziej
□ *Then **fold in** the rest of the sugar and flavoring.*

fold in one's arms përqafoj
□ *Father **folded** the tiny child **in his arms**.* □ *Mother **folded** her child **in her arms**.*

fold one's arms/hands kryqëzoj krahët (duart)
□ *One cannot **fold his hands** and stand idly by at a time when the others are working hard.*

fold up përthyhem, thyhem (këputem) në mes (nga dhembja, gazi etj.)
□ *From the moment he appeared on stage, the audience **folded up** in their seats.* □ *He jabbed me just once in the solar plexus and I **folded up**.*

follow in somebody's footsteps eci në gjurmët e
□ *We shall not recount the many experiments carried out by Rhine and by others who have **followed in his footsteps**.* □ *John is going to **follow in father's footsteps** and become a doctor also.* □ *She works in theatre, **following in her father's footsteps**.* □ *'I thought you had **followed in your fathers' footsteps**,' Pickering said... 'Geologist, wasn't he?'*

follow one's (own) bent ndjek (zhvilloj) shijet (prirjet, dhurëtitë etj.) individuale
□ *'The more differences the better. It's the same with people. The more*

*individuals there are **following their own bent** the healthier we are as a society.* □ *Several of the boys who had seemed stubbornly stupid under the former system showed plenty of common sense when allowed to **follow their own bent**.*

follow one's (own) nose 1. eci drejt përpara
□ *When you get to the main street, just **follow your nose**: your hotel is at the end of the street.* □ ***Follow your nose** and you will get to the place which you are looking for.*
2. veproj instiktivisht
□ *Since you don't know the language I can only suggest that you **follow the nose**.*

follow one's own way bën (vepron) si i thotë mendja (koka) e vet
□ *I could give good counsel to my descendants, but I know they'll **follow their own way**.*

follow sb's advice ndjek këshillën e
□ *You won't get well unless you **follow** your doctor's **advice**.*

follow sb's example ndjek shembullin e
□ *We learn from the book that he has **followed** his mother's **example** in diary-keeping: when it is eventually published, that may be his best book.* □ *I'm only talking to you like this because I don't want you to **follow my example** and rush into marriage with the wrong kind of man.*

follow sb's lead marr shembull nga, e marr si shembull
□ *Mind you, if we all **followed his lead**, the courses would be practically deserted.*

follow suit pasoj, bëj të njëjtën gjë, ndjek shembullin e
□ *The Ministry of Labor is already engaged on a campaign to make factories even safer; the Ministry of*

Education would be well advised to **follow suit.** □ *Jim decided to go for a swim and Jack* **followed suit.** □ *If he's going home early, I think I'll* **follow suit.**

follow the crowd shkoj pas berihasë

□ *Not wanting to make my controversial views known yet, I preferred to* **follow the crowd** *for a while.*

follow through ndjek (çoj) deri në fund

□ *'Don't keep breaking off. I'd like to hear you* **follow** *the argument* **through** *to a conclusion.'* □ *He takes several schemes in hand, but lacks the persistence to* **follow** *them* **through.**

follow up 1. vazhdoj, pasoj

□ *Don't rest on your laurels:* **follow up** *your success and start looking for new markets now.*

2. ndjek, hetoj nga afër

□ *The night editor decides which of the stories that are phoned in should be* **followed up.**

food for thought/meditation/reflection ushqim (shkak, arsye) për meditim (reflektim); ushqim për mendjen

□ *The teacher warned John that he would fail if he did not work harder and this gave John some* **food for thought.** □ *The long journey with its innumerable meetings provided me with much* **food for thought.** □ *The meetings had, they said uneasily, been interesting. They had provided much* **food for thought.**

fool's errand, a punë pa punë, punë e kotë, punë pa bereqet, punë e budallait

□ *No harm in trying, I suppose, but you're going on a* **fool's errand** *in my opinion.* □ *Every call and investigation goes down on the records—even*

the false alarms and the various **fool's errands** *that are part of the fireman's lot.*

fool about/around rri kot; e kaloj kohën kot

□ *I was meant to be working on Sunday, but I just* **fooled around** *all day.* □ *If you go to college, you must work, not* **fool around.**

foot the bill paguaj, heq shpenzimet

□ *We can have a party if you like, but who's going to* **foot the bill?** □ *Science has created the physical environment in which we conduct our lives. The effects are felt by everyone—and everyone* **foots the bill** *for the scientist's electron microscope, test-tube, jar of fruit flies and micro-analyser.*

for a bit për pak kohë

□ *I told him about you and he said that if you were in trouble he would be glad to look after you* **for a bit.**

for a certainty me siguri

□ *Know* **for a certainty** *that the Lord your God will no more drive out any of these nations from before you. (Joshua 23:13)* □ *He left two weeks ago, I know this* **for a certainty.**

for a change për variacion

□ *I suppose you'll be spending your holiday in Devon as usual. Don't you ever think of going somewhere else* **for a change?** □ *We usually go to France in the summer, but this year we're going to Spain* **for a change.** □ *Shall we have tea* **for a change?**

for ages (and ages) për shekuj; për një kohë shumë e gjatë

□ *I haven't seen you* **for ages!** □ *'You were with him last night, weren't you?' 'Yes, but Mother, he's going in less than three weeks.* □ *I shan't see him* **for ages and ages** *then.'*

for a little për pak kohë; një copë herë; një copë udhë
□ *We left the car and walked **for a little**.*

for all I know me sa di unë
□ *How was I to know you would come back tonight? **For all I knew** you were never coming back.* □ *'...my child is dying. She may be dead **for all I know**. And nobody is doing anything: nobody cares.'*

for all one's efforts me gjithë përpjekjet
□ ***For all his** courageous **efforts**, the image of the company is slightly less secure.*

for all (that) pavarësisht, megjithatë
□ ***For all** his talk about sports cars and swimming-pools he's just an ordinary bank clerk.* □ ***For all** his wealth and fame, he's a very lonely man.* □ *Mr. Jones was a rather lazy teacher but, **for all that**, he was still quite popular with his students.* □ *I turned to go indoors when I saw a girl waiting in the next doorway. I couldn't see her face, only the white silk trousers and long flowered robe, but I knew her **for all that**.*

for all one/it is worth me sa kam fuqi, me tërë fuqinë, me të gjitha forcat
□ *I think the last day the sun shone was when that dirty little train steamed out of that crowded, suffocating Indian station, with the battalion band playing **for all it was worth**.* □ *The next thing I saw of him he had climbed over the fence and was running down the road **for all he was worth**.* □ *Hold on, boy, hold on, **for all you are worth**.*

for all the world as if (like) tamam si, pikërisht si
□ *'That sounds **for all the world like** a lark,' she said in amazement.*
□ *When he came through that door he looked **for all the world like** his father when he was young.* □ *He's **for all the world** a man I knew 20 years ago, in looks, behavior, everything.*

for and/or against pro (ose) kundër
□ *Anything really worth saying could, in her opinion, be said in two minutes. And the same for any arguments **for and against**.* □ *He has at one time or another argued both **for and against** most of the big changes in the country over the past twenty years.*

for a moment (për) një çast
□ *He might have popped in **for a moment**, since he was passing this way.*

for a rainy day për një ditë të zezë, për një ditë të keqe
□ *It's always a good idea to save up **for a rainy day**.*

for a (mere) song badihava, fare lirë, për pesë para
□ *I had to sell the house at a very bad time, and so it went **for a song**.* □ *This table was going **for a song** at the market.* □ *All of these lovely things by which he had set great store... went **for a song**.*

for a spell për pak kohë, për pak minuta
□ *You hold on **for a spell** and I'll be back.* □ *Shall we rest **for a short spell**?*

for a start pikësëpari, së pari
□ *I'm not buying it—I can't afford it **for a start**.* □ *'Why don't you take your wife with you on this trip?' 'We couldn't afford it, **for a start**, and anyway, I don't think she'd like to leave the children with somebody else for so long.'*

for a time përkohësisht, për pak kohë, për një periudhë të shkurtër
□ *Our small fishing boat was used **for***

a time, but the boats now in use are much bigger and better equipped.

for a while për pak kohë

□ *She worked in a bank **for a while** before studying law.* □ *Let us sit in silence **for a while** and listen to the music.*

for a wonder (si) për çudi

□ *You are punctual **for a wonder**.*
□ ***For a wonder** he was not seasick.*

for better (or) for worse për ditë të mirë a të keqe

□ *... his other faithful ally, **for better and for worse**—the gout—darts into the old oak bed chamber... and grips him by both legs.*

for better or worse për mirë a keq

□ *It's been done, and, **for better or worse**, we can't change it now.* □ *I've just walked out on him, **for better or for worse**.*

forbidden fruit fryt i ndaluar

□ *Eve ate the **forbidden fruit**.*

forbidden ground/territory 1. zonë e ndaluar

□ *This document trespassed on **forbidden ground** in the opposite direction.*

2. fushë e ndaluar, aktivitet i ndaluar

□ *Whatever his motive I'm surprised he lent his presence. Surely the oculist is **forbidden territory** for clergymen.*

force of circumstance forcë (fuqi) madhore; shkaqe madhore

□ *The camp contained men from many backgrounds brought together through **force of circumstance**.* □ *It was **force of circumstance** that led to their getting married.*

force of habit forca e zakonit

□ *It's **force of habit** that gets me out of bed at 7:15 each morning.* □ *Three new murders, two new air crashes, one old fashioned strike; I don't know*

*why I buy the paper really—**force of habit** I suppose.*

force sb's hand detyroj (shtrëngoj) dikë të veprojë pa dëshirë

□ *The teacher said that he did not want to punish the students, but they would **force his hand** if they did not behave.* □ *Tony did not want to tell where he was going, but his friend **forced his hand**.* □ *We made that move in order to **force Larry's hand**.*

force one's way hap (çaj) rrugën me forcë

□ *... If we want to **force our way**, we've got to give the enemy battle.* □ *You need not **force your way** out, if you are in no hurry.*

for dear life për të shpëtuar kokën

□ *When the mountaineer felt himself slipping, he clung on to the ledge **for dear life**.*

forever (for ever and ever, forever and a day) përgjithmonë, për jetë; gjithmonë, vazhdimisht, kohë pa kohë

□ *The color TV boom is still strong though it will not keep up the pace of the last year **forever**.* □ *... With a general shaking of hands the assembly broke up **forever**.* □ *For a man who's **forever** grumbling about his electricity bills, you're pretty careless about switching off the lights when you leave a room.* □ *We waited **forever and a day** to find out who won the contest.* □ *Once he gets a drink in his hand he's here **forever and ever**.*

for example për shembull

□ *While the trumpet, the horn and the piano were being improved, and the clarinet invented, some instruments—varieties of keyboard, **for example**—were falling out of use.*

□ *I know many women who have a career and a family—Alison **for example**.*

for fear of nga frika se mos
□ *We spoke in whispers **for fear of** waking the baby.*

for free gratis
□ *Many fishmongers still give you an assortment of fishy bits and pieces **for free**. □ And what did the jolly porter tell him? He said he had the best job in the world. 'Travel anywhere in England, crossing Channel steamers, the Continent—for me, the missus and five kids, all **for free**.*

for fun/for the fun of it për qejf, për të qeshur, për shaka, për zbavitje (gallatë)
□ *I'd like to go back again some day **for fun**, say in about ten years' time, and see how it's all getting on. □ I'm learning to cook, just **for the fun of it**.*

for good (and all) përgjithmonë
□ *Alan's been away five years, but from what they say he's definitely coming home **for good**. □ If you borrow money once, you're on the slippery slope **for good and all**. □ As well as I could make out, she had come **for good**, and had no intention of ever going away.*

for good measure për më tepër; si dhe
□ *The pianist gave a long and varied recital, with a couple of encores **for good measure**. □ When we were buying the drinks for the party we bought ten bottles of red wine and, **for good measure**, ten bottles of champagne.*

for goodness/heaven's/Pete's sake(!) për Perëndi! në ke(ni) Perëndi!
□ *On meeting his friend again, Jack exclaimed: '**For Pete's sake**, I hardly recognised you after all these years!' □ Soames found her with a letter in her hand. 'That from Val?' he asked gloomily. 'What does he say?' 'He*

*says he's married,' said Winfred. 'Whom to, **for goodness' sake**?'*

for instance për shembull
□ *A warning system for earthquakes is probably worthwhile, since quite minor precautions should be able to reduce the number of casualties. **For instance** many of the 30,000 killed in the great Lisbon disaster of 1755, were buried by the collapse of the roofs of churches where they had gone for shelter. □ His many different hobbies include, **for instance**, skating and stamp collecting. □ The daily motion of the earth is very different in different parts -at the equator and at a pole, **for instance**.*

for keeps 1. përgjithmonë, për fare
□ *When the famous film star married for the fifth time, she said, 'This time it's **for keeps**.' □ Can I have it **for keeps** or do you want it back? □ He left town **for keeps**.*

2. për falje
□ *The played marbles **for keeps**.*

3. seriozisht, jo me shaka
□ *This is not a joke; it's **for keeps**. □ The policeman knew that the robber was trying to shoot him. He was playing **for keeps**.*

for lack/want of sth për mungesë të
□ *The project had to be abandoned **for lack of** funds. □ The ships were needed urgently back in England for the build-up of the army, and if they had been damaged on the beaches the whole venture might have met disaster a week later **for lack of** supplies. □ I cannot even decide whether to tell him I have spoken to you yet, or to lead him to suppose that I have deferred doing so, **for want of** opportunity for any other reason.*

for life për jetë e mot, përgjithmonë
□ *Scars of battle have marked this soldier for life.*

for my money sipas mendimit tim
□ *For my money, Ann's idea is better than Mary's.* □ *For my money it's the washing machine that takes pride of place over the deep-freeze.*

for nothing 1. kot, më kot, kot së koti
□ *I didn't tell you until I got the doctor's report: I didn't want to have you worrying for nothing.* □ *You see, Miss Wallace, I had to give you some story about our work you wouldn't feel you had come here for nothing.*
□ *'Then I had all that agony for nothing,' thought Dinny.*
2. falas, gratis
□ *There is very little art in hitch-hiking as Germaine Greer describes it. It seems rather to be one of the crudest ways of getting something for nothing.* □ *You may have these books for nothing; we give them to you as a gift.*

for once (in a way) një rast, në këtë (atë) rast
□ *On most occasions, and from most people, Isabel was pleased to hear Harold praised; but for this once she wasn't.* □ *'What on earth is the idea, Chris?' 'Oh, just a hunch, a crazy idea, I suppose. But, perhaps, you'll indulge me for once in a way.*

for one natyrisht
□ *I for one have no doubt that he's lying.* □ *He for one will never do such a thing.*

for one's (own) part nga ana ime, sipas meje, sipas mendimit tim, sa më takon mua
□ *Many people criticise Jim, but for my part, I think he has done very well.* □ *For my part, I don't mind where we eat.* □ *For my part I can*

give you definite assurance that the task assigned to me will be fulfilled ahead of schedule.

for one thing (...(and) for another thing) nga një anë ... nga ana tjetër; së pari ... së dyti; në radhë të parë ...në radhë të dytë
□ *There are lots of reasons for choosing Tony as chairman of the company: for one thing, he's worked harder than anyone else.* □ *'Are you going to give Shakespeare equal billing?' 'Why should I?' he buoyantly replies. 'For one thing, it's fairly well known that he is the author.* □ *For another thing, he hasn't got an agent.'*

for real me të vërtetë
□ *This isn't a practice game; we're playing for real.*

for sale për shitje
□ *These articles are displayed for sale in chaotic piles.* □ *She has put her house up for sale.*

for sb's benefit për të mirën e
□ *It's often necessary to be strict with children for their own benefit.*

for sb's/sth's (own) good për të mirën e
□ *Don't think I enjoy finding fault with people. I'm only talking to you like this for your own good.* □ *I'm giving you this advice for your own good.*

for sb's/sth's sake për hir të
□ *Maybe later he would realise that all she had done was for the children's sake, not her own.*
□ *'Please accept, Father,' she said, 'I'd be so proud of you.' 'I'd make a fool of myself.' 'You wouldn't. For my sake.'*

for shame! turp!
□ *You ought to be ashamed of yourself, I told them—at the first sign of intimidation you want to give in. For*

shame! I yelled at them—for shame!
□ *He picked up a handful of gravel and drew back his arm to throw at the hens. 'Stop it Patrick,' Jenny called. 'What do you think you're doing?' For shame. Leave them alone.'* □ *At which remark... Miss Caroline very properly said: 'For shame, Becky!'*

for short shkurt, shkurtimisht
□ *Her name is Philippa, but she's called 'Phil' for short.* □ *Her name is 'Frances', or 'Fran' for short.*

for show për t'u dukur
□ *She only has those books for show -she never reads them.*

for sure me siguri
□ *I don't know his age for sure, but I think he's about thirty.* □ *I think he lives there but I couldn't say for sure.* □ *Do you know that for sure?*

for that matter/for the matter of that sa i takon, lidhur me, për këtë, sa i takon kësaj çështje (pune)
□ *I don't know, and for that matter, I don't care.* □ *I don't know how old he is and, for that matter, I don't care.* □ *'Is that all the mystery you were to tell me?' '- No', said Tom: 'not all.' 'What's the rest?,' asked Martin. 'For the matter of that,' said Tom 'it's no mystery.'* □ *... he fought so long as anybody did, and followed the directions given him to the letter. For that matter, so did they all.* □ *Indeed, in New Jersey as elsewhere... I noticed and still do, for that matter, that editorially in the local newspapers, Big Business and Big Business alone, sounded the trumpet call.*

for the best për të mirë
□ *Your sister shouldn't have interfered, I agree. But she meant it for the best so I don't be too cross with her.*

for the life of one kurrësesi
□ *I cannot for the life of me*

remember her name. □ *I can't for the life of me think why he should want to give up his studies just a few weeks before his final exams.* □ *But for the life of him Bill could not imagine what that reason was.*

forlorn hope shpresë e kotë
□ *The young man thinks he may get a job here, but it is a pretty forlorn hope: there is a lot of unemployment.* □ *Going to their rescue in a rowing-boat is a bit of a forlorn hope.*

for love/for the love of sth/sb pa pagesë, pa shpërblim
□ *They're all volunteers, doing it just for the love of the thing.* □ *Well, I'd cleaned the cottage up all Friday, just for the love of the thing.*

for the moment hë për hë, tani për tani, për momentin
□ *Carry on for the moment with your own ideas and don't take any notice of your friends' criticism or advice.* □ *We're happy living in an apartment for a moment but we may want to move to a house soon.*

for the most part në tërësi, në pjesën më të madhe, në pjesën dërrmuese; kryesisht
□ *It is a very exclusive club: the members are wealthy businessmen and professional people, for the most part.* □ *Japanese TV sets are, for the most part, of excellent quality.* □ *The audience consisted for the most part of students.*

for the nonce përkohësisht; vetëm për këtë rast
□ *He let it be assumed for the nonce that he was one of the touring party.* □ *This is a very poor pen but it will do for the nonce.*

for the present hë për hë, tani për tani
□ *That, for the present, was all that Brigit could think.* □ *That will be*

enough for the present, if I need any more I will let you know.

for the time being tani për tani

□ *Evidence will be brought forward later on to show that this suggested usage agrees quite well with common usage in many ways; for the time being let us just note this new way of defying the concept.* □ *I am sorry I can tell you nothing more about this for the time being.*

foul one's (own) nest pëgër atje ku ha

□ *1972 will be remembered as a vintage year for doom merchants, the year when mankind realises that it cannot go on fouling its nest indefinitely, the year of the first United Nations conference on the environment.*

foul play 1. krim; dhunë kriminale

□ *The police suspect foul play rather than suicide.* □ *The body of an elderly man was found early this morning in the darkened doorway of a shop. According to a police statement, foul play is not suspected.*

2. mashtrim, gënjeshtër, batakçillëk

□ *He saw foul play going forward before his eyes and he felt bound to interfere.*

3. lojë e rëndë

□ *It seemed to the spectators that the referee was letting a fair amount of foul play go unchecked.* □ *Foul play in a football game is subject to penalties.*

foul up 1. prish, ngatërroj

□ *Everything was just fine until Fred came along and fouled things up.* □ *When everything is running smoothly, why must he step in and foul things up?*

2. katranos, djallos

□ *He fouled the whole play up by forgetting his part.*

3. gaboj

□ *Blue suit and brown socks! He had fouled up again.*

four corners of the earth/world, the në të katër anët e botës

□ *Former students of this school are now working in the four corners of the earth.* □ *There is only one industry here now, and that is tourism. Tourism has grown tremendously, and this place has become known in the four corners of the earth.*

frame of mind, a gjendje shpirtërore, në humor

□ *I'm not in the right frame of mind to start discussing money.* □ *He was in a cheerful frame of mind.* □ *As it chanced on this occasion, Short... was in an exceedingly jovial frame of mind.*

freak of nature gjë e çuditshme

□ *At the far end of the fairground stood the booths where dwarfs, a giant, a bearded woman, and other freaks of nature could be viewed for 20p a visit.*

free and easy i shpenguar

□ *He had a free and easy way of acting that attracted many friends.* □ *It was a very relaxing holiday: there was a very free and easy atmosphere.* □ *'I wouldn't like to call on your parents without an invitation.' 'Don't worry. They're very free and easy, and as long as you're willing to take them as you find them you'd be welcome any time.'* □ *...as for Kit, he looked at him in open-mouthed astonishment—wondering what kind of language he would address to him, if he talked in that free-and-easy manner to a notary.*

free fight, a përleshje (kacafytje, grindje) e përgjithshme

□ *By the time the bus came so many*

*people were waiting that it was **a free fight** to get on it.* □ *I thought this was to be a reasoned discussion about next year's plans. If it's going to degenerate into **a free fight**, I'm not going to stay.*

free hand 1. dorë e lirë, liri veprimi
□ *The teacher had **a free hand** in her classroom.* □ *The architect was given **a free hand** to design the house any way he liked.*
2. bollëk
□ *Tony put paint on the fence with **a free hand**.*

free of charge falas, gratis
□ *All goods are delivered **free of charge**.*

free speech liri e fjalës
□ *'What's on telly now?' 'Something about **free speech**,' Mariette said.*

free with one's money dorëshpuar, dorëdhënë, dorëlëshuar
□ *John earns more, in my opinion, than any man has a right to, but I've always found him very **free with his money** which is more than you can say of many in his position.*

fresh/new blood gjak i ri
□ *This company is badly in need of **new blood**.*

freshen oneself up freskohem
□ *I'll just go and **freshen myself up** before the interview.*

fret and fume shpreh padurim (ankth, irritim etj.)
□ *He spent ten minutes at the phone while the others **fretted and fumed**. At length he put the receiver down.* □ *I found the door open and Sadie **fretting and fuming** about the hall. 'My dear creature,' she said, 'thank heavens you've come.'*

friend in need (is a friend indeed), a shoku i mirë njihet në ditë të vështirë
□ *No, we don't see a lot of each other,*

*but I know she would always be **a friend in need**.*

frighten/scare sb to death tremb për vdekje
□ *The child was **frightened to death** by the violent thunderstorm.*

frighten sb out of his wits/frighten the life out of sb tmerroj, i kall frikën (tmerrin), i fus frikën në palcë
□ *You **frightened the life out of me/frightened me out of my wits** suddenly knocking on the window like that.*

from afar nga larg
□ *I know no other city so splendid **from afar** and so cosy from close quarters.*

from A to Z nga fillimi në fund, tërësisht, plotësisht; nga i pari tek i fundit
□ *Our carriage reached the porch units turn and we dismounted with as much ease and comfort as though we had been escorted by the whole Metropolitan Force **from A to Z** inclusive.* □ *Oh, he knew... them all **from A to Z**. He knows the subject **from A to Z**.*

from bad to worse keq e më keq
□ *We were hoping for an improvement but things have gone **from bad to worse**.* □ *The economic situation in the country is going **from bad to worse**.*

from beginning/start to end nga fillimi në fund, nga kreu në fund
□ *... a sober, clear, moving and singularly unbitter book which makes fascinating reading **from beginning to end**.*

from China to Peru kudo, gjithkund, në të gjitha vendet
□ ***From China to Peru** the transistor radio has become as necessary a part of the furniture of human life as the cooking-pot.*

from dawn/morning to/till dusk/ night nga mëngjesi deri në mbrëmje, gjithë ditën

□ *When the month of Ramadan comes round each year and Moslems have to fast from dawn to dusk, any display of energy depends upon the miraculous.*

from day to day nga dita në ditë

□ *The patient is improving from day to day.*

from first to last nga fillimi në fund, fillim e mbarim, fund e krye

□ *There is no truth whatever in the impression under which you labor. It is a delusion from first to last.*

from hand to hand dorë më dorë

□ *The box of candy was passed from hand to hand.* □ *June brought her engagement ring, and it passed from hand to hand until all the girls had admired it.* □ *Buckets of water were passed from hand to hand to put the fire out.*

from head to foot nga koka deri te këmbët, kokë e këmbë, fund e krye

□ *Every time the phone used to ring I used to shake from head to toe and felt sick in my stomach.* □ *He looked at me in return over the bar, from head to foot with a strange smile on his face.* □ *And with another explosion the water hit him from head to foot. He shook it from his face.*

from mouth to mouth gojë më gojë

□ *Rumors of various natures went still from mouth to mouth.*

from now on tash (këtej) e tutje, paskëtaj

□ *'Say Hello to Prissie, Nick,' said Fergus. 'She may be looking after you from now on.* □ *From now on you can work on your own.*

□ *From now on my address will be as follows.*

from one's heart nga zemra

□ *'I thank you from my heart,' he said.*

from pillar to post nga një vend te tjetri, gjithkund, gjithandej

□ *The escaped prisoner was hunted from pillar to post.*

from scratch nga hiçi, nga fillimi

□ *I don't know any French at all: I shall have to learn it from scratch.*

□ *Dick built a radio from scratch.*

□ *Mary already knew how to sew a little, but Jane had to start from scratch.*

from the bottom of one's heart nga fundi (nga thelbi) i zemrës (i shpirtit)

□ *'I love you. I shall always love you. You're my wife. I wouldn't have it any different.' I was speaking from the bottom of my heart.*

□ *In the office Luke and Martin were both sitting down. As Nora saw her husband she said, awkwardly, wishing from the bottom of her heart that she could let herself go.*

from the cradle to the grave nga lindja (nga djepi) deri në vdekje (varr)

□ *In olden times there was a saying that the Coop took care of you from the cradle to the grave, provided a pharmacy to delay the event, and then buried you.* □ *Jason is at your service from the cradle to the grave.* □ *I am also local agent for the never-never furniture company, a qualified midwife, a marriage broker, and undertaker. Jason is at your service from the cradle to the grave.*

from the first/from the start/from the beginning/from the outset qysh në fillim

□ *I knew from the first, that, if I could not do my work as well as any of the rest, I could not hold myself above slight and contempt.* □ *From the outset and for most of the time that Mrs Mackay was alive, the police refused finally to accept that she had been kidnapped.* □ *From the first, the Reformation had been quarrelling with the symbolism of Christianity, with all that connected it with the ancient, vanished, pagan world of Europe.* □ *The pundits and columnists have been wrong about Strauss from the beginning. Their assessment of his chances of nomination was wrong.* □ *Right from the start it was a lovely friendship. We went everywhere together.*

from the mouth of sb nga goja e

□ *My nephew entertains with so much suspicion any admonition coming from my mouth.*

from the word go qysh në fillim

□ *She knew right from the word go that it was going to be difficult.* □ *It's important to realise from the word go that broadcasters should get out and about among the people. They must take guidance from the local people.* □ *There's nowhere in the country where there's properly integrated accident service, where a seriously injured person can get absolutely first-class treatment from the word go.*

from/since time immemorial që kur s'mbahet mend, që në kohët e lashta

□ *This is a very ancient custom, which has been practised here from time immemorial.* □ *... the workshop benches, the equipment, and, indeed, the craftsmen, look as if they have been there since time immemorial.* □ *All the vegetable sedatives and narcotics, all the euphorics that grow on trees have*

been known and systematically used by human beings from time immemorial.

from time to time nga koha në kohë, herë pas here

□ *He read through the letter carefully, from time to time raising his eyebrows or emitting a long slow whistle.* □ *In the main the art of the potter has been a secular art. From time to time, however, this secular art has been placed at the service of religion.*

from top to bottom nga fillimi deri në fund; fund e majë, fund e krye; cep më cep

□ *She searched the house from top to bottom, behind sofas, in cupboards, under beds.*

from top to toe/from tip to toe nga koka te këmbët, kokë e këmbë

□ *A sweet warmth overtook Ashurst from top to toe.* □ *He was caught in the rain and so was wet from top to toe.*

full of beans/life i gjallë, aktiv, në humor të mirë, gjithë shëndet e energji

□ *John seems to have fully recovered from his illness: when I saw him, he was full of beans.* □ *After the first pint he remarked, 'You're looking full of beans, Richard. Hard work must agree with you, or something.'*

full of oneself mendjemadh, kryelartë, i duket vetja kush e di se ç'është, i pëlqen vetja

□ *I can't stand that man, he is so full of himself, always boasting and so on.* □ *His friends said he was too full of himself for what he had done.*

G

gain a livelihood siguroj jetesën
□ *'Well, well,' said the other clerk; 'we all have our various ways of gaining a livelihood...'*

gain an advantage of/on/over sb fitoj epërsi (avantazh)
□ *Absolute. Really, sir, you have the advantage of me, I don't remember ever to have had the honor.* □ *... and so **gained an advantage over** her rival.*

gain ground 1. përparoj, fitoj terren (në luftë)
□ *At last our men began to **gain ground**, forcing the enemy back towards the river.* □ *A glance behind confirmed his fears. His pursuer was **gaining ground** on him rapidly.*
2. përhapet, fiton truall (terren)
□ *His ideas are **gaining ground**.*
3. më zë (më pushton) një ndjenjë
□ *The feeling that after all she had won a sort of victory was every moment **gaining ground** in her.*
4. forcohem
□ *The sick man **gained ground** after being near to death.*
5. mësohem, ambientohem, ndjehem lirshëm me
□ *All this while I had been **gaining ground** with Mr. Rankeillor, and in proportion as I **gained ground**, gaining confidence.*

gain on/upon afrohem
□ *The runner was catching up with his rival, **gaining on** him with every step.*
□ *You'll have to drive faster—they are **gaining on** us.* □ *We were **gaining on** him towards the end of the race.*

gain one's end arrij synimin (pikësynimin)
□ *I must tell you that if you use such methods you'll never **gain your end**.*

gain sb's good graces fitoj simpatinë e
□ *During the progress of this memorable holiday, little Rawdon... has **gained the good graces** of his married and maiden aunts.*

gain sb's heart i fitoj zemrën
□ *It would be tedious... to develop the gradual approaches by which **the heart** of Richard Swiveller was **gained**.*

gain/get the upper hand (over sb) 1. fitoj (kam) epërsi; dal fitimtar; mund
□ *Our team **gained the upper hand** in the second half.* □ *After a fierce struggle we **gained the upper hand** of the enemy.*
2. kontrolloj
□ *Don't let your feelings **get the upper hand** over you.*

gain time fitoj kohë
□ *He tried to **gain time** by postponing his answer.*

game is not worth the candle, the s'e vlen barra qiranë
□ *We thought of smuggling some extra cigarettes in, but when we saw the penalties for smuggling, we decided that **the game was not worth the candle**.* □ *'What I mean is that it **isn't worth the candle**.'*

game is up/over, the ia djeg kartat (letrat) në dorë, ia zbuloj planet
□ *As soon as the police came through the door, the thief realized that **the***

game was up. □ *The game, in her opinion, was over in that little domestic establishment.* □ *'You had better be very careful. The game is up,' he said.*

game that two can play, a lojë me dy porta

□ *Sulking until you get your own way is a game that two can play, you know.* □ *You know Jack. He can't help chatting up any pretty girl he meets. It doesn't mean a thing, but if you don't like it why not show him it's a game that two can play?*

gasp for breath 1. gulçoj

□ *The low punch made him gasp for breath.*

2. mbetem gojëhapur nga habia

□ *The sheer insensitivity of his remarks leaves one gasping for breath.*

gather one's courage marr kurajo (guxim, zemër)

□ *It was difficult to speak to Minnie about this, but at last she gathered the courage.*

gather dust e ka zënë pluhuri, është harruar fare

□ *And then she played us an unfunny snatch from an old Victor Borge record that has been gathering dust on my shelves for the past 20 years.*

gather momentum fiton, merr vrull (forcë, inerci)

□ *The boulder seemed to slide almost reluctantly down the first few yards of the incline then, gaining momentum, it crashed through the sparse scrub and bounded off the rocky surfaces.*

gathered to one's fathers vdiq, shkoi me të shumtët

□ *I write to tell you that my dear old friend Jonathan, who suffered so uncomplainingly for so many years has at last been gathered to his fathers.*

gather way merr, shton shpejtësinë (anija)

□ *The steamer left the pier and slowly gathered way.* □ *A light breeze was blowing and the ship soon gathered way.*

get about 1. përhapet, qarkullon, shkon gojë më gojë

□ *I don't know how such a rumor got about. There's absolutely no truth in it.* □ *The news of his resignation soon got about.*

2. lëviz

□ *Considering his age, the old man gets about a great deal.* □ *Now that the traffic has been restricted in the center of the city, it's easier to get about.* □ *My father isn't able to get about since he had his stroke last year.*

get above oneself më rritet mendja, më hyn vetja në qejf

□ *That young man is getting above himself. He's only been in the firm two weeks and he's already telling his seniors how to do their work.* □ *She's been getting a bit above herself since winning her award.*

get abreast of shkoj (eci, vihem) krahas me

□ *As soon as the lifeboat got abreast of the foundering ship, the captain got a line aboard her and started to take the crew off.*

get abroad përhapet, qarkullon

□ *The news got abroad that the Chancellor had decided to make cuts in the VAT on some goods.*

get access to arrij, hyj

□ *The police are still not sure how the thieves get access to the safe. No damage seemed to be have been caused to the building.* □ *We realized too late that access could easily be got to stronghold by means of a long-forgotten tunnel.*

get across 1. kaloj, kapërcej, kaloj (hidhem) matanë
□ *Only half the company got across the bridge before it was blown up.*
□ *The frontier is so well guarded that no one can get across.* □ *The bridge was destroyed so we couldn't get across.*
2. transmetoj, përçoj, kumtoj
□ *The comedian didn't seem to be able to get his jokes across to his audience—they all fell flat!* □ *The teacher found it rather easy to get the ideas of the text across to the pupils.*
3. acaroj, irritoj, ngacmoj, fyej
□ *Those two men are so different in temperament that they were bound to get across each other.* □ *Be careful how you talk to Mr. Swann. He's an unpleasant man to get across.*

get ahead/ahead of eci, ia kaloj, dal mbi
□ *If you want to get ahead in life, you will have to work hard.* □ *As soon as he settled down to the routine of his new job, Alex got ahead splendidly.*
□ *By doing just a little extra homework each day, the girl got well ahead of the rest of the class.*

get a kick from/out of sth kënaqem, zbavitem, gjej kënaqësi
□ *I get a big kick from motor racing.*
□ *He gets a good deal of kick out of swimming.*

get a line on sth marr vesh, mësoj, informohem
□ *'Don't hang up, Mort. I'm calling because I got a line on your dear friend tonight.'*

get a load of/get a load of sb/sth shikoj, vërej
□ *Get a load of that chap just by the door: have you ever seen such strange clothes?* □ *Get a load of Tony's new car!*

get along 1. e nxjerr, ia dal me, jetoj me
□ *They could not possibly get along upon his wage alone.* □ *With his ninety dollars a week and her sixty they got along well enough.*
2. eci, ia çoj
□ *John's getting along in France better than he expected, considering he could hardly speak a word of French when he arrived.* □ *How is he getting along with his English?*
3. shkoj
□ *It's time we were getting along.*
□ *Well, I'd better be getting along, the train is due.*

get along/on with sb shkoj mirë me
□ *She got on well with aunt Ellen.*
□ *Her mother was quiet and good-natured—the easiest person in the world to get along with.*

get along/away with you! shporru! hiqmu sysh!
□ *'Get along with you! I don't believe you any more,' said Ona.*

get along without bëj pa, ia dal pa
□ *I don't know how Mr. Briggs gets along without domestic help in that large house.* □ *I have to get along without even proper equipment and work in a damned shack like this.*

get around/round 1. kaloj, kapërcej me sukses
□ *There seems to be no way of getting round the difficulty of keeping prices down when the cost of imports goes on rising.*
2. bëj për vete, i mbush mendjen, fitoj besimin (mbështetjen)
□ *The girl told her boyfriend that she would try and get round her father to lend them the car for the day.* □ *Mary knows how to get around her father.*
3. anashkaloj

□ *Some people try to get around the tax laws.*

4. bëhem mbarë, gjej kohë të

□ *When I finally got round to buying the Christmas cards it was too late. The shops were all sold out.*

get a move on luaj këmbët, shpejtoj, nxitoj

□ *Tell Jack to get a move on: we're going to be late.* □ *'John, get a move on, can't you?' a man's voice interrupted.* □ *'So you are back in time,' Essex said to him. 'We were about to leave. It's after one o'clock already. We'll have to get a move on.'* □ *'You'll have to get a move on if you want to get to the office in time.'*

get a rise out of sb ngacmoj pa të keq; xhindos, tërboj, e bëj si të tërbuar, e bëj të mos e përmbajë veten (të humbasë durimin)

□ *The boys get a rise out of John by teasing him about his girlfriend.* □ *'Look here! Are you trying to get a rise out of me because you won't succeed this morning?'*

get a slap in the face marr një shuplakë (goditje) të rëndë

□ *Bill assumed he was next in line for the editorship. He got a real slap in the face when they appointed an outsider.*

get at 1. arrij

□ *The bull was trying to smash the fence so that he could get at me.* □ *The book is on the top-shelf, I can't get at it.* □ *Always keep medicine where children can't get at them.*

2. mësoj, gjej, zbuloj

□ *The members of the official board of inquiry had great difficulty in getting at the truth of the matter: there seemed to be a conspiracy of silence.* □ *What I'm trying to get at is whether you want to marry the girl for her*

money or because you love her.

3. kuptoj, gjej (nxjerr) kuptimin e

□ *This book is very hard to get at.* □ *I could not get at the true meaning of the passage.* □ *It is not easy to get at the meaning of every idiom in English.*

4. dal, aludoj tërthorazi

□ *'I don't know what you're getting at exactly, but if you're suggesting that my brother is dishonest you'd better think again.* □ *'Don't you see what I'm getting at? If we shared an apartment we could each live more cheaply.*

5. kritikoj; i bie më qafë

□ *Olive is always getting at her husband because he doesn't keep the garden tidy.* □ *Whenever his mother-in-law started talking about men who drink too much he had a feeling he was being got at.*

6. ndikoj (me mjete të pandershme)

□ *The judge said that it was obvious from the man's behavior in the witness-box that he had been got at.*

get a view of shoh, vështroj, sodit

□ *He fanned away the smoke of his pipe, that he might get a better view of me, and soon recognized me with great delight.*

get away (as) clean as a whistle largohem pa lënë gjurmë (pa u vënë re, pa u kapur)

□ *I heard a door click, and then he was coming along the garden path, carrying one quite small suitcase. 'Got away clean as whistle,' he said chuckling.* □ *Despite the tip-off the police arrived too late. The bank-raiders got away as clean as a whistle, leaving nothing behind but an empty safe.*

get away (from) 1. largohem, iki, shkoj

□ *It was nice of you to invite me to tea tomorrow, but I'm afraid I can't get away from the office.* □ *It was impossible for us to get away earlier.* □ *I must get away before morning.*
2. shpëtoj
□ *Two of the prisoners got away from their captors.*
3. heq, shkëpus, rrëmbej
□ *'How are we going to get the ball away from the dog?'* □ *'You'll never get Doris away from Madrid now. She's fallen in love with the place.*
get away with 1. vjedh e iki
□ *Thieves raided the bank and got away with a lot of money.*
2. kaloj pa u ndëshkuar
□ *'Don't side with him, David, because if you side with him he knows he can get away with it.'*
get away with murder shpëton (lihet) pa kapur, pa ndëshkuar (edhe pse ka bërë diçka të keqe)
□ *That child is very badly behaved: her parents let her get away with murder.* □ *With that innocent, smiling face of his, he could get away with murder.* □ *Tony is scolded if he's late with his homework, but Robert gets away with murder.*
get a word in (edgeways/edgewise) them një fjalë
□ *My wife and her sister both talk too much; when they get together I can't get a word in edgeways.* □ *When Pickering starts shouting nobody can get a word in edgeways.* □ *The little boy listened to the older students and finally got in a word.*
get a word out of sb nxjerr një fjalë nga
□ *As for that architect chap, he was as gloomy as a bear with a sore head. Winifred could barely get a word out of him.*

get back 1. kthehem
□ *'When Tom gets back, please tell him that Jill phoned.'* □ *Johnny's mother told him that he was to get back home before dark.*
2. largohem
□ *The police had great difficulty in making the curious crowd get back and let the ambulance through.* □ *'Get back! There's a bomb in this building!*
3. kthej
□ *If you take Mary out for a drive you must promise to get her back for her music lesson.*
□ *I'm afraid we are very busy and can't get your camera back for this evening.*
4. marr sërish
□ *'Don't lend Bill your umbrella! If you do, you'll never get it back.'*
get back at sb marr hak, hakmerrem
□ *He hated meanness, and seems to consider it his duty to get back at those guilty of this.* □ *Civil servants have no way of getting back at individuals who criticize them, so they sometimes take it out of the public in general.*
get back to rifilloj, i kthehem
□ *The student was glad to get back to his books after a vacation that had seemed too long.* □ *But to get back to the question of your immediate plans. What are you doing next week?'*
get behind (with) mbetem prapa me
□ *Owing to his illness, Peter couldn't keep up with the rest of the class and got badly behind.* □ *Mr. Jones got behind with the payment on his car and had to surrender it to the garage.*
get blood from/out of a stone nxjerr dhjamë nga pleshti, nxjerr ujë nga guri
□ *It's no use asking your father for a*

159

*loan. You can't **get blood out of a stone**. □ Trying to borrow money from Jim is like **getting blood out of a stone**.*

get busy filloj nga puna

□ *We've only got an hour to do the job —we had better **get busy**. □ I thought I told you to clear up these papers. Come on now, **get busy**.*

get by 1. kaloj

□ *There was such a crowd outside the shop window that the young woman with the pram couldn't **get by**. □ I moved away from the doorway to let her **go by**. □ There's scarcely enough room for the car to **get by**.*

2. pranohem, kaloj pa u vënë re, pa u kritikuar

□ *John didn't possess a dinner-jacket, but he was told that he would **get by** in a dark suit.*

3. ia dal

□ *The old lady never seemed to have much money, but somehow she managed to **get by** though I don't know how. □ How does she **get by** on such a small salary?*

get by heart mësoj përmendsh

□ *He has **got** this poem **by heart**.*

get cold feet trembem, frikësohem, më dridhen leqet e këmbëve

□ *To this day I don't know how genuine that sudden bit of urgent business was; perhaps he just **got cold feet** and wanted me to go ahead and soften things up. □ Make up your mind—now decide to stay, you start **getting cold feet**. □ He... urged me to go ahead, not to faint or **get cold feet**.*

get control over vë nën kontroll

□ *The horse bolted out but the rider soon **got control over** it.*

get cracking shpejtoj, luaj këmbët (duart)

□ *There's a lot to be done, so let's **get**

*cracking. □ Come on, you guys, let's **get cracking**! □ Let's **get cracking**: we have ten miles to walk before lunch.*

get down 1. zbres

□ *The cat climbed to the top of the tree and then became afraid to **get down**. □ A man escaped from the burning building by **getting down** a ladder. □ I **got down** to Yarmouth in the evening, and went to the inn.*

2. marr shënim, shkruaj

□ *I didn't **get down** every word, but I certainly **got** a good deal of the conversation **down**. □ 'Make sure you **get** his confession **down**, and his signature at the bottom of it.*

3. gëlltis, kapërdij

□ *The little boy **got** his medicine **down** with the help of a spoonful of jam. □ I felt better yesterday, but I'm finding it hard to **get** food **down**.*

4. ngrihem (çohem) nga tavolina

□ *The children sat through the meal in complete silence and spoke only to ask permission to **get down**. □ 'Now, **down** you **get**!'*

5. përkulem, përgjunjem

□ *She **got down** on her knees and prayed that her husband would survive the storm.*

6. brengos, dëshpëroj, shkurajoj, ligështoj, shkaktoj depresion

□ *This wet weather is **getting** me **down**. □ Don't let the incident **get** you **down** too much.*

7. ul

□ *'Will you give me a hand to **get** this drunk **down**.' □ You'll never **get** the piano **down** the stairs.*

get down to i hyj (i përvishem, i shtrohem, i vihem)

□ *'Look! You'll never finish that job unless you forget everything else and **get down to** it.' □ Their eldest son is* returning from Britain to Australia for good, to **get down to** managing the estate. □ The holidays are over; we must **get down to** work again.

get down to brass tacks vij te thelbi i çështjes

□ *'It's time George stopped all this theorizing and **get down to brass tacks**. What we want to know is how much the job will cost, not how scientific the method is going to be.* □ *We had a few minutes of polite conversation, but then he **got down to brass tacks**, and asked me what salary I would want if I worked for him.*

get down to business i shtrohem punës

□ *The two men had a couple of drinks together, talked about their families and their holidays for a while, and finally **got down to business**.* □ *'I hope you don't mind if we **get down to business** straight away, as I've got to catch the four o'clock train.'*

get even with sb marr hak

□ *The prisoner swore he would **get even with** the judge who had sentenced him.* □ *During all my childhood I listened to her hating him and planning to **get even with** him. I was frightened of my mother. She was so bitter and unforgiving.* □ *They were trying to rob him. He would **get even with** somehow, he would creep up when they least expected it.*

get going 1. nisem (për udhë); nis (një punë)

□ *If we want to arrive on time, we'd better **get going**.* □ *The new hotel is open but it hasn't really **got going** yet, and won't until summer season.* □ *Let's **get going**. It's almost supper time.*

2. nis, organizoj, vë në funksionim (lëvizje)

□ *I'm sure with all these newcomers*

to the district we should be able to **get** the Football Club **going** again in the village this winter.

get hold of 1. kuptoj

□ *I cannot **get hold of** the meaning of this sentence.*

2. kap, zë, shtrëngoj, rrok, marr

□ *I threw the rope and he **got hold of** it.* □ *She seldom **got hold of** the newspaper, but she found something that she was certain Annie would like to see.*

3. kontaktoj, hyj në lidhje me

□ *'Where have you been? I've been trying to **get hold of** you all day.'* □ *I've been trying to **get hold of** her for days but she's never at home.*

4. gjej, shtie në dorë

□ *Do you know where I can **get hold of** a second-hand carpet?* □ *Little children sometimes **get hold of** sharp knives and cut themselves.*

get (hold of) the wrong end of the stick keqkuptoj, e marr një gjë mbrapsht (tjetër për tjetër)

□ *I'm afraid you've **got hold of the wrong end of the stick**; that man over there is not my brother.* □ *You've **got the wrong end of the stick**; he doesn't owe me money, I owe him!*

get home (to) 1. arrij në shtëpi

□ *'What time did you **get home** last night?'*

2. bëj të qartë; qëlloj (godas) në shenjë

□ *The TV program **got home** all right. The next morning, the papers were full of it.* □ *That remark of you about Sally **got home**.* □ *We left the meeting confident that we had at last **got** the essential part of our proposal **home** to the more conservative members of the Council.*

get in 1. hyj, futem

□ *He nearly knocked me over in his*

eagerness to get in the house. □ *I walked to the van, got in and drove away.*
2. vij, arrij
□ *When do you normally get in from work?* □ *The train got in five minutes early.*
3. mbledh (të lashtat etj)
□ *The farmers were delighted to get the hay in so early in the year.* □ *'Get the washing in quick! It's raining.'*
□ *The firm went bankrupt because their bad debts couldn't be got in.*
4. thërras
□ *When he saw how ill his mother was he told the doctor he would like to get a specialist in.*
□ *We'll have to get a plumber in to mend that burst pipe.*
5. ble
□ *Remember to get in some beers for this evening!* □ *We must remember to get some more coffee in.*
6. pranoj (në shkollë, universitet etj.)
□ *He took the entrance exam but didn't get in.*

get in contact/touch with hyj në kontakt (lidhje) me
□ *I've been intending to get in contact with you about a plan I had for opening a small shop as a side-line.*
□ *Bill and Sally miss each other badly. Somebody ought to get them in touch with each other again.*

get in/into sb's hair ngacmoj vazhdimisht
□ *Harry gets in my hair: he's always interrupting me.*

get in on the/sb's act hyj sa për figurë (sa për t'u dukur); hyj (futem) në valle
□ *She didn't want anything to do with organising the party until she saw it would be a success: now she is trying to get in on the act.*

get in (to) a jam bie ngushtë, bie në vështirësi (në pozitë të vështirë)
□ *He says if Roger has got in a jam he's only got himself to blame.*

get in the way (of) pengoj
□ *They say we'd just get in the way if we helped.*

get into 1. hyj, futem
□ *The bus was so full I couldn't get into it.* □ *He had only to walk up the avenue and read the signs, or get into a street car to obtain full information.*
2. fus, vesh
□ *At the end of six-hour flight, I couldn't get my feet into my shoes as they had swollen so much.* □ *I can't get into these shoes! They are three sizes too small.*
3. depërton
□ *The molten lava got into every nook and cranny on its downward path.*
□ *Spiders seem to get into every corner of the woodwork. They're everywhere.*
4. përftoj
□ *The children got into the bad habit of switching on the television as soon as they came in from school.*
5. angazhohem, i futem
□ *He was determined to get into politics.*

get into a fix ngatërrohem keq, futem në vështirësi (telashe)
□ *George has got himself into a fix by arranging absent-mindedly to take two girls out on the same evening.* □ *Trust him to get into a fix with his landlord; he never has been able to organize his finances.*

get into a mess hyj (futem) në telashe (në pozitë të vështirë)
□ *This young Bossiney, he's got himself into a mess. I know how it would be.*

get into a muddle hutohet, i turbullohet mendja, e humb toruan

□ *The old lady **gets** **into** **a** **muddle** trying to work the video.*

get into a rage inatosem, tërbohem, marr flakë

□ *'You needn't **get into a rage**,' he said. 'If I'm willing to put up with it, I suppose you needn't cry out.'*

get into a scrape futem (bie) në telashe (në pozitë të vështirë)

□ *The young man confessed to his father that he had **got into** a bit of a **scrape**: he had lost a lot of money through gambling.* □ *... and I knew I should **get into scrapes** there, if she put old Bounderby's pipe out.*

get into debt hyj (futem) në borxh

□ *They were borrowing money from Marija and eating up her bank account and they were even **getting into debt** to Tanasrius and letting him impoverish himself.*

get into deep water(s) bie në vështirësi, bie ngushtë, jam në hall (siklet) të madh

□ *He looked and looked, and the longer the situation lasted the more difficult it became. The little shop-girl was **getting into deep water**.* □ *'We'd better not talk about starting a new company before the first one is operating successfully, or we'll be **getting into deep water**.'*

get into difficulty ndesh (has) vështirësi, bie ngushtë

□ *Whenever I have not had you, Agnes, to advise and approve in the beginning, I have seemed to go wild, and to **get into** all sorts of **difficulty**.*

get into hot water futem në telashe të mëdha

□ *The young clerk **got into hot water** for handing over the documents without obtaining a receipt.* □ *'You'll be **getting** yourself and me **into hot water** if you take the car out again. The insurance doesn't cover a second driver.'*

get into one's stride futem në ritmin normal (në ritmin e duhur), ec me hap normal

□ *She found the job difficult at first, but now she's really **getting into her stride**.* □ *When the preacher **got into his stride** it became obvious that we were in for a long sermon.* □ *Now that I am **getting into my stride**, I think I can manage to do even more than ten pages of translation work in one day.*

get into sb's hands/the hands of sb bie në dorë (në duar të)

□ *A good dictionary has **got into my hands**.* □ *David tried hard not to **get into the hands** of the Murdstones.*

get into the habit of doing sth e kam bërë zakon, më është bërë zakon (shprehi)

□ *I've **got into the habit** of switching on the TV as soon as I get home.* □ *His frozen thumb gave him a great deal of trouble. While watching by the lake he **got into the habit** of taking his mitten off and thrusting the hand inside his shirt so as to rest the thumb in the warmth of his armpit.*

get into the way of mësohem, më bëhet shprehi

□ *Driving a car is easy once you've **got into the way of** it.*

get into trouble futem në telashe, bie në hall

□ *So Jurgis thought, and so he spoke, in his bold, free way; very much to his surprise, he found that it had a tendency to **get** him **into trouble**.* □ *You are just the type that **gets** the aged **into trouble**... Dinny.*

get it e pësoj, e ha keq
□ *You'll get it if your father finds you still in bed at this time.*
get it all together 1. e kam mendjen në vend
□ *You've sure got it all together, haven't you?*
2. mbledh veten
□ *A few minutes after the burglars left, he got it all together and called the police.*
3. organizohet, vihet nën kontroll
□ *She would be a very good player if she could get it all together*
get it in the neck/where the chicken gets the chopper e ha keq, e ha pas qafe
□ *They'll get it in the neck in real earnest one of these days.* □ *You sit here in Paris and send home some yards of silk and cases of cognac while we get it in the neck.* □ *That's another lesson of my life—the day anybody gets the whole story, you get it where the chicken got the chopper.*
get it into one's head fus në kokë, shtie në mendje, kuptoj qartë
□ *I can't get it into my son's head that he will have to work harder.* □ *'I wish you would get it into your head, once and for all, that I'm not made of money.'* □ *How did Tom get it into his head that Medicine is an easy profession?* □ *How it got into his head, I can't say; I can only say that it never got out.*
get nowhere s'është gjëkundi, nuk e ka punën në vijë, s'është asgjëkundi
□ *He was getting nowhere with his homework until his sister helped him.* □ *Seeing that he was getting nowhere with the experiment he decided to exchange notes with his colleagues.* □ *Philip's doing fine but George, the other son—well, he's getting nowhere.*

get off 1. zbres
□ *I'm getting off the train at the next station.* □ *Toward evening he saw an old lady getting off a street car and helped her down with her umbrellas and bundles.*
2. heq, zhvesh
□ *Her finger has swollen so much that she couldn't get her ring off.* □ *I can't get off my gloves; they are so tight.* □ *He cannot get his coat off.*
3. nisem, shkoj
□ *'What time are you leaving tomorrow?' 'We hope to get off before seven o'clock.'* □ *He was very busy all day, but got off by the evening train.*
4. dërgoj (me postë)
□ *He eventually got his letter off.* □ *We ought to get a cable off to him immediately.*
5. i shpëtoj (ndëshkimit)
□ *Considering his record, he was lucky to get off with a six-month sentence.* □ *It was her youth that got her off, not her innocence.*
6. shpëtoj (në një aksident)
□ *Fortunately the two cars did not crash head on, so Bill got off with nothing worse than a bad fright.* □ *The advanced party was ambushed but got off relatively lightly. They suffered only one killed and four wounded.*
7. iki, largohem
□ *I told them to get off the university playing fields.* □ *A cop would tell the noisy kids to get off the streets.*
8. vë në gjumë, më zë gjumi
□ *She got the baby off to sleep by rocking it.* □ *I had great difficulty getting off to sleep last night.*
9. lë bisedën (diskutimin) rreth një teme; ndryshoj muhabet
□ *Please can we get off the subject of dieting?*

get/start off on the right/wrong foot (with sb) e nis mirë (keq) me; e nis mbarë (ters) me

□ *The new student started off on the wrong foot with the teacher by answering back rudely.* □ *Sally and I got off on the wrong foot: I said that I hated dogs, not realising that she was a dog lover.*

get off easy shpëtoj me pak gjë, me dënim të lehtë

□ *Those ill-behaved students got off easy: the headmaster just gave them a warning.* □ *The children who missed school to go to the fair got off easy.*

get/go off scot-free dal pa lagur, pa u ndëshkuar

□ *Those criminals were not punished at all: they got off scot-free.* □ *If we could do that, she might go scot-free for aught I cared.*

get off the ground nis (fillon) të avancojë (të përparojë, të vihet në jetë)

□ *John has an idea for a new tennis club, but I don't know if it will ever get off the ground.*

□ *Our plans for a party didn't get off the ground because no one could come.*

get one's bearings orientohem

□ *No lights. A kind of clammy dark that stunned them. They stood still a moment to get their bearings, and then edged down along the wall, towards the dais.*

get one's dander up/gets one's Irish up nxeh; nxehem

□ *The boy got his dander up because he couldn't go to the store.* □ *The children get the teacher's back up when they make a lot of noise.* □ *...You've fair got my dander up. Now it's no use to bandy words.*

get oneself into shape vij (sjell) në formë

□ *I've been jogging a lot to get myself into shape.*

get one's fingers burnt digjem, e pësoj keq

□ *He got his fingers badly burnt dabbling in the stock-market.*

get one's hand in sth ia marr dorën

□ *You've got to learn to cane chairs, so the warden says... You're supposed to do ten of those a day. We won't count the next few days, though, until you get your hand in.* □ *You'll get your hand in sooner or later.*

get one's Irish (monkey) up nxehem, inatosem, zemërohem

□ *Come, come, don't get your monkey up for nothing.*

get one's knife into sb dëmtoj rëndë nga inati

□ *Walpole. ... Here: you'd better let me write the names down for you: you're to get them wrong... The Newspaper Man. Oh, I say: you have got your knife into us, haven't you? Walpole. I wish I had: I'd make a better man of you.*

get one's own back marr hak, hakmerrem

□ *If Kate ever smacked her little brother she knew that somehow he would get his own back—perhaps by scribbling all over one of her drawings or breaking one of her china dogs.* □ *Higgins... It is you who have hit me. You have wounded me to the heart. Liza (thrilling with hidden joy) I'm glad. I've got a little of my own back, anyhow.* □ *That is the man who dismissed me from my job: some day I'm going to get my own back on him.*

get/have one's own way bëj sipas kokës, bëj si dua (më pëlqen)

□ *He should not be allowed to get his own way. Its high time we call him to account.* □ *And arouse perhaps from* old Jolyon's perception of the quiet tenacity of the young man, of the secret doubt whether he could **get his own way** with him.

get one's rag out nxehem, inatosem

□ *'Now keep your hair on, Bill! There's no need to **get your rag out** every time Doris comes home late. She's a good girl and you must trust her.'*

get one's second wind marr frymë përsëri; e marr veten, rifitoj fuqinë, gjallërohem sërish

□ *I often feel sleepy after supper and then I **get my second wind** later in the evening.* □ *I was hoping my aunt had come to the end of her tirade, but no, she had just paused to **get her second wind**.* □ *Jim expressed a desire to go swimming. Tony had been talking to Dave, and I was just **getting my second wind**.*

get one's teeth into merrem (angazhohem) seriozisht, punoj i përqëndruar, jepem i tëri pas

□ *It was obvious that being put in complete charge of the office gave her something to **get her teeth into**.* □ *I don't like my new job at all. There doesn't seem to be anything that I can **get my teeth into**.* □ *The old chap should find that Charles was not to be defied, that when he **got his teeth into** a thing, he did not let it go.* □ *Most actors like the part of Hamlet, because it is a part you can **get your teeth into**.*

get on like a house on fire shkoj shumë mirë, shkoj grurë (mjaltë)

□ *It was a perfect marriage. They **got on like a house on fire**.* □ *'...We got on together like a house on fire... I think we'd make a pretty good team.'*

get on one's feet mëkëmbem, marr veten

□ *After the recent unrest the car industry will need time to **get on its feet** again.* □ *He rented a cheap room in a semi-respectable neighbourhood because he wanted to keep out of the run of intellectual life and hide until he could **get on his feet**.*

get on one's hind legs ngrihem, çohem në këmbë

□ *Soames... gathered that Alichael was to **get on to his hind legs** in the House at the first opportunity.* □ *Get on your hind legs and do some work!*

get on sb's nerves i ngacmoj, i ngre nervat

□ *Children **get on** their parents' nerves by being wakeful at night.* □ *'Is this a moment to **get on my nerves**, Charles, with your outrageous expressions?* □ *Tony and Bill discussed the idea of sharing an apartment but sensibly decided that, in view of their differing tastes and habits, they would soon **get on each other's nerves**.*

get on the high horse mbaj hundën përpjetë, mbahem me të madh

□ *'She's drawn herself up all stiff and rigid now, just like her mother. If she knew how much like her mother she looks and how much I hate Ma Rothwell I don't think she'd risk **getting on her high horse** so much.'*

get on the stick luaj duart, i përvishem punës

□ *All right, man, let's **get on the stick**.*

get on the wrong side of sb zemëroj, mërzis, krijoj marrëdhënie jo të mira me

□ *The unfortunate girl **got on the wrong side of** her mother-in-law from the start by refusing her offer of some old curtains.* □ *I would advise you not to **get on the wrong side of** Smith. He can be very awkward and* *is capable of making life very uncomfortable for you.*

get on to 1. kontaktoj, lidhem (me telefon etj.)

□ *If the fire station had been **got on to** at once, the hotel might have been saved.* □ *If you wish to lodge a complaint you'd better **get on to** the manager.*

2. gjej, gjurmoj, zbuloj

□ *The murder squad followed every bit of information and eventually **got on to** the wanted man's trail in a remote area of Scotland.* □ *The secret service **got on to** the enemy agent shortly after he arrived in the country and watched his every move.*

3. kuptoj, marr vesh

□ *When June **got on to** the real reason for her husband being 'kept late for the office,' it was not long before the whole affair was out in the open.*

4. kaloj në

□ *'Now that we've cleared up those necessary routine matters we can **get on to** what we've all been looking forward to.*

get on with 1. kaloj (shkoj) mirë, shkoj në harmoni

□ *'How do you think I shall **get on with** my mother?' 'Of course, you and your mother will get on capitally.'*

2. vazhdoj me

□ *'Put that novel away and **get on with** your work!'* □ *'Excuse me if I **get on with** this letter, but the post goes in twenty minutes. Then we'll have a cup of tea and a chat.*

go on without bëj pa

□ *How will Mr. Andrew **get on without** a housekeeper? He's never had to look after himself before.*

get out/out of 1. dal, largohem

□ *It's easy to get into a good seat at the theatre, but not so easy to **get out** if you want to leave early.* □ *As it is raining, I cannot **get out** for a walk.*

2. botoj, nxjerr (nga shtypi)

□ *Will we **get** the dictionary **out** by the end of the year?* □ *I **got out** the chess board and arranged the pieces.*

3. flas, shqiptoj, nxjerr nga goja

□ *The woman was in such a state of shock after the accident that she couldn't **get** a word **out**.* □ *Although the old man was deeply moved, he nevertheless managed to **get out** a short speech in which he thanked everyone for his retirement present.* □ *He managed to **get out** a few words of thanks.*

4. del, zbulohet (një e fshehtë etj.)

□ *Somehow the news **got out** that the film star was in the hotel, and a crowd gathered outside in the hope of seeing him.* □ *The secret soon **got out**.*

5. lë, pres, heq dorë

□ *'Can't you **get** this child **out of** the habit of repeating everything I say?'* □ *Smoking is a habit he can't **get out of**.* □ *I should **get out of** that bad habit if I were you.*

6. shmang

□ *Her sons were experts at **getting out of** hard work.* □ *I wish I could **get out of** that meeting.* □ *Don't try to **get out of** your duties.*

7. del, rrjedh

□ *'I don't know how the acid **got out**. The battery isn't broken, and it hasn't been moved.*

□ *The villagers were terrified when they heard that the lion had **got out of** its cage.*

8. nxjerr jashtë

□ *We had to find some way of **getting** the nurse **out of** the house for a few minutes so that we could talk freely.*

9. nxjerr, fitoj, siguroj

□ *'Don't imagine that I'm going to **get***

*a huge profit **out of** this deal. I'm probably going to lose money on it.'*
10. nxjerr (një pohim etj.)

□ *I held my breath. I had to step carefully now if I was to **get out of** him the full confession for which I thirsted; and as I inhaled slowly I could smell Hugo's thoughts.*

get out of bed on the wrong side/get up on the wrong side of the bed çohem (ngrihem) mahmur

□ *'What is the matter with Percy? He's cursing at everyone this morning.' 'I don't know. He must have **got out of bed on the wrong side**, or something.* □ *You must have **got out of bed on the wrong side** to be so cross about so small a matter.* □ *Bill must have **got up on the wrong side of the bed** today: he has been very nasty to me all day.*

get out of control del nga kontrolli

□ *Inflation has **got out of control.***

get out of hand del nga kontrolli, del dore

□ *I could see that the children were **getting out of hand** because of my presence, so I said goodbye and left.* □ *He tried to expand the firm too quickly. His staff did not have enough experience, production **got out of hand**, and he went bankrupt.* □ *The football fans have **got** completely **out of hand**.* □ *Unless you take James in hand now, he will **get out of hand** when he's older and will refuse to obey you.*

get out of one's mind/head heq nga mendja

□ *I wish I could **get** the picture of that awful accident **out of my head**.* □ *You must try to **get** your work **out of your mind**.* □ *'If you think I'm going to pay all your debts, you can **get** the idea **out of your head** now, because I'm*

not.* □ *Try as he would, Andrew could not **get** Christine **out of his mind**.*

get out of sb's sight heq sysh

□ *I'm going to **get out of your sight** as soon as I can get a bit of money in my pocket.* □ *'I wish you would **get** these quarrelling kids **out of my sight** for an hour or two.'* □ *'**Get out of my sight**, you wretch! I never want to set eyes on you again.'*

get/be out of one's depth është (del) jashtë aftësive të dikujt (për të kuptuar diçka)

□ *You are **getting out of my depth**. I don't understand a word you are saying.* □ *To speak the truth, sir, I don't understand you at all. I cannot keep up the conversation, because it has **got out of my depth**.* □ *When they start talking about economics I'm **out of my depth**.*

get out of order prishet

□ *The watch has **got out of order**.*

get out of sb's /the way heq, largoj nga udha; hap udhën

□ *'If you don't **get out of the way**, you're liable to be knocked down by a bicycle or something.* □ *'If your father comes home drunk, **get** the little children **out of the way** before he starts hitting them.'* □ *'Once I've **got** this pile of markings **out of the way**, I'll come for a walk with you.* □ *'**Get out of the way**,' the Colonel shouted and pushed him.*

get over 1. kaloj, kapërcej, hidhem matanë

□ *'How did the cattle manage to **get over** the road?* □ *We **got** ourselves safely **over** the wall.*

2. kaloj, shërohem, marr veten

□ *I'm glad to hear you have **got over** your cold.* □ *He had a bad illness, but he has **got over** it.*

3. kaloj, kapërcej (një vështirësi etj.)

□ *The negotiators had considerable difficulty in **getting over** the linguistic problems in the drawing-up of an agreed statement.* □ *In a week Jurgis **got over** his sense of helplessness and bewilderment in the rail mill.*

4. përshkoj, mbuloj (një largësi)

□ *The horse **got over** the distance in twenty minutes.* □ *The troops **got over** a wide area in their march.*

5. sqaroj, transmetoj

□ *She didn't really **get** her meaning **over** to her audience.* □ *The lecturer, though he knew his subject inside out, was quite incapable of **getting** anything useful **over** to the students.*

get rid of heq qafe

□ *Though I quite understand that the purpose of this announcement was to **get rid of** me, I have no distinct remembrance whether it pleased or frightened me.* □ *'Give him a sovereign, Hector, and **get rid of** him.'* □ *Some day we shall have to **get rid of** all that rubbish in the back garden.*

get round 1. mbuloj

□ *The runners **got round** the first lap in just under sixty-one seconds.*

2. bind, i kthej mendjen

□ *She knows how to **get round** her father.*

get sb in a (fine) pickle vë në pozitë të vështirë, fus në siklet

□ *'Tell me about him,' she urged. 'Perhaps I'll **get myself in a pickle**.' Martin debated humorously for a moment. 'Suppose you tell me first?'*

get sb into a corner fus në rrugë pa krye (në qorrsokak)

□ *At this difficult point of the conversation Bob gave in, and changing the subject to hard-bake: always his last resource when he found his little friend **getting him into a corner**.*

get sb into a hole vë në pozitë të vështirë, fus në siklet

□ *'Look here! Say you come to me and I advanced it... I've **got you into a hole**, and I'd like to get you out of it.'*

get/put sb's back up nxeh, zemëroj, i ngre nervat

□ *His offhand manner **put my back up**.* □ *'That's the kind of lie that **gets my back up**,' said Emery flushing.*

get sb's blood up nxeh, i nxeh (i ndez) gjakrat

□ *His insolent manner really **got my blood up** and for two pins I would have punched him on the nose.*

get sb's goat zemëroj, inatos

□ *What **gets his goat** about Desert is the look of his face. It is a deuced strange face.* □ *'All of you are against me. None of you had a good word for me when I was down and out, and now it **gets your goat** to see me make good.'*

□ *'I want to know what's the meaning of the expression '**got his goat**'?' 'Oh, raised his dander.'*

get sb under hand vë nën kontroll, bëj zap

□ *We can... **get him under hand** before he has the time to withdraw.*

get sb wrong keqkuptoj dikë

□ *'Clever, aren't you?' he said in a very unfriendly way, 'but we won't rest until we clear all this up.' 'Look,' I pleaded, as if about to sob my socks off because he'd **got me wrong**.*

get sth off one's chest shfrej, i zbraz (i them) të gjitha

□ *If you have any complaints, **get them off your chest** now.* □ *You're obviously worried about something; why not **get it off your chest**?*

get sth right/straight e kuptoj qartë (saktë, mirë)

□ *I want you to explain properly why*

Mira should have done a thing like that. I must get it straight, Joe, I must. □ *I feel I could stand if I could get it straight.* □ *Let's get one thing straight—I give the orders round here, OK?* □ *Now let's get this right before we pass on to the next point.*

get the ax 1. pushohem nga puna
□ *Poor June got the ax at the office yesterday.*
2. përjashtohem nga shkolla (për kopje)
□ *Joe got caught cheating on his final exam and he got the ax.*

get the best of mund
□ *Our team got the best of the visitors in the last quarters.* □ *'It's too bad, daughter,' he said quietly after a moment. 'I'm letting my anger get the best of me.'* □ *David wanted to study till midnight, but sleepiness got the best of him.*

get the best of it/the deal/the bargain fitoj, përfitoj, dal i fituar (në pazarllëk)
□ *I gave my concert ticket to Jim, but it seems that it was a very poor concert, so I got the best of the bargain.*

get the better of fitoj, mund, mposht
□ *She always gets the better of our quarrels.* □ *In the boxing match, Tony got the better of Jim, probably because Tony was stronger.* □ *'His feelings will soon get the better of it..'* □ *'Now and then his impatience would get the better of him, and he would try to get up.'*

get the bird 1. pushohem nga puna
□ *'When you were ill,' he said, 'I stole for you. I got the bird for it.'*
2. pritem me britma (fishkëllima etj.)
□ *It was a poor performance and the actors got the bird.* □ *The comedian got the bird.*

get the feel of sth mësohem, familiarizohem, ia marr dorën

□ *You haven't got the feel of the gears in this car yet.* □ *If you keep practising, you'll soon get the feel of it.* □ *He drove the car carefully at first until he got the feel of the controls.*

get the hang of sth mësoj, përvetësoj përdorimin e, ia marr dorën
□ *I'm trying to get the hang of the new telephone system.* □ *I have been trying to get the hang of this new electric typewriter.* □ *This machine looks very complicated, but you'll soon get the hang of it.*
2. kuptoj
□ *I didn't quite get the hang of his argument. 'One feels at sea coming home into all this.'* □ *'You? You get the hang of things so quick.'* □ *She began to get the hang of those little things.*

get the jitters nervozohem, bëhem nervoz
□ *I always get the jitters before I go on stage.*

get/take the measure of sb vlerësoj aftësitë (karakterin) e dikujt
□ *It took the tennis champion a few games to get the measure of his opponent.* □ *Lucy made no reply. She got the measure of that creature upon the sofa.*

get the message kuptoj, marr vesh
□ *When they saw their host appearing in his pyjamas, the guests who had stayed too long finally got the message.*

get the sack pushohem nga puna
□ *I suppose I have really got the sack.* □ *John got the sack at the factory last week.* □ *When the big company went bankrupt, thousands of workers got the sack.*

get the short end of the stick/deal dal i humbur
□ *My partner cheated me, but it was*

only later that I found I'd got the shortened end of the deal.

get/have the whip hand of sb kam pushtet të plotë mbi

□ *Their opponents had the whip hand and it was useless to resist.* □ *You were at my mercy. I had got the whip hand of you.*

get/have the wind up trembem, frikësohem

□ *When he saw the height of the mountain, one of the party got the wind up and went home.* □ *I happened to see his face in the sideboard glass as I went out. He's got the wind up all right.*

get/have the worst of it dështoj, mundem, pësoj humbje (disfatë)

□ *The dog had been fighting and had obviously got the worst of it.* □ *So far, Alice felt, she was getting the worst of the conversation. She changed the subject.* □ *'You know,' he said, 'I think I'm going to get the worst of it down there.'*

get through 1. kaloj nëpër

□ *You would wonder how such a large animal could get through such a small hole.* □ *The woman was so stout that she could not get through the door.* □ *The small fish got through the net.*

2. lidhem (me telefon)

□ *'Hello, Hello! Is that the doctor?—He got through at last.'*

3. kryej, përmbush, përfundoj, mbaroj, i jap fund

□ *My new secretary is very quick; she gets through a lot of work in a morning.* □ *As soon as I get through with my work, I'll join you.*

4. kaloj (provimin)

□ *I got through the written papers but failed in the oral examination.* □ *She has got through the examination.*

5. miratoj

□ *People began to doubt whether the Bill would ever get through.*

6. lidhem me radio (telefon etj.)

□ *The telephone operator told me that all the lines were engaged. That's why I couldn't get through to you.* □ *At the fifth attempt the operator got me through to New York.*

7. arrin

□ *If more supplies do not get through, thousands of refugees will die.* □ *I started as soon as your message got through to me.*

8. kaloj, kualifikohem

□ *How many times did Laver get through to the final of the men's singles at Wimbledon?*

get together 1. mblidhem, takohem

□ *The younger members of the staff decided to get together over the question of weekend duty.* □ *... every week they got together and compared notes.*

2. mbledh

□ *'I want you to get your things together, so that we can leave at a moment's notice.'*

get too big for one's boots kapardisem, mbahem më të madh (rëndë)

□ *Don't try to take that line with me, my lad. You're getting too big for your boots, taking to me in that tone.* □ *'You talk hard, and get too big for your boots, Ralph.'*

get to the bottom of sth i zbuloj rrënjët diçkaje, i nxjerr (i gjej) fundin diçkaje, e studioj thellë, e shqyrtoj me themel

□ *'I'm determined to get to the bottom of this outrageous rumor.'* □ *We must get to the bottom of this mystery.* □ *Some very strange things have been happening in this house, and I'm going to get to the bottom of it before I leave.* □ *The doctor made several tests to get to the bottom of the man's headaches.*

get to the heart of hyj në thelb të, hyj në brendësi

□ *You can often get to the heart of someone's unhappiness by letting him talk.* □ *'If you can find a topic sentence, often it will help you get to the heart of the paragraph,' said the teacher.*

get/come to the point hyj në temë

□ *Peter is a very boring person to listen to: it always takes him so long to get to the point.*

get under control vë nën kontroll

□ *You must get your spending under control.* □ *The firebrigade arrived within minutes of the alarm and quickly got the conflagration under control.*

get under sb's skin ngacmoj, irritoj, i ngre nervat

□ *After the session he told Eddie, 'It's no use letting those guys get under your skin.'* □ *Children who talk too much in class get under the teacher's skin.* □ *I finally had to stop working with Peter: he just got under my skin.*

get under way niset, fillon të lëvizë, niset për udhë

□ *He has proposed me that he shall go on board and get the brig under way.* □ *We get under way before the wind...* □ *After a few hitches and hindrances the van with its human freight got under way.*

get up 1. ngrihem, çohem

□ *'Oh, it's nice to get up in the morning. But it's nicer to lie in bed!'* □ *What time do you get up in the morning?*

2. çohem më këmbë

□ *I got up from the table and left the room as quickly as possible.* □ *He got*

up from his chair when I entered the room. □ *He got up to ascertain if the door was closed shut, before he replied, in a low voice.*

3. ngrihet, forcohet, egërsohet

□ *Although the wind was obviously getting up, and with it the sea, the foolish couple left the harbor in their flimsy catamaran.* □ *The sea is getting up.*

4. përgatis, studioj

□ *When we went to see John he was busy getting the Law of Torts up for his exam.* □ *What subjects have you to get up for the examination?*

5. organizoj

□ *Who's going to get up the concert?* □ *They got up a dramatic performance.*

6. vesh, zbukuroj

□ *He got himself up to the occasion.* □ *He was got up as a sailor.*

get-up-and-go entuziazëm, vitalitet, vendosmëri, kurajë

□ *You will find that Jane is a very good worker: she has lots of get-up-and-go.* □ *Andy has a lot of get-up-and-go and is working his way through school.*

get up steam 1. merr (rrit) shpejtësinë

□ *We saw the boat in the harbor getting up steam for the daily crossing to the island.*

2. përthej mbledh fuqitë (forcat)

□ *'Do you think you could get up enough steam to take these letters along to the post office for me?'*

3. shfryj, shpërthej

□ *Miss Mary, getting up the steam in her turn, asked whether Caroline had attended the Meeting.*

get wind of nuhas, marr vesh, bie në erë

□ *Our competitors must not be allowed to get wind of our plans.* □ *The students were going to have a* *demonstration, but the authorities somehow **got wind of** it and brought in the police. □ What did Soames want now? Had he **got wind of** Paris? □ 'I thought I was going to get on first rate. But one day, all of a sudden, the other clerks **got wind of** it.'*

get/put wise to sth kuptoj, marr vesh, bëhem i vetëdijshëm për

□ *One girl pretended to be sick when she had athletics, until the teacher **got wise** and made her go to gym anyway. □ It was that one careless remark of Paterson that **put me wise to** where he had really spent the evening.*

give a final touch/give the finishing touch to/put the finishing touches to i jap dorën e fundit

□ *Carrie was **putting the finishing touches** to her toilet when a commotion near the stage caught her ear. □ He is **giving a final touch to** his composition.*

give a good account of oneself shquhem, dallohem, nderoj veten

□ *Although he is quite small, John **gave a good account of himself** when he was attacked by those hooligans. □ Our team **gave a good account of themselves** to win the match.*

give/lend a (helping) hand ndihmoj, i jap dorën, i jap një dorë

□ *Would you mind **giving us a hand** with this case? □ **Give us a hand** here, Clyde, will you? Let's see if we can get her out. She has fainted. □ I say, you fellows, **give me a hand** with this load. □ You took me here as a caretaker. I was going to **give you a helping hand**.*

give a hard time shqetësoj, krijoj shqetësime, i hap telashe, vë në siklet

□ *June **gave** her mother **a hard time** on the bus by fighting with her sister*

*and screaming. □ Don't **give me a hard time**, boys. I'm doing my best on this job. □ When I first arrived in England as a child, the other children **gave me a hard time** because I was a foreigner.*

give a lead drejtoj, orientoj, udhëheq

□ *The church should **give** more than **a lead** on basic moral matters.*

give a look hedh një vështrim

□ *He **gave** her **a look**, half in remonstrance, half in approval, and went on. □ He **gave** her a sidelong **look**, and found she was giving him the same.*

give an affront fyej, ofendoj

□ *All that I dare claim is that I have as much sense of humor as other people. Any man will admit that his sight is no good, or that he cannot swim, or shoots badly with a rifle, but to touch upon his sense of humor is to **give** him a mortal **affront**.*

give/lend an ear to dëgjoj, i vë veshin

□ *He **gave an ear to** the conversation. □ Children should **give an ear to** their parents' advice. □ The government **lent an ear to** the complaints of the people.*

give an eye to shikoj, hedh një sy

□ *'**Give an eye to** the fire while I'm out, won't you? There's plenty of coal in the scuttle.*

give and take jap e marr; bëj lëshime të ndërsjella

□ *The headmaster told Mary that she could not expect everything to be arranged for her convenience: she would have to learn to **give and take**. □ For a marriage to succeed, both partners must learn to **give and take**.*

give away 1. jap, fal

□ *The young man **gave** his entire fortune **away**, and went to live in a small island. □ He **gave away** most of his money to charity.*

2. shpërndaj

□ *The mayor gave away the prizes at the school sports day.* □ *She gave away the prizes at the sports meeting.*

3. tregoj, zbuloj, nxjerr një të fshehtë (me ose pa qëllim)

□ *'Don't give away where we're going.'* □ *Love is its own torturer; and, like cruder tortures, it makes its victim want to tell the truth—the truth about itself. It is by nature self-betraying; if nothing else, the eyes give it away.* □ *She gave away state secrets to the enemy.*

4. humbas, lë të shkojë

□ *You've given away a good chance of winning the match.*

5. epet, lakohet

□ *It was no use to say that the floor of the wardrobe was rotten and had given way with Nurse Ellen's heavy body.*

give a wide berth qëndroj larg

□ *Victoria resolved to give this lady as wide a berth as possible. Something told her that inventing stories to satisfy that kind of woman was no easy job.* □ *Mary gave the barking dog a wide berth.* □ *After Tony got Andy into trouble, Andy gave Tony a wide berth.*

give back 1. kthej

□ *'Isn't it time you gave Mary her earrings back? She may want to wear them herself!'* □ *The photographic equipment was given back to the tourist when he proved that it belonged to him.* □ *The book isn't mine, I must give it back to the owner.*

2. rikthej

□ *There was nothing the doctors could do to give me back the use of my legs. The paralysis was complete and irreversible.* □ *'Give me back my*

husband!' the woman screams at the president. 'Don't leave him rot in jail.'

give birth to sb/sth lind

□ *Well, it is strange that I who gave birth to her... should be alive and merry now, and she lying there: so cold and stiff.* □ *His wife gave birth to a healthy baby last night.* □ *When the father was told that, as a result of a fertility drug, his wife had given birth to sextuplets, he said 'That's too much of a good thing.'*

give cause for jep (lë) shkak

□ *During the night the old lady took a turn for the worse and today her condition gives us cause for deep anxiety.*

give chase ndjek, gjëmoj, vihen në ndjekje

□ *After the robbery the police gave chase. Someone cried, 'Stop thief!' and immediately everyone gave chase.* □ *The dog gave chase to the rabbit.*

give/lend color to sth i jep ngjyrë reale (të besueshme), vërteton, pohon

□ *His expensive way of life gave color to the story that he was a millionaire.* □ *The scars on his body lent color to his claim that he had been tortured.* □ *His appearance, too, and manner somehow lent color to this distrust.*

give credence to besoj, i zë besë

□ *It was impossible to give credence to his story of hair-breadth escapes and heroic feats on the battlefield.* □ *But, then, the thought darted across his mind that it was barely eleven o'clock; and that many people were still in the streets; of whom surely some might be found to give credence to his tale.* □ *Little credence should be given to such wild rumors.*

give credit for lavdëroj; njoh, atribuoj

□ *The credit for the success of the concert should be given to the teacher who organized it.* □ *The police haven't been given sufficient credit for keeping essential services running.* □ *Harry's actions gave evidence of a will stronger than I would have given him credit for.* □ *I wouldn't have given him credit for such fine feelings.*

give credit to besoj

□ *Do you give credit to his story?*

give currency to përhap

□ *Newspaper stories gave currency to this scandal.* □ *Any newspaper that gives currency to such inflammatory reports should be brought before the Press Council.* □ *Don't give currency to idle gossip.*

give effect to sth zbatoj, vë në veprim, vë në jetë

□ *The new ruling gives effect to the recommendations of the special committee.* □ *The teachers urged the principal to give effect to the proposal.*

give evidence of provoj, dëshmoj

□ *The packing-cases which were examined by the foreman gave evidence of having been tampered with; that is why he sent for the police.* □ *If it were a sentient thing that would give evidence, I might appeal to it at this day to bear witness for me.* □ *The prosecution gave the court evidence of identification before proceeding with the case against the accused.*

give/allow free play/rein to i lë (i jap) dorë të lirë, i jap liri të plotë veprimi

□ *In this picture the artist certainly allowed his imagination free rein.* □ *She was a woman who gave free play to her emotions, one who both* laughed and cried a lot more than most people. □ *The millionaire invited the architect to give free rein to his imagination when designing the house.* □ *When she was gone he gave free play to his feelings. His face never easily controlled by him, expressed all the perplexity and disturbance which he felt.*

give forth nxjerr, lëshon

□ *The strange animal did not run away, but stood its ground giving forth a mooing sound.* □ *On summer evenings the flowers gave forth an almost intoxicating scent.* □ *The engine gave forth a horrible grinding noise, and stopped.*

give ground 1. tërhiqem, zmbrapsem

□ *The solders' position was under constant attack, but they refused to give ground.* □ *We launched a counter-attack and the enemy were forced to give ground.*

2. tërhiqem, heq dorë

□ *We must learn to give ground in order to gain further ground later.*

give heed i kushtoj vëmendje

□ *I was too attentive to the Doctor and his wife, to give any heed to this request.* □ *Give heed to what I am saying.*

give in 1. dorëzohem

□ *The rebels were forced to give in.* □ *The enemy troops gave in after a short fight.*

2. jepem, lëshoj, lëshoj pe, lëshoj udhë, bëj lëshime

□ *They will argue and fight against it, bur they will give in if they see that you are sure it's the right thing to do.* □ *All sorts of other things I've had— tempers, scenes, reconciliations, giving in sometimes, sometimes holding out.*

3. dorëzoj

□ *All papers should be **given in** before 12.30. Candidates disobeying this rule may be disqualified.* □ *Please **give in** your examination papers now.*

give it a try 1. provoj, përpiqem, bëj përpjekje

□ *How silly of him to decide he wouldn't qualify for a grant without ever **giving it a try**.* □ *'Here, let me **give it a try**,' Lawrence said.*

2. provoj; vë në provë

□ *Even if you don't think you'll enjoy listening, **give it a try**. You'll probably be surprised.* □ *'Bread sauce? Horrible stuff!' 'Not as I make it. Go on, **give it a try**.'*

give mouth/tongue flas, tregoj, shpreh

□ *And he chafed the more because his training and his disposition forbade him **giving tongue**.* □ *She **gave mouth** to her thoughts.* □ *I have an opinion of you to which it is not easy to **give mouth**.*

2. leh

□ *They expected every moment to hear Merrylegs **give tongue**, but the highly trained performing dog had not barked.* □ *The hound **gave mouth** when in sight of a quarry.*

give off lëshon, përhap

□ *The fire doesn't seem to **give off** much heat.* □ *Some flowers **give off** their richest fragrance at night.* □ *The boiling water was **giving off** steam.* □ *The acid **gives off** a characteristically pungent odor.*

give oneself airs/put on airs mbahem me të madh, mbahem rëndë

□ *Sally annoys a lot of people because of the way that she **gives herself airs**.* □ *He was in great demand. Consequently, he **gave himself airs**.* □ *They say that Glorvina **gives herself airs**, and that Peggy herself is intolerably domineering.* □ *Don't **put on airs** with me Jack, I know you too well.*

give one's heart to i fal zemrën, dua me shpirt

□ *She grew to womanhood, and **gave her heart to** one who could not know its worth.*

give/send sb one's love i bëj (i çoj, i dërgoj) dikujt të fala

□ *Please **give** your sister **my love**.* □ *Please, **give my love** to your kind grandmother.*

give one's mind to sth përqëndroj vëmendjen, i kushtoj vëmendje

□ *He reckoned up his advantages as an idle winner might count his gains. He was not at all bored for the time, and could **give his mind to** it.* □ *Whatever you do you must **give your mind to** it.*

give one's word premtoj, jap fjalën

□ *If you lend me your notes, I'll return them before the exam: I **give you my word**.* □ *'Wasn't aware you had a grand-nephew, I **give you my word**,' said Mr. Wickfield.* □ *The letter will arrive on time. I **give you my word**.*

give one's word of honor jap fjalën e nderit

□ *I **give you my word of honor**, Segura, that I didn't even know he existed until tonight.* □ *I will **give you my word of honor** that you may safely ride by my side, and I will accept yours.* □ *Will you **give me your word of honor** that you'll never do it again?*

give out 1. njoftoj, shpall, bëj të ditur

□ *It was **given out** that casualties from the air-raid had been very light.* □ *The doctor **gave out** that the patient was not quite well.* □ *The news was **given out** this morning.*

2. shter, mbaron, merr fund

□ *The engine spluttered ominously. We exchanged anxious glances. Our worst fears were about to be realized. The petrol was* **giving out**. □ *After a month their food supplies* **gave out**. □ *The oxygen* **gave out**.

3. nxjerr, lëshon, përhap

□ *The radiator is* **giving out** *a lot of heat*. □ *This flower* **gives out** *a sweet perfume*.

4. pëson avari

□ *They drove the old car a long way up the mountain but eventually the engine* **gave out**. □ *One of the plane's engines* **gave out** *in mid-Atlantic*.

5. mbaroj, thyhem, jepem, më shterin forcat (fuqitë)

□ *And so Jurgis turned out and staggered away. He didn't go very far; round the corner he* **gave out** *completely*.

give over pusho, mjaft më

□ **Give over**, *can't you? I can't work with you chattering away like that*. □ *'We want boiled eggs, too!—the twins said, as in one voice. 'Can we have boiled eggs?'* **'Give over**. *Can't you see I'm cutting the pineapple?'*

give over to 1. dorëzoj

□ *The ruthless officers* **gave** *the city* **over to** *their men, who raped and pillaged without mercy*.

2. jepem, zhytem

□ *I* **gave** *myself* **over to** *dreams for a few minutes*.

give pause to sb vë në dilemë (mëdyshje), bëj të hezitojë (të ngurrojë)

□ *Weather conditions were bad enough to* **give pause to** *even the most experienced climbers*. □ *And Jill Trumbull, sitting beside him, wanted to know where he came from, what his own home life and connections were like. Questions which* **gave** *Clyde* **pause**. *He did not feel that he could admit the truth in connection with his family at all*. □ *He may say that he is not interested, but when he hears how high the salary is, it may* **give** *him* **pause**.

give place to sb/sth i lëshon vendin

□ *Houses and factories* **gave place to** *open fields as the train gathered speed*. □ *It was now April, and the snow* **had given place to** *cold rains and the unpaved street in front of Aniele's house was turned into a canal*. □ *His surprise* **gave place to** *indignation*. □ *With the announcement of the ceasefire, despair at last* **gave place to** *hope*.

give rise to shkakton, jep shkas

□ *The government's economic policy* **gave rise to** *increased unemployment, though it is true that it produced a favorable balance of payments in the country's international trade*. □ *The fact that the president was not present at the parade* **gave rise to** *rumors that he was ill*. □ *Her disappearance* **gave rise to** *the wildest rumors*. □ *What* **gave rise to** *this humor?*

give sb a big hand duartrokas nxehtësisht

□ *Let's all* **give** *her* **a big hand**.

give sb a blank check i lë dorë të lirë, i jap liri të plotë

□ *The architect was* **given a blank check** *to design a new city centere*. □ *He looked expectantly at her, but she said 'I do not* **give blank checks**.'

give sb a chance i jap, i krijoj mundësi

□ *The woman had told her to come the next day and she would perhaps* **give** *her* **a chance** *to learn the trade of painting cans*. □ *'Will you and your* *sister come and see us at Conda-ford?' 'Give me a chance!' 'When do you go back to your ship?'*

give sb a dose/taste of his own medicine i përgjigjem (ia kthej, ia shpër-blej) me të njëjtën monedhë
□ *The smaller boys badly wanted to **give** the bully **a dose of his own medicine**.*

give sb a dressing down qortoj ashpër
□ *Delaney would not come back and in a case he should, there was half a hundred young men who would **give him a dressing down**.*

give sb a fair hearing dëgjoj me paanësi
□ *You would **give him a hearing**; let him explain—there's bound to be a reason.* □ *'All I am asking is that you should **give a fair hearing** to them.'*

give sb a free hand i jap liri të plotë veprimi, i lë dorë të lirë
□ *They must be **given a full free hand** to conduct their mission.*

give sb a kick kënaq, i jap dikujt kënaqësi
□ *'Look,' I said, pointing to the west, 'a good sunset always **gives me the hell of a kick**.'*

give sb a lead marr iniciativën; drejtoj, i jap drejtim
□ *He was emphatic that when the war was over, I must speak out and say these things, and **give a lead** in the matter.* □ *These people are ignorant, not lazy, and **given a lead**, could quickly improve the quality of their crops and livestock.*

give sb a lecture (a lesson) i jap një mësim të mirë dikujt
□ *In that very room he and Bosinney had talked one summer afternoon; he well remembered even now the dis-guised and secret **lecture** he had **given** that young man in the interest of June.*

give sb a leg up 1. ndihmoj të hipë në kalë (të kapërcejë një pengesë)
□ *The wall is very low, sir, and he will **give you a leg up**.*
2. i jap dorën, i jap një shtysë
□ *He was devoting all his energies to **give Emily a leg up**.* □ *Hugo began to put his money into films. He started to do this in a vaguely philanthropic way, in order to **give** the British film industry **a leg up**.* □ *Why not just keep on your regular patients and **give** that new young dentist across the square **a leg up** by recommending any new-comers to him?* □ *He is determined to achieve whatever he does achieve in life on his own terms. He doesn't want to be **given a leg up** by his family.*

give sb a lift marr në makinë
□ *'You won't get back unless you start now.' I added unwillingly, 'I'll **give you a lift** if you like.'* □ *'If you are going my way,' he said, 'I can **give you a lift**.'* □ *Can you **give me a lift** to the station?*

give sb an inch and he will take a mile i jep gishtin, të merr dorën
□ *'Jane asked me if she could use our phone occasionally.' 'I wouldn't advise it; **give** that woman **an inch and she'll take a mile**.'*

give sb a new lease of life përtërin, i jep jetë
□ *Far from being too much for her to cope with, the care of her grandchil-dren seems to have **given** the old lady **a new lease of life**.* □ *The good news **gave us a new lease of life**.*

give sb a piece of one's mind ia them copë (troç, hapur) mendimin
□ *I shan't be sorry to have the chance of **giving** the old windbag **a piece of my mind**.* □ *My wife got fed up with his self-pity and **gave** him **a piece of**

her mind. □ *I'll give him a piece of my mind when he does come.*
□ *'I'd give her a piece of my mind that she wouldn't forget. I'd tell her off proper.'*

give sb a rap on/over the knuckles qortoj; kritikoj; ndëshkoj
□ *I shall give some of these good people a rare rap over the knuckles for their want of charity.*

give sb a Roland for an Oliver i përgjigjem (ia kthej, e shpërblej) me të njëjtën monedhë, i jap përgjigjen e merituar
□ *Remember you have kept a secret from me, and if I give you not a Roland for your Oliver, my name is not Dickon Sludge!* □ *Comforted by the thought that he had given Mrs. Carr a Roland for her Oliver.*

give sb a warm welcome/reception i bëj dikujt një pritje të ngrohtë, pres ngrohtësisht
□ *The President was given a warm welcome when he landed at the airport.*

give sb/sth a wide berth mbaj larg, qëndroj larg, mbaj distancë nga
□ *He's so boring that I always try to give him a wide berth.* □ *I think that Brown is a complete bore. I always give him a berth when I see him in parties.* □ *If they are hard upon you, brother, as perhaps they are, give them a wide berth, sheer off, and part company cheerily.*

give sb carte blanche i lë dorë të lirë
□ *'I wish you 'd give me carte—blanche for all my patients and all their wants.'*

give sb his due i jap hakun, i jap atë që i takon
□ *He's a slow worker, but to give him his due, he does try very hard.* □ *And yet, give him his due, he always pays his share.*

give sb his marching orders 1. pushoj nga puna; pushohem nga puna
□ *He referred to a recent case where the directors of the company gave the guilty executives their 'marching orders'.* □ *Mr. Peter has been given his marching orders simply because he has been found guilty of the crime.*
2. udhëzoj, orientoj, drejtoj
The answer to the question,' Who, in a democratic society, is to give the scientists their marching orders? is quite simple: democratic society itself and its elected representatives.

give sb line on sth informoj, njoftoj
□ *He should be given line on it.*

give sb plenty of rope/some rope etc. i jap liri të plotë; i jap një farë lirie
□ *The police gave the suspect plenty of rope.* □ *We're an old-fashioned firm, Mr. Smith, but not hide-bound. We're are not averse to giving a man with ideas of his own some rope.* □ *You're absolutely hopeless about people you like or who you think like you. You—give them too much rope.* □ *Tony's nearly sixteen. You've got to give kids a bit of rope as they grow older.*

give sb the benefit of the doubt quaj dikë të pafajshëm për mungesë provash
□ *The magistrate was not entirely certain that the accused man was guilty, so he gave him the benefit of the doubt and set him free.* □ *By allowing her to go free the judge gave the accused the benefit of the doubt.* □ *George's grade was higher than usual and he might have cheated, but his teacher gave him the benefit of the doubt*

give sb the boot pushoj nga puna
□ *If you're late once more you're getting the boot.*

give sb the cold shoulder sillem ftohtë, i kthej krahët dikujt

□ *After Jack's rude behavior in the meeting, several people **gave** him **the cold-shoulder**.*

□ *He could not think that he had played a handsome part. Those who knew the story **gave** him **the cold shoulder**.*

give sb the creeps (jim-jams, the shivers, shudders) i fus frikën, i kall datën, i shtie dridhmën, ngjeth, bëj t'i ngjethet mishtë, t'i shkojnë të dridhura

□ *I don't like him; he **gives** me **the creeps**.* □ *'Who was that old buffer?'—she asked of the soft man; 'he **gave** me 'the jim-jams'.'*

□ *Having to make a speech always **gives** me **the shivers**.* □ *... he wouldn't stay by himself. The place **gave** him **the jim-jams**, he said.*

give sb the glad eye vështroj me dashamirësi (me sy të dashuruar)

□ *I think that the blonde girl over there fancies you; she's **giving** you **the glad eye**.* □ *I was surprised when Jack **gave** me **the glad eye**.*

give sb the push pushoj (shkarkoj) nga puna; hedh (flak) përjashta

□ *Soon, I suppose, they'll be wanting to **give** you **the push** from here. You must rehabilitate yourself, as they would say.*

give sb the sack pushoj nga puna

□ *June was **given the sack** for being lazy.*

give sb the slip përvidhem, shpëtoj, largohem (iki) pa më vënë re

□ *The hunters finally had to admit that the fox they were hunting had **given** them **the slip**.* □ *We managed to **give** our pursuers **the slip**.* □ *Mind what I say—he has **given** his friends **the slip** and persuaded this delicate*

young creature, all along of her fondness for him, to be his guide and travelling companion.

gave sb/sth the (whole/entire) works
1. trajtoj keq, dhunshëm; rrah, zhdëp në dru

□ *He's bleeding: someone has **given** him **the works**.* □ *And the cops were **giving** him **the works**. Determined to have him sign a document he hadn't seen.*

2. e qaj me lot, e shkrij

□ *They **gave** Jane **the whole works** at the hairdressing saloon: she looked terrific!* □ *When Jim's turn in the dance competition came, he **gave** it **the works** and won first prize.*

give sb up for lost/dead quaj të humbur/të vdekur

□ *When the climbers were three days overdue at the rendezvous, they were **given up for dead**. It was thought that no one could survive for so long without food on the north face of the mountain.* □ *When Sue's father—a pillar of the Church—heard that she had been living with an avowed atheist, he **gave** her **up for lost**.*

give sb warning paralajmëroj

□ *The least he could do was to **give** fair **warning** of a change of attitude.*

□ *You might **give** me some **warning** when you're bringing people home to dinner!*

give sth a whirl provoj

□ *The job doesn't sound very exciting but I'll **give** it **a whirl**.* □ *I'm prepared to **give** this **a whirl**, Senora, if things are done my way.*

give sth up as a bad job lë, heq dorë

□ *Every time we tried to put the tent up, it was blown down. Finally we **gave** it **up as a bad job**.* □ *I had been sitting there all the afternoon and had caught literally nothing... and I was* *just about **giving it up as a bad job** when I suddenly felt a rather smart pull at the line.*

give the devil his due kija inatin dhe foli hakun; të rrimë shtrembër e të flasim drejt!

□ *I don't trust Jack but, **give the devil his due**, he has a very good sense of humor.* □ *You're all talking about George's meanness, but **give the devil his due**, he's not a sponger like some I could name.* □ *To **give the devil his due** whatever racket Frank is engaged in, he's likely to make a success of it.*

give the game away nxjerr një të fshehtë

□ *It was supposed to be a surprise party, but I **gave the game away** and now everyone knows about it.* □ *I wish she wouldn't talk and **give the game away.***

give the go-by 1. injoroj, shpërfill, s'i jap të njohur, bëj sikur s'e shoh

□ *He **gave me the go-by** in the street yesterday.* □ *I am enough of a Forsyte to **give** them **the go-by**, June.*

2. shmangem, i largohem, i ruhem, i bëj bisht

□ *I don't feel like going to the pub tonight: I'll **give it the go-by** this time.*

give the green light i hap dritën e gjelbër, i hap udhë, i çel rrugë

□ *The Mississipi legislature **gave the green light** to the state to take over and develop any seaport in the state.* □ *They refuse to say which companies have been **given the green light** to increase their prices.*

give the lie to përgënjeshtroj, nxjerr të pavërtetë

□ *These figures **give the lie** to reports that business is declining.* □ *David's excellent performance in the game has **given the lie** to the story that he's too old to play.* □ *The words sounded foreign, difficult to understand in such a place; their easy politeness, formality **giving the lie** to what they said.*

give thought (to) mendoj mirë, vras mendjen, i kushtoj vëmendje

□ *Have you **given** any **thought to** which university you would like to attend when you leave school?* □ *It's high time that Millie **gave** serious **thought to** whether she is ever going to get married or not.* □ *Now that he had **given** the matter **thought**, he recalled that he had always liked this boy Belford.*

give tongue to shpreh me zë të lartë

□ *If I had **given tongue to** my doubts about the plan, we might all have been saved a lot of trouble.*

give to understand i jap të kuptojë, i le të kuptojë

□ *I lent him the money because he **gave me to understand** that I could have it back next week.* □ *I was **given to understand** that you might help me in my work.*

give trouble i krijoj shqetësime, i hap telashe

□ *The new computer's been **giving us** a lot of **trouble**.* □ *That has **given** him too much **trouble**.*

give up 1. lë, heq dorë, braktis

□ *For no apparent reason Matthew **gave up** his lucrative job in the city and emigrated to Canada.* □ *The truth is that she had **given up** the idea of cleaning anything.*

2. lë, shes, heq qafe

□ *Nothing could persuade her to **give up** her home; it was much too big for her, but it was where she had always lived.*

3. nxjerr, zbuloj

□ *It was not until the twentieth century that Tutankhamun's tomb* **gave**
its secrets **up** *to the world.*

4. dorëzoj; dorëzohem

□ *After a week on the run he* **gave**
himself **up** *to the police.* □ *The desperate man forced his hostages to
drive on through the night. He was
afraid, hungry and thirsty, but he had
no intention of* **giving** *himself* **up**.

5. heq dorë, lë, pres

□ *You ought to* **give up** *smoking.* □ *It
is easy to say that dairy products are
bad for the heart, but the eating habits
of a lifetime are not so easily* **given up**.
□ *I* **gave up** *smoking last month.*

6. quaj (konsideroj) të pashpresë
(shërimin, kthimin etj.)

□ *Everyone—the doctors, the nurses,
his own family—had* **given** *him* **up**,
*when he surprised them all by sud-
denly taking a turn for the better.*

give up all hope i humb të gjitha
shpresat, pres shpresën

□ *After three days of continuous
flights over the Atlantic,* **all hope** *of
finding the missing aircraft was* **given
up** *and the search abandoned.* □ *Even
though the woman had been missing
for three years, her mother refused to*
give up hope *that one day she would
walk into her home again.*

give up the ghost 1. jap shpirt

□ *When he finally* **gave up the ghost**,
he was over one hundred years old.
□ *A tiger shot through the heart is still
capable of killing half-a-dozen men
before* **giving up the ghost**.

2. merr fund

□ *The car seems to* **have given up the
ghost**.

give utterance to shpreh

□ *There was one dim unformed fear
lingering about his sister's mind, to
which she never* **gave utterance**.

give vent to sth shfaq, shpreh lirisht
(ndjenjat etj.)

□ *He pressed a penny into his hand
and* **gave vent to** *his feelings.* □ *She
stole away to bed as quickly as she
could, and when she was alone* **gave
free vent to** *the sorrow with which her
breast was over charged.* □ *She* **gave
vent to** *her opinions in the kitchen
where the cook was.* □ *He* **gave vent
to** *his feelings in an impassioned
speech.*

give voice to sth shpreh

□ *To their feelings of frustration and
dissatisfaction with the government,
the public were at last able to* **give
voice** *when a general election was
called.* □ *If I have any friend here,
who can* **give a voice to** *any suspicion
that my heart has sometimes whispered to me.* □ *Little Tony* **gave voice
to** *his pain by crying loudly when the
dog bit him.*

give way (to) 1. sprapsem, tërhiqem

□ *The enemy army is* **giving way**
before cannon fire. □ *When the battle
became fierce the enemy* **gave way**.

2. i hap rrugën, i lëshoj vendin

□ *The grey clouds gradually broke up
and* **gave way to** *a blue sky.* □ *But Mr.
Weller's anger quickly* **gave way to**
curiosity. □ *As winter* **gave way to**
spring the days began to lengthen.
□ *A common feeling of respect
induced passengers to* **give way to** *the
father and daughter.*

3. shpreh lirisht (ndjenjat etj)

□ *It was the first time he had* **given
way to** *anger with her.* □ *Left alone in
her strange abode Jennie* **gave way to**
her saddened feelings.

4. thyhet, këputet; bie, rrëzohet,
shembet, shkatërrohet

□ *The bridge* **gave way** *under the
weight of the truck.* □ *... As I turned the*

*silly branch **gave way**... and I was out midstream with a gallon of Thames water inside me before I knew what had happened.* □ *The joists were so eaten through by rot it was a wonder the whole floor hadn't **given way**.*

5. jepem, humb kontrollin e vetes, humb toruan

□ *Mrs. Jones didn't **give way** during the flood, but she was very frightened.*

6. lëshohem, këputem, më priten fuqitë (këmbët, leqet e këmbëve, gjunjët)

□ *His legs suddenly **gave way** and she fell to the floor.*

7. pushtohem, më mbërthen të tërin

□ *It was no use. She didn't shout, but she **gave way to** a low controlled anger.*

8. lëshoj, bëj lëshime

□ *We must not **give way** to their demands.*

give weight to përforcon

□ *The facts that he had not been seen in his usual haunts and that he had answered the phone at ten o'clock **gave weight to** his claim that he had not been out on the evening in question.* □ *To this speculation recent discoveries **give further weight**.*

glad rags rrobat ceremoniale, rrobat për festë

□ *Help yourself to a drink, Peter, and I'll go and put my **glad rags** on.* □ *We'll have to put on our **glad rags** tonight: we are going to a big party.*

glance one's eyes down/over/through sth i hedh një sy

□ *He **glanced** his **eyes over** the books and found that his favorite novel was among them.* □ *She **glanced** her **eyes over** the letter she'd just gotten.*

gladden sb's heart gëzon zemrën e

□ *I took out a tight wad of dividend*

*warrants ringed with a rubber band, and the records in the wad would have **gladdened the heart** of a broker.*

gloss over mbuloj, kaloj shkarazi, kaloj pa vënë re

□ *It is important that a politician's vices should be known and if necessary exposed. They should not be **glossed over**.* □ *I deplore the modern tendency to **gloss over** the low standards in some of our schools.* □ *It does not do to **gloss over** one's mistakes.*

gnaw away at 1. ha, gërryen, bren

□ *It was obvious from their appearance that the young trees had been **gnawed at** by some small creature.* □ *The tiger in the cage **gnawed** listlessly **at** an old bone.*

2. bren, mundon, ha për brenda

□ *Day in, day out, the feeling that he had been misjudged and punished for another man's crime **gnawed at** him until he became obsessed with the idea of revenge on society.*

go about 1. shkoj, shëtis, endem, sillem lart e poshtë

□ *Is it dangerous to **go about** bareheaded when it's raining?* □ *I would advise you not to **go about** criticizing your superiors.* □ *So for several days he had been **going about**... and going weaker and weaker.*

2. merrem, bëj, kryej

□ *She'll do anything for you if you **go about** it in the right way.* □ *You're not **going about** it in the right way.* □ *We shall have to **go about** it carefully.*

3. nis, filloj

□ *Peter hasn't the faintest idea of how to **go about** finding a better job.* □ *'Never mind me, my dear. **Go about** your work, and let me watch it for a while.'*

4. vazhdoj (punën)

□ *While the bombs were exploding daily, the housewives* **went about** *their everyday tasks of keeping their home going.* □ *I must* **go about** *my work or I shall be all behind.*

5. qarkullon

□ *The rumor is* **going about** *that John and Mary are getting married.*

6. ndryshon drejtim (kurs)

□ *As soon as the captain heard the cry 'Man overboard' he ordered the ship to* **go about** *and search for the missing man.*

go about one's business sheh punën e vet

□ *'If your brother comes here with any more criticism about how we bring the children up, I'll tell him to* **go about** *his business.'* □ *'You had better* **go about** *your business, Ralph.'*

go about with sb shoqërohet me

□ *I'm afraid your daughter is* **going about with** *a man who is old enough to be her father.*

go abroad shkoj jashtë shtetit

□ *The young widow felt that she wanted to get away for a while, so she decided to* **go abroad** *for a long holiday.* □ *He* **went abroad** *on business.*

go after 1. ndjek

□ *The police warned the public not to* **go after** *the escaped prisoner, as he was armed and dangerous.* □ *He* **went after** *the burglars.*

2. shkoj pas, orvatem të siguroj

□ *We're both* **going after** *the same job.* □ *Once Sam decided what he wanted, he* **went after** *it with a single-mindedness that reminded me of his father.*

go against 1. bie ndesh me, është kundër (në kundërshtim me)

□ *The idea of trying to cheat the income tax authorities* **went against**

his principles—he had a strong sense of civic responsibility. □ *That a man could be saved from disease by means of the injection of a serum seemed to* **go against** *logic.*

2. merr, kthehet kundër

□ *The thought that the battle could* **go against** *them never for a moment entered into the generals' calculations.*

3. kundërshtoj

□ *He* **went against** *the advice of his colleagues and resigned.* □ *Don't* **go against** *your parents wishes.*

go against the grain është kundër dëshirës, natyrës, prirjeve

□ *It really* **goes against the grain** *to have to go into the office at weekends.* □ *Staying in bed may* **go against the grain** *but that's what you must do if you want to get better.* □ *This prosecution* **goes** *very much* **against the grain** *with me.* □ *Dishonesty* **goes against the grain** *of an honest man.*

go against the stream/tide ecën kundër rrymës

□ *Teenagers often* **go against the stream.**

go a good/great/long way to/towards 1. ndikon (ndihmon) shumë, ka rëndësi të madhe, luan rol të madh

□ *It had a reasonable appearance of probability: at all events, Martin hoped so, and that* **went a long way.** □ *I had, to the best of my belief, a simple earnest manner of narrating what I did narrate; and these qualities* **went a long way.**

2. shkon gjatë

□ *However there was plenty of porter in a tin can; and the cheese* **went a great way** *for it was very strong.*

go ahead 1. vazhdoj

□ *Now that you've had the all clear from your doctor you can* **go ahead** *and start up your new shop.* □ *The*

*government has decided to go ahead
with its plans to develop the North.*
2. avancon, përparon
□ *With the strike settled, work on the
new bridge went ahead like wildfire.*
□ *He is going ahead on lessons.*
3. filloj
□ *'May I start now?' 'Yes, go ahead.'*
□ *Now then, go ahead.*
go all (to all) lengths bëj çmos, bëj
ç'është e mundur
*I was conscious that a moment's
mutiny had already rendered penalties, and like any other rebel slave, I
felt resolved in my desperation to go
all lengths.* □ *If your father hadn't
been against me they wouldn't have
gone to any such length in making
me the victim.*
go all out vë të gjitha forcat
□ *Our team is going all out to win the
championship.* □ *We'll go all out to
fulfil the plan ahead of time.*
go all to pieces e humbi fare
□ *After the car accident, she seemed
to go to pieces.* □ *He went to pieces
when they told him the tragic news.*
go along (with) 1. eci, shkoj
□ *I went along the corridor until I
found a door open.* □ *I meditated as I
went along.*
2. vazhdoj, vijoj, avancoj
□ *You may have some difficulty at
first, but you'll find it easier as you go
along.* □ *You'll get more skillful at
this job as you go along.*
3. përcjell, shoqëroj
□ *'I have to go to the dentist this
morning.' 'Would you like me to go
along with you?'*
□ *Master Davy, how should you like
to go along with me and spend a fortnight at my brother's at Yarmouth?*
□ *He'll go along with you as far as
the post office.*

4. bie dakord, pranoj
□ *I can't go along with you on that
point.* □ *I don't go along with her
views on nuclear disarmament.*
go at 1. sulmoj, vërsulem
□ *They went at each other furiously.*
□ *The two women lost their tempers
and went at each other tooth and
nail.*
2. nis, ia hyj një punë, i përvishem
punës
□ *The villagers went at the building
of a dam with a will, once they had
seen that the rising water could be
stemmed.* □ *Once John decided to do
something, he went at it for all he was
worth.*
go at it hammer and tongs 1. zihen,
grinden me të madhe; zihen si qentë
□ *We could hear the neighbours
going at each other hammer and
tongs.* □ *Bill slapped Tony's face and
now they're going at it hammer and
tongs in back of the house.* □ *Helen
and Mary have been arguing all day,
and now they are going at it hammer
and tongs.*
2. i hyj një pune me të gjitha fuqitë
□ *The farmer had to chop down a tree
and he went at it hammer and tongs.*
□ *Andy had a lot of homework to do
and he went at it hammer and tongs
till bedtime.*
go away 1. iki, largohem
□ *'I'm tired of your constant complaints: go away and leave me in
peace!'* □ *I plainly discerned that Mr.
and Mrs. Micawber and their family
were going away from London, and
that a parting between us was near
at hand.*
2. ikën, largohet, zhduket
□ *The smell still hasn't gone away.*
□ *Sometimes the fever lasts for a day
or two and then goes away.*

go back 1. kthehem

□ *The children have to* **go back** *to school next week.* □ *... So Ona* **went back** *to Brown's and saved her place and a week's wages.*

2. rikthehem, kthehem mbrapa

□ *Once we decide to emigrate, there will be no* **going back**. *Our decision will be final and irrevocable.* □ *To trace the origins of the Irish problem, we have to* **go back** *over three hundred years.*

go back on sth ha fjalën, shkel premtimin

□ *Promises are made to be kept, and not lightly to be* **gone back on**. □ *'You can't* **go back on** *a promise like that!'* □ *He is not the sort of man who would* **go back on** *his word.*

goes back to 1. rifilloj, rikthehem

□ *She's decided to* **go back to** *teaching.* □ *We have to* **go back to** *the early years of the industrial revolution if we want to trace the history of mass production.*

2. daton, zë fill

□ *How far does the tradition* **go back?**

go begging sëe do njeri, s'i duhet (lipset) kujt; është i lirë

□ *If that sandwich is* **going begging**, *I'll have it.* □ *Please take any of those tools which you think might be useful to you. They are* **going begging**, *because I have bought some new ones.* □ *'That flat over the stables,' Mrs. Middleton said, 'it seems such a pity that it should* **go begging**. *I thought perhaps you would like it.'*

go bankrupt falimentoj

□ *'It's a bad business for that young Bosinney, he'll* **go bankrupt**, *I shouldn't wonder.*

go before 1. ndodh para

□ *Each stage depends on what has*

gone before. □ *The present crisis is more than any that have* **gone before**.

2. dal para

□ *In my day, a boy who was caught smoking in school* **went before** *the headmaster and was probably beaten.*

3. paraqitet

□ *My application to add a room to my house* **goes before** *the planning committee next week.*

go beyond kalon, kapërcen

□ *His interests* **went beyond** *political economy.* □ *This year's sales figures* **go beyond** *all our expectation.*

go beyond one's duty kaloj kompetencat zyrtare, dal nga suaza e detyrës së

□ *It was clear that the Town Clerk had* **gone beyond** *his* **duty** *in ordering the new and very expensive street-lightning without authority.*

go beyond a joke kalon caqet e shakasë

□ *Your teasing of the new typist has* **gone beyond a joke** *and I advise you to stop it.*

go broke jam trokë, mbetem pa një dysh në xhep

□ *He gambled very heavily and eventually he* **went broke**.

go by 1. kalon (koha, etj)

□ *As time* **goes by** *my memory seems to get worse.* □ *Sometimes hours* **go by** *without him saying a word.* □ *As the months* **went by**, *the villagers gradually got accustomed to the stranger in their midst.*

2. kaloj (para, pranë etj.)

□ *As each contigent* **went by**, *there was a burst of applause from the watching crowd.* □ *The parade* **went by** *us, and soon silence descended once more on the square.* □ *In going to the Palace of Culture you'll* **go by** *the Post Office.*

3. gjykoj në bazë të

□ *It's often a mistake to* **go by** *appearances: that poor-looking individual is anything but poor. In fact, he's a millionaire.* □ *You can't* **go by** *appearance; you must have facts to go by.*
4. udhëhiqem, drejtohem; orientohem
□ *I shall* **go entirely by** *what my solicitor says.* □ *We had no compass, and only the distant gunfire to* **go by.** □ *In deciding that question you should not* **go by** *instinct.*
5. kalon (rasti etj.)
□ *Mr. Simpson hesitated just a little too long over the offer of a partnership in the firm; and when he finally made up his mind to accept, the opportunity had* **gone by.**

go by the board lë mënjanë, harroj
□ *I'm afraid the new car will have to* **go by the board**—*we can't afford it.* □ *After he took up golf, all his other sports* **went by the board.** □ *Tony had many chances to go to college, but he let them* **go by the board.**

go by the book veproj në bazë të rregullave
□ *Some of the managers allow us to leave early, but Jones* **goes** *strictly* **by the book.** □ *'If you* **go by the book** *you shouldn't have any trouble with the authorities.*

go by (under) the name of quhet, njihet me emrin
□ *This wild flower* **goes by the name** *of Old Man's Beard.* □ *'...who are you, if I may be so bold?' said Tom, 'Oh, I* **go by** *various* **names.'**

go cap in hand kërkoj përunjësisht
□ *The workers feel that they should get regular increase in salary without having to* **go cap in hand** *to their employers every time.*

go down 1. zbres, ulem
□ *Let's* **go down** *by the lift.* □ *As*

Andrew **went down** *to supper his thoughts were painfully confused.*
2. bie, rrëzohet
□ *The policeman hit the man once with his truncheon, and he* **went down** *like a felled ox.* □ *The glass* **went down.**
3. kapërdihet, gëlltitet, kalohet poshtë
□ *It was Portugese champagne and* **went down** *like mother's milk.* □ *The pill just won't* **go down.**
4. ulet (çmimi)
□ *It's a strange thing, but prices always seem to be going up. They never* **go down!** □ *The price of petrol is* **going down.**
5. fundoset, mbytet (anija)
□ *We watched amazed as the destroyer keeled over and* **went down.** □ *The ship struck a hidden reef and* **went down** *with all hands.* □ *In the tradition of the sea, the captain stayed on board until all the passengers and the crew had left; but he himself* **went down** *with the ship.*
6. perëndon (dielli)
□ *The sun comes up from the east and* **goes down** *to the west.* □ *They stood there while the sun* **went down** *upon the scene, and the sky in the west turned blood red, and the tops of the houses shone like fire.*
7. hyn, mbetet (në histori)
□ *He will* **go down** *in history as a great statesman.* □ *Scanderbeg's name has* **gone down** *in history as our national hero.*
8. shkruhet, regjistrohet
□ *Every word uttered in court* **went down** *for future reference.* □ *It all* **goes down** *in her notebook.*
9. zë fill, nis
□ *The event* **goes down** *to 1914.*
10. bie, qetësohet era
□ *If the wind doesn't* **go down** *before*

*three o'clock, we won't be able to
take off today.* □ *The wind had gone
down with the light, and the snow had
come on.*

go downhill keqësohet, shkon tatëpjetë, shkon gjithnjë e më keq
□ *This part of the town used to be
fashionable, but it's starting to go
downhill.*

go down to 1. mundem nga
□ *The reigning champion went down
to a hammer-blow in the twelfth
round.* □ *The Roman Empire went
down to the barbarians.*
2. arrin, shtrihet
□ *This book is no use to me; it only
goes down to the General Elections
of 1993.* □ *This volume only goes
down to 1945.*

go down (with) 1. pritet, pranohet
□ *'Well, I think she'll go down all
right with father, but I'm not sure
about mother.'* □ *Rude jokes don't go
down too well with the vicar.*
2. sëmurem, më kap (zë) një sëmundje
□ *Our youngest boy has gone down
with mumps.* □ *Mr. Armstrong was
unable to go into the office on Monday because he had gone down with
influenza.*

go down in the world bie nga dynjallëku
□ *Nor were there any wanting other
indications of the gentleman's having
gone down in the world of late.*

go down to history hyn në histori
□ *Winston Churchill will go down to
history as the man who rallied the
British people when they seemed to
be defeated.*

go Dutch paguajmë secili për vete
□ *Since Mary and John are both
earning the same salary, they always go Dutch when they dine out
together.*

go easy e marr shtruar
□ *You should go easy, you're getting
tired.*

go easy on/with sb/sth 1. veproj
(sillem) me të butë (me të mirë, me
kujdes)
□ *Go easy on the new neighbour
when you complain about the dog.*
□ *Go easy there! That furniture is
breakable.* □ *'Go easy with him, he is
only a child.'*
2. harxhoj (përdor) me nikoqirllëk
(me kursim)
□ *Most dentists recommend that children go easy on candy.* □ *You can
have yourself another slice of bread
but go easy with the butter, young
man, or there will be none left.*

go far 1. mjafton, arrin, del; shkon
gjatë
□ *$45 a week doesn't go very far
these days.*
□ *You only bought half a dozen bottles of wine! That won't go far among
thirty people.*
2. çan përpara në jetë
□ *His teachers used to say that the
boy would go far but I don't suppose
that even they thought a small village
school would produce a future Cabinet minister.*

go far to do sth/towards doing sth
ndikon shumë, luan një rol të rëndësishëm, ka rëndësi të madhe,
ndihmon shumë
□ *Their promises don't go very far
towards solving our present problems.*

go fifty-fifty ndaj përgjysmë, barabar
□ *They went fifty-fifty on expenses.*

go for 1. shkoj (të thërras, të marr)
□ *When she found that the baby still
had a high temperature after twelve
hours, the young mother decided to
go for the doctor.* □ *She's gone for
some milk.*

2. sulmoj, turrem, hidhem, sulem

□ *Just as the man was about to push his way into the house, the girl called out 'Come on, Fiso!* **Go for him!***',* *and the intruder fled.* □ *The news-paper really* **went for** *him over his defence of terrorism.*

3. ka të bëjë, i takon

□ *What I have said about Eddie goes for you, too. 'Your sister is a selfish girl—and that* **goes for** *you too.'*

4. zgjedh

□ *I think I'll* **go for** *the fruit salad.*

5. pëlqej, më tërheq

□ *I don't* **go much for** *modern art.* □ *I don't* **go for** *horror films, and I can't understand why anyone likes them.*

6. shitet

□ *The old cottage, dilapidated as it was,* **went for** *over $5000.* □ *'How much do you think these Chinese vases will* **go for?'**

go for a breather dal të marr ajër të pastër

□ *Outside in the damp October air she said, 'Let's* **go for a** *little* **breather***, Uncle, and get the smell of that court out of us.'*

go for broke rrezikoj gjithçka

□ *The racing car driver decided to* **go for broke** *in the biggest race of the year.* □ *The desperate gambler decided to* **go for broke** *by risking everything on one last throw of the dice.*

go for nothing shkon kot

□ *Because he turned up late for the exam, all the studying he had done* **went for nothing.** □ *We realized that all the care we had taken to bring up and educate our daughter had* **gone for nothing** *when she ran away with her French teacher.*

go for very little vlen pak, ka pak vlerë

□ *Philip's work* **went for very little.**

go forth del, shpallet, lëshohet

□ *We must call the whole people to our help, as partners in the battle; only from an inspired Nation can* **go forth***, under these conditions, an inspired Army.* □ *From Herod's palace the command* **went forth** *that all young children were to be slain.*

go forward avancoj, përparoj

□ *Work on the new hospital is* **going forward** *at a satisfactory pace.* □ *The committee decided to* **go forward** *with its plans for the compulsory pur-chase of the land, so that the road could be widened.* □ *The work is* **going forward** *well.*

go from bad to worse shkon keq e më keq

□ *We are afraid that the shop may have to close soon: the business situ-ation is* **going from bad to worse.** □ *With inflation and rising unemploy-ment, the situation is* **going from bad to worse** *for millions of people.*

go halves/go half and half ndaj përgjysmë

□ *The two partners agreed to* **go halves** *in the profits.* □ *That was an expensive meal let's* **go halves.**

go hand in hand with shkojnë krahas (paralelisht) me

□ *War and suffering* **go hand in hand.**

go hard for/with sb heq keq, e ka punën keq

□ *I'm sorry for Paul: things have* **gone hard with** *him these few years.* □ *He's very ill and it's* **going hard with** *him.* □ *It might have* **gone hard with** *him, had the mistake not been discovered.*

go haywire është prishur, s'punon më, ka dalë jashtë përdorimit

□ *Since I dropped it on the floor my watch has* **gone** *completely* **haywire.** □ *My electric typewriter has* **gone** *all* *haywire: I have to call the repair man.*

go heart and soul into sth jepem me mish e me shpirt, jepem i tëri pas

□ *I now go heart and soul, neck and heels, with Fred in all his scheme about little Nelly, and right glad he'll be to find me so strong upon it.*

go home 1. kthehem në shtëpi

□ *'It's terribly late! I must go home!'*

2. qëllon (godit) në shenjë, qëlloi aty ku duhet

□ *Rufford was a skillful debater, and his calculated sarcasm went home. His opponent flushed under the attack.*

go home to sb's heart hyn thellë në shpirt (zemër), prek në zemër, ndiej thellë në shpirt

□ *Now as he spoke, his voice trembled with that peculiar vibration which is the result of tensity. It went ringing home to his companion's heart.*

go in 1. hyj, hyn

□ *'We can't discuss your problems standing here in the rain. Let's go in and make ourselves comfortable.' □ I went in by the back door and found myself in the kitchen. □ He opened the door and went in. □ The key won't go in the lock. □ The cork's too big, it won't go in.*

2. hyn, futet, fshihet në re (dielli, etj)

□ *Just as we were ready to be photographed, and all saying 'cheese' to produce those smiles, the sun went in! □ The sun went in and it grew rather cold.*

3. marr pjesë në garë, konkurroj

□ *Which events is he going in at the Olympics? □ Go in, young fellow, and win if possible.*

4. hyn në kokë

□ *I've read and re-read the chapter on the life-cycle of the river fluke, but it won't go in!*

go in (at) one ear and out (at/of) the other i hyn në një vesh e i del nga tjetri

□ *I gave the candidates instructions to print their names clearly: but it seems to have gone in one ear and out the other. □ It's no use asking Tim to deliver any messages for you. Everything I say to him goes in at one ear and out at the other.*

go in for 1. hyj në garë (provim etj.)

□ *He went in for too many events, and so won none. □ I'm going to go in for an examination tomorrow.*

2. jepem pas, më tërheq

□ *'Why don't you go in for collecting antiques or something? You need something to take your mind off your work.' □ He is going in for collecting stamps.*

3. ushtroj, merrem me

□ *Do you go in for any kind of sports? □ I'm not one of those people who go in for dieting—I'm much too fond of eating!*

go into 1. hyj, futem

□ *The dog used to go into a corner of the room as soon as its master left the house, and stay there till he returned. □ I went into the garden and picked some grapes.*

2. godit

□ *The car must have gone into the side of the house at a tremendous speed. The car was unrecognizable and one side of the house was destroyed.*

3. hyj, merrem me

□ *Nothing would induce me to go into the family business! □ I would not be averse to going into business on my own account.*

4. diskutoj, shqyrtoj, konsideroj
□ *'I know you want to tell me about your father's illness; but please don't let's go into it now.'* □ *The chancellor said that these proposals would have to be gone into very carefully.*

go into action filloj operacionin
□ *The commandos went into action at night with their faces blackened for better concealment.*

go into detail(s) hyj në hollësira
□ *He refused to go into details about his plans.* □ *'Please don't spend too much time going into details of your case. Just let me know the main points.'* □ *Tell me what happened in a few words; don't go into details.*

go into effect hyn në fuqi
□ *The law went into effect on the first of January.* □ *This law has not gone into effect yet.*

go into operation hyn në fuqi, vihet në veprim (funksionim)
□ *The new regulations will go into operation on September first.* □ *This hydroelectric power station went into full operation in 1997.*

go into orbit 1. del në orbitë, zë një vend të dukshëm
□ *After he appeared on television, the actor's career went into orbit.*
2. marr zjarr, tërbohem nga inati
□ *Tony was afraid his father would go into orbit when he found out about the car accident.*

go into particulars hyj në hollësira
□ *I told Mr. Guest I would open the subject to you; and when you come back from this northern business, we can go into particulars.*

go into raptures ngazëllohem, më rrëmben hareja, fluturoj nga gëzimi
□ *Seeing the new successes in business we all went into raptures.*

go into the melting pot pëson ndryshime rrënjësore
□ *He had written two thirds of the composition when he found out he got on the wrong lines and the whole thing went into the melting pot.*

go it alone veproj më vete, veproj (bëj) një punë vetëm
□ *He put forward all sorts of schemes on how to capitalise on the unused assets of various companies, but his employers wouldn't listen. So he went it alone.* □ *In an age of motor manufacturing giants, it is not easy for the smaller company to go it alone.*

golden opportunity, a rast i shkëlqyer (i artë)
□ *Polytechnics present golden opportunities to a bright young lecturer. Starting salaries are higher than in universities, and there are unparalleled chances to experiment with new syllabuses.*

go like clockwork shkon (vete, ecën) sahat
□ *We're used to emergency catering, we all know our jobs and everything went like clockwork.*

go like hot cakes shiten shpejt, shiten si simite të ngrohta
□ *The tickets for the Radio and T.V. Song Festival went like hot cakes.*

go like the wind shkon me vërtik, u bë erë, ikën shumë shpejt (si era)
□ *Harry was on his bike and going like the wind in the direction of the beach.* □ *Pop only knew that the month at St. Pierre le Port seemed to have gone like the wind.*

good/great/vast deal, a shumë, tepër
□ *They followed it this time, as eager as children in sight of a circus menagerie—which, indeed, the scene*

a good deal resembled. □ *They knew... a vast deal about flowers.*

good feeling dashamirësi, mirëdashje

□ *For so old a man of the world Soames was singularly unaware how in that desirable sphere, called Society, everyone is slandered daily, and no bones broken; slanders and slanders dining and playing together with the utmost* **good feeling** *and the intention of reslandering each other the moment they are round the corner.*

go off 1. dal, iki, largohem

□ *They sold their house and* **went off** *to live in Canada with their married daughter.* □ *Our visitor* **went off** *at six o'clock.*

2. del nga skena

□ *Hamlet* **goes off.**

3. humb ndjenjat, më bie të fikët; më zë, më merr gjumi

□ *She* **went off** *into a faint.* □ *He didn't seem to* **go off,** *so he went into the kitchen and made himself a cup of tea.* □ *Hasn't the baby* **gone off** *yet?*

4. shkon, kalon

□ *The performance* **went off** *well.* □ *'How did the sports meeting* **go off?'** □ *Aunt Ellen had the operation this morning and it all* **went off** *quite well.*

5. shpërthen

□ *Then the first mine* **went off.** □ *They had barely reached the corner of Randon place when 'bang' the first cane* **went off.**

6. prishet, thartohet

□ *Meat and fish* **go off** *quickly in hot weather.* □ *This milk has* **gone off.**

7. ikën, kalon, zhduket

□ *I've got rather a headache, but it will probably* **go off** *when I've had a rest.* □ *The pain* **went off** *quite suddenly.*

8. ndërpritet (uji, drita etj.)

□ *Just as the weather turned cold, the electricity supply* **went off.**

9. s'më pëlqen

□ *I've* **gone off** *the South of France since it became so overcrowded.*

go off at a tangent ndryshoj papritur temën e bisedës

□ *We were talking about the cost of tomatoes when John* **went off** *at a* **tangent** *and started talking about the revival of wine-making in England.*

go off at half-cock/go off half-cocked flas (veproj) para kohe; filloj para kohe

□ *Mr. Jones was thinking about quitting his job, but his wife told him not to* **go at half-cock.** □ *Bill often* **goes off at half-cocked.** □ *The publicity for the new car* **went off at half-cock** *following a leak of information about all the novel features that it incorporated.*

go off one's head/nut luaj mendsh (nga mendtë)

□ *Poor old Tom* **went off** *his head, spent all his money in six months and ended up begging in the streets.* □ *Samuel seemed to have* **gone off** *his nut.*

go off the deep end pëlcas nga inati, xhindosem, më hipin kacabujtë

□ *When the teacher saw how badly the homework had been done, he just about* **went off the deep end.** □ *You should have heard the other night. You know what happened? Her wandering boy returned. He hadn't been home for two weeks. And she* **went off the deep end.**

go off the rails 1. del nga binarët, është shthurur

□ *It was odd how Harold, who had never since his marriage taken a step along the primrose path, never* **gone off the rails** *in any way or*

wished to, proved himself a past-master of intrigue.
2. s'është më në rregull, ka luajtur mendsh, është çmendur

□ *I think that Jim went off the rails because of the strain of overwork.*

go off the track 1. futem në rrugë të gabuar

□ *You'll never work it out by that method, you've gone off the track altogether.*

2. dal nga tema

□ *The student went a long way off the track.*

go on 1. eci, vazhdoj të eci, vazhdoj udhëtimin

□ *The party of explorers decided that they could not go on with darkness closing in.* □ *We all voted to go on despite the signs of a thunderstorm on the horizon.* □ *Go on until you get to the post office and then turn left.*

2. vazhdoj, kaloj, hidhem

□ *'We can't go on as though nothing has happened. You've broken your promise.'* □ *He gave her a look, half in remonstration, half in approval and went on.* □ *Let us go on to the next item on the agenda.*

3. kalon, shkon (koha)

□ *As the years go on, we grow both wiser and sadder.* □ *As the days went on he wanted anything, anything that offered a chance.*

4. ndodh, ngjet

□ *Something wasn't right there, and she wanted to know what was going on.* □ *'What's going on between that couple over there? There's something very odd about their behavior.'* □ *What's going on next door? There seems to be a good deal of noise.*

5. dal në skenë

□ *She doesn't go on till Act Two.*
6. ndizen dritat

□ *We had been sitting for a couple of hours in candlelight when to our relief the lights went on again.* □ *Suddenly all the lights went on.*

go on about flet pa pushim, flet si çakalle mulliri

□ *'Yes, yes! I admit I was wrong in not keeping you informed of my plans. But please don't go on about it!* □ *'That woman bores me stiff! The way she goes on about her paragon of a son!*

go on at ngacmoj, kritikoj, i bie më qafë

□ *'Why do you go on at that poor girl all the time? She does her best.'* □ *She goes on at her husband continually.*

go on for është gati, është afër, i afrohet

□ *'Good Lord! It's going on for one o'clock and I promised to see George at half past twelve!'* □ *It's going on for lunch time.*

go one better (than sb/sth) bëj diçka më mirë se; ofroj më shumë; ia kaloj

□ *I saw the other dealer was determined to have the picture: however I bid he would go one better. So I gave up.* □ *It hit the target 17 times out of 20, but Tom went one better and scored 18 hits.* □ *He tried to go us one better by bidding twice as much as we did for the antique.*

go one's own way bëj sipas qejfit, bëj si më thotë mendja, bëj sipas kokës

□ *As far as others are concerned, whatever they tell me to do, I usually go my own way.* □ *They didn't even pretend to like the lad, and their generosity towards him showed itself chiefly in... allowing him to go his own way...*

go on strike dal (bëj) grevë

□ *We are going on strike.*

go on the stage bëhem aktor(e)

□ *To her parents' dismay, Brigit*

decided to **go on the stage.** □ *She's wanted to* **go on the stage** *from an early age.*

go on with vazhdoj me

□ *The teacher told the class to* **go on with** *the exercise quietly while he was out of the room.* □ *If we don't finish painting the kitchen today, we can* **go on with** *it tomorrow.* □ *In a very little while he took his hand away and put it on his breast, and* **went on with** *his story.*

go out 1. dal jashtë, largohem, iki

□ *'What a pity you didn't arrive half an hour ago. Mary's* **gone out** *riding and won't be back until six o'clock.'* □ *He* **went out** *hatless, leaving the street door open behind him.* □ *Andrew* **went out** *to the call immediately with a queer sensation almost of relief.*

2. del jashtë mode

□ *'You can't wear that to the party! Miniskirts* **went out** *years ago.'*

3. fiket, shuhet

□ *We were looking forward to getting back to a warm house, but when we arrived the fire had* **gone out.** □ *His pipe* **went out** *and he put it away.* □ *My cigarette has* **gone out.** *Strike a match for me, will you?*

4. bie. zbret, ulet

□ *The sea, at certain parts of the coast,* **goes out** *so far that it can no longer be seen.* □ *The tide has* **gone out,** *but will soon return.*

5. bëj grevë

□ *Are we likely to gain anything if we* **go out** *on strike?*

6. përfundon, largohet

□ *When March comes in like a lamb, it* **goes out** *like a lion.*

7. humb ndjenjat, më bie të fikët

□ *After the sustained effort of the day I lay down on the bed and* **went out**

like a light. □ *One blow to the chin and the challenger* **went out** *for the count.*

go out of business ndërpres punën, falimenton

□ *A lot of small grocers have* **gone out of business** *since the advent of the supermarkets.* □ *Some people believe that it would be a good thing if certain manufactures were to* **go out of business.**

go out of date vjetërohet, i kalon koha, nuk është më i kohës

□ *Will denim jeans ever* **go out of date?** □ *That dictionary has* **gone out of date.**

go out of fashion del nga moda

□ *That style of dress* **has gone out of fashion.** □ *Miniskirts have* **gone out of fashion.**

go out of one's mind 1. më del nga mendja

□ *I'm sorry I forgot to turn up at the meeting. I fully intended to, but it* **went right out of my mind.** □ *'I should know his name but it's just* **gone out of my mind** *for the moment.'* □ *I know their telephone number quite well but it has* **gone out of my mind** *for the moment.*

2. luaj mendsh, çmendem

□ *'Annie, get up immediately, and don't disgrace everybody belonging to you by humbling yourself like that, unless you wish to see me* **go out of my mind** *on the spot.'* □ *When he heard how much his wife had paid for the furniture, her husband said,' Have you* **gone out of your mind?** *We have hardly any money left.'*

go out of one's way bëj çmos, bëhem copë (copa, copash)

□ *The people in this village are very*

helpful: if you are ever in trouble, they will go out of their way to help you. □ *You should be willing to go out of your way to oblige a friend.* □ *We went out of our way to make him feel at home.*

go out of sight/view zhduket nga pamja (sytë)
□ *The fog came down like a curtain and in a few moments the coastline had gone out of sight.*

go over 1. kaloj, kapërcej matanë
□ *A boat goes over to the island once a week with mail and provision.* □ *As your wife was going over the bridge, one of planks gave way.* □ *They went over the river by ferry boat.*

2. kontrolloj, rishikoj, rilexoj
□ *You'll have to go over the figures again; they don't balance out.* □ *Before you hand in your composition, you had better go over it.* □ *He carefully went over the whole account item by item.*

3. inspektoj, kontrolloj
□ *We are going over the whole area to look for ore.* □ *The prospective tenants went over the accommodation, but made no comment except to thank the old lady for her trouble.*

4. shqyrtoj
□ *We went over every detail of his story in an effort to discover whether it was true or not.* □ *The detective went over the facts in his mind for the twentieth time, but still the vital clue eluded him.*

5. kaloj
□ *'We're interrupting the programme to go over to our news desk for an important bulletin.'*

go phut 1. vete tatëpjetë
□ *The business went phut.*
2. prishet, dëmtohet

□ *The washing-machine has gone phut.*

go red (in the face) skuqem në fytyrë
□ *We can behold an outraged member of Women's Lib going red in the face and choking with anger so that she cannot find words to express her contempt.*

go right/wrong (for sb) shkon (ecën) mirë (keq)
□ *It was a tight schedule but everything went right for us.* □ *Nothing goes right for Noddy today.*

go round 1. rrotullohet
□ *The hand of the clock goes round.*
□ *I went to see the wheels go round.*

2. kaloj nga, bëj një vizitë
□ *'Let's go round and see Mary. She's always ready for a chat.'*
□ *'Michael would like to see you some time?' 'I'll go some time. I'll go round tomorrow.'*

3. vërtitet, vjen rrotull
□ *After a couple of glasses of whisky, the bar began to go round.* □ *His head seemed to go round, and he clutched at the nearest passer-by.*

4. i bie rrotull, i bie qark
□ *The front gate was shut so we had to go round.* □ *The main road to Worcester was flooded and we had to go a long way round.*

5. del. mjafton, ka (për të gjithë)
□ *The hostess didn't know what to do, as she hadn't got enough food to go round so many people.* □ *The meat won't go round, you must get enough to go round.*

6. vërtitem, sillem poshtë e lartë (në një vend)
□ *'While you're here, would you like to go round?'*

go round in circles vij rrotull
□ *We have been trying all day to find*

195

*a solution to this problem, bur we just
keep going round in circles.*

go scot-free shpëtoj paq (pa u
ndëshkuar), dal pa lagur
□ *Men like the Kray brothers or the
Richardson gang are often too canny
to get personally involved in the
crimes they are planning. It would be
wrong to let them go scot-free just for
lack of fingerprints.* □ *If we could do
that, she might go scot-free for aught
I cared.*

go (shares) share and share alike
ndaj barabar, ndaj përgjysmë
□ *'Any time you like to go shares,
Fleur, you've only to say so.'* □ *Let me
go shares with you in the taxi fare.*

go short (of sth) mbetem pa, privoj
nga
□ *If you earn well, you'll never go
short.* □ *The children must not go
short of food.*

go slow punoj më avash; ul ritmin, e
marr shtruar, tregohem më pak aktiv,
nuk nxitohem
□ *You ought to go slow until you get
well again.* □ *There's something
wrong with his lungs. Nothing immediately serous but he does have to go
slow.*

go steady with sb shkoj rregullisht me
□ *I have been going steady with a girl
for nearly two years, and we were
shortly to be engaged.*

go steady with sth tregohem i
kujdesshëm, i përkorë, i matur
□ *Here you two, just go steady with
that bottle!* □ *I'd go a bit steady about
calling the police if I were you.*

go the right/wrong way shkon (përfundon) mirë (keq)
□ *He had opened the bag of uncut
rubies meaning to cache the rest
where, if the war went the right way,
he could come back and collect them.*

□ *His lawyer advised him not to sue;
the case could so easily go the wrong
way and leave him worse than ever
before.* □ *... he had finished his ale in
a hurry and some of it had gone the
wrong way.*

go the rounds (of sth) vizitoj
□ *We went the rounds of all the pubs
in the town.*

go the round of qarkullon
□ *The news quickly went the round of
the village.* □ *There is a story going
round that the Greens are going to be
divorced.*

go the way of all flesh vdes
□ *Now that the greatest artist of
the first half of this century has
at long last gone the way of all
flesh, the small talents are doing
their best to discredit his phenomenal
achievements.* □ *He pardoned us
off—hand, and allowed us something
to live on till he went the way of all
flesh.*

go the whole hog çoj diçka deri në
fund
□ *Having bought the house, they
decided to go the whole hog, and buy
all the furniture in it as well.* □ *If one
promises to do a thing, the proper
thing to do is to go the whole hog.*

go the whole length çoj deri në fund
□ *Having decided to do that, he went
the whole length of it.*

go through 1. provoj, përjetoj, heq,
kaloj
□ *Before the days of anaesthetics
people had to go through dreadful
pain when they were operated on.*
□ *'After what he went through with
his first wife, you'd think he would
have steered clear of marriage for the
rest of his life.*

2. kaloj, shqyrtoj
□ *They went through the details of*

the plan over and over again to make sure that there was no possibility of failure. □ I cannot **go through** these letters in an hour.
3. përdor, harxhoj, shpenzoj, konsumoj
□ 'Do you mean to say that we've **gone through** all those envelopes I bought last week?' □ It didn't take Albert very long to **go through** his inheritance.
4. kryej, bëj
□ As he watched Leywellen **go through** the operation he could not repress a feeling of admiration.
5. rrëmoj, kontrolloj
□ The woman **went through** every drawer and cupboard in the house, but she could not find the missing silver. □ The police **went through** the building with a fine tooth comb, but they found no evidence that would help them to catch the thief.
6. kalon
□ This rope is too thick to **go through** the hole.
□ The piano **went through** the door easily, but the sideboard wouldn't **go through** at all.

go through fire and water kaloj çdo vështirësi (rrebesh)
□ The loyal soldiers were ready to **go through fire and water** for the king.

go through hoops/the hoop kaloj prova, vështirësi
□ We all had to **go through the hoop** of reading our essays aloud to the rest of the class.

go through the mill kaloj prova të vështira, jam regjur në punë
□ .. she had for him the fellow—feeling of one who had **gone through** the same mill. □ The best men at running industry are those who had to **go through the mill** themselves.

go to 1. i jepet, i kalon
□ The first prize for Biology **went to** the youngest child in the class. □ The family was furious when the old man's entire possessions **went to** his housekeeper.

go to bed bie (shtrihem) në krevat (shtrat)
□ Finally, she began to grow dull in her chair, and feeling the need of sleep, arranged her clothing for the night and **went to bed**.

go to blazes në djall të shkojë (vejë)
□ He told the annoying salesman to **go to blazes**.

go to earth/ground fshihem; futem (në strofkë)
□ The police search for the escaped prisoner has been unsuccessful: he has **gone to earth** somewhere in the city. □ A minute later the fox **went to earth** within a hundred yards of the leading hounds. □ When the master of the hounds realized that the quarry had **gone to earth** and the dogs had lost the scent, he called off the hunt.

go to extremes kaloj në ekstrem, kaloj çdo cak
□ Why should you **go to extremes**?
□ He is the kind of man who cannot do anything in moderation. If he drinks, he drinks too much; if he drives a car, he drives too fast; if he goes for a meal, he goes to the most expensive hotel. He always **goes to extremes**.

go too far e teproj, kaloj (kapërcej) çdo kufi (cak)
□ He's has always been rather rude but this time he's **gone too far**.
□ Don't **go too far** with your joke.

go to one's head 1. i ra në kokë
□ The wine I had at lunchtime seems to have **gone to my head**: I can't think properly. □ The wine **went to Susan's head**. What with that and the heat,

she simply passed out at the table.
2. i ra në kokë, ia mori mendjen
□ *Don't let the manager's congratulations* **go to your head.** *Next week he's just as likely to bite your head off.* □ *The girl's fame as a movie actress* **went to her head.**

go to pieces 1. thyhet, copëtohet, bëhet copë-copë
□ *When he dropped the glass on the floor it* **went to pieces.** □ *It's* **gone to pieces** *at the first touch.*
2. thyhem mendërisht (moralisht, fizikisht); humb kontrollin (shëndetin, vetëbesimin etj.); bie, lëshohem, këputem
□ *When he heard the news of his wife's death, he just* **went to pieces.** □ *At the sight of someone from home the big fellow nearly* **went to pieces**— *he had to steady himself by a chair.* □ *When Sam heard of his son's death he* **went to pieces;** *but as time passed he gradually returned to something like his old cheerful self.* □ *Mary* **goes to pieces** *when she can't have her own.*

go to pot rrënohet, shkatërrohet, merr të tatëpjetën
□ *The motel business* **went to pot** *when the new highway was built.* □ *His son is a very poor businessman; ever since he took over his father's business, it has* **gone all to pot.**

go to rack and ruin prishet, rrënohet, shkatërrohet, merr të tatëpjetën
□ *Nobody has lived in that house for many years, and it has been allowed to* **go to rack and ruin.** □ *And now the house was* **going to rack and ruin.** *Aunt Annabel patiently inquired how it could be expected to do anything else, with only a cook-housekeeper, one maid, and a daily.*

go to sea bëhem marinar
□ *The boy was tired of looking for a job near his home and eventually decided to* **go to sea.**

go/run to seed 1. nxjerr (zë) farë
□ *He and his Scotch wife were forced to migrate with their goods and their chattels, and left the stately comfortable garden to go to waste, and the flower beds to* **run to seeds.** □ *What a pity you let all those cabbages* **go to seed.** *They are no use now.*
2. bie, prishem, marr të tatëpjetën
□ *Mr. Monks is aware that I am not a young man, my dear, and also that I am a little* **run to seed,** *as I may say.* □ *He used to be a very athletic person, but since he started drinking heavily, he's really* **gone to seed.**

go to show tregon, provon
□ *When we started out the sun was shining, but when we arrived at the seaside it was pouring with rain: it just* **goes to show** *that you can never rely on the weather in Britain.*

go to sleep 1. bie të fle
□ *Aunt Juley recalled how he had* **gone to sleep** *on the sofa one day, when James was sitting.* □ **Go to sleep** *now, it's late.*
2. mpihet
□ *I've been sitting on the floor and my foot's* **gone to sleep.**

go to sb's heart mallëngjehet, preket thellë në shpirt, i dhemb shpirti
□ *It goes to Ma Parker's* **heart** *to see little Lennie suffer.*

go to the bad marr rrugë të keqe, shthurem (moralisht)
□ *'... it hurts Alice so much to see a son of hers'* **go to the bad.'**

go to the country shpërndaj parlamentin, thërras zgjedhjet e përgjithshme

□ *The Prime Minister said that if Parliament went against him on the crucial issue of our joining the Common Market, he would be forced to go to the country.*

go to the dogs shkatërrohet, merr të tatëpjetën

□ *From the way some people talk, you'd think that the country had been going to the dogs for the last fifty years.* □ *Everything costs three times as much as it did five years ago: the country is going to the dogs.* □ *I had to resign my membership because the club was going to the dogs.*

go to the heart of hyj në thelb të

'You are getting married?' 'Yes.' 'To whom?' asked Donna Rachele, who liked to go to the heart of a question. □ *Providing a few clinics for drug addicts may help, but it doesn't go to the heart of the problem.*

go to the wall dështon, falimenton, merr fund

□ *Business has been so bad recently that many companies have gone to the wall.* □ *Everything must go to the wall now except the providing of an extra pair of hands.*

go to waste shkon kot (dëm)

□ *She dropped her expensive bottle of perfume and it broke: it's a shame to think of all that money going to waste.* □ *'How can you let all this food go to waste when there are so many starving people in the world?'*

go to work (on) filloj nga puna

□ *The young architect went to work with a will on his first commission.* □ *Intelligence agents went to work and soon found the reason for the leak of information to the enemy.*

go under 1. zhytet

□ *Just as the would-be rescuer reached the drowning man, he went*

under *for the third time and was never seen again.*

2. dështon, falimenton

□ *Poor Donaldson had no head for business, and it was not long before he went under.* □ *The firm will go under unless business improves.*

go under the hammer shitet në ankand

□ *Everything that Joss possessed went under the hammer to pay his debts.* □ *We must do everything we can to prevent the old homestead from going under the hammer.*

go up 1. ngrihet, ngjitet

□ *Since the old lady fell, she's been unable to go up stairs.* □ *The squirrel went up the tree like greased lightning.* □ *Hush! The curtain is going up.*

2. ngrihen çmimet

□ *Everything seems to be going up these days: coal, groceries, busfares, rents.* □ *'Have you seen the paper today? Up go the prices again!'*

3. hidhet në erë, shpërthen

□ *The hill went up with a roar when the mine was exploded.*

4. ndërtohen, ngrihen

□ *'Everywhere you look, you can see glass and concrete monstrosities going up.* □ *New buildings are going up everywhere in Albania.*

go up in smoke/flames 1. digjet

□ *The house went up in flames.*

2. dështon, shkon kot, përfundon në hiç, bëhet tym, humbet si pluhuri në erë

□ *His hands were seriously injured when he fell, so all his plans for becoming a musician went up in smoke.* □ *When he crashed his car all his travel plans went up in smoke.*

go west 1. vdes

□ *'I'm afraid not', said Michael. 'You see, he was a Chinknot quite of the*

best period; but he must have gone west five years ago at least.'
2. humbet, zhduket, shkatërrohet, merr fund, shkon prapa diellit, shkon në humbësirë
□ *There was a fire, and five years of research work went west.* □ *The food mixer must have gone west along with my baking tins, when we moved house.*

go with 1. shoqëroj
□ *The younger children stayed with their uncle while the older ones went with their parents to Spain.* □ *He went with the man, who picked up several other newly landed immigrants, and took them all outside.*
2. shoqërohem, shkoj me
□ *How long has Alice been going with Steven? I thought Adam was her boyfriend.*
3. shkon, përshtatet, harmonizohet
□ *Her blouse doesn't go with her skirt.* □ *I need some new shoes to go with these trousers.*

go with the tide shkon pas rrymës
□ *Tom hasn't got a mind of his own on any matter of importance; he just goes with the tide.*

go without rri pa, bëj pa
□ *Millions of the refugees were given food, but thousands had to go without and died of starvation.* □ *The doctor willingly went without his dinner if by attending a patient quickly he could relieve his suffering.* □ *On rainy days umbrellas and rubbers are something we cannot go without.*

go without saying afërmendsh, kuptohet vetiu, s'ka dyshim
□ *Since you are our guests, it goes without saying that we shall pay all the bills for your accommodation.* □ *'We have to keep friends anyhow and hear of each other.' 'That goes*

without saying.' □ *When you visit England it goes without saying that you will be my guest.*

go wrong 1. dështon, shkon (përfundon) keq
□ *As long as nothing goes wrong with my other ear I won't be too deaf.* □ *She was feeling that it would serve Alec and the lawyers right if all went wrong.*
2. gaboj, bëj gabim në llogaritje (gjykim, manazhim etj.)
□ *Perhaps all you need to do to see where you went wrong is to read the instructions more carefully.* □ *With a skilled instructor to correct you each time you go wrong, bad driving habits don't get built in.* □ *They ask why the young take to drugs, they ask where they, as parents, might have gone wrong.*
3. prishet, pëson difekt
□ *His watch has gone wrong.*
4. marr rrugë të gabuar
□ *This chap came from a very good family, but he went wrong, and in 1996 he got a two-year sentence.*

grasp a (the) shadow and miss a (the) substance kapem pas çikërrimave dhe le mënjanë thelbësoren
□ *They knew so well what they wanted. They were almost Forsytes. They would never grasp a shadow and miss a substance.*

grasp at straws kapem pas fijes së kashtës, mbahem me shpresa të kota
□ *To depend upon one's memory without studying for a test is to grasp at straws.*

grasp the nettle i vihem (hyj) një pune të vështirë me guxim (me vendosmëri), e kap demin prej brirësh
□ *You are looked up to as a man who can manage his own affairs... we want a man of principle and common*

sense. We want a man that'll grasp the nettle—and that's you.

grass is always greener on the other side of the fence pula e tjetrit duket më e majme

□ *He wishes to give up teaching and become a lawyer like his brother: I think it's a case of the grass being always greener on the other side of the fence.*

grease/oil sb's palm i lyej rrotën (dorën, duart), i jap mitë

□ *The head waiter can get a table for you, but you will have to grease his palm first.* □ *Percy realized it pretty well that he could not be given a job without greasing first the master's palm.* □ *Some politicians will help you if you grease their palms.*

great and small të pasur e të varfër, shtresat e ulta e të larta

□ *Everyone, great and small, is affected by these changes.* □ *Cromwell, efficient policeman that he was, filed away all the reports he was sent concerning the treasonable utterances of great and small, up and down the country.*

green with envy gjithë smirë

□ *Alice's girl friends were green with envy when they saw her new dress.* □ *When Peter saw Bill's expensive new car, he was green with envy.*

grin and bear it duroj dhembjen (zhgënjimin etj.) pa u qarë; pranoj me kënaqësi diçka të pakëndshme

□ *He would grin and bear it, pretend he was pleased to act as a model to so great an artist.* □ *I had to grin and bear it.*

grind one's teeth kërcëllij dhëmbët

□ *Daniel came home slowly, on his fiery feet, grinding his teeth as each rod of pain probed upward from his toes into his forehead.* □ *He ground*

his teeth and forced himself down and the rock was so sharp against his knees that he reopened the wounds of the first day.

grist to/for sb's mill ujë në mullirin e

□ *He is interested in writing a book on the problems that foreigners have in learning English: anything you can tell him on that subject will be grist to his mill.* □ *Nearly everything is grist to his mill.* □ *I never refuse odd jobs to supplement my income— it's all grist to the mill*

grit one's teeth 1. shtrëngoj dhëmbët

□ *The swimming baths terrified me as a child. But rather than be made a fool by the other boys I would grit my teeth and jump in.*

2. bëj kurajë, bëhem burrë, shtrëngoj dhëmbët, mbledh të gjitha fuqitë

□ *When things get difficult, you just have to grit your teeth and persevere.*

grope one's way eci duke prekur

□ *The blind man groped his way to the door.*

□ *She was groping her way along the darkened corridor.*

grow away from sb shkëputem, largohem nga

□ *It often happens that a girl who in her early teens has been very close to her mother suddenly grows away from her as she makes new friends and her horizons widen.* □ *After only one term at the university, David was conscious that he had grown away from his old school friends and that things would never be the same again.*

grow into 1. bëhet, rritet

□ *We did not meet again for ten years. By then, the rather puny boy had grown into a six-footer weighing 220 pounds.* □ *The small family business grew into a company of international importance.*

2. mësohet, ambientohet

□ *She is a good actress, but still needs time to* **grow into** *the part she is playing.*

grow on 1. më tërheq, më pëlqen

□ *When I first went to live in Glasgow I found it rather a dreary place, but after a while it began to* **grow on** *me.* □ *This book seems uninteresting at first but it* **grows on** *you.*

2. rrënjoset, kultivohet

□ *The habit of early rising has* **grown on** *me with the years.*

grow out of 1. s'më bëjnë (nxënë) rrobat etj.

□ *'It's terrible the way Sheila's* **growing out of** *her shoes; she needs a bigger size every three months!'* □ *The child has* **grown out of** *his clothes.*

2. heq dorë, lë, pres (një zakon etj)

□ *'Don't worry about Johnny's tantrums. He'll* **grow out of** *them. Children always do.'* □ *He has* **grown out of** *the bad habit of smoking.*

3. zë fill, buron, vjen

□ *My interest in the art of India* **grew out of** *the time I spent there during the war.*

grow up 1. rritem

□ *'What are you going to do when you* **grow up**, *Annie?' 'I'm going to be a nurse.'* □ *When the boy* **grows up** *he will surely be very tall.*

2. burrërohem, piqem

□ *'It's not good, George. There's only one thing you can do about it, and that's* **grow up**. *Stop being the kind of person that people play practical jokes on.*

guard against ruhem nga, bëj kujdes të mos, marr masa që të mos

□ *A doctor must always* **guard against** *passing on disease to his family.* □ *They've been doing very well, but they should* **guard against** *over-confidence.*

gulp sth back gëlltit, kapërdij

□ *She* **gulped back** *her tears and tried to smile.*

H

hack off pres
□ *The cook **hacked off** a piece of the roasted carcass and handed it me in his fingers.*

hack one's way across/out of/through çaj rrugën nëpër, përmes
□ *We **hacked our way through** the undergrowth.*

had better/best më mirë të
□ *You'd **better** not say that.* □ *You **had better** finish your composition today, for tomorrow we shall have other things to do.* □ *I'm afraid you **had better** let us in.* □ *You **had better** leave us.*

had rather preferoj, pëlqej të
□ *I **had rather** walk than ride.* □ *In the way of exercise I'd **rather** undertake some physical labor than just take a walk.*

hale and hearty plot (tërë) shëndet, shëndoshë e mirë
□ *Being still **hale and hearty** in spite of his seventy years, my father was able to add to his pension by selling vegetables from his garden.* □ *That little boy looks **hale and hearty** as if he is never sick.* □ *He's a remarkable man: although he is in his seventies, he is still **hale and hearty**.* □ *They came on bicycle and on foot, all **hale and hearty**.*

half a loaf is better than no bread/none më mirë pak se aspak
□ *'You do understand, don't you, that the operation will only partially restore your eyesight?' 'Well even **half a loaf is better than no bread**.'* □ *Realising that they couldn't prevent raw materials coming in through the docks, the strikers decided that **half a loaf was better than none** and accepted a 10% wage increase instead of the 15% originally demanded.*

half a mo/moment/sec një minutë, një moment, një sekondë
□ *'**Half a mo**. Stay a few minutes.' But I was already on my feet.* □ *'There's no bus after 10 pm,' he said, studying the time table. '**Half a sec**. There's a later one on Saturdays and Sundays.'*

half and half gjysma ... gjysma ...; gjysmë për gjysmë
□ *'How do you like your coffee?' Mary asked. '**Half and half** please and no sugar.'* □ *Let's share it **half and half**.*

half as many/much again edhe një herë kaq
□ *There aren't enough chairs for the meeting—we need **half as many again**.* □ *The first price we were offered for the house was a good one, but the next buyer offered **half as much again**.*

half seas over/cut çakërqejf
□ *By the time he left the bar he was **half seas over**.* □ *Look at Frank **half seas over** already, and the party's hardly begun.* □ *He spoke with the careful enunciation of a man who knows he is **half seas over** but does not wish to be sought so.*

half the battle gjysma e punës
□ *When you write an essay for class, making the outline is **half the distance**.* □ *If you want to camp in a field, getting the farmer's permission is **half the battle**.*

hammer away at punoj me ngulm
- □ *They were all **hammering away at** their work.*

hammer sth into sb/sth 1. ngulit, ngul në mendje
- □ *We had Latin **hammered into** our heads for five years. How much of it do we still remember?*

2. ngul
- □ *First the pegs were **hammered into** the ground in a large circle, then the tent was raised and the ropes fastened.*

hammer sth into sb's head (into the head of sb) ia ngulit në mendje, ia fus në kokë
- □ *I found it hard to **hammer** the sums **into** the child's **head**.*

hammer sth out 1. rrafshoj, drejtoj me rrahje
- □ *That dent is not big enough to be worth **hammering out**; we can fill it in.*

2. arrij (nëpërmjet diskutimit etj.
- □ *After prolonged discussion, the delegates **hammered out** a form of words that was acceptable to everyone.*
- □ *The club members have **hammered out** an agreement between two groups.*

hand down 1. kalon, përcillet, transmetohet
- □ *In poor families, clothes may be **handed down** from one child to the next.* □ *These ceremonies have been **handed down** through the centuries, and remain practically unchanged.*
- □ *Popular medicine, as part of the national culture, has been **handed down** from one generation to another.*

2. marr vendim
- □ *After the jury had returned its verdict the judge **handed down** very heavy sentences ranging from fifteen to twenty-five years on all the accused.*

hand in dorëzoj
- □ *She **handed in** her resignation.*
- □ *The teacher asks every student to **hand in** his homework in time.*

hand in glove with sb bythë e brekë me, si mishi me thuan, në bashkëpunim të ngushtë me, lidhur ngushtë me
- □ *The energetic Sippens came after a few moments, and he and Van Sickle after being instructed to be mutually helpful and to keep Cowperwood's name out of all matters relating to this work, departing together. In ten minutes they were **hand in glove**...*
- □ *It was revealed in the newspapers that some policemen had actually been working **hand in glove** with the criminals.* □ *'You must speak to the doctor, Granny Barnacle,' said Miss Tailor, 'if you really feel you aren't getting the right treatment from the Ward Sister.' 'The doctor, my backside. They are **hand in glove**. What's an old woman to them I ask you?'*

hand in hand dorë për dore
- □ *One of the genial moments of the film finds them gazing raptly at an exploding helicopter before wandering off into the desert **hand in hand**.* □ *They walked along **hand in hand**.*

hand it to sb i jap dikujt lavdërimet që meriton
- □ *You have to **hand it to** Bill; he may not work very hard, but he always comes first.* □ *'She's been wonderfully cheerful, and interested in everything—you've really got to **hand it to** her.*

handle with gloves/with kid gloves trajtoj me takt, kujdes e butësi
- □ *Sally is such a baby that she cries if her teacher does not **handle her with gloves**.*

hand over 1. dorëzoj

□ *This was the day of the week that Uncle Saunders was expected to* **hand over** *the housekeeping money.* □ *Having expelled the student, the authorities almost literally* **handed** *him* **over** *to the secular arm.*

2. ia kaloj, ia dorëzoj

□ *The time had come for* **handing over** *power to a local, elected government.* □ *The stores were properly* **handed over** *to the new man—even the nuts and bolts were checked.*

hand over fist kollaj e pa hesap

□ *They're making money* **hand over fist,** *but anyone capable of counting up to ten can do that now.* □ *Ever since they opened their shop they have been making money* **hand over fist.**

hand over heart me dorë në zemër, çiltërisht, ndershmërisht

□ *I ask you, in a society which repeatedly declares,* **hand over heart,** *that the child's interests are always paramount in these disputes, how damned hypocritical can we be?*

hands off sb/sth larg duart nga

□ *I was going to touch the machine, but the man cried, 'Hands off!' and let it alone.* □ *So friends or no friends, Polly,* **hands off** *him.*

hand-to-hand fighting luftë trup me trup

□ *One scene taken from high ground for an attack over open ground, including* **hand-to-hand fighting,** *showed the horror, the courage, and the bravery of war.*

hang about/around rri e pres; endem kot, sorollatem, sillem vërdallë

□ *She was left to* **hang about** *the platform on her own.* □ *Desmond had spent several weeks* **hanging around** *the garage.* □ *We* **hung about** *until the shops opened.* □ *Almost at once the winter was upon them and* **hang about** *the streets.*

hang back ngurroj, hezitoj

□ *When the police came around asking questions, Peter* **hung back** *from giving information.* □ *He's a solitary child—always* **hangs back** *from any group activities.* □ *Most of the boys dashed across the road but two* **hung back.**

hang by a hair/thread varet në një qime, varet në fije (fill) të perit (të flokut)

□ *All Meg had built up, all she had earned by the shrewd work of her mind... was* **hanging by a thread.** □ *The success of John's application for the job is* **hanging by a thread:** *the committee is evenly divided.* □ *For three days Tom was so sick that his life* **hung by a thread.**

hang down one's head var (ul) kokën nga turpi

□ *As Mr. Pecksniff ceased to speak, she* **hung her head** *and dropped a tear upon his hand.*

hang fire 1. ecën (përparon, zhvillohet) avash (ngadalë); vonohet

□ *For a little while the conversation* **hung fire.**

□ *We were in bed by ten, for we wanted to be up and away on our tramp homeward with the dawn. I* **hung fire,** *but Harris went to steep at once.* □ *'Answer the gentleman, Thomas—don't be afraid.' Tom still* **hung fire.**

2. pres

□ *We can't start yet; shall we have to* **hang fire** *until the others arrive.*

hang heavy/heavily on one's hands mezi kalon (shtyhet) koha, etj.

□ *The weeks until her husband's return* **hung heavy on her hands.**

□ *Tom presently wondered that his coveted vocation was beginning to* **hang** *a little* **heavily on his hands**.

hang in the balance është (qëndron) pezull; është me dyshim

□ *The jury has not yet returned its verdict: the accused man's fate still* **hangs in the balance**. □ *If your heart begins to fail when the issue* **hangs in the balance***, your opponent will probably win.* □ *She was very sick and her life* **hung in the balance** *for several days.*

hang on 1. pres paksa

□ **Hang on** *a minute—I'm nearly ready.* □ *Mrs. Roth said she'd* **hang on** *a bit.*

2. mbahem fort; shtrëngoj fort

□ *Jack almost fell off the cliff, but managed to* **hang on** *until help came.* □ *'***Hang on** *with your knees. Don't let go.* □ **Hang on** *tight.* □ **Hang on** *to that rope and don't let go.*

3. varet

□ *The survival of the government* **hangs on** *tonight's crucial vote.* □ *On our ability to compete in difficult markets* **hangs** *our future as a trading nation.*

4. vazhdoj, këmbëngul

□ *The grocer was losing money every day, but he* **hung on***, hoping that business would improve.*

hang on sb's lips/words/ on sb's every word dëgjoj me vëmendje të madhe, përpij çdo fjalë, i bëj veshët pipëz

□ *The audience* **hung on** *the speaker's* **every word***.* □ *When he'd get started on art subjects Laura would just* **hang on every word***.*

hang out 1. var (rrobat)

□ *'I've just got one or two shirts to* **hang out***—then we can go shopping.*

2. jetoj, banoj

□ *'What did you say were doing? And where are you* **hanging out***?'*

3. sorrollatem, vij rrotull, shkoj shpesh

□ *Where does he* **hang out** *these days?* □ *The teacher complained that Joe was* **hanging out** *in poolrooms instead of doing his homework.*

hang over sb's head rri varur shpatë mbi kokë, është kërcënim i përhershëm për

□ *During the last years of the politician's life, the threat of imprisonment* **hung over** *his* **head***.*

hang together 1. ndihmoj, mbështes njëri tjetrin

□ *We can come through any crisis if we* **hang together***.*

2. formojnë një të tërë koherente

□ *Their accounts of what happened don't* **hang together***.*

hang up (on) mbaroj bisedën telefonike, ul receptorin

□ *Carol's mother told her she had talked long enough on the phone and made her* **hang up***.* □ *I didn't have a chance to apologize: she* **hung up on** *me.*

happen what may sido që të ndodhë

□ **Happen what may***, I'll make no move without your permission.*

hard and fast 1. i rreptë, i prerë

□ *It is a* **hard and fast** *rule that all the students must be back in their rooms by midnight.* □ *These stages may now be discussed in more detail but first it must be emphasized that they do not present* **hard and fast** *categories.* □ *We must make it a* **hard and fast** *rule not to allow any parent to enter a classroom without first speaking to the headmaster.* □ *There are no* **hard and fast** *rules in this game.*

2. fort, në mënyrë të palëvizshme

□ *The boulder was wedged* **hard and fast** *in the crevice and nothing short* *of an explosive charge could have moved it.*

hard/tough as nails 1. i fortë si çeliku, i kalitur, i fortë fizikisht

□ *After six months of training, the young soldiers were all as hard as nails.* □ *After a summer of work in the country, Jack was hard as nails, without a pound of extra weight.* 2. zemërgur

□ *I wouldn't like to annoy that barmaid: she looks as hard as nails.*

hard by shumë afër pranë

□ *Not a stone's throw from Whitehall, and hard by the River Thames, there stands an old, decaying building.* □ *Never assume a young animal has been deserted. The mother is probably concealed hard by, waiting for you to go.*

hard case, a rast i vështirë

□ *Everybody that comes to this Bureau is in trouble of some sort but I have seldom heard of a harder case than that poor woman's.* □ *'He'll lose his job as well as his license.' 'The court can't make exceptions for hard cases.*

hard cash monedhë, kartmonedhë

□ *I don't have that much money on me—not in hard cash anyway. Will you take a check?* □ *Victoria toyed hopefully with the idea that Mr. Chipp might press upon her a parting present in the form of hard cash.*

hard luck fat i keq

□ *So he didn't inherit a penny? That was hard luck, after all the years he worked for the old devil.*

hard/tough nut to crack, a problem i vështirë, situatë e vështirë; njeri i vështirë

□ *She's a tough nut to crack. I don't think she'll give us permission.* □ *The*

police have been trying to solve the case for weeks now, but it seems to be a tough nut to crack. □ *I've put all the facts and figures before you. Try to work it out, though I warn you it's a hard nut to crack.*

hard of hearing i rëndë nga veshët

□ *Since your father's getting so hard of hearing you must all learn to speak up instead of losing patience with him.* □ *Old as my grandfather is, he is by no means hard of hearing.*

hard on sb i ashpër me

□ *I don't like to be hard on an old man but I'm going to have to tell him, one of these days, what a lying old fraud he is.*

hard put to it to do sth e kam vështirë të

□ *Even with the three of us working, we were still hard put to it to cope with all the work.* □ *There are very good restaurants in this town: in fact, I would be hard put to it to name every one.*

hard to say/tell vështirë të thuhet

□ *'How old a man is he?' 'About my age, probably, though it's hard to say.'* □ *All this time Finn had been leaning against the door, looking abstractedly into the middle distance. Whether he was listening or not was hard to tell.*

hard to take vështirë të pranohet (të besohet)

□ *Be patient and kind with her, John. The loss of a young child is very hard to take.* □ *I joined the army when I was 17. The discipline was dreadful, and the loss of freedom hard to take.*

hard way, the në mënyrën (rrugën) më të vështirë

□ *As for the strike committee, they have found out the hard way who their real friends are.*

□ *Young people find it very easy to earn money these days; I earned all my money **the hard way**.*

hard words fjalë të rënda (të ashpra)

□ *There were some **hard words** between us, that I will admit. But if it came to threats, what could I do?* □ *Those who have nothing but **hard words** for the present generation of university students have little idea of how hard most of them work.*

hard/harsh world, a botë e vështirë

□ *This is **a hard world**—they've got to learn to give and take some hard knocks before they're very much older.* □ *Emily's protected upbringing had not equipped her for the realities of **a harsh world**.*

hard up ngushtë (keq) për para

□ *When I was a student, I was always **hard up**.* □ *Dick was **hard up** and asked Lou to lend him a dollar.*

harp on/about sth i bie një avazi, mbaj një avaz

□ *In his campaign speeches, John **harps on** his rival's wealth and powerful friends.* □ *She's always **harping on** the family's neglect of her.* □ *He's always **harping about** my faults.*

harp on one's string i bie kavallit (fyellit) në një vrimë, mbaj avazin e Mukës

□ *No matter what we say, he keeps on **harping on the same string**.* □ *They are sure still **harping on their old string**.* □ *That's a **string** that's been **harped on** many times before.*

hatch a plot/scheme etc. thur (bëj) një plan

□ *So the next time I ran into Ned we **hatched a scheme** for going to see Robert together.*

hate sb's guts urrej dikë për vdekje; kam antipati të thellë për

□ *I just had to tell someone. Funny it*

happened to be you, and you **hate my guts**. □ *Jim and Peter are not friends: in fact, they **hate** each others **guts**.*

hate sb/sth like poison urrej për vdekje

□ *Little Mr. Booker, his bristling eyebrows wrathed in angry smiles, was having a parting turn-up with old Scrubsole. The two **hated** each other **like poison**.* □ *The Earl and Gilles's father **hated** each other **like poison** I believe.*

hate/loathe the sight of sb/sth sëe shoh dot me sy

□ *'You don't love me any more, do you, Charles?' 'To be frank, Amanda, I **hate the** bloody **sight of** you.'*

hat in hand gjithë servilizëm (përulësi, temena)

□ *John Dennis was **hat in hand** to Mr. Congreve.*

haul over the coals i heq vërejtjen, qortoj ashpër

□ *'What was all the fuss about?' 'Oh, just the Old Man **hauling me over the coals** for borrowing his car again.'* □ *If this unpunctuality continues we shall have to **haul** him **over the coals**.* □ *He was **hauled over the coals** by the teacher for his carelessness.*

haul sb up nxjerr para gjyqit

□ *He was **hauled up** before the local magistrates for disorderly conduct.* □ *This is the second time that Matthew has been **hauled up** on a dangerous driving charge.*

have a bad nose (for) kam nuhatje të keqe

□ *'Can you smell anything unusual?' 'Not at all, I **have a bad nose**.'*

have a ball kënaqem, bëj qejf, e kaloj për mrekulli

□ *You should have come to Jim's party: we really **had a ball**.* □ *Johnny **had a ball** at camp.*

have a bee in one's bonnet e ka mendjen te, i rri (punon) mendja te, mendon vetëm për

☐ *Our teacher **has a bee in his bonnet** about punctuation.* ☐ *Everybody knew that 'young Mont' **had a bee in his bonnet** about child emigration.*

have a bone to pick with sb kam arsye (shkak) të zihem (grindem, hahem) me

☐ *I've got a **bone to pick with** you. Where's the money I lent you last week?* ☐ *I **have a bone to pick with** you about the rude way you spoke to me last night.* ☐ *Peter has gone over to see David at the library; he says he **has a bone to pick with** him.*

have a card up one's sleeve kam një gur të fortë në dorë

☐ *There was no question in Western capitals that the Russians **had** many **cards up their sleeves**. (New York Times)*

have a care bëj më shumë kujdes

☐ ***Have a care** not to slip when you climb on the roof.*

have a chip on one's shoulder është mbushur gjithë mllef

☐ *She's **got a chip on her shoulder** about not having gone to university.* ☐ *You'll get on all right with Carson if you take him the right way. He **has a chip on his shoulder** of course—feels he knows more about the business than the people he sees being promoted above him.* ☐ *He applied for a promoted post and did not get it: ever since then he **has had a chip on his shoulder**.*

have a clear conscience kam ndërgjegjen e pastër

☐ *'It must be a great burden nursing your old mother at home for so long.' 'Oh, I prefer to do that and **have a clear conscience**, than let her go in one of those 'homes'.'*

have a close/narrow call/shave shpëtoj për qime

☐ *Jean Robillard **had a close call** that summer. He never would have survived but for the way his mate nursed him.*

have a corner in sb's heart ruaj të gjallë në zemër

☐ *I am sure that the widow and the child you have ever protected and loved will always **have a corner in your heart**.*

have a crush on sb pëlqej, dua, dashuroj marrëzisht

☐ *Almost all the girls in the class **had a crush on** their handsome young teacher.* ☐ *'I am going to save my fares this week and buy Miss Cox flowers.' 'You **have a crush on** Miss Cox.'*

have a fancy for pëlqej

☐ *The children **have a fancy for** their teacher.* ☐ *I **have a fancy for** some wine tonight.*

have/get a/the feeling that kam parandjenjën se

☐ *She took the two bottles of whisky, half a bottle of brandy, and all the tins of soup. She **had a feeling that** she and Joe were going to need them.* ☐ *He was very pleasant but I **got the feeling that** he didn't much like me, all the same.*

have a/one's finger in the pie kam gisht në

☐ *The only annoying feature of the past few weeks had been the re-opening of the two rival totes. John West suspected that Brogan and Devlin **had a finger in the pie** somewhere.* ☐ *Jones is a very important man in our town: whenever anything is planned you can be sure he will **have a finger in the pie**.*

have/throw a fit/have fits 1. habitem, alarmohem; tërbohem nga inati
□ *You mother would* **have a fit** *if she knew you were here.* □ *Father will* **throw a fit** *when he sees the dent in the car.* □ *When Tony decided to drop out of college, his parents* **had fits.**
2. dridhem, kam të dridhura a rrënqethje
□ *Our dog* **had a fit** *yesterday.*

have a free hand kam dorë të lirë, kam liri veprimi
□ *My boss* **has given** *me* **a free hand** *in deciding which outside contractor to use.*

have a go at sth 1. provoj
□ *He had never played tennis before, but he decided to* **have a go at** *it, anyway.* □ *Let's* **have a go at** *it.* □ *He* **had** *several* **goes at** *it before he succeeded.* □ *Let's* **have** *another* **go.**
2. sulmoj; kritikoj
□ *Just because he's a politician, everyone seems to want to* **have a go at** *it.*

have a good head for sth ia them për, ma pret për
□ *I* **have no head for** *figures.*

have a good head on one's shoulders e ka kokën plot, ia pret mendja
□ *Your son will do well in business: he* **has a good head on his shoulders.**

have a (good) mind to do sth kam shumë dëshirë të
□ *I'd* **a good mind to** *smack him for being so rude!* □ *I* **have a good mind** **not to** *go to him really.*

have a good nose for kam nuhatje të mirë
□ *You* **have a good nose.** *Smell this and tell me what it is.*

have a good time kënaqem, e kaloj mirë, e kaloj për mrekulli
□ *Apparently he had taken an overdose of sleeping tablets. 'But why do*

it in Brighton? That's where one goes to **have a good time.** □ *Everyone* **had a good time** *at the party.* □ *The children went to the beach and* **had a good time** *there.*

have a grudge against e kam dikë inat
□ *John's been put into detention so many times that he's beginning to feel his form master must* **have a grudge against** *him.*

have/take a hand in sth marr pjesë; kam ndikim; kam dorë, kam gisht në
□ *I bet he* **had a hand in** *it.* □ *Almost everyone in the school* **had a hand in** *making the play a success.* □ *I thought myself it was a silly business, but I could not forget my father* **had a hand in** *it.* □ *The cookery was so good that it was clear Jane very seldom* **had a hand in** *it.* □ *It's pretty obvious that he has* **had no hand in** *this affair.*

have a hand like a foot i ka duart e thara
□ *You'll break the plate if you are not careful. There you are! You* **have a hand like a foot.**

have a heart tregoj mëshirë, tregohem i mëshirshëm
□ *'Have a heart, Jake,' he said. 'If you don't help me to get away now I may not be let out for days.'* □ *He dropped the window with a crash, and was staring angrily up the line when a rich husky voice from inside the compartment summoned him back. 'Have a heart, partner! I'm refrigerated to the marrow as it is!'* □ *When their father told them to have all the grass cut by noon, the children asked him to* **have a heart.**

have a heart of gold e ka zemrën flori
□ *Everyone behaved as if they were under the contract to live up to the tradition of the outspoken Yorkshireman*

with a heart of gold underneath a rough exterior. □ *You can rely on her: she has a heart of gold.*

have a heart of stone e ka zemrën gur

□ *It could not be said that she had a heart of stone for this usually implies some conscious rejection of pity.* □ *Anyone who can treat his children so badly must have a heart of stone.*

have a hide/skin like a rhinoceros e ka lëkurën shollë, i është bërë lëkura shollë

□ *Angrily the men returned 10 minutes later to tell their mates, 'We had no impact. These men have hides like a rhinoceros.'*

have a high old time kënaqem

□ *I'm a bit of an old fogy, but I still flatter I can rise to the occasion. We should have a high old time tonight and no mistake, heh?* □ *'Oh yes,' said Dollie,' we had a high old time all right. I enjoyed myself.'*

□ *The children had a high old time at the birthday party, and it took us ages to clean up the place afterwards.*

have/get a hunch that kam një parandjenjë se

□ *Purvis's description of him is right. Nationality, on the face of it, British. But I have a hunch that he might not be.* □ *So today I just had a hunch he might want a note on Waterman. Instinct.*

have a level head s'e humb toruan, ruaj gjakftohtësinë

□ *He has a level head in emergencies.*

have a lump in one's throat kam një lëmsh në grykë

□ *Several had a lump in their throat(s).* □ *Seeing him step out of the plane and down the gangway gave me such a lump in my throat that*

when we finally met I was quite unable to speak.

have a mind of one's own ka kokën e vet

□ *'I'd like to know who's been putting such ideas into your head.' 'What do you mean? I have a mind of my own.'*

have a thick head 1. jam kokëtrashë, jam i trashë nga mendja

□ *You could have worked that out for yourselves if you hadn't such thick heads.*

2. e kam kokën të rëndë

□ *No more brandy, thanks. I'll have a thick enough head as it is.*

have all one's marbles/buttons e ka mendjen në vend

□ *Mr. Green may be very old man, but he's certainly got all his marbles.*
□ *The uncle claims he was butted at a sèance by a goat which had died the previous October. John thinks his uncle may not have had all his marbles.* □ *He would not go to town barefooted if he had all his marbles.*

have all the marks of sb/sth ka të gjitha shenjat (gjasat) e

□ *Williams has all the marks of a successful and rather ruthless man.*
□ *I think he knew he was dying. At any rate, his last novel had all the marks of having been written in haste.*

have/keep an ace/card up one's sleeve ka në dorë një gur të fshehtë

□ *Even if he loses the election the President has another card up his sleeve: the army is ready to seize control to keep him in power.*

have an axe to grind ka një qëllim (synim, arsye) të caktuar

□ *He assures me his visit is quite disinterested: but why should he come if he has no axe to grind?* □ *She's only doing it out of kindness—she's got no particular axe to grind.*

have an edge on/have the edge 1. jam më i mirë se

□ *I can't beat you at tennis, but I have an edge on you in ping-pong.* □ *Peter and Philip are both good students, but I think that Peter has an edge on Philip.*

2. jam çakërqejf

□ *Joe sure had an edge on when I saw him last night.*

have an edge to one's voice flas me ton të acaruar (nervozuar), shfaq zemërim (nervozizëm etj.)

□ *'The facts, Robert, the facts! Ned cut in. There was an edge to his voice, this time, that revealed how sick of it all he was getting.* □ *'You have a ten-minute tea-break, don't you?' was all the manageress said, pausing at the canteen table. But her voice had and edge to it that sent the girls scurrying away to their work.*

have an eye for ka ndjenjën e, ia thotë për, jam në gjendje të vlerësoj (çmoj)

□ *I would advise you to go shopping with John: he has a good eye for a bargain.* □ *He has a good eye for beauty.*

have an eye on/have one's eye on e kam synë te

□ *I bought ice-cream, but Jimmy had his eye on some candy.* □ *Tony had his eye on a scholarship to go to college.*

have an eye to shikoj, kujdesem

□ *Have an eye to the children till I come back.*

have an itching palm më hanë duart për para

□ *Cussius, you yourself are much condemned to have an itching palm.* □ *The bellboys in that hotel seem always to have itching palms.*

have an old head on young shoulders është më i pjekur për vitet (moshën) që ka

□ *You appear to have an old head upon very young shoulders; at one moment to be a scampish boy ..., and at another a resolute man.*

have/keep an open mind jam i hapur ndaj

□ *I've an open mind. I have nothing against angels, for those who put their trust in them.* □ *I'm not convinced your idea will work, but I'll keep an open mind for the moment.*

have ants in one's pants s'më rrihet në një vend, s'më zë vendi, nuk rri dot në një vend nga shqetësimi

□ *She's had ants in her pants all week—waiting for the exam results.*

have a rough time kaloj vështirësi të shumta, kaloj (përjetoj) kohë të vështira

□ *She had a really rough time when her father died.*

have a screw loose ka një dërrasë mangut, i janë liruar vidhat, ka luajtur nga vidhat (burgjitë), ka një vidhë mangut

□ *She eats nothing but nuts: she must have a screw loose!* □ *You cannot simply discuss things with Jack. I suppose he has a screw loose.*

have a thick skin jam i pandjeshëm ndaj kritikës, e ka lëkurën e trashë, i është bërë faqja shollë

□ *Don't worry about hurting his feelings; he has a thick skin.*

have a way with one ka aftësinë të tërheqë (të drejtojë, të bindë etj.) të tjerët; ia gjej anën

□ *Quilp has such a way with him when he likes, that the best-looking woman here couldn't refuse him if he chose to make love to her.* □ *Dave has such a way with the campers that they do everything he tells them to do.*

have a way with ka sukses me, ka talent në trajtimin e

□ *Joan is a very good teacher: she has a way with children.* □ *It was Saturday, so they were early home from school; ... little rascals of seven and six, soon talkative, for Ashurst had a way with children.*

have a whale of a time kënaqem pa masë, e kaloj shumë mirë

□ *The children had a whale of a time at the funfair.*

have a word with sb about sth flas me

□ *'Could I have a word with you?— There's something I want to know.'* □ *Besides Bill had always been fond of Mercy, and he made up his mind to have a word with her as to what was wrong between her and Mac.* □ *Do you mind, Sergeant, if I have a word with this Frenchman before you let him go?* □ *'John's left his room in a mess again. You promised to have a word with him about it, darling.'*

have bats in the belfry jam i luajtur (i çmendur)

□ *He's not the first in the family to have bats in the belfry. His grandfather used to sit up half the night composing letters of warning to all his acquaintances about the end of the world, or whatever his current obsession happened to be.*

have blue blood (in one's veins) kam gjak fisnik (ndër deje)

□ *A young upstanding Tory's the romantic thing to be now, especially with any blue blood in your veins.*

have enough and to spare ka e tepron

□ *How many hired servants of my father's have bread enough and to spare, and I perish with hunger.* □ *'Listen, Findlay,' he babbled, 'there's money down here -millions of it. Be sensible, there's enough here and to spare for both of us.'*

have everything/it/things one's own way bën si i thotë mendja

□ *All right, have it your own way— I'm tired of arguing.* □ *Well, you must not have it your own way.*

have eyes in/at the back of one's head kam dy palë sy; i bëj sytë katër

□ *You need to have eyes at the back of your head to keep the kid out of mischief.* □ *How did you know I was behind you? You must have eyes in the back of your head.* □ *You cannot hoodwink us. We have eyes in the back of our head.*

have eyes in one's head i kam sytë në ballë

□ *Well, it's getting pretty obvious about you and Katie, and I've got eyes in my head as well as anyone else.* □ *There's a notice outside that says 'Please knock before entering.' Haven't you got eyes in your idiot head?*

have/have got sth on the brain më rri mendja; s'më hiqet nga mendja

□ *I've got the new tune on my brain all day but I can't remember what it's called.*

have had enough jam ngopur me, më ka ardhur në majë të hundës

□ *Tony: I'm waiting for that moment when you put your foot down about something and say you've had enough. But you never do.* □ *The work was hard but the pay was good. I had no complaint against the company, but I suddenly felt I had had enough.*

have had it mori fund, kaq e pat, e hëngri çairin

☐ *Sometimes I think I've* **had it**. *I really do. I get phases of desperation and my husband and I agree we'll manage to live somehow on his salary.* ☐ *'I've* **had it**,' *the injured soldier whispered. 'Leave me to die here.'* ☐ *His bicycle looks as though it* **has had it**. ☐ *I think this radio* **has had it**: *it will never work again.* ☐ *When the doctor examined the man who had been shot, he said, 'He* **has had it**.'

have had one's day ka rënë nga vakti, e hëngri çairin, i ka ikur koha; kaq e pati

☐ *'I'm afraid these shoes* **have had their day**.' *'They certainly have. Throw them out.'* ☐ *He was a great singer once but now he's* **had his day**. ☐ *Colonialism* **has had its day**.

have half a mind to do sth jam me dy mendje, e kam me mëdyshje

☐ *The service in this hotel was terrible and I* **have half a mind to** *write and complain about it.* ☐ *She* **had half a mind to** *reply 'Is that so strange?' But her respect for Harley stopped her.* ☐ *When you came on me in Hay Lane last night, I thought unaccountably of fairy tales, and* **had half a mind to** *demand whether you had bewitched my horse.* ☐ *I* **have half a mind to** *shut him up.*

have half a word with sb i them dikujt dy fjalë

☐ *'Miss Potterson! might I* **have half a word with** *you?' 'Well?' said Miss Potterson ...'say your half word.'*

have in hand përmbaj (zotëroj) veten

☐ *... he* **had** *himself well* **in hand**, *knew exactly how far he was going, and that when the time came he could and would stop.*

have in view kam parasysh

☐ *What the president* **has in view** *is a world without nuclear weapons.*

have it/sth coming to one 1. dëgjoj, marr vesh; kuptoj

☐ *I* **have it** *on the best authority that we will be paid for our work next week.*

2. thuhet se

☐ *Rumor* **has it** *that we'll have a new manager.*

3. e gjeta

☐ *'I* **have it**!' *said John to Mary. 'We can buy Mother a nice comb for her birthday.'*

4. meriton

☐ *I'm sorry that Jack has been dismissed: he's* **had it coming** *to him for a long time.* ☐ *Everybody said that Eve* **had it coming** *when she won the scholarship.*

have it in for sb kam halë në sy; dua t'i bëj keq dikujt

☐ *I see that Jim was beaten up last night: someone obviously* **had it in for** *him.* ☐ *She's* **had it for him** *ever since he called her a fool in public.* ☐ *George* **has it in for** *Bob because Bob told the teacher that George cheated in the examination.*

have it in mind to do sth kam ndërmend

☐ *I* **have it in the mind to** *ask her advice when I see her.* ☐ **Have** *you anyone* **in mind** *for the duty?*

have it out with sb zgjidh, sqaroj (një çështje) me

☐ *If you have got a complaint, the best thing is to see the person concerned and* **have it out with** *him.* ☐ *'I'm going round to Ned's. We've got to* **have this thing out**.' ☐ *Mr. Brown keeps interfering with my work: I'm going to his office now to* **have it out with** *him.* ☐ *The former friends finally decided to* **have it out** *in a free argument and they became friends again.*

have many irons/several in the fire
kam shumë punë në dorë
□ *He **had** too **many irons in the fire** to find time for original research.*
□ *I'm very busy at the moment because I **have several irons in the fire**.*

have no business to do sth/doing sth
s'ke punë të
□ *Actually he **had no business to** give you any orders at all. You're not part of his command.* □ *You **have no business to** be here—this is private property.* □ *You **have no business to** interfere.* □ *You will have to tell him to leave: he **has no business** being in here without official permission.*

have no head for sth s'më punon koka për, s'ma pret për
□ *He **has no head for** figures.*

have no heart to do sth s'më bën zemra
□ *He had the carriage closed now, he **had no heart to** look on gaiety.* □ *He **had no heart to** beg. And there he sat.*
□ *'I **have not the heart to** take it, Irot, tonight.'*

have no idea s'e ke idenë, s'e merr dot me mend
□ *You **have no idea** how talented that boy is.*
□ *You can **have no idea** of how happy we were.* □ *'Of course he speaks Welsh. It was his first language.' 'Really? I **had no idea**.'*

have no use for sb/sth 1. s'kam më punë me
□ *I've **no further use for** the typewriter, so you can have it.*
2. urrej, s'duroj dot
□ *I've **no use for** people who do not try.*

have not a leg to stand on është pa bazë, s'qëndron
□ *When he is through adding up his last column of figures, the notion of a coup d'ètat pulled off by big city bondholders **hasn't a leg to stand on**.*

have nothing in common s'kam gjë të përbashkët me
□ *I **have nothing in common** with Jane.*

have nothing on 1. nuk është aq i zgjuar (i aftë, i mirë etj.) sa
□ *Sherlock Holmes **has nothing on** you—you're a real detective.* □ *Dick is a good runner, but he doesn't **have anything on** his brother.*
2. s'ka prova, dëshmi kundër
□ *They've **got nothing on** me—I've got an alibi.* □ *I think that he will be released, because they really don't **have anything on** him.*

have nothing to do with sb/sth s'kam të bëj me, s'kam lidhje me
□ *I don't know why he keeps interfering: it **has nothing to do with** him.*
□ *He's a thief and a liar; I'd **have nothing to do with** him, if I were you.*
□ *I advise you to **have nothing to do with** him.*

have one foot in the grave është me një këmbë në varr
□ *He's **got one foot in the grave**: he can't live much longer.* □ *Some of us stay nymphs and satyrs till we **have one foot in the grave**.*

have oneself a ball kënaqem shumë, kënaqem pa masë
□ *We were subjected to Colin Davies **having a ball** teaching the Promenaders how to sing.*

have one's/both feet on the ground
jam me të dy këmbët në tokë, mbështetet në të dyja këmbët
□ *'If my brother hadn't been with me I dare say I would have been talked into lending them the money.' 'Yes, It's a good job John **has both feet on the ground**, since you haven't.'*

□ *Silvia: I want a home. Peter: I'll build one for you. Silvia: what, with dreams? I want a boy **with his feet on the ground**.*

have/drink/eat/take one's fill of sth ha (pi) sa ngopem

□ *The stag at eve **had drunk his fill**.* □ *They drank and drank until they **had their fill of water**.*

have one's fling bëj jetë të shthurur

□ *He's only young once. Let him **have his fling**. He'll settle down, you'll see.* □ *It's nice for a bride to be able to dress up and be the center of attraction, without having to feel guilty about it. And you never forget it, it's probably the last chance you get to **have a bit of a fling**.*

have one's hands full/one's hands are full jam i zënë deri në grykë

□ *I won't stay for coffee. I can see you **have your hands full** this morning.* □ *Somebody else will have to see to the curtains and lighting. I'll **have my hand full** helping with all the changes of costume.* □ *Dawney answered slowly: 'Never so happy as when **my hands are full**.'* □ *I'll talk to Hilary but **his hands are always full**.* □ *He **had his hands full** and could not take another job for two weeks.*

have one's head in the clouds i fluturon mendja; sheh ëndrra me sy çelë

□ *Mary never knows what is happening around her: she always **has her head in the clouds**.*

have one's head screwed on (the right way) e ka kokën në vend, e ka kokën mbi shpatulla

□ *George has done very well out of his investments: he certainly **has his head screwed on the right way**.*

have one's heart in one's mouth i ngriu zemra, i shkoi gjaku në fund të këmbëve

□ *All the time I was climbing on the mountain, **my heart was in my mouth**.* □ *I was so greatly started that I **had my heart in my mouth**.*

have one's heart in sth i kushtohem (i jepem) me shpirt

□ *He **had** so little **heart** in the affair that at last he dropped it, altogether.* □ *He is very listless, which shows that he **hasn't his heart** in his work.*

have one's heart in the right place është zemërmirë, e ka zemrën të mirë

□ *Your **heart is in the right place**; if only you had the right words on your tongue.* □ *He may seem cold but his **heart is in the right place**.*

have one's say them (shpreh) mendimin tim

□ *At Hyde Park Corner pacifist speakers were usually allowed to **have their say** along with everyone else.* □ *The work gets done in the best possible way, because everyone feels he has **had his say**.* □ *He began to talk like a man who has an unwilling audience but who will **have his say** whether anyone listens to him or not.* □ *Everyone will have a chance to **have his say**.* □ *Don't interrupt her: let her **have her say**.*

have one's tail between one's legs mbledh bishtin

□ *'I've always known Mr. Golding was that sort of man,' said Miss Flynn, ' and she sent him packing **with his tail between his legs**.*

have/keep one's wits about one rri (qëndroj) syhapët; e kam mendjen në vend

□ *You need to **keep your wits about you** when you're dealing with a man like that.* □ *He may be quiet and dreamy looking, but he **had all his wits about him**.* □ *If he **had had his*** *wits about him he would not have entered the wrong train.*

have one's work cut out (doing sth)
1. e kam vështirë të bëj diçka (brenda kohës së dhënë)

□ *You'll have your work cut out getting there by nine o'clock.*

2. jam i zënë deri në fyt

□ *Irene, looking at him again with that intent look, said quietly: 'Something he wanted me to do for him!' 'Humph!' said Soames. 'Commissions! You'll have your work cut out if you begin that sort of thing!'*

have/get other fish to fry kam punë tjetër më të rëndësishme (për të bërë)

□ *What? You're walking out on me? You've got other fish to fry? Is that it?* □ *He said that he could not attend to this job for he had other fish to fry.* □ *I've got other things in hand. I've got other fish to fry.*

have/take pity on sb kam (tregoj) mëshirë për

□ *... have no pity on him. He is a sworn enemy. I am to entreat that you well take pity of me.*

have recourse to sb/sth kërkoj ndihmën e, i drejtohem për ndihmë, përdor

□ *On the voyage one of the engines was disabled and the captain had recourse to the sails.* □ *He hoped the affair could be settled without either of them having recourse to legal proceedings.* □ *I hope the doctors won't have recourse to surgery.*

have seen/known better days kishte parë (njohur) ditë më të mira

□ *He was wearing a dirty shirt, cracked shoes and a suit that had seen better days.* □ *That coat has seen better days.*

have sb in one's pocket e ka në xhep, e ka në dorë, e ka në kontroll

□ *Even before he plunges in his program, he has his audience in his pocket.*

have/keep sb on a string mbaj nën kontroll

□ *She's had us all on a string for too long.*

have (got) sb/sth taped kuptoj (marr vesh) mirë; di se kush është; di ta vërtis

□ *It took me a while to learn the rules of the game but I think I've got them taped now.* □ *Jack can't fool me: I've got him taped.* □ *If you want to know how to arrange a successful party, ask Jim—he's got it all taped.*

have sth at heart e kam në zemër

□ *I really have been able my dear Copperfield to do all that I had most at heart.* □ *He has your welfare at heart.*

have sth at one's fingertips e di (e njoh) në majë të gishtave

□ *He has at his fingertips every stroke of the game.*

have sth on one's conscience e ka barrë në ndërgjegje

□ *He has several murders on his conscience.*

have sth on/at the tip of one's tongue e kam në majë të gjuhës

□ *But there was something I was going to tell you. What was it? I have it on the tip of my tongue.* □ *He had arguments at the tip of his tongue.*

have sth up one's sleeve kam (ruaj, mbaj) të fshehtë

□ *... he always has a trick up his sleeve.* □ *'Unless you've got something up your sleeve Mr. Forsyte, we're dished.' 'What should I have up my sleeve?' said Soames coldly.*

have sth/sb in mind for sth kam ndër mend për

□ *Don't give your confidence to others regarding a plan you* **have in mind**. □ *Who do you* **have in mind** *for the job?*

have sth in one's blood e kam në gjak
□ *Shirley Anne can reasonably claim to* **have betting in her blood**.

have the air of duket, ngjan, ka pamjen
□ *He picked up his tankard with a rather weary gesture, and drank from it. He* **had the air of** *a man who is turning a number of things in his mind.* □ *The house* **has an air of** *comfort.*

have the advantage of sb jam në pozitë më të favorshme se
□ *'You'll forgive me,' said Soames, 'it quite clearly refers to my daughter, Mrs. Michael Mont, and her husband. Indeed! You* **have the advantage of** *me, but what's the matter with it?'*

have the ball at one's feet ka rast (mundësi) të mirë
□ *You must decide what you want to do:* **the ball is at your feet** *now.*

have the courage of one's conviction ka kurajon (guximin) të veprojë sikundër mendon (beson, ndjen)
□ *If you feel so strong about this matter, then you must speak up: you must* **have the courage of your conviction**. □ *He* **had the courage of his own conviction**, *good luck to him.*

have the face/cheek to do sth ka sy e faqe, ka paturpësinë të
□ *After I paid for his meal and driven him home, he* **had the cheek to** *ask me for the loan of $5!* □ *How dare you* **have the face to** *say that?* □ *How can he* **have the** *face to ask for more money when he already owes me more than $1000?*

have the game in one's hands e kam fitoren në xhep; e kam situatën në dorë

□ *We have seen how Mrs. Bute* **having the game in her hands**, *had really played her cards too well.*

have the goodness to do sth kam mirësinë të
□ **Have the goodness** *to come this way, please.*

have the grace to do sth kam mirësinë të
□ *He might* **have had the grace to** *say he was sorry.* □ *I didn't* **have the grace** *to feel a bit ashamed when I got a picture postcard from a Chelsea address.*

have the guts to do sth kam kurajon (guximin) të bëj diçka
□ *I used to hope that one day, somebody would* **have the guts to** *slam the door in our faces.*

have the heart to do sth më bën zemra të
□ *I hadn't the heart to refuse.* □ **Have you the heart to** *say this of your own son ... !* □ *I groped my way out, and groped my way to my room in the dark, without even* **having the heart to** *say good night to Peggotty.*

have/get the key of the street kaloj natën jashtë
□ *You can't get in tonight, you* **have got the key of the street**.

have the last word ka (them) fjalën e fundit
□ *We can all make suggestions, but the manager* **has the last word**. □ *If the negotiations fail and the government says that the outcome is unsatisfactory, the people must* **have the last word** *in a referendum.* □ *I hate arguing with Mary: she must always* **have the last word**.

have/get the last laugh qesh i fundit
□ *All his relatives made fun of Charles when his grandmother left him only her old armchair, but he* **had**

the last laugh: it contained all her savings.

have the law on sb denoncoj; hedh në gjyq

□ *If you do that again I'll **have the law on** you.*

have the makings of ka të gjitha të dhënat (cilësitë)

□ *He **has** all **the makings** of a fine musician.*

have the nerve to ka guximin të; ka fytyrë të; ka paturpësinë të

□ *I worked with about five different guys before I **had the nerve to** tell Capitol that I wanted to leave unless they let me do it the way I wanted.* □ *He came in late this morning, and then **had the nerve** to ask to be allowed to go home early!* □ *She **had the nerve to** say I was cheating.*

have the time of one's life kaloj çastet më të bukura të jetës; kënaqem (zbavitem) pa masë

□ *The children **had the time of their lives** at circus.*

have time on one's hands/time to kill ka kohë të tepërt

□ *Young people sometimes get in trouble when they **have time on their hands**, and there is nothing for them to do.* □ *'Still here then, I see,' he said conversationally. 'You must **have plenty of time on your hands**.* □ *'Now that father's retired he'll **have more time on his hands**.' 'That's what worries me. He'll feel miserable with so little to do.'*

have to do with 1. kam të bëj me, kam lidhje me

□ *Some years ago I published an autobiographical book 'Double Lives'. It **had to do with** my progenitors and my own early life.* □ *What does that remark **have to do with** the subject we have been talking about?*

□ *I don't know why my feet are sore: I think it **has** something **to do with** these new shoes.* □ *What **has** it **got to do with** you anyway?* □ *I won't **have** anything **to do with** him.*

2. merrem me, tregoj interes për

□ *A man like Angus that's **had to do with** boats and these waters all his life does not need advice from you.* □ *I had never **had** much **to do with** children and I felt awkward with them.*

have under control kam nën kontroll

□ *It will be quite a blow to Sarah, sir, but she **has** all her feelings **under control**.*

have words with sb zihem, grindem, bëj (këmbej) fjalë

□ *John and Mary look rather upset: I think they **have been having words**.* □ *Mrs. Williams sprang out of bed and rescued it and we **had some words**.* □ *'If you fiddle with my camera again you and me are going to **have words**, young man!'*

head for shkoj drejt

□ *'If you go with him, Jinny, you're **heading for** disaster.'* □ *He **headed** straight **for** the bar.*

head off ndaloj, pengoj; devijoj

□ *They did well to **head off** that quarrel that was on the point of breaking out.* □ *'If you take the next turning to the right, you'll be able to **head** them **off** at the big crossroads.'* □ *Let's **head off** his departure by wiring him right away.*

heads or tails (?) kokë a pilë

□ *Since neither of us can make up our minds, we'll toss for it. **Heads** we go to the cinema, **tails** we stay at home.* □ *'**Heads or tails**?' their father asked, looking at Tony. 'Heads.' 'Heads it is, so you get the first service.'*

head over heels/ears 1. tërësisht, plotësisht, deri në grykë
□ *John is head over heels in debt and that's why he is selling the house.* □ *'But you would be absolutely right as Romeo,' said Jesica. 'Can you still say your lines?' 'I could to you,' said Ludovic, who was by now head over ears in love.* □ *For weeks after my discovery I was head over heels in work.*
2. laradashas, kollotumba, picingul
□ *You must all be aware from our ports that we are now tumbling along head over heels.* □ *The puppy made another rush at the stick and tumbled head over heels in its hurry to get hold of it.* □ *He caught his foot against a stone and fell head over heels.*

hear a pin drop nuk dëgjohet (ndihet) as miza, nuk pipëtin asgjë
□ *The audience was so quiet you could have heard a pin drop.*

hear of dëgjoj të flitet rreth; kam dijeni rreth
□ *'Do you know Patterson?' 'No, I've never heard of him.'* □ *I first heard of the firm, and had dealings with them, three years ago.*

hear from marr lajm nga
□ *Mother hasn't heard from you for quite some time. She's beginning to think you must be ill.* □ *How often do you hear from your sister?* □ *I hope to hear from you soon.*

hear tell of sth dëgjoj të flitet
□ *I've often heard tell of such things.*

heart and soul me gjithë shpirt, me mish e me shpirt
□ *Josephine Barstow throws herself heart and soul into the part of Natasha, singing the lyrical music beautifully.* □ *Miss Bates has dedicated herself to her profession heart and soul.* □ *I echoed with all my heart and soul that it was like himself.* □ *Amelia's maid... was heart and soul in favor of the generous major.*

heart go out to më vjen keq për, ndiej keqardhje për
□ *Poor Harry has not been chosen for the team after practising so hard; my heart goes out to him.*

heart to heart i përzemërt, me zemër të hapur
□ *The father decided to have a heart-to-heart talk with his son about smoking.* □ *The boy had a heart-to-heart talk with his father about what he should do for a career.*

heavy going i vështirë; i lodhshëm; i mërzitshëm
□ *She's heavy going.* □ *I find the work heavy going.*

help a lame dog over a stile ndihmoj dikë në ditë të keqe, në momente të vështira
□ *The charitable precept always to help a lame dog over the stiles is shared by the world's major religions.* □ *He would always help a lame dog over the stile, that was his boast.*

help oneself 1. marr (për të ngrënë etj.)
□ *The waitress only clears the table between courses. The food is all laid out on side tables and you help yourself.* □ *Did you see him helping himself out of my box of cigarettes all evening? Cheek!* □ *My host again and again bade me to help myself.*
2. ndihmoj veten
□ *The surgeons have done a wonderful job on your knee but you've got to help yourself.*

hen party, a mbrëmje femërore
□ *Mary held a hen party for her friends once a month.* □ *The first time I was asked to do an act for a hen party I nearly didn't accept.*

here and there aty-këtu, vende-vende
□ *The country is very fertile, with* **here and there** *a barren spot.* □ *We still have the Lord knows how many hydrogen bombs stored* **here and there**, *waiting for some madman to set them off.*

here below në këtë botë
□ *If his lot* **here below** *was miserable, he was encouraged to hope for pie in the sky. And he was freely allowed the consolation of religion.*
□ *I do not know the name of the lady who announces the trains at Victoria Station, nor do I expect to meet her* **here below**.

here is to sb/sth për shëndetin e
□ *You'll need a stiff whisky before your interview. Well,* **here's to** *you and I hope you get the job.* □ *He raised his glass. 'Your father,' he said. 'Here's to him.'* □ **Here is to** *you.... Yellowlery.* □ *Jennison stood beside Morgan, raised his glass and called. 'Here's how!'*

here, there, and everywhere kudo, gjithkund, gjithandej
□ *Rumors fly from ear to ear of apparitions* **here, there and everywhere**. □ *I think you should get yourself a big filing cabinet, instead of having your papers lying around* **here, there and everywhere**. □ *'Don't you have a regular run then?' 'No, just* **here, there and everywhere**, *wherever there's a load to be picked up.'*

high and dry në vetmi, në mëshirën e fatit, në mes të katër udhëve
□ *I saw, in the sharp silver light of the fool moon, that the mine was left* **high and dry** *by the ebbing tide.* □ *He left her* **high and dry** *in a strange country without any money.*

high and low 1. të të gjithë shtresave
□ *Listen, children of the world, both* **high and low**, *rich and poor. I shall speak the truth.* □ *Troubles, like death, come to* **high and low**.
2. gjithandej, gjithkund
□ *Anyway, we've hunted* **high and low**, *boy, believe me.*

high and mighty fodull, krenar, kryelartë, mendjemadh, kryepërpjetë, hundëpërpjetë
□ *He ought to stop doing nothing and criticizing everybody. If he had some work, he would be so* **high and mighty**. □ *If Jenny had not had the fear of being thought* **high and mighty**, *she would not have hoisted and edged her way on to Patrick's lap.*

hither and thither andej-këtej, tutjetëhu, poshtë e lart, në të katër anët
□ *The water was clear to the bottom and bright with tropical weed and coral. A school of tiny, glittering fish flicked* **hither and thither**. □ *We searched* **hither and thither**, *but could not find it.*

hit back at sth kundërpërgjigjem
□ *In a TV interview she* **hit back at** *her critics.* □ *As soon as an enemy battery opens fire fighter-bombers can be ordered into the air to* **hit back**.

hit it off (well) miqësohem, shkoj (mirë), merrem vesh me
□ *I don't think they* **hit it off**, *doctor. They're at daggers drawn the whole time.* □ *But from the time when... she brought Bosinney into his life to wreck it, he had never* **hit it off** *with June.* □ *We had soon become friends, in fact, we* **hit it off** *immediately.*

hit on/upon mendoj, gjej; zbuloj
□ *The committee eventually* **hit upon** *a formula that would be acceptable to all.* □ *Then an idea was* **hit upon** *that seemed the answer to all our problems.*

hit out (at) sulmoj egërsisht (me fjalë, grushta etj.)
- □ *The Bishop hit out at hippie culture.*
- □ *Ralph hit out; then he and a dozen others were rolling over, hitting, biting, scratching.*

hit sb/sth hard godit rëndë
- □ *The advent of commercially viable television hit the cinema very hard.*
- □ *The recent rise in National Insurance contributions for the self-employed will hit small shopkeepers hard.*

hit the bottle pi shumë
- □ *He seemed all right for a while after his marriage but I'm afraid he's hitting the bottle again.*

hit the bull's eye i ra pikës, qëlloi në shenjë, i bie në shenjë (shenjës)
- □ *Patricia Highsmith is a brilliantly talented novelist and she has hit he bull's eye often in the past.* □ *John hit the bull's eye with his first answer.*

hit the ceiling/roof tërbohem nga inati
- □ *John's father hit the roof when he discovered that John had borrowed his car without permission.* □ *Don't creep around so quietly! I nearly hit the ceiling when you spoke.*

hit the deck 1. shtrihem (bie) për tokë
- □ *The contender hit the deck twice in the fifth round.* □ *When the shots rang out, everyone hit the deck.* □ *All the people there hit the deck when they heard the sound of an explosion.*

2. çohem nga krevati
- □ *'Hit the deck, boys!' said the old seaman who awoke us.*

hit the hay/sack bie (shtrihem) të fle
- □ *I just said, 'Sure, lets hit the hay, James.' I set the clock to arouse us in ample time.* □ *I'm very tired; I think I'll hit the hay.*

hit the mark qëlloj në shenjë, i bie pikës

- □ *Your answer just hit the mark.*
- □ *'You are right!' said Mr. Jarndyce brightening. 'Your woman's wit hits the mark. He is a child—an absolute child.'*

hit the nail on the head i bie në shenjë, i bie shenjës, i bie pikës, qëlloj (godit) në shenjë
- □ *The report spoke of a period of unfulfilled promise. That hit the nail squarely on the head.* □ *Good, with that suggestion you've really hit the nail on the head.* □ *I thought that the chairman's suggestion hit the nail on the head.*

hit the road/trail 1. nisem; nisem për udhë
- □ *Let's go now: it's time we hit the road.*

2. marr udhët, endem rrugëve
- □ *When Jack's wife left him, he felt a desire to hit the road.*

hold back 1. mbaj, përmbaj, ndaloj, pengoj
- □ *Millions of tons of water are held back by a complex system of dykes.* □ *The thin cordon of police could do nothing to hold back the crowd; they flooded on the pitch.* □ *He was so eager to get going that I could not hold him back.* □ *'Well, what's holding you back?' Burton said. 'If you don't go north soon, it will be too late.'*

2. përmbahem, ngurroj, hezitoj
- □ *Because of the uncertain state of the market, buyers are holding back.* □ *She held back, not knowing what to do or say.*

3. mbaj, ndal, pengoj
- □ *Now that the end's in sight, nothing can hold him back.* □ *John felt that he was held back from further promotion because of his background.*

4. pengoj, vonoj (lëshimin, dhënien etj.)

□ *The laboratory has been advised to* **hold back** *any announcement of its findings.* □ *There will be sharp resentment if they have their salaries* **held back** *for too long.*

hold captive mbaj rob

□ *They were* **held captive** *by masked gunmen.*

hold court takohem me admiruesit

□ *The famous writer used to* **hold court** *in a nearby restaurant every evening.*

hold down 1. shtyp, mbaj të nënshtruar

□ *How long can a small force of mercenaries* **hold down** *an entire people?* □ *The people are* **held down** *by a vicious and repressive military regime.*

2. frenoj

□ *They were blamed for their failure to* **hold down** *expenditure.* □ *Last year we had to* **hold down** *student intake because of the cuts in the grants.*

3. mbaj (punën)

□ *He couldn't* **hold down** *a job after his breakdown.* □ *What's the longest she's* **held down** *a job?* □ *Father fixed him up with work when he came out of prison, but he couldn't* **hold** *the job* **down**.

hold good është i vlefshëm; është në fuqi

□ *Treat others as you expect them to treat you: that is a rule which* **holds good** *wherever you go.* □ *The same argument doesn't* **hold good** *in all cases.* □ *The contract* **holds good** *for two years.* □ *That used to be the rule, but it no longer* **holds good**.

hold in mbaj, përmbaj, kontrolloj

□ *Eventually these feelings could be* **held in** *no longer; there were outbreaks of violence everywhere.* □ *He's incapable of* **holding** *himself* **in**.

hold/keep in check përmbaj, mbaj nën kontroll

□ *The epidemic was* **held in check** *by widespread vaccination.*

hold off 1. vonohet, arrin vonë

□ *The rain* **held off** *just long enough for us to have our price.* □ *The monsoon* **held off** *for a month; then the rain fell in torrents.*

2. mbaj larg

□ *For several days a small force* **held off** *the attacks of a numerically superior enemy.* □ *He's been* **holding** *her* **off** *for years, but sooner or later he'll have to give in.*

3. druhem, stepem, përmbahem

□ *Perkings was a scholarly man who* **held off** *from people.*

4. vonoj

□ *Could you* **hold off** *making your decision until next week?*

hold on 1. pres

□ *'Just* **hold on** *a second while I get my breath back.'* □ *'Hold on!' John's father said. 'I want the car tonight.'*

2. qëndroj, mbahem

□ *The party cut off by the tide were told to* **hold on**; *help would soon reach them.* □ *It was hard to keep the store going during the depression, but Tony* **held on** *and at last met with success.* □ *At the height of the financial crisis, all they could do was* **hold on** *and hope that conditions would improve.*

3. mban, fikson

□ *Use special adhesive for this job: ordinary glue won't* **hold** *the handle* **on**. □ *This pin* **holds** *the wheel* **on**.

4. mbaj telefonin hapur

□ *Mr. Jones asked me to* **hold on** *while he spoke to his secretary.*

5. mbaj, shtrëngoj fort

□ *As Andy was pulling on the rope, it began to slip and Jane cried, 'Hold on, Andy.'* □ *'Don't panic; just* **hold on** *to that rock and I'll come and fetch you down.*

hold one's breath mbaj frymën
□ *He **held his breath** and waited, tightening his grip on the chain.* □ *The sky broke like an egg into full sunset and the water caught fire. He **held his breath**.* □ *We **held our breath** as we listened to his story of their experiences in the expedition.* □ *The child **held his breath** as he listened to his grandmother's tale.*

hold one's ground qëndroj në timen, qëndroj në pozitat e mia, mbroj pikëpamjet e mia
□ *The witness stoutly **held the ground** despite Defending Counsel's skilled efforts to confuse him and discredit his testimony.* □ *He couldn't **hold his ground** in the face of relentless opposition.* □ *Throughout the debate he firmly **held his ground** and won out in the end.*

hold/stay one's hand përmbahem, mbaj dorën, nuk veproj
□ *The Diamond Detectives **held their hand**. All went well, and de Graaf was on his way to the bus with a fortune in his pockets when the detectives pounced.* □ *The landlord was persuaded to **stay his hand** till other accommodation was found for the occupying tenants.*

hold/keep one's head above water qëndroj mbi ujë; jetoj me zgrip (me të keq); i shpëtoj falimentimit (borxheve etj.)
□ *There are many who, I fancy, believe that my pockets are lined with bank bills; but I assure you, you are all mistaken. If I can **hold my head above water** it is all I can do.* □ *I'm managing to **keep my head above water**, though I'm not earning much.*

hold one's head high mbaj kokën përpjetë, mbahem me të madh, mbaj kryet lart, mbaj hundën përpjetë.

□ *Now he and Lindsay feel we can **hold our heads high** again.* □ *... he will no longer boast and **hold his head high**.* □ *Now they can go about with **their heads held high**.*

hold oneself aloof from sb/sth rri (qëndroj) larg nga
□ *The people who really had a genuine interest in art couldn't scoff and **hold aloof** because his pictures really were the freshest and strongest thing we had to boast of.*

hold one's own qëndroj i paepur; bëj qëndresë të fortë, nuk jepem; ruaj pozicionin (epërsinë etj.); qëndroj fort në timen
□ *Strange superstitions still **hold their own** in many parts of the world.* □ *He is still **holding his own**.* □ *We have decided to **hold our own** to the last man.*

hold one's peace hesht, nuk flas, s'hap gojën
□ *Julius found himself under the cruel necessity of **holding his peace** about the subject which he most liked to discuss.* □ ***Hold your peace**, sir... and keep your own breath to cool your own porridge.* □ *Once or twice he **held his peace**, hoping that in silence her thought would take the colour of his own, but she had lightly continued the subject.*

hold one's tongue hesht, s'hap gojë, mbledh (rrudh, mbaj) gjuhën
□ *The boy's mother told him to **hold his tongue** when adults were speaking.* □ *'Obey your order and **hold your tongue**.'* □ *'Come! **Hold your tongue!**' she cried in sharp reproof... 'I wish you'd hold your noise!'* □ *The Daughter. Make her give you the change... The Mother. Do **hold your tongue**, Clara.*

hold out 1. rezistoj, qëndroj
□ *That so small a force was able to hold out against such odds is certainly proof of bravery.* □ *They held out bravely against repeated enemy bombing.*
2. jep, ofron
□ *Doctors hold out little hope of her recovering.* □ *Radio astronomy investigations seem to hold out the best hopes of obtaining such proof.*
3. del, vazhdon
□ *We can stay here for as long as our supplies of food and water hold out.*

hold out for sth vonoj arritjen e marrëveshjes (me qëllim përfitimi)
□ *Having won the first round, the unions are likely to hold out for more than their original demand.* □ *Union negotiators are holding out for a more generous pay settlement.*

hold out on sb refuzoj t'i jap të dhëna etj.
□ *I'm not holding out on you. I honestly don't know where he is.* □ *I couldn't hold out on him any more.*

hold over shtyj
□ *The matter was held over until the next meeting.* □ *Its proposals should be held over until everyone has got a good think.*

hold/keep sb at bay mbaj larg dikë, s'lë të afrohet
□ *The stag kept the hounds at bay.*

hold sb/sth dear çmoj (vlerësoj) lart
□ *I said farewell to those I hold dear.* □ *We hold his reputation dear.*

hold sb/sth responsible mbaj përgjegjës
□ *The first question is whether the scientist can be held responsible for the eventual misuse of his discoveries by others.* □ *If you take the car don't hold me responsible if you have a breakdown on the way.*

hold sth cheap nënçmoj
□ *I hold your dainties cheap, sir...*

hold sth in leash përmbaj
□ *I managed to hold my anger in leash until she had gone.*

hold sway over sb/sth dominon, ka ndikim (pushtet) të madh mbi
□ *James, our janitor, was the real boss of our school and held sway for thirty years while headmasters came and went.* □ *Among English playwrights, few would deny that Shakespeare holds sway.*

hold the purse strings mbaj qesen
□ *I hold the purse strings and they must come to me for money.*

hold the stage vihem në qendër të vëmendjes
□ *Jack likes an audience: he loves to hold the stage.*

hold true qëndron, është e vërtetë
□ *This theory of language teaching is supposed to hold true whatever the mother of the children.* □ *Yet the French police made no effort to prevent his leaving with the child, saying they could do nothing until an offence had been committed. The same apparently hold true in this country.*

hold to i përmbahem, i qëndroj besnik
□ *She always holds to her convictions.* □ *We shall hold firmly to what has already been agreed.*

hold together qëndroj i bashkuar
□ *The Party has held together wonderfully during the current crisis.* □ *A group can hold together unless there's a general exodus.*

hold up 1. jap, nxjerr si shembull
□ *She's always holding up her children as models of behavior.*
2. vonoj; ndaloj, pengoj
□ *Ships held up by the strike of dockers.* □ *Road works on the*

*motorway are **holding up** the traffic.*
□ *Our flight was **held up** by fog.*
3. grabis me dhunë, ndaloj me dhunë (për të grabitur)
□ *Masked men **held up** a wages van.*

hold water qëndron, është me bazë, është logjik
□ *The tempting theory that he was a double agent does not **hold water**. Gehlen was, and is, a Nazi.* □ *His argument can **hold water** all right.*

hole up fshihem
□ *The gang has **holed up** somewhere in the mountains.*

home in (on sth) drejtohet, shkon drejt
□ *The torpedo **homed in** on its target.*
□ *The fans are **homing in on** the concert site from miles around.*

hook, line and sinker tërësisht, kryekëput, plotësisht
□ *It was a poor excuse but Mary swallowed it **hook, line and sinker**.*
□ *What I said was untrue but he swallowed it **hook, line and sinker**.* □ *She gave her some unlikely excuse for his being late and swallowed it **hook, line and sinker**.*

hope against hope (that) mbaj veten me shpresë; besoj te mrekullia e madhe
□ *Even though the crash was a bad -one, we still **hoped against hope that** there might be some survivors.*
□ *There is another kind of truth, which counts blessings and **hopes against hope** and which has quite often been proved right in the long run.*

hope and trust (that) shpresoj gjithë besim, kam besim se
□ *We have observed the changes all over Africa as the result of the policies of your governments. We **hope and trust that** these changes will affect our own deplorable state.*

hope for the best shpresoj për më mirë
□ *Let us **hope for the best**.* □ *Virginia knew that Ellen came to see John; but there was nothing she could do about it, except **hope for the best**.*

horse of another color, a tjetër gjë, tjetër punë; tjetër njeri
□ *You can't have friends sharing the room for the same rent, but if you want your brother to stay for a week or so, that's **a horse of another color**.*

hot air fjalë (llafe, premtime etj.) boshe, mburrje kote; pordhë, pallavra, gjepura
□ *You should not pay any attention to his promises; they are just a lot of **hot air**.* □ *What John said was just a lot of **hot air**.*

hot under the collar i zemëruar, i nxehur, i mërzitur
□ *Don't say anything about lawyers to him: he gets **hot under the collar** when anyone mentions them.*

household name/word, a emër i dëgjuar (i njohur)
□ *The product was so successful that its name became a **household word**.*
□ *He talks about the big companies which are **household words** and of the smaller ones too.*

how/what about (doing) sth? a; sikur
□ *'**How about** having a cup of coffee with me?' 'All right,' she said..*

how come (that)? si ndodhi që; si shpjegohet që
□ *He was told that the whole edition had been sold out. He asked the bookseller: '**How come**?' And the man replied: 'These days people want to forget, so they read books.'* □ ***How come that** you are late?*

how do you do? tungjatjeta
□ *'Veronica, this is Mr. Lockwood whom you remember my having mentioned so often. This is Miss*

Roderick.' *'How do you do?'—said Lockwood bemusedly.* □ *When Mr. Smith was introduced to Mr. Jones, they both said, 'How do you do?'*

hue and cry zhurmë e madhe

□ *A terrific **hue and cry** was raised against the new tax proposals.* □ *In the **hue and cry** after the robbery was discovered, the thief was able to escape.*

hunger for digjem, vuaj shumë për, dëshiroj, kam dëshirë të madhe për, kam mall të madh për

□ *He **hungered for** some contact outside his own circumscribed world.* □ *The letters for which she **hungered** grew fewer, then stopped altogether.*

hunt sb/sth down ndjek

□ *Small detachments left hiding out in the forest were **hunted down** by our men.*

hunt sth out kërkoj

□ *I've got the picture for you somewhere, but it'll need some **hunting out**.*

hunt sth up gjurmoj, kërkoj

□ *He's **hunting up** details of Elizabethan household expenditure in a document of the time.*

hurry up nxitoj, shpejtoj

□ *'I wish the train would **hurry up** and come; I've been waiting here for hours.'* □ *She yelled down to Robbin to **hurry up**.* □ *I can't **hurry up**! Not if you keep shouting!*

hush sth up mbaj të fshehtë, lë (kaloj) në heshtje, s'e zë me gojë

□ *The government **hushed** the affair **up** to avoid public outcry.* □ *You can't **hush** a thing like this **up**.* □ *They tried to **hush up** the small matter of ten thousand being missing.*

I

I beg your pardon më falni (për të kundërshtuar me të butë mendimin e bashkëbiseduesit)

□ *'How that dangerous idiot ever got on the committee, I shall never know.' 'I beg your pardon', he happens to be a friend of mine.*

I bet that vë bast se, jam i sigurt se

□ *You ask anyone in this house what the secret is. I'll bet you find they've all got one.*

ice sth over/up mbuloj, mbulohet me akull

□ *When a road ices over it can be extremely dangerous, because drivers may mistake the coating of ice for dampness.* □ *The superstructure of the boat had iced up dangerously during the night, putting it in danger of capsizing.*

identify with 1. identifikohem, njëjtësohem; gjej veten te

□ *I found the play unsatisfactory: there wasn't a single character—hero or anti-hero—with whom I could identify.* □ *I found it hard to identify with any of the characters in the film.* 2. lidhem me, mbështes

□ *He refused to identify oneself with the new political party.*

I dare say ka të ngjarë, ndofta, besoj se, mbase; marr guximin të them, guxoj të

□ *He doesn't like me—I dare say he suspects me because I refuse to treat him either as a clown or as a tragic hero.*

idle one's/the time away kaloj kohën kot, vras kohën

□ *When you find yourself sitting in front of an examination paper you'll regret idling your time away in empty conversation.*

I mean (to say) (!) dua të them

□ *Of course you should type it out again! I mean to say, just look at it!* □ *We walked straight out again and found another hotel. I mean to say, if you're going to pay $30 for bed and breakfast you expect the place to be at least clean.*

I'm afraid (that...) më vjen keq por

□ *I can put you up for the night but you'll have to sleep on the sofa, I'm afraid.* □ *'Have you got two tickets for tomorrow night's performance?' 'I'm afraid not, madam.'*

impose on/upon sb/sth imponohem

□ *'Really, Mary! You must not be so generous towards everyone who comes asking you for money. Don't allow yourself to be imposed upon!'*

if my memory serves me right nëse e mbaj mend saktë, nëse nuk gabohem

□ *I think he had been married before—a short and unhappy affair in his earlier twenties, if my memory serves me right.* □ *I was paid, if my memory serves me right, six shillings for the mid-week meeting and seven shillings for Saturday nights.*

it need be në se është nevoja, po ta lypë nevoja

□ *'How many men were employed to erect it?' 'We would use a thousand, ten thousand if need be.* □ *There's always the food in the freezer if need be.*

if only sikur, nëse; në qoftë se
  □ *If only I could get away for a bit from all work and muddle!* □ *If only he arrives in time!* □ *If only she had known about it!* □ *If you could only have seen it!*

if so në rast të tillë
  □ *He will not die unless we abandon him, and if so, we are indeed answerable for his blood.*

if the cap fits, wear it po të dogji, mbaje
  □ *I have noticed that there are some classrooms where the pupils have been in at least five minutes before their teacher appears. I will name no names but, if the cap fits, wear it.* □ *'You shouldn't have ranted on so much. Jenkins might have thought you were getting at him.' 'Well if the cap fits, let him wear it; if not, he doesn't have to bother, does he?'*

if the sky fall (falls) we shall catch larks kur të bëhet deti kos
  □ *Lubin... I grant you that if we could live three hundred years we should all be, perhaps wiser, certainly, older. You will grant me in return, I hope, that if the sky fell we should all catch larks.*

if the worst comes to the worst në rastin më të keq
  □ *I'm told the show may be very boring: if the worst comes to the worst, we can leave early and come home.* □ *I adopted Paula's attitude, saying that if the worst came to the worst we could make our way across the river into Brazil.* □ *Even if worst comes to worst, I've got enough to live on for six months.* □ *You have everything to lose if worst came to worst.*

if you don't mind po të më lejoni, po deshët, po të mos keni ndonjë kundërshtim, nëse nuk bezdiseni

  □ *I'll have to leave a little of this, if you don't mind. You gave me an enormous helping.*

if you please ju lutem
  □ *Come this way, if you please.* □ *Now where shall we sit? Mrs. Johnston, over here if you please, and Andrew next to Mrs. Johnston!* □ *Pass me the salt if you please.*

if you will nëse preferon (dëshiron)
  □ *Mrs. Allen sat down again. 'You may bring me a small glass too, if you will.'* □ *'Oh, I nearly forgot, sir. Mr. Wickham said he had the Tranter documents ready for you to sign.' 'Good. Go and ask him to bring them in now if he will.*

I had (would) rather do të doja, do të pëlqeja (preferoja)
  □ *'Some more wine?' 'Thank you. I'd rather not. I have to drive home.'* □ *She'd rather die than lose the children.* □ *'Shall I go downstairs, sir?' inquired Oliver. 'No', replied Mr. Brownlow. 'I would rather you remained here.'*

ill at ease i shqetësuar, i paqetë, si mbi gjemba
  □ *A young man stood in a curious attitude, half arrogant and half obsequious, by the girl's side. He was obviously rather ill at ease.* □ *The last witness seemed very ill at ease when she was being questioned: do you think she was lying?* □ *I was sufficiently ill at ease. She was ill at ease in the presence of strangers.* □ *The newcomer was fidgeting with his tie and seemed ill at ease.*

I'll/I'd bet (you) my bottom dollar jam plotësisht i sigurt
  □ *I'll bet you my bottom dollar that Jane comes late.* □ *I bet you my bottom dollar that the Cubs will win this year.*

ill/bad feeling pakënaqësi, ndjenjë e pakëndshme; zemërim

□ *His rapid promotion caused much **bad feeling** among his colleagues.*

I ('ll) tell you what e di çfarë

□ *No, no, I never smoke a cigarette. **I'll tell you what**, though, I'll have a bit of that tobacco for my pipe if you like.* □ *'**Tell you what**!' he cried excitedly, 'Come to my place in town next Sunday night.'*

I am a Dutchman if e pres kokën, qofsha i poshtër

□ *That precious young thing will have something to say about this, or **I'm a Dutchman**!*

□ *'Then we've won?' said Fleur. 'Unless **I am a Dutchman**', answered Soames.* □ *'I'll have a glass of wine', said Kit, picking up a bottle and smelling it. 'Good stuff, or **I'm a Dutchman**'.*

impress/imprint on sb's memory ngulit në kujtesë

□ *The dying man's words were **impressed on my memory**, though I could not understand them; 'Look beyond the sunset ... beyond the sunset.'* □ *His words are strongly **impressed on my memory**.*

in a bad way shumë keq; shumë rëndë

□ *I'm afraid your uncle is **in a bad way**: he may not survive.* □ *The finances of the company are **in a bad way**: it may have to close down soon.*

in a big way seriozisht, gjerësisht, në shkallë të gjerë

□ *They are receivers of stolen goods **in a big way**, but the countries where they operate don't care, so long as they take a cut in taxes and import licences and so on.* □ *Our company is going into the motor-car business **in a big way**: we are investing millions of pounds in it over the next few*

years. *He's got himself in trouble **in a big way**.*

in a body të gjithë tok (së bashku), si një trup i vetëm

□ *As a kind of protest, the students left the hall **in a body** in the middle of the graduation ceremony.* □ *The audience rose **in a body** and cheered him to the echo.* □ *The protesters marched **in a body** to the town hall.*

in a brown study i kredhur (zhytur) thellë në mendime

□ *She begins to pace up and down the garden **in a brown study**.* □ *Her mother was inaccessibly entrenched **in a brown study**.* □ *They saw that he sat for a few minutes at a time like one **in a brown study**.*

in accordance with në përputhje (pajtim) me

□ *Trespassers may be prosecuted **in accordance with** the law.* □ *He always acts **in accordance with** the regulations.* □ *What he did was **in accordance** with what he said.*

in a crack sa hap e mbyll sytë, aty për aty, menjëherë

□ *I'll be with you **in a crack**.* □ *He was off **in a crack** before I could address him.* □ *He was on his feet again **in a crack**.*

in addition (to sth) përveç (veç) kësaj; për më tepër

□ *Two main kind of waves travel outward from the center of an earthquake. **In addition**, there are surface waves.* □ *On the first day over six hundred people visited the exhibition, **in addition to** those who were present at the opening ceremony.*

in advance me avancë, para afatit, që më parë, para kohës së caktuar

□ *The rent will be $20 a week, paid **in advance**.* □ *No one can possibly know **in advance** how he would react in cir-*

cumstances like these. □ There's always a great demand for tickets. You'd better book your seats well in **advance**. □ They were having winter racing in New Orleans and a syndicate was laying out each day's program **in advance** and its agents in all the northern cities were 'milking' the poolrooms.

in a/the family way shtatzënë
□ The wives will have a fine easy time when they are **in the family way**. □ Sue and Liz are happy because their mother is **in the family way**.

in/after a fashion njëfarësoj, në një farë mënyre, as mirë as keq
□ He speaks English **in a fashion**. □ He played the violin, **after a fashion**.

in a fix në pozitë të vështirë
□ He put himself **in a bad fix**. □ He is never at loss when he is **in a fix**.

in a flash aty për aty, menjëherë, në çast, sakaq, sa të hapësh e të mbyllësh sytë
□ He just looked at the maths problem once, and the solution came to him **in a flash**. □ Realization broke on Andrew **in a blinding flash**. □ You just have to call and he is here **in a flash**.

in a fog i hutuar, si nëpër tym
□ I've read his book twice, and I'm still **in a fog**. □ I confess that, until it came to light, I was **in a fog**. □ I am all **in a fog** over these accounts, perhaps you can explain to me your system of book—keeping.

in a good cause për qëllim të mirë
□ And when his Mum went away for a few days it was all **in a good cause**. □ Noel said his evening and his wife's digestion were going to be ruined, but he supposed it was **in a good cause**.

in agreement with sb/sth në një mendje me, në pajtim me, në përputhje me

□ I take it we are **in agreement**? □ I find myself so completely **in agreement with** your letter of 18 September that I cannot believe there is any great difference in our concepts. □ **In agreement with** this suggestion we all set off for Bournemouth the following morning.

in a flash sakaq, menjëherë
□ Flynn sliced through the defence of the two England centers. **In a flash** he was past them and clean over the England line. □ **In a flash** she realized how superficial, and in a sense how vulgar, her reaction to the book had been.

in a hole në gjendje (situatë) të vështirë (financiare); në borxh
□ When the restaurant cook left at the beginning of the busy season, it put the restaurant owner **in a hole**. □ I am **in a hole** and I thought you'd help me. □ Jack is rather **in a hole**.

in a hurry 1. ngutas, nxitimthi, shpejt e shpejt, me të shpejtë, me ngut, me nxitim
□ I made a mistake through doing it **in a hurry**.
□ They went there **in a great hurry**.
2. shpejt; kollaj
□ She won't forget it **in a hurry**. □ I shan't ask that rude man to dinner again **in a hurry**! □ It's not the kind of experience you forget **in a hurry**.
3. nuk më pritet, nuk më durohet
□ He was **in a hurry** to leave.

in a jiffy në çast
□ 'Where's Irma?' one of them asked. 'Just gone out to powder her nose, I think. She'll be back **in a jiffy**.' □ I won't take long to fix your radio. I'll have it ready for you **in a jiffy**. I know just what has to be done to it.

in a large/great measure në një masë të madhe

□ *His failure is* **in great measure** *due to lack of confidence.*

in all gjithsej, gjithë-gjithë, si total

□ *I did quite a lot of flying at the London Aeroplane Club. I did about a hundred hours* **in all.** □ *It seemed we were to be a cosy roundtable party, fourteen* **in all.** □ *There were twelve of us* **in all** *for dinner.* □ *How many are there* **in all?**

in all conscience 1. sigurisht, natyrisht, pa dyshim

□ *Half a dozen fools are,* **in all conscience,** *as many as you should require.* □ *You cannot* **in all conscience** *regard that as fair pay.* □ *He is a clever boy* **in all conscience.**
2. ndershmërisht, me ndershmëri

□ *I cannot* **in all conscience** *ask him to do that what I would not.*

in all honesty/sincerity ndershmërisht, në mënyrë të ndershme (të sinqertë)

□ *A few students answered this correctly, and a few abstained from answering, but the majority declared unhesitatingly and* **in all sincerity** *that the man returned the book to the shelf.* □ *Can you* **in all honesty** *claim that none of this has been your own fault?*

in all likelihood/probability ka shumë të ngjarë (mundësi); me sa duket

□ *Why should we go so far out of our way to visit somebody who* **in all likelihood** *moved out of the district years ago?* □ **In all likelihood,** *we shall be away for a week.*

in all/every respects në të gjitha drejtimet, në çdo drejtim

□ *He was* **in all respects** *a proper gentleman.* □ *They resemble one another* **in all respects.**

in all one's born days gjatë gjithë jetës

□ *A man who came level with them on the same side called out derisively: 'Did you ever see such a game?' 'Never* **in all my born days,'** *Fred replied.* □ *I have never seen anything so disgraceful* **in all my born days.**

in all weathers në mot të mirë a të keq

□ *He was a van boy on a dray working* **in all weathers** *for twelve hours a day.* □ *Her father was a powerful fifty-years-old, with the grain red brown complexion of a man accustomed to being out* **in all weathers.**

in a manner në një farë shkalle, në një farë mase (mënyre)

□ *He masters the language* **in a manner.** □ *The bread* **in a manner** *is common.*

in a manner of speaking në një farë mënyre; si të thuash

□ *His success is* **in a manner of speaking** *our success, too.* □ *'What are you doing hanging about there?' 'Well, sir, hanging about is my job,* **in a manner of speaking.** □ **In a manner of speaking,** *he is putting the cart before the horse.*

in a minute në çast, shpejt, në këtë minutë

□ *Our guests will be here* **in a minute.** □ *I'll come* **in a minute.** □ *I'll join* **in a minute.**

in a moment në moment, në çast

□ *Just rest, dear. The doctor will be here* **in a moment.** □ *Oh, please come in and wait for Jack. He'll be back* **in a moment.** □ **In a moment** *the house was in flames.*

in and out brenda e jashtë

□ *He was very busy Saturday and was* **in and out** *all day.* □ *He's always* **in and out** *of the hospital.*

in answer/reply to në përgjigje të

□ *'Fergus hasn't given me anything yet,' she said lightly,* **in answer to**

Guy's question. □ *I threatened to set the dogs on them and after flinging a few ill-aimed stones in reply, they scrambled back over the fence.*

in a nutshell shkurt, me dy fjalë

□ *We have very little time left: could you please explain your point of view in a nutshell?* □ *'You never told me that yet.... But here it is in a nutshell. About a year ago...'* □ *I'll give you the facts in a nutshell.* □ *...this problem which, in a nutshell, is a problem of the relation between body and mind generally.*

in any case sidoqoftë, sido që të ndodhë, sido që të jetë puna

□ *It may rain tomorrow, but we are going home in any case.* □ *'It was no business of yours, Jack, in any case.' 'No business of mine!'* □ *We shall call on him in any case, though we may not be able to stay long.*

in any event sidoqoftë, për çdo rast

□ *Admittedly his microphone was not working, but in any event most of the delegates did not seem in the mood to listen to him.* □ *In any event I have several pressing matters waiting for me.*

in any shape or form në çfarëdolloj forme

□ *Never again did he sample tobacco in any shape or form.* □ *You can give me eggs as often as you like. I'm very partial to them in any shape or form.*

in a round-about way tërthorazi, larg e larg

□ *When one has something to say, it's best to come to the point directly instead of saying it in a round-about way.*

in a row me radhë

□ *This is the third Sunday in a row that's rained.*

in a rush me nxitim, me ngut

□ *He is always in such a rush that he never thinks of anything.* □ *I'm in a dreadful rush.*

in a sense në një kuptim, deri diku

□ *I know that Jones is very strict with his workers: but, in a sense, he is doing them good, because his business is efficient and their jobs are secure.* □ *What you say is true in a sense.* □ *In a sense, Beaverbrook was not a character of the first importance. He wasn't a serious character.*

in a shake/in a couple of shakes/in two shakes shpejt e shpejt, fët e fët

□ *'Hurry up and get a fire going and I'll have the lunch ready in two shakes.'* □ *'Billy's finished your coat.' '—Let it be,' Dallow said. 'I'll fetch it in a shake.'*

in a small way 1. thjesht, në mënyrë modeste

□ *She lived with her daughter in a very small way.* □ *His family were not utterly without funds, sufficient to live in a small way.*

2. në masë (shkallë) të vogël

□ *He is in business in a small way.* □ *He collects antiques in a small way.*

in a tick në moment, në çast

□ *I'll be down in half a tick.* □ *'I'll be ready in a tick.'*

in a trice menjëherë, sakaq, në sekondë, në çast, sa të hapësh e të mbyllësh sytë

□ *You thought you were as dead as a herring two hours since, and you are all alive and talking now. I'll make you decent in a trice.* □ *In a trice Weston had picked up his own special piece of equipment, and nipped swiftly up the steps in time to bring up the rear of the party. I'll be with you in a trice.*

in a way/in a sort of way në një kuptim, në një drejtim, në një farë mase

□ *Orinthia. I believe you would sign my death warrant without turning a hair. Magnus. That is true in a way.* □ *'I advised you to go back, Marcie.' 'In a sort of way: not in the right tone.'* □ *He was a big, strong man, and many women must have liked him. She liked him, too, in a way.*

in a whisper duke pështpëritur

□ *'Don't you find it awfully irritating?' 'Actually I do,' Aunt Annabel confided in a whisper, giving a quick nervous glance towards her husband.* □ *'I'll tell you, mate; only keep it under your hat,' he said in a hoarse whisper.*

in a word me një fjalë, shkurt, në mënyrë të përmbledhur

□ *You certainly picked the right person for that job, James. In a word, she's the best engineer this firm's ever employed.* □ *Another night elapsed; another morning came, but no wife. In a word, she was never heard of more.* □ *In a word, a happy thriving atmosphere pervades both the cities and the countryside.* □ *In a word, Professor Jones, what are your views on the present financial crisis?*

in bad humor në humor të keq

□ *He had been in bad humor even since his dear wife's death.*

in bad odor me nam (emër) të keq

□ *Jack has been in bad odor with the management since the last strike: they think he caused it.*

in bad/good repair në gjendje të keqe/të mirë

□ *Tony keeps his car in good repair.*

in bad shape në formë të keqe

□ *We lost the game for most of our players were in bad shape.*

in black and white me shkrim

□ *This letter's from your mother saying she agrees to your coming with me. Now we have it in black and white.* □ *This view, indeed, has become so much a commonplace that one feels almost ashamed of putting it down in black and white.* □ *'Perhaps I could have it all in what's called black and white from the family solicitor,' he said.* □ *Look here, here it is in black and white.*

in brief shkurt, shkurtimisht, me një fjalë

□ *It would take a long time to go into all the details, but I can give you the facts in brief.* □ *Time is limited, please tell the story in brief.* □ *It would need a book to tell properly but, in brief, she started an extramural diploma course and got a place at Bedford College, London, four years later.*

in broad daylight në mes të ditës

□ *'Nothing happens to a woman in broad daylight,' he said. 'She'll turn up.'* □ *Criminals used to rob people only when it was dark, but now they are doing it in broad daylight.* □ *... it took place in broad daylight.*

in case of sth në rast se

□ *Ham Peggotty had been for some days past secreted in the house, unknown to my mother, as a special messenger in case of emergency, to fetch the nurse and doctor.* □ *In case I forget, please remind me of my promise.* □ *You had better take your umbrella in case it rains.* □ *In case of fire, ring the alarm bell.*

in character (with) në karakter, në natyrë

□ *John was very rude at the party, and that was not in character, because he is usually very polite.* □ *He*

was an extremely kind man: the fact that his last thoughts were for his friends completely in character.
2. i përshtatshëm, i natyrshëm
□ *The fat actor in the movie was in character because the character he played was supposed to be fat and jolly.*

in charge of sb/sth përgjegjës për
□ *Who is in charge here?* □ *He was left in charge of the shop while the manager was away.*

inch by inch pak e nga pak, ca nga ca, dalëngadalë
□ *They climbed the steep mountain inch by inch.* □ *Inch by inch he crawled away.*

in cold blood me gjak të ftohtë, me gjakftohtësi; me mendje të qetë
□ *The ambushes and pitched battles were fought in fury. And afterwards, prisoners were shot in cold blood.* □ *I think that anyone who murders another person in cold blood should be hanged.* □ *Secondly, thank you for all you say about my new adventure in the East. In cold blood I'm sometimes a little terrified when I think of the immensity of the task.*

in common bashkë, bashkërisht, së toku, së bashku; të përbashkët
□ *The language which everyone in the group has in common is English.* □ *The land is owned in common by the residents.*

in common with sb/sth tok (bashkë) me
□ *Tony, in common with many of his generation, had no very clear idea of what he wanted to do in life.* □ *In common with many others, she applied for the job.* □ *You deserve to be blamed in common with the rest.* □ *In common with other students he had very good results.*

in company with sb së bashku me, tok me, në shoqëri me
□ *I, in company with many others, feel this decision was wrong.* □ *But neither Peggotty nor I had eyes for him, when we saw, in company with him, Mr. Murdstone.* □ *He came in company with a group of boys.*

in/by comparison with sb/sth në krahasim me
□ *The tallest building in London are small in comparison with those in New York.*

in concert with sb/sth në bashkëpunim me
□ *He is working in concert with his colleagues.* □ *They did not act in concert with one another.*

in connection with sb/sth lidhur me, në lidhje me
□ *I am writing to you in connection with your job application.* □ *'I want to see the manager,' she said, laying an envelope on the counter, 'in connection with this letter I received from him yesterday.'*

in confidence në mirëbesim
□ *'Naturally,' she added, 'all that I say to you now is in confidence.'* □ *Olive had promised to write and tell Eric in strictest confidence about his difficulties with Mrs. Pettigrew.* □ *'That would make a good story for your paper.' 'Too true, it would. But I cannot use information given me in confidence in that way.'*

in confusion 1. lëmsh e li, rrëmujë
□ *The room had been thoroughly ransacked and the contents of drawers and cupboards lay in confusion on the floor.*
2. i hutuar
□ *'They've altered this part of the town completely since I was here*

last,' he complained, peering through the windscreen in confusion.'

in conjunction with sb/sth tok (bashkë) me

□ *At least two other preschool centers built and financed by private trusts and administered in close conjunction with the Inner London Education Authority are in the pipeline.* □ *We are working in conjunction with the police.*

in consequence of sth si (për) rrjedhim

□ *She was found guilty, and lost her job in consequence of it.* □ *In consequence, an ill-natured story got about, that Emily wanted to be a lady.*

in consideration of 1. për shkak të

□ *In consideration of his wife's health, he moved to a milder climate.* 2. në këmbim (kompensim)

□ *Mr. Bounderby being a bachelor, an elderly lady presided over his establishment, in consideration of a certain annual stipend.*

in contrast to/with sb/sth në dallim (kontrast) me

□ *In contrast to the subterranean life which Granny Walton lived, Granny Trill's cottage door was always open and her living room welcomed us daily.*

in course of sth në ... e sipër

□ *The house is in course of construction.*

in default of sb/sth në mungesë të

□ *He was acquitted in default of strong evidence of his guilt.* □ *The committee will not meet in default of a chairman.*

in defiance of pa përfillur, duke shpërfillur

□ *She wanted him to stay, but he left in defiance of her wishes.* □ *He jumped into the river to save the drowning child in defiance of the icy water.*

in depth në thellësi

□ *In this fourth lecture I have decided to interpret the problem broadly rather than in depth.* □ *I think that everybody who has helped other people with personal problems, and who has pursued the study in any depth comes to the conclusion that there are interactions going on within the mind itself.*

in despite of megjithë, pa marrë parasysh, pa përfillur

□ *William persisted in his conduct in despite of repeated warnings.* □ *The seized my hand in despite of my efforts to the contrary.*

in detail me hollësi (imtësi), hollësisht (imtësisht)

□ *In future, a claim for expenses must be rendered in detail and accompanied by receipts.* □ *He explained to us in detail the plan he has drawn for the coming action.* □ *Will you please explain the matter in detail?* □ *It is not possible to treat the matter in detail in a short speech.*

in dispute në diskutim

□ *The exact cause of the accident is still in dispute.* □ *The reliability of the evidence is in dispute.*

in doubt në dyshim

□ *Their acceptance of the contract is still in doubt.* □ *When in doubt about the meaning of a word, consult a dictionary.*

in drink çakërrqejf

□ *It was spoken in drink, but it happened to be true. Half drunk myself, I loved him for it.* □ *'Was he drunk at the time of his accident?' 'Not what you'd call drunk. I would say he was in drink—a bit happy, may be had a glass or two.'*

in due course në kohën e duhur

□ *Sopphy arrives at the house of Dora's aunts in due course.* □ *I will consider the matter and let you know my answer in due course.* □ *Sow the seed now and in due course you will have the flowers.* □ *Your request will be dealt with in due course.*

in due time në kohë, në kohën e duhur

□ *Mr. Micawber immediately descended to the bar, where he appeared to be quite at home, and in due time returned with a steaming jug.* □ *In due time the doctor came.*

in earnest seriozisht, me seriozitet

□ *The snow did not start to fall in earnest until after the darkness had set in.* □ *Are you in earnest or are you joking?* □ *I just wanted to give the boy a fright, but I'll be angry in earnest if he does it again.* □ *For a long time he did nothing, but now he has started working in earnest.*

in effect 1. në të vërtetë, në fakt

□ *The procedure could in effect deprive parents of their right to be represented legally before a court.* □ *The factory is going to be modernized: this means, in effect, that there will be fewer jobs.* □ *We had, in effect, been trying hard to accomplish the task successfully.*
2. në fuqi, në veprim, në përdorim

□ *Some ancient laws are still in effect.*

in essence në thelb (esencë)

□ *The two arguments are in essence the same.* □ *The two stories were in essence the same.*

in every way në të gjitha drejtimet

□ *This is in every way better than that.* □ *They support our proposal in every way.*

in fact në fakt, në të vërtetë

□ *You believe that you are careful and efficient but in fact you are not good at organization.* □ *'You look tired, Jilly.' 'I am tired, in fact.'* □ *I want your frank opinion. Is he in fact likely to recover?* □ *'Quite correct. In fact, I have no particular notice at all.* □ *In fact she was not jealous at all.*

in favor of sb/sth për, në favor të

□ *I am sure, headmaster, it would help if you would speak in his favor when Tom's case comes up.* □ *... as fairly and persuasively as a scientist will present the case in favor of a particular belief he holds.* □ *All of us were in favor of his suggestion.* □ *Was he in favor of death penalty?*

in fear of sb/sth i frikësuar (i trembur) nga

□ *The thief went in constant fear of discovery.*

in/with fear and trembling gjithë frikë e drithërima

□ *... but now much more in my absence, work out your salvation with fear and trembling.* □ *I arrived in fear and trembling. I was also followed everywhere by the sound of breathing, the heavy breathing of the Secret Service.*

in fine shkurt e saktë

□ *In fine, I would say that this book is the best one on the subject that has ever been written.*

in fine/full/good/great/high feather në formë të shkëlqyer, në humor shumë të mirë

□ *She was her old self again, her blues were gone, she was in high feather.* □ *The next week she was in even greater feather.* □ *Below stairs, he halted in the lobby to look for a barbershop. For the moment he was in fine feather.*

in fine/good fettle në formë të shkëlqyer, në gjendje shumë të mirë shpirtërore

□ *Harry has completely recovered from his illness and you will find him in good fettle.* □ *He had evidently woken up feeling in fine fettle: his song was loud and persistent.*

in force 1. në fuqi

□ *Laws to make sure that one's car is safe to drive have been in force for many years now.* □ *The regulation is no longer in force.*

2. në numër të madh

□ *The police were present at the demonstration in full force.*

in front of 1. para, përpara

□ *There are some trees in front of the house.* □ *The children streamed into the zoo, with their teacher in front of them.*

2. në faqe të, para, në prani

□ *Please don't talk about it in front of the children.*

in full plotësisht, tërësisht

□ *Anything he has ever borrowed from me he has always repaid in full.* □ *He decided to publish the report in full.* □ *Write your name in full.*

in full blast me kapacitet të plotë

□ *The plant started building the iron foundry only last autumn, but now is in full blast.*

in full sail me vela të ngritura

□ *The racing yacht was a magnificent sight as it came into the harbor in full sail.*

in full swing në kulmin (vlugun) e vet

□ *The meeting was in full swing when he arrived.* □ *When I got to the playground the football game was already in full swing.*

in fun me shaka

□ *Grandpa didn't mean he was going to eat your ice cream, you silly girl. He only said it in fun.* □ *'I know Celia will never see forty again.' 'Oh, come,' I said. 'She was exaggerating when she told you that. She was in fun.'* □ *Things said in fun are not to be taken seriously.*

in future/in the future që sot e tutje; në të ardhmen

□ *'You could have insured your luggage, you know, for quite a small sum.' 'I know, and that's what we'll do in future.'* □ *He foresaw that he was going to have some anxious times, some very awkward moments in the near future.* □ *Try to do it better in the future.* □ *I don't want this to happen in the future.*

in general në përgjithësi, përgjithësisht

□ *I don't like historical novels in general, but this particular one is very interesting.* □ *About midnight I came to and realized we'd been talking about the world in general and nothing in particular.* □ *In general, I agree with your remark.*

in good faith ndershmërisht, me ndershmëri; sinqerisht; me mirëbesim

□ *The police would have found it difficult to inspire confidence unless they were negotiating in good faith.* □ *They could perfectly well defend this suit, or at least in good faith try to.* □ *I am sure he acted in good faith.*

in good/capable hands në dorë të mirë (të aftë)

□ *I've left the department in Bill's very efficient hands.*

in good heart 1. në kushte të mira

□ *My garden, lying over solid chalk,*

needs constant organic enrichment to keep it in good heart.
2. në gjendje të mirë shpirtërore
□ *The Times, this year, has found most industrialists in surprisingly good heart.*

in good humor me humor, në ditë të mirë, në qejf
□ *Harold was in high good humor: Isabel had seldom seen him so pleased.* □ *... and likely to be in good humor.*

in good time 1. me kohë, para kohe
□ *I tell you in good time to keep clear of me. The students finished their schoolwork in good time.* □ *We arrived in good time to catch the train.*
2. në kohën e duhur
□ *'Tell me all about yourself and Spencer and your house and everything.' 'I will in good time. Right now, I'm, only interested in getting out of this pigsty.' □ 'Oh Harold,' she exclaimed, 'why all this mystification?' 'You'll find out in good time.'*

in good tune në qejf; ka qejf (dëshirë)
□ *Are you in a good tune for playing football today?* □ *I don't feel in good tune for discussing that matter now.*

in hand 1. në dorë
□ *I complained to the Ministry because they had not replied to my letter, but they assured me that the matter was in hand.* □ *He gave his whole attention to whatever he had in hand.* □ *He had much business in hand.*
2. në dispozicion
□ *The supplies are not finished; we still have some in hand.* □ *There is only another mile to go, and we have still twenty minutes in hand.*
3. në shqyrtim
□ *This is the great subject now in*

hand. □ *He congratulated his honorable friend on his able and well-delivered effort, he only regretted that it had nothing to do with the business in hand.*
4. nën kontroll
□ *The police have got the situation in hand.* □ *The principal was happy to find that the new teacher had her class in hand.*

in/into harness në punë
□ *I hate having nothing to do: I can't wait to get back in harness again.*

in haste 1. shpejt
□ *Bring the doctor in haste.*
2. shpejt e shpejt, nxitimthi, me nxitim
□ *Replying in haste, he gave the wrong answer.*

in high spirits në humor të mirë, shend e verë, shend e gaz
□ *The children are always in high spirits on the last days of the school term.*

in high places në sferat e larta
□ *She has friends in high places.* □ *I had sacked a peculiarly incompetent and indolent officer who had friends in high places.* □ *Insurance agent Kirby stumbled on corruption in high places—information he can sell to the British Civil Service.*

in itself në vetvete
□ *Not only is the success an honor in itself, but it means that the team will be Albania's representative in next season's European Cup competition.* □ *Jullien's conducting was an exciting performance in itself.*

in Indian file për një, njëri pas tjetrit
□ *The path between the trees was so narrow that we had to walk in Indian file.* □ *They climbed up the mountain in Indian file.*

in jest me shaka
 □ *His reply was taken half seriously, half in jest.* □ *Many a true word is spoken in jest.* □ *I only said it in jest.*

in keeping with në pajtim me
 □ *I don't think that what the government is doing now is in keeping with what it promised before it was elected.*

in kind 1. në natyrë
 □ *He's paid $70 a week beside what he receives in kind—a rent-free cottage, firewood, milk and potatoes, and so on.*
2. me të njëjtën monedhë
 □ *Abba Eban is probably just the right kind of figure to stand up to the extreme provocation of some of the hotter challenges. He never replies in kind and always tries to diffuse the situation.*

in league with në aleancë me, në bashkëpunim me
 □ *It was then we realized that one of our generals was in league with the enemy.*

in memory of në kujtim të
 □ *He founded the charity in memory of his late wife.* □ *The building was named Ford Hall in memory of a man named James Ford.*

in name only vetëm me emër
 □ *He is a leader in name only: his deputy has effectively taken over.* □ *He is the manager in name only; most of the work is actually done by his son.* □ *Well, he may be a minister, but he's a Christian in name only if that's how he treats people.*

in no case kurrsesi, në asnjë mënyrë
 □ *In no case should you panic.* □ *I will in no case accept his proposal.*

in no sense në asnjë drejtim, në asnjë pikëpamje
 □ *It is in no sense right.*

in no time menjëherë, sakaq, në çast, sa hap e mbyll sytë
 □ *When the entire class worked together they finished the project in no time.* □ *In no time she had cleared the table...* □ *Only just a minute; me Cokane and will be back in no time to see you home.* □ *The experiment proved successful and in no time the firm introduced the new method of production.* □ *Why don't you dance? It's easy. You could learn in no time.* □ *George: I'm all right, I'd like a cup of tea though.* □ *Mrs. Elliot: It's all ready. And I'll get you something to eat in no time.* □ *I'll give you a hand! We'll put up that shed together! See? Get it done in next to no time.*

in no way në asnjë mënyrë, aspak
 □ *He was influenced to give a certain degree of attention to this new proposition. He in no way countenanced it.*

in one's cups i pirë tapë
 □ *I've come to know him pretty well these last ten or twelve years. And odd facts drop out when a man's in his cups.* □ *My mother was merely a horrified looker-on, my father in his cups already predicted the gallows for me.*

in one's eyes/in the eyes of në sytë e, sipas vlerësimit të
 □ *He was quite right in the eyes of everybody.*

in one's heart of hearts/in one's heart's heart thellë në shpirt, në thellësi të shpirtit
 □ *In his heart of hearts he sympathized with the strikers and hated this 'scab'.* □ *'Oh, I knew you'd take it like this,' Milly said, 'I knew it in my heart of hearts.'* □ *In his heart he wept for his own guilt and failure and for the echo of her words which he would spend the rest of his life trying*

to refute. □ *Yet* **in my heart of hearts** *I feel your might.*

in one's mind në mendjen e

□ *Prissie would make a wonderful wife for guy. No doubt already* **in her mind** *she was admiring this house as its mistress.*

in one's/the mind's eye me sytë e mendjes

□ *Hamlet. ...My father,—me think I see my father... Horatio. O! Where my lord? Hamlet.* **In my mind's eye,** *Horatio.* □ *The summers I look back on myself all,* **in my mind's eye,** *turn into 1959 which was so hot for so long that reservoirs turned into patches of cracked mud.* □ *Although our old house was knocked down a long time ago, I can still see it* **in my mind's eye.**

in one's opinion/in the opinion of sb sipas mendimit të

□ **In my opinion** *and* **in the opinion of** *most people, it is a very sound investment.* □ *But a surgeon specialist at the same hospital said later that he disagreed. He said:* '**In my opinion,** *the vertebra is compressed not fractured.'* □ *I have now much pleasure in announcing the winner of the entry which was,* **in the** *unanimous* **opinion of** *all the judges, the best.* □ **In our opinion** *his suggestions were useful.*

in one's own time në kohën e lirë

□ *I'll do it* **in my own time.**

in one's senses në gjendje normale, me mendjen në vend

□ *No one* **in their right senses** *would let a small child go out alone.*

in sb's sight sipas mendimit (opinionit) të

□ *Do what is right* **in your** *own* **sight.**

in one piece shëndoshë e mirë, pa pësuar gjë

□ *We never mixed it with German fighters if we could avoid it, for our main duty was to get home* **in one piece.** □ *I was so glad to see the car back* **in one piece** *that I forgot to ask him if he had filled up the tank again.*

in one's tracks në vend; befas, papritur

□ *He fell dead* **in his tracks.** □ *Your question stopped him* **in his tracks.** □ *John West stopped dead* **in his tracks** *and looked around.*

in one's true colors me fytyrën (karakterin) e vërtetë

□ *Once he achieved power he showed himself* **in his true colors.**

in opposition to sb/sth 1. në kundërshtim me

□ *We found ourselves* **in opposition** *to several colleagues on this issue.* □ *If Jenny chooses to marry you* **in opposition to** *my wishes, I cannot of course prevent her.* 2. në opozitë me

□ *The conservative party was* **in opposition** *for the first time in years.* □ *The two wing of a political party would not do so well separately and* **in opposition to** *each other in an election as they have done together.*

in order në rregull

□ *Is your passport* **in order?** □ *He put his papers* **in order** *before going out.*

in order that/to që, me qëllim që

□ **In order to** *make these calculations it is essential to have as much information as possible about the terrain through which the road is to go.* □ *'Why did we leave so early?'* '**In order that** *the old man might go to bed.'* □ *You must take measures* **in order that** *such mistakes may never be* *made again.* □ *You must work hard in order to succeed.*

in other words me fjalë të tjera

□ *Pressure on the surface of an object varies with the depth of the object below the surface of the water. In other words, the farther down you go, the greater the pressure.*

in part pjesërisht

□ *We planted the garden in part with flowers. But in large part we planted vegetables.* □ *The story is in part autobiographical and in part fictitious.*

in particular në veçanti, sidomos, veçanërisht

□ *The whole meal was good but the wine in particular was excellent.* □ *'Is there anything in particular you would like for dinner?' 'No, nothing in particular.'* □ *I remember one of them in particular.*

in passing rastësisht, kalimthi; në udhë (ecje) e sipër

□ *He just happened to mention in passing that he had met you before.* □ *I don't remember the address, he only mentioned it in passing.* □ *I have not come on a visit, I have just called in passing.*

in peace në paqe, qetësisht

□ *The main object of the couple's lives, the one thing they still had to do before they could die in peace, was to guide Robert into a job where he'd be safe from the sack.* □ *'Oh, there's a man sweeping leaves.' 'That's all, dear, just a man with a barrow. So you can sleep in peace.'*

in person vetë, personalisht

□ *You must go yourself. Dr. Kingsley will be flattered if you go to see him in person.* □ *The winner will be there in person to collect the prize.* □ *You may apply for tickets in person or by*

letter. □ *I'd like to talk to him in person instead of over the telephone.* □ *I'll be present at the meeting in person.*

in place 1. në vend

□ *The children tidied up the room and left everything in place.* □ *She likes everything to be in place before she starts work.*

2. i udhës, i përshtatshëm

□ *A little gratitude would be in place.* □ *Do you think it would be in place if I left early?*

in place of sb/sth/in sb's/sth's place në vend të

□ *Even grafting new blood vessels in place of the diseased coronary arteria has been tried.* □ *Jill has gone to another job. Whoever comes in her place will find it hard to match her efficiency and flair.* □ *The chairman was ill so his deputy spoke in his place.*

in plain English/Saxon shqip, troç, copë, haptas

□ *If you wanted me to go why didn't you say so in plain English instead of making vague hints?* □ *What I mean in plain English was that it would be easier to stand him a meal if he was on the spot: but I didn't put it that way.* □ *If you want the flat to yourself for some reason this afternoon, why don't you say so in plain English?* □ *He equivocates; in plain English, he lies.*

in play me shaka

□ *The remark was only made in play.*

in point në fjalë

□ *That's a case in point.*

in point of lidhur me, në lidhje me, përsa i takon

□ *States were busy with their laws and too negligent in point of education.* □ *'Was it an unequal marriage, sir,* ***in point of*** *years?' asked Mrs. Sparsit.*

in point of fact në fakt, në të vërtetë

□ *There had been rumors of a Turkish invasion. Now* ***in point of fact*** *the rumor of the arrival of the Turks was entirely true.* □ *He said he would pay, but* ***in point of fact*** *he has no money.* □ *This last averment was a slight alternation* ***in point of fact.***

in/into position nëpër vende, në vendet e duhura

□ *The orchestra were all* ***in position,*** *waiting for the conductor.* □ *The runners got* ***into position*** *on the starting line.*

in possession of sth në zotërim (posedim)

□ *Their opponents were* ***in possession*** *of the ball for most of the match.* □ *He was caught* ***in possession of*** *stolen goods.*

in power në fuqi, në pushtet

□ *The government has been* ***in power*** *for two years.*

in principle në parim

□ *There is no reason* ***in principle*** *why people couldn't travel to Mars.* □ *They have agreed to the proposal* ***in principal*** *but we still have to negotiate the terms.* □ *We agree with the scheme* ***in principle,*** *but we think it needs modifications in certain details.*

in print 1. në qarkullim, në shitje

□ *Is that volume still* ***in print?*** □ *I am not sure whether the work you mention is still* ***in print.***

2. i botuar

□ *It is delightful to a young author to see himself* ***in print.*** □ *It was the first time he had seen his work* ***in print.***

in private vetëm për vetëm, privatisht

□ *It's when a man—or woman—starts to drink a lot* ***in private*** *that he's in danger of becoming an alcoholic.* □ *I*

could feel that he was waiting for Luke to leave. He had something to say to me ***in private.*** □ *May I speak to you* ***in private*** *for a few moments?*

in process (of) në proces, në ... e sipër

□ *The author has just finished one book and has another* ***in process.*** □ *Many new buildings are* ***in process*** *of erection.* □ *While the road was still* ***in process of*** *construction much damage was done to it by the subsidence of the earth beneath.*

in proportion në proporcion

□ *Her features are* ***in proportion.*** □ *It's a model village in which everything is* ***in proportion.***

in proportion to sth në proporcion (përpjesëtim) me

□ *The room is wide* ***in proportion to*** *its height.* □ *Payment will be* ***in proportion to*** *the work done, not the time spent doing it.* □ *It's wide* ***in proportion to*** *the height.* □ *It's a model village in which everything is* ***in proportion.***

in public në publik, publikisht, hapur, botërisht

□ *She could have thrashed both James and Bernard for losing their tempers* ***in public.*** □ *He had made his views known* ***in public*** *on many occasions, so his decisions not to vote along party lines should have come as no surprise.* □ *He made that remark* ***in public.***

in pursuance of në ndjekje të, në kryerje të, në zbatim të, në realizimin e

□ ***In pursuance of*** *his duties, the policeman risked his life.* □ ***In pursuance of*** *the plan to transform the barren hills into green orchards, the farmers set to work promptly.*

in quest of në kërkim të, për të kërkuar

□ *He emigrated* ***in quest of*** *employment.* □ *She had come* ***in quest of*** *advice.*

in question në fjalë; në shqyrtim
- □ *The job* **in question** *is available for three months only.* □ *The lawyer said that the house* **in question** *had already been sold.* □ *Let us stick to the point* **in question.** □ *That is not the subject* **in question.**

in reality në realitet, në të vërtetë
- □ *The house looks very old, but* **in reality** *it's quite new.* □ *We thought he was serious, but* **in reality** *he was joking.* □ *In reality our team should have won.*

in/with reference to në lidhje me
- □ *I am writing* **with reference to** *your job application.*

in/with regard to sth në lidhje me, lidhur me, për sa i përket
- □ **With regard to** *your request for an additional assistance, I can only say at this stage that this is being considered.* □ *I have nothing to say* **with regard to** *your complaints.*

in respect of për sa i përket, lidhur me
- □ *Substantial increases can be now expected* **in respect of** *gas and water costs.* □ *On our approaching the house where Spenlow lived, I was at such a discount* **in respect of** *my personal looks and presence of mind, that Traddles proposed a glass of ale.* □ *The book is admirable in* **respect of** *style.* □ *The letter is undated both* **in respect of** *time and place.*

in response to sth në përgjigje të
- □ **In response to** *Brigit's question he admitted that they had had fun catching the kitten.* □ *If you treat a child with consistent care and kindness you are bound to get some trust and affection* **in response.**

in return for sth në përgjigje, si përgjigje; në këmbim të; si shpërblim për
- □ *Let me buy the gin* **in return for** *all your kindness while I have been staying here.* □ *Sarah, plump and placid, gave her a wide friendly smile* **in return.** □ *What can we do for them* **in return for** *all the help they have given us?*

in revenge for sth si hakmarrje për
- □ *Terrorists bombed the police station* **in revenge for** *the arrests.*

in revolt në revoltë
- □ *The people rose* **in revolt.**

in round numbers/figures afërsisht, përafërsisht
- □ *You don't have to give the exact number; you can give the answer* **in round numbers,** *if you like.* □ *In round numbers, the population of this city is 50.000.*

in ruins në rrënim të plotë
- □ *An earthquake left the whole town* **in ruins.**

in safe hands në duar të sigurta
- □ *'Don't fret. The child is* **in safe hands** *now.'*

ins and outs, the detaje, hollësira, imtësi
- □ *I know more of* **the ins and outs** *of him than any person living does.* □ *There were so many* **ins and outs** *to this financial life.*

in search of sb/sth në kërkim të
- □ *Scientists are* **in search of** *a cure for the disease.* □ *Because baboons roam widely during the day* **in search of** *food we do not use hides.* □ *Blearney and several others of the guests came* **in search of** *him.* □ *The more people who visit the island* **in search of** *peace and quiet, of course, the less likely they are to find it.*

in season në sezon
- □ *Apples are expensive just now because they are not* **in season.** □ *Strawberries are* **in season** *now.*

in season and out of season vend e pa vend; kohë e pa kohë
□ *He would discourse on his favorite topic in season and out of season.*

in secret në fshehtësi
□ *First in secret she had to practice walking until she was reasonably strong.* □ *They pretended that they had broken off their relationship but continued to meet in secret.*

in short shkurt, shkurtimisht, me një fjalë
□ *'In short, you are provided for,' observed his sister, 'and will please to do your duty.'* □ *My address, said Mr. Micawber, is Windsor Terrace, City Road. I—in short, said Mr. Micawber with the same genteel air, and in another burst of confidence—I live there.* □ *He is greedy, lazy, untruthful, and boastful: in short, a very nasty person.*

in short order shpejt, sakaq, pa humbur kohë
□ *The sergeant was very efficient; in short order, he had his men fully armed and ready to march.*

in short supply me pakicë
□ *Because of the bad weather, fresh food is in short supply.* □ *The cookies are in short supply, so don't eat them all up.*

inside out 1. së prapthi; përmbys
□ *He put his socks on inside out.* □ *The wind blew her umbrella inside out.* □ *The burglars turned everything inside out.*
2. katërcipërisht, në mënyrë të gjithanshme; në të gjitha anët (drejtimet)
□ *David knows the parts of his bicycle inside out.*

in sight në fushëpamje, në fushën e shikimit
□ *Bothwell Bridge was at a little distance, and also in sight.*

in silence në heshtje, në qetësi
□ *She handed him the manuscript in silence, with her remarks written between the lines and on several attached loose sheets.* □ *They sat there a moment in silence. 'I suppose' he began. 'We'd better go' she said at the same moment.* □ *The students were listening to the teacher in silence.*

in single file një nga një, në rresht për një
□ *The pupils entered the classroom in single file.*

insinuate oneself into hyj (futem) fshehurazi (tinëz)
□ *The cat somehow insinuated itself into the larder, and feasted off a large joint of meat.* □ *The few remaining days on the boat were spent by Tollifer in planning and executing such moves as might insinuate himself into Allien's good graces.*

in so far as në atë që, në kuptimin që; me aq sa
□ *This is the truth in so far as I know.* □ *This small boy was something of an exception to the rule in so far as he appeared to seek knowledge rather than profit.*

in so/as many words tekstualisht, fjalë për fjalë; me këto fjalë; qartë, në mënyrë të qartë
□ *The Lord Mayor had threatened in so many words to pull down the old London Bridge and build up a new one.* □ *He didn't say that in so many words, but that's what he meant.*

in sb's favor në favor të
□ *The exchange rate is in our favor today.* □ *The court decided in his favor.*

in sb's place në vend të
□ *The chairman was ill so his deputy spoke in his place.*

in sb's/sth's stead në vend të
□ *I can't attend the meeting but I'll send my assistant in my stead.*

in spirit me shpirt
I shall be with you in spirit.

in spite of pavarësisht nga, me gjithë, pa marrë parasysh
□ *I confided all to my aunt when I got home; and in spite of all she could say to me, went to bed despairing.* □ *In spite of all the differences, Joan and Ann remained friends.* □ *I believe in you in spite of everything.*

in step (with) me një temp; me një hap
□ *Try to keep in step when you are marching.* □ *They were moving in step with the music.*

in stock gjendje
□ *I asked the shopkeeper if he had any butter in stock.*

in store 1. në ruajtje, mënjanë
□ *Keep these supplies in store: they may be needed for future use.*
2. ruan, pritet të ndodhë; e shkruar
□ *I wonder what fate has in store for us next?*
□ *I think that there is trouble in store for him.*

in (full) strength 1. me tërë forcën;
□ *If Rommel attacked in strength, as we expected soon, the Eighth Army would fall back on the Delta.*
2. me gjithsej; në numër të madh
□ *You'll meet my family at the party tonight: they'll be there in strength.*
□ *The civilian population used to turn out in strength every evening to watch our guard mounting parade in the town square.* □ *The Robinsons from Westhill were there in full strength down to the latest grandchild.*

in style sipas modës së fundit
□ *He and his wife live in style. He is proud of his children.*

in substance në thelb
□ *It was a long speech, but what he was saying in substance was that taxes should be reduced.* □ *I agree in substance with what you say.*

in succession radhazi, njëri pas tjetrit, me radhë
□ *The tray of drinks came past again, and this time I took a couple. In rapid succession I tossed them back.* □ *This'll be the fourth year in succession that we've not had a proper holiday.* □ *Our team won three games in succession.*

in sum shkurt, me pak fjalë
□ *In sum, that is what it really adds up to.* □ *In sum, I seriously protest that no man ever had a greater veneration for Chaucer than myself.*

in support of sb/sth në përkrahje (mbështetje) të
□ *He spoke in support of a ban on arms supplies.*

in sympathy with sb në mbështetje të; duke shfaqur simpatinë (miratimin) për
□ *If she could shed tears in sympathy with a child she would not be able to lie in her own bed and listen to him cry.* □ *The steel workers came out in sympathy with the miners.*

in terms of në gjuhën e, në pikëpamje, në kuptimin e
□ *Even his love for his own mother expressed itself in terms of money.* □ *It is difficult to express it in terms of science.* □ *It's a better job in terms of money.* □ *Have you thought about these plans in terms of what they would cost.*

in the absence of sb/sth në mungesë të
□ *The formulas of politeness tend to become meaningless in the absence of good will.* □ *In the absence of more solid evidence most of his*

admirers will prefer to think her mistaken—if not, indeed, malicious.
□ *The difficulties of bringing up a pair of spirited boys in the absence of a father were beginning to weigh her down.* □ *Our typewriter was frequently in pawn and in its absence we had to make do with pen and paper.*

in the abstract teorikisht
□ *Harold paused in his unexpectedly sympathetic analysis of Alec's character to consider emotion in the abstract.* □ *Consider the problem in the abstract .*

in the affirmative në mënyrë pohuese
□ *He answered in the affirmative.*
□ *When asked if they wanted to plead guilty, the accused men all replied in the affirmative.*

in the aggregate në total, në tërësi
□ *The tax increases will, in the aggregate, cause much hardship.* □ *No one of his faults was very serious but in the aggregate they made him an unbearably irritating person to live with.* □ *Domestic consumption of coal has certainly decreased in the aggregate, however, demand is still high.*

in the air 1. në hava, pezull
□ *These expressions and points of view were not peculiar to Philo. They were, so to speak, in the air.* □ *His plans are still quite in the air.* □ *Plans for the picnic are still in the air since we can't decide where to go.*
2. ndihet gjithkund
□ *Spring is in the air.*
3. qarkullon, përhapet
□ *There's a feeling of unrest in the air.* □ *Wild rumors were in the air.*

in the altogether lakuriq, nudo
□ *The model posed in the altogether.*
□ *She had no compunction. It was her secret, her surprise: if by sitting in or out of 'the altogether', not yet*

decided, she could make their passage money—well, she could tell him she had won it on a horse.

in the bag i sigurt, në xhep
□ *We shall certainly win tomorrow's game: the result is in the bag.* □ *His re-election is in the bag.*

in the clear 1. jashtë rrezikut
□ *She was very ill for a few days but doctors say she's now in the clear.*
2. i pafajshëm, i çliruar nga faji, dyshimi etj.
□ *After John told the principal that he broke the window, Martin was in the clear.*
3. i çliruar nga borxhet
□ *We've been paying back our debts and at last we are in the clear.* □ *Bob borrowed a thousand dollars from his father to start his business, but at the end of the first year he was in the clear.*

in the course of gjatë
□ *These tidal waves have hardly any effect on ships in the open sea, since there is only a very gradual rise of perhaps a few feet on the sea's surface in the course of several minutes.*
□ *She took so kindly to me, that, in the course of a few weeks she shortened my adopted name of Trotwood into Trot.* □ *This time he talked for ten minutes at a stretch and in the course of the speech he told Jurgis all of his family history.*

in (the) course of time me kalimin e kohës, me kohë
□ *Be patient: you'll be promoted in the course of time.* □ *It wears out in course of time.* □ *In course of time I got to know him better, and we became close friends.* □ *He is only a beginner at tennis; his game will improve in the course of time.*

in the dead/depth of night në mesnatë
□ *Awakening in the dead of night, I opened my eyes on her disk silver-white and crystal—clear.* □ *She walked among them with my child, minding only her, and brought her safe out, in the dead of night, from the black pit of ruin.*

in the dead of winter në palcë të dimrit, në kulm të acarit
□ *'It's a wonderful house, Frank,' he said 'with great gardens ablaze with all the colors in the rainbow.' 'That's not likely in dead of winter, said Frank, and his little mouth pursed tightly.* □ *If you had to live here in the dead of winter, you wouldn't think it so delightful. We were snowed up for weeks on end last year—that's why we store up fuel and provisions every autumn.*

in the dolddrums 1. në gjendje të keqe shpirtërore, në humor të keq
□ *He's been in the dolddrums ever since she left him.*
2. në amulli, në gjëndje amullie
□ *Business is in the dolddrums because most people have no money to spend.* □ *Despite the measures, the economy remains in the dolddrums.*

in the dumps i trishtuar, i mërzitur, i dëshpëruar
□ *After she crumpled the car fender she was really in the dumps.* □ *'Well', blustered Mr. Bounderlb, 'what's the matter? What is young Thomas in the dumps about?'*

in the end më së fundi, më në fund, tekembramja
□ *I hope everything will turn out all right in the end.* □ *'Listen to me', said the old woman to Jurgis. 'If you get me you will be glad of it. I will save your wife and baby for you, and it will not seem like much to you in the end.*

□ *But, in the end, a compromise was affected and Mrs. Crupp consented to achieve this feats, on condition that I dined away from home for a fortnight afterwards.*

in the event sikundër ndodhi në të vërtetë
□ *She was afraid that she wouldn't like living in London but, in the event, she thoroughly enjoyed it.* □ *I was worried about the hotel bill, but in the event I had enough money to pay it.*

in the event of/that në rast se, nëse
□ *In the event of your being late, we shall start without you.* □ *In the event of his death Sheila will inherit the money.*

in the extreme në kulm, në ekstrem
□ *Seaman has been conducting for many of the world's top soloists. It's no easy task either. They can be capricious and eccentric in the extreme.* □ *Time and again movements broke down through passes going astray, and much of the play was scrambling in the extreme.* □ *This is inconvenient in the extreme.*

in the eyes of në sytë e, sipas vlerësimit (mendimit) të
□ *You may not think it very serious, but theft is still an offence in the eyes of the law.* □ *In your father's eyes you're still a child.*

in the face of 1. përballë
□ *We are powerless in the face of such forces.*
□ *He had resolved to be patient in face of the many difficult situations that he knew must arise during the Christmas visit.* □ *No such view can be maintained for one moment in the face of the evidence.* □ *In primitive times, men found themselves powerless in the face of nature which*

appeared to be a mysterious force.
2. me gjithë, pavarësisht nga
□ *The factories were taken over by the government in face of opposition from the factory owners.* □ *He succeeded in the face of great difficulties.*

in the family way shtatzënë
□ *'She says she is in the family way again' Phyl whispered when she returned, 'Please do be kind to her.'* □ *She has to relax a bit; she is in the family way.* □ *Fran always referred to her pregnancy as, 'your condition', Gerald had been wont to say delicately 'in the family way', when he had to mention such matters.*

in the final/last analysis në analizë të fundit, në fund të fundit
□ *Plants get it from sunlight, and animals get it from plants, or from other animals of course. So in the last analysis the energy comes from the sun.* □ *Is not peace, in the final analysis, a matter of human rights?* □ *Willoughby sat back and folded his hands. In the final analysis, it would be up to Farish. Let him decide!* □ *In the final analysis I think our sympathy lies with the heroine of the play.*

in the first instance fillimisht, në fillmin
□ *The problem was solved by heating alone, and refrigeration was used to dry out the buildings in the first instance.* □ *It was very good of you to come to the rescue like this. Why I didn't ask you to take charge of the arrangements in the first instance I can't imagine.* □ *In the first instance, I was inclined to refuse, but then I reconsidered.*

in the first place para së gjithash, në radhë të parë; si fillim, si hap të parë; qysh në fillim

□ *They were punished by being ignored and excluded. Of course, they needn't have gone there in the first place.* □ *In the first place, as Boswell urged, Christ's death was intended to appease God's wrath and thus to reconcile Him to admitting sinners to Heaven.* □ *In the first place he feared another act of treachery.*

in the flesh vetë, personalisht, dora vetë
□ *Their idol is appearing for only 10 or 12 minutes, but their appreciation of him in the flesh is such that they have converged on Belle Vue tonight from Newcastle, Peterborough, London, Bristol, Birmingham.* □ *You will have a chance to see your favorite film-star in the flesh today: he is coming to visit our school.*

in the fullness of one's heart në thellësi të shpirtit
□ *What boastful father in the fullness of his heart ever related such wonders of his infant prodigy as Kit never wearied of telling Barbara in the evening time, concerning little Jacob?*

in the heyday of sth në lulëzimin e, në kulmin e suksesit, popullaritetit etj.
□ *She was a great singer in her heyday.*

in the hope of sth/that me shpresë se, duke shpresuar se
□ *The American company has been drilling in the Western Desert in the hope of striking large reserves similar to those in the neighbouring Libya.* □ *Writers will write what they want, in answer to the need within them and in the hope that there is an audience who wants to see their plays.*

in the innermost recesses of the heart në skutat më të thella të shpirtit
□ *Now, the fact was, that in the innermost recesses of his own heart,*

Mr. Gremwig was strongly disposed to admit that Oliver's appearance and manner were usually prepossessing.

in the interim ndërkohë

□ *'My new job starts in May.' 'What are you doing in the interim?'*

in the lap of luxury në mes të luksit

□ *He won a lot of money in a competition and since then he has been living in the lap of luxury.*

in the last resort si mjetin e fundit, në rastin më ekstrem (më të keq), në fund të fundit, në analizë të fundit

□ *In the last resort we can always walk home.*

□ *In the last resort the battle is won by the initiative and skill of regimental officers and men.* □ *In the last resort we shall have to turn to him for help, though I hope that will not be necessary.*

in the light of në dritën e, duke u mbështetur në, nisur nga

□ *In the light of what happened last year, I think we must plan things more quickly this year.* □ *When people are going through difficult times they don't always see things in the light of reason.* □ *In the light of our own general expectations about events, we construct, out of a few elements, an account of what was likely to have occurred.* □ *He made his decision in the light of what he had heard.*

in the line of duty në shërbim e sipër, duke kryer detyrën, në krye të detyrës

□ *The policeman was shot in the line of duty.*

□ *I thanked the policeman for all his help, but he just said, 'It's all in the line of duty.*

in the long run në fund të fundit, tekembramja; me kalimin e kohës

□ *It may look hard now but you are going to feel better about it in the long run.* □ *Dublin, London and Belfast are all concerned in Northern Ireland's future and in the long run tripartite agreement must be sought.*

□ *These changes are making things very inconvenient now, but they should improve matters in the long run.* □ *It pays in the long run to buy goods of high quality.*

in the main kryesisht, në pjesën më të madhe, përgjithësisht

□ *In the main, the art of the potter has been a secular art.* □ *Some days of course, she's still very unwell. But in the main she is hideously bored, I'm afraid.* □ *He can lose his temper at times, but in the main, he is a good man to work for.*

in the making në ngjizje (krijim, formim etj.)

□ *Dickens' depiction of the American scene in 'Martin Chuzzlewit' was deeply resented over there, and indeed he did not allow for the fact that he was observing a nation in the making.* □ *I could have taken a different literary example—namely, what a critic does when he looks at a first novel and says: 'Here is a great writer in the making.'*

in the manner of sb në stilin e

□ *That's a painting in the manner of Raphael.*

in the meantime ndërkohë, ndërkaq

□ *The next program starts in five minutes: in the meantime, here's some music.*

in the name of sb/sth në emër të; për hir të

□ *I greet you in the name of the President.* □ *I arrest you in the name of the law.* □ *They did it all in the name of friendship.*

in the nature of në karakterin e, në natyrën e; një lloj (mënyrë)

□ *Of course, underground explosions are more **in the nature of** simple outward pushes on to the surrounding rock.* □ *I hoped they would look upon me **in the nature of** an adviser and helper rather than as an overseer or critic.* □ *His speech was **in the nature of** an apology.*

in the nature of things në natyrën e gjërave, është e natyrshme

□ *Some productions were, **in the nature of things** less good than others and occasionally a kindly critic would give a timely warning.*

□ *It is **in the nature of things** that as people get older they become less active.*

in the negative negativisht, në mënyrë mohuese

□ *When asked if he wanted to make any statement, the prisoner answered **in the negative**.*

in the neighbourhood of rreth, pak a shumë, afër, afërsisht

□ *It was a sum **in the neighbourhood of** $5000.*

in the nick of time pikërisht në kohë

□ *Jack grabbed the little girl in the nick of time, otherwise she would have fallen in the pool.* □ *'It is come just **in the nick of time**', said Smith, 'I suppose Crawley had not a shilling in the world.'* □ *... she had been saved **in the nick of time**.* □ *I nearly cooked a chicken for supper last night but I remembered **in the nick of time** that Jack's a vegetarian, so we had a cheese soufflé instead.* □ *You got here **in the nick of time**; the train is just leaving.*

in the ordinary way zakonisht, normalisht

□ *You were lucky to find me in. **In the ordinary way** I'd have been off to work by now.*

□ *And although **in the ordinary way** these books would cost $15 or more, members of the club are privileged to buy them for only $1.*

in the pink of condition/health kuq si molla, si kokërr molle

□ *The children all looked **in the pink** after their holiday.* □ *I wasn't well last month, but I'm now **in the pink**.*

in the public eye në qendër të vëmendjes, në sytë e publikut, në mbikqyrjen e publikut

□ *But a penitentiary record, for whatever reason served coupled with previous failure, divorce and scandal ... served to whet public interest and to fix Cowperwood and his wife **in the public eye**.* □ *They have got Sommerville to clinch the frame-up. They always set someone like that. Someone who looks good **in the public eye**.*

□ *Any successful politician or filmstar is going to be very much **in the public eye**.*

in the raw 1. në gjendje të egër (të paqytetëruar); në gjendje të papërpunuar; në kushte natyrore

□ *George Orwell was a writer who lived among very poor people for a long time: he really saw life **in the raw**.* 2. lakuriq, zhveshur, nudo

□ *It was so warm that he slept **in the raw**.*

in/into the red me humbje

□ *A large number of American radio stations operate **in the red**.* □ *We have been trying to pay back our debts, but we are still **in the red**.*

in the right me të drejtën, ke të drejtë

□ *You are **in the right**: your neighbours are not entitled to walk across your land without permission.*

in the rough në dorë të parë

□ *We only saw the new painting **in the rough**.*

in the same breath 1. me të njëjën gjuhë

□ *He admits that I can't be blamed and in the same breath. He blames me and absolves me by taking the blame upon himself.* □ *They are not to be mentioned in the same breath.*
2. me të njëjtën frymë

□ *He told us what a wonderful party it would be and, almost in the same breath, said that he would not be coming to it.*

in the same way në mënyrë të ngjashme, po ashtu

□ *She swears she didn't mean to leave Nurse Ellen down there to die. In the same way she says she only pretended to kidnap the children.*

in the shape/form of sth/sb në formën e

□ *I received a nasty surprise in the shape of a letter from the taxman.*

in/into the small hours në orët e para të mesnatës

□ *So far I had not mentioned to anyone the signal I had received in the small hours of that morning.*

in the soup në telash, në vështirësi, në pozitë të vështirë

□ *Charles Ventor might be in the soup—a position which he deprecated both by nature and profession.* □ *What if she declared her real faith in Court and left them all in the soup.* □ *If your Mum finds out what you have done, you'll really be in the soup!* □ *The police misunderstood Harry's night errand, and arrested him, which put him in the soup with the boss.*

in the teeth of përballë, kundër; në kundërshtim me, pavarësisht nga

□ *We'd be quicker trying a zig-zag course than rowing in the teeth of this wind.* □ *She won a travelling*

fellowship to Turkey in the teeth of stiff competition from fifteen men. □ *The ship struggled back to port in the teeth of the gale.* □ *We were walking in the teeth of the wind and we made slow progress.* □ *The new policy was adopted in the teeth of fierce criticism.*

in the thick of sth në mes të, në zemër të

□ *Wherever there was fighting, the captain could be seen there in the thick of it.*

in the twinkling of an eye sa të hapësh e të mbyllësh sytë

□ *Her moods could change from sweet to sour in the twinkling of an eye.* □ *We got our packets together in the twinkling of an eye, and made off, running with the best will in the world.* □ *Having emptied the glass in a twinkling, Mr. Pell smacked his lips and looked complacently round on the assembled coachmen.* □ *All this happened as it were in the twinkling of an eye.* □ *We got our packets together in the twinkling of an eye.*

in the vicinity of sth në afërsi të

□ *He is in the vicinity of sixty.*

in the wake of 1. në gjurmët e

□ *'Come and talk to her,' said Lucy, and she clove a way through the crowd, Lord Mellings following in her wake.* □ *Outbreaks of disease occurred in the wake of the drought.* □ *With these three, but walking independently behind, was a girl of fifteen, a boy of twelve and another girl of nine, all following in the wake of others.*
2. fill pas

□ *Many troubles follow in the wake of war.* □ *In the wake of recent outbreak of food-poisoning, people are being more careful about what they eat.*

in the way zë (pengon) udhën, bëhet pengesë

□ *Please remove these boxes: they are in the way.* □ *I cannot get the door open, the chair is in the way.* □ *He is cast as an irritating gadfly, standing in the way of Lloyd Georges's efforts to win a peace that would give Germany its just due.*

in the way of 1. në pozitë të favorshme

□ *He put me in the way of a good investment.*

2. si për shembull, të tilla si

□ *We have a small stock in the way of hats.*

in the wind në përgatitje (mbrujtje) e sipër

□ *Changes in top management of the company had been in the wind for weeks.* □ *Things may be different from now on: some changes are in the wind.*

in the world 1. në botë

□ *He was the most retiring man in the world.* □ *Nothing in the world would please me more.*

2. po kush, në fund të fundit

□ *And if they don't know how to do this sort of thing, who in the world does.*

in time 1. me kohë, me kalimin e kohës

□ *You will learn how to do it in time.* □ *This is a sad and rather comic misunderstanding, but one which will no doubt be cleared up in time.* □ *Fred and Jim didn't like each other at first, but in time they became friends.* □ *It'll be crystal clear to you in time.*

2. në kohë

□ *By hurrying, we were just in time to catch the train.* □ 'Your parents must be very glad to see you come home again.' I nodded. 'I'm glad I came in time to help them out with this.' □ *The*

realisation came—somewhat belatedly but still in time. □ *The journey may seem long, but we shall get there in time.* □ *We arrived in good time.*

in token of sth në shenjë

□ *I am offering you this book, in token of my friendship for you.* □ *Please accept this gift in token of our affection for you.* □ '1 wish you all good night now', said he, making a movement of the hand towards the door in token that he was tired of our company, and wished to dismiss us.*

in total si total

□ *In total there must have been twenty vehicles in the pile-up.*

into/in the bargain përveç kësaj, gjithashtu, po ashtu

□ *She was a distinguished scientist— and a gifted painter into the bargain.* □ *We got away all right, and had a good feed into the bargain.* □ 'I don't mind telling you', said Francis. 'Though it's nothing to do with the business and you'll probably laugh at me into the bargain.'*

in touch (with) në kontakt me

□ *It is necessary to be in touch with the recent developments in our subject.* □ *John kept in touch with his school friends during the summer.* □ *We have not seen each other since he left here about five years ago, but I have always been in touch with him.*

in trust në besim

□ *When the girl's father died, his money was kept in trust for her until she was twenty-one.*

in truth në të vërtetë

□ *These people pretend to blame him, whereas in truth they ought only to blame themselves.* □ *It was in truth a miracle.*

in tune 1. në akord
□ *Before you start playing the music, you must make sure that all the instruments are in tune with one another.* □ *The violin is not quite in tune with the piano.*
2. në përputhje, në harmoni me
□ *I am afraid that Mr. Brown's ideas are not in tune with mine.* □ *Bessie's mind was not quite in tune with the profundities of that learned journal.* □ *Quiet settled over the little colored community of Stillveld, a quiet that was in tune with the stillness of the night.*

in turn me radhë, njëri pas tjetrit
□ *Each of the children took it in turn to read a part of the story aloud.* □ *The younger children came forward in turn to be given a present from the Christmas tree.* □ *I shall hear each one of you recite the passage in turn.*

in two në dysh, në dy pjesë
□ *The vase fell and broke in two.*

in/by twos and threes dy nga dy e tre nga tre
□ *Applications for the job are coming in slowly in twos and threes.*

in two twos/ticks fët e fët, shpejt e shpejt, menjëherë, aty për aty, sakaq
□ *I don't like to hear people sneering at positions and titles they'd have accepted in two twos if they'd got the offer.* □ *Jim didn't expect the water to be so cold. He was in and out in two twos.* □ *Every one sprung to his feet and the work was over in two twos.* □ *Wait just a moment! I'll be with you in two twos.*

in two shakes (of a lamb's tail) shpejt e shpejt, fët e fët, menjëherë
□ *It won't be long: I'll be with you in two shakes.* □ *As though, it's just a loose connection. I'll have it fixed up for you in two shakes of a lamb's tail.* □ *Don't worry about the money. In two shakes I can be on to Fred about a loan.* □ *I'll be back in two shakes of a lamb's tail.*

in unison në të njëjtën kohë, në harmoni, në unison; në akord me
□ *Once in a while they would act in unison and move a spanner on a particularly difficult nut and bolt.* □ *The last verse will be sung in unison.*

in vain më kot
□ *A poor and young literary beginner had tried in vain to get his manuscripts accepted.* □ *We knocked at the door for ten minutes, but in vain: no one answered.* □ *In vain Sarah had striven to reassure him.* □ *It's an enchanted place—I rack my memory in vain for its counterpart in literature; perhaps you can think of one.*

in view of duke patur (marrë) parasysh
□ *In view of your departure tomorrow, can you spare me a few moments?* □ *In view of the success you were having, why didn't you stay there?* □ *In view of the numbers expected to attend, special parking facilities have been arranged.* □ *I think we ought to cancel our holiday in view of what was said on the news about probable transport strike.*

in weal and/or woe në të mirë e në të keq, në gëzime e hidhërime, në ditë të mira e të këqia
□ *In weal and woe I have ever had the true sympathy of all my people.*

in word and (in) deed me fjalë e me vepra
□ *He's just another of these hypocrites who are pacifists in words but not in deed.* □ *...let us not love in word, neither in tongue; but in deed and in truth.*

iron out sheshoj
□ *The company and its workers ironed out their differences over hours and pay.*

J

jack of all trades mjeshtër për gjithçka, ç'i sheh syri ia bën dora, i zë dora gjithçka, i zoti për gjithçka
□ *Wolfenden described the background of a typical rural police man. 'He has to be* **a jack of all trades**. *For minor crimes like petty theft, he sometimes has to change into civilian clothes.* □ *You are right, he is* **a jack of all trades**. □ *But you have got to be a* **jack of all trades** *under our system.*

jack of all trades but master of none i zoti për të gjitha, mjeshtër për asgjë
□ *I had two hundred jobs all told... Reckon I'm* **a jack of all trades and master of none**. □ *I was* **a jack of all trades and master of none**, *but General Papers (in exams) went down before me like ninepins.*

jack sth in lë, braktis
□ *I can't take any more of the nightwork. I'll have to* **jack** *it* **in**.

jack sth up 1. ngre, rrit
□ *'We know you're not happy about the money you're getting. We think it could be* **jacked up** *a bit.'* □ *If they* **jack up** *the wage rates they'll have to cut down on expenditure somewhere else.*
2. ngre me krik
□ *'* **Jack** *her* **up** *a bit more. The wheels are still touching the ground.'*
3. rregulloj, organizoj
□ *That about your holiday? Have you got everything properly* **jacked up**? □ *We didn't need to worry about tickets or reservations. The Travel Section* **jacked** *the whole thing* **up** *for us.*

jam sth on mbaj (shtrëngoj) frenat menjëherë
□ *I had to* **jam on** *the brakes sharply to avoid hitting two schoolchildren.* □ *As soon as she saw the child in the road, she* **jammed on** *her brakes.*

jog along/on ecën, përparon ngadalë
□ *He just* **jogs along** *contentedly from year to year without any thought of promotion.* □ *The industry is happy to* **jog along** *in the old way.*

jog sb's memory ndihmoj për ta kujtuar, për të sjellë ndër mend; kujtoj, ia sjell ndër mend
□ *He tied up a string around his finger to* **jog his memory**. □ *Never heard of anybody called Mary Woodson, eh? Well, here's a snapshot of her and you together at Newmarket that might* **jog your memory**. □ *He mentioned it to* **jog her memory**.

join battle with sb filloj luftën me
□ *Battle was* **joined**, *shortly after ten o'clock,* **with** *advance elements of two enemy divisions.* □ *And there went out the king of Sodom, and the king of Gomorrah ... and they* **joined battle with** *them in the vale of Siddim.*

join forces (with sb) bashkoj forcat me
□ *The two armies* **joined forces** *to fight against the common enemy.* □ *Two of our battalions* **joined forces** *to attack the enemy.*

join hands with bashkohem me, veproj së bashku
□ *'We are not through with those sharpers', he declared to Cowperwood. 'They'll fight us with suits. They may* **join hands** *later.'* □ *The leading troops of the English Army* **joined hands with** *the right flank of the Fifth U.S. Army.*

□ *Let's join hands in the work and finish it ahead of schedule.*

join in sth/doing sth marr pjesë në

□ *A group of bystanders was invited to join in the game.* □ *'Who said you can join in?'*

join issue with sb hahem, diskutoj me

□ *I am ready to join issue with you on this point.*

join the (great) majority vdes

□ *'Think I'm going to join the great majority, eh?'*

join up marr pjesë në forcat e armatosura

□ *He joined up as a private in a country regiment.*

joking apart/aside t'i lëmë shakatë

□ *Joking apart, I think we should do something to make the path outside safer.* □ *Joking apart, we have to begin discussing the problem.*

jolly sb along mbaj dikë në humor, mbaj gjallë

□ *You'll have to jolly him along a bit, but he'll do a good job.* □ *The job won't be finished on time unless you jolly the men along with an occasional bonus.*

jot sth down mbaj shënim

□ *He had jotted down the license number.* □ *I'll just jot down their phone number before I forget it.*

jump at sth pranoj pa ngurrim (një propozim etj.)

□ *If he offered me a job sweeping out the theatre I'd jump at the chance.* □ *He is ready to jump at the proposal that is made to him.*

jump down sb's throat kritikoj, i flas ashpër dikujt, i hidhem përsysh

□ *'How are you getting?' he asked cheerily. 'What does that matter to you?' she asked in reply.* □ *Philip could not help laughing. 'Don't jump*

down my throat, I was only trying to make myself polite.' □ *When I told him a joke about lawyers, he just about jumped down my throat: it was then I discovered he was a lawyer himself.* □ *The teacher jumped down Billy's throat when Bill said he did not do his homework.*

jump for joy hov (hidhem përpjetë) nga gëzimi

□ *The children are jumping for joy at the thought of an extra day's holiday.*

jump on qortoj, fajësoj, kritikoj rëndë

□ *My maths teacher really used to jump on us when we got our answer wrong.* □ *His wife jumped on him if he seemed to be taking Virginia's side.* □ *I object to being jumped on for a trivial matter like this.*

jump out of one's skin hidhem përpjetë (nga frika, habia etj), trembem, habitem pa masë

□ *When I heard the explosion I just jumped of my skin.* □ *The lightning struck so close to Bill that he almost jumped out of his skin.*

□ *The sudden noise made her jump nearly out of her skin.* □ *The door slammed to with such a bang that I nearly jumped out of my skin.*

jump the gun 1. startoj para sinjalit të nisjes

□ *The runner was disqualified for jumping the gun.* □ *The runners were called back because one of them jumped the gun.*

2. veproj para kohe, nisem para të tjerëve

□ *I had to open veins and things, which worried me a bit, because the last doctor I knew who did the same thing jumped the gun and ten minutes later the blood was running down the stairs.* □ *We are not supposed to go*

home until tomorrow, but some people have **jumped the gun.**
□ *The new students were not supposed to come before noon, but one boy* **jumped the gun** *and came at school at eight in the morning.*

jump the track 1. del nga shinat (treni)
□ *The train* **jumped the track.**
2. hidhem degë më degë, kaloj sa andej -këtej
□ *Bob didn't finish his Algebra homework because his mind kept* **jumping the track** *to think about the new girl in class.*

jump the queue kapërcej radhën, dal para të tjerëve në radhë
□ *The sailor looked, and was very strong. If someone* **jumped the queue** *he would give them a sharp crack on the head with his enormous wooden spoon.* □ *Under half found work, and even this represented an achievement. How was it done? 'To be quite frank,' said one genial manager, ' we* **jump the queue.** *Otherwise our chaps wouldn't stand a chance in hell.'*

jump to a (the) conclusion dal (arrij) në një përfundim të nxituar (të shpejtuar)
□ *Don't* **jump to the conclusion:** *wait until I have finished speaking.* □ *Jerry saw his dog limping on a bloody leg and* **jumped to the conclusion** *that it had been shot.* □ *Why did you* **jump to the conclusion** *that we couldn't change any note that you might happen to be carrying around. On the contrary, we can.* □ *From this they immediately* **jumped to the conclusion** *that it was I... who was making an exhibition of myself.*

jump to it nxitoj, luaj këmbët
□ *The bus will be leaving in five minutes, so* **jump to it!**

just about 1. thuajse
□ *I'll be with you shortly: I've* **just about** *finished what I'm working on.*
□ *I've met* **just about** *everyone.*
2. afërsisht
□ *He should be arriving* **just about** *now.*

just as tamam, pikërisht
□ *This is* **just as** *good as the other.*
□ *Leave everything* **just as** *you find it.*

just in case për çdo rast
□ *The sun is shining, but I'll take an umbrella* **just in case.**

just now tani, posa, sapo
□ *He can't be far away: he was here* **just now.** □ *I'll phone him at home: he should be there* **just now.** □ *I'll take a note of that* **just now** *if you can give me a slip of paper. I don't trust my memory.* □ *'Want one?' he asked, holding up the bottle. 'Not* **just now.** *Tell me something darling. Where did you get the typewriter?'* □ *Tom came in* **just now;** *he's probably upstairs.*

just so 1. tamam, pikërisht ashtu
□ *'Your name is Smith, is it?' 'Just so.'* □ *'I ordered the carpet four months ago, you know.' 'Just so, madam, but I'm afraid we've been having delivery problems because of the transport strike.'*
2. tamam, ashtu siç duhet
□ *I told her that her friends were coming to see her, not to inspect the house. But you know mother, she always has to have everything* **just so.**

just the same 1. njëlloj
□ *These two pictures are* **just the same.**
2. megjithatë
□ *The sun's out, but I'll take a raincoat* **just the same.**

just the thing tamam ajo që duhet (nevojitet, është më e përshtatshme etj.)

□ *Also I had a curious faith in Finn's intuition. It often happened that Finn made some unexpected suggestion which when I followed it up turned out to have been* **just the thing**.

□ *I've got some homemade soup in the pan.* **Just the thing** *to warm you up.*

just what the doctor ordered tamam ajo që nevojitej, duhej

□ *I really enjoyed that long sleep: it* **was just what the doctor ordered**.

□ *'Oh, isn't it lovely,' Rose said, the minute they were in park. 'Yes', said Stanley, accepting compliment, 'very refreshing.* **Just what the doctor ordered**.

K

keel over bie, rrëzohet, shembet; përmbyset

□ *After a couple of drinks he just **keeled over** on the floor.* □ *John walked into the room unsteadily, fixed me with a glazed stare, uttered the words 'I think I'm going to ...' then **keeled over** and fell unconscious at my feet.* □ *The old Queen Elizabeth liner burnt out and **keeled over** while anchored off Hong Kong in January 1972.*

keen on i dhënë pas, i interesuar për; i apasionuar pas, entuziast

□ *He rarely switches on to hear any of the classical music he professes to be **keen on**.* □ *My girlfriend and I would like to go on a holiday together abroad next summer but our parents are not **keen on** the idea.* □ *He is very **keen on** photography.* □ *I am not particularly **keen on** going out.*

keep abreast of azhurnohem, mirinformohem, jam në korrent; eci krahas me (në një hap me)

□ *Is the opera company's first duty to make available the acknowledged operatic masterpieces ... or should it concentrate on **keeping** the public **abreast of** current developments?* □ *What young doctors needed to do was to **keep abreast of** the latest medical development.* □ *In the strong breeze the catamaran skimmed over the water, **keeping abreast of** the motor-launch.*

keep a civil tongue in one's head flas me mirësjellje (me respekt, njerëzishëm)

□ *He replied that he would do exactly as he liked and would just thank her*

*to **keep a civil tongue in her head**.* □ *Mrs. Dudgeon. What does she want troubling me at this hour, before I'm properly dressed to receive people? Christy. You'd better ask her. Mrs. Dudgeon (threateningly) You'd better **keep a civil tongue in your head**.* □ *Remember to **keep a civil tongue in your head** when you are speaking to older people.*

keep a close/sharp look-out vëzhgoj (ndjek) nga afër; përgjoj

□ *I was forgetting all his faults, for which I had once **kept a sharp look-out**.* □ *On all accounts we **kept a close look-out**.*

keep a cool/level head mbaj (ruaj) gjakftohtësinë, nuk e humb toruan

□ *Even in the middle of the fire he **kept a level head**.* □ *I gather that isn't too difficult, though you'll want to **keep a cool head**.* □ *It's not so hard to get out of a skid if you **keep a cool head**.* □ *'Now', said Soames in a low voice, 'we must **keep our heads**. He'll deny it, of course.'*

keep a good heart mbaj veten, bëhem burrë, tregohem trim

□ *The sheriff soon arrived and took the twins away to jail. Wilson told them to **keep heart**, and promised to do his best in their defence when the case should come to trial.* □ ***Keep a good heart!***

keep an eye on shikoj, vëzhgoj, ruaj, ndjek me sy, mbaj në mbikqyrje

□ ***Keep an eye on** the stove in case the coffee boils.* □ *Mother told June to **keep an eye on** the baby while mother was in the store.* □ *Would you mind* *keeping an eye on this parcel for me for a few minutes?* □ *'Do you know where he is staying? 'At the Bristol'. 'It might', said Sir Lawrence slowly, 'be worth while to* **keep an eye on** *him.'* □ **Keep** *your* **eye on** *this door, Mangan, I'll look after the other.*

keep an eye open/out for sb/sth shikoj, kontrolloj (për të gjetur)

□ *I have lost my ring—could you* **keep an eye out for** *it when you clean the house?*

keep a quiet/still tongue in one's head hesht, kyç gojën, mbaj gjuhën mbledhur

□ *'You'll* **keep a quiet tongue in your head**, *will you?' said Monks, with a threatening look. 'I'm not afraid of your wife.'* □ *I'll tell you what I know, because I believe you can* **keep a still tongue in your head** *if you like.*

keep a record of regjistroj, mbaj shënim

□ *He* **kept** *a careful* **record of** *all expenses.*

keep a secret ruaj sekretin

□ *'I wonder if you can* **keep a secret?' 'Me, keep a secret?** *What, I'm the grave's only good rival with a good secret, I'm.'* □ *If you like to tell me, I assure you I can* **keep a secret.**

keep a stiff upper lip qëndroj i fortë, tregoj burrëri, nuk e lëshoj veten, tregohem (mbahem) burrë

□ *He was very much worried about his sick daughter, but he* **kept a stiff upper lip.** □ *'Keep a stiff upper lip, Matt, dear. Be brave, and nothing can hurt you, and don't forget your own, loving sister.'* □ *... I know that you're really not guilty, I know that now I believe it. See! So* **keep a stiff upper lip** *before Mason and everybody.*

keep a straight face mbaj të qeshurit

□ *He has such a strange voice that it's*

difficult to **keep a straight face** *when he's talking.* □ *I knew he couldn't be feeling as funny as he looked, all covered with mud and dripping weeds, so I managed to* **keep my face straight.** □ *The story was so funny that it was impossible to* **keep a straight face.** □ *The situation was so humorous that I found it difficult to* **keep a straight face.**

keep a tight hand/rein on sb mbaj nën kontroll, nën mbikqyrje të rreptë

□ *'My young lady', thought Mrs. Thornton to herself. 'You've a pretty good temper of your own. If John and you had come together he would have had to* **keep a tight hand over you**, *to make you know your place.*

keep at sth 1. punoj me ngulm

□ *The only way to get a dictionary written is to* **keep at it**, *day after day.* □ *Come on,* **keep at it**, *you've nearly finished!* □ *He* **kept at** *his work all day.* □ **Keep at it.** *Don't give up.* □ *If he* **keeps at** *his job he will soon finish it.*

2. shtrëngoj (detyroj) dikë të punojë

□ *The old professor was a martinet. He* **kept** *his students* **at** *their studies when they would have preferred to be at the discotheque. But in the end they all thanked him.* □ **Keep** *the children* **at it**, *don't let them get lazy.*

keep at arm's length/a distance mbaj larg, mbaj distancë

□ *If you're wise, you'll* **keep Mrs. Jones at a distance.** *She's the worst gossip in the village.* □ *All her relations were insupportable to her, and she* **kept them at arm's length.** □ *I always end up quarrelling with that name so I try to* **keep him at a distance.** □ *Carrie took his love upon a higher basis than he had anticipated. She* **kept him at a distance** *in a rather earnest way.* □ *I had none of the frus-*

*tration that Luke felt and perhaps Martin also, because they were being **kept at arm's length** from a piece of scientific truth.*

keep at bay mbaj larg

□ *When fiddling about with lens and exposure meters I found it essential to have someone stand over me with a hat, to **keep** at least some of the insects **at bay**, otherwise it was impossible to concentrate and my temper frayed rapidly.* □ *Industry as a whole is trying to **keep** rising costs **at bay**.*

keep away from sb/sth qëndroj (rri) larg, mbaj larg

□ *'What's been **keeping** you **away**? You haven't been around to see us for ages.'* □ *If Jo doesn't **keep away from** that woman, he's going to regret it. Her husband is a jealous and violent man.* □ ***Keep away from** the fire.*

□ *First he went to the steel mill and the harvester works, and found that his places there had been filled long ago. He was careful to **keep away from** the stockyards.*

keep a weather eye open for i bëj sytë katër, shikoj me kujdes të madh, rri syhapët

□ *There are some holes in that fields which are quite dangerous: **keep a weather eye open for** them.* □ *The fishermen **kept a weather eye open for** bears as they moved upstream.*

keep a whole skin dal pa lagur, shpëtoj lëkurën

□ *We'll assume... that your anxiety to **keep a whole skin** justified you in taking to your heels.*

keep back (from) 1. fsheh, mbaj të fshehtë

□ *The specialist recommended that the exact nature of the woman's illness should be **kept back from** her.*

□ *Duane did not even bother to **keep back** names and places—he told all his triumphs and his failures.* □ *I'll **keep** nothing **back from** you.*

2. rri (mbaj) larg, mbaj në distancë

□ *The crowd was so great that the organizers of the demonstration could not **keep** them **back** when they reached the barriers.* □ *'Now then stand away there, please—we can't have you round the body. **Keep back**—clear out now.* □ ***Keep back** there. The dog is dangerous.*

3. mbaj, përmbaj

□ *She was unable to **keep back** her tears.* □ *She was choking with tears which she tried hard to **keep back**.*

4. mbaj, nuk paguaj

□ *It is quite normal to **keep back** ten percent of the cost of a building for a period of six months or so, in case faults are found in it.* □ *We agreed to let our employer **keep back** twenty pence a week **from** our wages to go into a special fund for welfare purposes.*

keep bad company kam shoqëri të keqe

□ *Counsel said that the youth was of weak character and had been **keeping bad company**.*

keep (bad) time shkon (keq) sahati

□ *My watch **keeps bad time**. It needs repairing.*

keep late/early hours bie të fle vonë (herët)

□ *'What are you doing here? You should be in bed. You **keep** too **late hours**!'* □ *His friends do not **keep late hours**: he left their house soon after ten.*

keep body and soul together mbaj frymën gjallë

□ *Nearly the end of their long journey there was hardly enough food left to **keep body and soul together**.* □ *John*

261

was unemployed most of the year and hardly made enough money to **keep body and soul together.** □ *Six shillings a week does not* **keep body and soul together** *very unitedly.* □ *Trench, your fortune has been made out of a parcel of unfortunate creatures that have hardly enough to* **keep body and soul together.**

keep clear of qëndroj larg nga; shmang, evitoj

□ *The train slowed and Eddie and Uncle Jennison, to* **keep clear of** *the company police, dropped off as they reached the edge of the yard.* □ *All that day Kit* **kept clear of** *his mother's house.* □ *Try to* **keep clear of** *trouble.*

keep close 1. mbaj të fshehtë, mbaj sekret

□ *'Then what does he do it for, and why does he* **keep** *it so* **close** *from you?' said Mrs. Nubbles.* □ *'Nay! I'm not going far to tell more. I've may be gotten them into mischief already, for they* **kept** *it very* **close.**

2. qëndroj, rri fshehur

□ *He decided to* **keep close** *for some time.*

keep company with sb shoqërohem me

□ *Jane was lonely, so Mary stayed with her and* **kept** *her* **company** *until midnight.* □ *... and the kinder I felt it that you came away from there, purposely to comfort me, and* **keep me company.** □ *A person may be known by the* **company** *he* **keeps.** □ *I'll keep you* **company** *as far as the end of the lane.*

keep cool mbaj (ruaj) qetësinë (gjak-ftohtësinë)

□ *'Shall you be in court during your sister's case, Dinny?' 'I must.' 'I'm afraid it may make you very wild.*

They've briefed Brough, and he's particularly exasperating when he likes... Clare must try and **keep cool.'**

keep dark/keep sth/it dark from sb mbaj (ruaj) të fshehtë

□ *'Annete's going on with the idea of taking Elspeth's job when she gives it up.' I stared at him. Elspeth had been* **keeping it dark from** *me.* □ *Anyway, Strether wanted his identity* **kept dark** *and for Hiscock that meant* **keeping it dark from** *everybody, including the other directors and his own wife.* □ *It's no less than natural he should* **keep dark:** *so would you and me, in the same box.* □ *Harris and I say* **keep it dark.** *Don't let the Press get on it.* □ *He hid himself...* **kept** *himself* **dark.**

keep down 1. ulem

□ *'There's somebody coming!* **Keep down** *and don't make a sound!'* □ *'When we reach the footbridge over the canal,* **keep down** *or you'll bang your head on it!'* □ **Keep down** *or they will see you.*

2. ul, mbaj ulur

□ *My father's parting words as I left to join my unit were '* **Keep** *your head* **down** *and your eyeballs moving!'* □ *'I wish you two would* **keep** *your voices* **down.** *I can hardly hear myself think!'* □ *The government seems to be making little effort to* **keep** *the cost of living* **down.** *Prices have gone up by fifteen per cent in the last year.*

3. shtyp

□ *The people have been* **kept down** *for years by a brutal regime.*

4. pëmbaj, ndrydh, mposht, vë nën kontroll, shuaj

□ *He couldn't* **keep down** *his anger.* □ *It was all I could do to* **keep** *my anger* **down** *when I heard how the visitor had been treated in my absence.*

□ *The firemen kept the fire down with their hoses.*
5. pengoj (zhvillimin, rritjen)
□ *Sodium chlorate will keep the weeds down on your paths.* □ *If you want good crops of flowers and vegetables you must keep the weeds down.*
6. mbaj (ushqimin, etj.)
□ *Unless we can find a way of making the baby keep its food down, it is simply going to starve to death.* □ *He couldn't keep his food down.* □ *'Can you prescribe something else for me, doctor? I can't keep the powders down at all.'*
7. ul, pakësoj (shpenzimet)
□ *We must keep down expenses.*

keep hold of mbaj, shtrëngoj
□ *Keep hold of the rope.*

keep house mbaj, qeveris shtëpinë
□ *Since their mother died, Mary and her brother keep house for their father.* □ *In his own small room Martin lived, slept, studied, wrote and kept house.* □ *She had been keeping house all the time.*

keep in 1. rri (qëndroj) brenda
□ *It's best to keep in while the temperature is so far below freezing point, unless you have to go out to earn your living.* □ *The rabbits kept in their burrows most of the day, and only came out to eat as darkness fell.*
2. mbaj, detyroj të rrijë brenda
□ *'Our teacher was in a bad temper today. She kept us all in for half an hour.* □ *I was kept in by a bad cold.* □ *To our regret, we were kept in by the rain.*
3. mbaj, furnizoj
□ *Such jobs as he had from time to time barely kept him in drink and cigarettes.* □ *He won first prize in a lottery—enough to keep him in beer for a year.*

4. përmbaj, ndrydh (ndjenjat etj)
□ *The policeman was provoked by the hostile crowd but he managed to keep his anger in, and dealt with the situation coolly and competently.* □ *He couldn't keep his indignation in.*

keep in check frenoj, mbaj (vë) nën kontroll
□ *Unless imports are kept in check we are in danger of losing our favorable balance of trade.* □ *If I hadn't kept myself in check, I might have said something that I would have regretted later.* □ *By prompt action the authorities managed to keep the threatened epidemic of typhus in check.* □ *The enemy was kept in check by the floodwater, which made the terrain impossible for armoured vehicles.* □ *She had a great gift of mimicry which ordinarily she kept in check.*

keep in hand ruaj, përmbaj veten, mbaj nën kontroll
□ *He's deeply in love with my sister, and yet he's kept himself in hand.* □ *'How about the sheep?' 'The dogs will keep them in hand, and I shall not be gone long.'* □ *He kept his feelings well in hand.*

keep in mind mbaj ndër mend, kam (mbaj) parasysh
□ *'We've got to keep in mind how very small a disturbance—small from the astronomical point of view— could still wipe us out of existence.* □ *'You'll keep my son in mind, won't you—just in case a vacancy should occur in your firm?'*

keep in the dark i fsheh dikujt diçka, nuk informoj (vë në dijeni) për
□ *'Let me tell you that I don't like being kept in the dark about matters that affect me as closely as my daughter's future life.'* □ *It's as if they*

were all in a conspiracy to keep you in the dark. □ *'Mr. Micawber has his faults, I do not deny that he is improvident. I do not deny that he has kept me in the dark as to his resources and his liabilities, both,' she went on... 'but I never will desert Mr. Micawber.'* □ *We were kept completely in the dark about his plan to sell the company.* □ *He must keep Bunder absolutely and permanently in the dark about Dogson and his mission to reveal the secrets of the drug traffic.*

keep in touch with mbaj lidhje me
□ *It's a pity you are going to Australia. But, anyway, let's keep in touch, shall we?* □ *As they were both radio enthusiasts they were able to keep in daily touch with each other over the air.* □ *We shall be away for two years. Try to keep in touch with us.* □ *When you leave New York I hope you will keep in touch with me.*

keep in view mbaj (kam) parasysh
□ *Try to keep the teacher's advice in view as you try to improve your work.* □ *This should always be kept in view.*

keep in with sb mbaj marrëdhënie të mira me, shkoj mirë me
□ *We'll have to keep in with her in case we can't ever pay the rent.* □ *In wartime people who before were always ready to accuse the butcher of giving short weight went to great lengths to keep in with him.* □ *He will keep in with her.*

keep mum hesht, mbaj qetësi; qep gojën
□ *Keep mum during all his favorite TV programs—don't chatter when he's playing his best-loved disc.* □ *I want you to keep mum. If it comes out, it can't be helped, but I beg that you'll neither of you say anything.*

□ *Oh, one snub's enough for me. I'm keeping mum now, thank you.*

keep off 1. nuk lë të afrohet
□ *'How can I keep the flies off the jam?'* □ *They made a big fire to keep wild animals off.*

2. rri, qëndroj larg
□ *I put him away. 'Stay,' I said. 'Keep off.'*

3. shmang, evitoj
□ *The only way to get your weight down is to keep off fattening foods, and cut out alcohol altogether.*

keep on 1. vazhdoj
□ *Keep on with your work, don't waste time.*
□ *He kept on talking.* □ *Why do the dogs keep on barking?*

2. mbaj veshur
□ *'I have told you before not to keep your socks on if they get wet.'* □ *Keep on your overcoat as it is cold.*

3. mbaj në punë
□ *Only half of the workforce will be kept on after this order has been completed.*

4. vazhdoj udhëtimin
□ *The climbers had a long discussion about their position. Some were for returning to their base camp, others were for keeping on in the hope of reaching the top with one last efforts.*

keep one's balance mbaj (ruaj) drejtpeshimin
□ *It's difficult to keep one's balance on an icy pavement.* □ *When walking on a tight rope you should try to keep your balance.* □ *A small child has to learn to keep its balance before it can walk far.*

keep one's breath to cool one's porridge kursej frymën, harxhoj frymën kot
□ *'Hold your peace, sir... and keep*

your own breath to cool your own porridge. □ *When they are as old as us, mother, they'll* **keep their breath to cool their porridge.**

keep one's chin up mbaj ballin lart, ngre ballin lart

□ *I know things are going badly for you now, but you will just have to* **keep your chin up** *and hope that they will get better.* □ *She put her finger under Jan's chin and tilted her face up so she could look into her eyes.'* **Keep your chin up**, *Jannie.'*

keep one's countenance e mbaj veten, e zotëroj veten; mbaj gazin, qëndroj serioz

□ *She* **kept her countenance** *and made no semblance of sorrow.* □ *It was as much as I could to* **keep my countenance** *at the figure he made.* □ *He looked so funny that I found it difficult to* **keep my countenance.**

keep one's distance qëndroj larg prej

□ *They have a large fierce-looking dog: I always* **keep my distance** *from it.* □ *He was asked many times to join the party, but he always* **kept his distance.**

keep oneself in hand përmbaj veten

□ *He's deeply in love with my sister, and yet he's* **kept himself in hand.** □ *It's all my fault in a sense, but I have tried to* **keep myself in hand.**

keep one's end up nuk thyhem, nuk jepem (para vështirësive)

□ *'How is Dinny?' 'Very low in her mind. But she* **keeps her end up.'**

keep one's eye on the ball përqëndroj (ngulit) vëmendjen te esencialja; rri syhapur

□ *In spite of the many different jobs he had to do, Jack always managed to* **keep his eye on the ball.** □ *There are good times and bad times... We just*

have to **keep our eye on the ball.**

□ *Tom is just starting on the job but if he* **kept his eye on the ball,** *he will be promoted.*

keep one's eyes/weather eye/open mbaj sytë hapur

□ *I want you to* **keep your eyes** *and ears* **open** *to see if anyone said anything about Coombargana, but I haven't heard anything.* □ *He had taken me aside one day, and promised me a silver fourpenny on the first of every month if I would only* **keep my weather eye open** *for a seafaring man with one leg and let him know the moment he appeared.*

keep one's eyes peeled/skinned i mbaj sytë hapur, i hap sytë

□ *The soldiers were told to* **keep their eyes peeled** *for enemy planes.* □ *Don't move,* **keep your eyes peeled,** *and be prepared to wait for several hours— then you might catch a glimpse of Rumpelayer's Blue-backed Seathrush.* □ *Keep your eyes skinned for any movement in the house opposite. The police think it's a terrorist cell and they want our help.* □ *Keep your eyes peeled, Lil, and tell me if you see a blink of sun on those hills ahead.*

keep one's feet ruaj ekuilibrin

□ *Although the ship was rolling badly, the captain managed to* **keep his feet.**

keep one's hair/shirt/wig on e marr shtruar, ruaj qetësinë, rri urtë, nuk nxehem, nuk inatosem

□ *She told the impatient customer to* **keep his hair on,** *and he would be served along with the others.* □ *You just* **keep your hair on** *and listen to me.* □ *... But at that moment all my pain, anger, and temper exploded in a screaming oath. Jack Cotery was taken aback.* **'Keep your shirt on,'** *he said.*

keep one's hand in stërvis (ushtroj) dorën

   □ *I am not a very good golfer, but I try to* **keep my hand in** *by having an occasional game on the weekend.* □ *He plays violin everyday to* **keep his hand in**.

keep one's head ruaj qetësinë

   □ *If your father hadn't* **kept his head** *and switched off at the mains they'd have both been electrocuted.* □ *He was torn in two between the desire to win and the desire to* **keep his head**, *but his head was clouded by anger as well as whisky.* □ *As always she has* **kept her head** *while others around her have been losing theirs.*

keep one's head above water mbahem, rri mbi ujë

   □ *It's difficult for the common people to* **keep their heads above water** *with the rising cost of living.* □ *We had had many heavy expenses to pay in running the business, but so far we have* **kept our heads above water**.

keep one's mind on sth përqëndrohem, kam mendjen

   □ **Keep your mind on** *what you are doing.* □ **Keep your mind on** *the job!*

keep one's mouth closed/shut mbyll (kyç gojën)

   □ *'What are you yammerin' about? Are you talking or am I? If you've nothing to say then* **keep your mouth shut** *and don't interrupt.'* □ *The thieves told the watchman that if he* **kept his mouth shut** *no harm would come to him.* □ *Charles began to tell Barry how to kick the ball, and Barry said angrily,* **'Keep your mouth shut!'**

keep one's nose clean s'përzihem në telashe

   □ *The police released him but warned him to* **keep his nose clean** *or else he would be arrested again.* □ *I'll tell him to* **keep his nose clean** *when he goes out of prison, but I know he will be back.* □ *The boss said Jim could have the job as long as he* **kept his nose clean** *and worked hard.*

keep one's nose out of sth nuk fus hundët në, nuk përzihem në, nuk ndërhyj në

   □ *'It happens to be nothing to do with Ed, but you* **keep your nose out of** *it, anyway.* □ *She could never learn to* **keep her nose out of** *her son's private life, though she was always made unhappy by what she discovered.* □ *'When will you learn to* **keep your nose out of** *my affairs?'*

keep one's nose to the grindstone punoj pa pushim, punoj me këmbëngulje, s'ngre kokën nga puna

   □ *He kept his* **nose to the grindstone** *and eventually built up a prosperous business.* □ *He* **kept his nose to the grindstone** *and accomplished the task successfully.* □ *Only by* **keeping one's nose to the grindstone** *can one hope to improve one's standard of living.* □ *Miss Pennington was one of the teachers who enjoyed seeing that children's* **noses** *were* **kept to the grindstone**.

keep one's own counsel mbaj të fshehta mendimet, planet etj.

   □ *In writing it is wise to* **keep your own counsel**, *otherwise people may steal your ideas.* □ *John listened to what everyone had to say in the discussion, but he* **kept his own counsel**. □ *He listened to all the suggestions put forward, took notes from time to time, and* **kept his own counsel**. □ *Return to me tomorrow and* **keep your own counsel** *on this subject.* □ *He was evidently secretive and* **kept his own counsel**.

keep one's pecker up bëj kurajë, mbaj frymën lart, qëndroj i fortë moralisht

□ *'Sorry, Bicket, Mr. Desert has been in, but, it's no go.' 'No, sir?' 'Keep your pecker up, you'll get something.'* □ *I'm going to keep in touch with you. I'll see what can be done. And in the meantime keep your pecker up.*

keep one's powder dry mbaj barutin të thatë

□ *It doesn't sound like business for a long time. Still it won't do any harm to watch out and keep our powder dry.* □ *No man was ever more fit than the Afrikaner to hold the motto: Have faith in God but keep your powder dry.*

keep one's promise mbaj premtimin

□ *Jos promised, but didn't keep his promise.*

keep one's temper përmbaj veten, ruaj gjakftohtësinë

□ *Querry was not angry with him when he spilt water; he kept his temper when one of his drawings was smeared by ink from a broken bottle.* □ *For once Red had kept his temper; he talked fairly quietly to Jarvis, telling him the Lodge intended to enforce its seniority rules.* □ *His behavior was very rude but, fortunately, I managed to keep my temper.*

keep one's tongue between one's teeth kafshoi gjuhën, mbledh gjuhën, i vë fre gjuhës

□ *'But he knew his place and managed to keep his tongue between his teeth.'* □ *Roy regretted his outburst. His anger and his surprise passed with the additional effort of keeping his tongue between his teeth.*

keep one's wits about one hap sytë, kam mendjen në vend

□ *You need to keep your wits about you when you're dealing with a man like that.* □ *You were looking at a rainbow like a damned silly fool instead of keeping your wits about you.* □ *During the fire, the young boy kept his wits about him and got out by one of the less crowded exits.* □ *He soon found that if he kept his wits about him he would come upon new opportunities.*

keep one's word mbaj fjalën

□ *I promised not to go out of his territory and I kept my word.* □ *Rosamond Oliver kept her word in coming to visit me.* □ *'Then will I have the first bath myself!...' In two days we had it all done and the water in ... He kept his word and was the first to try it.* □ *They must trust him, he would keep his word, come what might.*

keep on tenter-hooks lë si mbi gjemba

□ *Why do you keep me on tenter-hooks like this?* □ *Grierson was in a haste to divulge his secret information and still smiled sleekly, keeping them on tenter-hooks.*

keep open house e mban derën hapur (çelur)

□ *Well, it's very nice to be able to keep open house, I suppose. But it's not everybody that can afford to be hospitable.* □ *In the evening, he'd keep open house for his cronies with endless champagne and caviar and half a dozen girls that some agent used to procure for him.*

keep out of sth 1. lë jashtë, nuk lë të hyjë

□ *I do not at all complain of having been kept out of this property.* □ *The butler held the chair at the opposite side of the table, and Jurgis thought it was to keep him out of it.*

2. shmang, rri larg

□ *He learned early in life that it was best to keep out of other people's* quarrels. □ *Half of all morality is negative and consists in* **keeping out of** *mischief.*

keep pace with sb eci krahas, në një hap me

□ *It's important for a firm to* **keep pace with** *the changes in the market.* □ *When they go for a walk, Johnny has to take long steps to* **keep pace with** *his father.* □ *The long-legged young man rattled away at such a rate, that I walked much as I could do to* **keep pace with** *the donkey.* □ *He walked very quickly and she had to run a little to* **keep pace with** *him.* □ *I cannot* **keep pace with** *him in physics.*

keep quiet about sth hesht, mbaj të fshehtë, nuk flas për

□ *I have decided to resign but I'd prefer to* **keep quiet about** *it.*

keep silence mbaj qetësi

□ *Carrie did not stir at the words. She was bound up completely in the man's atmosphere. He would have* **silence** *in order to express his feelings, and she* **kept** *it.*

keep step with mbaj hapin

□ *Soldiers must* **keep step** *in marching.*

keep tab/tabs/a tag on 1. ndjek, mbikqyr; kontrolloj

□ *'Alec seems to be* **keeping a tab on** *his wife these days. Does he think she's got a lover?'* □ *I've* **kept** *a pretty close* **tab on** *most of what he's said these last twenty years.*

2. regjistroj

□ *The government tries to* **keep tabs on** *all the animals in the park.*

keep the ball rolling ushqej, mbaj gjallë, nuk e lë të shuhet

□ *The important thing with young children is to* **keep the ball rolling** *from one activity to another; otherwise they become bored.* □ *Most of*

the group had nothing to say, but Mary and Peter **kept the ball rolling**. □ *He inquired whether we had known Powell. Then there was a pause... To* **keep the ball rolling** *I asked Merlo if this Powell was remarkable in any way.*

keep the flag (Union Jack) flying ngre flamurin, valëvit flamurin

□ *British golf fans tend to Jacklin as something of a standard-bearer, playing for Queen and country and* **keeping the Union Jack flying** *in a foreign land.*

keep the home fires burning kujdesem për punët e shtëpisë, mbaj shtëpinë hapur (çelur)

□ *While Tony was in the army, Mary* **kept the home fires burning**.

keep the peace ruaj qetësinë, rendin

□ *Those two children are always fighting each other when their mother is not there to* **keep the peace**. □ *The government had made plans for a mounted force to* **keep the peace** *on the prairies.*

keep the pot boiling 1. fitoj sa të mbaj shpirtin gjallë, sa të siguroj bukën e gojës

□ *Even with the bits of gardening and house-jobbing I do in the evenings It's not easy to* **keep the pot boiling**. □ *Sometimes he's lucky and sells a picture for a good price and we think, 'Oh, well, that'll* **keep the pot boiling** *for a bit.'* □ *If John cannot go out to work, I shall have to, the* **pot** *has to be* **kept boiling** *by some means or the other.*

2. vazhdoj energjikisht, mbaj gjallë

□ *Mr. Pickwick paused ... took two or three short runs, baulked himself as often and at last took another run and went slowly and gravely down the slide ..'* **Keep the pot boiling**, *sir,' said*

Sam. □ *The audience **kept the pot boiling** by shouting encouragement to the players.* □ *It was not for nearly half an hour that he did arrive and in the meantime someone had to **keep the pot boiling.***

keep the wolf from the door i shpëtoj urisë (skamjes, varfërisë)

□ *Their wages are barely enough to **keep the wolf from the door.*** □ *When we were young, our family was very poor, and sometimes it was difficult to **keep the wolf from the door.***

□ *Many unemployed people are forced to do all kinds of odd jobs to **keep the wolf from the door.***

keep time mbaj ritmin (kohën, tempin)

□ *When you are learning to dance, the main thing is to **keep time** to the music.* □ *The dancers in the hall **kept time** with the music.*

keep to the point/subject i përmbahem temës (çështjes në fjalë)

□ *Do please, **keep to the point.***

keep track 1. ndjek këmba-këmbës, s'ia ndaj sytë

□ *The man suspected of the murder travelled about so much that it was difficult for the police to **keep track** of him.*

2. azhurnohem, jam në korent, jam në dijeni

□ *We read the newspapers to **keep track** of current events.*

keep under 1. shtyp, mbaj nën kontroll

□ *The army managed to **keep** the population of the occupied country **under** for a few months, and then trouble began to break out.*

2. mbaj në

□ *The plainclothes officers were told to **keep** the suspected man **under** constant observation.*

keep under control mbaj nën kontroll

□ *The threatened epidemic of smallpox*

was **kept under control** by the authorities' vigorous action.* □ *He had learned to **keep** himself **under control.*** □ *He kept his feelings **under control.***

keep under observation mbaj në vëzhgim (mbikqyrje)

□ *The patient is seriously ill and is being **kept under** continuous observation.*

keep under one's hat mbaj të fshehtë, mbaj sekret

□ *Mr. Jones knew who had won the contest, but he **kept** it **under his hat** until it was announced publicly.*

□ ***Keep** this **under your hat**, but I hear that we are to have a new manager.*

keep up 1. ruaj, mbaj, vazhdoj

□ *He pretends to consider himself bound to **keep up** the tradition.*

□ *They entered into a correspondence which was **kept up** for almost ten years.* □ *The troops' spirits were **kept up** by the occasional visit of well-known entertainers to their camps.*

2. qëndron në nivel të lartë

□ *In spite of strikes, the national output managed to **keep up**. It even increased a little beyond the previous year's.* □ *So long as the cost of raw materials **keep up**, prices of consumer good will **keep up**, too.*

3. vazhdon, nuk pushon (ndalon, bie)

□ *If this rain **keeps up**, all the crops will be ruined.* □ *The hurricane **kept up** for several days and left a swathe of destruction across the country.*

keep up appearances mbahem sa për sy e faqe, sa për sy të botës

□ *She would rather go hungry and **keep up appearances** than eat properly and wear last year's fashions.*

□ *His family is not as wealthy as it used to be, but they **keep up appearances** by running a big car and living in the same large house.* □ *Even when* the Johnsons fell on evil times and money was short they always tried to **keep up appearances**.

keep up one's courage mbaj frymën (moralin) lart

□ We talked to him and gave him our advice, hoping that it might help him **keep up his courage**.

keep up with 1. eci krahas me, arrij

□ The main cause of industrial unrest is that the workers' incomes are not **keeping up with** rising prices. □ 'This was called 'speeding up the gang', and if any man could not **keep up with** the pace, there were hundreds outside begging to try. □ You are walking so fast. I can't **keep up with** you.

2. ruaj (mbaj) lidhje

□ Between whiles—for Alec was writing hard -she visited her old friends. She had scarcely **kept up with** them at all, so alien had been the mere thought of them to the life she led at Marshport. □ For some years after his retirement he **kept up with** a number of his old workmates, but as time went by he dropped them one by one.

3. ruaj standard të njëjtë social e material

□ Most people, in this competitive society, think they must **keep up with** their neighbours. □ 'it's no use asking me for a fur coat just because Mavis has got a new fur coat. My salary is only about half of her husband's, and we can't just **keep up with** them, that's all.

keep watch/and ward ruaj, bëj roje; mbikqyr

□ Mrs. Pipchin had **kept watch and ward** over little Paul and his sister for nearly twelve months. □ They took it in turns to **keep watch** after that, in case Simmons should come back to continue his search. □ She came so quickly after him that she might have been **keeping watch**—and almost at once there was another constraint in the room.

kick against sth shpërfill; ngre zërin kundër, protestoj kundër; hedh shqelma kundër

□ It's no use trying to **kick against** the rules; you'll be the sufferer in the end. □ 'Don't **kick against** fate. What will be, will be.'

kick against the pricks i bie murit me kokë

□ He will have to learn to accept certain things in life, instead of **kicking against the pricks** all the time. □ 'I'm not going back to that school. I hate it! I hate it!' 'Look, dear! It's no use **kicking against the pricks**. Everyone has to stay at school to the age of sixteen. You'll just have to grin and bear it.'

kick around 1. sillem keq; trajtoj keq

□ John likes to **kick around** the little boys.

2. vij (sillem) vërdallë

□ Harry has **kicked around** all over the world as a merchant seaman. □ He **kicked around** for several years before he settled down to work.

3. diskutoj lirshëm

□ After the clinical examination, the consultant invited his students to put forward any suggestions they had about the nature of the disease, so that they could **kick** them **around** for a while. □ We'll **kick** some ideas **around** and make a decision to-morrow.

kick downstairs shtyj, hedh nga shkallët (me shkelma)

□ The irate husband seized his wife's lover and **kicked** him **downstairs**.

kick in thyej, çaj me shkelma

□ *As the door was locked, and I could hear someone screaming for help, I kicked it in and rushed into the house.*

kick off shkelmon topin e parë (në futboll); fillon ndeshja

□ *A television personality was invited to kick off at the final.* □ *The center forward kicked off at four p.m.* □ *The match is due to kick off at 2:15.*

kick one's heels pres gjatë

□ *'Why didn't the chap come? Can't kick my heels here for ever,' thought Soames.* □ *... to let your uncle kick his heels in your hall.*

kick out/out of nxjerr jashtë me forcë, i jap shkelmin; përzë (dëboj) me forcë

□ *'You're only allowed one mistake in this firm. If you slip up a second time, they kick you out without any hesitation.* □ *A group of directors tried to kick the young tycoon out of his position as Chairman, but he turned the tables on them.*

kick the bucket vdes

□ *'I hope I shall kick the bucket before I'm as old as grandfather,' he thought.* □ *The old man finally kicked the bucket at the age of 89.* □ *Mr. Wickham, their agent for many years past, said that if he kicked the bucket Mrs. Merton could run the place standing on her head.* □ *They slept so well I think that every scruffy head's kicked the bucket in the night and I'm the only one left.*

kick the habit shkelmoj, flak tej një zakon të keq

□ *Formerly a 20-a-day smoker, Dr. John Dunwoody kicked the habit when he was a general practitioner.* □ *Doctors should try to persuade smokers to kick the habit.*

kick upstairs ngre në pozitë (për ta hequr qafe)

□ *The only way for us to get rid of old Smith is to kick him upstairs; then we'll be able to appoint Brown, and get some life into business.*

kick up a fuss/raw bëj zhurmë, potere; hap telashe, bëj skandal

□ *When he discovered that his room had been given to someone else, the tourist kicked up quite a fuss.* □ *When the teacher gave the class five more hours of homework, the class kicked up a fuss.* □ *He is the kind of person who will kick up a fuss about a very trivial matter.* □ *The prisoners at a pre-arranged signal, began to kick up a hell of a raw with the aim of attracting the attention of the people passing the prison.*

kill off vras, zhduk, heq qafe, shfaros

□ *A late frost killed off nearly all the apple-blossom, with the result that we had a very poor crop this year.* □ *Since the mosquitoes were killed off, the island has become a far pleasanter place to live in.* □ *The frost killed off most of the insect pests.*

kill time vras kohën, harxhoj kohën kot

□ *He did not want to stay and filled in the puzzle 'only to kill time'.* □ *To kill time before the train left, we went to a movie, after which we returned to the hotel.* □ *To kill time until the exhibition opened, we looked round the shops.*

kill two birds with one stone me një gur vras dy zogj

□ *If a get a job in London, I shall be killing two birds with one stone. I shall be near my parents and I shall also be in the best place for advancement in my career.* □ *'Why don't you come and discuss your idea when you're next in Edinburgh?' 'Well, I have to see my solicitor there next week, so perhaps I could drop in and have a chat with you while I'm there.' 'That's right.* **Kill two birds with one stone.'**

kind of paksa; njëfarësoj, në një farë mënyre; gati-gati, për pak; mënt
□ *I* **kind of** *thought this would happen.* □ *This seemed* **kind of** *unfair.* □ *I'm not sure why, but I feel* **kind of** *sorry for him.*

kith and kin miq e të afërm; farefis
□ *The French troops were given orders no longer to pamper their '***kith and kin'.*** □ *My grandfather is his cousin, so he's* **kith and kin** *to me somehow.*

knit one's brows(s) rrudh (ngrys) vetullat
□ *The prince's rude reply caused the king to* **knit his brows.**

knock about 1. bredh, endem sillem poshtë e përpjetë
□ *When he was a child, he used to* **knock about** *the market, trying to find a little work to earn a few coppers.* □ *'Our elder son has been* **knocking about** *the continent for several months. We don't know exactly where he is or what he's doing.'*
2. godit, rrah vazhdimisht; trajtoj egërsisht
□ *The young woman tried to conceal her damaged eye behind dark glasses, but it was obvious to everyone in the office that her husband had been* **knocking** *her* **about** *again.* □ *She gets* **knocked about** *by her husband.*

knock back rrëkëllej, pi me njëherë
□ *The stranger ordered a double rum and* **knocked** *it* **back** *in three second flat. 'That's better,' he said, as he rubbed his hands together. 'Same again, please!'*

knock down 1. hedh, rrëzoj për tokë
□ *He* **knocked** *his opponent* **down** *three times in the first round.* □ *Half an hour later he had been violently attacked,* **knocked down,** *and almost chocked to death.* □ *He was* **knocked down** *by a lorry.*
2. shemb
□ *When the slum property has been evacuated it will be* **knocked down** *and replaced by modern blocks of flats.* □ *These old houses are to be* **knocked down.**
3. zbërthej, çmontoj
□ *The machines will be* **knocked down** *before being shipped.*
4. shes në ankand
□ *The painting was* **knocked down** *to an American dealer for $5,000.*
5. ul
□ *I managed to* **knock** *his price* **down** *from $500 to $450.* □ *She is never happy unless she succeeds in* **knocking** *the bill* **down** *by a few pence.*

knock in/into ngul, mbërthej
□ *The child tried hard, but couldn't* **knock** *the nail* **in.** □ *He* **knocked in** *a nail.* □ *I* **knocked in** *the top of the barrel.*

knock off 1. lë (ndërpre) punën, pushoj
□ *'I'll meet you at the factory gate after work.' 'O.K. What time do you* **knock off?'** □ *'We always* **knock off** *early on Christmas Eve. Nobody's in the mood to do any work, and we usually have a drink and a bit of an office party before we go home.'*
2. hartoj, shkruaj, bëj shpejt e shpejt
□ *This script shows every sign of having been* **knocked off** *in great haste. It is very badly written.* □ *That composition was* **knocked off** *in about thirty minutes.*
3. zbres, ul
□ *The greengrocer always* **knocked** *a*

little off the price of his fruit for the old age pensioners. □ *'Did you pay the full price for this book?' 'No. The girl knocked twenty-five pence off because it was shop-soiled.'*

knock off one's feet befasohet, habitet shumë, mbetet pa mend

□ *The announcement that John and Mary were to be married just knocked me off my feet: I didn't even know that they were going out together.* □ *When Charlie was given the first prize, it knocked him off his feet for a few minutes.*

knock oneself out bëhem, bie copë

□ *He really knocked himself out to get the repairs done on time.* □ *Mrs. Ross knocked herself out planning her daughter's wedding.*

knock out 1. shkund (pipën etj.)

□ *I heard him knock out his pipe on the mantel piece.*

2. nxjerr nokaut

□ *Joe Frazier knocked his inexperienced opponent out in the first round of the contest.*

3. befasoj, lë gojë hapur

□ *For a moment I was completely knocked out by the news of my friend's death. It was some time before I could convince myself that it had really happened.* □ *The letter informing the manager that his services would no longer be required knocked him right out. He refused to see anyone all day.*

knock the bottom out of sth përmbys

□ *The unexpected evidence of a passer-by knock the bottom out of the youth's statement that he was nowhere near the scene of the crime.* □ *She knocked the bottom out of our argument.* □ *This day's news has knocked the bottom out of my life.*

knock the spirit/the stuffing out of ligështoj, demoralizoj

□ *No amount of bombardment seemed to knock the spirit out of the guerrillas. They always reappeared, ready to strike at the enemy in the most unexpected places.* □ *I released his shoulder, letting my hand fall helplessly to my side as if his words had knocked all the spirit out of me.*

knock together bëj, sajoj, përgatis shpejt e shpejt

□ *I don't pretend to be much of a handyman, but if need be I could knock a rough table together.* □ *The hut looked as if it had been knocked together by someone in a great hurry.* □ *The bookshelves had obviously been knocked together.*

knock up 1. zgjoj (duke trokitur)

□ *'Would you mind knocking me up at about 7 o'clock tomorrow, as I must catch an early train to London?* □ *Run to the doctor's house and knock him up.* □ *Tell mother to knock me up at half past five.*

2. sajoj shpejt e shpejt

□ *My mother was a marvel at knocking up a meal for an unexpected guest. There always seemed to be something in the larder.*

3. lë me barrë

□ *'Why ever did she let him knock her up? Now I suppose she'll have to have an abortion.*

know all the answers i di të gjitha

□ *The researchers say: 'The broadcaster often seems to give the impression of knowing all the answers.'*

know a thing or two është njeri me mend (me përvojë); di shumë rreth

□ *She's been married five times, so she should know a thing or two about men.* □ *I think it would be foolish to try to trick Tom: he knows a thing or two.*

know best e di më mirë
- □ *'I want to get up.' 'But the doctor said you were to stay in bed, and surely he know best?'*

know better (than to do sth) e di, e kupton shumë mirë që s'duhet të ....
- □ *There was hardly any light but he knew better than to waste time because of what was coming.*

know by sight njoh si fytyrë
- □ *I know the man you are looking for by sight, but I'm afraid I don't know his name.*

know one's own mind di se ç'duhet të bëj, di se ç'dua, di se ç'vendim duhet të marr
- □ *Ralph turned to him quickly. This was the voice of one who knew his own mind.* □ *'Well,' her mother replied calmly, 'you are twenty-five and old enough to know your own mind.'* □ *She ought to have known her own mind, no dependable woman made this mistake.*

know/keep one's place di (mbaj) vendin që më takon
- □ *I've seen better days than you have, man. I'll be all right as long as you keep your place.* □ *Just you keep your place, that's all.*

know one's stuff di, njeh mirë punën (zanatin) e vet
- □ *Professor Brown is a real expert in his subject: he certainly knows his stuff.*

know one's way about/around di të mbaroj punë; njoh shumë mirë një vend (një temë, një proçedurë etj.); jam i aftë e i mirëinformuar
- □ *Jack is friendly with all sorts of important people: he knows his way round.* □ *Joe looks well, a bright complexioned curly-haired young man... with a cheerful air of knowing his way about.* □ *Harry, who knew*

his way about, had supplied us with glasses of stone ginger beer.

know on which side one's bread is buttered on di ku del (fitimi, leverdia etj.)
- □ *You can be sure that Tom will not offend the new manager: Tom knows which side his bread is buttered on.* □ *Her mind twisted. 'You're a timid soul, aren't you?' 'I know which side my bread is buttered on,' I said.* □ *Bossiney looked clever, but he had also—and it was one of his great attractions—an air as if he did not quite know on which side his bread were buttered.*

know sb/sth as a person knows his ten fingers njoh shumë mirë; njoh në pëllëmbë të dorës
- □ *He knew his assets and his liabilities, as he knew his ten fingers.*

know sb/sth like a book e njoh shumë mirë, i njoh dhëmbë e dhëmballë
- □ *I know him like a book. And I tell you the man is in love with you.*

know sb/sth like the palm/back of one's hand njoh në majë të gishtave
- □ *All I got to do is to go down to Sidcup tomorrow. I got all the references I want down there. I know that place like the back of my hand.* □ *I know Warley like the palm of my hand. In fact, much better, because I don't know the palm of my hand.* □ *He knew the passage like the palms of his hand.*

know the ropes di (njoh) të fshehtat (marifetet, kleçkat) e zanatit etj.
- □ *Everything will be confusing for you at the beginning, but you will soon get to know the ropes.* □ *Besides Bannal's knowledge of the theatre is an inside knowledge; we know him, and he knows us. He knows the ropes.* □ *Miss Williams will look*

*after you well because she knows
the ropes.* □ *Anywhere from Tonga to
the Admiralty Isles, he knew the
ropes and could lie in the native
dialect.*

know the score njoh mirë situatën
(gjendjen); di si qëndrojnë punët; di
si është e vërteta

□ *If you want information, ask Jim:
he knows the score.*

know what's what ndaj shapin nga
sheqeri, të keqen nga e mira (të padobishmen nga e dobishmja)

□ *You are old enough now to know
what's what.* □ *I had so much claret. I
did not much know what was what.*

□ *'Some day I'll have a dress like
hers, Miss Todd's, I mean. Satin it
was and real lace edging. She knows
what's what, I'll be bound.*

L

labor under sth gabohem, kam mendim të gabuar për

□ He is **laboring under** a wrong delusion if he thinks that we have any prejudice against him. □ Our political opponents **labor under** the delusion that support for our policies is dwindling.

labor the point specifikoj, përpunoj, trajtoj me hollësi

□ The speaker **labored the point** so long that we lost interest. □ 'It has always seemed to me, and I fear that I have **labored the point** more than once in print.'

land on one's feet/both feet bie në këmbë, në të dyja këmbët

□ Jack was dismissed one day, and the following day he had got a much better-paid job: he always **lands on his feet**.

land sb/oneself in sth fus dikë, veten në vështirësi (telashe etj.)

□ Your rush to find out what had become of me has **landed you in** a pretty fine pickle!

larger than life në madhësi të mbinatyrshme

□ The hero appears as a **larger-than-life** character.

last but not least i fundit, por jo më pak i rëndësishëm

□ And **last but not least**, there is the question of adequate funding.

last lap, the xhiroja e fundit (në një garë); faza, etapa e fundit

□ As they entered **the last lap** Johnson was still running third. □ We are on **the last lap**, so don't slacken! □ It has been a hell of a business completing this contract. Thank God, we're on **the last lap** now. □ Here in Basarah, in sight of safety, he felt instinctively sure that the danger would be greater than during the wild hazards of his journey. And to fail at **the last lap**— that would be hardly bear thinking about.

last word in sth, the fjala e fundit

□ She's always going on about women's feelings and intuitions as though she was **the last word in** women. □ Don't talk to me about untidy kids; I've got two at home that are **the last word**. □ The superintendent has **the last word** in ordering new desks. □ Ten years ago this dress was considered **the last word** in elegance.

late in the day vonë, me vonesë

□ I'm an old man. Your offer has come too **late in the day** for me. □ I feel, however, that it is rather **late in the day** to call in new technical advisers.

later on më vonë

□ James had to visit a patient but he hopes to join us **later on**. □ 'He doesn't mention a price.' 'Oh, yes he does, but **later on**, near the end of the letter.' □ At first things went well, but **later on** we ran into trouble. □ We shall discuss that matter **later on**.

laud/praise/extol to the skies ngre në qiell, lëvdoj shumë, e mburr sa s'ka ku të shkojë më

□ The comedian was **lauded to the skies** for his sense of humor. □ You were **extolled to the skies**, I assure you.

laugh at 1. qesh me
□ *He laughed at all the jokes she told him.* □ *He laughed at the way the clown kept falling over their big feet.*
2. tall, vë në lojë
□ *Thoughtless children sometimes laugh at beggars and tramps.* □ *We all laughed at Jane when she said she believed in ghosts.* □ *It's unkind to laugh at a person who is in trouble.*
3. shpërfill
□ *He laughs at the difficulties, while they just spur him on to further effort.* □ *His mother's pleas to be careful were just laughed at.*

laugh away heq, largoj, kaloj me të qeshur
□ *He tried without success to laugh her fears away.* □ *'I know you are brave, but you can't just laugh a toothache away. You will have to see a dentist.'* □ *Jane had this tremendous fear of the dark, and her husband would try to laugh it away, saying it was just her overdeveloped imagination.*

laugh off kaloj me të qeshur
□ *This is a mistake that can't easily be laughed off.* □ *'Don't worry,' he said, trying to laugh off his resentment at the intrusion.* □ *The young man simply laughed off the embarrassing situation in which he found himself...*

laugh on the other side of one's face/mouth qesh e qan, kalon nga gëzimi në trishtim, nga gazi në vaj
□ *He may think that throwing stones at my windows is amusing, but he'll be laughing on the other side of his face soon. I've just reported him to the police.* □ *He may laugh at our discomfiture now, but before long he'll be laughing on the other side of his face.* □ *'Laugh as much as you like. I've got some news here that will*

make you laugh on the other side of your face.
laugh one's head off qesh me gjithë zemër, qesh me të madhe, shkulem së qeshuri
□ *As he picked himself up from the floor, he saw a couple of boys laughing their heads off.* □ *'If I had any sense of humor I'd just laugh my head off,' she cried. 'It's the most priceless joke I've ever heard.'*
laugh till one's sides burst/shake/ split qesh sa më dhembin ijët
□ *I can imagine a group of men laughing till their sides split.*
laugh up one's sleeve qesh nën hundë
□ *Although they didn't dare show it, most of the audience were laughing up their sleeve at the politician's silly remark.* □ *She knew the truth all along and was laughing up her sleeve at us.* □ *We had a feeling that he was laughing up his sleeve at us.*
launch out (into) i futem, i hyj
□ *Why must a dancer launch out as choreographer as well?* □ *You'll want to launch out into something with a proper salary.*
law of the jungles, the ligji i xhunglës
□ *The Robens Committee of 1972 had been told, in written evidence, by W H Thompson, a leading union solicitor: 'The only law that rules in factories is the law of jungle, and it is a jungle where innocent persons are maimed and mutilated and their lives laid waste.'*
lay a finger on sb prek, vë dorë
□ *Anyone who lays a finger on that child will be reported to me.* □ *If you lay a finger on that boy, I'll never forgive you.* □ *We have firm discipline, but the staff never lay a finger on the boys.* □ *'Nobody has laid a finger on me, yet.'* □ *Don't you dare*

lay a finger on that vase! □ *If you so much as lay a finger on* my boy, I'll call the police.

lay aside 1. lë, vë mënjanë

□ *I laid my book aside, turned off the light and went to sleep.* □ *She laid aside her knitting to rest her eyes for a moment.* □ *The students laid aside their books to watch TV.*

2. largoj, heq dorë, braktis

□ *Now that his sons are growing up, some of his responsibilities can be safely laid aside.* □ *Now lay aside all those thoughts and look to the future.* □ *After receiving the letter, he had laid aside all thoughts of Carrie for the time being.*

3. ruaj, vë mënjanë

□ *We must lay something aside for the boy's education.*

lay bare zbuloj, nxjerr në shesh; hap, zbraz

□ *The police laid bare the plot to rob the bank.* □ *He was not laying bare his desires for anyone to see.* □ *He is near and dear to them, he often lays bare his heart to them.* □ *He laid bare his soul to her in a way he would not willingly have done had he been entirely sober.*

lay claim to sth kërkoj kthimin e, rivendikoj; kërkoj njohjen e të drejtës mbi; pretendoj për

□ *I'm afraid I can lay no claim to your compliment.* □ *I undoubtedly lay claim to both of these characteristics.*

lay down 1. vendos, përcaktoj si rregull, parim etj.

□ *We had to lay down the general direction in which the answer lay.* □ *Follow the procedure laid down in our booklet.* □ *It is laid down that all applicants must sit a written exam.*

2. nis të ndërtoj

□ *Several of the new-type tankers are*

being laid down on Tyneside. □ *A new ship was laid down last month.*

3. depozitoj, vë mënjanë (në qilar)

□ *Father laid down a few good bottles before the war.*

lay down one's arms dorëzoj armët, dorëzohem

□ *The majority of their soldiers simply laid down their arms.* □ *After a fierce battle the enemy troops were forced to lay down their arms.*

lay down one's life (for) jap jetën për

□ *Young men flocked to the recruiting offices, willing to fight, and if need be to lay down their lives.* □ *This is a cause for which he is prepared to lay down his life.*

lay down the law bëj ligjin

□ *The children behaved badly today: I'm going to have to lay down the law about their behavior.* □ *He concluded this sentence with a self-important cough as one who has laid down the law in an indisputable manner.* □ *It is not right for the soldier to lay down the law in political matters.*

lay emphasis on sth theksoj, vë theksin te

□ *Some schools lay great emphasis on language study.* □ *'What's the matter with you of late? Can't I talk with you any more?' 'Certainly, you can talk with me,' she replied laying emphasis on the word.*

lay eyes on shoh

□ *'Do you deny having spoken to the witness on the day in question?' 'Yes, sir. I do. In fact I've never laid eyes on him before.'* □ *'He's a hooligan. When I first laid eyes on him, I thought he's certainly not the type for my Cairy. Too damn rough.'* □ *'How do you know?' he demanded. 'You never laid eyes on me before.'* □ *I've hardly laid eyes on you all summer.*

lay hands/one's hands on 1. vë dorë
□ *How dare you lay hands on me?*
□ *They were afraid that if they left him alone in his disturbed condition he would lay hands on himself.*
2. fus, shtie në dorë
□ *His primary concern was to catch, kill, stuff and describe as many kinds of beasts as he could lay his hands on.* □ *For weapons, the mob used anything they could lay their hands on.* □ *When everybody had eaten as much as possible, the waiters withdrew to 'clear away', or in other words to appropriate to their own private use and emolument, whatever remnants of the eatables and drinkables they could contrive to lay their hands on.*
3. kap, zë, arrestoj
□ *If the police lay hands on him, they will put him in jail.* □ *The place is swarming with policemen just waiting to lay their hands on some of us.*
4. gjej
□ *I arranged these shelves, and I could lay my hands on anything.*

lay/put heads together këshillohem, konsultohem, shkëmbej mendime
□ *You didn't put your heads together as to what you would say to us?* □ *And the two gentlemen were laying their heads together, and consulting as to the best means of being useful to Mrs. Becky.* □ *You didn't put your head together as to what you would say to us?*

lay hold of kap, zë, mbërthej me dorë
□ *We laid hold of the rope and he pulled lustily.* □ *Michael was firmly laid hold of by the collar and shaked till his teeth rattled.* □ *So saying, he laid hold of the branch.*

lay it on (thick) e teproj me lavdërime (komplimente, lajka), lavdëroj

(fajësoj) jashtë mase, përdor lavdërime të ekzagjeruara
□ *To call him a genius is laying it on a bit too thick.* □ *Lammence was not impressed with Barney's ideas of publicity. 'Lays it too thick.'* □ *He exaggerates. I wish he would not lay it on so.*

lay off 1. lë, heq dorë, pres
□ *I've smoked cigarettes for years, but now I'm going to lay off.* □ *You must lay off alcohol for a while.* □ *I was told that I should lay off these visits.*
2. lë rehat; pushoj, ndërpres (ngacmimin etj.)
□ *'Take it easy, then he'll soon lay off you.'* □ *'Lay off my tie and give me a kiss.'*
3. pushoj nga puna
□ *The factory was laying people off.* □ *He is a skilled worker laid off from his job.* □ *Hundreds of thousands of workers are being laid off every day while others are being threatened with wage cuts.*

lay on 1. organizoj, rregulloj
□ *It's his birthday. That's why I laid on a party.* □ *The reception at the Town Hall was well laid on*
2. bëj lidhjen e ujit, dritës etj.
□ *We can't move in until the electricity has been laid off.* □ *We have electricity laid on all over the house.*
3. ekzagjeroj
□ *He was laying it on a bit, with all this talk of wanting to help the poor.*

lay one's account for/on/with sth var shpresat te, shpresoj te
□ *Lay your account with having it to bear, and put no trust in being set right by me.*

lay/put one's cards on the table hap letrat në tavolinë
□ *I'm not going to lay my cards on*

the table and tell you everything about this affair. □ *How did Alec know that Harold wouldn't take advantage of these confidences? How foolish to* **lay** *all* **his cards on the table!** □ *The negotiators felt they had nothing to lose by* **laying** *some of* **their cards on the table** *at the beginning of the talks.* □ *In talking about buying the property, Tom* **laid his cards on the table** *about his plans for it.*

lay oneself out bëj çmos, bëhem copë
□ *Larry wanted to win a medal for his school, so he really* **laid himself out** *in the race.* □ *The doctor* **laid himself out** *to be polite and social.* □ *She* **laid herself out** *to make her guests comfortable.*

lay oneself open to sth jam i hapur ndaj, vë veten, vihem
□ *Not to defend oneself would be to* **lay oneself,** *and one's children,* **open to** *oppression, slavery or extermination.* □ *One can, however, admire a researcher who* **lays himself open to,** *and suffers, attack from his subjects.*

lay open zbuloj, nxjerr në shesh
□ *The repetition to any ears—even to Steerforth's—of what she had been unable to repress when her head* **lay open** *to me, by accident, I felt I would be a rough deed.*

lay out 1. shtroj, hap, ndej
□ *The drill is to* **lay out** *the clothes he'll be wearing in the evening.* □ *His dinner jacket was already* **laid out** *on the bed.*
2. rregulloj, sistemoj
□ *The gardens and parks in our cities are well* **laid out.**
3. shpenzoj, harxhoj
□ *He had to* **lay out** *all he had on the airline tickets.* □ *They must have* **laid out** *a large sum for that project.* □ *My*

brother had **laid out** *all his strength and is weary.*
4. nxjerr nokaut
□ *A stiff right to the jaw* **laid** *the boxer* **out** *in the second round.*
5. projektoj
□ *The architect* **laid out** *the interior of the building.*

lay siege rrethoj
□ *Frederic the Great* **laid siege** *to Prague, but he was defeated on the battle of Kolin.* □ *In the year 1474 a large Turkish army* **laid siege** *to Shkodra and bombarded it throughout a whole month with artillery, but the citadel resisted.*

lay sb/sth low 1. rrëzoj; vë poshtë
□ *Many trees were* **laid low** *by the storm.* □ *Crops had been destroyed and many buildings* **laid low.** □ *Influenza has* **laid** *him low, forcing him to stay in bed for quite a few days.*
2. vras
□ *The hunters* **laid low** *seven pheasants.*

lay sth at sb's door ia lë dikujt në derë, ia ngarkoj dikujt
□ *The blame for the disaster has been* **laid** *firmly* **at** *the company's* **door.** □ *But there is one thing that can never be* **laid at the door of** *Francis Bruke; he never turned his back on a friend.* □ *He was in so bad a state financially, that to have this charge,* **laid at his door** *was very destructive.* □ *Hence her flight from her own family would be* **laid** *more to the* **door** *of a lovely temperamental peevishness than anything else.*

lay sth to sb's charge ia vë (hedh) përgjegjësinë dikujt; padis, akuzoj
□ *She* **laid** *the offense* **to his charge.**

lay stress on sth theksoj, e vë theksin në, nënvizoj

280

□ *Serene in her own judgement of what was worth while, she was like to* **lay stress on** *any silly mood or fact; thinking it exquisite—the last word.*

lay/put the blame (for sth) on sb fajësoj, ia hedh fajin dikujt

□ *To be sure, he had written a letter,* **laying all the blame on** *himself.* □ *Whenever these qualities involved mother and daughter in some unpleasant dilemma they both concurred in* **laying the blame on** *the shoulders of Mr. Nupkins.* □ *These politicians were trying to* **put the blame** *of their own evil deeds* **on her** *Frank.*

lay to rest 1. varros

□ *In a simple ceremony, the victims of the disaster were* **laid to rest** *in the village churchyard.* □ *He was finally* **laid to rest** *in the village he had been born in.*

lay up 1. vë, lë mënjanë, rezervoj

□ *We'll need to* **lay up** *a good supply of feed if this winer's going to be like the last.* □ *These old pieces of wood have been* **laid up** *for years, but at last we can use them.*

2. heq nga përdorimi

□ *He's had to* **lay** *his car* **up**: *he can't afford the insurance premiums.* □ *If you* **lay up** *a car for the winter, you should take out the battery.*

3. bllokoj në shtrat

□ *A bout of malaria had* **laid me up** *for a few weeks.* □ *Furthermore, he was* **laid up** *with a bed knee.*

4. vë, mbledh, grumbulloj

□ *Bees* **lay up** *honey for the winter.*

lay sth waste shkatërroj, shkretoj, rrënoj

□ *The emperor vanished with his army into the wilderness of the Ethiopian plateau, murdering, torturing and* **laying waste** *the country*

as he went along. □ *The invading army* **laid waste** *the countryside as they advanced.* □ *In a very few minutes Mr. Swiveller was asleep, dreaming that he had married Nelly Trent and come into her property, and that his first act of power was to* **lay waste** *the market garden of Mr. Cheggs and turn it into a brick field.*

lead a dog's life bëj jetë qeni

□ *His wife is a horrible woman; they say she* **leads** *him* **a dog's life.** □ *Since he got married to her, he's been* **leading a dog's life.**

lead astray çoj në rrugë të gabuar

□ *He* **led** *many girls* **astray** *with his easy, superficial charm.*

lead by the nose tërheq për hunde

□ *Jack is very much under Mary's influence; she just* **leads** *him* **by the nose.** □ *Don't let anyone* **lead you by the nose.** *Use your own judgment and do the right thing.*

lead nowhere s'jep rezultat, s'ka fryt

□ *Your planless work seems to be* **leading nowhere.**

lead off nis, filloj

□ *Ned, the General Editor,* **led off** *with a general survey of the objectives to be aimed at.* □ *He* **led off** *by making an apology.* □ *The town band* **led off** *by playing the National Anthem.* □ *She* **led off** *by saying that we must work harder than before.*

lead on nxit, i mbush mendjen (të besojë, të ndjekë një rrugë të gabuar); fus në rrugë të gabuar

□ *Travel brochures do* **lead** *you* **on** *with their promises of five-star treatment in luxury hotels.* □ *'Haven't you noticed the predatory gleam in his eyes? He's probably* **leading** *you* **on.'**

lead sb a (merry) dance/chase i hap (i nxjerr) punë, telashe

□ *The thieves led the police a merry chase all over the city before they were finally caught.* □ *They marvelled that a man so brilliant could be so difficult. He led them a hell of a dance.* □ *Helen, the youngest, led her family a dreadful dance in which drink, opium and conversion all figured.* □ *He looked at the bronze face; and the philosopher looked back from his hollow eyes, as if saying: 'What do you know of the human heart, my boy? A pretty dance the heart will lead you yet!'*

lead sb a dog's life ia nxij jetën dikujt, ia bëj jetën të padurueshme

□ *She waged fierce war against her dear papa; she led her parent what is usually called for want of a better figure of speech, the life of a dog.*

lead sb up the garden path mashtroj

□ *When he said he was an expert car mechanic, he was leading you up the garden path. He really knows nothing about cars.* □ *Someone posing as a television reporter has been leading us up the garden path.*

lead the way prij, udhëheq udhën, i tregoj udhën; eci përpara, shkoj në ballë (në krye)

□ *The boys need someone to lead the way on their hike.* □ *He led the way with Michael retailing the events of the morning.* □ *She led the way up the spiral stairs, and Dinny followed.*

lead up to sth çojnë në

□ *The report describes the negotiations which led up to the settlement.* □ *Every event in Oswald's life led up to that moment.*

leaf through shfletoj

□ *I can't claim that I've read the article at all carefully: I've just leafed through it.* □ *Mary leafed idly through some old magazines as she waited for her taxi to arrive.*

leak out merret vesh, del në shesh

□ *The details were supposed to be secret but somehow leaked out.* □ *The news leaked out.* □ *Stringent precautions were taken to prevent the details of the wedding leaking out.*

lean on sb ushtroj presion (trysni) mbi dikë (me dhunë, kërcënim etj.)

□ *I would gladly do what you ask if you would only stop leaning on me so hard! 'Joe's soft. He'll co-operate. He just needs leaning on a little.'*

lean on/upon sb mbështetem te

□ *In a crisis, the headmaster tends to lean overmuch on senior members of staff.* □ *It was reassuring to have someone upon whom he could lean for a while.*

lean towards sth priret drejt

□ *He leans towards more light-hearted subjects in his later works.*

leap/shot in the dark, a ndërmarrje e guximshme, hap i guximshëm

□ *We are calling for a halt to progress, for prevention and preservation for safety first and no leaps in the dark, because it's all that we are capable of.* □ *It has always been usual for a new kind of work to be considered in an unacademic manner, realizing that a just estimate requires a certain generosity, a readiness to take a leap in the dark, or risk a rash generalization.* □ *We're going to open up a hotel, and it's really a leap in the dark; we've never done this sort of thing before.*

leap at sth pranoj pa mëdyshje (pa hezitim)

□ *If he offered me a small part in his new production, I'd leap at chance.* □ *The opportunity was laid before him and eagerly leaped at.*

learn (off) by heart mësoj përmendsh
□ *All the students are required to* **learn** *the poem* **by heart.** □ *The pale and trembling candidate had to recite three times over the little speech... which he had been a month* **learning by heart.** □ *'Learn these words off by heart.'*

learn a/one's lesson nxjerr, marr një mësim të mirë
□ *The trouble was that he expected everybody to be as honest as himself, but I think he's* **learned his lesson** *now.* □ *But he had* **learned his lesson.** *Never since then had he speculated.*

least of all aq më pak
□ *Nobody can complain, you* **least of all.** □ *Nobody need worry, you* **least of all.**

leave sth aside lë mënjanë, shpërfill, nuk llogaris, nuk marr parasysh
□ *Leaving the matter of cost* **aside,** *we still have to find time off from other work.* □ *I don't see how you can* **leave aside** *his neglect of his family.*

leave/let sb/sth alone lë të qetë, lë rehat; nuk prek, nuk ngas, nuk trazoj
□ *Some of the spectators went out to meet the cricketers, Horace's mother in the lead. He told her, several times and loudly, to* **leave him alone.** □ *Site wants to think things out for herself, so we'd better* **leave her alone.** □ *Leave the cat* **alone.**

leave a bad/bitter/nasty taste in one's mouth lë shije të keqe (të hidhur) në gojë
□ *His rudeness to the teacher* **left a bad taste in my mouth.** □ *I was shocked at her remarks; they* **left a bad taste in my mouth.**

leave behind 1. harroj të marr, lë pa marrë, nuk marr me vete
□ *'It's a fine day: you can* **leave** *your mac* **behind!'** □ *In their withdrawal,*

much of the heavy equipment had to be **left behind.** □ *Oh! Dear! The bag has been* **left behind.** □ *If you stand here talking much longer, the train will leave without you. You'll be* **left behind.**
2. lë prapa
□ *The cyclone* **left behind** *it a trail of destruction.* □ *Some rulers have* **left behind** *no lasting memorial.*

leave go of sth lëshoj
□ *Leave go of my harm—you're hurting!* □ *Leave go of my hand.*

leave it at that lë me kaq
□ *We'll never agree, so let's just* **leave it at that.**

leave its/one's mark lë gjurmët e veta
□ *War has* **left its mark** *on the country.* □ *Two unhappy marriages have* **left their mark** *on her.* □ *You have worked very hard and the scare of the last few days has* **left its mark.** □ *The gentry took over the house in turn; a painter, a mad poet, then someone retired from the City. Each* **left his mark,** *brick floors were covered with boards, doorways blocked up or altered to make way for unheard of luxuries such as bathrooms.*

leave no avenue unexplored s'lë mjet pa përdorur (shfrytëzuar)
□ *The minister said he would* **leave no avenue unexplored** *in his attempt to improve the standard of education.*

leave no stone unturned s'lë gur pa lëvizur
□ *Mr. William Whitelaw promised that* **no stone** *would be* **left unturned,** *but again this did not soothe all doubts.* □ *Don't* **leave a stone unturned.** *It's always something to know you've done the most you could.* □ *This has given him time to breathe, time to* **leave no stone unturned** *to*

find her. □ *If instead you choose to make trouble, to force this matter into the daylight I shall **leave no stone unturned** to protect myself.*

leave much to be desired lë shumë për të dëshiruar

□ *The way in which the evidence was handled may **leave much to be desired** but this does not necessarily mean that evidence is unconvincing or that the 'allegation' is fake.* □ *'We'd best get ourselves seated,' Graham said. 'I should suggest near the back. The acoustics of this place **leave much do be desired**.* □ *'The condition of the people **leaves much to be desired**.'*

leave of absence leje

□ *She would go to her native village if she got her **leave of absence** now.*

leave off 1. lë, ndërpres, pushoj, ndaloj

□ *Ned **left off** talking about the firm.* □ *It's time to **leave off** work now.* □ *Has the rain **left off** yet?* □ *We **left off** at the end of Chapter Five.*

2. heq, nuk vesh më

□ *I **left off** my woollen underwear when the weather got warm.* □ *Do not **leave off** your overcoat, it is cold.*

leave out/out of 1. lë përjashta

□ *If you **leave** your bicycle **out** at night, you'll soon have trouble with rust.*

2. lë jashtë

□ *My name can be **left out of** this; I don't want to be involved.* □ *When you wrote the invitations, did you **leave** anyone **out**?* □ *In copying this document, be careful not to **leave out** any words.*

3. lë jashtë (konsideratës)

□ *Make sure that nothing is **left out of** account.* □ *He had **left out of** consideration the resentment of his former colleagues.*

leave over shtyj

□ *I regret that these matters will have to be **left over** until our next meeting.* □ *We shall just have to **leave** the matter **over** till the next meeting.*

leave sb cold s'i bën përshtypje, s'e ngacmon

□ *Instrumental music, oddly enough, **left** me rather **cold**.* □ *He was then the guest of Lord Rothschild, who's invited him over to view several fine gardens, which **left** Mr. Streeter **cold**.* □ *Her emotional appeal **left** him completely **cold**.*

leave sb high and dry lë si peshku në zall (pa ujë)

□ *To take the love of a man like Cowperwood from a woman like Aileen was to **leave her high and dry** on land, as a fish out of its native element.* □ *'Do you know Sir Charles Denbury?' 'I have had that privilege.' 'He seems to be **left high and dry** too.*

leave sb holding the baby/bag ia lë (ia hedh) barrën (përgjegjësinë) dikujt

□ *My boss has made a mess of the arrangements for next week's conference; now he's going abroad, and I'm **left holding the baby**.* □ *'And you would **leave us to hold the baby**?' Dave was incoherent with indignation. 'You go off to Paris and leave here your stolen property to be found by the police, no?'*

leave sb/sth hanging (in the air) lë varur

□ *The committee did not have time to discuss the matter, so it has been **left hanging**.*

leave sb in the lurch lë në baltë (batak), lë në pikë të hallit (në vështirësi)

□ *The town bully caught Eddie, and Tom **left him in the lurch**.* □ *If I could have hoped it could have brought in* *nearly the sum wanted I'd have sold all long ago. Don't believe that I'll **leave you** or yours **in the lurch**, Mat. I'd sell myself first.* □ *How does he come not to have been taken too? Did he run away and **leave Rivarez in the lurch?*** □ *She has had a hard life: after she had her third child, her husband walked out and **left her in the lurch.***

leave sb to oneself/to his own devices lë në punë të vet, lë vetëm

□ *When my aunt and I were **left to ourselves** by Mr. Dick's going to bed, I sat down to write my letter to the two old ladies.* □ *To our amazement, our host went away and **left** his guests **to their own devices.** □ I'll **leave you to yourself** now. I'm off to town.* □ *He **left us to our own devices;** he didn't mind how the work was done as long as it was finished when'd promised.* □ *Altogether I was not in the most jovial of moods, and Jacquie had long since **left me to my own devices.*** □ *He **leaves** his staff **to their own devices** as long as the work gets done he's happy.*

leave sb speechless lë pa gojë

□ *'Yes, it's for sale if you can afford it,' the dealer replied, mentioning a sum that **left** him **speechless.** □ 15-year-old Adrian Dannat has amazingly adult views on everything from girls to money. Since he **left** me **speechless,** I'll leave him to explain in his own words.*

leave sb to his own resources lë të kaurdiset me dhjamin e tij, lë vetëm (të zgjidhë një punë), lë në punë të vet

□ *Left entirely **to his own resources** I doubt whether Jeffries would last a week in this job.* □ *Don't organize the children all the time: **leave them to their own resources** once in a while.*

leave sth out of account/consideration s'e vë në hesap, nuk e përfill fare, nuk e marr parasysh

□ *There is one important fact that has been **left out of consideration.***

leave/let well alone lëre të mirën rehat, të mirën lëre mos e nga; më mirë prishet

□ *Our car used to go fine until my husband started trying to improve its performance. He doesn't have the sense to **leave well** enough **alone.*** □ *The living room is well furnished, and almost aggressively expresses Mrs. Harrington's personality. We are let know by it that she is a person of taste; but also that she does not often **let well alone.***

leave word (with sb) lë fjalë me

□ *If you have any news for me, **leave word with** the janitor; he will let me know.* □ *Please **leave word** at the office as to where I can find you.* □ *Please **leave word with** the secretary if you get a reply.*

left, right and center gjithkund, gjithandej, në të gjitha anët

□ *I've been looking for it **left, right and center**—where did you find it?* □ *The poor were sacrificed **left, right and center** to make money for a privileged few.*

lend sb a (helping) hand with sth ndihmoj, jap një dorë

□ ***Lend me a hand** in moving this table, won't you?*

lend an ear/one's ear to sb/sth dëgjoj me durim e simpati

□ *Most people are only too keen to talk about their disabilities to anybody willing to **lend an ear.*** □ *Friends, Romans, country men, **lend** me **your ears....** (W. Shakespeare)*

lend itself to 1. është i përshtatshëm

□ *The play **lent itself** admirably **to***

presentation on an open stage.
2. është objekt i, është i prirur ndaj
□ *Any system of taxation* **lends itself** *to manipulation by clever or unscrupulous men.* □ *The various malpractices* **to** *which the election arrangements could* **lend themselves** *were pointed out by neutral observers.*

lend wings (to) jep krahë
□ *... this sound of danger* **lent me** **wings.**

let alone 1. jo mo, aq më pak
□ *I am surprised that Jack has joined the Royal Air Force: he can't drive a car,* **let alone** *pilot an airplane.* □ *No hot drinks,* **let alone** *sandwiches, were available.* □ *You would not harm an earthworm,* **let alone** *a dog.*
2. pa përmendur, pa marrë parasysh
□ *There were seven people in the car,* **let alone** *a pile of luggage.* □ *There isn't enough room for us,* **let alone** *dogs and cats.*

let bygones be bygones të shkuara të harruara
□ *The two enemies agreed to* **let** **bygones be bygones** *and become friends again.* □ *After a long angry quarrel the two boys agreed to* **let** **bygones be bygones** *and made friends again.* □ *Don't you go worrying your little head about that. That's all over—finished and done with, as they say. Let's* **let bygones** **be**—*what's the word? Oh yes!* **Bygones.** □ *Sender hasn't* **let bygones** **be bygones** *without a murmur. He has laid down stringent conditions for the end of his self-imposed exile.* □ *What happened is a very long time ago. I'm going to ask her to* **let bygones be** **bygones.**

let down 1. ul poshtë, lëshoj
□ *She* **let down** *the bucket into the*

well. □ *The fisherman* **let down** *their nets and brought them up again with fish.* □ *The hem of your dress needs to* **let down** *an inch.*
2. lë në baltë; zhgënjej
□ *'You won't go to jail. I fixed it up. I didn't* **let** *you* **down.**' □ *He has been* **let down** *so much in the past that he trusts no one.*
3. shfryj
□ *'Some joker has* **let down** *the back tires of my car!'*
4. bie shpirtërisht
□ *He felt at once relieved and* **let down.**
5. çlodhem, relaksohem
□ *The team* **let down** *in the fourth quarter because they were far ahead.*

let fly (at sb) with sth shkreh, zbras; shtie, qëlloj, gjuaj; godas; shfrej
□ *When Newcombe held a game point for it, Smith* **let fly with** *an ace so fast and accurate that the Australian had no chance to return it.* □ *His voice was louder as he* **let fly at** *Francis Getliffe, Luke, me and all liberal-minded men.* □ *He aimed carefully and then* **let fly at** *the ducks.*

let (oneself) go shpërthej, lë ndjenjat të shfaqen lirisht
□ *Victoria had been entertaining the three other typists and the office boy with a vivid performance of Mrs. Greenholtz paying a visit to her husband's office. Secure in the knowledge that Mr. Greenholtz had gone round to his solicitors, Victoria* **let** **herself** *go.* □ *I cried for about ten minutes when I got back to the Wrenner but I suppose it does one good to* **let go.** □ *Myrtle was a little vulgar, and I must say that I like it. People who cannot* **let themselves go** *on occasion will not do for me.*

let sb/sth go lëshoj, liroj
□ *I took the wrist with the watch upon*

it, and twisted it. 'Jake,' you're hurting me,' said Anna. I **let** *her* **go**. □ *The police had taken Bates in for questioning but, after having established his identity and made a few routine inquiries, they* **let** *him* **go**. □ *Mr. Headstone,* **let** *me* **go***! Mr. Headstone, I must call for help.* □ *Keep hold of the reins and don't* **let** **go** *the horses.* □ *You must not* **let** **go** *any good chance of practicing the language.*

let/leave go of sb/sth lëshoj, lë të lirë
□ *You're mad, Roberts! For heaven's sake* **leave** **go** *of me!* □ *You cross the road with Granny, Sue—and don't* **let** **go** *of her hand till you're on the other pavement.* □ *Will they* **let** *the hostages* **go***?*

let in fut, lë të hyjë
□ *Air is* **let in** *through vents at the side of the car.* □ *'We asked him to call this afternoon. Go and* **let** *him* **in**.*' □ *Jane opened the window to* **let in** *the soft May air fresh from the sea.* □ *These shoes* **let in** *water.*

let into a/the secret i tregoj një të fshehtë
□ *Don't* **let** *Peter* **into the secret***; it won't remain a secret for long.* □ *I began to feel the warmth of being* **let into** *a family* **secret**.... □ *I'll* **let** *you* **into a secret***: I'm being sent abroad.*

let it go (at that) lë me kaq
□ *Either the slight gloss of irony which I put on the words had escaped him altogether, or he preferred to* **let** *it* **go***; I could not tell which, at the moment.* □ *I went carefully through the dead man's personal records yet Waterman was still a man in a mist as far as I was concerned. But something attempted, something done, I told myself and thought I would* **let** *it*

go at that*.* □ *He must put the best face on it, and* **let** *it* **go at that***.*

let loose liroj, lëshoj, lë të lirë
□ *Don't* **let** *the dog* **loose** *among the sheep.* □ *Just close your eyes and* **let** **loose** *your imagination.*

let me see pa të mendohem, pa ta shoh
□ *If the insurance company pays up I might invest in—***let me see***—Guy, what do you think of these Bolivian oil rigs?* □ *I think it was August, '64 we were there. No,* **let me see***, that was the summer Julia was expecting our eldest and we didn't go abroad at all. It must have been '63.*

let no grass grow under one's feet/not let/allow the grass (to) grow under one's feet veproj pa humbur kohë, veproj energjikisht
□ *Ay! They've* **not let grass grow under their feet** *in hunting out the man that did it!* □ *He was a real attorney. He had not '***allowed any grass to grow under his feet***', you bet.*

let off 1. shtie, qëlloj; shpërthej, plas, ndez
□ *A brass cannon was* **let off** *dangerously with real gunpowder.* □ *I told you that you were not to* **let off** *any more fireworks.*

2. fal, lëshoj pa ndëshkuar
□ *He was charged with petty larceny, but the court* **let** *him* **off***.* □ *'I'll be lenient this time, but you won't get* **let off** *again.'*

3. liroj nga një detyrë e pakëndshme
□ *'Is he on guard duty tonight?' 'No, he's been* **let off***.'*

let off steam 1. shpreh ndjenjat
□ *'No damage was done... Dinny said, and the outburst did the men good; gave them a chance to* **let off steam***.'* □ *We had better hold a public meeting, because people will want to* **let off steam** *on this issue.*

2. shkarkohem, shfrej dufin
□ *Still fuming with frustration, I sat down and applied for the vacancy, rather as a means of **letting off steam**.* □ *I **let off steam** by mimicking and muttering silently.*
3. derdh energjitë
□ *At the end of the term the students **let off steam** by having a big parade.* □ *The children ran around the playground at recess, **letting off steam**.*
let on nxjerr një të fshehtë
□ *It doesn't do to **let on** too much.* □ *He knew where the boy was but he didn't **let on**.* □ *If I tell you a secret, you won't **let on** to anybody, will you?*
let oneself/sth go 1. lëshoj veten
□ *He has **let himself go** a bit since he lost the job.* □ *'You're **letting yourself go**, my girl!' her father told her, eyeing the dowdy skirt and jumper, her lusterless hair.*
2. shfaq hapur ndjenjat, dëshirat etj.; lë të shpërthejnë ndjenjat, dëshirat etj.
□ *Go on, enjoy yourself, **let yourself go**.* □ *There's nobody but me, you can **let yourself go**. Don't try to control yourself. Have a good cry.*
let out 1. lëshoj, liroj, nxjerr
□ *At seven o'clock the next morning Jurgis was **let out** to get water to wash his cell.* □ *Don't **let the dog out**.* □ *How can we **let the water out**?*
2. lëshoj, zgjeroj (fustanin, pantallonat etj)
□ *I've got so fat that I'll have to **let the waistband out** several inches.* □ *The trousers need to be **let out** round the waist.* □ *This coat is rather tight. Do you think you could **let it out** for me?*
3. jap me qira
□ *Farm machinery is **let out** by the week.* □ *Boats are **let out** from the boathouse by the lake for $3 per hour.*

4. nxjerr, bëj të njohur
□ *Who **let out** the details of the reshuffle in the department? It was confidential now.* □ *Keep that to yourself—don't **let it out** to the press.*
let sleeping dogs lie nuk shtyj (trazoj, ngacmoj) urët
□ *We decided to **let the sleeping dogs lie** and not take them to court.* □ *For the time being there was no fear of public alarm, and for this reason he resolved to **let the sleeping dogs lie**.* □ *You say that he took part in a bank robbery when he was a young man. I say it all happened a long time ago, and we should **let sleeping dogs lie**.*
let slip 1. lë të shkojë (rasti etj.)
□ *He's a born cadger—never **lets slip** an opportunity of getting something for nothing.* □ *But you've always wanted to see Venice! It would be crazy to **let** a chance like this **slip**.* □ *Well, you've **let the opportunity slip** this time.* □ *For fear of **letting** something **slip** that he might otherwise secure, he was physically unable to make up his mind.*
2. nxjerr, më shpëton pa dashur
□ *Now remember that you told Carsons you'd be out of town last Friday, and don't **let it slip** that you weren't.*
let sb down easy ia them ëmbël (një lajm të keq)
□ *When you tell him that he hasn't got the job, **let him down easy**; he expected to get it.*
let sb/sth through lë të kalojë
□ *Most of their party were **let through** customs without an examination.* □ *A number of mistakes in the proofs were **let through**.* □ *I'm a hopeless driver, but the examiner **let me through**.*
let the cat out of the bag nxjerr një të fshehtë

□ *We were planning a surprise birth-day party for Mary, but Jack **let the cat out of the bag**, so now she knows about it.* □ *I've **let the cat out of the bag** already, Mr. Corthell, and I might as well tell the whole thing now.* □ *Her father kissed her when she left him, with lips which she was sure had trembled ...From the warmth of her embrace he probably divined that he had **let the cat out of the bag** for he rode off at once.* □ *Peter was rampant, boisterous, and—(this last epithet I choose to suppress, be-cause it would **let the cat out of the bag**).*

let the grass grow under one's feet rri duarlidhur (duarkryq)

□ *As soon as he heard that the post was vacant, he applied for it: he cer-tainly doesn't believe in **letting the grass grow under his feet**.* □ *Mr. Plowden was not a suitor to **let the grass grow under his feet**...* □ *And he would not **let the grass grow under his feet** either, he would go there at once and take very care...*

let things ride i lë gjërat të ecin vetiu, të marrin udhën e tyre

□ *Sometimes that night we had to discuss tactics; but just for this brief space we put the tactics out of our minds, we gave ourselves the satis-faction of **letting it ride**.* □ *Could the doctor after all be depended on to understand Rose? Might he not take it too seriously and have her taken away? It might be better just to **let things ride** for the moment.*

let things slide i lë gjërat të marrin tatëpjetën, sëe çaj kokën, sëe vras mendjen, s'më bëhet vonë

□ *She got depressed and began to **let thing slide**.* □ *'I'm terribly nervous that he has **let things slide**.'* □ *You*

may have some problems in running this office; the previous manager was often ill and **let things slide**.

lick one's chops/lips lëpin buzët, mprihet për të shtënë në dorë diçka

□ *The children, **licking their lips**, watched while the cake was carefully cut into equal portions.* □ *Maybe the old man has left all his money to charity. It's too soon to be **licking your lips**.* □ *The home team are sure they are going to win, so they are **licking their chops** in anticipation of tonight's game.*

lick one's wound lëpin plagët; mbledh (merr) veten

□ *'Where's George?' 'Gone off home to **lick his wounds**, I expect. You were pretty severe with him.'* □ *We have got to have peace—peace to **lick our wounds** and make a new world, and to do that we must try to understand each other.*

lick sb/sth into shape formoj, mbruj, i jap formë (trajtë); sjell në formë

□ *After a few months' training, the recruits had been **licked into shape**.* □ *They're not a very promising bunch but we'll soon **lick them into shape**.* □ *Now that we have got most of the material it can very soon be **licked into shape**.*

lick sb's boots/arse i lëpihem dikujt, i lëpij (i puth) këmbët (çizmet), i kreh bishtin dikujt, e laj dhe e lyej dikë

□ *He caved in straightaway. If you just spoke roughly to that chap, he was **licking your boots** the next moment.* □ *I am not interested in get-ting a promotion if it means to have to **lick the boss's boots**.*

lick sth up lëpij

□ *'Don't mop up the spilt milk; the cat will **lick it up**.* □ *The cat **licked up** the milk.*

lie at sb's door bie, i takon

□ *At whose door does the blame lie?*
□ *I accept that the responsibility for this lies squarely at my door.*

lie at anchor/its moorings qëndron e ankoruar

□ *The fleet lay at anchor half a mile off the headland.*

lie back shtrihem

□ *You don't have to do anything, just lie back and enjoy the journey.* □ *She was so weak and exhausted she had to lie back.*

lie behind sth qëndron prapa

□ *What lies behind the recent Cabinet changes is the need to get rid of certain unpopular ministers.* □ *I'm not sure what lay behind his remarks, but it wasn't good will.*

lie doggo rri fshehur; rri si i vdekur; rri pa lëvizur; rri pa u ndjerë

□ *... a snake clambering along a length of twig, blissfully unconscious the twig is another kind of insect lying doggo.* □ *This is all strictly for your ear only. Promise to lie absolutely doggo, Dinny, or I shan't say anything.*

lie down shtrihem

□ *He was lying down on the sofa when he came in.* □ *You're going to lie down for a bit.*

lie heavy on sth më bie rëndë

□ *The rich meal lay heavy on his stomach.*

lie in 1. rri në shtrat

□ *It's a holiday tomorrow, so you can lie in.* □ *They let us lie in, but I got up for breakfast.*

2. rri në shtrat (për të lindur)

□ *Normally, a woman will lie in a few hours before the birth of her child.*

lie in ambush rri në pritë

□ *The hunters lay in ambush for the tiger.*

lie in one's teeth/throat gënjej sy për sy, gënjej pa pikë turpi

□ *Thou comest to the Lady Olivia; and in my sight she uses thee kindly; but thou liest in my throat; that is not the matter I challenge thee for. (W. Shakespeare)* □ *'Nephew!' retorted Denis, 'you lie in your throat,' and he snapped his fingers in his face.* □ *If he says he never struck his wife, he is lying in his teeth: he was seen striking her many times.*

lie in state vendoset në sallën e përmortshme

□ *After the king died, his body lay in state for two days in the cathedral.*

lie in/on the bed one has made for himself ç'të mbjellësh, do korrësh; ç'kërkoi e gjet; si shtroi, fjet

□ *Don't accuse me. She has made her own bed—let her lie on it.* □ *'After all, mama, it is Louisa's affair,' said Mary distinctly, 'and we must remember—As she makes her bed, she must lie—but she'll regret it,' interrupted Mrs. Lindly.*

lie in wait zë pusi (pritë)

□ *A small group of rebels were lying in wait at the side of the road for the general's car.* □ *The habit of questioning and being questioned had given him a suspicious manner, or a manner that would be better described as one of lying in wait.* □ *The driver of the stagecoach knew that the thieves were lying in wait somewhere along the road.*

lie low rri fshehur e palëvizur; rri gojëkyçur

□ *He had been telling tote workers and customers that he was just 'lying low' for a while; now his idle boast that 'he would show the bloody traps something before long would come true.'* □ *But nobody up here believes that our dear old monster was killed by this flying saucer. We think it's* **lying low***.* □ *After committing the robbery, the thieves agreed that it should be a good idea to find a safe place to stay and* **lie low** *for a while.* □ *He's been* **lying low** *ever since I asked him for the money he owes me.*

lie one's head off kërdis me gënjeshtra

□ *Dad never did know all the details. Bill and I helped cover things up. On occasion we* **lied our heads off***.*

lie out of the whole cloth gënjej pa pikë turpi

□ *Cowperwood was* **lying out of the whole cloth** *in regard to bringing Sterner with him.* □ *He was* **lying out of the whole cloth** *about Frieda, but Angela didn't know and he knew she didn't know.*

lie up 1. rri në shtrat (gjatë një sëmundje)

□ *John must* **lie up** *for a few weeks until his leg mends.*

2. fshihem

□ *Nobody saw him all through the war. I think he* **lay up** *in the mountains.*

life and/or limb jetën

□ *Fire-fighters risk* **life and limb** *every day in their work.* □ *Meanwhile, the burnings go on. Teenagers throw bottles at firemen as they risk* **life and limb***.*

life and soul (of), the frymëzuesi, shpirti

□ *But resolved in his usual phrase, to 'come out strong' under disadvantageous circumstances, he was* **the life and soul** *of the steerage.* □ *Last week we had an office get-together and, as Joan was ill, she wasn't able to come. Tom was there, though, and was* **the life and soul** *of the party.* □ *With a grin that dares you to keep glum*

when he's around, Bruce Forsyth is, every affable inch of him, the **life and soul** *of the party, the host who keeps pouring even if you're not thirsty.*

life is not a bed of roses jeta nuk është fushë me lule

□ *I felt I should explain to them that* **life is not a bed of roses***.* □ *'Life is not a bed of roses,' they assume, but tomorrow will take care of itself. On this scale the working classes have been cheerful existentialists for ages.* □ *A parochial life is not* **a bed of roses***, Mrs. Mann.*

lift a finger luaj gishtin e dorës

□ *All worked hard except June. She wouldn't* **lift a finger***.* □ *He turned out to be a very poor friend: when I was in trouble he didn't even* **lift a finger** *to help me.* □ *They wouldn't even* **lift a finger** *to save their own grandmother without orders in triplicate.*

lift a weight off sb's mind qetësoj, i heq shqetësimin

□ *'Oh, a wonderful pudding!'... Mrs. Cratchit said that now* **the weight off her mind had been lifted***, she would confess she had her doubts about the quantity of flour.*

lift/raise one's hand against sb ngre dorën kundër

□ *When she* **lifted her hand against** *his life, he dared not openly charge her with the attempt, much less punish her for it.*

lift up one's eyes ngre sytë

□ *... and then Allar* **lifted up his eyes***.*

lift/raise one's voice ngre zërin, protestoj

□ *The workers are ever more forcefully* **lifting their voice** *against their bad living and working conditions.*

light on/upon sb/sth gjej rastësisht

□ *Luckily, I* **lit on** *a second-hand copy of the book.*

light up 1. ndez (cigaren, çibukun etj.)
□ *He settled comfortably in an arm-chair and **lit up**.* □ *Pop had **lit up** one of his best Havanas.*
2. ndez dritat e makinës etj.
□ *It's seven o'clock, and still one or two cars haven't **lit up**.*
3. gjallërohem, çelem në fytyrë
□ *His face was **lit up** with sudden excitement.*
□ *Marta's face **lit up** when she saw her old friend.*

like a bad penny sa paraja e kuqe
□ *I purposely didn't introduce you to my sister-in-law at the party, because once she gets an entry into anybody's home she keeps turning up **like a bad penny**.* □ *The conditioned response, once it is firmly in place, will always return, **like** the proverbial **bad penny**.*

like a bat out of hell si rrufe, si plumb, vetëtimthi
□ *When someone shouted 'Fire!', I got out of that house **like a bat out of hell**.* □ *When I saw him tearing out of his front door **like a bat out of hell** and into the telephone booth I thought his wife or one of the kids have taken ill or something.*

like a bird flutur; flutur e shpejtë
□ *My new car goes **like a bird**.*

like a bull in a china shop i ngathët si buall
□ *I wish I could mark everything fragile, that's how I feel, trucked in here. Listening to her, I feel **like a bull in a china shop**.*

like a bullet out of/from a gun si plumb, si vetëtimë, vetëtimthi
□ *Well, as soon as I read that bit in the 'Daily Tale' about the Loch Ness Monster being sent in Little Todday and Great Todday I was off **like a bullet out of a gun**. I mean to say,*

I don't want to miss seeing this monster. □ *'Would you care to take on the job yourself?' His 'No!' came **like a bullet from a gun**.*

like a cat on hot bricks si mbi gjemba (ferra)
□ *Suddenly Sugar screwed up his face in pain and grabbing one foot in his hands, hopped around **like a cat on hot bricks**. 'Can't we get a tram, Jack? My feet is givin' me hell in this new shoes.'* □ *Jenny, you're **like a cat on hot bricks**. I wish you'd either sit down with a book or some sewing, or go out for a walk.* □ *I don't know when he'll get the results of the exam, but he'll be **like a cat on hot bricks** until he does.*

like a lamb si qengj, i urtë si qengj
□ *He went up to his solicitor's office **like a lamb**, while Mrs. Pettigrew waited in the car below.* □ *Billy's been such a good boy, Mrs. Smith—never once got out of bed and took his medicine **like lamb**.*

like a shot 1. si veriu, si era, me vërtik
□ *That dog is getting deaf. He used to be off down the path **like a shot** when Charlie tooted his horn.* □ *When the headmaster said 'You may go now,' the student left the room **like a shot**.* □ *Of course I'll go **like a shot** if I'm in the way.*
2. me shumë dëshirë
□ *If I could hear of any chance of employment elsewhere. I'd take it **like a shot**.* □ *Young people like to be together, don't they. At least in the stage you two are at the moment. Anyway—I'd be into that flat **like a shot** if I was in your shoes.*

like/as sheep to the slaughter si cjapi te kasapi
□ *He was led **as a sheep to the slaughter**.*

like/as a thief in the night si hajduti natën

□ *'Oh,' he said to himself,' these erotic throes that come **like thieves in the night** to steal my High Churchmanship.'* □ *One day, perhaps, you glimpse a figure in a mirror, and realize, with a shock, that the funny little woman is you. The years, **like a thief in the night**, have stolen what you were.*

like a ton of bricks me forcë, me furi, me tërbim

□ *The fondest father does not welcome his offspring landing on his bed **like a ton of bricks** at 5:30 in the morning.* □ *If I print it, I shall have the Home Office down on me **like a ton of bricks**.*

like father, like son si i ati dhe i biri, bëmë o babë të të ngjaj

□ *George and his father never miss going to a football match on Saturdays: **like father, like son**.* □ *It was intellectual dishonesty again. **Like father, like son**. I bet you he knew all about it.* □ *Jean-Claude is acquiring the respectability that quite right eluded his father. But if there is any real threat to the power of the Duvalier, no one doubts that it will be a case of **like father, like son**.*

like it or not/no do apo s'do, e pëlqen apo jo

□ *Mr. Stewart should be made to realize, **like it or not**, that he is fifty years behind the times.*

like mad/crazy/blazes/hell si i çmendur, jashtëzakonisht shumë

□ *Most of us have experienced that excruciating pain when our calf muscles double up into a knot. We rub the calf **like mad** and the pain gradually eases.* □ *Everybody was rushing about **like mad**.* □ *They pushed the car **like mad** to get it moving.* □ *When*

*I rose at seven the next morning the wind was still blowing **like blazes**.* □ *Don't blame me. I tried **like hell** to dissuade him.*

like the look of sb/sth më pëlqen pamja e

□ *Silltoe **liked the look of** Desdemond and believed him.* □ *I **like the look of** your assistant—she should do very well.*

like water off a duck's back pa efekt

□ *Advice and correction roll off him **like water off a duck's back**.* □ *There is no use complaining to him; it's **like water off a duck's back**.*

line one's (own) pocket(s) mbush xhepat, pasurohem

□ *Just as in the 1914-1918 war, the merchant princes of France and Germany were continuing to **line their pockets** by trading with each other in war materials across Belgium.* □ *They used public appointments to **line their own pockets**. They combined fraudulently during elections to keep the plum jobs in the hands of their families and their friends.* □ *They say that, when he was Commissioner of Police, he **lined his pockets** with bribes from criminals.* □ *But what incensed his contemporaries was that he accused Sir Humphry Davy of **lining his pocket** at the Society's expense.*

line up 1. zë radhë; futem në radhë

□ *Fans began **lining up** early in the morning to buy their cup-tie tickets.*

2. rreshtoj, radhit; radhitem, rreshtohem

□ *The sergeant **lined** his platoon **up** on the parade-square.* □ *The trucks were **lined up**, ready to move off.*

link up with sb/sth bashkohet, lidhet

□ *The two spacecraft will **link up with** each other in orbit.*

lion's share of sth, the pjesa e luanit, pjesa më e madhe

□ *As usual, **the lion's share** of the budget is for defence.* □ *Polanski subscribes to the view that life is a jungle and so long as society makes sure that none of its members is actually starving, he sees no reason why **the lion's share of** the spoils should not go to the most talented.* □ *This misuse of the nation's money is partly due to the determination of specialists—the aristocrats of the profession—to keep **the lion's share of** medical practice under their control and within the hospitals where they reign supreme.*

listen in (to sth) 1. dëgjoj radion

□ *He likes to **listen in** late at night.* □ *I just don't find such programs worth **listening in to**.*

2. përgjoj; më zë (kap) veshi

□ *She loves **listening in to** other people's gossip.*

little by little pak nga pak, dalëngadalë

□ *His English is improving **little by little**.* □ *Little by little the flood waters receded.*

little or nothing gati (thuajse) asgjë; pak ose aspak

□ *She said **little or nothing** about her experience.* □ *'Besides, whether I am or no,' he added, 'that has **little or nothing** to do with his thinking me ungrateful.'*

live and learn sa të rrosh do mësosh

□ *I have been in the habit of leaving my door unlocked, and last night someone walked in and stole my wallet: you **live and learn**.* □ *'Don't be surprised,' he told me. '**Live and learn**.'*

live from hand to mouth rroj me të keq, me zgrip

□ *After he lost his job, the whole family had to **live from hand to***

mouth. □ *Ellie... Are you very rich?* □ *Captain Shatover. No, **living from hand to mouth**.* □ *Livens. I've got no home. I'm **living from hand to mouth**. I've got no work to keep them on.* □ ***Living** as he does **from hand to mouth**, nothing is too good for him to eat, and he will eat it.*

live in clover rroj në mirëqënie (luks, bollëk); rroj me të gjitha të mirat; notoj në bollëk

□ *I got you the place where you are now **living in clover**, and yet not a word of gratitude, or even acknowledgement, have you offered in return.*

live in the hope of jetoj me shpresën e

□ *The prisoner **lives in the hope of** an early release.* □ *The future looks rather gloomy, but we **live in hope**.*

live in the past jetoj me të kaluarën

□ *'Time passes. You are **living in the past**, Taylor*

live off/on the fat of the land jetoj me gjitha të mirat

□ *He is as vulgar as a hog, as awkward as an elephant, and as ugly as an ape. I believe he never had a friend. And yet for thirteen years he has **lived on the fat of the land**; for five years he has been in the Parliament and every man in the city has been willing to shake hands with him.* □ *The poor people starved, while a few **lived off the fat of the land**.* □ *He couldn't get out of London, **living on the fat of the land** in George's house.*

live on/off jetoj me

□ *You can't **live on** 200 calories a day.* □ *I can't **live on** that wage.*

live on one's own jetoj vetëm

□ *I don't think I'd have the courage to **live on my own** again.* □ ***Living on your own** is certainly better than life with a man you can't stand.*

live out one's days/life ngrys jetën, mbyll ditët

□ *These two old men had **lived out** their lives as industrial laborers.*

□ *No doubt he would **live out his days** in the same Welsh valley.*

live through përjetoj e mbijetoj

□ *He had **lived through** the worst years of the depression.*

live up to jetoj (veproj, sillem) sipas, në përputhje me

□ *He didn't **live up** to his reputation.*

lock in kyç brenda

□ *'Open the door, you idiot! You've **locked** me in.'*

lock out/out of lë, kyç jashtë; i mbyll derën

□ *Father threatened to **lock** us **out** if we didn't get back from the party before midnight.* □ *I went to empty the bins and found that I'd **locked** myself **out**.*

lock, stock and barrel me gjithçka, me laçkë e me plaçkë; tërësisht, plotësisht

□ *'So you're moving out tomorrow?' '**Lock, stock and barrel**. Leave me a trace behind!'* □ *He has sold the whole business, **lock, stock and barrel**, to his main competitor.* □ *I will agree to this year's dividend on condition we drop this foreign business in the future, **lock, stock and barrel**.*

lock sth away vendos në kyç

□ *He switched off the heating and **locked away** the food whenever he left the house.* □ *Take good care to **lock away** your jewellery before going away on holiday.*

lock the stable door after the horse has bolted pas pilafit, pas së vjelash, si kofini pas së vjeli

□ *Also, although the family's remaining valuables are now lodged with the bank, he has installed an electronic 999 dialing system. 'It can be expensive, **locking the door after the horse has bolted**.'*

lock up 1. burgos, mbyll në burg

□ *The idea of being **locked up** in jail filled her with terror.* □ *He was **locked up** for trying to break the Official Secrets Act.*

2. kyç, mbyll me kyç

□ *He always **locks up** last thing at night.* □ ***Lock** everything **up** securely before going away on holiday.*

lodge a protest protestoj, bëj protestë

□ *'I will have to **lodge a protest** against you, Mr. Annixter, in the matter of keeping your line fence in repair.'*

long shot, a qitje e largët (që synon larg, që ka synime të largëta)

□ *Cuspalt and Pforzheim are both very keen to start other excavations that might throw up the same thing, though it's **a** very **long shot**.* □ *Their committee had read 'Journey's End' and were lukewarm, but one man urged Sheriff to send it to George Bernard Shaw for an opinion. It was **a long shot**, but worth the risk.*

long and the short of it, the shkurt hesapi, me një fjalë, përmbledhtas

□ *Hector. Violet and I are married: that's **the long and the short of it**.* □ *'So we are to expect no help from the council?' 'That's **the long and the short of it**, I'm afraid.'*

long haul, a punë e gjatë; udhëtim (fluturim) i gjatë

□ *My forces were based on Benghazi and Tobruk, and it was **a long haul** by road from them.* □ *That's something which is only just beginning. It's all going to be **a long haul**, but I know of no more worthwhile and exciting challenge.*

long in the tooth i moshuar, i ka ikur mosha

□ *In my opinion, they are a bit **long in the tooth** for climbing the mountain.* □ *'Journalism is great fun when you're young,' he said. 'But I'm getting a bit **long in the tooth** to be jumping in and out of airplanes.'*

look after 1. kujdesem për

□ *He knows how to **look after** himself.* □ *The nurses **look after** their patients very well.* □ *The neighbours **looked after** the children when their mother was in the hospital.*

2. ndjek me sy

□ *Every man at his tent door **looked after** Moses, until he was gone into the tabernacle.* □ *They **looked after** the train as it left the station.* □ *He stood at the gate and **looked after** us.*

3. përgjigjem për

□ *Our neighbours are **looking after** the garden while we are away.*

look a gift horse in the mouth i shoh dhëmbët kalit të dhuruar, i qis bishta gjësë së dhuruar

□ *He thanked us for the watch but said he would have preferred a leather strap: talk about **looking a gift horse in the mouth**!* □ *John gave Joe a baseball but Joe complained that the ball was old. His father told him not to **look a gift horse in the mouth**.* □ *It was one of my mother's maxims never to **look a gift horse in the mouth**.*

look alive nxitoj, shpejtoj, luaj këmbët

□ *I say, **look alive**! We've only a couple of minutes left.*

look around/round 1. shikoj përreth

□ *I **looked around** the crowded amphitheatre, hoping to find an empty seat.* □ *'Say, **look around**. Isn't it a nice little room?' 'I have been*

around,' he answered, sweeping the room with a series of glances.

2. këqyr, vëzhgoj

□ *'Was there anything you particularly wanted, sir?' 'No, I'm just **looking around**.'* □ *'Have you got a good job yet?' 'No, I'm having a good **look round** before committing myself.*

look at 1. shqyrtoj

□ *The implications of the new legislation will need to be **looked at**.* □ *The committee wouldn't even **look at** my proposal.* □ *We must **look at** the question from all sides.*

2. kontrolloj

□ *Your ankle is badly swollen: I think the doctor ought to **look at** it.* □ *Will you please **look at** the battery of the car?* □ *My washing machine has gone wrong. I must get someone to **look at** it.*

3. shoh, konsideroj

□ ***Looked at** from that point of view, the job becomes easy.*

look back rikujtoj; hedh sytë (shikimin) prapa (në të kaluarën)

□ *When she turned away from the house, there were tears in her eyes, but she never **looked back** at it again.* □ ***Looking back**, I don't remember any inward struggle at all.* □ *An era in its history has ended. It may be worthwhile at this moment to **look back** and try to see what has happened.*

look before you leap matu pa hidh hapin

□ *In choosing a career, it's very important to **look before you leap**. You may regret it if you make the wrong decision.* □ *But all the same, go slow, go easy, **look before you leap**.* □ *The virtues and faults of both writers are those of their protagonists: Emily* *watchful, fastidious, ruthless but lacking in life; the vital, vivacious Vivienne, needing to **look** more carefully before she leaps.* □ *He will always feel annoyed when asked to **look before he leaps**—one cannot help that.*

look black duket e pashprese, s'ka asnjë fije shprese

□ *His wife is still seriously ill: things are **looking black** for him at the moment.* □ *'I know things **look black** at the moment,' said William, seeking to console his son. 'But who knows what's round the corner?'*

look daggers at sb shikoj gjithë inat (vëngër)

□ *He **looked daggers at** me when I told him he was lazy.*

look down on/upon përçmoj, përbuz

□ *Parents scrape and save and sacrifice themselves, and then their children **look down on** them.* □ *He was **looked down on** because of his humble background.* □ *All people with a sense of decency will **look down on** such conduct as that.* □ *Standing hand-in-hand, they both **looked down upon** the solemn countenance.*

look down one's nose at sb e sheh nën hundë dikë, sheh me përçmim (përbuzje)

□ *She **looks down her nose at** anyone who hasn't been to university.* □ *'It simply mustn't come out,' said Michael violently. 'I loathe the idea of a lot of swabs **looking down their noses at** you.'* □ *I gave the dog some lovely steak, and he **looked down his nose at** it!* □ *I've had a bellyful of being **looked down on** since I came to Hillchester. But when folks start **looking down their noses at** my daughter, I'm going to know the reason.*

look for 1. kërkoj

□ *'What are you **looking for**?' 'A little sympathy.'* □ *The chance which he had **looked for** was now freely offered to him.*

2. shpresoj, pres

□ *We shall be **looking for** an improvement in your work this term.* □ *It's too soon as yet to **look for** results.* □ *I **look for** important news by the next mail.*

look for a needle in a haystack kërkoj gjilpërën (qimen) në kashtë (në bar, në mullar), kërkon kallëza në borë

□ *Larry. No, it's such a big place that looking for a man there is like **looking for a needle in a haystack**.*

look for trouble kërkoj vetë belanë, kërkoj belanë me para

□ *You could see from his face that he was **looking for trouble**.* □ *There is no sense coming into a new place just **looking for trouble**.* □ *Everyone who wanders round the streets after dark is just **looking for trouble**.* □ *I must say that you are **looking for trouble**.*

look forward to pres me padurim, mezi pres

□ *She had been **looking forward to** leaving the hospital wards for a holiday in the Orkneys.* □ *'You'll be **looking forward** to the concert tonight.'* □ *We are so much **looking forward** to seeing you again.*

look full in/into face shikoj drejt në sy

□ *You'll meet difficulties, you must **look them full in the face** and devise ways and means to grapple with them.*

look here dëgjo

□ *'But **look here**, Alfred, you don't mean I ought to take it seriously, do you?'* □ *Now **look here** young man, I shall not accept the same excuse again.* □ ***Look here**, my good fellow, I* *told you that you'd got to put your nose to the grindstone. That means this kind of thing has got to stop.* □ *'Just a minute, dear—let me fix your tie for you.' 'Look here, honey, lay off the tie, and give me a kiss.'*

look in (on sb/at...) bëj një vizitë të shkurtër, kaloj nga

□ *I may look in at the party on my way home.* □ *Won't you look in on us next time you are in town?* □ *The doctor will look in again this evening.*

look into shqyrtoj, hetoj, studioj

□ *After what you have said I shall certainly look into the matter at the very first opportunity.* □ *Police are looking into the disappearance of a quantity of uncut gems.* □ *Perhaps you wouldn't mind looking into it for me?*

look on/upon 1. shikoj, vështroj, bëj sehir

□ *Most people aren't good enough to take part in first-class matches; they have to be content to look on.* □ *Don't look on passively but take an active part in the work.* □ *Why don't you play football instead of just looking on?*

2. quaj, konsideroj

□ *I look upon him as the betrayer of his country in its darkest hour.* □ *He is looked upon as something of an authority on rare books.* □ *Do you look on him as the best pupil of the class?*

look one's age tregon moshën e vërtetë, tregon vitet që ka mbi supe

□ *She doesn't look her age.* □ *You do not look your age at all.*

look out 1. kujdes, ki mendjen, ruaju, hap sytë

□ *'Look out! The train is starting; you're going to miss it.'* □ *'Look out,*

Peter, that step's not safe. □ *'Tell them to look out, the ceiling's threatening to fall in.*

2. kërkoj (të gjej)

□ *The policemen are looking out for burglars.* □ *I was looking out, as may be supposed to Mr. Spenlow's house.*

look over 1. shikoj me kujdes, shqyrtoj, inspektoj, hetoj

□ *We must look over the house before we decide to rent it.* □ *Will you please look over this essay of mine, and tell me what you think of it?*

2. kaloj, shikoj një për një

□ *Here's the correspondence; I've looked it over.* □ *Here's the mail; I've looked it over.*

look round 1. shikoj përreth (qark, përqark); kthej kokën

□ *She looked round when she heard the noise behind her.* □ *The other man looked round, and then wrinkled up his nose.* □ *Don't look round, I don't want him to notice us.*

2. peshoj mirë, studioj (shqyrtoj) të gjitha opsionet (mundësitë)

□ *We're going to look round a bit before deciding to buy a house.* □ *Don't make a hurried decision; look round well first.* □ *Look round carefully before you take the step.*

3. vizitoj

□ *Shall we look round the cathedral this afternoon?* □ *Have we time to look round the town before lunch?*

look sharp 1. nxitoj, shpejtoj

□ *'Finish it later,' he said with a threatening look. 'The fire needs making now, so come, look sharp and get some coal from the cellar.'* □ *Kit ordered him to bring three dozen oysters, and to look sharp about it!* □ *You had better look sharp, if you want to be in time.*

2. hap sytë, i bëj sytë katër

□ *'Do look sharp for old Bounderby, Loo!' said Tom with an impatient whistle.* □ *'He'll be off if you don't look sharp!'* □ *But look sharp, for they will be here in a couple of minutes.*

look through 1. studioj, rishikoj, shqyrtoj me kujdes

□ *'Have you read the man's references?' 'I haven't finished looking them through.'* □ *Look through your notes before the examinations.*

2. kaloj, hedh një sy

□ *He looks through several newspapers before breakfast.*

look to 1. mbështetem, var shpresat te

□ *Many people are looking to the new government to reduce unemployment.*

□ *'I have four children looking to me for their bread.'* □ *I look to you for help.*

2. kujdesem për

□ *Just look to it that this does not happen again.* □ *You should look to your health.*

look to one's laurels mbroj emrin e mirë (pozitën, titullin etj.)

□ *Bill is a very good runner. The champion will have to look to his laurels.* □ *One or two younger scientists are challenging him in this field, so he must look to his laurels.*

look up 1. përmirësohet

□ *Inflation is coming down; unemployment is coming down; things are definitely looking up.* □ *Prospects for the small builder are looking up.*

2. kërkoj në fjalor etj.

□ *He comes back with an enormous dictionary, sits down and looks up the word.* □ *I don't know the meaning of that word but I'll look it up in the dictionary.* □ *In the card catalogue*

she looked up the books she wanted.

3. ngre sytë

□ *He didn't look up from the newspaper when I entered the room.*

4. vizitoj, bëj një vizitë, kontaktoj, takoj

□ *Jack Duane gave Jurgis his address, or rather the address of his mistress, and made Jurgis promise to look him up.* □ *I'll come round and look you up.*

look up to respektoj, admiroj

□ *She has always looked up to her father.* □ *He was still a leading member of the local organization, much looked up to for his maritime war experience.* □ *His friends look up to him.*

loosen the purse strings zgjidh qesen

□ *Widespread loosening of the buying public's purse strings is bringing better business.*

loosen sb's tongue ia zgjidh gjuhën

□ *Wine soon loosened his tongue.*

loosen sth up shtendos muskujt, nervat etj.

□ *He loosened up with a few exercises before the big match.*

lord it over tiranizoj, sillem si tiran; dominoj, komandoj

□ *He likes to lord it over the junior staff.* □ *She'd be queen and lord it over all the other servants, and live in luxury.* □ *The office manager lorded it over the clerks and typists.*

lose an opportunity humb rastin

□ *She lost the opportunity of coming with us to see the old castle.*

lose color i iku çehrja, u zbeh, u prish në fytyrë

□ *He lost color when we told him about the accident.*

lose countenance humbas gjakftohtësinë (kontrollin)

□ *At that question he instantly* **lost countenance**. □ *He was afraid of* **losing countenance** *before the examiners.* □ *Though he was subjected to severe provocation, he did not* **lose countenance**.

lose count humb (ngatërroj) numrin

□ *So many came at once that I* **lost count** *of them.*

lose face turpërohem, humbas nderin, më nxihet faqja; bëj figurë të keqe

□ *The businessman was furious because his secretary's carelessness had caused him to* **lose face** *with his colleagues.* □ *So if they want to go through the highway they'll have to fight for it. But we guess they'll want to stick to the main route so as not to* **lose face**—*you follow?*

lose (give) ground 1. tërhiqem, humb terren, humb tokë

□ *The soldiers' position was under constant attack, but they refused to* **give ground**. □ *The enemy was steadily* **losing ground**.

2. mbetem mbrapa, humb avantazhin

□ *The leader is* **losing ground** *as the rest of the runners accelerate.*

lose heart dëshpërohem, demoralizohem, shkurajohem, bie moralisht, më thyhet zemra

□ *She is doing quite well, I must admit that—but so was Golding, and one day something like this will happen to her, and she'll* **lose heart** *like the rest of us.* □ *The team had won no games and it* **lost heart**. □ *He seemed to* **lose heart** *in the business after that.* □ *No matter what difficulties may come our way, we must* **never lose heart**.

lose no time in doing sth nuk humb kohë në

□ *Ford was coming, the papers said, and would be recruiting Irish technicians, for this was to be the start of an* Irish film industry. *I* **lost no time in** *seeking out the Irish producer of the film.*

lose one's balance humb ekuilibrin (drejtpeshimin)

□ *He cycled too fast round the corner,* **lost** *his* **balance** *and fell off.*

lose one's bearings humb orientimin; hutohem, humb toruan, s'di nga t'ia mbaj

□ *They* **lost their bearings** *in a snowstorm.* □ *It's easy to* **lose one's bearings** *in the woods.*

lose one's breath më merret (më zihet) fryma

□ *He ran too fast and nearly* **lost his breath**.

lose one's cool humb qetësinë

□ *He was extremely insulting—and very silly too. I don't know how I managed not to* **lose my cool**.

lose oneself in sth humb, zhytem i tëri në

□ *I soon* **lost myself in** *the excitement of the film.*

lose one's footing më rrëshqet këmba

□ *He* **lost his footing** *on the wet floor and fell.*

lose one's grip on sth humb kontrollin, më del nga dora (situata)

□ *Ahead by 2-1, Barrows show no signs of* **losing their grip**. *It's Newport who lack the effort and are doing all the flustered, careless, bad things.*

lose one's head humb toruan (mendjen)

□ *A lot of things went wrong during the meal, and finally the head-waiter simply* **lost his head** *and started screaming at other waiters.* □ *'Don't* **lose your head**—*keep calm!* □ *'I can't make that out,' said Michele. It's not like Rivarez to* **lose his head** *at a crisis.'*

lose one's heart to dashurohem cmendurisht pas, lë mendtë pas

□ *She **lost the heart to** the young man who had rescued her from drowning.*
□ *You might pass Eleanor Harding in the street without notice, but you could hardly pass an evening with her and not **lose your heart**!* □ *Tess's heart ached. There was no concealing from herself the fact that she loved Angel Clare all the more passionately from knowing that the others had also **lost their hearts to** him.*

lose one's life humb jetën
□ *As a young man he had nearly conquered Kanchenjunga, where he had failed to prevent fellow climbers from **losing their lives**.*

lose one's marbles çmendem, marrosem, më ikin mendtë, luaj nga mendtë
□ *The old chap is behaving very strangely: I think he's **lost his marbles**.* □ *'Maybe I am an old woman,' she says, 'but that doesn't mean I've **lost all my marbles**.'*

lose one's mind/senses luaj nga mendtë
□ *Young Amelia felt that she would die or **lose her senses** outright if torn away from her last consolation.*

lose one's nerve humb kurajën (guximin), e lëshoj veten, trembem
□ *He had climbed almost to the top of the rock, but **lost his nerve** and turned back.* □ *Anthony Butt's death had been doubly horrible, in its cause and in its details. To the very last he never **lost his nerve**.* □ *Dave felt Jennison's fear and confusion from the fact that he had apparently **lost the nerve** even to make a statement, he asked a question 'You're out of order, ain't you?'*

lose one's rag shpreh zemërimin (acarimin, padurimin etj.)
□ *His wife says: 'Barry's really very good-tempered. It's very rarely that*

he **loses his rag**. And I pick at him a lot, especially after a hard day with the hotel and the kids.*

lose one's shirt humb gjithçka (në bixhoz etj.)
□ *Uncle Joe spent his life savings to buy a store, but it failed and he **lost his shirt**.* □ *The same people who hopefully predicted that my father would **lose his shirt** now say that he had the Midas touch.* □ *He **lost his shirt** at the casino.*

lose one's temper humb qetësinë (durimin, vetëpërmbajtjen)
□ *When he realized how badly he had been treated, he **lost his temper**.* □ *She frowned. 'I shall **lose my temper**.* □ *You'll make me **lose my temper**. Why do you hide to so much from me?'* □ *Alice said nothing: she had never been so much contradicted in all her life before, and she felt that she was **losing her temper**.* □ *And the delegate, who was an Irishman and only knew a few words of Lithuanian, **lost his temper**.*

lose one's tongue humbi gojën, iu lidh (iu pre gjuha, goja)
□ *He was so astonished that he **lost his tongue**.* □ *'Now,' she went on, 'you must call me Aunt Flo and we shall be great friends.' But the boys, faced with this flamboyant and somewhat terrifying figure, had **lost their tongues**.* □ *Have you **lost your tongue**, Jack?*

lose one's way humb rrugën
□ *...you seem to me like one who has **lost his way** and made a great error in life.* □ *We **lost our way** in the dark.*

lose sight of 1. humb nga sytë
□ *'Drive on!' he shouted to the driver, 'and don't you **lose sight of** that fellow in front.'* □ *We followed at a distance: never **losing sight of** her but never caring to come very near,*

as she frequently looked around.
□ *We **lost sight of** the enemy in some thick scrub about half a mile to our front.*
2. harroj, nuk mbaj parasysh
□ *By all means, play sports at the University, but don't **lose sight of** your main reason for being there.* □ *My mind could take such decisions without **losing sight of** the main question.*

lose the thread of humb fillin e
□ *He stopped and, for a moment, appeared to have **lost the thread of** his remarks.* □ *Stop, please. I seem to have **lost the thread of** your argument altogether.* □ *The lecturer was not a very clear speaker and I soon **lost the thread of** his argument.*

lose the use of humb përdorimin e
□ *The doctors did what they could, but he **lost the use of** both legs.*

lose touch with humb lidhjet me
□ *It's difficult to keep up with events when you live in the country, you tend to **lose touch**.* □ *Do write me as often as you can. I don't want to **lose touch with** you.*

lose track of sb/sth 1. humbas fillin
□ *I **lose track of** the number of times he repeated what he had already said.*
2. humb gjurmët (kursin)
□ *I can follow his career up to 1996, then quite abruptly I **lose track of** him.* □ *His plane was **lost track of** about two hours out from London Airport.*

lost cause, (a) kauzë (çështje) e humbur
□ *He will never be a successful politician: he supports too many **lost causes**.*

lost in thought i kredhur, i zhytur në mendime
□ *At four in the afternoon Miss Aldclyfte was sitting in her study, clothed in mourning and **lost in thoughts**. She had sat erect for more than an hour utterly unconscious of every thing around.*

love is blind dashuria është e verbër
□ ***Love is blind** and lovers cannot see the pretty follies that they themselves commit.* □ *'His wife's not just plain. Where were his eyes when he met her?' 'Ah well, **love is blind**.'*

M

make a beginning/start filloj, nis, bëj hapin e parë, ia hyj një punë

□ *The only practical way is to* ***make a small beginning*** *and then try to extend it.* □ *You've* ***made a start***, *anyway. If your clients are satisfied they're likely to bring you more business.*

make a beeline for i bie drejt (shkurt)

□ *We were very thirsty so, as soon as we arrived at the hotel, we* ***made a beeline for*** *the bar.* □ *The path was a regular will-of-the-wisp. He must* ***make a bee line*** *for it.* □ *He was now* ***making a beeline for*** *indoors to discover what Steve was doing.*

make a bolt/dash/run for ia mbath, iki me të katra, ia mbath këmbëve

□ *I became oblivious of the passage of time and I had to* ***make a bolt for*** *it to get the bus.* □ *The prisoner* ***made a dash for*** *the open window while their guard's attention was distracted.* □ *'I wanted to ask you about Dartie.' 'Flitted,* ***made a bolt*** *to Buenos Aires with the fair Lola.'*

make a break for it iki, arratisem nga burgu

□ *He was looking at her frequently, perhaps to make sure of catching her if she decided to* ***make a break for it.*** □ *I'm not so daft as to* ***make a break for it*** *on my long-distance running.*

make a call bëj një vizitë të shkurtër

□ *He* ***made a*** *short* ***call*** *to his medical adviser.* □ *He soon* ***made a call*** *at Fieldhead.*

make a change ndryshoj, bëj një ndryshim

□ *You haven't half* ***made a change*** *here, Mrs. Black. You must have worked very hard to get the place cleaned up like this.* □ *Having checked over the leadership problem and* ***made*** *the necessary* ***changes***, *I was satisfied that I had a team which would collectively handle the task.* □ *We should necessarily* ***make a change*** *in our plan.*

make a clean breast of sth hap zemrën, tregoj (rrëfej me sinqeritet, me zemër të hapur)

□ *If worst came to the worst, he could* ***make a clean breast of*** *it to Butler and receive aid.* □ *'I wonder, Roger never told me.' 'He never told me either,' said the Squire. 'It was Gibson, who came here and* ***made a clean breast of*** *it, like a man of honor.'* □ *The criminal* ***made a clean breast of*** *everything he had done.*

make a clean sweep spastroj, i vë fshesën

□ *We shall have to* ***make a clean sweep*** *of all these old books and papers.* □ *Why should you* ***make a clean sweep*** *of your old furniture?*

make a day of it kaloj gjithë ditën

□ *If we are going to London this morning, we might as well* ***make a day of it*** *and go to a show in the evening.*

make a decision marr vendim

□ *'Sorry,' he would say in answer to questions about his future, 'but I'm not* ***making*** *any major* ***decision*** *just now.'* □ *I advise you not to* ***make*** *any* *hasty decision.* □ *Have you made a decision yet?*

make a difference 1. ka rëndësi; ka efekt (ndikim)

□ *A person's appearance makes a difference in how others judge him.* □ *It makes a difference how you do it.*

2. bën dallim

□ *She makes no difference between her two sons.*

make a face/faces at sb ngërdheshem, shtrembëroj fytyrën e përdredh buzët

□ *The schoolboy made a face at his teacher's back.* □ *Joe took a drink of whisky and made a face. He was at the stage when alcohol is repulsive and essential at the same time.* □ *Wormold began to make faces in the glass. 'What on earth are you doing, Father?' 'I wanted to make myself laugh.'* □ *Mr. Bailey had been trying his cravat, getting on his coat, and making hideous faces at himself in the glass.* □ *Miss Shepherd makes a face as she goes by and laughs to her companion.*

make a fool of oneself/sb bëhem budalla, sillem si budalla; vë në lojë, bëj budalla

□ *Your friend, the Buccaneer has made a fool of himself, he will have to pay for it!* □ *I went there, I suppose, to make a fool of myself, and I am quite sure I did.*

make after sb/sth ndjek

□ *The rabbit shot from its burrow and two dogs made after it at top speed.* □ *The policeman made after the burglar.* □ *They made after him in the car.*

make a/one's fortune vë pasuri, bëj para

□ *He has made a fortune, bought his family a fabulous house.* □ *He made a*

small fortune, intent on marriage and settling.

make a fuss of/over sb/sth 1. bëj zhurmë, bëj potere

□ *She said: 'I shall say nothing about it. I don't see any use in making a fuss.'* □ *'Oh!... You make such a fuss over everything,' Uncle Podger would reply.*

2. tregoj vëmendje të veçantë për

□ *A lot of fuss was made of the play, but it wasn't a success.*

make a go of sth i dal mbanë, i dal në krye, arrij sukses, më vete mbarë

□ *We don't know whether it will be successful, but we are going to try to make a go of it anyway.* □ *He undertook the task and has made a go of it.* □ *He was sure he could make a go of the filling station.*

make a hash of sth e bëri çorap, e bëri rrëmujë, e bëri lesh e li

□ *The clumsy workman made such a hash of the job that it had to be done over.*

make a hit 1. pëlqehet shumë, ka sukses

□ *The young playwright made a hit with his first play.* □ *Mary's new dress made a hit at the party.*

2. bë përshtypje të mirë te

□ *You've made quite a hit with Bill.*

make a hole/dent in dhjetoj, ha një pjesë të madhe

□ *The holiday will make quite a dent in our savings.* □ *The hospital bills made a big hole in his savings.*

make a joke about/of sb/sth qesh me, bëj shaka me

□ *I want to be with you, to watch you unfold out of sadness and see you laugh at any silly stupid joke I make.*

make a laughing stock of oneself
bëhem gazi i botës

□ *'If you go on behaving like that you'll **make a laughing stock of yourself**.'* □ *When he talked, he talked nonsense, and **made himself the laughing stock** of his hearers.*

make a/one's living nxjerr bukën e gojës

□ *Sarah: Dave is making furniture by hand. Monty: He **makes a living?** Sarah: They live! They're not prosperous but they live.* □ *The outer world is what we wake up to every morning of our lives, is the place where, willy-nilly, we must try to **make our living**.* □ *He was **making a bare living** at times...*

make allowance (for) marr parasysh

□ *The financing of road improvements is just as much of a burden to one place as another when **allowances** are **made for** size and revenue.* □ *The jury were asked to **make all allowances for** the age of the accused.* □ *Now that I had seen this attitude abroad, I was even less ready to **make allowances for** it.*

make a long story short/make short of a long story i bie shkurt

□ *To **make short of a long story**, I am afraid I have wanted an object.*

make amends to sb for sth laj, shlyej, shpaguaj, kompensoj

□ *The young man **made amends for** the damage he caused by paying for it out of his wages.* □ *He promised to **make amends to her for** his carelessness.*

make a mess of sth bëj lëmsh, bëj lesh e li, bëj rrëmujë

□ *'Not one man in a hundred can sharpen a quill properly. You must have done it before.' 'No.' 'Then you must have good hands. I usually*

make a mess of them myself.' □ *I must say you've, certainly, **made a mess of things**.* □ *'I suppose your father had no head for business, and **made a mess of it**.'* □ *If you interfere in such a matter, you'll **make a mess of it**.*

make a mountain out of a molehill e bën mizën (pleshtin) buall (ka), e bën qimen tra

□ *You are **making a mountain out of a molehill**. They never have epidemics here.* □ *I can see you have bruised your knee but don't **make mountains out of molehills**, you certainly are not badly hurt.* □ *Mary is still complaining about the trick that Jack played on her last week: she is **making a mountain out of a molehill**.* □ *You're not hurt badly, Johnny. Stop trying to **make a mountain out of a molehill** with crying.*

make a move 1. nisem

□ *It's getting dark, we'd better **make a move**. It was time to go home, but no one **made a move**.* □ *Unless we **make a move** soon, we shall not get there in time.*

2. veproj

□ *We are waiting to see what our competitors do before we **make a move**.*

make an agreement bëj marrëveshje

□ *To Elizabeth it appeared that her family had **made an agreement** to expose themselves as much as they could during the evening.* □ *They went and told him that they were ready to **make an agreement**.*

make a name for oneself bëj emër

□ *The Prime Minister favored Gott, who had **made a** great **name for himself** in the desert.* □ *He's **made** quite a **name for himself** as an after-dinner speaker.*

make answer/reply përgjigjem
- □ *'What did you do before?' she asked. 'I was a student of history,' I made answer.*

make an attempt on orvatem të thyej rekordin etj.
- □ *A fresh attempt is being made on the land speed record later this year.*
- □ *The Kenyan runner made two further attempts on the 5000 meters record that summer.*

make an attempt on sb's life orvatem të vras
- □ *Last night a fresh attempt was made on the life of the Crown Prince.*
- □ *Further attempts have since been made on his life.*

make an effort përpiqem, bëj përpjekje
- □ *He smiled as did the others in the room, who however made some slight effort to conceal their humor.*
- □ *Far down the room he saw Elisabeta and Katrina, risen from their seats, staring in fright; he made one effort to go to them.*
- □ *James made a great effort and rose to the full height of his stork-like figure.*
- □ *Some woe appeared to be weighing her down, though she was clearly making an effort to bear up.*
- □ *Ned realized that he had been a fool to start provoking Robert by insinuating that he had no time for his old friends, and he made a lame effort to back out.*

make an end of sth përfundoj, i jap fund
- □ *'And there is not another word to tell Agnes,' said I when I had made an end of my confidence.*

make an example of sb e bëj shembull dikë
- □ *The headmistress decided to make an example of the pupil and expel him from the school.*
- □ *I shall make an example of any student who misbehaves.*

make an exhibition of oneself tregon se kush është, i nxori bojën vetes, u bë palaço
- □ *'Pull yourself together, man.' 'Don't make an exhibition of yourself in the street.'*
- □ *People at the party were embarrassed when Frank got at the party and made an exhibition of himself.*

make an issue (out) of sth bëj problem një çështje të parëndësishme
- □ *It's only a small disagreement— let's not make an issue of it.*

make a mental note of sth ngulit (fiksoj) në mendje
- □ *I made a mental note of the phrase.*
- □ *Here is another point that ought to be made a mental note of.*

make a monkey out of bëj budalla (palaço)
- □ *Those children have been trying to make a monkey out of me.*

make a noise about sth ankohem me të madhe, bëj zhurmë rreth
- □ *She made a lot of noise about the poor food.*
- □ *It can't be helped, you know. He is not the only one in the same fix. You mustn't make a noise about it!*

make a note of shënoj, mbaj shënim
- □ *I must make a note of that.*

make a parade of bëj një paradë të
- □ *He's always making a parade of his knowledge.*

make a point of doing sth bëj çmos, bëj kujdes të veçantë (të bëj diçka të rëndësishme, të domosdoshme); këmbëngul, e bëj rregull (normë)
- □ *Do you make a point of being on time for work and social appointments?*
- □ *She makes a point of having someone around to sort things for her.*
- □ *He always makes a point of*

checking that the back door is locked before he leaves the house. □ *Very good. I'll* **make a point of** *clearing this up.* □ *He* **makes a point of** *getting up early.*

make a practice/habit of sth e bëj zakon

□ *You may occasionally use the emergency exit if you are in a hurry, but don't* **make a practice of** *it.* □ *He* **made a habit of** *taking a nap after lunch.* □ *'Use my telephone by all means, but don't* **make a habit of** *it.'* □ *He* **made a practice of** *doing his exercises in front of an open window.*

make a rod for one's own back e kërkoj vetë belanë

□ *By putting the former president in prison, the new president may be* **making a rod for his own back.**

make a scene bëj sherr, bëj potere

□ *I could hardly face the thought of seeing Magdalena at once. She would expect me to* **make a scene** *and I didn't feel energetic enough to* **make a scene.** □ *She was terrified she would burst into tears and* **make a scene.** □ *I thought of complaining about the service in that restaurant, but I didn't want to* **make a scene.** □ *If they had to part, he would not* **make a scene.** □ *He lighted his cigarette. After all Irene had not* **made a scene.**

make a secret of mbaj të fshehtë

□ *Uncle Saunders had* **made no secret of** *his disapproval and disappointment.* □ *You knew I was doing that at the club. I never* **made a secret of** *that.*

make a show of sth bëj sikur, shtirem

□ *But he sat perfectly quiet and took his breakfast at his leisure, or* **made a show of** *doing so, for he scarcely ate*

or *drank, and frequently lapsed into long intervals of musing.*

make a song and dance about sth bëj shumë zhurmë; shqetësohem pa masë

□ *You may be a bit upset, but it's really nothing to* **make a song and a dance about.** □ *Kay's parents* **made a** *dreadful* **song and dance about** *her being out after midnight.*

make a spectacle of oneself lë nam; tërheq vëmendjen e të tjerëve

□ *He* **made a spectacle of himself** *by arguing with the waiter.*

make a splash bën sensacion, bën bujë

□ *She has* **made quite a splash** *in literary circles with her first book.* □ *The big party he threw for his friends* **made** *quite* **a splash** *in the local newspapers.* □ *He hadn't much appetite for the feast he had insisted on providing. It wasn't simply self-indulgence, the wish to compensate himself for the lean times he'd been having; nor was it wholly, the desire to* **make a splash** *and assert himself.*

make a stand against/for bëj qëndresë

□ *'We'd like to have you on our platform.' Bernard thought that the moment had come to* **make a stand.** *'I'm afraid that's quite unlikely,' he said.* □ *If you only* **make a firm stand** *against these builder chaps, you'll get them down.* □ *Paul was dreadfully frightened, but still he* **made a stand** *for the absent Glubb, though he did it trembling.*

make at sb sulmoj; i turrem, i sulem dikujt

□ *His attacker* **made at** *him with a knife.* □ *He* **made at** *the man with a heavy ruler snatched from the table.* □ *The child* **made at** *the dog with a stick.*

make away with sb/sth 1. vras, zhduk

□ *'You don't think she had any motive*

*for **making away with** herself,
Mother?'*
2. rrëmbej, grabit
□ *While we were having coffee two
small boys **made off with** our suitcases.*
make believe e zë, hiqem, përfytyroj
veten si
□ *'Inside me,' she said, 'I've been
making believe I was a little girl
again, I've been acting the part.'*
□ *The children **made believe** that
they were cowboys and Indians.*
make bold to do sth guxoj, marr guximin; rrezikoj
□ *Dobbin **made so bold** as to bring
her refreshments.* □ *I **made so bold** to
say Bobby Jones's feat of the so-
called Grand Slam will not happen
again because today golf has turned
into a money-making industry.* □ *I
make bold to give you a piece of
advice.*
make both ends meet prish (shpenzoj)
me zgrip, e nxjerr muajin me të keq, e
shtyj si mundem, bëj hall me ato që
kam
□ *I have to keep writing if I'm to
make both ends meet and when I am
homeless I can settle down to
nothing.* □ *What was it like to be a
Roman legionary? Just how did a
medieval peasant **make ends meet?**
□ *I also took odd jobs—telephonist,
clerk, so on. Eventually, I just
couldn't **make both ends meet** and I
had to go back home.* □ *'And Con
says,' went on Lady Mont, 'that he
can't **make two ends meet.'** □ *I shall
probably have enough to do to **make
both ends meet**,... now my occupation's gone.*
make bricks without straw bëj diçka
pa mjetet e nevojshme, bëj petulla
pa vaj

□ *Ye shall no more give the people
straw to **make bricks**, as heretofore:
let them go and gather straw for
themselves. (Exodus, V7)* □ *Teaching
English with no books is like **making
bricks without straw**.* □ *Sheila has
lovely hair anyway. The best hair-
dresser in the world couldn't do much
with mine. You can't **make bricks
without straw**.*
make capital (out) of sth fitoj kapital
nga
□ *The opposition parties **made** political **capital out of** the disagreements
within the Cabinet.*
make certain sigurohem; siguroj
□ *'I think Mr. Brown has gone out,'
the landlady said, 'but I'll run
upstairs and **make certain**.'* □ *It is
said that the show begins at seven,
but you ought to **make certain**.
□ **Make certain** he comes at once.*
□ *'Simpson has withdrawn.' 'Then
that **makes** Edward's election certain. Most of our members distrust
Bolton's radical views.*
make conversation bëj bisedë
(muhabet)
□ *He didn't say anything interesting:
we were just **making conversation**.*
make (sheep's) eyes at sb perëndoj
sytë (për dikë që dua), e ha me sy,
shikoj me dashuri
□ *The lovers were **making sheep's
eyes at** each other over the table.*
□ *Do you think I don't know what a
woeful day it was for the soft little
creature when you first came in her
way—smirking and **making** great
eyes at her.* □ *I'll be bound, as if you
couldn't say boh! To a goose! He was
handsome that all the girls **made eyes
at** him.*
make for 1. shkoj, drejtohem
□ *'I can't listen to anymore of this*

rubbish!' he said, and **made** *for the door.* □ *It's late, we had better turn and* **make** *for home.* □ *Dinny* **made** *for Melton Mews and met her sister on the doorsteps.* □ *The clerk* **made** *resolutely for the door.*

2. turrem, sulem

□ *Two sentries* **made** *straight for him with drawn swords.* □ *When he was halfway across the field the bull* **made** *for him and he had to run.*

3. mundëson, kontribuon

□ *Does early rising* **make** *for good health?* □ *Industrial development* **makes** *for a rapid improvement in agricultural technique and a rise in agricultural production.*

make free with marr (përdor) lirisht, pa pyetur (si gjënë time)

□ *He kindly* **made** *free of his library for my research.* □ *While your friends were here they* **made** *free with our food supplies, so now there is hardly any food left.* □ *Bob* **makes** *free with his roommate's clothes.* □ *He seems to have* **made** *free with my oil while I was away.*

make friends with sb miqësohem, zë miqësi me

□ *If you want to* **make** *friends with them, you must be frank and modest.* □ *David finds it hard to* **make** *friends with other children.* □ *Jurgis had* **make** *friends with some men by this time.*

make fun of tallem me, vë në lojë

□ *The students* **made** *fun of the professor's strange way of speaking.* □ *We all* **make** *fun of him behind his back, of course.* □ *'You're* **making** *fun of me,' she said in a low voice. 'I'm quite serious.'* □ *His efforts to improve himself are constantly* **made** *fun of.*

make game of tallem, qesh, vë në lojë

□ *She had all the talents which qualified her ... to* **make** *game of his scruples.* □ *There was another boy, Tommy Traddles, who I dreaded would* **make** *game of me and pretended to be dreadfully frightened to me.* □ *Julia. I couldn't bear it any longer. Oh, to see them sitting there at lunch together, laughing, chatting,* **making** *game of me.*

make good realizoj, përmbush, mbaj

□ *He made many other fine promises that have still to be* **made** *good.* □ *He* **made** *good his word and arrived in time.* □ *'You can see that I'm prepared to* **make** *good my promise.'*

2. plotësoj mungesën e, zëvendësoj, kompensoj; rregulloj

□ *Dr. John is much concerned at the underequipment, and regards* **making** *good the lack of a stretcher as particularly important.* □ *In addition to the fee, any expenses incurred by me really ought to be* **made** *good.* □ *We'd like to borrow these glasses; if any are broken, we shall* **make** *good the loss.* □ *We must* **make** *good the days we lost when rain prevented us from working in the fields.*

3. shkon (ecën) mirë, përparon

□ *It is probably due to his protection and advice that I remained at Sanburst, turned over a new leaf, and survived to* **make** *good.* □ *He was the white-collar one of the family, the one who was going to* **make** *good and redeem all their fortunes.* □ *He* **made** *good in high school.*

make good time udhëtoj shpejt

□ *We* **made** *good time in spite of the poor state of the roads.*

make great/rapid etc. strides bëj progres të mirë, të shpejtë; bëj hapa përpara, përparoj

□ *Tom has **made enormous strides** in his maths this term.* □ *The country is **making rapid strides** in the development of its educational system.* □ *I thought Johnny was just stupid but he's **made** such **tremendous strides** since he went to his new school. I'm sure the teaching must have been at fault before.*

make haste nxitoj, shpejtoj

□ *I shouted 'Hey!' and Finn came slowly on. He never **makes haste**.* □ *'I'm not ready.' 'Well then you had better **make haste** and be ready.'* □ *I wish she'd **make haste** to finish it. He said her father had gone and he must **make haste** and get himself ready.* □ ***Make haste** now, or we shall miss our train.* □ *There's folks **making haste** all one way afore the window; I doubt something's happened.*

make havoc prish, dëmton, rrënon, shkatërron

□ *She began **making havoc** in the old arrangements.* □ *Then I changed and bicycled off down the hill, with the wind **making havoc of** my hair.*

make hay of 1. ngatërroj, bëj lesh e li, bëj lëmsh

□ *Who has been **making hay of** these papers? I left them in a good order and now look at the mess they are in.* □ *Oh! Father, how you are **making hay of** my things!*

2. rrah paq

□ *The champ has **made hay of** every opponent he has faced.*

3. përmbys

□ *He **made hay of** the careful arguments of opposition speakers.*

make hay while the sun shines hekuri rrihet sa është i nxehtë

□ ***Make hay while the sun shines**: enjoy yourself while you are young.* □ *I've heard about **making hay while**

the sun shines but it's a bit mean to start chatting up your brother's girlfriend while he's in hospital.*

make head çaj (eci) përpara

□ *They **made head** against the wind.*

make head or tail of sth kuptoj, marr vesh, i jap dum

□ *Jack's handwriting is terrible: I can't **make head or tail of** this letter he has written.* □ *He was for some time completely unable to **make head or tail of** the blotted scrawl.* □ *She'd take some notes, which she subsequently could not **make head or tail of**.* □ *He spoke so rapidly and in such a confused way that I could **make neither head nor tail of** his meaning.* □ *Then there are those new styles of barometers, the long straight ones. I never can **make head or tail of** those.*

make headway përparoj, eci (çaj) përpara; bëj përparime, bëj hapa përpara

□ *In the meanwhile we had been **making headway** at a good pace for a boat so overloaded.* □ *The ship was **making headway** against the heavy seas.* □ *You have been trying to persuade him for three hours. Did you **make** any **headway**?* □ *The police have been working hard on the case, but there are few clues, and so they have not **made** much **headway**.* □ *On some narrow stretches they **made** such feeble **headway** against the current that it saved time to carry the canoes and walk.*

make history hyn në histori

□ *'Some people are going to **make history** and some aren't,' Taffy said. 'I think this'll go down in the history books. It deserves so.'* □ *Floyd Patterson **made** boxing **history** at the Polo Grounds here tonight by sensationally defeating Sweden's Ingemar Johansson and becoming* *the first man to regain the world heavyweight.*

make it arrij, realizoj, përmbush me sukses; kam sukses

□ *He's never really made it as an actor.* □ *I should be up at half past seven tomorrow morning. I'll never make it. I'll just have to be late.*

make it hot for sb ndëshkoj, ia rregulloj qejfin; i flas ashpër

□ *The teacher said that she would make it hot for the next student who wasted her time*

make it snappy bëj shpejt, luaj duart

□ *Micky slapped a pound note down on the counter. 'Make that three,' he ordered. 'And make it snappy.'* □ *'May I ask a favor of you?' 'Ask away, but make it snappy.* □ *I should have been out of here five minutes ago.' Two cups of coffee, and make it snappy; we're in a hurry.*

make it one's business to do sth ia vë detyrë vetes

□ *He made it his business to check every day that his elderly neighbours were well.* □ *If Ned had known you were in this kind of state, he'd have made it his business to help you.*

make light of nuk i jap rëndësi, e marr lehtë

□ *The cut in his finger seemed quite deep to me, but he made light of it: 'It's nothing,' he said.* □ *He makes light of his illness.* □ *The doctor waved his hand, as if to make light of it.* □ *The old woman was so decent and contented, and made so light of her infirmities that they both took an interest in her.*

make little of 1. s'i jap rëndësi

□ *She made little of her troubles.*

2. kuptoj fare pak gjë

□ *I studied the letter for a long time, but could make little of it.*

make love (to) bëj dashuri

□ *He refused to make love before they were married.* □ *Casanova was supposed to have made love to dozens of women.*

make mention of përmend, zë ngoje

□ *He made mention of a book he read recently.* □ *In his letter he made no mention of your work.* □ *She made no mention to Frank of her recent discovery.*

make merry argëtohem, dëfrej, bëj qejf, e kthej përmbys

□ *We made merry about Dora's wanting to be liked and Dora said I was a goose and she didn't like me at any rate...* □ *Jason: Wake up, make it lively. This is a wedding. Bring out the bunting, make merry, look alive, if you can.*

make mincemeat of sb/sth dërrmoj, bëj pluhur e hi

□ *He made mincemeat of his opponent's arguments.*

make/do mischief ndez sherrin, shtie në grindje, fut spica

□ *Don't let her make mischief between you, she's only jealous.* □ *He had never in the past hesitated to make mischief if it served his curiosity.* □ *She had a tactless tongue, but it came from an honest heart, not from a desire to do mischief.*

make money bëj para

□ *The way he saw it, Ned was making him a bit of a sermon, to clear his own conscience for being a business man and making money.* □ *You are a Templar. You must know ways of making money. They all did, didn't they?* □ *I like the way you edit this magazine, but you'll never make any money.*

make/earn money hand over fist fitoj para me thes

□ *Ever since they opened their shop they have been **making money hand over fist**.*

make much of sth/sb 1. i kushtoj shumë vëmendje, i jap shumë rëndësi, e vlerësoj (respektoj) shumë; theksoj

□ *In conversation he **makes much of** his aristocratic connection.* □ *Running has always been **made much of** in our family.* □ *They talk together constantly, and sit long at meals **making much of** their meal.* □ *A child, a little girl, she hoped—for he always liked little girls and **made much of** them—would quiet him. If she could only have a little girl now.*

2. jam në gjendje të kuptoj

□ *I couldn't **make much of** his speech. It was all in Russian.* □ *I listened to his lectures, but I didn't **make much of** them.*

make no bones about nuk hezitoj, nuk më vjen zor; pranoj menjëherë; them hapur (pa hezitim)

□ *If only Bounderby of Coketown had been in question, you would have joined and **made no bones about** it.* □ *He **made no bones about** the matter, he despised the captain.* □ *He **made no bones about** how boring he found the meeting; he kept yawning and looking at his watch.* □ *She **made no bones about** telling her husband she wanted a divorce.*

make no difference s'ka rëndësi

□ *It **makes no difference** whether you go today or tomorrow.* □ *It **makes no difference** to me what you say; I'm not going.*

make no mistake të jesh i sigurt; pa dyshim

□ *Make no mistake, swimming is the best all-round exercise you can take.*

make nothing of 1. s'kuptoj gjë fare, s'i jap dum

□ *Bella could **make nothing of** it but that John was in the right.* □ *He heard what was said, but could **make nothing of** it.*

2. kapërcen me lehtësi; e quan gjë të lehtë, sëe ka për gjë

□ *'She comes round again to take that fence and of course **makes nothing of** it.'* □ *She **makes nothing of** leaping over a six-bar gate.*

make off ikën, largohet me të shpejtë; ia dha (mbathi) vrapit

□ *Suddenly Myrtle slid down from the gate and quietly **made off** beside the hedgerow.* □ *The child **made off** when he saw the dog approaching him.*

make one's adieu(s) përshëndetem, i lë shëndetin, i jap lamtumirën

□ *The old man rose and **made his adieus**.*

make one's appearance del, duket, shfaqet

□ *Already a very ill man, he **made his** last public **appearance** at a Campaign for Nuclear Disarmament.* □ *As Jurgis came in, the first cattle of the morning were just **making their appearance**, and so, with scarcely time to look about him, and none to speak to anyone, he fell to work.* □ *I rang, and my younger brother **made his appearance** at the door.*

make one's bed and lie in it si shtron, ashtu gjen; siç e bëre, hiqe

□ *Billy smoked one of his father's cigars and now he's sick. He **made his bed**; now let him **lie in it**.* □ *Don't accuse me. She has **made her** own **bed**, let her **lie on it**.*

make one's dèbut debutoj, dal për herë të parë në skenë

□ *It was not till her father's death that, at the age of eighteen, she **made her dèbut** in a small part at the Lyceum.*

312

make one's departure iki, largohem, nisem

□ *They made their cheerful departure yesterday.*

make oneself at home rri si në shtëpinë time

□ *'Take off your hat and make yourself at home.'* □ *It will perhaps seem a matter of no very great wonder that he should have been rather out of sorts and unable to make himself quite at home.* □ *Will it do? There's a couch. You'll find some washing things. Make yourself at home, see!*

make oneself understood kuptohem, merrem vesh, bëj të qartë

□ *He doesn't speak much English but he can make himself understood.*

make one's exit dal

□ *Precisely as Mr. Bobster made his entrance by the street door, he and Noggs made their exit by the area gate.*

make one's farewells lë lamtumirën, jap lamtumirën

□ *As he was making his farewells, a photographer leaped out of what looked like a cupboard in the Senator's office.* □ *By the evening she had made all her farewells, including the most difficult of all.* □ *He shook hands with them as he made his farewells.*

make one's hair stand on end iu drodhën flokët (qimet e kokës, leshrat e kokës); iu ngritën flokët përpjetë

□ *Steve and Jack gave a talk about their trek across the Polar ice cap. It was very interesting but it made my hair stand on end just to hear about the dangers they faced.* □ *Jane's gone rock climbing with her new boyfriend once or twice. She says that it makes her stand on end when she looks down at hundreds of feet of empty air.*

make one's mouth water më lëshon (më shkon) goja lëng

□ *That food smells good, it makes my mouth water.* □ *You should see the beautiful jewels she is wearing: they would make your mouth water.*

make one's peace with sb pajtohem me, bëj paqe me

□ *Meg was making her peace with him.* □ *Johnson had no intention of making his peace with his superiors simply to give an impression of harmony within the department.* □ *'Have you made your peace with your wife yet?' 'I have certainly tried, but she refuses to talk to me.'*

make one's point sqaroj plotësisht propozimin

□ *All right, you've made your point; now keep quiet and let the others say what they think.* □ *Dr. Bothwick with the air of a debater who has made his point, sat back in his chair complacently enough.*

make one's way to/towards sth 1. shkoj, eci

□ *He made his way quickly to the other end of the hall.* □ *The morning before I went home I made my way once more up the evil-smelling stairs to my friend's garret.* □ *When he was again told to move on he made his way to a 'tough' place in the Lêvêe district.* □ *Tamosziu begins to edge in between the tables, making his way towards the head, where sits the bride.*

2. çaj (në jetë)

□ *After school, you will have to make your way in the world, and it will be easier to do that if you have good results.*

make out 1. kuptoj, marr vesh

□ *I could never make out if they wanted our help or not.* □ *As well as I*

could **make out** she had come for
good. □ Whenever the story was
plain enough for Jurgis to **make out**
Antanas would have it repeated to
him, and then he would remember it.
2. shquaj, dalloj, lexoj, deshifroj
□ I see something in the distance, but
cannot **make** it **out**. □ I could just
make out the mountains afar off.
□ He could not **make out** my writing.
□ We could not **make out** the inscription on the gravestone.
3. plotësoj, shkruaj, mbush, përpiloj
□ Applications have to be **made out** in
triplicate. □ He picked up a laundry
list **made out** on the back of the envelope. □ He was instructed to **make
out** an account of all the sums paid.
□ She had **made out** the document in
duplicate. □ **Make out** a list of books,
please.
4. shkoj, çoj, shpie, kaloj, eci
□ I wonder how John is **making out**
in his new practice? □ How are you
making out with Mary? □ How are
things **making out**? □ I was just
asking how you've been **making out**
recently.

make over 1. ndryshoj, konvertoj,
transformoj
□ The basement has been **made over**
into a workshop. □ Though you say
you've **made over** your outside in a
week, no one can do that with the
inside.
2. kaloj, transferoj
□ The best farming land was **made
over** to the younger son. □ To which of
his partners is he **making over** the
residue of his estate?

make progress përparoj, avancoj, bëj
hapa përpara, bëj përparime; përmirësohet
□ The snow here was firm and smooth
but not icy and so we **made** better

progress. □ At the hospital, the two
survivors were **making progress** but
were not well enough to be questioned. □ Jordan Jules had never been
able to **make** any satisfactory
progress in his fight on Cowperwood
in connection with the city council.
□ Are you **making** any **progress** with
your report?

make ready përgatit; përgatitem
□ We must **make** the hall **ready** for the
conference. □ His companions **made
ready** to fight.

make room for liroj vend, bëj vend
□ Mr. Owen had **made room for** me,
and placed a chair. □ Can you **make
room for** me?

make sense 1. ka kuptim
□ Often, what a child tries to say at
that age **makes** no **sense** to anyone
but his mother. □ It just doesn't **make
sense**. □ What he says doesn't **make
sense**.
2. është e arsyeshme, e logjikshme
□ It doesn't **make sense** to buy that
expensive coat when these cheaper
ones are just as good. □ They all have
their peculiar notions of reward and
punishment which never seem to
make sense to the outside world.

make shift bëj si bëj, mbaroj punë,
rregullohem
□ We haven't really got enough food
for everyone but we'll have to **make
shift** with what we have got.

make short work of sth/sb heq qafe, i
jap fund fët e fët, mbaroj punë shpejt
e shpejt
□ 'The thing wants tackling,' he
grumbled; 'the Chairman's not the
man for the job!' Shades of old Uncle
Jolyon. He would have **made short
work of** this! It wanted a masterful
hand. □ The children **made short
work of** the trifles and jellies. □ If the

Tynes had been an average sociable couple one knows only because leisure must be got through somehow, I would have **made short work of** *that special invitation.* □ *Harris: 'There's one more charge, Mr. Mayor— poaching. I told them to keep that back till after.' Chantrey: 'Oh, well, we'll* **make short work of** *that. I want to get off by eleven.'*

make sb a present of sth i bëj dikujt një dhuratë

□ *I'll* **make you a present of** *my dictionary.* □ *I* **made him a present of** *it.*

make sb's acquaintance/make the acquaintance of sb njihem me

□ *'Your daughter, I presume?' 'No, my niece.' 'Is that so? I am honored to* **make your acquaintance, Ma'am.'** □ *I* **made his acquaintance** *at the party.*

make sb's blood boil bëj t'i hipë (t'i kërcejë) gjaku në kokë

□ *Trench, it used to* **make my blood boil** *to think that such things couldn't be prevented.* □ *Uncle Rogers has a really terrific manner. Things* **make his blood boil** *and then he hardly knows what he is doing.* □ *When someone calls me a liar it* **makes my blood boil.**

make sb's flesh creep/crawl bëj t'i ngjethet mishtë

□ *I was woken up in the middle of the night by a weird, high-pitched, monotonous wailing that* **made my flesh creep**, *sent my heartbeat rocketing and caused me to break out into a cold sweat.* □ *He* **makes my flesh crawl.** *His cat-like walk, his husky voice, his black clothes, his perpetual grin- there's something really sinister about him.* □ *'Tom, why didn't you wake me sooner? Oh, Tom, don't! It*

makes my flesh crawl *to hear you. Tom, what's the matter?'* □ *Jinny Oates, the cobbler's daughter, being more imaginative, stated not only that she had seen the earrings too, but that they had* **made her blood creep.**

make sb's heart bleed bëj t'i pikojë zemra gjak

□ *But you should have seen poor old Jim. It would have* **made my heart bleed**, *if I hadn't guessed he'd been such a sodding fool, getting wed with a nice tart and then making a mess of it all.* □ *The quiet pain and loneliness he suffered after his wife's death* **made** *his daughter's* **heart bleed.**

make sport of sb tallem, vë në lojë

□ *Don't* **make sport of** *somebody who doesn't understand something.*

make sth clear/plain to sb ia bëj të qartë dikujt

□ *We* **made** *it quite* **clear to** *him that they must include a visit to all or any diamond mines in Liberia.* □ *Once the intention to do no such thing was* **made clear**, *they gave all the help they could.* □ *He has certainly* **made clear** *the principles on which the budget had been designed.*

make sure sigurohem

□ *I want to* **make sure** *of the time of his arrival.* □ *After they were through, the carcass was again swung up, and a man with a stick examined the skin, to* **make sure** *that it had not been cut and another rolled it up and tumbled it through one of the inevitable holes in the floor, and the beef proceeded on its journey.* □ *The old man looked cautiously at the door to* **make sure** *no one was listening.* □ *I think there's a train at 7:40, but you'd better* **make sure.**

make terms with arrij (bëj) marrëveshje, bie në ujdi, merrem vesh, arrij në mirëkuptim

□ *'Steady!' said Soames; 'You're thoroughly upset. I'll go back with you.' 'What's the use?' 'We ought to make terms with him.' 'Terms!'*

make the bed shtroj krevatin

□ *We made the beds for the guests.*

make the best of (a bad bargain/job) bëj ç'është e mundur, bëj maksimumin në një situatë të pafavorshme

➪ *The living conditions are not very good. I'm afraid you'll just have to make the best of a bad bargain.*

make the grade arrij standardin e dëshiruar (në aftësi, arsim etj.)

□ *Every year we train about twenty young people to be managers, but only about half of them make the grade.*

make the most of shfrytëzoj (përfitoj) në maksimum nga

□ *Mr. Bounderby in his desire to make the most of it, really seemed mortified by being obliged to reply.* □ *Make the most of your life— because life is a holiday from the dark.* □ *'I never met a girl like you, so I might as well make the most of having you here.'* □ *Not many people get a chance to study at university, so make the most of it.*

make the/one's round(s) of kaloj për kontroll

□ *The night watchman makes his rounds every hour.* □ *On the contrary a large majority of the boys were visited with similar instances of notice as Mr. Creecle made the round of the classroom.*

make the running udhëheq garën; udhëheq muhabetin etj.

□ *Johnson after having made most of the running previously had left himself with nothing in reserve for the last sprint.* □ *At dinner he talked little; but he opened up readily if you made the running.*

make tracks (for) iki, shkoj, largohem

□ *It's getting late; we'll have to make tracks.* □ *He made tracks straight for the bar.* □ *As soon as Ed released him, the kid made tracks away from there.* □ *It's time we made tracks for home.*

make trouble bëj, shkaktoj rrëmujë

□ *'You seem to have come here,' the professor said 'with the sole purpose of making trouble.'*

make up 1. përgatit (ilaçet etj)

□ *The doctor writes out a prescription and you get it made up at the chemist's.* □ *He made up a medicine from the juice of berries and applied it to the wound.* □ *Make up a bottle of medicine for me, please.* □ *Ask the chemist to make this up for you.*

2. mbledh, paketoj, përgatit

□ *He made up a package of books and sent it off by train.* □ *She made up a basket of food for the picnic.*

3. shpik, trilloj, sajoj

□ *These entertainers make their stories up as they go along.* □ *You can't go around making up things about being assaulted by people who don't exist.* □ *That story isn't true. You've made it up.* □ *There isn't any little girl called Clementine. He's just made her up.*

4. grimohem, bëj grim

□ *It took Lawrence Oliver more than one hour to make up for the part of Othello.* □ *Actors make up before going on stage.* □ *Her hair is dyed platinum blonde and she is heavily made up.*

5. zëvendësoj, kompensoj, vë në vend

□ *I missed several lessons owing to illness so I am trying hard to make up for lost time.* □ *By hard work they made up for the loss of time.*

*They hurried on to **make up** for lost time.* □ *Our losses will have to be **made up** with more loans.* □ *You must **make up** the time you wasted this afternoon by working late tonight.*

6. shtroj, asfaltoj

□ *Half the roads in the estate are still to be **made up**.*

7. bëj, formoj

□ *What are the qualities that ideally should **make up** a man's character?* □ *Society is **made up** of people with widely differing abilities.*

8. shtroj krevatin

□ *Sister sat down on the springs of the bed. I had not had time to **make** it **up** yet.* □ *I had a bed **made up** for me on the sofa.*

9. plotësoj

□ *We still need $1000 to **make up** the sum required.* □ *We have ten players, so we need one more to **make up** a team.*

10. i hedh dru, qymyr etj. zjarrit

□ *The fire needs **making up**.* □ *If the stove isn't **made up**, it'll go out.*

11. faqos

□ *He has just **made up** a page of type.*

12. pajtohem

□ *After having **made** it **up** with my mother, she kneeled down by the elbow-chair, to **make** it **up** with me.*

make up for lost time kompensoj kohën e humbur

□ *So, now that we are practically neighbours, we must **make up for lost time**.* □ *We came into this field late, so we must work hard to **make up for lost time**.*

make up one's mind vendos, mbush mendjen

□ *'Look, I've **made up my mind**. I want to have the party here.'* □ *They **made up their minds** to sell the house.*

make use of përdor, shfrytëzoj

□ *We must **make** full **use of** every kind of advanced experience.* □ *The apothecary's apprentice, having completed the manufacture of the tooth-pick, planted himself in front of the fire and **made** good **use of** it for minutes or so.*

make way for i hap (liroj, lëshoj) rrugën

□ *Don't think to frighten me as you have done others. **Make way**, Sir, and let me pass.* □ *The people crowded round the injured man, but they **made way for** the doctor when he reached the scene of the accident.* □ *All traffic has to **make way** for a fire engine.*

man in the street, the njeriu i thjeshtë, njeriu i rrugës

□ *The miners are talking about the possible necessity of strike action to defend their industry. This puzzles **the man in the street**.* □ *All major brands of gas have comparably high quality. **The man in the street** cannot discern the difference and doesn't want to be able to.*

man of his word, a njeri i fjalës

□ *If Jack promises to help you, then he will. He is **a man of his word**.*

man of letters, a njeri i letrave; shkrimtar

□ *Jack's detective stories are very popular, but you wouldn't call him **a man of letters**.*

man to man hapur, çiltërisht, si burri me burrin

□ *Let's talk **man to man**.*

many hands make light work bashkimi bën fuqinë

□ *If we can get some others to help us, the job won't take nearly so long. **Many hands make light work**.* □ *We'd have to clear the lounge for the painters coming in the morning.*

*The children can help too. **Many hands make light work.***

many a time shpesh, shumë herë

☐ *I have been here **many a time**.*

☐ *That mailbox has always been there. You must have passed it **many a time**.*

march past kaloj në revistë

☐ *The battalion **marched past** their commanding officer.*

mark down 1. shënoj, mbaj shënim

☐ *Now just **mark** that **down** in your notebook.*

2. ul çmimin

☐ *Many household articles are **marked down** during summer sales at the big stores.* ☐ *All the goods have been **marked down** by 15%.*

3. i ul notën

☐ *The boys at the top of the form were **marked down**, as the gap between them and the rest did not reflect their true merits.*

mark my words vëri veshin fjalëve të mia

☐ ***Mark my words**, the son of yours will be a famous politician one day.*

mark off ndaj me vijë (me kufi)

☐ *An area at the end of the site was **marked off** as a future playground.* ☐ *The boundaries are clearly **marked off** on the map.*

mark out vijëzoj

☐ *The sports field is **marked out** for an athletic meeting by the ground staff.* ☐ *They **marked out** the basketball court.*

mark time bën në vend-numëro; në vend-numëroj

☐ *After all, life is a matter of taking risks, stretching yourself to limits and maybe finding you can go further than you first thought. The rest is **marking time**.* ☐ *We often think we are doing some vastly important*

thing, whereas in reality we are merely **marking time**. ☐ *The officer made the soldiers **mark time** as a punishment.*

mark up 1. i ngre notat (studentit etj.)

☐ *If we **mark up** Jones on two or three papers he will just scrape a pass.*

2. ngre çmimin

☐ *Spirits have been **marked up** following price increases announced in the Budget.*

marry in haste, repent at leisure martesa e nxituar, pendim i gjatë

☐ *Thus grief still treads upon the heels of pleasure. **Marry in haste**, we may **repent at leisure**.* ☐ *'**Marry in haste, repent in leisure**,' she thinks. But how much and how often will she disappoint him?*

marry money martohem me një njeri të pasur, martohem me paranë

☐ *'She made a fortune,' Godfrey remarked. 'Retired and **married money** both times. I wonder what she has left?' ☐ 'Money **marries money**, lad. Be careful she doesn't break your heart.'*

master in one's own house zot në shtëpinë e vet

☐ *The garden is to be closed. No one may enter, and no one from the house may leave. Please note that I am not joking, and that from now on I intend to be the **master in my own house**.*

match against/with matem, hahem

☐ *He's prepared to **match** his skill and strength **against** all comers.* ☐ *You've been **matched with** one of the best amateur fighters.*

match up kombinoj, harmonizoj; përputh

☐ *'Have you noticed how well the blouse goes with my long skirt? The whole outfit **matches up** beautifully.'* ☐ *'I can't **match up** the two halves of* *the photograph.* □ *The two statements do not* **match up**.

matter of course gjë e zakonshme (e natyrshme), kuptohet vetvetiu

□ *He thought it would be* **a matter of course** *for the sons of former pupils to receive preferential treatment instead of having to compete on equal terms with other entrants.* □ *I thought that the chairman's behavior was extraordinary, but the committee members seem to take it as* **a matter of course**. □ *I thought your coming was* **a matter of course**.

matter of opinion, a çështje opinioni

□ *'The sprouts are half-cooked again.' 'I call them perfectly cooked, nice and crisp. It's all* **a matter of opinion**.' □ *'She's a fine singer.' 'That's* **a matter of opinion**.'

matter of time, a çështje kohe

□ *He became more and more daring as the path got worse, until I felt it was only* **a matter of time** *before he fell.* □ *She talks of getting better but I think she knows it's just* **a matter of time**.

mean business e ka seriozisht, flet seriozisht

□ *He says he will blow up the bank unless we give him all the money in it. I think he* **means business**. □ *He* **means business**; *he really will shoot us if we try to escape.*

means to an end mjeti për të arritur qëllimin

□ *For me, money is only* **a means to an end**; *I spent most of mine on enjoying myself.* □ *Harold felt that conversation should either be* **a means to an end**, *or a business deal.*

mean well ka qëllim të mirë, është i prirur për të mirë, e ka për mirë

□ *I don't think she intended to insult you by offering you money: she* **means well**. □ *I find her terribly interfering. It's not enough that she* **means well**.

measure off mat

□ *The assistant* **measured off** *a dress-length from the roll.* □ *'How much shall I* **measure** *you* **off**?'

measure one's length bie për tokë sa gjerë gjatë

□ *The dog's leash got round my ankle somehow and I* **measured my length** *in the mud.*

measure up to sth arrin (standardin e kërkuar)

□ *The discussions didn't* **measure up** *to my expectations.* □ *Differentiate between the genuine private detectives and others who do not* **measure up** *to our standards.*

meet sb half-way i bëj lëshime, bëj kompromis me

□ *My view of what should be done differed somewhat from his and I was unwilling to yield and* **meet** *him* **half-way**. □ *The owner said he was prepared to* **meet** *the striker's* **half-way**.

meet one's death gjej vdekjen

□ *My brother* **met his death** *heroically in the fight against the fascists.*

meet one's match has (ndesh) rivalin (kundërshtarin) e denjë

□ *As a chess player my friend has yet to* **meet his match**. □ *The fellow was not as flabby as he looked and I began to fear I had* **met my match**. □ *In me he'd* **met his match** *and I'd never give in to questions no matter how long it was kept up.* □ *If she hoped to rouse her father by this slight impertinence she had* **met her match**, *as Lord Pomfret paid no attention to her at all.*

meet one's Waterloo pësoj disfatë të plotë

□ *He won every fight until the world championship. Then he* **met his Waterloo.**

meet sb's eye kryqëzoj shikimin, shoh drejt në sy
□ *The child was afraid to* **meet his** *mother's* **eye.**

meet the ear zë (kap) veshi
□ *All sorts of strange sounds* **met my ear.**

meet the eye shoh, zë syri
□ *When I went into the room, the first thing that* **met my eye** *was a large red cupboard.*

meet with sb/sth 1. takohem me
□ *The President* **met with** *senior White House aides at breakfast.*
2. has, ndesh; përjetoj
□ *They* **met with** *stubborn resistance.*

meet up with takoj rastësisht
□ *When he ran round the tree, Bob suddenly* **met up with** *a large bear.*

melt in one's mouth shkrihet në gojë
□ *The chicken was so tender that it* **melted in your mouth.** □ *The birthday cake simply* **melts in the mouth.**

mend one's manners rregulloj mënyrën e sjelljes (të folurit etj.)
□ *I will implement my promise to send you twenty-five pounds, but not until you write to me in a proper and civil strain. So come off your high horse and* **mend your manners,** *and send me something remotely publishable.*

mend one's ways ndreq (korrigjoj) sjelljen
□ *The little child was told to stay indoors until he would* **mend his ways.** □ *There's no sign of him* **mending his ways.**

mince matters përtyp fjalët
□ *I didn't* **mince matters.** *I said he was an idiot.* □ *Don't* **mince matters,** *but speak plainly.*

□ *'It's of no use* **mincing matters,** *or making secrets, is it?' added Mrs. Lupin. 'I know all about it, you see!'*

mind one's own business shoh punën time
□ *He earned his bread at an honest, useful craft that he had taught himself without being helped, and* **minded his own business,** *and looked the world in the eyes.* □ *Tony (slowly): 'He's staying here?' Myra: 'Tony,* **mind your own bloody business.** *I've never interfered with anything you did.'* □ *He is always telling me what to do—why doesn't he* **mind his own business?** □ *'Mr. Smith says that if he were in your position he would have acted differently.' 'I wish Mr. Smith would* **mind his own business.'** □ *'Minding your own business** is the shortest way to make yourself sick.'*

mind/watch one's p's and q's tregohem i kujdesshëm (në sjellje, në të folur etj.)
□ *If he doesn't* **mind his p's and q's** *again, he will soon find himself in a difficult position.* □ *Matro's not very keen on a man for this job, so you'd better* **mind your p's and q',** *if you want to keep it.* □ *If we had been* **minding our p's and q's** *we would have been referring to Mr. Hislop as Professor Hislop, for that is his correct title in Sweden.*

mind/watch one's step sillem, veproj me kujdes
□ *You'll be in trouble if you don't* **watch your step.**

miss one's footing më shket këmba
□ *He was climbing a steep side of the mountain when he* **missed his footing** *and fell.*

miss out harroj, lë jashtë
□ *Through an oversight his name was*

missed out from the list of guests.
□ *The printers have missed out a word.*

miss the boat/bus humb rastin, nuk arrij të shfrytëzoj rastin
□ *You should have applied for the job when it was advertised; now it's too late and you've missed the bus.* □ *I have an intense awareness of the opportunity the Open University offers to chaps who, like me, have perhaps missed the boat.* □ *Mr. Brown missed the boat when he decided not to buy the house.*

miss the mark nuk i bie në shenjë, nuk i bie shenjës
□ *His answers missed the mark every time.*

miss the point nuk kap thelbin e
This capacity for missing the point has, of course, always been characteristic of philosophers.

mix one's drinks ngatërroj pijet
□ *He had consumed so much vodka, and had mixed his drinks to such an extent that it was considered by experts that it would be two days before he 'surfaced'.* □ *He wanted more than anything in the world to get drunk. Perhaps if he mixed his drinks sufficiently it might be enough. After the whisky, he could have a gin, and then, if he had any money left, a glass of stout ought to finish him off.*

mix up in/with 1. ngatërrohem
□ *He was mixed up in that horse-doping case.*
2. ngatërroj
□ *He's forever mixing me up with my brother.*
□ *The porter got our bags mixed up. I nearly walked home with someone's else's.* □ *Even the twins' mother mixes them up.*

money for jam/rope para të siguruara lehtë; para pa djersë
□ *In this job you only have to work about ten hours a week; it's money for old rope.*

more and more gjithmonë e më shumë, akoma më tepër (më shumë)
□ *I am becoming more and more irritated by his selfish behavior.* □ *He speaks more and more openly about the problem.* □ *The story gets more and more interesting.*

more or less pak a shumë, gati-gati; afërsisht
□ *The station lies a mile more or less from the village itself, so someone will come to meet you.* □ *It took more or less a whole day to paint the ceiling.* □ *It's an hour's journey, more or less.*

move heaven and earth to do sth s'lë gur pa luajtur, s'lë gjë pa bërë, tund dheun, bëj të pamundurën, bëhem copash
□ *I am already in debt again, and moving heaven and earth to save myself from exposure and destruction.* □ *I moved heaven and earth to get him out of town and did not succeed.* □ *'I have two possible buyers coming this afternoon—one is from a national collection.' 'How much do you want? I'll move all my bit of heaven and earth.'* □ *John moved heaven and earth to be sent to Washington.*

move house shpërngulem me shtëpi
□ *At the time he was moving house, he had just been appointed to the BBC Scottish Orchestra.* □ *They felt they simply couldn't face the bother of moving house again so soon.* □ *We are moving house next week.*

much the same pothuajse njëlloj
□ *The patient's condition is much the same.*

mum's the word kyçe (qepe)
□ *'Ed Treasdale was in town yesterday.' (This with a knowing eye, as much as to say '**Mum's the word.**')*
□ *Remember that Betty's party is meant to be a surprise one, so **mum's the word**.*

N

nail one's colors/flag to the mast
ngre, shpalos flamurin; shfaq hapur
qëndrimin (pikëpamjet etj) e mia
□ *I shall speak up at the meeting; I'm
not afraid to* **nail my colors to the
mast.** □ *The Home Secretary* **nailed
his colors** *firmly* **to the mast** *on the
question of arming the police.*

name names përmend emra
□ *He said someone had lied but
wouldn't* **name names.** □ *Now it is
easy enough to write about such-and-
such a politician's supporters but it is
more convincing to* **name names.**

narrow escape, a shpëtim për qime
□ *Returning to the mountain hut for
the night, the climbing party had a*
narrow escape *from falling rocks.*
□ *Tim had a* **narrow escape** *from the
clutches of Barbara last year. I had*
an *even* **narrower one** *this Christmas
after she claimed I proposed to her
at the office party.* □ *'That was a*
narrow escape,' *said Alice a good
deal frightened at the sudden change,
but very glad to find herself still in
existence.*

narrow shave/squeak shpëtim për
qime
□ *We just managed to get out of the
burning building in time: it was a*
narrow squeak.

near miss, a 1. shpëtim për një fije
floku (për një fill, për një qime)
□ *He did survive but whether he lives
to be fifty or a hundred he'll never
have a* **nearer miss.** □ *'Your Aunt Ada
was here till a few minutes ago.'*
'Wow! That was a **near miss.** *Thank*
God she walked up from the station.'
□ *Luckily the van ahead of us skidded
off the road on our left, but it was a
very* **near miss.**
2. goditje (e shtënë) gati në shenjë
□ *In his state he almost derailed a
nearby couple, and when the man's
hand shot out for revenge he felt the
wind of a* **near miss** *blowing by the
side of his face.* □ *'That's such a* **near
miss,'** *the quiz master said, 'that I
think we'll give you a mark. The correct answer is 3982 miles.'*

necessity is the mother of invention
kush i thërret nevojës, gjen ndihmë
gjithmonë; thirri nevojës se të përgjigjet
□ *Art imitates Nature, and* **necessity
is the mother of invention.** □ *Necessity may* **be the mother of invention**
in evolutionary processes too.

neck and crop trupërisht; tërësisht,
plotësisht, me gjithsej
□ *She was a Victorian servant girl
who had been turned out* **neck and
crop** *by her employers when they discovered she was going to have a
baby.*

neck and neck 1. hap më hap
□ *Deerstalker and his own out from
the rest...—***neck and neck***—Docker
riding like a demon.* □ *They used to
call it a draw, when two horses finished* **neck and neck.**
2. njësoj, barabar, në mënyrë të
barabartë
□ *'You see, I was a week or so behind
you, but I mean to catch up to you
and come* **neck and neck** *into the*

winning—post,' he continued. □ *Sales analysis shows these two products still vying* **neck and neck** *to corner the market.*

neck of the woods vend, zonë, rajon; rrethinë

□ *We haven't seen you in this* **neck of the woods** *for a while: where have you been?* □ *We visited Illinois and Iowa last summer, in that* **neck of the woods** *the corn really grows tall.*

neck or nothing o fitore, o hiç fare

□ *'Well, it's* **neck or nothing,** *' he thought to himself as he set his horse at a high windbreak hedge in the hope of outdistancing his pursuers.* □ *A good climber takes only carefully calculated risks. The urge to go at it,* **neck or nothing,** *in a spirit of bravado is not uncommon in beginners, and is the first thing they have to unlearn.* □ *For a bare living he would have to sell—why, three dozen big and four dozen small balloons a day... But it was* **neck or nothing** *now—he must try it, and in off hours go on looking for a job.* □ *I am risking all the money on the success of this invention; if it fails I'm ruined: it's* **neck or nothing**

needless to say është e tepërt të thuash; natyrisht; kuptohet vetiu

□ *I've thought the thing out pretty carefully—***needless to say.** □ **Needless to say** *he kept his promise.* □ *The playing of the English Chamber Orchestra is superb.* **Needles to say,** *Peter Pears give a highly perceptive account of the hero himself.* □ **Needless to say,** *I survived.*

needs must/must needs to do sth duhet doemos

□ *'A laborer! Your parents didn't send you to Oxford for that!' 'Honors*

degrees are ten a penny now, it seems. And even a philosophy graduate **needs must** *eat.* □ *... if Cowperwood were convicted, Stener* **must needs** *be also.* □ *She shall go, if* **needs must.** □ *He* **must needs** *to do it.*

neither fish, flesh nor good herring/fresh meat; neither fish nor fowl; neither fish, flesh, nor fowl as mish as peshk

□ *A man may consider himself an atheist, an agnostic or a believer, and good luck to him. But to call yourself a religiously-minded man without professing a religion is to be* **neither fish, flesh nor good herring.** □ *As a business man, journalist and writer, I was* **neither fish, fowl nor fresh meat.** *So at the age of 45, I packed it all in and we came up here.* □ *The book he has written is* **neither fish nor fowl:** *it's not exactly a poem and it is not really a novel, but something in between.*

neither here nor there i parëndësishëm; i pavend; nuk ka lidhje, nuk ka të bëjë me; as në qiell as në tokë

□ *'I have come here with a letter,' I said. 'From whom is it?' asked the man with the blunderbuss. 'That is* **neither here nor there,** *' said I, for I was growing very angry.* □ *Don't pay any attention to what he says: his opinion is* **neither here nor there.** □ *He talked for two hours but his remarks were* **neither here nor there.**

neither hide nor hair of sb/sth gjë prej gjëje; kurrgjë; asnjë shenjë (gjurmë)

□ *'What do you mean? Hasn't he been in?' 'I have seen* **neither hide nor hair** *of him.'* □ *Yet he's disappeared these last three years now. I've heard* **neither hide nor hair of** *him.*

□ *The place seemed to stink of cats, but I never saw **hide or hair of** one all the time I lived there.*

neither... nor as... as

□ *Neither you **nor** I can leave now.* □ *He **neither** knows **nor** cares what happened.* □ *The hotel is **neither** spacious **nor** comfortable.*

never mind 1. nuk prish punë, s'ka gjë; mos u shqetëso

□ *Never mind the cases: someone else will get them.* □ *You're a naughty boy to frighten Sarah like that, and to tell lies. But **never mind**, it was just a game, wasn't it?* □ *You might as well take the clothes away now. Never mind if you can't spare the money at the moment. You can pay me later.* □ *We've missed the train, but **never mind**, there will be another one along shortly.* □ *Never mind returning the book you borrowed from me.*

2. s'ka ç'të duhet; mos pyet

□ *'How much was the bill?'—'Never mind -what you don't know won't hurt you.'* □ *We got hold of a copy of the letter—**never mind** how—before it left the solicitor's office.* □ *'Where are you going?' Sue repeated, running out after him. 'Never mind,' he answered roughly.*

never say die mos u dorëzo

□ *'Never say die!' the mountaineer muttered to himself as he climbed the last section of the cliff.*

new/fresh blood gjak i ri

□ *Into this somewhat hidebound 'staff atmosphere' it was vital to inject **new blood**.* □ *It's some six months since I last saw 'Coronation street', and what a change for the better are the recent episodes. There's **new blood** in the show, and Ray and*

Deirdre's marriage has brought into the programme an element of realism.

new deal, a 1. program i reformave politike, sociale e ekonomike

□ *At the start of 1935, Lloyd George launched his 'New Deal,' which proposed a National Development council to revive the British economy and, by slum clearance, road building and restored agriculture, to eliminate unemployment.*

2. ndryshim rrënjësor; fillim i ri

□ *People had been on the job too long: **a new deal** was needed to change the old bad habits.*

3. një mundësi tjetër

□ *The boy asked for **a new deal** after he had been punished for fighting in school.*

new lease of/on life, a mundësi (perspektivë) për një jetë më të mirë (më të lumtur, më të gjatë)

□ *He was not well for a long time, but then he took up painting as a hobby, and seemed to take on **a new lease of life**.* □ *Since recovering from her operation, she's had **a new lease of life**.*

next door to 1. në hyrjen ngjitur

□ *Next door to us there's a couple from USA.*

□ *He lives **next door to** me.* □ *The child **next door** is noisy.*

2. gati njësoj si; afër, pranë

□ *I had given her the manuscript to read and I strongly suspected that she had not read it. For Myrtle not to have read it seemed to me **next door to** perfidy.* □ *... an inclination to that indulgence which is **next door to** affection.*

next to nothing thuajse (gati) asgjë, gati hiç

□ *'Did I understand, that, being*

rejected by one employer, he would probably be rejected by all? I thought he said as much?' 'The chances are very small, young lady—next to nothing for a man who gets a bad name among them.' □ *He now sleeps for an hour or two in twenty-four and does rigorous exercise for five. He reads voraciously and writes copiously. He eats next to nothing.* □ *... an unmarried man can live on next to nothing.*

night after night për netë me radhë, çdo natë
□ *Airplanes fly out of that airport night after night.* □ *Night by night she sat by the bed of her sick child.*

night and day/day and night ditë e natë, pa pushim
□ *Father worked night and day to earn enough money for the family.* □ *They travelled night and day for four days.*

nip sth in the bud mbys (shtyp, eliminoj) që në embrion (që në vezë, pa nxjerrë krye)
□ *It looked as if there was going to be some trouble at the meeting, but the police nipped it in the bud quickly arresting a few of the trouble-makers.* □ *He sat down with the air of having nipped some possibly dangerous nonsense in the bud.* □ *His new found inimicality with his son had been nipped in the bud.* □ *We must nip this bad habit in the bud.*

no call to s'kishte arsye që të
□ *He had no call to get up and interrupt the speaker: it wasn't necessary.*

no doubt pa dyshim, me siguri, patjetër
□ *No doubt, he's the finest boxer alive.* □ *You will, no doubt, be coming to the meeting?* □ *No doubt Susan was the smartest girl in her class.*

□ *No doubt that he'll come with us.* □ *I have no doubt that you'll succeed.*

no end (of) 1. tepër, shumë, pa masë, pa hesap, së tepërmi
□ *I enjoyed myself no end at the concert.* □ *Jim was no end upset because he couldn't go swimming.* □ *She has been boasting no end about how wealthy her husband is.* □ *Since he appeared on television, there has been no end of people wanting to meet him.* □ *He has no ends of books.* □ *There will be no end of trouble if you do not wipe out the insect pests now.*
2. pa pushim, vazhdimisht
□ *The baby cried no end.*

no end of a fuss shumë zhurmë
□ *Dad likes his steak grilled two minutes on each side and he makes no end of a fuss if it's not just right.*

no fear jo, natyrisht që jo
□ *'Are you coming climbing?' 'No fear!'* □ *'Did you see Robert safely off?' 'At half past six in the morning? No fear? We said goodbye last night.'* □ *'Don't tell me you paid $100 for that old wreck!' 'No fear. Twenty dollars, I said, take it or leave it.'*

no fewer/less than sth jo më pak se
□ *Out of 200 candidates no fewer than 180 gained their certificates.* □ *Crimes involving robbery rose 3 percent. This is disappointing as during 1996 there had been a drop of no less than 7 per cent.*

no go e pamundur
□ *A child could wriggle through the 20 inch gap, but it was clearly no go for a man of his weight.* □ *I tried very hard to make him take some money for the fish, but it was no go.* □ *As far as my parents were concerned, for me to hitchhike across the Sahara was definitely no go.* □ *You want to trot me*

out, but it's **no go.** □ *Nor, although he made a great effort to be as encouraging as possible, could he prevent his head from shaking once involuntarily, as if it is said, in the vulgar tongue, upon its own account.* **'No go!'**

no great shakes jo shumë i mirë; mediokër

□ *She's* **no great shakes** *as an actress.* □ *I can play golf a little, but I'm* **no great shakes** *at it.*

no joke s'është shaka

□ *Preparing fourteen pounds of meat when the temperature is over a hundred in the shade is* **no joke.**

no laughing matter s'është për të qeshur, s'është shaka

□ *For actors, the craft of creating comedy is often* **no laughing matter.** □ *Pat laughed, but you could see it was* **no laughing matter.** □ *It's not a good joke, I admit, but you must blame Julius for it, not me. In any case, I don't need telling that income-tax is* **no laughing matter.** □ *It's* **no laughing matter**—*we must take it very seriously.*

no/not any longer jo më, jo më gjatë

□ *He took off his spectacles. Deprived of them, his eyes seemed paler and larger and older; his round red face wasn't jolly* **any longer.** □ *I'm sure you're all hungry. I don't think we should wait* **any longer** *for Bob. I can keep his meal warm in the oven.* □ *I am* **no longer** *a young man.* □ *I shall wait* **no longer.**

no matter s'ka rëndësi, s'ka gjë, s'prish punë

□ *'I may not be able to leave the office in time to get your coat from the cleaner's.'* **'No matter.** *I can pick it up tomorrow.'* □ **No matter** *what he says, you must do as you think best.*

'This fellow's behavior, Mr. Peck-niff's, I mean. You saw it?' '*No, indeed I did not,'* cried Tom... *'It is* **no matter,'** *said Martin.* □ *'Come! Let us make haste back.'* It's **no matter** *whether you get there early or late.*

no matter what 1. sido që

□ *I'm going to take next week off,* **no matter what** *happens.* □ *But* **no matter** *how he turned his head he could see nothing but a patch of darkness.*

2. çfarëdo që, pavarësisht se

□ *'There, my darlings!' she crooned to her cats. 'There! You shan't starve,* **no matter what** *your wicked master says.'*

no more jo më

□ *I bore the pain till I could bear it* **no more** *and had to ask for another injection.* □ *It's* **no more** *than a mile to the shops.* □ *My grandmother is* **no more.**

none but vetëm

□ **None but** *the brave deserves the fair.* □ **None but** *geologists can understand it.*

none the less megjithatë, prapseprapë

□ *'It's a bit early to send a child of ten to bed.' 'She'll go when I tell her to,* **none the less.'** □ *He is quite old,* **none the less** *he works like a young man.*

no room to swing a cat s'ke ku të hedhësh mollën

□ *I'd rather live in this old house with all its inconveniences than in one of those pokey bungalows where you haven't* **room to swing a cat.** □ *It was supposed to be my workshop but there isn't* **room to swing a cat** *now, my wife's filled it so full of household gear.* □ *'At London I am pent up in frowzy lodgings, where there is* **not room to swing a cat...'**

nose about/around/into kërkoj, rrëmoj
  □ *I wish I could stop him **nosing about** he's not wanted here.* □ *In Grandmother's attic, Sally spent a while **nosing about** in the old family pictures.*

no smoke without fire s'ka tym pa zjarr, ku ka zë s'është pa gjë
  □ *Soon after sunrise the first column of smoke stood upright on the eastern horizon. My pulse quickened. **No smoke without fire**; no fire without man! Could it, by some miracle, be a sign of River Bushman?* □ *Everybody is saying that he was involved in robbery, so he probably had something to do with it: there's **no smoke without fire**.* □ *'There is **no smoke without fire**,' Glen used to say.*

no sooner... than sapo, posa, me të
  □ *His head had **no sooner** touched the pillow **than** he fell asleep.* □ ***No sooner** had he arrived home **than** he was asked to go shopping.* □ ***No sooner** had he arrived **than** he was asked to leave.*

not a bit (of it) aspak, asnjë grimë, hiç fare
  □ *'Are you cold?' '**Not a bit**.'* □ *He is **not a bit** better.* □ *You'd think she'd be tired after such a long journey, but **not a bit of it**!*

not a cat's/dog's chance asnjë mundësi, as mundësinë më të vogël
  □ *Young Mont said imploringly: 'Oh! No, sir, I simply must hang around or I shouldn't have **a dog's chance**.'*

not as black as it/one is painted nuk është aq i zi sa duket (sa thuhet)
  □ *'I am glad for my own sake, that he is **not so black as he is painted**,' said Agatha.*

not at all aspak, s'ka gjë, ju lutem
  □ *'It's very kind of you.' '**Not at all**.'*

not a whit aspak, asnjë grimë
  □ *The patient is **not a whit** better today.*

not bad jo keq
  □ *'**Not bad** for a beginner,' Andrew said as they left the court. 'We'll make a tennis-player of you yet.'* □ *'Nice place you have here, Mr. Liversedge,' he said admiringly. '**Not too bad, not too bad**,' Jack said modestly.*

not/never bat an eyelid nuk i bën syri tërr, nuk i dridhet (nuk i luan) qerpiku (qepalla, bebja e syrit)
  □ *The condemned man listened to his sentence **without batting an eyelid**.* □ *The rock nearly hit him, but he **didn't bat an eyelid**.* □ *They threatened him with death, but he **didn't bat an eyelid**.* □ *The sound of the crash brought everyone to their feet—except John who **never** even **batted an eyelid** and stolidly went on eating his dinner.*

not breathe a word of/about sth to sb nuk nxjerr zë, nuk hap gojë
  □ *Promise me you won't **breathe a word of** this to anyone.* □ *She had never let him know—**never breathed a word**.*

not for nothing jo pa shkak
  □ *It is **not for nothing** that this is carried out in strict secrecy, protected by Acts of Parliament.*

not for (all) the world në asnjë mënyrë, kurrsesi, kurrën e kurrës, sikur të më fshësh gjithë botën
  □ *When she was gone, Ashurst thought: 'Did she think I was chaffing her? I wouldn't **for the world**.* □ *Daphne, usually loquacious, felt as if she could not have spoken **for the world**.* □ *I wouldn't sell that picture **for all the world**.* □ *She wouldn't have it known that she*

had said so, for the world. □ *Oh, hide me! Don't let me be seen for the world.* □ *Her eyes were strange. They seemed to ask me a question. But I couldn't have spoken for the world.*

not half 1. shumë, jashtëzakonisht shumë, s'ka ku të shkojë më, pa hesap □ *'You will be glad when you've finished that job, I'm sure.' 'Not half! What a bore it's been.'* □ *'Was she annoyed?' 'Not half.'* □ *'Are you thirsty? 'Not half.'* 2. aspak □ *It's not half bad, your new flat.*

not have a bean s'kam asnjë grosh (asnjë dysh) □ *'You know there is a young man hanging around?' 'Yes. He hasn't a bean.' Dinny smiled.* □ *'Have you money left, Jack?' 'Not a bean. I didn't realize it was going to be such an expensive evening.'*

not half bad/badly mjaft i mirë; jo i keq □ *He is not half bad when you know him.* □ *I say, Daphne, this cake isn't half bad! You must bake another soon.* □ *Johnny's getting to be quite a little musician. He was playing A Chopin Study just before you came in, and not half badly either.*

nothing but vetëm, asgjë tjetër përveç □ *The boys in the workhouse received for dinner nothing but a very thin gruel.* □ *Nothing but a miracle can save her now.*

nothing doing jo, aspak, në asnjë mënyrë, kurrsesi □ *He had, however, less intention even than before of moving for a meeting of the shareholders... No. Nothing doing—as they said nowadays.* □ *'Will you lend me a dollar?' 'Nothing doing!'*

not know where/which way to turn s'di nga t'ia mbaj □ *Every line of investigation had brought me to a dead end and I didn't know where to turn.* □ *The prospective parents objected to blood transfusion, and the surgeon did not know which way to turn in order to save the child.* □ *A service to Jura would require Government assistance. The islanders do not know which way to turn next, but they still live in hope that ships will again call at Craighouse on a regular basis.* □ *Oh, this is awful—I don't know what to do nor which way to turn!*

nothing less than tërësisht, plotësisht □ *His negligence was nothing less than criminal.*

nothing of the kind/sort aspak i tillë, asgjë të tillë □ *People had told me she was very pleasant but she's nothing of the kind.* □ *'Did he apologize?' 'Nothing of the kind.'*

nothing out of the common asgjë e veçantë □ *'How do you like this song?' 'Well, it is nothing out of the common.'*

nothing short of gati, thuajse □ *It is nothing short of a miracle.*

nothing to speak of nuk ia vlen t'i përmendsh, t'i zësh në gojë □ *She has saved a little money, but nothing to speak of.*

not in the least aspak □ *'Am I troubling you?' 'No, not in the least.'* □ *'Would you mind if I put the television on?' 'No, not in the least.'*

not mince matters/not mince one's words flas hapur, troç; sëi përtyp fjalët □ *I didn't mince the matter with him.*

329

I am never mealy with them. □ *She spoke in a decided voice, and did **not** **mince her words**.* □ *I didn't **mince matters**: I said he was an idiot.*

not much good at sth jo shumë i mirë, jo kushedi se çfarë

□ *I'm **not much good at** tennis.*

not only ... but also jo vetëm ... por edhe

□ *He **not only** read the book, **but also** remembered what he read.* □ *He is **not only** a good teacher **but also** a good educator.*

not (quite) right in the/one's head s'e ka mendjen në vend, s'është në të, s'është në rregull nga trutë e kokës

□ *Perhaps after all it was only a freak, and she had gone to the seaside for a few day's change.... She was evidently **not quite right in her head**.*

not to be sneezed at s'duhet shpërfillur (përçmuar)

□ *His opinion is **not to be sneezed at**.* □ *A prize of $5,000 is **not to be sneezed at**.*

not to mention pa përmendur

□ *There were three of us there, **not to mention** the child.* □ *He has a big house and an expensive car, **not to mention** a villa in France.*

not to say për të mos thënë

□ *It's warm, **not to say** hot.* □ *Sam was irreverent, **not to say** rude.*

not turn a hair nuk i lëviz as një fije floku, nuk tregon kurrfarë frike, habie etj.

□ *'What do you think of her?' 'Fascinating.' 'I'll tell her that, she won't **turn a hair**.'* □ *It was a swingeing sentence he got but he didn't **turn a hair** as he sat in the dock. You'd have thought the judge was talking about somebody else.*

not worth a damn, a straw, a red cent, a tinker's cuss etc. s'vlen asnjë grosh, nuk vlen fare

□ *This mediocre painting isn't **worth a damn**.* □ *So long as you and your opinions can be taken seriously, Harold's position isn't **worth a damn**.*

now and again kohë pas kohe, herë pas here

□ *Now and again he shook his head, as if to clear it like a boxes recovering from a knock-out.*

now and then kohë pas kohe, herë pas here

*I like to go to the opera **now and then**.*

no wonder s'është për t'u çuditur (habitur)

□ *No wander few people are drinking coffee: look at the price of it.* □ *It's **no wonder** that he didn't want to go.*

now that tani që

□ *Now that you mention it, I do remember.* □ *Now that the rain has stopped, we can leave.*

now then atëhere; pra

□ *Now then, why don't you volunteer?* □ *Now then, are there any comments on this report? I must say I enjoyed that.*

O

odd fish/bird, an njeri i çuditshëm

□ *This is not to say that Mr. Hughes is anything but **an** extremely **odd fish**, if we are to believe what we have been told. He has not been seen in public for 16 years.* □ *It would be smug and vain of me to suggest that he was merely **an odd fish** I took pity on.* □ *'He was **an odd bird**,' I said. 'I only saw him about a half dozen times.'*

odd jobs punë të rastit

□ *They await him for the first hand of cards, yet sometimes he busies with **odd jobs** about the house.* □ *At the of 17 he went out to New Zealand. Before long—it was during the slump—he was wandering about the country getting **odd jobs**.* □ *... John made his living by doing **odd jobs**.*

odds and bobs/sods çikërrima, vogëlsira; vogëlima

□ *The papershop window is a litter of **odds-and-bobs**; if the light is kept on at nights the children make it a meeting place.* □ *So I was a breadwinner when I was nine. I did **odds and sods** to get things by any means.*

odds and ends çikërrima, vogëlsira; copëra; mbetje

□ *Down right is heavy chest of drawers, covered with books, neckties and **odds and ends**, including a large, tattered toy teddy bear and a soft, woolly squirrel.* □ *It is of those thoughts which make you realize how long it is since you rearranged the lumber in the attic of your brain, and threw out all the **odds and ends** you've been saving.* □ *Time hurried away, and soon it was time for Lanny to go. He slipped the few **odds and ends** that he had not packed into his bags into his attache case.* □ *The tailor made a suit for the boy out of the **odds and ends** of the cloth.* □ *The packers were always originating such schemes they had what they called—boneless hams—which were all the **odds and ends** of the pork stuffed into casings.*

odds are (that), the ngjasat janë se, ka shumë mundësi që

□ *In the old days a pop star would approach his 30s with some trepidation, because **the odds were that** he would be abandoned by his public.* □ *Don't wait for Jack; **the odds are that** he has slept in again.*

of age në moshë

□ *His wealth is divided equally between his two sons, who will get it when they come **of age**.* □ *Mary will be **of driving age** on her next birthday.*

of a kind/sort/of sorts njëfarësoj, njëfarëlloj, çka, jo dhe aq keq

□ *There's a road **of a kind** from the lakeside to the forester's hut. A jeep could do it but not the car you have here.* □ *The Channel Islands and the Isle of Man have independence **of a sort**. So why not Cornwall?* □ *To protect themselves against the rain, they made a roof **of sorts** from branches.* □ *He plays football **of a sort**.*

of course natyrisht, sigurisht

□ ***Of course** you know that girl: she's in your class.* □ *Where are you going,*

Mother?—To the drawing-room, of course. □ *'Do you study hard?' 'Of course, we do.'* □ *Of course, this is just speculation. He may not be the right man.*

of late kohët e fundit

□ *I noticed that Jack has been working less hard of late.* □ *You've been very irritable of late. If you feel tired or unwell you should do something about it.*

of moment me rëndësi

□ *It is an affair of great moment.*

of necessity doemos; në rast nevoje; pashmangshmërisht, në mënyrë të pashmangshme

□ *Though of necessity accepting the need for new roads through the central area, it put these on a more model scale.* □ *We don't of necessity have to attend all these functions but it doesn't do any good to be thought anti-social.*

of one's/its own accord vullnetarisht, me dëshirën e vet; vetiu, spontanisht

□ *Meanwhile in the drawingroom Edith had, of her own accord, told her cousin Sally that she was sorry.* □ *He could not stop his mouth twitching; but it would stop of its own accord, he believed, once he was in the fresh air.* □ *Brought into the open, such difficulties have a happy knack of going away almost of their own accord.* □ *She had come back then of her own accord....*

of one's own free will vullnetarisht

□ *Do you take part, of your own free will, in any social or political organization outside your ordinary work?* □ *He walked straight into the prison of his own free will and shut the door behind him.* □ *... threaten to torture them until they agreed to come with us of their own free will.*

of one/the same mind i një mendje

□ *We get on very well together because in most matters we are of the same mind.* □ *Are they of the same mind about this today as they were last week?*

of that ilk i të njëjtit vend; i të njëjtit lloj

□ *At the crossroads about a mile from Monboddo the travellers' carriage was met by His Lordship of that ilk who invited them to dine and rest at his house that night.* □ *Hundreds of that ilk are produced every year by printers down cobbled alleys.*

off and on/on and off nganjëherë, kohë pas kohe, herë pas here, nga koha në kohë

□ *Of course, I haven't met her but being famous as an author off and on, she gets all the sympathy.* □ *You're kind of out of touch with real life, being a chess player. I have thought of giving it up off and on, but I always considered: what else could I do?* □ *I see him off and on.* □ *Joan wrote to a pen pal in America off and on for several years.* □ *It was raining off and on all day*

off balance gafil, në befasi, në gjendje të papërgatitur

□ *The teacher's surprise test caught the class off balance, and nearly everyone got a bad mark.*

off color/off-color 1. i prerë në fytyrë, çehrevrarë, me çehre të keqe (të verdhë), pa qejf, i pamundur

□ *I feel a little off color and I am off my food.* □ *'To tell you the truth, dear Laurie.... I've been a little off color lately.' 'I'm terribly sorry. What is it?' 'Oh, just a bit out of sorts. I'm sure I'll be all right soon.*

2. i pakripë, bajat, i dalë boje

□ *I thought that some of his jokes*

were rather **off-color**. □ When Jack finished his **off-color** story, no one was pleased.

off duty pas pune; në pushim; i lirë, i pazënë me punë

□ The nurse said that she would meet us later, when she was **off duty**.
□ Sailors like to go sightseeing when they are **off duty** in a foreign port.
□ While the workers were **off duty**, they cleaned up the factory's backyard. □ He goes on duty at 7 a.m. and comes **off duty** at 2 p.m.

offer one's hand (in marriage) i kërkoj dorën (për martesë), e kërkoj për grua

□ I **offer** you **my hand**, my heart, and a share of all my possessions.

offer (sb) one's hand i zgjat dorën dikujt (për ta takuar)

□ He came towards me, smiled and **offered his hand**.

off one's hands nga duart

□ I'm selling these things cheaply just to get them **off my hands**. □ Ginny was glad to have the sick dog taken **off her hands** by the doctor.

off/out of/ one's head/chump/nut/ rocker i çmendur, i marrë, i shkalluar, i luajtur nga mendtë

□ He transferred an inspector from one plant after Mr. Rubin had complained that the man was **off his head**. □ Anyone who thought of such a crazy plan must be **off his head**. □ 'I think he's a little **off his nut**.' □ In the morning when Andrew Masters came to see how he felt, Pledger was half **out of his head**.

off one's own bat vetë, pa ia kërkuar kush, pa e urdhëruar (këshilluar, drejtuar etj.) kush, me iniciativën e vet

□ But Joan was enthusiastic. **Off her own bat**, at home, she worked out the whole operation—vehicles, staff,

finance, building. □ Nobody asked him to help: he helped **off his own bat**. □ Since your builder put the window in **off his own bat** I don't see that I'm responsible.

off (one's) guard gafil, në befasi, në bef, bosh, pa mendje

□ Our sudden attack caught the enemy **off guard**. □ He struck while I was **off my guard**. □ Tim's question caught Jean **off guard**, and she told him

off one's mind (heq) nga mendja

□ I am glad you have got that affair **off your mind**. □ And he had felt so happy; he had not felt like for months. His confession to June was **off his mind**.

off the beaten track i parrahur, që nuk shkelet shumë nga njerëzit; i mënjanuar; i panjohur

□ He likes to go for his holidays to places that are **off the beaten track**.
2. i pazakontë, i veçantë

□ You will find his plays strange: they are about subjects that are a bit **off the beaten track**.

off the cuff aty për aty; pa parapërgatitje

□ I did not have time to prepare a speech so I just made out one **off the cuff**. □ Some presidents like to speak **off the cuff** to newspaper reporters.

off the hook (nxjerr, shpëtoj) nga sikleti

□ I didn't want to go to the meeting, but Jack got me **off the hook** by going in my place. □ Thelma found she had made two dates for the same night; she asked Sally to get her **off the hook** by going out with one of the boys.

off the point jashtë teme

□ The student received low marks for his essay, as much of it was **off the point**.

off the rails jashtë binarëve

□ ... *John used to be a very steady and reliable person, but he has gone* **off the rails** *recently.*

off the record konfidencial(isht), në konfidencë, jozyrtar(isht), jo për botim

□ *One of the committee members, whom I won't name, told John* **off the record** *the appointment was as good as his.* □ *Please understand that what I am telling you now is strictly* **off the record.** □ *He turned full face to Karen. 'I trust you Kid', he said. 'This is* **off the record.'** □ *The President told the reporters his remarks were strictly* **off the record.**

off the reel me një frymë; fët e fët; tak-fak

□ *The story seems to me to be so constituted as to require to be read* '**off the reel'.** □ *He won five races* **off the reel.**

of no avail pa dobi

□ *Letters had proved* **of no avail**— *personal inquiry shall replace them.*

of no effect pa efekt, pa rezultat, pa dobi, pa fryt

□ *My warning was* **of no effect.** □ *All Sam's efforts were* **of no effect.**

of repute me emër

□ *John is a doctor* **of repute.**

of the deepest dye i llojit më të keq

□ *Don't trust him: he is a villain* **of the deepest dye.**

of the first water/order i cilësisë më të lartë; i llojit më të mirë

□ *Because it was a diamond* **of the first water,** *it was insured for thousands of pounds.*

old hand, an njeri me përvojë

□ *Get James to help you with selling the house; he is* **an old hand** *at that sort of thing.*

old hat gjë e vjetër (e njohur, e vjetëruar); diçka që i ka kaluar koha

□ *It's a mistake to try mixing up checks; this is now* **old hat** *in the fashion world.* □ *He has no time for the school of contemporary musicians who, as far as he can see, think that anything done last week is* **old hat.** □ *We did not find the lecture very interesting; the ideas were a bit* **old hat.**

on account of nga shkaku, për arsye

□ **On account of** *the high winds the fishing vessel had not put out to sea.* □ *We delayed our departure* **on account of** *bad weather.* □ *The parents were anxious* **on account of** *their son's illness.* □ **On account of** *the rain, our visit was postponed.*

on a firm footing mbi baza të shëndosha

□ *The first time they started the business it failed, but the next time— having learned from their mistakes -they started it* **on a firmer footing.**

on a large scale në shkallë të gjerë

□ *Only on 28 July did the President formally announce his decision to commit American troops* **on a large scale.**

on all fours këmbadoras

□ *Harold encouraged the children; the beach seemed to go to his head as it did to theirs, he crawled about* **on all fours,** *or lay prone or supine while mounds of sand were heaped upon his body.* □ *Lotte was still* **on all fours,** *reddening the tiles.* □ *The baby approached its mother* **on all fours.**

on all hands nga të gjitha anët, nga të katër anët, gjithandej

□ *But finding me well-employed, and bearing a good character, and hearing* **on all hands** *that I rose fast* *in the school, she soon discontinued these visits.* □ *Debts there were on* **every hand**. *They haunted him, robbed him of his sleep.* □ *The old man was surrounded on all hands by children anxious to listen to his story.*

on all sides/every side nga të gjitha anët (drejtimet); nga të gjithë

□ *On all sides the importance of training youth is recognized.* □ *His refusal to convene an extraordinary session of Parliament is criticised on all sides.*

on an empty stomach pa ngrënë, me barkun bosh

□ *Oliver Gillie writing on hangovers points out that it is unwise to take aspirin-based products on an empty stomach.*

on and on pa pushim, pa u ndalur

□ *We walked on and on.* □ *He kept moaning on and on.*

on a par with njësoj me, në një nivel (shkallë) me, barabar me

□ *His performance was very good today: it's on a par with anything he has done before.* □ *What we did in the previous case is no guide to what we ought to do in this, as the two are not on the par.* □ *As a writer he was on a par with the great novelists.*

on a shoestring me pak pare

□ *The couple was seeing Europe on a shoestring.*

on behalf of/on sb/sth's behalf në emër të; në favor (mbështetje) të

□ *She knew it was useless to attempt to speak to him about her misgivings on his behalf.* □ *It had been sought, on behalf of the defendant, to show that no limit of expenditure was fixed or intended to be fixed by this correspondence.* □ *It was stated on behalf of the prisoner that he had a record of*

good behavior and had been under considerable strain at the time of his outbreak.

on call i gatshëm, në gatishmëri

□ *One of the doctors has to be on call over the weekend.*

on credit me kredi

□ *They run their business on credit.*

on condition that me kusht që

□ *You can go out on condition that you wear an overcoat.*

on business me shërbim, me punë

□ *'I came here on business.' 'I never knew you would go anywhere for anything else.'* □ *Bowes had got to know the place a bit from having been there on business—he was a salesman for nautical gear of all sorts.* □ *'I'd like to come,' George smiled at her. 'But I've got to go out on business.'*

once again/once more edhe një herë; sërish

□ *'That was better,' said the conductor. 'Let's have it once again from the bar twenty, and then you can go.'* □ *If you say that once more, I shall scream.* □ *I'll tell you how to do it once again.* □ *Let's sing it once more.* □ *'Only three weeks to go,' he wrote,' and we'll be together once more and making up for wasted time.'*

once and again vazhdimisht

□ *That good woman would open the door once and again in the morning and put her head through.*

once and for all një herë e përgjithmonë, një herë e mirë

□ *Stanley. Now you listen to me, my boy. You get this through your head once and for all; I'm in business to make money.* □ *We may as well get the matter settled once and for all.* □ *I tell you once and for all that I will not allow such conduct.*

once bitten, twice shy u dogj nga qulli, e i fryn dhe kosit
□ *'He never married again?' 'No, once bitten, twice shy, I suppose— though that hasn't deterred some others I know.'* □ *'Do you always check applicants' references?' 'Once bitten, twice shy. I always do now.'*

once in a blue moon rrallë e për mall, një herë në hënë
□ *I used to see him a lot but now we meet only once in a blue moon.* □ *He consulted the script once in a blue moon.* □ *Honegger's huge dramatic oratorio has been performed only twice before in London, once with Ingrid Bergman as Joan.* □ *'It's a once in a blue moon sort of thing,* said one of the violinists. □ *'Did he initiate?' 'Once in a blue moon.'* □ *One did not reach him, or so it was reported by members of the family who, would drive up once in a blue moon and ask after their surviving uncle....*

once in a lifetime një herë në një jetë të tërë
□ *She was brought to believe you fell in love and got married once in a lifetime.* □ *You haven't really achieved anything as a player unless you play in a Cup Final. It's usually once-in-a-lifetime experience—unless you play for the Celtics or the Rangers.*

once in a while/way nganjëherë, rrallë e tek, rrallëherë, më të rrallë, rrallë e për mall
□ *There isn't much upkeep with the hearses except to give them a lick of paint once in a while.* □ *Even the most reputable actresses had to suffer that thankless role of the dutiful wife of the 'great man' once in a while.* □ *'Don't you ever drink coffee?' 'Oh, once in a way I might. But I prefer tea or fruit juice.'* □ *He does write a letter once in a while.* □ *If he could come down once and a while after work hours, it would kind of reconcile her.*

once or twice një apo dy herë; disa herë
□ *I don't know the place well, I've only been there once or twice.* □ *We met only once or twice.*

once upon a time na ishte ç'na ishte; një herë e një kohë
□ *This is an older story, as old as Genesis. May be it could even start in the old way, and that, as I remember, was 'Once upon a time.'* □ *'Once upon a time there was a wife who ran her house with the organized precision of an electric clock. Everybody hated her and her husband ran away with a girl who couldn't tell the time.* □ *Once upon a time, in a very small country town, at a considerable distance from London, there lived a little man named Nathaniel Pipkin...*

on condition that me kusht që, po qe se, në qoftë se
□ *Mrs. Crupp consented to achieve this on condition that I dined from home for a fortnight afterwards.* □ *You may borrow the book, on condition that you return it in no time.* □ *The doctor told his patient that he would prescribe him some patent medicine on condition that he strictly followed his instruction.*

on duty në shërbim, në punë, në krye të detyrës
□ *The policeman refused to offer of a drink because he was on duty.* □ *I arrive at the hospital at eight o'clock, but I don't go on duty until nine.* □ *'Who is on duty today?' asked the teacher.* □ *They are not allowed to smoke while they are on duty.*

one and all secili, çdonjëri, të gjithë pa përjashtim

□ *I bid you* ***one and all*** *good night.*
□ *Woodgate or Hopalong as he was known to* ***one and all*** *shut the door carefully like a man whose doors were always slammed by other people.* □ *I thank you* ***one and all*** *for your kindness to me.* □ *And* ***one and all*** *they had a longing to get away from this painfulness, this ceremony.*

one and only i vetëm

□ *You have always been my* ***one and only*** *true love.* □ *Charles, whose nerves had been sorely tried by inactivity and pain, made his* ***one and only*** *scene with me.*

one and the same i njëjtë

□ ***One and the same*** *idea occurred to each of them.* □ *I can't be in the kitchen and running backwards and forwards at* ***one and the same*** *time.*

one another njeri tjetrin, shoku shokun

□ *'I think we ought to see more of* ***one another*** *and come to know one another better.'*

one by one një nga një

□ *John went over the items on the list* ***one by one.***

one could/might hear a pin drop; you could/might have heard a pin drop s'pipëtinte asgjë, nuk dëgjohej (ndihej) as miza

□ *The speaker let the ovation continue for a few minutes then with a single motion of his arms stopped the uproar instantaneously and you* ***could have heard a pin drop.***

one day një ditë

□ *And she was really connected— would likely make somebody a good wife* ***one day.*** □ ***One day*** *people wake up to the experience that what was important yesterday no longer matters in the same way.*

on edge nervoz, i irrituar, i ngacmuar

□ *She was a bit* ***on edge*** *till she heard he was safe.* □ *She was very much* ***on edge*** *until the doctor told her that her son had come through the operation successfully.*

one drop of poison infects the whole bottle of wine një mollë e kalbur prish gjithë shportën; një dru i shtrembur prish gjithë stivën

□ *It is very true that* ***one drop of poison infects the whole bottle of wine.*** *That's why we should criticize him sharply.*

one good turn deserves another nderi lahet me nder

□ *That* ***one good turn deserves another*** *was an axiom with Harold; he would not have dreamed of doubting it.* □ *I'll dig over that patch for you on Saturday. You've just about kept us in fresh vegetables these last two months, and* ***one good turn deserves another.***

one in a thousand/million një në një mijë (milion), shumë i rrallë

□ *'What's your new secretary like?' 'Reasonably competent—not a patch on Jean.' 'Ah, but she was* ***one in a thousand.'***

one looks as if butter wouldn't melt in one's mouth duket si qengj, duket sikur nuk turbullon ujë

□ *When she comes in she smiles and languishes, you'd think that* ***butter would not melt in her mouth.***

on end parreshtur, me radhë, pa pushim, pa ndërprerje, vazhdimisht; i tërë

□ *Sometimes for an hour* ***on end*** *she sat staring at a page, listening to the liquid summer sounds that floated through the windows.* □ *It rained for two days* ***on end.*** □ *That dog has been barking for two hours* ***on end.*** □ *For* five miles **on end** the road was bordered with apple orchards.

one of these days një ditë, një ditë prej ditësh; shpejt

□ *One of these days he'll realize what a fool he's been.* □ *If he goes on wasting his money, **one of these days** he is going to find himself a poor man.* □ *In our profession we know something of human nature and take my word for it, that the fellow will show himself **one of these days** in his true color.*

one's blood is up i hipën gjaku në kokë

□ *After being insulted like that, **my blood is** really **up**!*

one's cup of tea gjëja që më pëlqen, më tërheq

□ *'Got anything for me to read?' I said. 'What's that?' 'Oh, I don't think that's **your cup of tea**,' he said.*

one's days are numbered i ka ditët të numëruara (të shkurtra), nuk do ta çojë gjatë

□ *He has a serious illness, and **his days are numbered**.* □ *The factory is no longer profitable, so its **days are numbered**.*

one's own flesh and blood gjak, farefisni, fis, farefis

□ *I'll have to go to my aunt's funeral -she was **my own flesh and blood** after all.* □ *'And **your own flesh and blood** might come to want too, might they, for anything you cared?'* □ *And all the deeply rooted clanship in him, the family feeling and essential clinging to **his own flesh and blood** which had been so strong in Old Jolyon- was so strong in all the Forsytes....*

one swallow does not make a summer me një lule (dallëndyshe) s'vjen pranvera (behari)

□ *Could I say yet that everything was all right? **One swallow did not make a summer**, though I conceded that most people would think it meant they could reasonably look forward to a warm spell of weather.*

one way or another 1. në një mënyrë a në një tjetër, në një farë mënyre

□ *If you help a neglected, deprived child, he or she may well grow up to do you credit. They may not actually show you, though quite often they do, but the chances are that you will get thanks **one way or another**.* □ *The writer may feel on reflection that he has been pressed **in one way or another**, to change what should have been left as it was.* □ *The housekeeper who saw it all ... seemed to have no opinion about it, **one way or another**.* □ *You shall have to do it **one way or another**.*

2. sido që të ndodhë, sido që të vijë puna

□ *Before I met you I didn't care **one way or another**—I didn't care whether I lived or died.*

on foot 1. më këmbë

□ *We have missed the last bus and we shall have to go home **on foot**.* □ *I packed up my manuscripts in a brown paper parcel, and left **on foot**.* □ *We creep out to see as much as we can of this wonderful city **on foot** before the 'real' sightseeing of the day begins by coach.*

2. në lëvizje

□ *The scouts had brought in word that flank movement of the enemy was **on foot**.*

on guard 1. në gatishmëri, në beft, syhapur, vigjilent

□ *They say that there are some thieves about, so be **on guard**.* □ *We shall have to be **on our guard** against mistakes like that in the future.*

338

2. në shërbim, në rojë

□ *We have several soldiers on guard at the gate.*

on hand 1. në dispozicion; në disponim; në dorë

□ *If you need extra help, we have some people on hand to help you.*

□ *He longed to compare experiences with him, even though there was on hand a more exciting matter still.*

2. afër, pranë

□ *Always have your dictionary on hand when you study.*

3. i pranishëm

□ *Mr. Blake's secretary is always on hand when he appears in public.*

only too shumë, tepër

□ *I shall be only too pleased to get home.*

only too aware/conscious of sth/that tepër i vetëdijshëm se

□ *The boy is only too aware that he is less able than others of his age.*

on no account; not on any account në asnjë mënyrë, kurrsesi

□ *Don't on any account leave the prison unguarded.* □ *This patient must on no account be left unattended, even for one minute.* □ 'Would you consider taking on the editorship yourself?' 'On no account.' □ The students are on no account to leave the school ground after 9 p.m.* □ *I whispered to Catherine that she mustn't on any account accede to the proposal.*

on occasion me rast, kohë pas kohe, nganjëherë

□ *I know the park you mean; I used to go there for a walk on occasion.* □ *If on occasion he mistrusted his own powers, it was not a mistrust that he intended others to share.* □ *We no longer keep up the close friendship of a few—years ago,*

though we still visit each other *on occasion.*

on one's hands në zotërim; nëpër duar

□ *I'm trying to sell off these books; I don't want them on my hands any longer.*

on one side... on the other nga një anë... nga ana tjetër

□ *Dick, in addition to genuinely lovely mental interests, was a most romantic person on one side, a most... complaining soul on the other.*

on one's knees i gjunjëzuar, i përgjunjur; i përulur

□ *Better die standing than live on one's knees.*

on one's last legs mezi mbahet (qëndron) në këmbë

□ *When the contest ended, the champion was on his last legs.* □ *The blacksmith's business is on its last legs.* □ *People had grown tired of saying that the 'Disunion' was on its last legs.* □ *The dog is old and sick. He is on his last legs.*

on one's/its own 1. vetë, pa ndihmën e të tjerëve; vetiu

□ *I'll give my wrist a day or two to see if it gets better on its own before I go to the doctor.* □ *'But nobody comes here who would steal them or borrow them without asking.' 'I wouldn't have thought so either, but books don't walk off shelves on their own.'* □ *The little boy had painted the whole picture on his own.*

2. në vetvete

□ *A bowl of soup, thick with meat and vegetables, was a meal on its own.* □ *The thought of the voyage was enough on its own to make her feel sick without ever going on board.*

on one's own account 1. më vete, i pavarur nga të tjerët, me llogari (aktivitet) më vete

□ *All the customers want their car jobs done by Brian. It's a pity he can't find the capital to set up **on his own account**.* □ *He tried to show an intelligent interest in the family. What school did Glad go to? Did Stan think of starting **on his own**?*
2. në emrin tim; nga ana ime
□ *I am not making the complaint **on my own account**, but on behalf of others.*

on one's part/on the part of sb nga ana e
□ *The agreement has been kept **on my part** but not on his.* □ *It's hardly proper **on your part** to speak like that.* □ *I apologize for any mistake **on my part**.*

on one's side nga ana e
□ *...he was, **on his side** too, very anxious to see Osborne.* □ *In declaring your trust in me, you have done what is... in no way undeserved **on my side**.* □ ***Whose side** are you on, anyway?*

on one's toes gati për veprim; më këmbë; gjithnjë gati
□ *The successful ball player is always **on his toes**.*

on order i porositur
□ *I've got two books **on order** at the bookshop.*

on paper 1. me shkrim
□ *Could you put a few ideas down **on paper**?*
2. në letër
□ *It's a fine scheme **on paper**, but will it work in practice?*

on principle në parim, parimisht
□ *Many people are opposed to the sale of arms **on principle**.* □ *... I object to the whole thing **on principle**.*

on purpose me qëllim, qëllimisht, enkas
□ *Jo: How could you give me a father*

*like that? Helen: I didn't do it **on purpose**. How was I to know you'd materialize out of a little love that lasted five minutes?* □ *'Did he break it accidentally?' 'No, **on purpose**.'* □ *She seems to do these things **on purpose**.* □ *I came here **on purpose** to see you.* □ *He has left the book here **on purpose** for you to read.*

on record i regjistruar, i shkruar, i dokumentuar
□ *This is the worst earthquake **on record**.* □ *It is **on record** that the winter was the wettest for ten years.*

on reflection duke e menduar hollë, duke reflektuar
□ ***On further reflection**, I saw that she might be right, after all.* □ *I thought of telephoning elsewhere for assistance, but **on reflection** I decided that there was no one to whom I felt inclined to speak frankly of my predicament.* □ *The suspicion did cross my mind, even as he spoke, that the man was lying and **on further reflection** I was sure of that.* □ *She decided, **on reflection**, to accept the offer.*

on schedule në kohë, në afat
□ *Most of the trains arrive **on schedule**.* □ *I think we shall manage to complete the work **on schedule**.*

on second thought duke e rimenduar (peshuar) mirë (sërish)
□ *I was going to say something about what had passed between me and Mrs. Reed, but **on second thought** I considered it better to remain silent.* □ *I was intending to go at once, but **on second thought** I decided to wait for a few days.* □ ***On second thoughts** I think I'd better go now.*

on Shanks's mare/pony më këmbë
□ *If you won't drive me, I'll have to get there **on Shanks's pony**.* □ *We*

shall have to go on Shanks's mare, I suppose.

on sight me të parë; me shikimin e parë
□ *The sentry has orders to shoot looters on sight.* □ *Alison: Hugh and I disliked each other on sight, and Jimmy knew it.* □ *A couple of thugs were sent after him with orders to shoot on sight.* □ *She plays music on sight.*

on sb's account/on account of sb/sth për hir të, për shkak të, për arsye të
□ *Please don't worry on my account: I shall be quite safe.* □ *The Browns will be higher up the housing priority list on account of their children.* □ 'Then it was on my account that your home was broken up. Mother, I am sorry.' □ *That would be a greater calamity than ever now, Ona continued, on account of the baby.* □ *They would all have to work harder now on his account.*

on sb's back (i bie) në (më) qafë, e ngacmoj, e mërzit
□ *I'm tired of working for my present boss; he's always on my back for something or the other.*

on that score për atë, për atë shkak
□ *I'll make sure that everyone is on time, so you needn't have any worries on that score.* □ *You need have no anxiety on that score.* □ *He absented himself from the class without permission. He would be criticized on that score.*

on the air në transmetim radiofonik (televiziv)
□ *The President is making a broadcast to the nation tonight: he'll be on the air at 8 o'clock.* □ *His show is on the air at six o'clock.* □ *This channel comes on the air every morning at 7 a.m.*

on the alert në gatishmëri, në beft
□ *When the prisoner escaped, all police in the area were put on the alert.* □ *The night watchman was on the alert all the long hours he was on duty.* □ *You must be on the alert so as not to be taken by surprise.*

on the/an average mesatarisht
□ *Each of us uses, on average, 180 pounds of paper products every year.* □ *My husband enjoys an occasional three or four course blow-out but he eats on average much less than I do.* □ *We fail one student per year on average.*

on the basis of sth në bazë të
□ *It may be that some countries are sending more students to the universities than they should send on a basis of ability.*

on the cards i mundshëm, që mund të ndodhë
□ *By way of going in for anything that might be on the cards. I call to mind that Mr. Micawber composed a petition... □ I must think over this. I have known for years past that it was on the cards. □ An early general election is certainly on the cards.*

on the carpet për diskutim, për shqyrtim
□ *He planned to bring that subject on the carpet.*

on the (off) chance of me shpresë se
□ *I didn't think you would be at home, but I just called on the off chance.*

on the cheap me të lirë
□ *It is perfectly possible to make films of high technical finish on the cheap using first takes and actors working at weekends for a percentage.* □ *He bought it on the cheap.*

on the contrary përkundrazi
□ *There was none of the bitterness that has so often broken out in the*

past. **On the contrary,** *friend and foe treated each other with a respect that has been absent these many years.*
□ *It isn't true that Jack is no good at music:* **on the contrary,** *he plays the piano well.* □ *It doesn't seem ugly to me;* **on the contrary,** *I think it's rather beautiful.* □ *'You have nothing to do now,' I think. '***On the contrary** *I have a hundred and one things to attend to.'*

on the cuff me kredi
□ *Peter lost the money that mother gave him to buy meat, and the store would not let him have meat* **on the cuff.** □ *Many people buy cars and television sets* **on the cuff.**

on the dot saktësisht, në mënyrë të përpiktë; pikërisht, tamam në kohë
□ *He arrived at seven o'clock* **on the dot.** □ *He's very punctual—always arrives* **on the dot.** □ *They must show up promptly—***on the dot**—*and in good condition for the work every day.*

on the face of it siç duket, në dukje, në pamjen e jashtme
□ *Jack's school results have been very good so,* **on the face of it,** *he should do well at the university; but he has chosen a very difficult subject for his degree.* □ **On the face of it,** *he seems to be telling the truth though I suspect he's hiding something.* □ *His argument appears quite convincing* **on the face of it.** □ *Dave was constantly making this suggestion; I can't think why, as there were few pieces of advice which,* **on the face of it,** *I was likely to follow.* □ *The idea is absurd* **on the face of it.**

on the ground/(the) grounds of sth falë, për arsye (shkak) të; mbështetur në, bazuar në

□ *The board agreed to Jenkin's retirement* **on ground of** *ill-health without loss of pension rights.*

on the hop në lëvizje
□ *I've been* **on the hop** *all day.*

on the horns of a dilemma para një dileme
□ *Jim is* **on the horns of a dilemma:** *he has received invitations to two parties for the same evening, and he cannot decide which to attend.*

on the house nga lokali; nga pronari
□ *Oscar was the first customer at the dinner, so his lunch was* **on the house.** □ *At the opening of the new hotel, the champagne was* **on the house.** □ *The owner of the bar said, 'Today is my birthday, so the drinks are* **on the house.'**

on the job duke punuar; në punë, në aktivitet, në veprim
□ *She was* **on the job** *every minute until the cottage was 'on wheels'.*

on the level i ndershëm, i sinqertë; ndershmërisht
□ *I don't trust him: how do we know he is* **on the level?** □ *I'm glad you came here and told me, but why don't you tell everybody? If you're really* **on the level.** □ *Bud acted* **on the level.**
□ *... You better not get too stuck on that Hortense Briggs. I don't think she's* **on the level** *with anybody.*

on the move në lëvizje
□ *The Smiths are very fond of travel: they always seem to be* **on the move.** □ *Don't jump off a train when it's* **on the move.** □ *The army is* **on the move.**

on the nail menjëherë, aty për aty, në dorë
□ *I want cash* **on the nail.** □ *He bought the car and paid all the money* **on the nail.**

on the occasion of me rastin e

□ *A ceremony was held on the occasion of signing the treaty.*

on (the) one hand ... on the other (hand) nga një anë ... nga ana tjetër

□ *I don't know whether John will pass his degree exams or not: on the one hand, he is certainly very clever; on the other hand, he doesn't work very much.* □ *On the one hand it is a movement very much in tune with the general social changes which have gained enormous ground during the seventies: and, on the other, it is an antidote to the instant, throw-away fashion styles which dominated the sixties.* □ *On the one hand I admire his gifts, but on the other I distrust his judgment.*

on the point of doing sth gati të

□ *I was on the point of going to bed when you rang.* □ *I was so much the more discomposed by this unexpected behavior that I was on the point of slinking.* □ *He was just on the point of giving up hope when we came to rescue him.*

on the quiet/q. t./QT privatisht; fshehurazi, vjedhurazi, pa u vënë re, pa i thënë njeriu

□ *'I've been meaning to have a word with you as a matter of fact.' 'Well, here I am.' 'I'd like it more on the quiet, you know.'* □ *I warned a few of my regular customers, strictly on the QT, that they'd better fill their tanks now because there would be no petrol by the weekend.* □ *I shall let you in without a pass but, remember, it's strictly on the q.t.* □ *'Enter him on the quiet. Don't say a word to anyone.'* □ *'And the man from whom I got it told me on the strict Q. T.*

on the qui vive vigjilent, syhapur

□ *There is going to be trouble yet in London about these Canadians and we ought to be on the qui vive.*

on the right track në rrugë të drejtë

□ *We haven't the solution yet, but I'm sure we're on the right track.*

on the rocks 1. i rrënuar, i falimentuar, i dështuar, që ka marrë fund

□ *It has been a very bad year for trade: I'm afraid that our business will soon be on the rocks.* □ *I realize now that the grandiose plans for making me an educated man had gone on the rocks.* □ *After a year of high costs and poor sales the business found itself on the rocks.*

2. me akull

□ *He ordered a scotch on the rocks.* □ *Here's where I discovered rum on the rocks.*

on the run 1. në lëvizje, në aktivitet, s'më zenë këmbët vend

□ *I have been on the run all day and I'm exhausted.* □ *I have been on the run ever since I got up.*

2. largohem me vrap, ua mbath këmbëve (për t'i shpëtuar ndjekjes, kapjes)

□ *He's on the run from the police.* □ *We have the enemy on the run now.*

on the same line në linja të njëjta

□ *Could you write another programme on the same lines?*

on the shelf 1. mënjanë; në dosje, në raft

□ *We produced a plan but it has been left on the shelf.*

2. beqare, pa martuar

□ *She married him because she was afraid of being left on the shelf.*

on the side 1. jashtë (pune)

□ *He makes some money working on*

the side. □ *Many producers of lon-run shows are lenient about letting members of their casts earn money on the side.*
2. fshehurazi; privatisht
□ *Unknown to his wife, he had a love affair on the side with his secretary.*

on the sly fshehtazi, vjedhurazi
□ *We found that he was selling information about our products on the sly to our competitors.* □ *She says she has given up smoking but I think she goes to her room and has one on the sly sometimes.* □ *Mary's mother did not approve of lipstick, but Mary used it on the sly.* □ *Next Clarence found that old Merlin was making himself busy on the sly among these people.*

on the spot 1. në vend, në vendngjarje
□ *The police were on the spot within a few minutes of my telephone call.*
2. aty për aty, menjëherë, përnjëherë
□ *Greatly to the astonishment of the passengers in the street, as well as of her relations going on before, the good soul was obliged to stop and embrace me on the spot.* □ *He took off his coat and set to work on the spot.* □ *Now do, Lawson, just finish up this job, and I'll pay you down right on the spot; and you need the money.* □ *I asked him for the loan of $500 and he gave me it on the spot.*
3. në pozitë të vështirë
□ *Henry's conduct has put me on the spot: I really don't know what to do.* □ *Jones is on the spot because he cannot pay back the money he borrowed.*

on the spur of the moment i shtyrë nga momenti, impulsivisht, në mënyrë impulsive; rrëmbimthi
□ *I've taken a job at Coombargana, as a parlormaid. I did it on the spur*

of the moment without really thinking. □ *The intention to kill or do grievous bodily harm was possibly conceived only on the spur of the moment.* □ *We hadn't planned to go to London: we just went on the spur of the moment.*

on the square i ndershëm; ndershmërisht
□ *Is their business on the square?* □ *I've always been on the square with you.*

on the strength of sth në bazë të, mbështetur në
□ *I got the job on the strength of your recommendation.* □ *On the strength of many successful performances, he was chosen to play the leading role in an important film.*

on the surface në pamje të jashtme, nga ana e jashtme, pa i hyrë në thelb a në brendësi; në sipërfaqe
□ *The scheme seems on the surface to be quite practical.* □ *The results of the conference appeared on the surface to be gratifying.* □ *On the surface he doesn't appear to be a miser, but you find out about him, really.*

on the threshold of në prag të
□ *He is on the threshold of a successful career as a writer.*

on the tip of one's tongue në majë të gjuhës
□ *His name was on the tip of my tongue, but it has gone again.*

on the understanding that me kusht që, po qe se, në rast se
□ *I shall allow you to go out tonight, on the understanding that you will be home by midnight.* □ *I'll take it on, on the understanding that everybody helps me.* □ *I lent him $1,000 on the understanding that he would repay me today.*

on the up and up 1. në rritje, lart e më lart, nga suksesi në sukses
□ *Jim's career as a businessman is on the up and up: they say he will be the next manager.* □ *Attendances and sales at recent exhibitions have been on the up and up.*
2. i ndershëm, i sinqertë, i besueshëm
□ *We felt that he was honest and could be trusted. This information is on the up and up.*

on the upgrade në përmirësim
□ *I am glad to see that his health is on the upgrade.* □ *This business is now on the upgrade.*

on the verge of sth në prag të; gati të
□ *When I went into the room I found him on the verge of departure.* □ *She was on the verge of bursting into tears.*

on the wane në rënie, në ulje
□ *The team's fortunes seem to be on the wane: they may have to go down to a lower league.* □ *The actor's popularity has been on the wane lately.*

on the warpath gati të zihet, të ndeshet
□ *You had better be punctual for your meeting with Mr. Smith: he's on the warpath.* □ *Look out—the boss is on the warpath again!*

on the way/on one's way 1. rrugës për; në rrugë e sipër
□ *I'll buy some on my way home.* □ *We saw a number of nice houses on the way here.* □ *My friends have not arrived yet, but they are on the way.*
2. në udhën e
□ *He is on the way to success.*

on the whole në përgjithësi, në tërësi
□ *I think that the plan has some weaknesses but, on the whole, it's worth doing.* □ *To pretend, however, that the struggle to gain his own way had been wholly unpleasant would*

be untrue. *He had, **on the whole**, enjoyed it.* □ *On the whole, it had been a successful evening.* □ *'How are they taking the news?' 'Pretty calmly on the whole.'* □ *We have had quite a good summer on the whole.* □ *On the whole our stay there was quite enjoyable.*

on the wing në fluturim
□ *He tried to shoot a bird on the wing.* □ *He photographed the bird on the wing.*

on tick me kredi
□ *We used to buy our groceries on tick and pay for them at the end of the week.*

on time në kohë
□ *Fortunately the supplies were not late, and arrived on time.* □ *Do you set great store by punctuality and make a point of being on time for work and social appointments?* □ *Blake, British Rail's construction engineer in charge of the Scottish section of the program, says with quiet confidence that work will be finished on time.* □ *The train arrived on time.*

on top 1. në krye
□ *The horse that everyone had expected would be on top actually came in third.* □ *Although John had been afraid he was not prepared for the exam, he came out on top.*
2. mbi, sipër, përsipër
□ *The green book is at the bottom of the pile and the red one is on top.*

on top of 1. veç, përveç; mbi
□ *He is working very hard at the moment because he has to do a lot of corrections on top of his normal teaching duties.* □ *He gets commission on top of his salary.* □ *Mrs. Lane had many expenses and on top of*

everything else her baby became ill.
2. përsipër, mbi krye
□ *There is no privacy when the houses are built on top of each other.* □ *The elevator was so crowded that everybody was on top of each other.*
on trial në provë; në sprovë
□ *This new method is on trial for a month to see if it is any good.* □ *Take this machine on trial for a week.* □ *Democracy itself is on trial as the country prepares for its first free elections.* □ *The driver was found on trial to be competent.*
on trust 1. në mirëbesim
□ *You'll have to take all what I say on trust.* □ *You'll have to take my statement on trust.*
2. me kredi
□ *We bought goods on trust.*
on view i ekspozuar, i paraqitur
□ *Our entire range of cars is now on view at your local showroom.* □ *Have you seen the new tools and machines on view?* □ *The exhibits are on view from 9 a.m. to 5 p.m.*
open an account hap llogari bankare
□ *I'm just going along to the bank to open an account.*
open and above board i ndershëm, i çiltër, i hapur
□ *No one will try to cheat you: the whole thing is open and above board.*
open fire at/on hap zjarr mbi
□ *He ordered his men to open fire.* □ *It would not have surprised me if someone had opened fire on us from an upstairs window.* □ *A searchlight picked the ship up, and fire was opened on her from the shore.*
open its doors hap dyert
□ *It was some time before the medical profession opened its doors to women doctors.* □ *The store opened its doors for the first time yesterday.*

open one's eyes (to) i hap (çel) sytë dikujt
□ *It was the inspector's report which opened our eyes to what was going on.* □ *Foreign travel opened his eyes to poverty for the first time.* □ *What he told me opened my eyes to the true state of affairs.* □ *He took pity on this greenhorn of a nephew, and wanted to open his eyes too.*
open one's heart to sb ia hap zemrën dikujt
□ *He wanted to open his heart seriously to him.* □ *After going around worrying, June opened her heart to her mother.* □ *Mrs. Smith opened her heart to the poor little boy.*
open one's mouth hap gojën
□ *Everything I say is wrong this morning. I'm frightened to open my mouth.* □ *If you so much as open your mouth about it to her—you can pack your bags and go.*
open out 1. hapet, zgjerohet
□ *The river opens out suddenly into a broad estuary.* □ *At that point, the road opens out and becomes a dual carriageway.*
2. shpalos
□ *He opened the road map out and laid it on his knee.*
3. zhvillohet
□ *She opened out a good deal while she was with us.*
4. hapet, çel
□ *In the warmth of the room, the roses opened out in a few days.*
open question, an pyetje e hapur
□ *Whether any adolescent would have benefited from a kind of upbringing he didn't actually have is always an open question, isn't it?*
open secret e fshehtë e njohur
□ *It's an open secret that John is going to resign soon.* □ *It's an open*

secret that Joan and June are engaged.

open the door hap dyert

□ *The successful operation on his leg open the door to a new life for him.*

open up 1. hap derën (portën)

□ *Mother! Open up! Let me in, I'm home.* □ *'Open up in the name of law!'* □ *We told them to open up or we'd break the door down.*

2. hapem, flas hapur (lirshëm)

□ *She hoped that he would open up at once about his visit, but he didn't.* □ *It was only after he had a few drinks that he could open up.*

3. hap, çel

□ *Paul opened up his tiny store and cafe as usual.* □ *He never opens up shop on a Sunday.*

or else ndryshe, përndryshe

□ *Hurry up or else you'll be late.* □ *You must work or else you'll lose your job.* □ *You'd better give me that book—or else!*

or rather apo më saktë

□ *We stayed at my friend's house, or rather at my friend's parents' house.* □ *'You're going to say I must go,' I said. 'You must,' said Anna, 'or rather I must.'*

or so nja, rreth, afro

□ *'Ah! Young Mont!' he said: 'sit down.' Sir Lawrence took a chair. He found it pleasing to be called young Mont at sixty-six or so.* □ *The losses so far reported have come from only a half-dozen or so companies.* □ *I'll keep on for another hour or so. Then if there's no improvement I'll turn in.* □ *He was here a month or so ago.*

order of the day rendi i ditës

□ *He looked at the order of the day to see if there was anything interesting in it.* □ *Handouts were issued to the delegates, giving the order of the day for each session of the conference.*

other than sb/sth veç, përveç

□ *Does anybody other than yourself know this?* □ *Games should normally require no equipment other than a ball or stick.* □ *He had never once thought of himself as a man whom a woman other than his wife could fall in love.*

out and away pa krahasim

□ *'Who's the best shot?' 'Mr. Trelawney, out and away!'* □ *She was out and away the most intelligent student in the class.*

out-and-out i madh, me nam, me damkë; i plotë

□ *Don't believe him: he's an out-and-out liar.*

□ *They managed to steer the conference into throwing out a resolution expressing out-and-out opposition.*

out in the cold i shpërfillur, i mënjanuar, i lënë jashtë

□ *They chatted to one another but, being the only stranger, I was left out in the cold.* □ *All the other children were chosen for parts in the play, but Johnny was left out in the cold.*

out of a clear sky krejt papritur (papandehur), si rrufe (si bubullimë) në qiell të kaltërt (të kthjellët)

□ *He dropped upon me suddenly out of a clear sky and began asking questions which I had to answer.* □ *For, assuming that Clyde persisted in denying that he had carried a camera ... then how damning in court, and out of a clear sky, to produce this camera.*

out of character jashtë natyrës (karakterit) të

□ *It's out of character for Jim to tell lies: he is usually very honest.* □ *It is out of character for him to say a thing like that.*

out of circulation jashtë lidhjeve shoqërore, i shkëputur nga shoqëria

□ *I think John is ill; he has been* ***out of circulation*** *for days.* □ *Tony has a job after school and is* ***out of circulation*** *with his friends.*

out of date i vjetëruar, i ka kaluar koha, i dalë mode

□ *We ought to buy some new office equipment: the stuff we've got is* ***out of date.*** □ *This kind of fashion is now* ***out of date.*** □ *Much of the information in that book is now* ***out of date.***

out of doors jashtë (në natyrë)

□ *It's cold* ***out of doors,*** *put an overcoat on.*

out of hand 1. menjëherë, aty për aty, sakaq

□ *The plan needs careful preparation, we cannot put it into effect* ***out of hand.*** □ *He... ordered him to marry her* ***out of hand*** *as he would have ordered his butler to draw a cork, or his clerk to write a letter.* □ *Martin's proposal to get rid of that man* ***out of hand*** *was indefensible.* □ *His request for another trial was dismissed* ***out of hand.***

2. jashtë kontrollit

□ *The police have been called in, in case the demostration gets* ***out of hand.***

out of humor në humor të keq (të prishur), me qejf të prishur

□ *Julia was probably still* ***out of humor*** *over that affair in the morning, but that could easily be straightened.* □ *What's the matter with him today? Something seems to have put him* ***out of humor.***

out of joint 1. e nxjerrë nga vendi (kocka)

□ *He fell and put his knee* ***out of joint.***

2. në çrregull (çorganizim) të plotë

□ *The delays put the whole schedule* ***out of joint.***

out of keeping (with) në mospërputhje me

□ *His recent statement is* ***out of keeping with*** *what he promised us earlier.*

out of line (with sb/sth) 1. jashtë rreshtit

□ *If you look along the row of chairs, you will see that one is* ***out of line.*** □ *One of the soldiers is* ***out of line.***

2. i papërshtatshëm, i papëlqyeshëm, i pahijshëm

□ *Those remarks you made about me were* ***out of line,*** *and I want an apology.*

3. në mospërputhje

□ *The judge's latest verdict is* ***out of line with*** *his previous verdict.* □ *For some time it has been felt that the share capital of the company was* ***out of line with*** *the capital employed in the business.*

out of luck i pafat

□ *If you're looking for a cigarette, you're* ***out of luck:*** *I've just smoked my last one.*

out of (one's) reach i paarritshëm

□ *The shelf is so high, it is well* ***out of my reach.*** □ *Such highly-paid jobs are* ***out of his reach.***

out of one's wits nuk është në të, nuk është në rregull

□ *During the whole of this time Scrooge had acted like a man* ***out of his wits.***

out of place 1. i pavend

□ *I thought that some of his remarks were* ***out of place.*** □ *Your remarks were rather* ***out of place.***

2. i pazakontë, i pazakonshëm

□ *I didn't notice anything* ***out of place*** *about his behavior, did you?*

out of pocket pa një dysh në xhep, me xhepat bosh

☐ *You won't be out of pocket: I'll pay for all expenses.*

out of print i shitur plotësisht

☐ *The book you are looking for has been out of print for many years.*

out of proportion to sth në shpërpjestim me

☐ *The figures of the horses in the foreground are out of proportion.*

out of season jashtë sezonit

☐ *Apples are very expensive just now; they are out of season here, so they have to be imported.*

out of shape jashtë forme

☐ *He will have to train hard for his next fight: he is a bit out of shape.*

☐ *Take exercise if you are out of shape.*

out of sight, out of mind larg sysh, larg zemrës

☐ *Such instances of recall are, however, by no means frequent and it still seems to be largely a question of 'out of sight, out of mind.'* ☐ *The end is still unhappy. Out of sight, out of mind, I say, or would if it weren't for those redeeming bits of humor and madness before brutality sets in.* ☐ *'Good,' said Rose, 'who's talking about good? I don't want to do her good, I just want to keep her out of sight and mind, thank you very much.*

out of sorts pa qejf; pa humor

☐ *I'm not going out tonight: I feel a bit out of sorts.* ☐ *She looked confused and out of sorts.* ☐ *He's always out of sorts early in the morning.*

out of spite nga inati

☐ *They reported him to the police out of spite, because they hated him so much.* ☐ *He did it out of spite.*

out of step 1. jo me një hap

☐ *As the soldiers marched past we noticed that one or two of them were out of step.*

2. në mospajtim (mospërputhje)

☐ *Just because you don't smoke, it doesn't mean you are out of step with other boys and girls of your age.*

out of stock s'ka gjendje, janë mbaruar

☐ *We have no cigarettes left: they are out of stock.*

out of the blue papritur, papandehur, befas

☐ *I hadn't expected to be promoted: it just came out of the blue.* ☐ *At the last minute Johnny came out of the blue to catch the pass and score a touchdown.*

out of the corner of one's eye me bisht të syrit

☐ *I kept my face to the front but, out of the corner of my eye, I could see that someone was creeping up on me.* ☐ *Out of the corner of my eye I saw Reggie take Susan away, and the next ten minutes were a blur of new faces and half-heard names.* ☐ *I turned my attention to the package. I had already noticed out of the corner of my eye.* ☐ *Even when he was writing on the blackboard he'd be watching you out of the corner of his eye.*

out of the frying pan (and) into the fire nga shiu në breshër

☐ *He joined the army to escape the strict discipline of his home: but it was a case of out of the frying pan into the fire.*

out of the ordinary i veçantë, i pazakontë

☐ *The police searched the missing man's room but they couldn't find anything out of the ordinary.* ☐ *Her new house is certainly out of the ordinary.* ☐ *His behavior is nothing out of the ordinary.*

out of the question nuk diskutohet, s'ka asnjë dyshim; as që mund të mendohet, jashtë çdo dyshimi, është e pamundur
□ *Missing school to watch the football match is **out of the question**.* □ *A new bicycle is **out of question**— we can't afford it.* □ *We can't go out in this weather, it's **out of the question**.* □ *'You must be quite aware that what you propose is **out of the question**.'* □ *The drawback was that I was often sleepy at night or out of spirits and indisposed to resume the story for to disappoint or to displease Steerforth was of course **out of the question**.*

out of the race/running jashtë gare
□ *Either Jim or Bill will get the job: Jack is **out of the running**.*

out of the way/out-of-the-way 1. larg; i largët
□ *This village is very much **out of the way**.*
2. i veçantë, i pazakontë, i rrallë, i jashtëzakonshëm
□ *He has done nothing **out of the way** yet.* □ *'What an extraordinary meeting!' said Tom. 'I should never have dreamed of seeing you two together here.... Such an **out-of-the-way** place for you to have met in,' pursued Tom, quite delighted.* □ *This picture is nothing **out of the way**.* □ *... nor did Alice think it was so very much **out of the way** to hear the rabbit say to itself, 'Oh dear! Oh dear! I shall be too late!'*

out of the whole cloth kryekëput, kokë e këmbë, krejt
□ *He was lying **out of the whole cloth** about Frieda, but Angela didn't know and he knew she didn't know.* □ *There*

*was considerable bickering between Mr. Steger and Mr. Shannon, for the former was very anxious to make it appear that Mr. Stener was lying **out of the whole cloth**.*

out of the wood(s) jashtë rrezikut
□ *'She's been visiting that American with pneumonia...' 'Fransis Wilmot?' 'Yes, He's **out of the wood**, now.'* □ *'Not **out of the woods** yet,' he remarked to a group of his adherents.* □ *She's regained consciousness, but she's not **out of the woods**.*

out of tune 1. i çakorduar
□ *This piano sounds terrible: it's **out of tune**.*
2. në mospërputhje, në disharmoni
□ *His ideas are **out of tune** with what most people think.* □ *What Jack said was **out of tune** with how he looked; he said he looked happy, but he looked unhappy.*

out of work pa punë
□ *He has been **out of work** for a year.* □ *There are 5,000 men **out of work** in this town.*

over a barrel në pozitë të pashpresë (të pambrojtur)
□ *I'm **over a barrel**: I must do what I'm told.*

(all) over again 1. përsëri, edhe një herë; nga e para, nga fillimi
□ *He did the work so badly that I had to do it **all over again** myself.* □ *I'll tell you what you have to do and then you'll say it **over again** after me.* □ *I was adding up this long column of figures when some idiot phoned, so I had to start **all over again**.*
2. gjallë, krejt, njësoj si
□ *Even if you hadn't written I'd have known who you were. You're your mother **all over again**.*

over and above përveç, veç
□ *He was formally hired at an annual income of six pounds **over and above** his board and lodging by Mr. and Mrs. Garland.* □ *I denied being too busy, because **over and above** any consideration of courtesy, I was genuinely pleased to see him.*

over and over (again) herë pas here, kohë më kohë, vazhdimisht
□ *He's been warned **over and over** by his doctor to stop smoking, but will he?* □ *I've told my children **over and over** to be careful crossing the street.*
□ *I've warned you **over and over again** not to do that.*

P

pace off/out mat me hapa

□ *'Pace off about four feet along the side of the marquee and knock in a peg. Then pace the same distance off again, and so on all the way round.'*
□ *She paced out the length of the room.* □ *He paced out the length and width of the room again, and so on all the way round.*

pack sth away fus, vë në kuti (dollap etj.)

□ *All the glass and china was carefully packed away in cases and stored in the attic.*

pack sb/sth in 1. lë, braktis punën; pres, ndërpres marrëdhëniet me

□ *She's packed in her job.* □ *I've packed in this telephone-answering service so anyone can get me personally any time of day or night.*
□ *Smoking is no good for your health: it's time you packed it in.* □ *The girl had only worked for Mr. Touchitt for a week when she packed him in. It would be the same old story: he couldn't keep his hands to himself.*

2. tërheq publik të madh

□ *'Do you remember the way we used to pack them in at the old Alhambra?'* □ *That show has been packing them in for months.*

pack one's bags ngre (mbledh) plaçkat

□ *After their row she packed her bags and left.* □ *Believe me, if I'd been married to that woman I'd have packed my bags years ago.* □ *Almost every week she's been here the cook's threatened to pack her bags over some trifling incident or other.* □ *The delegation's bags were packed and*

they were all set to leave when they received new instructions from the government. They unpacked and stayed.

pack sb off nis, largoj

□ *She packed the children off to their aunt's for a few days while the house was being cleaned through.* □ *As they got up late they were packed off to school after a hurried breakfast.* □ *I packed them off with notes to the appropriate hospitals.* □ *When the children knocked on Mr. Ransby's door and asked for a penny, he packed them off with a flea in their ear.*

pack sb like sardines shtyp (ngjesh) si sardele, ngjesh në pak vend

□ *Even packing them like sardines into wards planned for half the number of beds, many cases requiring hospital treatment could not be admitted.* □ *The passengers were packed like sardines into the carriages.*

pack sth out mbush plot e përplot

□ *Opera houses were packed out whenever she was singing.* □ *The Festival Hall was packed out for Menuhin's first concert.*

pack the house mbush plot e për plot

□ *The fact that 'Peter Pan' still packs houses with delighted kids says a lot for Barrie, or for the staying-power of the Victorian imagination, or both.*

pack up 1. lë, braktis, heq dorë

□ *If you don't know where you are going you might just as well pack up.*
□ *Business is terrible—I might as well pack up.*

2. paketoj, mbledh plaçkat
□ *He **packed up** his things and left.*
□ *He **packed up** the few possessions he had and moved out.*

paddle one's own canoe luaj këmbë e duar, eci vetë, çaj vetë, mbështetem në forcat e veta
□ *I decided that it was best not to depend on anyone else, but to **paddle my own canoe**. □ Why don't you let the girl alone? You take my advice and let her **paddle her own canoe**. □ Birkett made his way up fast, thanks to his father's influential friends. My achievements were less spectacular but at least I could say I had **paddled my own canoe**. □ The boy's been featherbedded at home long enough—at 19 he should be learning to **paddle his own canoe**.*

pad the hoof eci, shkoj në këmbë
□ *At length Charley Bates expressed his opinion that it was time to **pad the hoof**. □ Nothing remained for thousands of them but to '**pad the hoof**' back to London.*

pain in the neck, a njeri i bezdisshëm; gjë e bezdisshme
□ *I hate meeting that man: he's **a pain in the neck**. □ Writing letters is **a pain in the neck** to me, and I arrange everything I possibly can by telephone and I think the expense well worth it. □ Picnics are a treat to some and **a pain in the neck** to others.*

paint the town red përmbys, bëj qejf (me zhurmë), e kthej përmbys
□ *When our exams are over we're going to go out and **paint the town red**. □ Two thirds of the crew went on shore leave. They spent too much money, **painted the town red**, and one or two of them got themselves locked up and had to be bailed out next morning.*

pal up (with sb) miqësohem, bëhem shok me
□ *Two or three of us who'd **palled up** went off on weekends to the sea. □ In the first form he **palled up with** a boy from the same village.*

palm sb off (with sth) ia hedh
□ *He tried to **palm me off with** some excuse about the bus being late.*

palm sb/sth off (on sb) ia ngec, ia lë në dorë
□ *John wanted to **palm off a horse on** him but just when he was going to close the bargain the man found that the horse was blind in one eye. □ He's the kind of dealer **on** whom anything can be **palmed off**.*

part and parcel of sth pjesë e pandarë
□ *Freedom of speech is **part and parcel of** the liberty of a free man. □ Do I fight or flee? Do I conform or rebel? Do I put my foot down or let my children do as they please? These are fairly usual day-to-day decision that are **part and parcel of** being human. □ Assault and robbery, cattle-driving and train wrecking were **part and parcel of** his terrorizing tactics. □ Keeping the accounts is **part and parcel of** my job.*

part company (with sb/sth) 1. ndahem me
□ *He had been his college friend and always his close companion; in the first shock of his grief he had come to console and comfort him, and from that time they had never **parted company with** each other. □ I'll go with you to the end of the street, and then I'm afraid we shall have to **part company**. □ I regretfully **parted company with** my fellow-climbers at the end of the first stage of the ascent.*

2. ndahen, nuk përputhen
□ *We are in agreement on most issues,*

*but we **part company** on the subject of capital punishment.* □ *It's on political questions that their views **part company**.*

part with sth ndahem nga

□ *Despite his poverty, he refused to **part with** the family jewels.* □ *He's not the sort who's happy to **part with** hard-earned cash.*

pass an opinion jap mendim (vlerësim)

□ *The research student asked his supervisor to **pass an opinion on** the material he had collected.* □ *There are few matters **on** which our friend will not **pass an** unsolicited **opinion**.* □ *He read my article, but did not **pass any opinion** on it.*

pass away 1. vdes, jap shpirt

□ *After the look at the old face, the doctor announced that Miss Forsyte had **passed away** in her sleep.* □ *His mother **passed away** last year.* □ *Mr. Richard Williams **passed away** at the great age of ninety years.*

2. zë, kaloj kohën

□ *He **passed** the evening **away** looking at his collection of stamps.*

3. kalon (koha etj.)

□ *The morning mist **passed away** quickly.* □ *His illness will soon **pass away**.* □ *Three weeks had **passed away** after this conversation.* □ *One day is **passed away** like its defunct predecessor.*

4. zhduket, merr fund

□ *When automobiles became popular, the use of the horse and buggy **passed away**.*

pass by 1. kaloj, lë në heshtje, lë të kalojë

□ *If you try to **pass** the problems **by**, they will remain to dog you.* □ *I cannot **pass** the matter **by** without saying a few words.*

2. kalon pa kurrëfarë ndikimi mbi, kalon pa u vënë re

□ *The whole business **passed** him **by**.*
□ *The great drama and passion of the world had already **passed** him **by**.*

3. shmang, evitoj

□ *He had a feeling that his friends were **passing** him **by**.*

pass muster kalon provën, është i përshtatshëm, përmbush kërkesat, pranohet

□ *The figures were before them, a somewhat colorless show, appearing to disclose a state of things which would **pass muster**, if within the next six months there were no further violent disturbances of currency exchange.* □ *This work of yours is not good enough to **pass muster**.* □ *Double dealers may **pass muster** for a while, but all parties wash their hands of them in the conclusion.* □ *Faulty arguments, which the statistician would recognize as such immediately, often **pass muster** in the popular press because they are disguised in such a way that their statistical nature is not recognized.* □ *Though my work at school was never as good as it could have been, it **passed muster** and I even did well.*

pass down përcillet, transmetohet nga një brez te tjetri

□ *The skill has been **passed down** over four generation.* □ *Our sense of the past is developed by our knowledge of history, by the accumulated heritage of art, music, literature, and science **passed down** to us through the years.*

pass into 1. pranohem

□ *He **passed into** Sandhurst by the narrowest possible margin.*

2. kalon, bie

□ *Patients under hypnosis* **pass into** *a trance-like state.*

pass off 1. kalon

□ *'How did the demostration* **pass off?'** *'Without incident.'* □ *The concert* **passed off** *well.* □ *The day* **passed off** *quite well.*

2. pushon, kalon, zhduket, ikën (dhembja etj.)

□ *Your numbness in your foot will soon* **pass off.** □ *The pain* **passed off** *quickly after the tooth was extracted.* □ *At the moment I have a slight headache, but it will probably* **pass off** *after I have had a rest.*

3. hiqem, mbahem, e mbaj veten, shtirem

□ *He has been* **passing** *himself* **off** *as a deaf mute.* □ *He* **passed** *himself* **off** *as a doctor until someone checked his record.*

pass on to sb kaloj, transmetoj

□ *The news was* **passed on** *by word of mouth.* □ **Pass** *the book* **on to** *me when you've finished with it.* □ *I* **passed** *her message* **on to** *his mother.* □ *If you can't do the job yourself,* **pass** *it* **on to** *someone who can.*

pass one's lips vë (fus) në gojë; ha, pi

□ *My head swam as I stood erect: I perceived that I was sickening from excitement and inanition: neither meat nor drink had* **passed my lips** *that day, for I had taken no breakfast.* □ *No food had* **passed my lips** *all day.*

2. më del (shpëton) nga goja, them padashur

□ *Then endeavouring by every little artifice to prepare her mind for what must come... they told him, at last, the truth. The moment it had* **passed their lips** *he fell down among them like a murdered man.* □ *I have recalled his words. I wish that he should know*

how true they were, although the least acknowledgement to that effect has never **passed my lips,** *and never will.*

pass out 1. shpërndaj bujarisht

□ *He's a generous spender: when he wins money at the races, he starts* **passing out** *the beer and cigarettes.*

2. më bie të fikët

□ *'I'd only have to point a gun at him and say bang, bang, and the little twerp would* **pass out** *cold from fright.*

pass out of mind harroj; më del (ikën) nga mendja

□ *This incident* **passed out of mind** *long ago.*

pass over 1. lë në heshtje, nuk zë në gojë, s'hap gojë

□ *'Now, look here, Michael, if I* **pass** *it* **over** *will you give me your word not to try it on again?'*

2. shmang, kaloj pa vënë re, pa i kushtuar vëmendje

□ *If small offences are* **passed over** *they may lead to more serious ones.* □ *We may* **pass over** *the details.* □ *You can't* **pass over** *these painful sources of conflict, and hope they'll disappear.*

pass through 1. kaloj në një qytet

□ *'Why don't you stay the night?' 'No, thank you: we're just* **passing through.'**

2. përjetoj

□ *John* **passed through** *a difficult period shortly after his marriage broke down, but after a year or so his health and spirits picked up.* □ *The astronauts* **passed through** *an anxious hour when the onboard computer started to malfunction.*

pass the buck ia hedh përgjegjësinë dikujt

□ *Jates had no desire to go to the*

*kitchen. He **passed the buck** to Bing.* □ *I spent all day trying to find an official who would deal with my complaint; but each one **passed the buck** to someone else.* □ *If you lose a race, it's always a question of **passing the buck**. The owner blames the trainer, because the trainer told him the horse would win. The trainer can't admit he's wrong, so who's he going to blame? The jockey.*

pass (the) time kaloj kohën
□ *I suggested that we should perhaps fish—to **pass the time** I said, but of course we all realized that it was for our next meal.* □ *I fell in with anything anybody suggested, chiefly because one way of **passing time** seemed as good as another till I could get back to London and see Philip again.* □ *Inevitably, therefore, television is in perpetual danger of being turned into a mere domestic appliance for **passing the time**, painless and undemanding.* □ *How do you **pass the time** now you are retired?*

pass the time of day (with sb) përshëndetem, shkëmbej përshëndetje
□ *I gave it to one of the priests there. He knows me. I've **passed the time of day with** him on street. You know the way they'll talk to anybody.* □ *I wonder if there really is anything in the wind, or whether this man has just dropped in to **pass the time of the day**.* □ *I didn't know him well: when we met, we would just **pass the time of the day**.* □ *They **passed the time o'day** to one another.*

pass up refuzoj të pranoj; lë të shkojë
□ *Imagine **passing up** an offer like that!*

paste up ngjit
□ *There were posters advertising the bullfight **pasted up** all over the town.*

pat sb on the back përgëzoj, uroj, i rrah krahët (shpatullat, supet) dikujt
□ *We **patted him on the back** for his good work.* □ *The whole class **patted him on the back** because of his good play in the final game.*

pave the way for sth përgatit terrenin, hap rrugën për
□ *The continual rioting in the streets **paved the way for** the army taking over the government.* □ *The discovery of electricity **paved the way for** many inventions.*

pay a call/visit vizitoj, shkoj për vizitë, bëj një vizitë
□ *I **paid** him **a visit** early one morning.* □ *At last, Jurgis found work... And he fell to work, and toiled like a Trojan till night. Then he went and told Elizabeta, and also, late as it was, he **paid a visit** to Ostrinski to let him know of his good fortune.*

pay a compliment to sb/pay sb a compliment i bëj një kompliment dikujt
□ *'What a charming man!' 'He sets out to be a great one for **paying compliments** to the ladies and all that.'* □ *Of course I don't object. I haven't taken out copyrights on my teaching methods. If a colleague **pays** me **the compliment** of adopting any of them, I am only too pleased.* □ *He on his side **paid** him appropriate **compliments** and then... entered upon a matter which was on his mind.*

pay attention to i kushtoj vëmendje, i jap rëndësi
□ *Then I would commence a practical demonstration, to which Dora would **pay** profound **attention**, perhaps for five minutes.* □ ***Pay attention** to the instructions you are about to hear.* □ *Close **attention** is being **paid to** present movements in the money market.*

□ *'Please pay no attention to her, my lady,'* Briggs *interrupted, obviously distressed.* □ *The circus man paid no attention to her, didn't even seem to see her.*

pay back 1. kthej paratë

□ *Have you paid me back the money you owe me yet?* □ *The sum was paid back to the bank with interest.*

2. shpaguaj, ia marr hakun

□ *She paid him back for his casual infidelities.* □ *I'll pay him back for the trick he played on me.*

pay back in kind i përgjigjem (ia kthej) me të njëjtën monedhë

□ *Don't get sarcastic with him; he can pay back in kind.*

pay court to 1. i vardisem, i vij rrotull (një femre), i bëj korte

□ *Many young men came to pay court to his daughter.*

2. mikloj, lajkatoj; trajtoj me respekt (admirim)

□ *He represented the power of money as Jack did: he was another king. As I watched them paying court to him, I wondered how on earth he came to marry Alice.*

pay heed to tregoj, kushtoj vëmendje për

□ *It is all to the good that the school is to pay greater heed to the voice of the youth.* □ *She paid no heed to our warnings.*

pay homage to sb bëj homazhe, bëj nderime, nderoj

□ *We went to the Martyr's Graves to pay homage to the finest sons and daughters of our country.* □ *We pay homage to the genius of Shakespeare.*

pay lip service to shpreh mbështetjen (miratimin) vetëm me fjalë

□ *He pays lip service to feminism but his wife still does all the housework.*

□ *Trade unionists pay only lip service to the need for research.*

pay off 1. del me sukses, ka sukses, jep rezultat, shpërblen

□ *Sinatra fought like a tiger for the part of Maggio in the film—a gamble which paid off with an Oscar.*

2. paguaj rrogë të plotë dhe pushoj nga puna

□ *The crew of the merchant ship were paid off at the end of the trip and a fresh one engaged.* □ *It's all most regrettable but it looks as though I'm compelled to pay you off for your caretaking work.*

3. shlyej, laj borxhin etj.

□ *You'll have to pay off your old loan before being allowed a new one.* □ *All his outstanding debts have been paid off.*

4. paguaj

□ *The men were paid off just before quitting time, the last day before holiday.*

5. sjell fitim

□ *At first Mr. Harrison lost money on his investments, but finally one paid off.*

6. shpaguaj, ia marr hakun

□ *When Bob tripped Dick, Dick paid Bob off by punching him in the nose.*

7. paguaj

□ *Publicans are known to have paid off one gang of terrorists to stop their pubs being blown up by another.*

pay/settle an old score qëroj (laj) hesapet e vjetra

□ *He was pleased to think that he was being given a chance to pay up old scores and to do large things; he was really grateful.*

pay one's (last) respects i bëj respektet e fundit

□ *All his friends went to the funeral to pay their last respects.*

357

pay one's way mban veten, përballon harxhet (shpenzimet) e veta, tiganiset me dhjamin e vet

□ *'Look here, old man. You're bound to get into debt; mind you come to me at once. Of course, I'll always pay them. But you must remember one respects oneself more afterwards if one pays one's own way.'* □ *I never earned much money, but I always had enough to pay my way.*

pay sb back in his own coin/in the same coin ia shpërblej me të njëjtën monedhë

□ *He was but paying back Hugh and William in their own coin.* □ *We turned up half-an-hour late for Jims's meeting: he always keeps us waiting, so we thought we would pay him back in his own coin.*

pay sb (off) scot and lot laj (shlyej) plotësisht, qëroj hesapet

□ *It's all very well now—it keeps one on somehow, and you know it but I'll pay you off scot and lot bye and bye.*

pay through the nose paguaj shtrenjtë, paguaj si frëngu pulën

□ *'He pays well, I hope?' said Steerforth. 'Pays, as he speaks, my dear child—through the nose,' replied Miss Mowcher.* □ *That fellow would make his family pay through the nose to keep out of bankruptcy or even perhaps gaol!* □ *The shopkeeper knew that we needed the supplies badly, so he made us pay through the nose.* □ *There was a shortage of cars; if you found one for sale, you had to pay through the nose.*

pay tribute to nderoj, i bëj nderime

□ *By erecting the statue we have paid tribute to the memory of the founder of our school.* □ *His colleagues paid generous tribute to the outgoing president.*

penny for your thoughts, a çfarë po mendon? na një pare, nxirr (fol) një fjalë

□ *You have been silent now for quite a few minutes. A penny for your thoughts. Neverout.* □ *... Come, a penny for your thoughts. Miss. It is not worth a Farthing; for I was thinking of you.* □ *'A penny for your thoughts,' Muriel said suddenly. 'My thoughts?' Bill ejaculated with a startled expression. 'Oh, my thoughts? I really don't know. Not worth a penny anyway.'* □ *You are looking very worried: a penny for your thoughts.*

penny wise (and) pound foolish i lirë në miell, i shtrenjtë në krunde

□ *Janet is penny wise and pound foolish: she buys cheap food, and then spends all her savings on expensive clothes.* □ *'I never waste food.' 'But you're often penny wise and pound foolish even in that.'* □ *Mr. Smith's fence is rotting and falling down because he wouldn't spend money to paint it. He is penny wise and pound foolish.*

perish the thought qoftë larg; është larg mendsh, as mund të mendohet

□ *'I was afraid you might leave me.'—'Perish the thought: I would never do anything like that.'*

pick and choose zgjedh me kujdes, me merak

□ *Persons can make up their own minds with whom they will work because there are plenty of people close at hand from whom to pick and choose.* □ *She liked to pick and choose books.* □ *I spent days picking and choosing before deciding on the wallpaper and curtains.* □ *We had to find an apartment in a hurry—there was no time to pick and choose.*

pick a fight/quarrel with sb kërkoj (hap) sherr, kërkoj të grindem, lëshoj brezin i pari

□ *When he is drunk he goes about* **picking quarrels with** *people.* □ *He tried to* **pick a quarrel with** *me about it but I refused to discuss the matter.* □ *It was foolish of you to* **pick a fight with** *a heavyweight boxing champion.*

pick holes in gjej të meta, nxjerr bishta (yçkla, kleçka)

□ *It is easy enough to* **pick holes in** *other people's work.* □ *His arguments were not well thought out: the students were easily able to* **pick holes in** *them.* □ *They* **pick holes in** *everything I suggest.* □ *It's easy for an outsider to* **pick holes in** *our program. What you don't understand is the technical difficulties we face.*

pick oneself up ngrihem, çohem më këmbë (pas rrëzimit)

□ *He was knocked down in the scramble, but he quickly* **picked himself up** *and dusted himself down.* □ *She slipped and fell, but quickly* **picked herself up.**

pick one's steps/way zgjedh rrugën, eci me kujdes

□ *The ground was covered with broken bottles: so he had to* **pick his way** *carefully to get to the exit.* □ *The street was somewhat muddy and we had to* **pick our way.**

pick one's words zgjedh fjalët

□ *I didn't want to make the audience angry, so I had to* **pick my words** *carefully.*

pick out 1. gjej, shquaj, dalloj, veçoj

□ *Can you* **pick out** *your father from amongst the group on that photograph?* □ *His house is easily* **picked out** *from the rest: it has a large blue door.*

2. zgjedh, veçoj, seleksionoj

□ *She was* **picked out** *from thousands of applicants for the job.* □ *He* **picked out** *the ripest peach.* □ *I'll go through the pile of magazines and* **pick out** *those I want.* □ *The pile on the left are the ones that have been* **picked out** *for the library.*

pick sb's brains marr mendje (mendim)

□ *I hope you'll allow me to* **pick your brains** *on this subject: I know very little about it.* □ *'Oh Jack, before you ring off, do you mind if I* **pick your brains** *on a minor legal matter?'* □ *If you have time, I'd like to* **pick your brains** *about home computers.*

pick sb's pockets i vjedh xhepat dikujt

□ *'He's just asking to get his* **pockets picked,'** *said Larry as they watched him stuff the notes into a hip pocket and turn to lean his elbow on the bar again.*

pick up 1. kap e ngre nga vendi

□ *She* **picked up** *the half-finished letter and put it on the mantelpiece.* □ *'You dropped the plate on the floor; now you* **pick** *it* **up.'**

2. marr, fitoj

□ *There are men in that factory* **picking up** *sixty pounds a week.* □ *'He earns good money, he does. He* **picks up** *a packet.'*

3. marr në makinë etj.

□ *You can walk or ride the mile or two to the crossroads where the school bus will* **pick** *you* **up.** □ *He* **picked up** *two students outside Doncaster and dropped them off in Central London.*

4. shpëtoj nga mbytja (në det)

□ *Air-Sea Rescue* **picked up** *the downed airman after receiving an SOS message.* □ *Survivors of the air disaster were* **picked up** *by small boats.*

5. marr, kap, interceptoj

□ *'Point all our aerials upwards. Then we'll* **pick up** *reflections of our own transmissions.'* □ *It should have been possible to* **pick up** *signals telling us more about the moon itself.*

6. dëgjoj, më zë (kap) veshi

□ *He'd* **picked up** *some tale that we were to have a cut in wages.* □ *She's always on the prowl,* **picking up** *scraps of gossip.* □ *'I hear that Buckingham Palace is to be turned into a museum.' 'Where did you* **pick** *that* **up***?'*

7. nxë, përftoj

□ *I* **picked up** *scraps of knowledge from a variety of sources.* □ *He* **picked up** *knowledge of radio just by standing around the radio station.*

8. kap, nxë, zotëroj, përvetësoj

□ *Jurgis had* **picked up** *a few words of English by this time, and a friend would help him to understand it.* □ *She isn't very quick at* **picking up** *the language.* □ *Young children soon* **pick up** *words their elders use.*

9. marr veten, shërohem, bëhem mirë

□ *You'll soon* **pick up** *after a day or two in bed.* □ *His health and spirits* **picked up** *after a week at the seaside.* □ *She is* **picking up** *wonderfully since she came out of hospital.* □ *You'll soon* **pick up** *health when you get to the countryside.*

10. vazhdoj, rifilloj sërish

□ *We'll* **pick up** *where we finished yesterday.* □ *The class* **picked up** *the story where they had left before the holiday.*

11. njoh rastësisht

□ *He* **picked up** *the girl at a college disco.* □ *She's living with some men she* **picked up** *on holiday.*

12. ndaloj, arrestoj

□ *The police* **picked** *him* **up** *as he was trying to leave the country.* □ *He was* **picked up** *and taken for questioning*

13. qortoj

□ *She* **picked** *him* **up** *for using bad language.*

14. marr (një sëmundje)

□ *Billy* **picked up** *a cold at the school.*

15. kap, ble lirë

□ *They* **picked up** *most of the furniture at auctions in country towns.* □ *She* **picked up** *a valuable first edition at a village book sale.*

16. marr, mbledh (të dhëna etj.), hetoj

□ *I was anxious to know what was going to be done with me and so was Peggotty, but neither she nor I could* **pick up** *any information on the subject.* □ *He had* **picked up** *rare coins in seaports all over the world.*

17. mbledh veglat

□ *When the carpenter finished making the cabinet, he began* **picking up** *his tools.*

18. pastroj, rregulloj

□ *Pick up* *your room before Mother sees it.*

pick up speed merr, fiton shpejtësi; ec më shpejt

□ *About a mile out of the station the train began to* **pick up speed***.* □ *The train moved slowly from the station, but* **picked up speed** *as it reached the open country.* □ *We reached the outskirts of the town and began to* **pick up speed***.*

pick up the threads/pieces 1. vë në fije (në fill), vë në rregull

□ *Their lives were shattered by the tragedy and they are still trying to* **pick up the pieces***.*

2. rilidh (rregulloj) fijet, i vë fijet mbarë, rregulloj (gjej) telat

□ *'You must realize that I've been away from the job for five years. It'll take me a little time to* **pick up the threads** *again.* □ *With some lingering mistrust on both sides Bill and Jane set about* **picking up the threads** *of their marriage again.*

pick up with sb njihem, takohem
□ *He's liable to bring home any odd character that he* **picks up with** *in a pub.* □ *Where did you* **pick up with** *him?* □ *She's* **picked up with** *some peculiar people.*

pie in the sky shpresa të kota
□ *Their ideas of reforming the prison system are just* **pie in the sky.**

piece by piece pjesë pjesë
□ *The bridge was moved* **piece by piece** *to a new site.*

piece of cake, a gjë e lehtë, e kollajtë; si bukë e djathë
□ *I won the race easily: it was* **a piece of cake.**
□ *The exam paper was* **a piece of cake.** □ *Persuading him to give us the day off won't be* **a piece of cake.**

pigs may/might fly fluturon gomari
□ *'Perhaps he'll let you have it cheap, since you are a relative.' 'Oh yes, and* **pigs may fly.'** □ *Jim might arrive on time, and* **pigs might fly!**

pin down 1. zë
□ *They seemed to have* **pinned** *his legs* **down** *under a heavy weight.*
□ *Mr. Jones's leg was* **pinned down** *under the car after the accident.*
2. përcaktoj, shpjegoj qartë e saktë
□ *The police tried to* **pin down** *the blame for the fire in the school.*
□ *And—this is the part I can't* **pin down** *in words—he had conveyed, to the right onlooker, that he knew what he was doing.* □ *It was difficult to* **pin down** *exactly what it was in her that pleased him so much.*
3. lidh, detyroj
□ *He's a very difficult man to* **pin**

down: he seems to enjoy being all things to all men.

pin one's ears back hap veshët, dëgjoj me kujdes
□ *You'd better* **pin your ears back.** *I've got important news for you.*

pin one's faith/hopes on mbështetem, var shpresat; kam besim
□ *My father is very ill but we are* **pinning our faith** *on a new method of treatment he is getting.* □ *Some* **pinned their faith on** *the emergence of a new national leader, others on a religious revival.*

pin sth on sb ia hedh fajin (përgjegjësinë) dikujt
□ *He tried hard to* **pin** *the responsibility* **on** *Alice, but to no avail.* □ *The bank manager was really to blame, though he tried to* **pin** *it* **on** *the clerk.*

pipe down pushoj, hesht
□ *She told the children to* **pipe down** *while she was talking on the telephone.* □ *'Have you come to see Mariete?' 'No,* **pipe down,** *you loony. Nobody knows anything about that.'*

pipe one's (the) eye qaj, nxjerr (derdh) lot
□ *He had got it into his head that his own peculiar mission was to* **pipe his eye** *which he did perpetually.*
□ *We had a minute together. I gave her your love, and she sent you hers, and said: 'Well, I'm very nearly over, Uncle dear. Wish me luck!' I felt like* **piping my eye.** □ *The rest of the smoke eddied about the house, and kept us coughing and* **piping the eye.**

pitch in/into 1. i shtrohem, i futem
□ *After a day in the fields, they* **pitched into** *the food with a rare appetite.* □ *We had prepared supper for the team and they all* **pitched in.**
2. sulmoj égërsisht

□ *Lewis hardly expected to be **pitched into** that way.*

3. i futem, i përvishem, i shtrohem (punës etj)

□ *They all **pitched in** and soon finished the job.* □ *We **pitched into** the work.*

4. ndihmoj, jap ndihmë; kontribuoj

□ *Local businessmen **pitched in** with an offer to meet advertising costs.* □ *We all **pitched in** a quarter to buy Nancy a present.*

place in the sun, a qoshe e ngrohtë; pozitë e favorshme

□ *Nations that have been oppressed for centuries were now fighting for **a place in the sun**.*

play about/around (with) luaj, tallem, trajtoj në mënyrë të shkujdesur e të papërgjegjshme

□ *Don't **play about** with my expensive tools!* □ *It's time he stopped **playing around** and began to take life seriously.*

play a/one's trump/winning card luaj kartën e duhur; luaj kartën e fitores

□ *'Oh, it doesn't matter if you don't want to go to the dance,' he said and **played his winning card**. 'There'll be lots of other pretty girls there.'*

play all one's cards luaj të gjithë gurët

□ *'Is there nothing you can do to avoid bankruptcy?' 'Not any more. I've staved it off for a couple of years but I've **played all my cards** now.'* □ *'The prisoner is bound to be convicted, isn't he?' 'Don't be too sure; the defense haven't **played all their cards**.'*

play a joke on sb vë në lojë, tall

□ *Felix did not notice what was happening and the wind, which takes such delight in **playing jokes on** absent-minded people, seized his hat and flung it gaily overboard...*

□ *We **played a joke on** him but he laughed all the time.*

play a part in sth luaj një rol

□ *He had a **part to play in** ensuring the success of the experiment.* □ *She plays an active **part in** local politics.* □ *She **played a** major **part in** the success of the scheme.* □ *We all have a **part to play in** the fight against the crime.*

play a trick on sb ia punoj, i punoj (i luaj) një rreng dikujt

□ *Sometimes they **played tricks on** him but they never know how he felt about them, and shrunk up, when he was alone with them.*

play a wrong card bëj një hap të gabuar, bëj një veprim të gabuar

□ *'How could you come?' she said. 'You've been a false friend to me!' Again Irene laughed. June saw that she had **played a wrong card**, and broke down.*

play back vë për dëgjim (shikim)

□ *The discussion was recorded on tape and then **played back**.*

play ball punoj së toku; bashkëpunoj, kooperoj

□ *It's often good business to **play ball** with a political machine.*

play ducks and drakes with shpenzoj pa hesap, bëj rrush e kumbulla

□ *He was sacked because he was **playing ducks and drakes** with the company's money.*

play fair (with sb) bëj lojë të ndershme, luaj (veproj) ndershmërisht (sipas rregullave të lojës)

□ *A well-turned out young lady of seventeen was a vast improvement on the heavily-laden gaunt man, but we had to **play fair** and, taking a coin, we tossed it for the place, and the lady won.* □ *Come on, you're not **playing fair**.*

play fast and loose tallem, qesëndis, luaj teatër me

□ Stop *playing fast and loose* with that girl's feelings. □ 'It's a shame by Heavens,' said George ... 'to *play fast and loose* with a young girl's affection.' □ James. ... You can't *play fast and loose* with morality and hope to go scot-free. □ And forcibly replying: 'My name's Clyde Griffiths all right, but the rest of this isn't true.' 'Oh, come now, Mr. Griffiths! Don't begin by trying to *play fast and loose* with me...' □ You can't *play fast and loose* with law, however much you may have lied to me.

play havoc with dëmton, prish, shkatërron, rrënon

□ Miserable food had *played havoc with* bone and muscle. □ An unhappy marriage, Jon can *play* such *havoc* with other lives besides one's own. □ The bad weather *played havoc with* our plans for the weekend.

play into sb's hands bëj lojën e dikujt, çoj ujë në mullirin e dikujt

□ 'No,' he said: 'it's just *playing into your hands* to loose temper with you. Make me angry if you can. □ And trade union leader who understates the profits being earned is *playing into the hands* of the wage-cutters. □ In the basketball game, Jerry's foul *played into* the opponents' *hands*. □ By ordering our soldiers to leave the higher ground, we *played into* the enemy's *hands*.

play one's cards well i luaj mirë gurët, shfrytëzoj mirë mundësitë (rrethanat)

□ People liked Harold, and he *played his cards well*—and soon he began to get ahead.

play one's last card luaj kartën (gurin) e fundit

□ Madge looked at me through her real tears. She *played her last card.* 'If it's Anna,' she said, 'You know that I wouldn't mind. I mean, perhaps I'd mind but that wouldn't matter. I just want you near me.' But, alas, when she turned again to the audience, many other people had risen to support the vicar in his signal for departure. □ Mrs. Middleton *played her last card.* 'I know, children,' she said 'The vicar is hungry, that is what it is. Now all of you, off! Then,' she added,' we will all be ready to sing again.'

play on words, a lojë fjalësh, kalambur

□ The advertising slogan was *a play on words.*

play politics bëj lojë politike

□ The Principal said that the student leaders were not really concerned with solving the problem, but just *playing politics.*

play safe nuk rrezikoj

□ You can climb to the summit by a more direct route, but we shall *play safe* and go up an easier way. □ True the team *played safe.*

play second fiddle to sb jam vartës i; jam i dorës së dytë; kam (luaj) rol dytësor

□ When young Jones was appointed head of the department, I left. I wasn't going to *play second fiddle* to someone much younger than myself. □ I was asked to stay on as housekeeper after he married but I couldn't bear the idea of *playing second fiddle to* another woman after having been in charge for all those years.

play sb/sth false gënjej, mashtroj, i hedh hi syve

□ Why should I trust you? You promised my family safe conduct across the border and you *played them false.* □ I think Fritz Spiegl's memory must have *played him false when he recounted the story of his discovery and reconstruction of the Donizetti opera.* □ *'Well', returned the other...'follow me if you must, but if you* **play** *me* **false***, it shall but little advance you, mark you that.* □ *Was he the sort of man to be allowed to* **play** *her* **false** *with impunity?* □ *If my memory does not* **play** *me* **false***, I have seen it somewhere.*

play sb's game luaj lojën e
□ *He's trying to needle you into saying something rash. You'll only be* **playing his game** *if you lose your temper.* □ *No, if* **playing his** *dirty* **game** *is the only way of winning an election I'd rather lose.*

play the game respektoj rregullat e lojës; veproj ndershmërisht
□ *Jack should not have repeated what Jim told him in private: it's just not* **playing the game.** □ *He spoke of a generation of peace, and his other goals—progress, prosperity. He then stated: 'The important thing in our process is to* **play the game.'**

play truant vidhem nga shkolla etj
□ *Always* **playing truant***; wouldn't learn Latin and that. Besides, my mind was always on other things, like football and swimming.* □ *They went everywhere together. Elizabeth* **played truant** *from her office and Terence let important contacts go unheeded.* □ *He had never had courage to* **play truant** *from the Academy...* □ *The teacher supposed that the absent pupil was ill, but some of his friends suspected he was* **playing truant.**

play up 1. bezdis, mërzit, i shkakton dhembje
□ *My shoulder's* **playing up** *horribly.*

2. i kushtoj vëmendje; flas më shumë për; theksoj
□ *The coach* **played up** *the possibilities and kept our minds off our weaknesses.* □ *Depend on him to* **play up** *to the full his own part in reaching the settlement.*

play upon words luaj me fjalë
□ *Shakespeare liked to* **play upon words** *in his plays.*

play with luaj
□ *'Where's Stephen?' 'Up in the attic* **playing with** *his toy railway, I expect.'*

play with fire luaj me zjarrin
□ *Guy. ...Well, let's see how it looks, any way. Athenes. Don't* **play with fire***, Guy.* □ *She's inviting trouble if she gets involved with that circle; but some people like* **playing with the fire.**

plead guilty njoh, pranoj fajësinë
□ *Both men cheerfully* **pleaded guilty** *and paid a fine of $330 without turning a hair.*

please yourself bëj si të duash
□ *You can either go to town or stay here: just* **please yourself.** □ *'I don't want to come with you today.' 'Oh,* **please yourself** *then!'*

pleased as Punch shumë i kënaqur (i lumtur)
□ *He was* **as pleased as Punch** *when he won first prize.*

pledge one's honor jap fjalën e nderit
□ *'There, I'll* **pledge my honor** *to you, Tom, you don't see me so again,' he said. And Tom went off, wiping his eyes with great satisfaction.*

plough a lone/lonely furrow punoj vetëm, pa ndihmë
□ *He didn't go out much, one didn't meet him at parties—he* **ploughed his own furrow***. Contemporaries*

assumed that his cocoon was a chosen protection rather than a prison. □ Arthur Blessit was a 30-year-old Louisiana-born preacher who for years **ploughed a lonely furrow** among the drug-users of Hollywood.

plough (one's way) through sth hap, çaj rrugën, eci përpara

□ A fresh breeze blew from the shore, and the boat **ploughed through** the heavy waves.

plough the sand(s) mih (prashit) në ujë, rrah ujë në havan, hedh farë në ujë (në lumë, det, shkëmb)

□ 'I suppose, we are not **ploughing the sands.**'

pluck up (one's) courage to do sth bëj kurajë, mbaj veten, bëhem burrë, marr zemër e guzim, bëhem trim

□ I shall have to **pluck up courage** and speak to her about it. □ I suppose, dear, we must **pluck up courage**, and get that ceremony over. □ Who should present himself but that very Kit who had been the theme of Mr. Chuckster's wrath! Never did man **pluck up his courage** so quickly or look so fierce, as Mr. Chukster when he found it was he. □ At last he **plucked up** enough courage to go to his boss and demand more wages.

pluck up (one's) heart marr zemër, bëhem trim

□ 'Yes, it's a toothache...' 'Why don't you **pluck up your heart** and have it out.'

ply a/one's trade ushtroj zanatin

□ They had pulled down the old smithy where his grandfather had **plied his trade** and a metal shed with petrol pumps in front now occupied the site. □ Though their work was cleaning, and dishing up food, few of

them were the ordinary charwoman type; mostly they were obviously welcoming the chance to earn a little extra money by **playing the** only **trade** they knew.

pocket one's pride ul hundën, heq dorë nga krenaria

□ I knew he would harm my career, so I had to **pocket my pride** and apologize to him.

point of honor, a çështje nderi

□ I always pay my debts punctually; it's **a point of honor** with me.

point of view, a pikëpamje, pikëvështrim; qëndrim, mendim

□ This is unacceptable from my **point of view.** □ What's your **point of view** on nuclear power? □ You have given me quite a new **point of view.** I never thought of that side of the question at all. □ Miss Bawden explains about writing for children. 'You need only to have a different **point of view.** Children are as emotionally sophisticated as adults, but they just don't know so much.'

point sth out to sb 1. vë në dukje, sqaroj, shpjegoj

□ When the mistake was **pointed out** to him he hastened to correct it. □ Not that he wasn't quick to see his own advantage, when it was **pointed out** to him. □ I must **point out** that further delay would be unwise.

2. tregoj

□ The guide **pointed out** the best known paintings in the gallery.

point up 1. theksoj, nënvizoj

□ The recent wage increases **point up** still further the difference between this government and the last. □ This admission only serves to **point up** an aspect of police work that the public fails to understand.

2. tregon qartë

□ *The recent disagreement **points up** the differences between the two sides.*

poison-pen letter, a letër anonime shpifëse

□ *She was busy addressing **poison-pen letters**. □ The police have been trying to find out who wrote the **poison-pen letters** which have caused so much bad feeling in the village.*

poke about/around kërkoj, rrëmoj

□ *They toured the parlor, then tramped loudly and indifferently through the house... peering, **poking about** into every room. □ What are you **poking about** among my papers?*

poke fun at sb tallem me, vë në lojë, përqesh

□ *They **poked fun at** him because of his queer accent. □ He enjoyed **poking fun at** others. □ He was often **poked fun at** school because of his shabby clothes.*

poke one's nose in/into fus hundët në

□ *'Why don't you mind your own business, ma'am?' roared Bonnderby. 'How dare you go and **poke your** officious **nose into** my family affairs?' □ I wish he'd stop **poking his** long **nose into** my affairs. □ If you'd stop **poking your nose in** where it's not wanted, we could get some work done. □ He's always **poking his nose into** other people's business.*

poles apart antipodë, krejt të kundërt, krejt ndryshe

□ *Although they are brothers, they are **poles apart** politically: one is very left-wing and the other is very right-wing. □ A young man once said to me, during a discussion about the impact of television on society, that at least it had made it possible for him to talk to his own father. Before they had been **poles apart**: now they had a shared*

experience about which they could argue.

polish off 1. mbaroj shpejt e shpejt

□ *I can **polish off** the rest of the typing in no time. □ The rest of the Christmas pudding was **polished off** by the children.*

2. mund lehtësisht; eliminoj

□ *His opponents in the eliminating rounds were quickly **polished off**.*

polish up 1. rifreskoj

□ *I'll have to **polish up** my Italian: it's getting a bit rusty.*

2. shndrit, lustroj

□ *These old pieces of brass have **polished up** beautifully. □ The silver need to be **polished up** for the dinner party.*

poor man's sb/th, the i fukarait

□ *Sparkling white wine is **the poor man's** champagne. □ 'I forget what it is called—something Norwegian out of a tin. I've tested it before, **a** sort of **poor man's** caviar.'*

poor old sb/sth i varfëri, i shkreti, i gjori, fatkeqi

□ *I've got a feeling sometimes that if the money lasts five years it may be long enough. **Poor old** Ma. □ We have just got Rover back. The **poor old** chap's been in quarantine. □ It's not their fault that postal services cost us so much but I bet **the poor old** postmen don't get many tips at Christmas now.*

poor thing, (the) i gjori, i varfëri

□ *'Your sister was tired and upset,' Prissie said. 'The doctor came and I don't think he gave her much hope of walking, **poor thing**. Just imagine that. Never being able to walk again.' □ Cathy didn't pass her exam, did you know? **Poor thing**, she was terribly disappointed.*

pop across/along/ away/into etc. sjell, çoj

□ *'I'll just **pop** this letter **into the post**.*

pop along/around/down/in/over/ round bëj një vizitë të shpejtë; kaloj nga

□ *'There's a meeting tonight, and I was thinking of popping along for half an hour or so. □ He had just popped over to the grocer's.*

pop off 1. vdes

□ *'Now you can all stop talking about my money: I've no intention of popping off yet.'*

2. shtie, qëlloj, shkreh

□ *There were children running all over the place, popping off toy guns.*

pop the question i kërkoj dorën për martesë

□ *What about that young man you've been going out with so long? Hasn't he popped the question yet? □ Tom and June have been going together for years now, but he hasn't popped the question.*

pop up shfaqem papritur

□ *Just when the coach thought he had everything under control, a new problem popped up. □ He seems to pop up in the most unlikely places.*

pot calls the kettle black, the shan i shari të sharin; shan tenxherja kusinë

□ *Marry me now, Sonia, we have witnesses—we could become one here and now. Sonia. Don't be a dirty old man, you dirty old man. Jason: Huh, the pot calls the kettle black. □ She accused us of being extravagant— talk about the pot calling the kettle black! □ No one is lazier than Harry, and yet he criticized Jack for coming late: it was a case of the pot calling the kettle black.*

pour oil on the fire/flames i hedh benzinë zjarrit

□ *Stop your remarks please, they would be pouring oil on the fire.*

pour oil on troubled waters ul (ftoh, zbut) gjakrat

□ *My two neighbours were quarrelling so badly that I went along to see if I could pour oil on troubled waters. □ The fight between the boys had become so fierce that the teacher had to come to pour oil on troubled waters. □ The groups were nearing a bitter quarrel until the leader poured oil on troubled waters. □ They seemed to calm down as I spoke, and I was glad that I was able to pour oil on troubled waters.*

pour out zbras (hap) barkun, i zbras (i them) të gjitha

□ *Mary poured out her troubles to her pal.*

pour out one's heart to sb i hap zemrën dikujt

□ *She longed to pour out her heart, and tell people her opinion of Marjorie Ferrar. □ As he had always poured his heart out to her, this was highly amusing. But Christine did not smile as he continued.*

practice what one preaches bëj si them

□ *One does not have to be very old to see that not everybody practices what he preaches. □ Why don't you practice what you preach?*

praise sb to the skies ngre në qiell, mburr sa s'ka ku të shkojë më

□ *You shouldn't praise Ketty to the skies...*

prepare the ground for përgatit terrenin për

□ *Early experiments with military rockets prepared the ground for space travel.*

prepare sb for sth përgatit dikë për

□ *'Prepare the children for the good*

news. □ *Prepare* yourself *for a nasty shock!*

presence of mind mendjeshkathtësi, shkathtësi

□ *When he saw the accident, he had the presence of mind to get the police immediately.* □ *The child showed great presence of mind by grabbing the falling child.*

prevail on sb to do sth kandis, bind, i mbush mendjen dikujt (të bëjë dicka)

□ *He prevailed upon Arthur to write an article for the magazine.* □ *The judge was prevailed upon to show clemency.* □ *At dinner he prevailed on her to take some wine.*

pretty much/nearly/well gati, thuajse

□ *The two are pretty much the same.* □ *Though still struggling on they were pretty nearly exhausted.* □ *Pretty well every country in Western Europe has had a motor-boom.*

prey on sb's mind e mundon, ia ha (bren) shpirtin

□ *Fear of consequences preyed on her mind.* □ *They say that he killed himself because his wife's tragic death had been preying on his mind.* □ *Was it the accident with the car and the blackmailing letters that were preying on his mind?* □ *It would appear that his impending trial played on his mind.*

prey on/upon 1. gjuaj

□ *Owls prey on small rodents, especially mice.*

2. bëj pre

□ *The villagers were preyed on by the bandits from the hills.*

prick up one's ears i ngreh veshët, i mban veshët ngrehur, i bën veshët pipëz, i bën (i mban) veshët bigë

□ *He pricked up his ears, but still he could not catch the drift of the conversation.* □ *The children pricked up*

their ears *when the heard the word 'ice cream'.* □ *The horse seemed so interested in what was going on that after being led away some paces she turned, pricked up her ears, and looked around.*

pride oneself on/upon krenohem me

□ *He had always prided himself on tact in handling such crises.* □ *He prided himself justly on his skill in negotiation.* □ *On this ability to learn new languages he had always prided himself.*

promise (sb) the earth/moon ia bën fushë me lule, premton qiell e tokë

□ *Never trust politicians: they will promise you the moon in order to get your vote.* □ *'And then Lettie,' said Chairmain, 'has been so cruel about her wills. Always promising Eric the earth, and then retracting her promises.'*

promise well premton, ngjall shpresa

□ *The sales policy promises well.*

prop up 1. mbështet, i vë një mbështetëse (shtyllë, furkë etj.), përforcoj

□ *The gardener propped up the apple tree with a stout plank.* □ *The baby cannot sit unaided—-she has to be propped up on pillows.*

2. mbështet, përkrah, ndihmoj

□ *The government refused to prop up inefficient industries.* □ *The regime had been propped up by the foreign aid.*

propose a toast ngre një shëndet

□ *I should like to propose a toast to the bride and bridegroom.*

provide for siguroj, furnizoj, pajis

□ *He's always provided well for his family.* □ *They worked hard to provide for his large family.*

puffed up i krekosur, i fryrë, i ngrehur

□ *Don't be puffed up over your success.*

puff and blow shfryn, gulçon

□ *You're in poor trim. A man of your age shouldn't be **puffing and blowing** after climbing one flight of stairs.*

pull a face/faces at sb ngërdheshem, shtrembëroj fytyrën e përdredh buzët

□ *The clowns **pulled funny faces**.*

□ *When I said that we were going for a walk, John **pulled a long face**: he hates going for walks.*

pull a long bow ekzagjeroj

□ *What is it makes him **pull the long bow** in that wonderful manner?* □ *He was on the point of **pulling** some dreadful **long bow**.*

pull ahead/ahead of kaloj para

□ *'That driver is trying to overtake. Slow down a bit and let him **pull ahead**.* □ *Liverpool has **pulled ahead** of Arsenal in the race for the League leadership.*

pull apart 1. zbërthej, çmontoj

□ *The table is so made that you can easily **pull** it **apart**.*

2. kritikoj ashpër

□ *There's nothing more dispiriting than having your essays **pulled apart** in front of other students.*

pull back tërheq

□ *The battalion **pulled back** two miles during the night and took up prepared positions.* □ *The army **pulled back** after the battle.*

pull down 1. shemb, shkatërroj

□ *A row of back-to-back houses is being **pulled down** to make way for new apartments.* □ *The cinema she used to visit had been **pulled down**.*

2. dobëson, vë poshtë (sëmundja etj)

□ *An attack of fever soon **pulled** the old man **down**.* □ *That long spell in hospital **pulled** him **down** a lot.*

3. ul poshtë

□ *His hat was **pulled** well **down** over his eyes so that nobody should guess*

his true identity.

pull in one's horn i uli veshët, i uli pendët

□ *Since my salary has been reduced, I may have to **pull in my horns** as far as expensive holidays are concerned.*

□ *He tried to bully her at first, but she soon forced him to **pull his horns**.*

pull in/into 1. arrin, mbërrin, hyn në stacion (treni)

□ *Our train **pulled into** Paddington dead on time.* □ *As we **pulled in**, an hour later, our connection to Rome was pulling out.*

2. lëviz, afrohem, shkoj (eci) drejt

□ *The steamer **pulled in** towards the quay side.* □ *The boat **pulled in** to the bank.*

3. marr, fitoj

□ *He's **pulling in** a regular salary.*

□ *They're **pulling in** a lot of overtime on that job.*

4. tërheq

□ *'We used to **pull in** a good Saturday crowd at the Palace Theatre.'* □ *They need to have a high rate of interest in order to **pull in** money from investors.*

pull oneself together përmbahem, mbledh (zotëroj) veten, marr veten në dorë

□ *She had her ups and downs, but she had always managed to **pull herself together** and have a good time.*

□ *Under their patronizing and hostile stares he **pulled himself together**, walked into the kitchen, and sat down on a chair.* □ *A painful sob shook Andrew. 'I know you didn't! But it's the truth. All the cases I've given you up till now have been child's play.' '**Pull yourself together**, you hysterical fool. You'll be heard!'* □ *Ona would **pull herself together** and fling herself into his arms, begging him to stop, to be still.*

pull oneself up by the/one's (own) bootstrap/bootlaces çaj me forcat e veta

□ *He came from a poor home, and had very little education, but he* ***pulled himself up by his own bootstraps****, and now he is a doctor.* □ *Unable to borrow to repair and modernize its plant, the company was forced to* ***pull itself up by its own bootlaces****.*

pull one's weight përpiqem me mish e shpirt, jap maksimumin; kryej punën që më takon, bëj timen

□ *If each one of us does his duty, and* ***pulls his full weight****, then nothing can stop us.* □ *If we want this job be done in time, then everyone will have to* ***pull his weight****.* □ *All these good people displayed toward me a kindness and indulgence which I tried to reply by* ***pulling my weight*** *in my new team, in short, by a conscientious attention to my work.*

pull out/out of 1. heq, nxjerr

□ *I was afraid he was going to* ***pull out*** *one of those big molars.*

2. shqit, shkëpus

□ *The map is at the back of the book, and may be* ***pulled out*** *for easy reference.*

3. ikën, niset, largohet, del (nga stacioni, skela)

□ *We arrived on the platform just as the train was* ***pulling out of*** *the station.* □ *The three-thirty was* ***pulling out of*** *platform five as I ran into the station.*

4. tërheq

□ *I had lain in the grass and impotently watched the enemy* ***pulling out*** *below me.* □ *They are* ***pulling*** *their troops* ***out of*** *the battle zone.*

pull over hap krahun

□ *I shouted to the driver of the tractor*

to ***pull over*** *and let me through.* □ *Having stopped the driver, the traffic policeman asked if he would kindly* ***pull his car over*** *to the side of the road.*

pull sb's chestnuts out of the fire i nxjerr gështenjat nga zjarri me duart e tjetrëve (e botës), bën një punë duke përdorur si mashë a si vegël të tjerët

□ *You can't make me your cat's paw to* ***pull your chestnut out of the fire....*** □ *'More and more I see the big cities turning to the suburbs to* ***pull their chestnuts out of the fire.'***

pull somebody's leg tallem (me shaka)

□ *You don't suppose, do you, that our friends here are in earnest. They have just been* ***pulling our legs*** *very wittily.* □ *They told him his car had fallen into the river, but they were only* ***pulling his leg****.* □ *For a moment I actually believed that his wife had royal blood. Then I realized he was* ***pulling my leg****.*

pull (the) wires/strings luan telat

□ *The rich man's son was released from prison because his father was able to* ***pull strings****.*

pull the wool over sb's eyes bëj sylesh, i hedh hi syve, mashtroj

□ *'You're talking a lot of damned lies,' he said roughly, 'don't think you can* ***pull the wool over my eyes*** *like that.'* □ *Yet all the corporations heads, I am sure, will deny that this oligarchical rule of the few is true. They will produce proof that thousands of people own stock in their concerns. Yet this is merely to* ***pull the wool over the eyes*** *of the people, for frequently portions of that stock are non-voting and almost the controlling stock-ownership is held under the management of the oligarchy.* □ *'I'm afraid you can't* ***pull the wool over*** *the eyes of Tax Inspectors. They have ways of finding out.* □ *'She's had the wool pulled over her eyes for years. You don't imagine he always travels to London on business, do you?'*

pull together bashkërendoj forcat, bashkëveproj

□ *If we all pull together, we should be able to get the country out of the mess it's in.* □ *We must all pull together, or the experiment will not succeed.*

pull to pieces 1. kritikoj ashpër, gjej të meta serioze në; hedh poshtë plotësisht

□ *The new theory of the universe was pulled to pieces by many of the world's leading astronomers.* □ *The poor woman was pulled to pieces by her neighbours. Her hairstyle, her clothes, her make-up, her accent, her political opinions; nothing escaped criticism.*

2. bëj copë-copë

□ *A tiger can pull a roebuck to pieces in a matter of minutes.* □ *The rags are washed and pulled to pieces by machine.*

pull up 1. ndaloj, qëndroj

□ *More slowly than usual he drove towards his office. At last he pulled up.* □ *The driver pulled up when the lights changed.* □ *He pulled up the bicycle at the gate.*

2. qortoj; korrigjoj

□ *He was pulled up by the chairman.* □ *He was pulled up by all his comrades.*

pure/plain and simple s'është gjë tjetër veçse, thjesht, vetëm

□ *It's madness pure and simple to race wildly on a bicycle down a country road, chasing a motorcar.* □ *He told the police that his friendship with the accused man was a business partnership, pure and simple.*

push about/around urdhëroj; vras e pres

□ *'I won't be pushed around by him any longer!'* □ *'I wish he'd stop pushing people about as though they were children.'*

push ahead/forward/on with vazhdoj me vendosmëri (zbatimin)

□ *We are pushing forward with our plan to complete an inner ring road.* □ *Now that problem is solved, there is nothing to stop us pushing ahead.*

push along iki, largohem

□ *'It's time I was pushing along.'* □ *I'm afraid it's time I was pushing along.*

push for sth këmbëngul, kërkoj me ngulm

□ *They are pushing for electoral reform.* □ *A small faction is pushing hard for new talks.*

push off iki, largohem, hiqem sysh, zhdukem

□ *He comes into town periodically, looks up a few friends, and then pushed off again.* □ *We must push off soon, it is getting late.* □ *Is it ten o'clock? It is time we were pushing off.*

push on vazhdoj me vendosmëri, me këmbëngulje

□ *We must push on with our work.* □ *It's getting dark, we must push on to our destination.* □ *After a short rest the travellers pushed on towards the coast.*

push/press one's luck provoj fatin

□ *The policeman said to the motorist who had been driving to fast: 'I'll let you off this time, but don't push your luck!'* □ *But Ashmore was cleverer than that. He came into more money and wisely didn't press his luck after that. Directors are like alchemists, their hour is brief.*

push one's way hap, çaj rrugën (me
bërryla, me të shtyrë)
□ *We had to push our way through
the crowd.*
push sb to the wall vë me shpatulla në
(pas) murit
□ *'And finally Ivory was pushed to
the wall.'*
push through kaloj, përfundoj shpejt
□ *We are trying to push legislation
through before the Christmas recess.*
put about 1. ndryshoj drejtimin,
kursin (e anijes), marr tjetër drejtim
□ *The captain put the ship about.*
□ *The skipper put us about to avoid
submarines that had been reported in
that area.*
2. hap, përhap, qarkulloj, kaloj gojë
më gojë
□ *Somebody has put the story about
that the department is being closed
down.* □ *I should like to know who put
that rumor about, anyhow, it's completely without foundation.*
put above vë mbi
□ *Above such considerations of cost
we should put the welfare of the men
who work the machines.* □ *The investigations revealed that few men were
determined to put the integrity of
Administration above its survival.*
put a bold/brave/good face on sth
marr një pamje të gëzuar (të
kënaqur); marr një pamje sikur s'ka
ndodhur gjë, mbahem sa për sy e faqe
□ *'Brazen it out', he commanded. 'It
doesn't amount to anything... Put a
good face on it, more depends on
your manner than on anything else.'*
□ *Nobody liked the meal, but nobody
complained, they put a good face
upon one and all, and made great
chattering of knives and forks.* □ *After
the election shock, he turned to put*

*as brave a face on it as he could
manage.* □ *There's not much optimism
in the air, but at least both sides
are putting a brave face on proceedings.* □ *Her exam results were disappointing but she tried to put a brave
face on it.*
put a bridle on i vë fre
□ *He must put a bridle on his tongue.*
put across 1. transmetoj, komunikoj,
përçoj
□ *John is a teacher who quickly puts
his ideas across to his students.* □ *The
lecturer had a thorough knowledge of
his subject and put it across to the
audience.* □ *He may be a very clever
research worker, but he's very poor at
putting the stuff across to a class.*
2. realizoj me sukses
□ *The new librarian put across a
drive for a new library building.* □ *He
put across a big sales campaign.*
put a damper on fashit, pres (vrullin,
gjallërinë etj.); frenoj
□ *It was a hard job but the thought of
it did not put a damper on our spirits.*
□ *The argument put a bit of a damper
on the party.* □ *The fact that the headmaster was there tended to put a
damper on the party.*
put all one's eggs in/into one basket i
vë të gjitha vezët në një shportë, vë
gjithçka në rrezik, i luaj të gjitha në
një dorë
□ *Because he never cared to put all
the eggs in one basket, in the organization of the Hyde Park Company
Cowperwood, he decided to secure a
second lawyer and a second dummy
president.* □ *'That is acting like the
man who put all his eggs in one
basket,' Jenny said.* □ *This car company used to sell several different
models but now it has decided to put*

all its eggs in one basket, and produce only one model.

put an end to sth mbaroj, përfundoj, i jap fund

□ *She now observed to me, aloud, resuming her former restraint, that it was useless to hear more, or to say more, and that she begged to put an end to the interview.* □ *Madame Lamotte put an end to that colloquy. Soames did not stay long.* □ *I am going to put an end to their bad behavior.*

put a foot wrong gaboj, bëj gabim

□ *I've never known him to put a wrong foot, no matter how delicate the issue.*

put a new face on sth hedh dritë të re mbi

□ *What he's said puts quite a new face on the whole matter.*

put a premium on sb/sth i jap (kushtoj) rëndësi të veçantë

□ *The examiners put a premium on rational argument.*

put a price on sb's head vë një çmim për kokën e

□ *A price has been put on robber's head.* □ *The authorities put a price on the outlaw's head.*

put aside 1. vë, lë, heq mënjanë

□ *She put her needle work aside, and we had a talk.* □ *He put aside his textbooks when he left school and never reopened them.* □ *They put aside their rifles and packs and resumed a peaceful life.*

2. kursej, heq mënjanë

□ *I have a nice little sum of money put aside for a rainy day.* □ *'If you'd like to pay me a small deposit, I'll put the suit aside for you, sir.'*

3. harroj, lë mënjanë

□ *At such a time of crisis, we must try to put aside all differences of party or*

class. □ *Put aside all that has happened and try to start again.*

put a spoke in sb's wheel pengoj, i nxjerr pengesa, i vë (i fut) shkopinj në rrota

□ *Jack wants to be elected chairman, but I'm going to see if I can put a spoke in his wheel.* □ *He ought perhaps to have put a spoke in the wheel of their marriage, they were too young...* □ *'No, you can't get out of it as easily as all that, Miss Richards—it's about time that someone put a spoke in your little wheel.'* □ *She did not spare him, and if he lost his flicker of self assurance, she welcomed it. She had put a spoke in that wheel, anyway.*

put a stop to i jap fund

□ *It's high time this leakage of information was put a stop to.* □ *Is there any hope of putting a stop to this mad triple arms race?* □ *The announcement of supper put a stop to the game.*

put at vlerësoj, llogarit

□ *I'd put the weight at about fourteen pounds.*

□ *'What would you put the price of that car at?'*

put away 1. izoloj, mbyll

□ *He was put away for ten years for armed robbery.* □ *He was put away for attacking young children.*

2. kursej, heq mënjanë

□ *I'll have to put something away for my retirement.* □ *She's got a few thousand pounds put away for his retirement.*

3. heq, vë, vendos

□ *The correspondence was all put away in numbered files.* □ *Put your toys away in the cupboard, when you've finished playing.*

4. konsumoj

□ *I don't know how he manages to put*

*it all **away**.* □ *He **put away** half a dozen cakes while my back was turned.*

put back 1. kthej, rivendos, vë në vendin e mëparshëm

□ ***Put** the reference books **back** on the shelf when you've finished them.* □ *'Kindly **put** the book **back** in its proper place.'* □ *She had **put back** her pork and onions on the stove.*

2. kthej, çoj prapa (orën)

□ *My watch was ten minutes fast so I **put** it **back**.* □ *All the clocks should have been **put back** one hour last night.*

3. vonoj

□ *The truck drivers' strike has **put back** our deliveries by over one month.*

4. shtyj

□ *The date has been **put back** from March to April.*

put before vë para

□ *He **puts** his children's welfare **before** all other consideration.* □ *The determination of the six is to **put** the development of the community **before** all other consideration.*

2. paraqis për shqyrtim

□ *Proposals for sweeping reforms were **put before** the ministers.*

put by kursej, vë mënjanë

□ *She has a fair amount of money **put by**.* □ *Have a bit **put by** for a rainy day.*

put down 1. shkruaj, marr (mbaj) shënim

□ *He took my various dimensions, and I **put** them **down** in a book.* □ *When the lists were first drawn, I **put** my name **down** mechanically.*

2. shtyp, nënshtroj (me forcë)

□ *The military junta is determined to **put down** all political opposition.* □ *In 24 hours the general had entirely **put down** the rebellion.*

3. vë

□ *She had **put** the sewing needle*

down *on the chair by the window.* □ *'**Put down** the knife before you hurt someone!'*

4. ul

□ *He **put** the glider **down** in a corn field.* □ *The helicopter hovered over us looking for a place to **put down**.*

5. zbres

□ *The bus stopped at the station to **put down** one or two passengers.*

6. vë në qilar (depo etj.)

□ *I **put down** a couple of cases of claret last year.* □ *When you see what you're charged for French wines now I'm glad I **put down** a couple of cases of claret and three dozen chablis last year.*

7. fus në rendin e ditës

□ *Some MPs are in favor of **putting down** a resolution.*

8. i jap fund

□ *She had patiently **put down** unkind talk by living a good life.*

9. vesh, atribuoj, quaj

□ *He **put** the odd weather **down** to nuclear explosions.*

put down in black and white shkruaj, hedh në letër

□ *He has only to **put it down in black and white** using it as a theme of a story.*

put forth lëshojnë, çelin

□ *Spring has come and the hedges are **putting forth** new leaves.*

put forward, to 1. parashtroj, paraqit

□ *Can I **put** your name **forward** for golf club secretary?* □ *She **put forward** a constructive proposal at the meeting.*

2. lëviz, shtyj, çoj përpara (orën)

□ *My watch was slow and I have **put** it **forward** to the correct time.*

3. avancoj

□ *We've **put forward** the day of our wedding by one week.*

put heads together mblidhem kokë më kokë, konsultohem, këshillohem

□ We shall have to sit down sometime and *put our heads together* and think about ways and means. □ If only the leaders would *put their heads together* we might find a way out of our difficulties.

put in 1. ndërhyj, ndërpres

□ 'But what about us?' he *put in*. □ 'It's the firm's time,' Baxter insisted. 'He's carrying out an experiment,' I *put in*.

2. zgjedh

□ Labor was *put in* with an increase majority at the last General Election. □ The electorate *put the Torries in* with an increased majority.

3. harxhoj, kushtoj

□ Harold consciously tried to *put in* a quarter of an hour each day improving his French. □ We've *put in* a great deal of time and effort into this project.

4. vë, vendos, instaloj

□ We're *putting in* a completely new system of wiring and switches. □ We have pulled out the old pipes and *put in* copper ones.

5. shtoj

□ While the boys were discussing the car accident, Ben *put in* that the road was icy.

6. mbjell

□ He *put in* a row of radishes.

7. hyn, futet, ndalon (në port)

□ The ship *put in* at Durrës for repairs.

put in an/one's appearance dukem, shfaqem, dal

□ Jeremy *put in* a brief *appearance* towards the end of our party, and was then wafted off somewhere more important. □ 'Wait five minutes—just to show you've *put in an appearance* —and then go for a drink.' □ He

waited for the right moment to *put in his appearance*—just as supper was about to be served. □ For a whole week he hasn't *put in an appearance* at my house. □ They had been waiting for a long time but suddenly he *put in an appearance*.

put in action vë në veprim

□ At daybreak troops were *put into action*.

put in an awkward/difficult position vë në pozitë të pavolitshme

□ The support given to the rebels by local officials *put the government in a difficult position*. □ This then is *the difficult position in* which we are *put* by their refusal to cooperate. □ Is that all you can say? 'I'm sorry'? Such *an awkward position I put you in*, didn't I?

put in a (good) word for sb them një fjalë të mirë

□ 'But when she married again did no one *put in a word for* the boy at that time?' □ I wondered if you'd mind *putting in a word for* him—old Dan won't listen to me. □ The head was always prepared to *put a good word in* for his former pupils. □ As it happens, the chairman of the company you are trying to get a job in is an old friend of mine: I'll *put in a good word for* you.

put in jeopardy rrezikoj, vë në rrezik

□ The chances of an important representative match at Twickenham are *put in jeopardy* by the weather. □ The hold-up in the supply of fuel *puts* our whole advance *in jeopardy*. □ A fall in demand for oil tankers has *put* thousands of jobs in shipbuilding industry *in jeopardy*.

put in mind kujton, sjell ndër mend

□ Sudden and grateful immersion in country air and country silence *puts*

me *in the mind of* an observation by
Norman Douglas. □ *Look at that old
car: it put me in mind of the one my
father used to have.*

put in motion vë në lëvizje
□ *They put the new campaign in
motion.*

put in order rregulloj, vë në rregull
□ *His study is a chaos: his housekeeper has long since given up trying
to put his papers in order.* □ *Congress has suggested that the union
should put its affairs in order.*

put into effect vë në veprim (përdorim, zbatim)
□ *It was only a random idea... but I
shouldn't be altogether surprised if
he had put it into effect.* □ *The new
system will soon be put into effect.*

put into execution zbatoj, vë në
zbatim, vë në jetë
□ *The worthy plan was adopted and
put into execution without a
moment's delay.* □ *He was literally
afraid not to put his design into execution at the first possible moment...*
□ *The plans were finally put into
execution.*

put into sb's hands lë veten në duart e
□ *And now comes the story!—Jeanie,
I put my life into your hands...*

put into words shpreh me fjalë
□ *He could not now put into words
his intense fear of the witch doll in the
cupboard.* □ *Though they could not
have put it into words, their objection
to him was that he did not wear a uniform.*

put off 1. shtyj, vonoj
□ *Their translation into reality is
put off until the Greek Calends.* □ *I put
off going to the dentist.* □ *Never put
off till tomorrow what you can do
today.* □ *Owing to the state of the
ground, the match has been put off.*

2. zhvendos, largoj vëmendjen
□ *Little Jeannie began to tell the
guests some family secrets, but Father
was able to put her off.* □ *He was
trying to write, but the continuous
noise outside his window put him off.*

3. niset (anija)
□ *No man in his senses and out of
them, would put off in such a gale of
wind, least of all Ham Peggotty who
had been born to seafaring.* □ *We put
off from the pier.*

4. mbyll, fik (radion, dritën etj)
□ *We forgot to put off the radio before
we went out.* □ *Could you put the
lights off before you leave.*

5. shkurajoj, pengoj
□ *Maybe he had put her off too often
when she wanted to talk.* □ *The grocer
won't be put off with airy promises
any longer; he wants his money.*

6. vë në gjumë
□ *'What about a nice cup of tea to put
you off to sleep again?'* □ *A whiff of
gas will soon put you off.*

7. hedh, flak; heq, lë mënjanë
□ *The war was over but Harold was
still in khaki; he never looked so
nearly a gentleman again when he
put it off.*

put/throw off the scent humbas
gjurmët
□ *The false alibi threw the police off
the scent.*

put on 1. vesh, mbath
□ *I don't know what dress to put on.*
□ *What dress shall I put on for the
party?* □ *Jurgis had nothing to put on
but his shoes...*

2. prezantoj, paraqes, vë në skenë
□ *We shall put on this play before
long, let us do our best to know all
our lines.*

3. shtoj në shërbim
□ *They put on extra buses during the*

rush hours. □ *Southern Region are* **putting on** *ten extra trains to cope with the holiday traffic.*

4. shtoj (në peshë), vë (mish, dhjamë)

□ *In the month she had been with them she hadn't* **put on** *any weight.* □ *How many pounds did you* **put on** *over Christmas?*

5. hap, çel

□ *'Half a tick and I'll* **put on** *the light.'* □ *He* **put on** *the light.*

6. rris, shtoj (shpejtësinë etj.)

□ *The driver* **put on** *speed.* □ *When we had got clear of the station we began to* **put on** *speed.*

7. vë

□ *He* **put** *a hand* **on** *my shoulder.* □ *When it was all ready, she* **put** *it* **on** *the tray.*

put on airs krekosem, ngrehem, mbahem me të madh, kapardisem

□ *Don't* **put on airs** *with me Jack. I know you too well...* □ *I don't like you to talk that way to me. You're too young to* **put on** *such* **an air** *with your mother.*

put one's back into sth i vë gjoksin (shpatullat), vë të gjitha forcat

□ *If you want to accomplish the job in time you've to* **put your back into** *it.*

put one's best foot/leg forward/foremost i jap këmbëve, eci me të shpejtë

□ *'Now you must* **put your best leg foremost**, *old lady!' whispered Sowerberry in the old woman's ear; 'we are rather late...'*

put one's cards on the table hap (zbuloj) letrat, flas hapur (troç) me

□ *'Let's* **put our cards on the table**, *Father Schlemm!' The benevolence was gone from the priest's rosy face.*

put oneself out of the way bëj cmos, mundohem së tepërmi, përpiqem shumë

□ *Why should Lady Castlewood* **put**

herself out of the way *to welcome the young stranger?* □ *Anything that's handy, Miss, don't* **put yourself out of the way**, *on our account.*

put one's faith/trust in besoj, i zë besë

□ *There's something about you that makes me burn to help you. I'd* **put all my trust in** *you.*

put one's finger on vë gishtin mbi

□ *I knew there was something wrong but I couldn't just* **put my finger on** *it.* □ *At those committee meetings it is always you who* **put your finger on** *the weak spot...* □ *I thought there was a contradiction somewhere, as there was in most of Tom's counsels, but I could not* **put my finger on** *it.* □ *I can't* **put my finger on** *the flaw in her argument.*

put one's foot down këmbëngul, ngul këmbë

□ *Mother let us go to the party, but when it came to staying overnight, she* **put her foot down** *firmly.* □ *He* **put his foot** *on our staying for dinner.* □ *The children wanted to stay up late, but I* **put my foot down** *and insisted on their going to bed at the usual time.*

put one's foot in it lajthit, bëj një gabim (gafë, budallallëk, proçkë)

□ *'...I beg your pardon, Lady Julia,'* cried the inopportune Jack Belsize. *'I'm always* **putting my foot in it**.' *'Putting your foot into what? Go on, Kew.'* □ *I really* **put my foot in it** *when I asked Jane how she had got on in her exam: she said that she had completely failed, and then she burst into tears.*

put one's hand in one's pocket paguaj, fus dorë në xhep

□ *If Manson was down and out Mr. Page never minded* **putting his hand into his pocket**.

put one's hand(s) to (the plough) i përvishem (futem) punës
□ *'Well—well. To the main point—the departure with me from England, the cooperation with me in my future labors—you do not object. You have already as good as **put your hand to the plough**: you are too consistent to withdraw it.'* □ *The first day the young workers arrived, they **put their hands to the plough**.* □ *Whatever he **put his hand to**, he did it exceedingly well.* □ *He had **put his hand to the plough**, and he was not the man to turn back.*

put one's head into the lion's mouth vë kokën në rrezik, jam në gojë të ujkut
□ *'The project is perfectly a mad one,'* he exclaimed. *'It is simply **putting one's head into lion's mouth.'***

put one's heart and soul into i kushtohem me mish e shpirt
□ *If each of us **puts his** whole **heart and soul into** this next contest, then nothing can stop us.* □ *Into the work of rebuilding their cities after the devastation of war, the peoples of Europe **put their heart and soul**.*

put one's (own) house in order rregulloj punët e veta, rregulloj shtëpinë e vet
□ *These companies must first **put their own houses in order**; then they may qualify for development grants.* □ *After a serious illness, he decided to **put his house in order**, by making a proper will, and so on.*

put one's last hand to sth i jap dorën e fundit
□ *He **put his last hand to** the article.*

put one's mind to i kushtoj kujdes (vëmendje)
□ *I'm sure we can get it all sorted out if we **put our minds to** it.* □ *He'll do*

well in the exams if only **his mind** was **put to** his studies.

put one's nose in dukem, shfaqem
□ ***Put your nose in*** here every now and then, to see if I want anything.* □ *He stood on the landing outside his patient's bed and dressing rooms, debating whether or not to **put his nose in** and say a reassuring word.*

put/pocket one's pride into one's pocket kapërdij një kafshatë të hidhur; mposht sedrën (krenarinë, kryelartësinë)
□ *Housework was what she wanted... She even **pocketed** the last of **her pride** and tried with Mrs. Ramage.*

put one's shoulder to the wheel i vë gjoksin punës
□ *This has been made a test case, all must **put a shoulder to the wheel**.* □ *We would be soon a rich company if every employee **put his shoulder to the wheel**.* □ *Come on, everyone, **shoulders to the wheel**—we've got a lot to do.*

put one's oar in përzihem, ndërhyj, fus hundët
□ *He stayed in his armchair thinking: '**Putting my oar in**! A nasty mess, and going to be nastier!'*

put on the map bën të njohur, i jep emër
□ *Her performance in that play really **put her on the map** as a comedy actress.*

put out 1. shuaj, fik (zjarrin, dritën etj.)
□ *Jurgis would smoke a pipe, after which he would crawl into his bed to get warm, after **putting out** the fire to save coal.* □ *Have you **put the light out** in the dining-room?*
2. dal në det
□ *We **put out** to sea on the early morning tide.*
3. heq, nxjerr me forcë

□ *The next time he brings his noisy friends to the club we'll have them **put out.***
4. nxjerr, çel, lëshoj
□ *The plants **put out** early shoots.*
5. nxjerr, lëshoj, botoj
□ *The department of Social Security have **put out** a pamphlet explaining the new rates of pension for retired people.*
6. inatos; irritoj, ngacmoj; trazoj, shqetësoj
□ *This rather **put** me **out**, very often.*
□ *It **puts** the teacher **out** to be lied to.*
□ *Father was **put out** when June spilled grape juice on his new suit.*
□ *The least thing **puts** him **out**.*
7. transmetoj
□ *They clustered around the radio, listening to the news of the invasion **put out** by the BBC.*
8. prodhon, nxjerr, lëshon
□ *The engine of a wartime fighter aircraft **put out** more than one thousand horsepower.*
9. ushtroj, demonstroj, vë në veprim
□ *The speech ended in an appeal to party workers to **put out** all their energy and enthusiasm during the electoral campaign.*
10. nxjerr
□ *He fell off a horse and **put** his shoulder **out**.*
11. investoj; huaj para
□ *He **put out** all his spare money at ten percent or better.*
12. shqetësoj, krijoj shqetësim
□ *The hotel was seriously **put out** by the sudden cancellation of holiday bookings.*
put out of action nxjerr jashtë luftimit
□ *Two hundred enemy soldiers were **put out of action.*** □ *Accurate gunnery had already **put** three of the leading tanks **out of action.***

put out of (one's) mind heq nga mendja, harroj
□ ***Put it out of your mind** altogether.*
put paid to i jap fund
□ *If I fail these exams, it will **put paid to** my hopes of becoming a doctor.*
put pen to paper nis të shkruaj
□ *But in a moment of confidence she **put pen to paper** for my sisters...*
□ *His Newark pupils just wouldn't **put pen to paper**.* □ *All the evidence would have to be assembled before he could **pen to paper**.*
put pressure on sb ushtroj trysni (presion) mbi
□ *The birth of twins **put pressure on** them to find a bigger apartment.* □ *I don't want to **put pressure on** you to make a decision, but we haven't much time left.*
put sb in his (proper) place ia tregoj dikujt vendin
□ *He tried to kiss her but she quickly **put him in his place.*** □ *He tried to boss my mother around, but she soon **put him in his place.***
put sb in mind of sb/sth më kujton, më sjell ndër mend
□ *Her way of speaking **put me in mind of** her mother.* □ *Please, **put** my young friend **in mind** that he promised me to do it.*
put sb in the way of doing sth fus dikë në rrugën (hullinë) e
□ *She **put him in the way of** doing a good research work.*
put sb in the wrong fajësoj, ngarkoj me faj
□ *They tried to **put me in the wrong.***
put sb/sth in/into the shade eklipsoj, lë në hije
□ *I thought that Jack's car was nice, but Jim's new car **puts it in the shade.***
put sb on trial for sth padis, hedh në gjyq

□ *She was **put on trial for** fraud.*

put sb on/under oath vë në be

□ *The witnesses were **put under oath**.*

put sb out of breath lë pa frymë

□ *The fast walk **put him out of breath**.*

put sb out of heart ligështoj, dekurajoj, demoralizoj

□ *You have come here on some design of improving your fortune, I dare say; and I should grieve to **put you out of heart**. I am some years older than you, besides and may, on a few trivial points, advise you, perhaps.*

put sb out of temper nxeh, zemëroj, inatos, ngacmoj nervat

□ *It would **put me out of temper**, which is a state of mind I can't endure.*

put sb's back up nxeh, inatos; ofendoj

□ *His offhand manner **put my back up**.* □ *If you had pressed him for a reply, you would have **put his back up**.* □ *After having to listen to these jeers and catcalls for half an hour **their backs** were really **put up**.* □ *What's the use of **putting your back up** at every trifle?*

put sb's mind at ease/rest qetësoj

□ *Yes, father, **put your mind at ease**; go on with this expedition with a light heart.*

put sb's nose out of joint e bëj me turp; turbulloj, shqetësoj; ia punoj keqas dikujt

□ *The next time he comes around cadging, I'll remind him of the five pounds he owes us. That'll **put his nose out of joint**.* □ *She didn't expect you to stand up to her as you did; her nose was **put badly out of joint**.* □ *Barbara. ... It's a pity you're too late. The new bloke has **put your nose out of joint**.*

put sb to shame: turpëroj, bëj me turp

□ *The behaviour of the younger children **put** the older **ones to shame**.*

put sb to the blush bëj të skuqet nga turpi, bëj t'i skuqet faqja

□ *His remarks **put me to the blush**.*

put sth out of sb's head heq, largoj nga mendja

□ *You said something just now that **put** everything **out of my head**.* □ *You had better **put** the idea of going there **out of your head**.*

put sb/sth to rights rregulloj, vë në rregull

□ *It took me ages to **put** things **to rights** after the workmen had finished.* □ *One of her worries was that the conjugal bedroom had not yet been **put to rights**.* □ *It will be some time before the wrongs suffered over many years are **put to rights**.* □ *When Maria Labbs had stowed them away, and **put** the room **to rights**, they opened the street door...*

put sth into sb's head fus në kokë

□ *Who's been **putting** such ideas **into your head**?*

put sth to the proof provoj, vë në provë

□ *You have said that your car is faster than mine. Tomorrow I wish I might have a chance to **put** that statement **to the proof**.*

put the cart before the horse i bëj punët së prapthi

□ *By acting so, Arthur is **putting the cart before the horse**.* □ *They **put the cart before the horse** and took the effect for the cause.*

put the final/finishing touches i jap dorën e fundit, përfundoj

□ *Carrie was **putting the finishing touches** to her toilet... when a commotion near the stage door caught her ear.* □ *While **the finishing touches** are **put to** the dinner, we'll stroll* *round the garden.* □ *The centerpiece was to be a massive cake, to which the caterers were now putting the final touches.*

put through 1. përfundoj, përmbush

□ *Whatever the difficulties, we are determined to put through this work ahead of schedule.* □ *At the moment we are trying to put through a mass literacy program.*

2. paguaj për shkollimin e

□ *He managed to put each of his four children through boarding school.*

3. lidh me telefon

□ *'An outside call, Mr. Murdoch.' 'Oh, put him through.'*

put through the mill i nxjerr ujë (në stërvitje etj.)

□ *Most of his present officers were put through the mill; he considers battle experience more valuable than college training.*

put to 1. përçoj, shpreh, transmetoj

□ *It might be put to the delegation that any reasonable demands would be heeded.* □ *Your proposal will be put to the board of directors.*

2. paraqis, parashtroj, drejtoj

□ *'The audience is now invited to put its questions to our visiting speaker.*

3. vë, fut

□ *I do hope we're not putting you to too much trouble.*

put to death vras, ekzekutoj

□ *The prisoner was put to death at dawn.*

put to flight vë përpara

□ *The enemy was put to flight by the advancing army.* □ *Our men in a sharp counterattack had put the enemy to flight.*

put together bashkoj, montoj

□ *He took the machine to pieces and then put it together again.*

put to sea lë portin, niset për lundrim

□ *The ship will put to sea at dawn.*

put to shame turpëroj, bëj me turp

□ *That she had not been put to shame and made to feel her unfortunate position seemed remarkable.* □ *The behaviour of the younger children put the older ones to shame.* □ *This little man with his variety of games and complex music puts many other so-called 'superior' cultures to shame.* □ *The face was dominated by a pair of tremendous eyes that would have put any self-respecting owl to shame.*

put to the proof/test vë në provë

□ *You have often said that your car is faster than mine. Tomorrow we shall have a chance to put that statement to the proof.*

put to good use shfrytëzoj efektivisht

□ *He will be able to put his experience to good use in the new job.* □ *The third division certainly put that first winter to good use and trained hard.*

put two and two together nxjerr përfundime (nga të dhënat etj.), arrij në përfundim se

□ *Putting two and two together, as the saying is, it was not difficult for me to guess who he was.* □ *The police can put two and two together, you know; they will be on his track in no time.* □ *There was a theft from the safe just before he went on an expensive holiday: it's only a matter of time before somebody puts two and two together.* □ *I saw his car in the garage and a light at the window, so I put two and two together and guessed that he was still at home.*

put up 1. ndërtoj

□ *Many ugly blocks of buildings were put up in the 1960's.* □ *They put up a tent near Lura's lakes.*

2. ngre

□ *He **put up** his hand to protect his face...*

3. rrit, shtoj, ngre

□ *Every time a new tenant moves into the apartment, he **puts up** the rent a bit more.*

4. ofroj

□ *The smuggler **put up** a fight but was finally overcome and carried off to jail.* □ *Very little resistance was **put up** by the surrounded men.*

5. zë vend në hotel etj.

□ *We **put up** for the night at an inn.*

6. paraqes si kandidat

□ *The green Party hopes to **put up** a number of candidates in the General Election.*

7. financoj, vë fonde

□ *A group of industrialists have **put up** a large sum towards the new school.*

put up for auction nxjerr në ankand

□ *He's **putting** the family jewels **up for auction**.*

put up for sale nxjerr në shitje

□ *That corner site is being **put up for sale** next week.*

put up with duroj, bëj durim

□ *The air would be full of steam, from the hot water and the hot blood, so that you could not see five feet before you ... All this inconvenience they might have **put up with**, if only it had not been some places where they might eat.* □ *There are some things that are not easily **put up with**—and his damned impertinence is one.*

Q

quarrel with one's bread and butter
i bie së mirës (bukës) me shkelm
(këmbë)

□ *Lord, she was crying! ...Clasping
her heavy shoulders, he said desperately: 'Cheerio, my dear, can't
quarrel with bread and butter. I
shall get a job, this is just to tide us
over.'*

queer fish, a njeri i çuditshëm

□ *I never like Jones: I always thought
of him as a queer fish.* □ *All sort of
cultists and queer fish teach all kinds
of techniques for achieving health,
contentment and peace of mind.*
□ *One of the last man to join this expedition was Denon, a queer fish in
this amphibious operation, since he
was a civilian and already aged.*

queer sb's pitch i nxjerr pengesa, i
prish planet

□ *'If I didn't see you otherwise, Clare,
you look so lovely!' 'That, if true, is
not a reason for queering my pitch at
home.'* □ *I think I'm likely to get the
job, but if Bob applies for it too he
could queer my pitch.* □ *I want to go
home before the end of term; but if
one of the other students asks first, it
may queer my pitch.*

quite a few mjaft, jo pak

□ *Quite a few people came to the lecture.* □ *'Are there many like you?'
'Yes, quite a few.'*

quite a lot (of) mjaft; goxha

□ *We drank quite a lot of wine.*

quite so tamam ashtu

□ *'We shouldn't have booked our
flight before the prices went up.'
'Quite so, my dear, but it's a bit late
thinking about it now.'*

quite the fashion/rage hiqet shumë;
është në modë

□ *Black leather trousers seem to be
quite the rage these days.*

quite the thing pikërisht ajo që duhet,
ajo që më pëlqen, që është e modës

□ *A cup of tea would be quite the
thing.* □ *This dress material produced
in our country is quite the thing.*
□ *Suddenly it was quite the thing to
wear one's hair long.*

R

rack one's brain(s) vras (lodh) mend-jen

□ *I have been **racking my brains** trying to remember his name.* □ *All night I have been tossing and turning, **racking my brains** to think what could have possessed that poor young man to kill himself.* □ *I **racked my brains** and tried hard to picture the feelings of anger and indignation.* □ *Bob **racked his brain** trying to remember where he left the book.* □ *He had to **rack his brains** to solve that complicated problem.*

rags and tatters lecka, rrecka, rroba të vjetra e të grisura

□ *They found several hundred pounds in the house when he died—enough to show that there had been no need for him to half-starve himself and go about in **rags and tatters**.*

rain cats and dogs/rain buckets/rain pitchforks/rain in torrents bie shi me gjyma (me shtamba, me rrëshekë), bie shi litarë-litarë

□ *I won't go out tonight; it's **raining buckets**.* □ *We'll meet at the parking place in the village about nine o'clock, and decide then whether it's a day for the boat, or for walking. If it's **raining cats and dogs**, of course, we won't expect you to turn up at all.* □ *We went to Ireland but we can hardly say we saw it. It **poured cats and dogs** every single day.* □ *'The sky's overcast and surely it's **raining cats and dogs** on the mountains...'* □ *A thunderstorm might blow up any day and rain fall in torrents... 'and it was **raining pitchforks**.'*

□ *When the ground was dry, he scanned every floating cloud before he descended into the mine at noon and hoped that it might be **raining pitchforks** when he came up again.*

rain or shine në kohë të mirë apo të keqe, sido që të jetë moti

□ *The athletic meeting will be held five days from now, **rain or shine**.* □ *He always goes for a walk on Sunday, **rain or shine**.*

raise a dust bëj zhurmë (rrëmujë, potere)

□ *The child was asked not to **raise a dust**. There were visitors in the sitting room.* □ *'Bad-tempered bitch! Where's she gone, anyway?' 'Probably to the manager's office to **raise a dust** about your using her typewriter.'* □ *Any day now, your wife's going to find out about your girlfriend and **raise the dust** accordingly.* □ *'There'll be threats of staff resignation, protest meetings by parent groups, and a whole lot more besides.' 'Oh well, you can't reorganize a whole school without **raising** some **dust**.'*

raise a laugh/smile shkaktoj të qeshura (buzëqeshje)

□ *When a plush circular couch in the center of the stage alarmingly started to spring to pieces, the audience took it in good humour—perhaps too good—it **raised** more **laughs** than any other part of the operetta.* □ *Baby was usually full of chuckles but that morning I couldn't **raise** even **a smile**.*

raise an objection to ngre një kundër-shtim kundër; shpreh kundërshtimin ndaj

□ *'If you won't* **raise any objections,** *I'm going to buy the champagne ... OK?'* □ **To** *this part of the scheme several* **objections** *were* **raised.**

raise a question bëj, ngre një pyetje

□ *That explanation should satisfy, but if anyone* **raises an** *awkward question, refer him to me.* □ *Another speaker* **raised the question** *why it was, if social workers were already in contact with the household, the more effective steps had not been taken to avert the tragedy.* □ *The 'marriage' made world headlines and here was a chance for the principal character to explain everything. Unfortunately, her account* **raises more questions** *than she answers.*

raise a racket turbulloj, bëj zhurmë (rrëmujë, potere)

□ *'Well, Mayella was* **raising this racket.'**

raise Cain/hell 1. bëj namin

□ *And keep that puppy off the sofa. Your mother will* **raise Cain** *if he piddles on it again.* □ *If I were the headmaster of that school, I'd* **raise hell** *with the education office till they got those potholes in the playground filled in.*

2. bëj zhurmë

□ *She seems so quiet usually—I got quite a shock seeing her* **raising** *merry* **hell** *with the rest of us at the party last night.*

raise from the dead ngre nga varri

□ *Among the tribal elders was one credited with the power of* **raising** *people* **from the dead.** □ *A common theme in horror stories is of a monstrous creature* **raised** *by supernatural power* **from the dead.**

raise hopes ngjall shpresa

□ *'You'll be rung if there are any fresh developments. Mustn't* **raise your**

hopes, though,' he added. *'She may never recover consciousness again.'*

□ *The fall, over the last week, in the number of notified cases has* **raised hopes** *that the epidemic is running itself out.* □ *It's true that the experiment hasn't worked according to plan, and Luke was right to tell us so. I'm not going to* **raise false hopes,** *so I shan't say any more about that.*

raise (the) money siguroj të holla (fonde)

□ *I'm sorry, Aunt, I'd much rather you took the check back. I'll* **raise the money** *somehow to pay off this lot.* □ *The campaign brought into being committees not only to* **raise money,** *but also to show the unity of purpose of the country with the army in the task which lay ahead.*

raise one's (sb's) dander up zemërohem, inatosem; zemëroj, inatos

□ *Soames stared. ' ... Oh! I want to know, what's the meaning of that expression 'got his goat'?—'Got his goat'? Oh,* **raised his dander,** *if you know what that means, it was before my time.'*

raise one's glass to ngre gotën për shëndetin e, pi për shëndetin e, ngre një dolli për

□ *He* **raised his glass to** *his old grandfather.* □ *'Mr. Charlton, I think we should* **raise a glass to** *our hostess.* □ *We* **raised our glasses to** *the memory of a great man.*

raise one's hand against ngre dorën kundër

□ *If you dare* **raise your hand against** *the innocent child, we'll teach you a good lesson.*

raise one's voice against ngre zërin kundër

□ *Not many* **voices** *were* **raised**

against that decision. □ *He raised his voice against the lack of provision for the mentally ill.* □ *This was an undoubted social evil against which many voices were to be raised.*

raise one's eyebrows at sth ngrys, rrudh vetullat

□ *Our more conventional archaeological friends sometimes raised their eyebrows and sniffed a little plaintively at all this publicity of Wheeler's!*

raise one's hat to i heq kapelën dikujt

□ *If you're prepared to work in that hospital for so little money, I raise my hat to you.* □ *That was a fine gesture, something worth raising one's hat to.*

raise sb's spirits ngre humorin (besimin), ngre moralin

□ *My win at chess raised my spirits a little.* □ *Your telling us how well your friend got on after the very same operation has raised Donald's spirits considerably.*

raise the roof 1. bëj zhurmë të madhe

□ *The audience raised the roof with their applause.*

2. bën namin

□ *Your father will raise the roof when he sees that you've broken another window.*

rake about/around for sth rrëmoj, kërkoj me kujdes

□ *We raked around in the files, but couldn't find the letter.* □ *He spent the afternoon raking around in the attic for some old family photographs.*

rake over old ashes ringjall kujtime të vjetra (të pakëndshme)

□ *'I don't want to rake over old ashes, Norah, but while we are discussing personal matters, have you heard from Jim at all lately?*

rake up rrëmoj, rikujtoj

□ *'Why did you have to rake up his*

political past? He's a reformed character now.'

ram sth down sb's throat i imponoj dikujt mendimet, pikëpamjet e veta

□ *'He wants to ram his notions down my throat,' he thought....* □ *I do dislike having her extreme ideas rammed down my throat.* □ *There is no point in trying to ram abstract information down the throats of young children.*

rank and file, the ushtarë të thjeshtë; njerëz të thjeshtë

□ *But this must surely be the same rule for all its members, and to be so no less for officers than for rank and file.* □ *Before the year is out they will once again take their place among the rank and file of the church of Scotland's ministers.* □ *The rank and file, however, were either foisted upon the city or else lived off the populace directly.* □ *The rank and file of the union have decided to go on strike, although the union leaders asked them not to.*

rap sb on/over the knuckles qortoj

□ *Don't leave early without the manager's permission otherwise you may be rapped over the knuckles.* □ *Uncle Jolyon in his later years—indeed, ever since the strange and lamentable affair between his granddaughter June's lover young Bosinney, and Irene...—had noticeably rapped the family's on the knuckles; and that way of his own... had begun to seem to them a little wayward...* □ *The fact is someone ought to speak to Bosinney and ascertain what he means. I am afraid of this myself for I should certainly rap him over the knuckles.*

raring to go mezi pret të niset (të shkojë)

□ *Fundamentally these boys are good. My boy was* **raring to go** *to work to help the home.*
ration sth out racionoj
□ ***Ration*** *the remaining water* ***out*** *among the survivors.*
rattle away/on llomotit, dërdëllit
□ *He* ***rattled on*** *about his job, not noticing how bored she was.*
rattle sth off them, përsëris mekanikisht
□ *'Now read the poem again, and this time don't* ***rattle*** *it* ***off*** *like a machine-gun.* □ *The child* ***rattled off*** *the poem he had learned by heart.*
rave about sb/sth flas (shkruaj) me adhurim (entuziazëm)
□ *She* ***raved about*** *her little dress-maker, who could copy a Paris model for next to nothing*
ray of sunshine, a rreze drite
□ *In the years of economic and social depression, 'Dr. Who' has been* ***the*** *only* ***ray of sunshine*** *in our lives.*
reach rock bottom arrin pikën më të ulët
□ *Congregational attendance had dwindled to handfuls. A few Sundays ago it* ***reached rock bottom*** *when the minister preached to his wife, the organist and the two presiding officers for the date.*
reach the top of sth arrij kulmin (majat) e
□ *Starting as a clerk in a shop which peddles rags, he rips through the garment jungle to* ***reach the top of*** *his outwardly glamorous profession.*
read between the lines lexoj në mes të radhëve (rreshtave)
□ *His letter is full of implications, so I have to* ***read between the lines.***
□ *You must* ***read*** *what he writes* ***between the lines*** *in order to get the full meaning.* □ *Some kind of poetry make you* ***read between the lines.*** □ *In*

this letter that Jack has written he does not actually say that he needs money but, if you ***read between the lines,*** *you will see that he does need more cash.*
read sb like a book kuptoj (lexoj) qartë mendimet, i njoh mirë karakterin (synimet, reagimet etj.), i njoh dhëmbë e dhëmballë, e njoh me rrënjë e me degë
□ *Mary told me that he was going to the library to study but I can* ***read him like a book:*** *I was pretty sure that he was going to the cinema with her girlfriend.* □ *'I'm not really very expert at this beating about the bush.' 'No,' she smiled. 'Any woman can* ***read you like a book,*** *James.'* □ *God-frey looked across the fireplace at Mabel Pettigrew and decided to give her the slip again this afternoon and go to see Olive. Mabel Pettigrew thought: I can* ***read*** *him* ***like a book.***
read sb a lecture/lesson i jap një mësim të mirë
□ *Soames stared. Was this young fellow* ***reading him a lesson*** *against pessimism?* □ *What* ***a lecture*** *she* ***read*** *me on having asked him home to lunch one day, when she had seen the Arley carriage in the town, and thought that my lady might call.*
read sb's mind/thoughts i lexoj dikujt mendimet
□ *Once or twice the lawyer looked up and asked a question of Szedvilas, the other did not know a word he was saying but his eyes were fixed upon the lawyer's face, striving in an agony of dread to* ***read his mind.***
□ *She must, he thought, be as clever as she was pretty to have* ***read his thoughts*** *so accurately.* □ *I didn't precisely feel guilty, but that's how you do tend to act when someone* ***reads***

your thoughts. □ *I was trying to think of a polite excuse for leaving, but my hostess* **read my mind** *and said, 'I mustn't keep you any longer: it's getting late.'*

ready cash/money para në dorë

□ *I cannot pay you now as I have no* **ready cash***.*

reap the benefit(s) of sth korr përfitimin e

□ *You had better slow down a bit. What's the point of all this toiling and saving if you don't live to* **reap the benefit** *of it?*

reason into bind (të bëjë diçka)

□ *Let me try to* **reason** *him* **into** *joining us.*

reason sth out arrij në përfundim (nëpërmjet arsyetimit)

□ *The police* **reasoned out** *that if the men had left by the midday train, it would be easy to pick them up at the terminal.* □ *It's easy to* **reason out** *what the consequences of that action will be.*

reason with sb diskutoj (debatoj, hahem) për t'i mbushur mendjen dikujt

□ *She* **reasoned with** *me for an hour about the shortcomings of my experiment.*

recall sb to sth ndërgjegjësoj, bëj të vetëdijshëm

□ *The danger* **recalled** *him* **to** *a sense of duty.* □ *The dangers that suddenly threatened* **recalled** *him* **to** *a sense of duty.*

recall to life sjell, kthej në jetë

□ *The doctors tried hard and* **recalled** *the seriously wounded patient* **to life***.*

recall to mind kujtoj, sjell ndër mend

□ *After so many years I find it hard to* **recall** *all their names* **to mind***.* □ *I can't* **recall to mind** *that he said anything about payment.*

receive sb with open hands/arms pres krahëhapur

□ *'He, my friend Professor Sinnott waiting to* **receive** *me* **with open arms...'**

reckon on/upon sb/sth mbështetem, var shpresat

□ *He will always help in time of need; on this you can* **reckon***.* □ *Can I* **reckon on** *you to help?* □ *I hope I can* **reckon on** *your support.*

reckon sth in përfshij (fus) në llogari

□ *Did you* **reckon in** *the cost of the taxi?* □ *When you submit your claim, don't forget to* **reckon in** *the money spent on petrol.* □ *'Don't bother to tip: the service charge has already been* **reckoned in***.*

reckon sth up llogaris; nxjerr shumën

□ *When Jurgis saw the despair of his family and* **reckoned up** *the money he had spent, the tears came into his eyes...* □ *A mechanic* **reckoned up** *the cost of repairing the damage to my car.*

reckon with sb 1. laj besapet me

□ *The strike is over, we'll* **reckon with** *scabs...* □ *Anyone not obeying the decrees of the new military junta could expect to be* **reckoned with***.* □ *The police* **reckoned***, in a horrible fashion,* **with** *all those suspected of supporting the government in exile.*

2. llogaris, marr në konsideratë

□ *I had not* **reckoned with** *the facts of my temperament, training and habits.* □ *He is a man to be* **reckoned with***.* □ *I hadn't* **reckoned with** *the possibility of his turning up so soon.*

3. trajtoj, zgjidh, kaloj, kapërcej

□ *When you consider all the petty irritations and shortages they had to* **reckon with***, it's a wonder they kept their sense of humor.* □ *All these* problems had to be **reckoned with** as they arose, before they grew large enough to hinder progress.

reckon without sb/sth nuk përfshij; nuk llogarit

□ *The organizers of the garden party had clearly **reckoned without** the possibility of a freak thunderstorm.* □ *We wanted a quiet holiday, but we had **reckoned without** the children.*

reckon without one's host i bëj hesapet (llogaritë) pa hanxhinë

□ *The old English proverb tells us that 'they that **reckon without their host** are to reckon twice.'*

red letter day, a ditë feste; ditë e përkujtueshme, e paharrueshme

□ *Bevill was looking forward to it like a child. 'I believe tomorrow is what I should call **a red letter day**,' he said earnestly, as though he had invented the phrase.*

red tape formalitete (proçedura) **administrative** (burokratike), burokraci

□ *Beaverbrook simply wanted to get things done. He hated **red tape**.* □ *Cuspatt was all right but in the last resort these museum fellows were as much bureaucrats as they were scholars, tied by a lot of **red tape**.*

reduce sb to tears bëj dikë të qajë (të përlotet)

□ *His angry words **reduced** her **to tears**.* □ *His emotional language **reduced** many of that open-air audience **to tears**.* □ *While she was feeling so overwrought, the slightest cross word or ill-judged remark could **reduce** her **to floods of tears**.*

reduce to order vë në rregull

□ *He employed an accountant to **reduce** his money affairs **to some semblance of order**.* □ *All these details must be **reduced to order** before the annual inspection.*

reduce to silence bëj të heshtë

□ *The dignity of his appeal **reduced** the loudest of critics **to silence**.* □ *His appearance on a platform could **reduce** even the professional hecklers **to total silence**.*

reel sth off them (tregoj, përsëris) shpejt e rrjedhshëm

□ *The little girl **reeled off** the verses of a long poem.* □ *Without apparent effort, he **reeled off** the names of those who had been associated with him in those early days.*

reflect credit on/upon sb nderoj, ngre lart emrin e mirë të

□ *The success of the meeting **reflected** the greatest **credit on** all concerned.* □ *His outstanding performance at the athletic meet **reflected credit upon** our faculty.*

refresh one's memory freskoj kujtesën

□ *'I hope that little document has **refreshed your memory**?'* □ *Just **refresh my memory**: were you born in New York?*

regain one's feet rimbahem në këmbë

□ *The boxer managed to **regain his feet**, but he was obviously not going to be able to fight much longer.*

regardless of sb/sth pavarësisht, pa marrë parasysh

□ *He continued speaking, **regardless** of my feelings on the matter.*

relieve one's feelings shfrej, nxjerr dufin

□ *Again a file drawer was noisily closed. 'Ethel,' Miss Jenkison said, 'unless you can **relieve your feelings** more silently, I shall return you to D3.'* □ *I called her the worst names I could think of, repeating them again and again under my breath, but it didn't **relieve my feelings** very much.* □ *Her feelings were **relieved** by a good cry.*

relieve sb of sth liroj, çliroj, lehtësoj
□ *Let me relieve you of your suitcase: it looks terribly heavy.* □ *I helped to relieve him of his anxiety.*

remember sb to sb i bëj të fala
□ *Remember me to everyone at home.* □ *He asked to be remembered to all his friends in the department.*

render an account jap llogari
□ *It's high time he renders account of his behavior.*

render (sb) a service i bëj dikujt një shërbim
□ *If you're ever in a position that I can be of any help to you, don't hesitate to ask. When a man renders me a service at a considerable inconvenience to himself, I don't forget it.* □ *I'm sure he gets a good few payments on the side 'for services rendered' that don't go through the books.*

resign oneself to pranoj, i nënshtrohem
□ *The team refused to resign themselves to defeat.* □ *He resigned himself to the idea that he would never be a world-class tennis player.*

rest assured rri i qetë, të siguroj se; të jesh i sigurt se
□ *You may rest assured that we shall do everything we can to help.* □ *You may rest assured that everything possible is being done.*

rest on one's laurels fle mbi dafina
□ *He hasn't done much since he wrote his first book some years ago: he's been resting on his laurels.* □ *There is no sense in resting on your laurels. You still have difficult problems to face.* □ *It might be better for his reputation if he stopped writing and rested on his laurels, as some other novelist had.*

rest on sth mbështetet
□ *His fame rests more on his plays than on his novels.*

rest with sb to do sth varet nga, është në dorën e, e ka në dorë
□ *It rests with the committee to decide.* □ *The choice rests entirely with you.*

retrace one's step kthehem në gjurmët e lëna
□ *When they realized that they were lost, they tried to retrace their steps through the forest.*

return like for like ia shpërblej me të njëjtën monedhë
□ *'Well, in all this I must own there is some frankness. Now I will return like for like.'*

return the compliment 1. ia kthej komplimentin
□ *When he praised my speech, I returned the compliment about his.*
2. bëj të njëjtën gjë
□ *He emptied all his rubbish into my garden, so I just returned the compliment.*

revenge oneself on marr hak
□ *In some societies it is a point of honor to revenge oneself on somebody who has insulted a member of one's family.*

ride for a fall kërkoj vetë belanë, kërkoj belanë me para, kërkoj të thyej qafën (kokën, turinjtë), veproj pa mend në kokë, kërkoj të keqen e vetes
□ *'From the way Walter behaved we knew that he was riding for a fall.'* □ *If he keeps up his reckless spending, he is riding for a fall.* □ *Jack's proud behavior is losing him a lot of friends; he's riding for a fall.* □ *He has survived many escapades, but this will be his last: he's riding for a fall.*

ride high gëzon popullaritet, ka sukses
□ *Politically, at the age of 42, she is riding high.* □ *Jim is riding high at the moment, but I don't know how long his success will be.*

ride one's high horse mbahet rëndë, mbahet me të madh, kapardiset, tundet e shkundet
□ *Jenkins rides a high horse with style and on this occasion rhetoric gave it wings.*

ride roughshod over sb nëpërkëmb, marr nëpër këmbë; shpërfill, injoroj; tiranizoj, sillem si tiran
□ *We shall see if you can ride roughshod like this.* □ *'Oh you take that tone,' he said, '—do you? You think you can ride roughshod over everything? Well, you're very much mistaken.'* □ *The people protested against the new road, but the authorities rode roughshod over their complaints.*

right and left gjithandej, kudo, gjithkund
□ *He is very popular. He has been making friends right and left since he arrived here.*

right/straight away/off tani; menjëherë, sakaq, në atë çast, pa vonesë
□ *I want it typed right away, please.*
□ *If you find any clue to the problem, let me know right away.* □ *'Have you remembered to phone your sister?' 'Oh no—I'll do it right away.'*

right now tani, në këtë çast
□ *'You should take a packet of sandwiches with you.' 'Common sense tells me so, although, right now, I never want to see food again.'*
□ *'Whom are you looking for?' 'June.' 'Oh, I saw her right now. She's probably upstairs.'*

ring a bell më ngjall kujtime, më kujton (më sjell ndër mend) diçka; tingëllon i njohur
□ *No, I don't know the person you mention, though the name seems to ring a bell.* □ *'Have you ever heard of a man called Armas? Castillo Armas?' 'The name rings a bell,'*

Mark said. 'He was in the news a few years ago, wasn't he?' □ *I don't recognize his face, but his name rings a bell.* □ *Not even the cat's meowing seemed to ring a bell with Judy. She still forgot to feed him.*

ring down the curtain on sth mbyll, i jap fund
□ *A few more matters will be accomplished and then the curtain will be rung down on the session.*

ring off mbaroj (mbyll) bisedën në telefon
□ *He said what he had to say, and then, before I could reply, he rang off.*
□ *My wife tells me there is someone who wants to see me, so I shall have to ring off.*

ring the changes krijoj variacione (kombinime)
□ *Traditionalists will tell you to drink red wine with meat, dry white wine with fish, and sweet wine with desert. But there's no reason why you shouldn't ring a few changes.* □ *The cook tried to ring the changes by preparing the food she had in different ways.*

ring true/false tingëllon i vërtetë/i gënjeshtërt
□ *This piece of agonized juvenile self-analysis rings true.* □ *Spies are trained to keep their mouths shut and they don't often lose the habit. That's why true spy stories are extremely rare, and personally I have never seen one in print that rang completely true.*

ring up 1. telefonoj, marr në telefon
□ *Please ring him up tomorrow morning.* □ *Has anyone rung up while I have been out?* □ *'I do wish he'd get out of the habit of ringing me up at mealtimes.'*
2. regjistroj

□ *In the village store our weekend groceries were **rung up** on an old-fashioned cash register.*

rinse sth down shtyj

□ *A bought a sandwich and a beer to **rinse it down**.*

rise and fall ngrihet e ulet; hipën e zbret

□ *Toynbee spent his life comparing the way civilizations **rise and fall**. He chose a career which made him almost inevitably a prophet of doom.* □ *The decades passes, administrations **rose and fell**, reputations were made and lost, successive Chancellors eased and squeezed the economy.*

rise from the dead/grave ngrihem nga varri

□ *Jones had disappeared at sea a week before—now here he was, as if **risen from the dead**. □ No one could emerge from that avalanche alive, unless one believed that men could **rise from the grave**.*

rise in the world eci përpara në jetë

□ *The customs officer explained, but it was difficult to understand whether he had **risen** or fallen **in the world** by local standards. □ He has **risen** far **in the world**, financially, without however widening his interests or his sympathies.*

rise to a/the bait bie brenda, e ha karremin, bie në grackë

□ *They left food and ammunition on the track—but would the enemy **rise to so obvious a bait**?*

rise to one's feet ngrihem në këmbë

□ *Someone **rose to his feet** to question the chairman on a point of order.* □ *He **rose** unsteadily **to his feet** to reply to the speech of welcome.*

rise to the occasion ngrihem në lartësinë e situatës

□ *Her breath was clean and fresh. I*

rose to the occasion like a shot. 'Kiss me, my sweet,' I said.

rise with the lark çohem menatë (pa gdhirë mirë, herët)

□ *He usually goes to bed very early and **rises with the lark**.*

risk one's neck rrezikoj kokën (jetën), vë jetën në rrezik

□ *The car in front was weaving about the road as if the driver was drunk or ill and I wasn't going to **risk my neck** by trying to pass him.* □ *'Summer of 77 recalls the official and volunteer rescue team **risking their necks** to save the luckless, often the plain stupid, who get themselves capsized, on fire, marooned by the tide or stuck up cliffs.*

rob Peter to pay Paul mbyll një vrimë e hap një tjetër

□ *He got the money to pay his income tax debts by borrowing from a moneylender: it was just a case of **robbing Peter to pay Paul**.*

rock bottom pika më e ulët

□ *No one is buying cars these days so their prices have hit **rock bottom**.* □ *Prices have reached **rock bottom**.*

rock the boat krijoj (nxjerr) pengesa (vështirësi), hap punë (telashe)

□ *The staff are going to put in a claim for higher wages to the management: Jack said that he would be willing to accept less than the others, but he was told not to **rock the boat**.* □ *Things are progressing well—don't **rock the boat**. □ The other boys said that Henry was **rocking the boat** by wanting to let girls into their club.*

roll in money notoj në para

□ *He's well off: in fact, he's simply **rolling in money**.*

roll up one's sleeves përvesh mëngët

□ *If you want to finish the job before Monday, then you will really have to roll up your sleeves.* □ *When Paul took his science examination, he saw how little he knew about science. He rolled up his sleeves and went to work.*

rolling stone gathers no moss gur që rrokulliset nuk zë myshk
□ *Uncle Willie was a rolling stone that gathered no moss. He worked in different jobs all over the country.*

Rome was not built in a day Roma nuk u ndërtua në një ditë
□ *Only about a month ago Mr. Shore's successor answered a question in the House of Commons on this very point by saying he hoped to make an announcement shortly. What could be fairer than that? Rome was not built in a day, old boy.*

room for improvement vend për përmirësim
□ *You have written a very good essay, but I think that there is still some room for improvement.*

room (and) to spare (for sb/sth) (ka) vend e tepron, (ka) vend me bollëk
□ *'But you use the garage yourself, don't you?' 'That's all right. There's room and to spare for another car.'*
□ *Only the parents were invited though I am sure she has room and to spare for all of them.*

root and branch krejtësisht, plotësisht, fund e krye, me rrënjë e me degë
□ *The Prime Minister decided to get rid of all the opposition to his ideas, root and branch.* □ *Was it really so reprehensible to oppose their policies root and branch?*

root cause of sth, the shkaku bazë i
□ *He argues that one of the root causes of crime is poverty.*

root out çrrënjos, shkul nga rrënjët (me rrënjë)

□ *Agents were sent to root out elements hostile to the regime.* □ *He was determined to root out corruption in his department.*

root up nxjerr me gjithë rrënjë
□ *They cut down the big trees and rooted up the stumps.*

rough and ready 1. shkel e shko, dosido, me ngut, shpejt e shpejt, pa kujdes
□ *Probably things were managed in a very rough and ready fashion out there.* □ *I have done the job in a rough and ready way: I shall do it properly when I have time.*
2. i pranueshëm; adekuat
□ *Breath-analysers and blood tests will be more reliable than the old rough and ready ways of judging a driver's sobriety or insobriety.*
3. i ashpër, i vrazhdë, i papërpunuar (por gjithë energji)
□ *He had a rough and ready face, all roughened and reddened and lined in his long travels.*

rough it bëj një jetë të vështirë, jetoj pa komoditet, duroj vështirësi
□ *I want a man who knows Upper Burma, who is prepared to rough it and who can drive a jeep.* □ *When I travel abroad, I don't like staying in hotels: I prefer to rough it.*

rough sth out bëj (skicoj, formuloj) në dorë të parë; planifikoj në vija të trasha
□ *He roughed out a plan for us.* □ *I have roughed out the article, but I have still to revise it and put it into its final form.* □ *I've roughed out some arrangements for the move tomorrow.*

rough sb/sth up keqtrajtoj, sillem keq; sulmoj, lëndoj fizikisht; rrah
□ *Three boys were sent home for a week because they roughed up a*

player on the visiting team. □ *While Peter was walking in a strange part of town, some boys **roughed** him **up** and told him to stay out of their territory.*

round robin, a peticion, protestë, letër ankimi (me firmat në formë rrethi)

□ *The members of the committee were so upset by the chairman's action that they sent him **a round robin** about it.*
□ *The people in our neighbourhood are sending **a round robin** to the Air Force to protest the noise the jet planes make flying over our houses.*

round on/upon i kthehem, i vërsulem, sulmoj me fjalë

□ *She was amazed when he **rounded on** her and called her a liar.* □ *Stanely was irritated and **rounded on** his son: 'Why were you so late last night?'*

round sth off mbyll, përmbyll, përfundoj

□ *He **rounded off** his career by becoming Home Secretary.* □ *This somewhat abstract description is **rounded off** with a number of examples.*

round the clock gjithë ditën e natën

□ *On Monday he worked **round the clock**.* □ *Surgeons are working **round the clock** to save his life.*

round the corner shumë afër

□ *Her house is just **round the corner**.*
□ *'You're round the corner now,' cried Alliss Pecksniff.*

round up mbledh, grumbulloj

□ *Cowboys **round up** their cattle in the springtime to brand the new calves.* □ *I have asked for the whole squad to be **rounded up**.* □ *The guide **rounded up** the tourists and led them back to the coach.* □ *Dave **rounded up** many names for his petition.*

rub along with sb/together jetoj miqësisht me

□ *They are **rubbing along** the same*

as ever. □ *She and her boss have **rubbed along together** for years—for all the world like an old married couple.*

rub away heq (me fërkim të vazhdueshëm)

□ *The paint had been **rubbed away** from the arms of the chair.* □ *You need a good course of massage to get the aches and pains **rubbed away**.*

rub down fshihem, fërkohem me peshqir

□ *'**Rub** yourself **down** properly after your swim; I won't have you catching cold.'* □ *The players paused to **rub** themselves **down** between games.*

rub elbows/shoulders with njihem, miqësohem, zë (lidh) miqësi me, shoqërohem; krijoj lidhje me

□ *Nevertheless, the fact that here men gather, here chatter, here have to pass and **rub elbows** must be explained upon some grounds.* □ *He had freely ventured into the very heart of the industrial provinces and **rubbed shoulders with** the aborigines.* □ *It is a very expensive club: if you join it, you will find yourself **rubbing shoulders with** some wealthy people.* □ *City people and country people, old and young, **rub elbows** at the horse show.*

rub it in i vë në dukje, i përmend herë pas here (një gjë të pakëndshme)

□ *I know I behaved foolishly but you needn't **rub it in**.* □ *There's no need to **rub it in** that we lost by three goals.* □ *Father never failed to **rub it into** the family how much they depend on his money.*

rub sb/sth out 1. vras, zhduk, eliminoj

□ *The gangsters **rubbed out** four police men before they were caught.* □ *A couple of mobsters were **rubbed out** in a fracas with the law.*

2. fshij, heq

□ *If you spill coffee on the carpet try to **rub** it **out** immediately with a damp cloth.* □ *She tried to remove the mark from his jacket with a cleansing fluid, but it wouldn't **rub out**.*

rub sb (up) the right way trajtoj me kujdes; qetësoj

□ *It's good of him to **rub** his friends **the right way**.* □ *He was careful to **rub** Mason **up the right way**, saying how invaluable his services had been to the club.*

rub sb (up) the wrong way mërzis, ngacmoj, nervozoj, inatos

□ *You've only got to stick in with the man to get the right side of him. It's not good **rubbing him the wrong way**.* □ *He doesn't like me: I must have **rubbed him the wrong way** on some occasion.* □ *He's so easily **rubbed up the wrong way**: everything you say he seems to take offence at.* □ *'Don't **rub** me **up the wrong way**: I'm in a foul temper this morning.'*

rub sth up 1. shndrit, ndrit (duke fërkuar)

□ *Those spoons look much better now they have been **rubbed up**.* □ *'Dust the mantelpiece and **rub up** the ornaments.'*

2. freskoj (njohuritë)

□ *Your shorthand is a bit rusty: you'd better **rub** it **up**.* □ *Your English grammar needs to be **rubbed up**.*

rule of thumb rregull i thjeshtë empirik; metodë (mënyrë) praktike (matjeje, vlerësimi etj.)

□ *You want a real explanation and not a mere **rule of thumb**.* □ *It is impossible to calculate all these factors because they vary widely from one share to another. As **a rule of thumb**, the bigger the company the easier it is to buy and sell.* □ *He knew*

nothing save by **rule of thumb** of navigation.* □ *If you want to turn degree Centigrade into degree Fahrenheit, a **rule of thumb** is to double the Centigrade figure and add 30.*

rule sth out përjashtoj

□ *The bad weather conditions **ruled out** any chance of hunting that day.* □ *That's a possibility that can't be **ruled out**.* □ *He was **ruled out** as a possible candidate.*

rule with a rod of iron/with an iron hand/with heavy/high hand sundoj, qeveris, drejtoj me despotizëm (me dorë të hekurt)

□ *Determined to ride the fore-horse herself, Meg would admit no helpmate..., she **ruled** all matters **with a high hand**.* □ *A small kingdom **ruled** by herself **with a rod of iron** was what she liked.* □ *He did not know what sickness was, never had an ache or pain, ate his food with gusto, and **ruled** his brothers **with a rod of iron**.* □ *Our parents were very strict: as children we were **ruled with a rod of iron**.*

run a chance/a hazard/a risk rrezikoj, vë kokën në rrezik

□ *They **ran a big risk** setting sail in such stormy weather.* □ *He **ran the risk** of losing his own life to save the little child.* □ *Unless you dress warmly in winter, you **run the risk** of catching a chill.*

run across sb/sth has, ndesh, zbuloj, gjej, takoj rastësisht

□ *I **ran across** an old friend in the street last week.* □ *I **ran across** one of his earliest recordings in a secondhand shop.*

run after sb/sth 1. ndjek, vrapoj pas

□ *The boy **ran after** the carriage.* □ *The dog was **running after** a rabbit.* □ *Mary **runs after** every spark of knowledge of mathematics.*

2. shkoj pas

□ *She had never before run after a man, and she was not very good at doing it seriously.*

run along ik, shko

□ *'Be a good girl and run along: Daddy's busy.'* □ *'For God's sake run along,' Robert snapped. 'You're dissipating my creative mood.'*

run amok/amuck tërbohem, harbohem, bëhem si i marrë

□ *As the mediamen run amok in this quiet backwater, literally millions of ordinary hard working people will be forced to pay up every day to subsidize their so-called activities.* □ *She saw that he resented her shrinking; but it seemed to excite him to run amuck the more.*

run a temperature ka temperaturë

□ *The doctor says that Jane is running a slight temperature, but she is not seriously ill.*

run at sb i turrem, sulem dikujt (për ta sulmuar)

□ *A big fellow ran at me with a big knife.*

run away (with) 1. iki, largohem

□ *Don't run away, I've something to say to you.* □ *Don't bother me while I'm reading, run away and play.* □ *'Don't run away. I shan't eat you!'*

2. iki nga shtëpia

□ *John has run away with the boss's daughter.* □ *The maid run away with the duchess's jewels.*

3. marr, vjedh (dhe largohem)

□ *A cashier ran away with the day's takings.* □ *Someone in the office ran away with the plans of the new engine.*

4. harxhon, konsumon shumë

□ *Those new heaters run away with a lot of electricity.* □ *My new car really runs away with the gas.*

5. fitoj lehtë

□ *The Brazilian team run away with the first match in the series.* □ *The champion run away with the match.*

6. fitoj kontroll të plotë mbi, dominoj

□ *You tend to let your feelings run away with you.* □ *Don't let your temper run away with you.*

run away with the idea/notion shkoj me mendimin (besimin) se

□ *Because I've overlooked your mistake this time, don't run away with the idea that you can always do this kind of thing.* □ *When I say that he doesn't work very hard, you mustn't run away with the idea that he is lazy: it is just that his health is not very good.* □ *Don't ever run away with the idea that bankruptcy is a joke.*

run back (over) 1. rikthej (filmin)

□ *'Just wait a minute while we have that sequence run back.'* □ *'Run that excerpt back to the beginning and replay it in slow motion.'*

2. i rikthehem, rishikoj, rishqyrtoj

□ *'I should like to run back over the past term, singling out events of particular importance.'* □ *I'll run back over the procedure again.*

run counter to sth kundërshton, bie ndesh me

□ *So Mr. Osborne, having a firm conviction in his own mind did not run counter to his fate, but yielded himself up to it quite complacently.* □ *This result runs counter to a very basic principle of human learning.* □ *The situation runs counter to ordinary logic.* □ *I am amazed at what you told me about Jim: it runs counter to everything I have heard about him.*

run down 1. i lodhur, i dërrmuar, i rraskapitur

□ *'You look thoroughly* **run down***. Why don't you take a week's holiday?'*
2. shtyp
□ *The cyclist was* **run down** *by a truck.* □ *I didn't get to her before she died. She had been* **run down** *by a truck.*
3. përplaset
□ *The liner* **ran down** *a fishing boat during the dense fog.*
4. kritikoj; poshtëroj, përçmoj, ul
□ *It's not good to flatter a person to his face and then* **run him down** *behind his back.* □ *'The food had better be good after all that talk.' 'That's enough for* **running down** *my cooking,' she said.* □ *She's always* **running** *her husband* **down** *in public. I'm surprised he puts up with it.*
5. bie, harxhohet, konsumohet
□ *The battery has* **run down***, it needs recharging.* □ *'If you leave the car lights on all night you'll* **run** *the battery* **down***.'*
6. bie, zbret, ulet, pakësohet
□ *The farm labor force is* **running down** *steadily.*
7. gjej (pas një kërkimi të gjatë)
□ *The suspect was finally* **run down** *at the home of one of his associates.*

run for it iki me të katra, ua mbath këmbëve, ia jap vrapit (për të shpëtuar)
□ *One jump and we'll* **run for it** *like antelopes.* □ *At first he was a bit suspicious and ready to* **run for it***, should the animal attack him.* □ *'Never mind your bloody boots.* **Run for it***.'* □ *The prisoner decided to make a* **run for it***.*

run for one's life /for dear life iki me të shpejtë (për të shpëtuar kokën)
□ *With pieces of burning masonry falling all around him, he* **ran for dear life***.* □ *Office workers* **ran for the**

their lives *as an earth tremor shook the centre of town.*

run high 1. trazohet (deti)
□ *The sea* **runs high** *and the boat may be dashed to pieces on the rocks.*
2. ndizen, marrin flakë (ndjenjat etj.)
□ *Feelings are* **running too high***.* □ *Passions* **ran high** *as the election approached.* □ *After the football match, the feelings of both groups of supporters were* **running high***.*

run in 1. arrestoj dikë dhe e çoj në rajonin e policisë
□ *Trevor was* **run in** *for dangerous driving on Saturday night.* □ *He was* **run in** *for drunk and disorderly behavior.*
2. shtroj (motorin etj.)
□ *'Don't expect me to get you home quickly—I'm still* **running** *my car* **in***.'* □ *Don't drive your new car too fast until I've* **run in***.*

run in the family vazhdon në familje (nga brezi në brez)
□ *We expect him to go into the navy. The tradition* **runs in the family***.* □ *Musical ability* **runs in the family***. They have always been good musicians for as far back as anyone can remember.*

run into 1. përplasem
□ *He lost control of his car and* **ran it into** *a lamp-post.* □ *The bus went out of control and* **ran into** *a shop front.*
2. has, takoj rastësisht
□ *I* **ran into** *an old schoolfriend at the supermarket this morning.* □ *I* **ran into** *an old friend at the race-meeting.*
3. has, ndesh (vështirësi etj.)
□ *The project is* **running into** *financial difficulties.*
4. hyj, futem
□ *They would sell their furniture, and then* **ran into** *debt at the stores, and then be refused credit.* □ *Climbing*

*higher, we **ran into** a patch of thick mist which blotted out our route.*

run into a brick wall has pengesa të pakapërcyeshme

□ *I have been trying to obtain the information you requested but I keep **running into a brick wall**. Everyone refuses to talk about it.*

run into debt futem borxh (në borxhe)

□ *If you don't spend your money wisely, you will soon **run into debt**.*

run into the ground 1. çoj në ekstrem

□ *You have a good idea but I hope you won't **run it into the ground**.*

2. këput, rraskapit, sfilit

□ *By working 13 hours a day she is **running herself into the ground**.*

3. prish pak nga pak, konsumoj

□ *I'm not going to buy a new car. I'm just going to **run the car I have into the ground**.*

run its course 1. merr fund, mbaron, përfundon

□ *Dave waited smiling, until the formalities had **run their course**.*

2. mbush (kalon) ciklin e plotë të zhvillimit, bën të vetën

□ *Don't worry. The disease will **run its course**. □ We can't cure the disease; it must **run its course**. □ I don't believe in swallowing all that chemist's muck for a cold. Go to bed, or stay indoors anyway and let it **run its course**.*

run low (on sth) mbaron

□ *The gas is **running low**.*

run of bad/good luck periudhë (gjendje) fatkeqe/fatlume

□ *My brother would like to borrow some money from you; he's had a **run of bad luck** in his business deals.*

run off 1. iki me nxitim, me vrap

□ *The child heard the noise and **ran off**. □ She gave a brief wave and **ran off** across the lawn.*

2. iki (nga shtëpia)

□ *She **ran off** to Paris with a chap ten years her junior.*

3. zhvillohet

□ *The heats of the 200 metres are being **run off** tomorrow.*

4. zbraz, derdh

□ *He asked his brother to **run off** the water from the tank. □ Why don't you ever **run** the water **off** after you've had a bath?*

5. kopioj, riprodhoj; shumëzoj; shtyp

□ *Could you **run off** twenty copies of the agenda? □ 'Run me off some copies of his electoral address.' □ The press can **run off** two thousand copies every hour.*

run off one's feet/legs u bien këmbët

□ *At the New Year sales rush, the girls in the clothing departments are **run off their feet** all day.*

run off sb (like) water off a duck's back s'bën asnjë efekt

□ *Her scoldings **ran off him like water off a duck's back**.*

run on 1. vazhdoj pa pushim (të flas)

□ *He will **run on** for an hour if you don't stop him. □ In her talk she **ran on** so that no one could get in a word. □ On he **ran**, until most of his audience were restless with impatience.*

2. ka të bëjë me, ka si objekt (temë); sillet rreth

□ *Her talk **ran on** the developments of computer softwares. □ His talk **ran on** recent developments in the industry.*

run one's eye over shikoj, këqyr, kontrolloj, i hedh një sy

□ *'Just **run your eye over** these materials and tell me if there are any you like.' □ I had the chance of **running my eye over** the new members of the company during rehearsal.*

run one's head against/into a brick wall i bie murit me kokë

□ *To try to change the political convictions of these people would be like* **running your head into a brick wall.**
□ *You may get your proposal accepted next year; at the moment you're* **running your head against a brick wall.**

run out (of) 1. iki, dal me vrap
□ *Kristoforas died, little Katrina, who was alone with him,* **ran out** *screaming for help.* □ *I* **ran out** *and slammed the door.*
2. derdhet, rrjedh
□ *Water is* **running out.** *Go and turn the tap off.*
3. mbaron
□ *The gas is* **running out.** □ *Could I have a cigarette? I seem to have* **run out** *of them.*
4. mbaron, skadon, është i pavlefshëm
□ *The lease on their London apartment* **runs out** *in a few months.*

run over 1. i hedh një sy, lexoj shpejt e shpejt
□ *He* **ran over** *his notes before starting his lecture.*
2. shtyp
□ *The dog was nearly* **run over** *by a car.* □ *The children were* **run over** *at that road junction last month.*
3. derdhet
□ *'You had better fetch the plumber; the cistern is* **running over.'** □ *'Don't fill the kettle too full: it'll* **run over.'**

run riot harbohet, tërbohet, harliset, shpërthen me furi
□ *Where had he gone? Why had he not let her know? Her scepticism* **ran riot.** □ *They had to call the police because the students were* **running riot** *through the town, frightening the passers-by.* □ *If by that time the population was not fed, and housed, famine and disease would* **run riot**

through the country. □ *'It's the thought of Alice,' Teddy said, 'unchaste thoughts are* **running riot.'**

run short (of) shteron, mbaron
□ *They were so numbed that they did not even suffer much from hunger now; only the children continued to fret when the food* **ran short.** □ *We're* **running short of** *sugar; we'll have to buy some tomorrow.* □ *Tell your mummy I'm sorry. I've not a drop of milk I could give her. We've* **run short** *ourselves this weekend.* □ *Time is* **running short,** *ladies and gentlemen and we won't be able to allow encores for the remaining items on the program.*

run sb/sth close është po aq i mirë (i shpejtë, i suksesshëm etj.) sa dhe
□ *'Thomson in the lead as they come round the bend,' went on the excited voice of the commentator, 'but the lanky Dutchman* **running** *him* **close!'**
□ *I don't know what year my dad's car is but it must* **run** *yours pretty* **close.**

run the gauntlet (of sb/sth) sulmohem nga të gjitha anët, kritikohem ashpër; pranoj (sprovoj) vuajtje (sulme, kritikë etj.)
□ *Those who wanted to work in the factory had to* **run the gauntlet of** *opposition from those who were on strike.* □ *Between me and the railway line there now stretched a thin but regular cordon of police. To* **run the gauntlet of** *both police and trains was more than I could bear.* □ *She had to* **run the gauntlet of** *her mother's liking for her company and her father's wish for her to go with him to Richmond.* □ *The consequential legislature will, he promises, force the Government to* **run** *a far severer* **gauntlet** *than the vote after a six-day debate.*

run through 1. kalon me të shpejtë nëpër

□ *Thoughts of revenge kept* **running through** *his mind.* □ *A snatch of their conversation kept* **running through** *his head.*

2. përshkon

□ *A deep melancholy* **runs through** *his poetry.*

3. prish, shpenzoj pa hesap; i bëj paratë rrush e kumbulla

□ *On the second branch of the question, I will only remark that unless I* **ran through** *that part of my inheritance while I was still a baby, I have not come into it yet.* □ *The money inherited from his father was quickly* **run through.**

4. përmbledh

□ *Let's* **run through** *the main points of the Budget so far.*

5. lexoj, shikoj me nxitim

□ *I had to* **run through** *the book in an hour.*

6. luaj, interpretoj, bëj prova

□ *'I'd like to* **run through** *that scene you have with Paula.'*

run to 1. arrin, kap (shumën etj)

□ *The book* **runs to** *just over three hundred pages.*

2. del, është i mjaftueshëm (për të përballuar shpenzimet etj.); përballoj

□ *The budget would not* **run to** *champagne.* □ *We can* **run to** *a long trip round the country this summer.*

run to earth/ground gjej (pas një kërkimi të gjatë)

□ *The police looked for the witness everywhere and finally* **ran** *him* **to earth** *in London.* □ *We* **ran** *the bird shop* **to earth** *eventually, on one side of an enormous square.*

run to fat ngjallem, shëndoshem, shtoj në peshë, majmem

□ *Her mother was wealthy and discontented,* **running to fat** *and losing her looks from idleness.* □ *After a year at a desk job, and only occasional weekend exercise, he was starting to* **run to fat.**

run up 1. ngre (flamurin etj.)

□ *Then the white flag was* **run up;** *the post had surrendered.*

2. bëj, sajoj shpejt e shpejt

□ *She hadn't been able to get a swimsuit to fit her. She had consequently* **run up** *two for herself.*

3. lë të rritet

□ *You'll* **run up** *a huge gas bill if you leave the heater on.*

run up against sth has, ndesh ballë për ballë

□ *These were some of the snags we expected to* **run up against.** □ *The same opposition had been* **run up against** *when we last tried to introduce the measures.*

run wild harbohet, tërbohet, del dore; harliset

□ *When they first arrive, the children* **run wild** *for a week, exploring every corner, climbing every tree.* □ *It's disgraceful the way she lets her children* **run wild.** *They should be kept under firmer control.* □ *The violets are* **running wild** *in the flower bed.*

run with the hare and hunt with the hounds bën lojë të dyfishtë

□ *Serve him right, say the heartless in either camp; no good ever comes from trying to* **run with the hare and hunt with the hounds.** □ *They think it is due less to sensitivity than to a shrewd instinct for* **running with the hare, hunting with the hounds.** □ *The man who through force of circumstances had tried to act as a bridge between the avant-garte and* *traditional culture was simultaneously rejected by both sides after a long and honorable career. Serve him right, say the heartless in either camp; no good ever comes from trying to* **run with the hare and hunt with the hounds.** □ *Others look less indulgently on Shirley Williams's apparent lack of toughness, her dislike of being disliked. they think it is due less to sensitivity than to a shrewd instinct for* **running with the hare, hunting with the hounds.**

rush into print botoj me nxitim

□ *I deplore the writing of so-called military history by people concerned with* **rushing into print** *so as to catch a market that is still fresh.*

rush to conclusions arrij në përfundime të nxituara

□ *'You were there last night. I saw your hat and coat.' 'Now don't start* **rushing to conclusions.'** □ *'You were talking to Stevens at lunch. I wouldn't mind betting he offered you a job.' 'That would be* **rushing to conclusions.'**

401

S

sacred cow, a totem; gjë (njeri, send) i paprekshëm (i pacënueshëm, i pakritikueshëm)

□ *It seems from your correspondence column that Harold Wilson is a **sacred cow**.* □ *We can't afford **sacred cows**.* □ *Let's not make a **sacred cow** of the monarchy.* □ *Education is one of the **sacred cows** of our modern civilization.*

safe and sound shëndoshë e mirë

□ *Anyway, everything of yours is still where you left them inside the house. Everything's all **safe and sound**.* □ *'I don't think we shall ever see them again. I feel it.' 'Come, come, dear. They'll be back **safe and sound**, you'll see.'* □ *His mother was overjoyed to hear that her little boy had been found, **safe and sound**.* □*The rescuers brought the climbers back **safe and sound**.*

sail close to/near the wind veproj në mënyrë të rrezikshme (gati të paligjshme)

□ *He never actually tells lies, but he often **sails** pretty **close to the wind**.* □ *I would not say that Jack is a crook, but he sometimes **sails close to the wind** in his business dealings.* □ *... he's **sailing near to the wind**, with those large contracts that he makes.* □ *He realized that he was **sailing** rather **close to the wind** financially.*

sail in/into hyj me zjarr (në diskutim, debat etj.)

□ *Ann then **sailed in** with a furious attack on the chairman.*

sail into sb sulmoj me fjalë

□ *He **sailed into** the witness, accusing him of lying.*

sail under false colors lundroj me flamur të rremë; fsheh identitetin e vërtetë

□ *I had so much wisdom as to **sail under false colors** in this foolish jaunt of mine.* □ *Cowperwood has decided that he did not care to **sail under** any **false colors** so far as Addison was concerned.*

salt of the earth njeri flori; flori në mushama; kripa e tokës

□ *I like him. I always have. He's the **salt of the earth** and all that.* □ *The villagers here may not be rich or well-educated but, in my opinion, they are the **salt of the earth**.*

same here unë gjithashtu, edhe unë gjithashtu; edhe unë jam i një mendjeje

□ *'I hate this book.' '**Same here**.'* □ *'I'm nearly falling asleep.' '**Same here**. I think I'll put this work away and go to bed.'* □ *'Paul distrusts him.' '**Same here**,' put in Sophie unexpectedly, 'though I don't know why.'* □ *'We thought that the service in our hotel was dreadful.' '**Same here**: we are going to complain to the manager.'* □ *'Mr. Mont! Often thought I'd like to see you again, sir.' '**Same here**, Bicket.'*

same old story, the e njëjta histori

□ *The villain of the piece—as is often the case in the theatre—is the box-office: 'It's always **the same old story**, money, money, money.'*

save appearances nuk fëlliqem në sytë e botës; mbahem sa për sy (sa për faqe) të botës

☐ *The meeting had to be abandoned because hardly anyone turned up. But, to* **save appearances***, it was announced that it had been abandoned because of bad weather conditions.*

☐ *So long as a Forsyte got what he was after, he was not too particular about the means, provided* **appearance** *was* **saved***.*

save one's bacon shpëtoj lëkurën (kokën)

☐ *With this lie I'd temporarily* **saved my bacon***, perhaps for long enough to escape.* ☐ *Instead of helping the passengers when the ship hit the rocks, the crew members were only interested in* **saving** *their own* **bacon***.*

☐ *I was nearly bankrupt, but your loan* **saved my bacon***.* ☐ *He sold his investment and* **saved his bacon***.*

save one's breath (to cool one's porridge) kursej frymën

☐ *Ask him what he wants and if it's not important the little runt can* **save his breath to cool his porridge***.* ☐ *I wanted to ask what they were, but so furious was her assault upon the slope, I thought it wiser to* **save my breath***.* ☐ *If you are thinking of asking him not to climb the mountain, you might as well* **save your breath***; he is determined to go.* ☐ *His incomprehension was getting me down. 'Make some effort to follow me or I'll* **save my breath***.* ☐ *In the end, of course, a civil outfit can't fight a government, and a month later we were thrown out. I might have* **saved my breath to cool my porridge***.* ☐ *If it's the job he wants me to see about, tell him he can* **save his breath***.*

save one's face shpëtoj nderin, ruaj emrin e mirë

☐ *To* **save face***, the company said in public that it was not to blame, but privately paid large sums of money to people making claims against it.* ☐ *Though she had lost her job, she* **saved face** *by saying that she'd left it willingly.* ☐ *We must tread very carefully. We must 'save face'.*

save one's/sb's life shpëtoj kokën; i shpëtoj jetën (kokën) dikujt

☐ *I might go up there to* **save my life** *but not for much less.*

save one's (own) neck/skin/hide shpëtoj kokën, shpëtoj lëkurën

☐ *When the rest of the gang was arrested, he* **saved his own skin** *by giving evidence against them.* ☐ *The fighter planes* **saved our skins** *while the army was landing from the ships.*

☐ *They behaved in a very cowardly way; they were only interested in* **saving their own necks***.* ☐ *The enemy adopted those emergency measures in order to* **save their own necks** *but to no avail.*

save sth for a rainy day kursej për një ditë të zezë (për kohë të vështirë)

☐ *But he wrote her regularly, as he confessed to me, and, I believe sent her a part of his earnings, which were to be* **saved** *by her for him* **against a rainy day***.*

save the day përmbys (shpëtoj) situatën (gjendjen); siguroj fitore (suskses)

☐ *'George', he said, 'there's no use being angry with me for going to Butler. I had to do it to* **save the day***.'*

☐ *As cavalry, the Mamelukes had no equal in the world. Once unhorsed, however, they were heavily encumbered by their arms, and it was left to their Bedouin infantry to* **save the** *day*. □ *We thought that we were going to lose the game, but the two goals that were scored in the last five minutes saved the day*.

save the situation nxjerr nga situata; shpëtoj situatën (gjendjen)

□ *We saved the situation and now it's up to those chaps not to let us down.*
□ *Disagreements threatened to wreck the peace talks, but the president's intervention saved the situation.*
□ *Luckily, the waiter came up with the bill just then and the situation was saved.* □ *None of us knew what to do until Danniel came up with an idea which saved the situation.*

saving your presence më fal për shprehjen

□ *Some of the members of your organization are unscrupulous schemers, saving your presence.*

saw off the bough on which one is sitting i bëri gropën vetes, i hapi varrin vetes

□ *You are acting like the proverbial man who sawed off the bough on which he was sitting.*

saw sth off sharroj, pres (me sharrë)

□ *If you saw six inches off the legs of the table, you can use it to rest the television on.* □ *Who did saw the branch off the tree?*

saw sth up sharroj (në pjesë)

□ *The timber should be sawn up.*

say adieu/good-bye lë lamtumirën

□ *As the train will start in a minute, he has to say good-bye to his friends.*

say a good word for sb them një fjalë të mirë për

□ *'Don't you have a good word to say for me?'*

say a mouthful them një llaf (fjalë) të vërtetë

□ *The man who said we'd be frozen up in mid-January said a mouthful.*

□ *'They say that he is the richest man in the town.' 'Whoever said that, said a mouthful. He has more money than everyone else put together.'*

saying and doing are two things me të thënë e me të bërë shkon në mes një lumë i tërë

□ *'You promised but never kept them, Giles. You should realize that saying and doing are two things.'*

say no to sth i them jo

□ *If you don't invest in these shares, you are saying no to a fortune.*

say nothing of sth/sb, to pa përmendur

□ *... failed to justify the hopes and efforts (to say nothing of the cost) which have been expended upon it.* □ *Glasgow has fine buildings and botanical gardens, and the great river Clyde with its' tradition of shipbuilding, to say nothing of the glorious scenery as the river unfolds.* □ *He had to go to prison for a month, to say nothing of the fine.* □ *She has been a creative worker and has played an important role in raising the production, to say nothing of her contribution to sporting and cultural activities.*

say one's piece shfaq hapur mendimin

□ *I got up at the beginning of the meeting, said my piece and left.* □ *Helen: I brought you some money. Jo: You know what you can do with that. Helen: All right! You've said your piece. I'll leave it on the table.*

say (out) one's say them fjalën time, shpreh mendimin tim

□ *I have done my best, and said my say.*

say the last word them fjalën e fundit

□ *I don't think I was treated unfairly, but I've said my last word on the subject so we can forget about it, if you don't mind.* □ *Neither Professor A.K. Cairncros nor the Government spokesman had* **said their last word** *on this figure.* □ **The last word** *has not yet been* **said** *on this subject.*

say the least of it më e pakta që mund të thuhet

□ *To be stranded in the middle of Buenos Aires with a truckload of animals and nowhere to keep them was,* **to say the least,** *a trifle disconcerting.*

□ *... a thoughtful and readable novel which is,* **to say the least of it,** *a pleasant change from some of the squalid muck and pretentious pornography which is flooding the market.*

say the right/wrong thing them diçka me vend/pa vend

□ *Poor Grandmother! She tried so hard to like me, poor dear, and she was so careful to* **say the right thing.**

□ *She looked at me rather strangely when I said it must be quite a challenge to have such a handsome and talented husband. Did I* **say the wrong thing?**

say (speak) the word fol, hape gojën, kërko

□ *If you ever need any help, just* **say the word.** □ **Say the word** *and it'll be done.* □ *Davies: I'd look after the place for you. I'll be your man, you* **say the word,** *just* **say the word.**

□ *Jack's the one who thinks it's sensible to wait but he has only to* **say the word** *and she'd marry him tomorrow.*

scare away/off bëj të largohet (duke e trembur); mbaj larg (nga frika)

□ *Strangers never call at that house. I think the bulldog* **scares** *them* **away.**

□ *A lot of potential visitors are* **scared off** *by the look of the place.*

scarer sb into doing sth i fus dikujt frikën që të bëjë diçka

□ *They* **scared** *him* **into** *handing over the keys.*

scare sb out of his wits i kall tmerrin (datën)

□ *'Don't go through the cemetery at night—it* **scares** *the girls* **out of their wits.'** □ *'Never take me to a horror film again. I was* **scared out of my wits.** □ *What do you mean by* **scaring the wits out of** *a man?*

scare sb stiff lemeris, i shtie (kall) tmerrin

□ *The children refuses to walk along the narrow bridge; they were* **scared stiff.** □ *'You don't seem worried,' Pyle said. 'I'm* **scared stiff**—*but things are better than they might be.'*

scare the daylights out of frikësoj tej mase

□ *Pete's ghost story* **scared the daylights out of** *the smaller boys.* □ *The howling sound she heard outside just about* **scared** *the living* **daylights out of** *her.*

scorched earth policy, a politikë e tokës së djegur

□ *I rebelled against the* **scorched earth policy** *which had advocates in Whitehall. Their reasoning was that as the Germans advanced inland towards London, so we would burn and destroy the countryside as we retreated.*

scrape a living nxjerr (siguroj) me zor bukën e gojës

□ *I manage to* **scrape a living** *by selling pictures.*

scrape along/by on sth mbahem gjallë, mbaj frymën gjallë

□ *I can't just* **scrape along** *on what my parents give me.*

scrape in/into futem me zor (në shkollë etj.)

□ *If he just **scraped into** secondary school, he'll be lucky to get a place at university.* □ *'How on earth did he get into Foreign Service?' 'He must have **scraped in** by the barest margin, or perhaps he has influence among the selectors.'*

scrape (the bottom of) the barrel mbledh, kruaj (marr, përdor) fundin e (kazanit)

□ *The country is so short of teachers that the government has been **scraping the bottom of the barrel**. Some of the new teachers have very poor qualification.* □ *'That was Sue on the phone. She wanted to know whether all seven of them could come round for lunch tomorrow. I said it would be okay.' 'But that's impossible! Even if **we scraped the barrel** it wouldn't be nearly enough.* □ *'They must have really **scraped the bottom of the barrel** to dig him up.'*

scrape through sth kaloj me vështirësi (provimin etj.)

□ *She only just **scraped through** the test.* □ *He got a comfortable pass in zoology, but barely **scraped through** in botany.*

scrape together/up mbledh (kursej, grumbulloj) me vështirësi

□ *If they know how I had **scraped** my half pence **together** for the purchase of my daily saveloy...* □ *'Well, you'll have to **scrape** the money **up**. I'm not going to dip into my funds to save you from a scandal.'* □ *'Can't you just try to **scrape together** a few pounds for a holiday?'*

scrape up an acquaintance with sb me zor arrij të njihem (të prezantohem) me

□ *'What makes you want to get on stage?' 'I need to make a living.' 'Oh,' he answered, rather taken by* her trim appearance, and feeling as if he might **scrape up an acquaintance with** her. □ *I slowly **scraped up an acquaintance with** neighbours.* □ *I managed to **scrape up an acquaintance with** some of the single passengers, but the married ones tended to keep to themselves.* □ *He would nod over the garden wall once in a while and after a month we'd **scraped up** some kind of **an acquaintance**.*

scratch my back and I'll scratch yours njëra dorë lan tjetrën, të dyja lajnë fytyrën (faqet)

□ *There was a political ring in Philadelphia in which the mayor, certain members of the council, the treasurer and others shared. It was a case generally of 'you **scratch my back and I'll scratch yours**'.* □ *I think we should do everything we can to help the new manager. If we **scratch his back, he may scratch ours**.*

□ *The contract went to a friend of the chief accountant. It's a case of you **scratch my back and I'll scratch yours**.*

scratch one's head kruaj kokën

□ *He glanced at my acquaintance who was **scratching his head** in a faintly worried fashion.* □ *We have been **scratching our heads** for a solution to the problem.* □ *He **scratched his head** and an idea was born.*

scratch sb's eyes out i nxjerr sytë

□ *'Be careful, Harry. She'll **scratch your eyes out** if you so much as glance at another woman.'* □ *'You'll stop fooling around with Mike if you don't want to have **your eyes scratched out**!'*

scratch the surface of sth cek (prek) kalimthi, trajtoj përcipazi

□ *They say they are only **scratching the surface of** the subject, but*

406

already they are surprised by the quality and diversity of the material available. □ *Despite the numerous attempts to induce industry to move into the development areas and to decentralize offices from Central London, we have only scratched the surface of the problem.* □ *Allport, who has written the classic introduction to this field, discusses some fifty definitions without doing more than scratching the surface.*

scream/yell blue murder bërtas me zë të lartë (me të madhe); bëj zhurmë (rrëmujë) të madhe

□ *He'll scream blue murder if you promote Jack Simpson instead of him—but Jack'll do the job better.* □ *One of them came over and tried to turn my face round with his hands and before I knew what I was doing, I was yelling blue murder.*

screw sth out of sth/sb 1. shtrydh, nxjerr me të shtrydhur

□ *Screw the water out of the sponge.* 2. nxjerr me të mirë a me të keq

□ *He's so unscrupulous that he'd screw the last penny out of a widow.* □ *'Can't you manage to screw a bit extra out of your parents?'*

screw up 1. bëj shuk

□ *With an impatient exclamation Peter screwed up the second draft of his letter to the bank and threw it into the wastepaper basket.* 2. tkurr, rrudh, mbledh

□ *Even under the broad brim of my hat I had to screw up my eyes against the ferocious glare.* □ *Janice screwed her face up into an expression of the utmost seriousness.* 3. nervozoj, tensionoj

□ *The last minutes before going on stage always screws him up, so he has a cigarette and a chat with someone*

in the dressing room to help him relax. □ *'Going to the dentist never seems to bother my wife, but I get terribly screwed up at the mere thought.'* 4. bëj rrëmujë; manazhoj, drejtoj keq

□ *'We should never have left the arrangements to Smithers. He screwed the whole thing up from start to finish.'*

screw up one's courage marr guxim (kurajo); bëhem burrë

□ *But Peter said he would teach Felix to swim, and Felix screwed up his courage to the point of assenting.* □ *I screwed up my courage and went to the dentist.* □ *I've been screwing up my courage to tell you.* □ *'Don't stand there—screw up your courage and jump.'*

scrub sth away/off heq duke fërkuar

□ *'Scrub that mud off your fingers before you sit down to lunch.'* □ *I got paint on my hands and it won't scrub off.* □ *He managed to scrub away the grease.*

scum of the earth, the llumi, fundërria e njerëzve (e shoqërisë)

□ *'Scum of the earth is what we are,' said a huge man in a club near Smithfield meat market, with heavy sarcasm.'*

seal off izoloj, bllokoj, mbyll kalimin

□ *It did not seem to occur to the police to seal off the entrances or order nobody to leave.*

seal one's lips/mouth mbyll (kyç) gojën

□ *Her inclination had been to ask Edward frankly, but he had potently sealed his lips upon the subject.* □ *And there and then began to form in his mind a plan by which he could escape exposure and seal Roberta Alden's lips for ever.*

seal sb's fate vulos fatin e

□ *I had received a card to say my application was being considered but*

*was still awaiting the letter that
would seal my fate.* □ *'That's the man
I'm going to marry,' Esther told her
friend. 'He may not know it now but
his fate is sealed.'*

seal up mbyll; vulos
□ *They sealed up the cracks in the
window to stop the icy wind from
blowing in.* □ *Make sure the parcel
of examination scripts is properly
sealed up.*

seamy side of sth, the ana e zezë
(e errët) e
□ *When a man had seen as much of
the seamy side, you know, as Bill, it
could hardly be expected that he was
going to be upset.* □ *Mr. Skipton
knows a lot about Flemish domestic
life. The seamy side, I believe.* □ *I
suppose even this delightful city has
its seamy side.*

search one's heart/soul rrëmoj
ndërgjegjen
□ *I'd get tired of listening to mother
searching her soul when I knew
damn well that she'd always do
exactly what suited her best, in
the end.*

search me nuk e di, nuk kam as idenë
më të vogël
□ *'I thought Ailsa Craigs were onions,'
said Hopalong. 'Are they?' 'Search
me, mate.'* □ *'Where has my book
gone?' 'Search me: I gave it back to
you about a week ago.'*

search sb/sth out gjej, zbuloj, nxjerr
në dritë (duke kërkuar me kujdes)
□ *We've searched out some of your
favorite recipes.* □ *He went through
drawer after drawer and eventually searched out a dusty portfolio.*
□ *Did you search out your former
neighbour?*

second best, (the) i dytë, më poshtë se
dikush a diçka

□ *He has had a number of fights with
the champion, but he has always
come off second best.*

second nature natyrë e dytë
□ *She's the kind of person who isn't
very good at doing nothing, to whom
work is second nature.* □ *Profession-
alism is already second nature to
Michel. He has been acting since the
age of two.*

second to none nuk ia del njeri, nuk
mbetet prapa askujt, nuk ia gjen
shokun, nuk ka shok
□ *For convenience, shopping at the
supermarket is second to none, but,
compared with the general shop
around the corner, it is a most impersonal institution.* □ *You should go to
that restaurant, their food is second
to none.* □ *In mathematics he is
second to none in the class.*

see about ndjek, kujdesem, merrem
me (një çështje)
□ *I shall see about the matter.* □ *Have
you seen about the railway tickets?*
□ *I must see about getting the television set repaired.*

see after shikoj, kujdesem, përkujdesem
□ *Here Tom, see after the luggage.*

see an end of shoh fundin e
□ *Perhaps with the appointment of
our new managing director we would
see an end to the inter-departmental
rivalries and quarrels of the previous
year.*

see daylight kuptoj, marr vesh, arrij ta
shoh (kuptoj) zgjidhjen
□ *I struggled with the problem for
hours before I saw daylight.* □ *'I begin
to see daylight,' broke in McNeil.*

see eye to eye (with) (about/on) jam i
një mendjeje me, kam të njëjtin
mendim me
□ *He said he could see eye to eye with
us in this affair, and would do all he*

could to help us. □ *We really see eye to eye on this thing and that is important.* □ *I guess they didn't see eye to eye on certain matters.* □ *Jack and Mary don't see eye to eye on this matter.* □ *Stanley: Clive, as you know, your mother and I didn't see eye to eye about sending you to college.* □ *Though we did not usually agree, we saw eye to eye in the matter of reducing the taxes.*

see fit (to do sth) e shoh të udhës, e shoh me vend

□ *We didn't see fit to adopt his suggestion. Do as you think fit.* □ *You can either come yourself or not, as you see fit.* □ *The newspaper did not see fit to publish my letter.*

see for oneself shoh vetë, shoh me sytë e mi

□ *If you don't believe me, go and see for yourself.* □ *If you don't believe that it's snowing, go and see for yourself.*

see here dëgjo

□ *'See here,' he exclaimed ...'You are in quite as delicate a situation as I am, if you only stop to think.'*

see/watch how/which way the cat jumps shoh nga fryn era; shoh si zhvillohen ngjarjet, si rrjedhin punët

□ *It will be interesting to see which way the cat jumps, now that his profit-making can no longer be reconciled with a clear conscience.*

□ *There's nothing for it but to wait and see how the cat jumps.* □ *'We expect you to help us,' said Annette, 'but, you English, we never can rely on. You always wait to see how the cat jumps.'*

see how the land lies shoh si qëndrojnë punët, shoh (studioj) situatën

□ *Bunder and Simons had given him addresses that they recommended,*

but to accept either would have meant the end of his policy of strict neutrality, and he was determined to preserve it until he saw how the land lay; so he found a place for himself. □ *... by this time I saw very clearly how the land lay between my patron and his wife.* □ *It was about half past six on a cool summer evening, but the bar was thick with smoke; it took him a moment or two to see how the land lay.*

see how/which way the wind blows shoh nga fryn era

□ *Why not wait and see which way the wind is blowing, with the flexibility to jump in quickly?* □ *Wiser men knew which way the wind was blowing, cut their losses and got out before the regulations blocking currency were enforced.* □ *I've expected it all along. You needn't worry about me. I know all about this. I've seen which way the wind is blowing and I know how to trim my sails.*

seeing is believing ta shikosh pa ta besosh, duhet parë pa ta besosh

□ *'Ultimately, anyone's experience of the unknown has to be personal.' In other words, seeing is believing and you either believe or you don't.* □ *Some people make fun of his supernatural powers, but I have seen the amazing things he can do, and seeing is believing.*

see in a new/different light shoh diçka në një dritë të re, shoh diçka me sy tjetër

□ *'We are all under somewhat of a strain, and in the morning we will probably see things in a totally different light.'*

see into shqyrtoj, analizoj; kuptoj (karakterin e vërtetë, qëllimin e fshehtë)

□ *The solicitors will **see into** your claim to property.* □ *I've **seen into** that problem.* □ *He promised to **see into** the matter for us.*

seek a hare in a hen's nest kërkoj qiqra në hell, kërkoj kallëza në borë, kërkoj të pamundurën

□ *By so acting you are simply trying to **seek a hare in a hen's nest**.*

seek a quarrel with sb kërkoj sherr (grindje)

□ *Are you **seeking a quarrel**?*

seek one's fortune kërkoj fatin

□ *Jurgis emigrated to America to **seek his fortune**.*

seek sb/sth out kërkoj të gjej

□ *Laura used to **seek** Gillian **out** when she had quarrelled with all her friends.* □ *I used to **seek** her **out** on her way home from school.* □ *When Marlowe returned from lunch the secretary **sought** him **out**. 'Cable for you, Dr. Marlowe.'*

see land shoh frytin e punës (rezultatin e përpjekjeve)

□ *Stephen worked the next day, and the next, uncheered by a word from anyone, and shunned in all his comings and goings as before. At the end of the second day he **saw land**.*

see life bëj jetë të pasur (të larmishme); njoh jetën

□ *We haven't much money but we do **see life**.* □ *With all that money in his pocket, an impulse to '**see life**' beset him.* □ *Vicky began to like the place and her company less and less. She had to remind herself that at least she was **seeing life**.* □ *We know all the people on the estates. We try to look after them, and we go and talk to them, and they tell us about their problems. I mean, you do **see life**.*

see little of sb shoh dikë rrallë

□ *We have **seen little** of him lately.*

see much of sb shoh dikë shpesh

□ *I don't **see much of** you these days.* □ *Aunt Ann sighed, 'Perhaps' she said, 'it will be just as well for her not to **see so much of** June.'*

see no further than one's nose s'sheh më larg se hunda e vet

□ *Immature as he was, Kevin could **see no further than his nose**.*

see off 1. përcjell

□ *We all went to the airport to **see** her **off**.* □ *A number of friends and well-wishers came to **see** him **off** at the airport.*

2. përzë, ndjek

□ *Some boys came round hoping to steal apples, but the farmer **saw** them **off** with a few well-chosen words.* □ *The farmer **saw** the boys **off** with a heavy stick.*

see one's way (clear) e shikoj të mundur, të volitshme; jam i gatshëm

□ *I can't **see my way clear** to finishing the work this year.* □ *If you could **see your way** to say nothing further on the subject, I should be very much obliged.* □ *He did not **see his way** as yet, but had little doubt that before long he would.* □ *He did not **see his way clear** to allow their names to remain upon the register.*

see out of the corner of one's eye shoh me bisht të syrit

□ *'I thought it was you,' said Dick 'though I **saw you** only **out of the corner of my eye** as you passed.'*

see over/round shkoj të shikoj

□ *I shall need to **see over** the house before I can make you an offer.*

see reason ha arsye, veproj (mendoj) në mënyrë të arsyeshme

□ *He's a thorough tiresome fellow, but*

he will **see reason**. □ *From then on, one just had to live from day to day, always hoping that it wouldn't be so long, that reason would be seen by the higher authorities.*

see red tërbohem, më hipën gjaku në kokë

□ *When he found the thieves in his bedroom, he just saw red and attacked them with his fists.* □ *It's just that I see red when I think anyone is trying to muscle in on my property.* □ *What made most of them see red was their assumption that we were somehow downgrading the scientist from the place where he belongs.* □ *Charles saw red. His livelihood was in danger, and after so much fatigue his nerves were raw.* □ *Mayor: When you spoke of the defendant seeing red, what exactly did you mean? Maud: I mean that my father was so angry that he didn't know what he was doing.*

see sense ha arsye, mendoj (veproj) në mënyrë të arsyeshme

□ *Sam: Maybe you can help him. Help him to see sense; persuade him to give up his crazy ideas.* □ *'I'm not going to take on more than one public engagement a week this winter.' 'Well, I'm glad you've seen sense at last.'*

see sb (all) right kujdesem, përkujdesem

□ *If you need anything, just get in touch with my father; he'll see you all right.* □ *Old man Barnett said that his son would never get a penny of his money but that he was very fond of his daughter-in-law and the children and would see them all right.*

see sb through ndihmoj dikë të kalojë një vështirësi (një periudhë të vështirë)

□ *'Come on,' he said, 'I'll see you through all right. Get yourself some clothes.'* □ *His courage and good humor has seen him through worse times than these.*

see stars i bëjnë sytë xixa

□ *My God, what a lump! You must have seen stars when you got that.* □ *I didn't feel a thing at the time. There was a bang, I saw stars, and then I woke up lying on the floor of the cut.* □ *When the piece of wood fell on his head, he saw stars for about a minute afterwards.* □ *Standing up suddenly I gave my head such a bang on the door of the cupboard that I saw stars for a moment.*

see sth through çoj deri në fund

□ *He said that whatever happened he would see it through.* □ *Together the whole team will see this thing through to the end.*

see sth with the naked eye shoh me sy (pa mjete optike)

□ *'The most short-sighted man could see that at a glance, with his naked eye,' said Martin.*

see the last of sb/sth shoh për herë të fundit

□ *I shall be glad to see the last of this job.* □ *That was the last I ever saw of her.*

see the light kthjellohem, më kthjellohet mendimi (mendja)

□ *One of the most deeply committed Christians I know was a rabid atheist before he saw the light.* □ *What brings you here, anyway? Thought you were a red-hot Labor man. Seen the light, eh?*

see the light (of day) 1. bëhet realitet

□ *We have some plans for a new type of car, but we don't know whether it will ever see the light of the day.*
2. botohet, sheh dritën e botimit

411

□ *His writings never saw the light of the day.*

3. lind, vjen në jetë

□ *The children visited the old house where their great-grandfather first saw the light of the day.*

see the red light shikoj një rrezik eminent

□ *He used to drink very heavily, but he saw the red light, and now he doesn't take any drink at all.*

see the sights shoh, vizitoj qendrat me interes (të një qyteti)

□ *The mystery and history of his religion made him see the sights and hear the sounds of the city with eyes and ears that never took anything for granted.* □ *'I suppose you've finished seeing the sights for a bit now?' 'Oh, no, there's a lot of stuff in and around Lisbon we've still got to see.'* □ *'You look hot,' she added to Victoria. 'I've been walking around seeing the sights.'*

see the world shoh botë

□ *I adore seeing the world and when you read this, I'll be in the middle of a hectic cabaret tour of Teheran, Hong Kong and Australia which lasts three months.* □ *You've seen so much more of the world than I have.* □ *Join the Navy and see the world!*

see the world through rose-colored/ rose-tinted/rosy glasses/spectacles e shoh botën me syze me ngjyra të trëndafilta

□ *Ever since he fell in love, he has been seeing the world through rose-colored glasses.*

see things i shfaqen (i faniten) shajni (halucinacione)

□ *Peter says there's a lion in our back garden; he must be seeing things!* □ *I had not seen him for twenty years and when we met on the street I thought I was seeing things.* □ *She woke her husband to tell him she had seen a face at the window, but he told her she was seeing things.*

see things in their true colors i shoh gjërat në dritën e tyre të vërtetë

□ *I shall tell the story of my life as a journalist in Europe, since this may help the reader to see in its true colors the anti-democratic policy of those who are betraying peace and dragging mankind to new sufferings in a new world war.*

see through sth/sb kuptoj natyrën e vërtetë të

□ *She learnt to see through the smooth exterior to the real person underneath.* □ *'Don't think you can fool me—I can see right through you!'* □ *We see through your little game.*

see to kujdesem, ndjek, merrem me

□ *Large sums of money would continue regularly to be moved, and their security must be seen to.* □ *You won't be put to this trouble again. I'll see to that.* □ *There is something wrong with this washing machine. I must get someone to see to it.* □ *Something has gone wrong with my electric iron. Could you see to it for me?*

see to it that sigurohem që

□ *See to it that you are ready on time!* □ *Matron has seen to it that the nurse did day duty only.* □ *'I promise to get everything finished on time.' 'Well, see to it you do!'*

see with half an eye shoh qartë, shoh me një të hedhur të syve, shoh me sy mbyllur

□ *She's as fond of me as she can be. Anybody can see that with half an eye.* □ *I saw with half an eye that all was over.* □ *You can see with half an eye that he isn't sober.*

see with one's own eyes shoh me sytë e mi, shoh vetë

□ *Many foreign friends have **seen with their own eyes** the positive effects of the large-scale privatization in our country.*

seize on/upon kap, shfrytëzoj

□ *He quickly **seized on** a basic flaw in the argument I was developing.* □ *Any weakness in their position will be **seized upon** and exploited.*

sell like hot cakes shiten (kërkohen) shumë

□ *I translate Breteuil because it's easy and because it **sells like hot cakes** in any language.* □ *Made from the first-class material, it retails at more than $250. At the moment it is **selling like hot cakes** in Switzerland but it is slow in Britain.*

sell off heq, shes (një mall që mezi shitet, një linjë prodhimi jofitim-prurëse)

□ *He had to **sell off** his cattle at a derisory price.* □ *We are going to **sell off** some of the lines which have been cluttering up our storeroom for so long.*

sell oneself to sb shitem te

□ *The police had **sold themselves to** the gang leaders.*

sell one's soul (to the devil) ia shes shpirtin shejtanit (djallit)

□ *She'd **sell her soul to the devil** to get the job.*

sell out of sth mbaroj së shituri, i shes të gjitha

□ *'I'm sorry, all the Sunday papers have gone; we've **sold out**.'* □ *'We seem to have **sold out of** your size. Can you come back next week?'*

sell out to sb shitem

□ *They spoke of people who had **sold out to** the enemy.* □ *The union leaders were accused of **selling out to** the employers.*

sell sb a pup mashtroj, ia hedh (në tregti)

□ *He began, however, to tell her how someone had tried to **sell him a pup**!* □ *Supposing I lend you what's necessary to buy a partnership somewhere? I won't **sell you a pup**, and I'll even send business your way.* □ *He had to buy the house quickly without examining it properly; when he did examine it, he realized that he had been **sold a pup**.* □ *That car's caused you nothing but trouble—you were **sold a real pup** there.*

sell sb down the river tradhtoj, pres dikë në besë

□ *When the thief entered the house, he discovered the police waiting for him; then he realized that someone had **sold him down the river**.* □ *At a mass meeting of car workers called by shop stewards the official leadership was accused of **selling** the rank and file **down the river**.*

sell sb out shes, tradhtoj

□ *They have **sold us out** by agreeing to work during the strike.*

sell the pass tradhtoj kauzën (aleatët)

□ *It would seem that the self-appointed leaders of the pupils have **sold the pass** to the enemy.* □ *At some point this vital **pass** in the battle of communication was **sold** and it would be fascinating to know just when and where.*

sell up shes gjithçka (për të larë borxhet apo arsye të tjera)

□ *They're **selling up** next week, so go round if there's anything you want to collect before the sale.*

send for 1. dërgoj për, dërgoj të kërkoj

□ *A doctor advises at what stage parents with ailing children should **send for** professional advice.* □ *'The plumber's been **sent for**. In the meantime help me mop up the water.'*

2. bëj kërkesë, porosi

□ *Don't delay.* **Send** *now* **for** *a free catalogue.*

send off 1. nis, dërgoj, postoj

□ *'Why haven't you got my letter? I* **sent** *it* **off** *last week.'* □ *Mother makes sure the children are* **sent off** *with a good breakfast inside them.*

2. përcjell, lë lamtumirën

□ *Many of his friends went to the airport to send him* **off**. □ *The whole family arrived on the quay side to* **send** *him* **off**.

3. nxjerr jashtë loje

□ *'Now don't try arguing with the ref. You'll only get* **sent off**.*

send out 1. lëshon

□ *The sun* **sends out** *light and warmth.*

2. bulon, bulëzon, nxjerr

□ *The trees* **send out** *new leaves in Spring.*

send sb about his business/send sb packing i them dikujt të shikojë punën e vet (të mos përzihet në punët e të tjerëve); largoj, përzë; ndjek (dëboj) nga puna

□ *He was trying to sell me some things that were obviously stolen, so soon I* **sent** *him* **about his business**. □ *Jean: I thought he's certainly not the type for my Cairy. Too damn rough, I* **sent** *him* **packing** *last year.* □ *The pay is good but you have no job security. If you don't bring enough orders you're soon* **sent packing**. □ *Magnus.... If the English people* **send** *me* **packing** *and establish a republic, no man has a better chance of being the first British president than you.* □ *She talked to her perpetually about Major Dobbin,* **sent about his business**.... □ *On our return home, we found some boys we did not*

know playing in our garden; we **sent** them **packing**.

send sb crazy çmend; i marr mendtë

□ *The Group have many better singles to their credit, yet this is the one that* **send** *the fans* **crazy** *wherever they perform.* □ *Lack of sleep was what* **sent** *people* **crazy**.

send sb down 1. përjashtoj nga universiteti

□ *Several students were* **sent down** *after incidents during the visit of a foreign Prime Minister.*

2. dënoj me burgim

□ *He was* **sent down** *for ten years for armed robbery.*

send sb in dërgoj në

□ *Soldiers were* **sent in** *to quell the riots.*

send sb to sleep vë në gjumë

□ *The gentle lapping of the waves against the side of the boat* **sent** *him* **to sleep**. □ *If there's anything calculated to* **send** *me* **to sleep** *it's a party political broadcast on television.* □ *The medicine soon* **sent** *the old man* **to sleep**.

send up 1. çon, ngre

□ *Any increase in production costs is bound to* **send up** *prices.* □ *A rise in temperature will* **send up** *the pressure inside the casing.*

2. shpërthen

□ *A convoy of gas trucks a mile to the rear was* **sent up** *in flames.*

send word dërgoj fjalë

□ *'The program has been changed.' 'I know, Sire; the Queen* **sent word** *altering it late this evening.'* □ *You should have* **sent** *us* **word** *that you were coming.*

separate/tell the wheat/grain from the chaff/separate/tell the sheep from the goats ndaj bykun (kashtën)

414

nga kokrrat; ndaj (dalloj) egjrën nga gruri; ndaj dhentë (delet) nga dhitë; ndaj shapin nga sheqeri; dalloj të padobishmen nga e dobishmja; dalloj të keqen nga e mira

□ We have to sift through the application forms very carefully to separate the wheat from the chaff. □ At the end of the year we have a test which separates the sheep from the goats.

serve/sail/ship before the mast shërbej si marinar i thjeshtë

□ Subsequently I shipped before the mast and sailed for the Japanese coast on a sea-hunting expedition.

serve sb right mirë t'i bëhet; mirë e gjeti; mirë e pësoi; sipas kokës edhe festen; ajo kokë atë feste do; atë kokë ka, atë feste do

□ Helen wanted everything. It would serve her mother right if she ran straight back to Felix and said, 'Forgive me, I will marry you.' □ His wife has left him, and serve him right: he treated her very badly. □ He failed his exam; it served him right because he had not studied. □ 'Serve him right, he should arrange his affairs better.'

serve one's/the purpose është i përshtatshëm, i shërben qëllimit; kryen punë; plotëson kërkesat

□ We have found a meeting-place that will serve our purpose. □ I believe this table will serve the purpose until we can get new one. That book should serve your purpose excellently.

serve one's/its turn plotëson (përmbush) kërkesat, kryen punë, bën punën e vet; është i nevojshëm për një qëllim apo periudhë të caktuar

□ I want something to keep the rain off and this old raincoat will serve my turn. □ I think this book will serve my turn. □ It served its turn well, did that little car, because John developed into a very fine driver. □ Now that the cleaning woman had served her turn, they'd be happy to get rid of her.

serve out shërbej, shpërndaj

□ Shall I serve out the soup or would you like to help yourself? □ We spent about two hours a day serving out the children's dinners.

serve sb's turn bën, hyn në punë, vlen; i shërben qëllimit të

□ A reliable lad that'll do what he is told will serve my turn perfectly well.

serve up 1. shërbej

□ They serve up far more food than could possibly be eaten. □ Mother was just serving up the meal as I walked in.
2. ofroj

□ She served up the usual excuses for being late.

set about 1. nis një punë, i hyj një pune

□ We then set about the job of putting the animals into their travelling boxes. □ I recommend you to set about your work. □ As soon as they arrived they set about tidying up the room. □ I don't know how to set about my job.
2. sulmoj (me grushta, fjalë)

□ 'I'd set about them with this custard-ladle if we have any trouble,' said Mrs. Fountain. □ A gang of boys set about a supporter of the other team.

set against kundërvë, vë ballë për ballë

□ The Dreyfus Affair divided many families, setting father against son and brother against brother. □ She accused her husband of setting their children against her.
2. ballafaqoj, krahasoj

□ Set against her virtues, her faults don't seem nearly so bad. □ You must set the initial cost of a new car against the saving you'll make on repairs.

set a lot/great/much store by/on sb/sth vlerësoj shumë, çmoj së tepërmi

□ *All the lovely things by which he had* **set great store**, *things which were of high value then, went for a song.* □ *Martin* **set more store by** *official honors than I did.* □ *It is odd that one so susceptible to the clash and glare of the theatre should* **set so much store by** *personal privacy.* □ *'My wife, too,* **sets great store on** *the boys being at home.'*

set an example jap shembullin, bëhem shembull për

□ *He seemed nervous lest, in thus announcing his intentions he should be* **setting** *his grand-daughter a bad* **example**. □ *We expect the older pupils in the school to* **set an example** *to the younger ones.* □ *'Is she in? She usually is by now.' 'She's certain to be, I think.' 'Yes,' said Miss Flynn, 'she certainly* **sets us all a good example**.*' □ *They are following the good* **example set** *by their teachers.*

set apart (from) veçon, dallon, shquan

□ *Her clear and elegant prose* **set** *her* **apart** *from most other journalists.* □ *Exceptional gifts* **set** *him* **apart from** *other sculptors of his generation.*

set aside 1. lë, heq mënjanë

□ *Peter* **set aside** *the papers he was marking and reached for his cigarettes and matches.* □ *Work on the library extension had to be* **set aside** *while labor was diverted to more urgent projects.*

2. anulloj; rrëzoj, hedh poshtë

□ *The judges's verdict was quashed and their prison sentences* **set aside**. □ *The judges's decision was* **set aside** *by the Appeal Court.*

3. shpërfill, lë mënjanë

□ *In dealing with the man, he tried to* **set aside** *an instinctive mistrust of him.* □ *Let's* **set aside** *your personal feelings.*

4. kursej, vë mënjanë

□ *She* **sets aside** *a bit of money every month.* □ *Don't eat all the tinned food.* **Set** *something* **aside** *for a possible emergency.*

set at defiance përbuz, shpërfill

□ *Your influence, sir, is evidently potent with him. He will never* **set** *you* **at defiance**. □ *'How he would bother the commissioners! He'd* **set** *them* **at defiance** *if they talked of committing him Sir.'*

set at large/liberty liroj

□ *The Doctor tried hard, and never ceased trying to get Charles Darney* **set at liberty**.

set at naught përbuz; shpërfill

□ *Her feeling that Cowperwood needed her, was hereby* **set at naught**. □ *Madame Defarge was not likely to follow their idiomatic remarks in detail, but she so far understood them as to perceive that she was* **set at naught**. □ *I am an aristocrat and it's my whim to* **set** *good manners* **at naught**.

set a trap/snare for sb/sth ngre kurth (për)

□ *They descended in all directions down the hill, and straightway several of the party fell into* **the snare set** *by nature.*

set back 1. pengoj, vonoj

□ *Financial problems have* **set back** *our building program.* □ *Work on the new theatre has been* **set back** *three months.*

2. kushton

□ *The meal is likely to* **set** *us* **back** *$15*

each. □ *His daughter's wedding set him* **back** *a few pounds.*

set/put back the clock kthej prapa rrotën e historisë

□ *The new censorship law will* **put the clock back** *by 50 years.*

set down 1. zbres

□ *'Would you mind* **setting** *me* **down** *at the next corner?'* □ *The bus stops regularly to* **set down** *and pick up passengers.*

2. shënoj, hedh në letër

□ *I'll* **set down** *one or two points while they are fresh in my mind.*

3. vendos, caktoj

□ *The day* **set down** *for the trial has still to be announced.*

set eyes on shoh, më zë syri

□ *I never* **set** *my* **eyes on** *so wonderful a sight.* □ *'How do you know?'* he demanded. *'You never* **laid eyes on** *me before.'*

set fire to sth/set sth on fire i vë zjarrin (flakën)

□ *'How many times have I got to warn you against* **setting** *the place* **on fire?'** □ *The blaze was fanned by a stiff breeze and in this way all the farm outbuildings were* **set on fire**. □ *'Stop emptying your pipe into the wastepaper basket: you'll* **set** *the house* **on fire**.'

set foot in/on shkel, vë këmbën në

□ *Don't ever* **set foot in** *this house again.* □ *Alan sat down by the doorway and resolutely refused to* **set foot** *outside the house.* □ *Not until I reached that first aim of my journey and actually* **set foot in** *the town itself, on the sixth day of my flight, did it desert me.*

set forth 1. nisem

□ *We* **set forth** *on the last stage of our climb.* □ *David* **set forth** *to do battle*

with Goliath.

2. paraqes, parashtroj, skicoj

□ *These figures are more clearly* **set forth** *in tabular form.* □ *The Prime Minister* **set forth** *the aims of his government.*

set free liroj

□ *I want to stop the whole thing and* **set** *the slaves* **free**.

set in nis, fillon, vjen

□ *The rainy season has* **set in**. □ *On account of his carelessness, blood poison* **set in** *and his arm had to be operated on.* □ *Go to dentist before decay of the teeth* **sets in**.

set in motion vë në lëvizje

□ *The price increases* **set in motion** *demands for further wage increases.*

set little/small store by sth i jap pak rëndësi, vlerësoj pak

□ *Like most men of strong character old Jolyon* **set small store by** *the class to which he belonged.*

set off 1. nisem

□ *Having said farewell to their friends, they* **set off** *for home.* □ *What time are you planning to* **set off** *tomorrow?*

2. shpërthej

□ *Do be careful with those fireworks; the slightest spark could* **set** *them* **off**.

3. nxit

□ *The threatened action by miners may* **set off** *sympathy strikes by transport workers.*

4. evidencon, thekson, përvijon, nxjerr në pah

□ *That jumper* **sets off** *the blue of her eyes.*

set one's cap at ia vë syrin (për ta marrë për burrë)

□ *The willy old fellow said to his son, 'Have a care, Joe, that girl is* **setting** *her* **cap at** *you.'* □ *Mary seems to be paying a lot of attention to Jack these* days. *Do you think she's set her cap at him?*

set one's (the) eyes at flow zë e qaj me ngashërim (me dënesë)

☐ *And set my eyes at flow. (W. Shake-speare)*

set one's face against sth kundërshtoj, jam kundër; kundërvihem

☐ *I am an honest man, seeking to do my duty in this carnal universe, and setting my face against all vice and treachery.* ☐ *Old Jolyon had from the first set his face against the press.* ☐ *The new government has set its face against any changes in the way the elections are run.*

set one's face/nose to/towards drejtohem, marr rrugën drejt

☐ *On that momentous mid October afternoon, Mont set his fine nose towards the east wind, and moved his thin legs with speed.*

set one's hand to sth nis (filloj) punë, vë dorë në një punë

☐ *'I won't set a hand to such tom-foolery for one,' replied Tommy.* ☐ *Once you have set your hand to a work you should persevere until you have finished it.* ☐ *He set his hand to the task and carried it through in no time.*

set one's heart/mind at ease/rest qetësoj

☐ *As soon as you hear that your father is out of danger, let me know; it will set my heart at rest.* ☐ *'If Mr. Nickleby has doubted that.... he may set his mind at rest.'*

set one's heart on sth dua shumë, dua me gjithë shpirt, dua pa masë, më digjet (qan) zemra për

☐ *... it's a sad thing, my dear, to lose so much when we had set our hearts upon it.* ☐ *She was mad on show-jumping; her heart was set on horses.*

☐ *Her husband worked hard to save up for the house she had set her heart on.* ☐ *To take part in the Olympics—this was an ambition on which he had set his heart.*

set one's (own) house in order vë punët (e veta) në rregull

☐ *He could wish Mr. More to set his house in order...* ☐ *'Our brothers in the docks industry should set their own houses in order before ven-turing to criticize the members of this union.'* ☐ *The Press must set its own house in order before the ultimate disaster of having imposed upon it.*

set one's mind to përqëndrohem, i kushtoj vëmendje (kujdes) të plotë, i kushtohem me zell, i vë veshin

☐ *You can do anything if you really set your mind to it.* ☐ *I can do anything when I set my mind to it.* ☐ *'Now just you set your mind to meeting these orders on time.'*

set one's sights on ka si objektiv (pikësynim)

☐ *It was not that Virginia had a con-suming passion to work on a women's magazine. She had set her sights on it because there was a chance for her in this place.* ☐ *John's sights were set on acquiring the controlling interest in a group of stores.*

set one's teeth on edge i ngre (i prish) nervat

☐ *The laugh, the first they have heard from him, sets Trench's teeth on edge.* ☐ *It set my teeth on edge to think of it.* ☐ *'You say things that set these people's teeth on edge. You make them feel you're getting at them.'* ☐ *The small boy was scraping a nail across glass, and the noise set my teeth on edge.*

set out 1. nisem

☐ *Ona set out to hunt for work.* ☐ *They set out on the last stage of*

their journey. □ *It was raining when we set out, but after about half an hour the weather cleared up.*
2. vë, vendos, rregulloj, sistemoj
□ *Michael set out the pieces on the chessboard.* □ *We'll need to set out the chairs for the meeting.*
3. deklaroj
□ *He set out his objections to the scheme.* □ *She set out the reasons for her resignation in a long letter.*

set out to do sth filloj, nis të
□ *She set out to break the world land speed record.* □ *They succeeded in what they set out to do.*

set right rregulloj
□ *When Soames said: 'Leave it to me' he meant it, of course; but it was really very trying that whenever anything went wrong he and not somebody else, had to set it right!* □ *There is a mistake in the wording of the telegram, I will set it right.*

set sail niset për udhëtim (me anije); niset për lundrim (anija)
□ *My friend set sail the other day.* □ *The ship set sail for Europe.* □ *With this he married Prudence, and set sail for Bendigo.*

set spurs to grah (kalin); nxis, cys, shpoj
□ *The Captain proceeded to set spurs to her resolution.* □ *Hawker set spurs to his noble chestnut horse.*

set the pace përcakton ritmin (e garës); i jep tonin; bëhet shembull (model) për
□ *With Roddy setting the pace, the boys tore uphill and arrived with bursting lungs.* □ *It was he who set the pace and established the style of a very agile and pert production.* □ *The champion set a rapid pace for the other racers.* □ *Jack set the pace for most of the race.*

□ *This company is setting the pace in the home computer market.*

set the seal on i vë vulën
□ *We had a meeting next which set the seal on our new business partnership.* □ *This award has set the seal on a successful stage career.* □ *'Once a man marries a girl like you, I find it impossible to think of him as a fellow citizen. He'll set the seal on his success today.'*

set the table shtroj tryezën
□ *She set the table for five people.* □ *In order to save time in the morning, we always set the table for breakfast on the previous evening.*

set the Thames/world on fire bën çudira; ngre ujin përpjetë; ndez zjarrin në ujë; nxjerr ujë nga guri
□ *He is a very ambitious student but, in my opinion, he will never set the Thames on fire.* □ *John works hard, but he will never set the world on fire.* □ *'Take young Jeffries, now. You wouldn't say he's the kind to set the Thames on fire, would you?'*

set the tone (of/for sth) përcaktoj tonin e
□ *His obvious boredom at the entire proceedings set the tone for what promised to be a remarkably cheerless Christmas dinner.* □ *The first party political broadcast of the election clearly sets the style and tone of the government campaign.*

settle a score/an old score/old scores with sb laj një hesap të vjetër me; laj hesape të vjetra me
□ *Now, we have cleared off old scores, and I have before me thy pleasant trusting, trusty face again.* □ *I think you should avoid him if you can; he said he had some old scores to settle with you.* □ *John*

settled an old score with Bob by beating him.

settle down to sth i përvishem, i shtrohem

◻ *The constant interruptions stopped me settling down to work.* ◻ *It's high time to settle down to work.*

settle for pranoj

◻ *She was not prepared to settle for being an ordinary housewife.* ◻ *He wants to make a quick sale, so he'll settle for a low price.*

settle one's/an account with sb qëroj (laj) hesapet me

◻ *As soon as Sir Sagramor got well, he notified me, that there was a little account to settle between us...* ◻ *She insulted my mother, so I have an account to settle with her.*

settle on sth zgjedh, vendos (të marr, të ble etj.)

◻ *After some discussion we settled on a date in early June.* ◻ *'Now that the meeting-place has been settled on, can we talk about the agenda?*

settle sb down qetësoj

◻ *The chairman tried to settle the audience down.* ◻ *Wait until the children have settled down before you start your story.*

settle sb's hash ia ndreq samarin dikujt, ia rregulloj qejfin dikujt

◻ *If he misbehaves again, I'm going to settle his hash.* ◻ *Promising herself she would soon settle the janitor's hash, Miss Murphy strode off down the corridor with the requisition sheet in her hand.* ◻ *He hasn't any claim on you at all. Don't worry. A good lawyer will soon settle his hash.*

settle sb into sth hyj, sistemohem (në shtëpi të re); sistemoj

◻ *We're a little disorganized after the move, but do come and see us when*

we have **settled in.** ◻ *We'd hardly settled the children into a new school when we were posted to another district and had to uproot them again.*

settle up with paguaj, shlyej llogarinë

◻ *I've already settled up with the waiter.* ◻ *'I'm tired of this place: let's settle up and go.'* ◻ *'I'm short of cash. Have you enough to settle up with the waiter?'*

set to 1. filloj, nis, i shtrohem, i përvishem

◻ *Wherefore Mr. Micawber set to work at the petition, invented it, engrossed it on an immense sheet of paper, spread it out on a table, and appointed a time for all the club and all within the work if they chose, to come up to his room and sign it.* ◻ *The engineers set to on repair work to the bridge.*

2. nis (të zihem, hahem me fjalë)

◻ *The boys set to and had to be separated by a teacher.*

set/put to rights rregulloj, vë në rregull

◻ *'Ah, so it is,' said Mrs. Weller setting her cap to rights.* ◻ *When Maria Labbs had put the room to rights, she opened the street door....*

set to work filloj punën

◻ *After breakfast we set to work and made a cage for the armadillo.* ◻ *The floor was so encumbered with objects that I had to set to work to clear myself a space.*

set up 1. krijoj, ngre, ndërtoj

◻ *Police set up road-blocks on routes leading out of the city.* ◻ *A fund was launched to set up a monument in memory of the dead camping site.*

2. shkaktoj, provokoj

◻ *I wonder what has set up this irritation in my throat?* ◻ *Smoking sets up an irritation in the throat and bronchial passages.*

3. furnizoj, pajis

□ *All the pupils are* **set** **up** *with the necessary text books.*

4. shëndosh, përtërij, gjallëroj

□ *Her holiday in the country has* **set** *her* **up** *again.* □ *'Alice says that the sea air'll* **set** *me* **up**. *But I don't know.'*

5. mbudh, inicioj, fus

□ *Her father* **set** *her* **up** *in business.*

6. vendos një rekord

□ *She* **set** **up** *a new world record time in the 100 meters.*

7. radhis (shkronjat)

□ *The book will be published shortly, the type is being* **set** **up** *now.*

shadow of doubt fije (pikë dyshimi)

□ *He is guilty, without* **a** **shadow** **of** **doubt**.

shadow of one's/its former self, a hije e vetvetes

□ *She used to be a great player, but now she's only* **a** **shadow** **of** **her** **former self.**

shake a leg shpejtoj, luaj këmbët

□ *Come on,* **shake** **a** **leg**, *we're late already.* □ **Shake** **a** **leg** *now, Ginger, there's a good sort. There's all that pile to be priced, and you know it's my half day.* □ *They certainly had plenty to do and would have to* **shake** **a** **leg** *the remainder of the night.*

shake down 1. shtrohem; përshtatem, harmonizohem; sistemohem

□ *The new office staff are* **shaking** **down** *well.* □ *Following extensive modifications after the accident to the turbine blades, the liner underwent trials at sea to ensure that everything* **shook** **down** *properly.*

2. i marr dikujt pare (me dhunë, kërcënim etj.)

□ *The gangsters* **shook** **down** *the store owner every month.*

3. kërkoj gjithandej

□ *Police* **shook** *the club* **down**, *looking for narcotics.*

shake hands with sb/shake sb's hand/ shake sb by the hand shtrëngoj duart me, i shtrëngoj dorën

□ *Sit down, sir, said Mr. Boffin,* **shaking hands with** *him.* □ *When he and the Micawbers cordially* **shook** **hands** *as comrades and his brow face brightened with a smile I felt that he would make his way, establish a good name, and be beloved, go when he would.*

shake in one's shoes dridhem nga frika, më dridhen leqet e këmbëve

□ *He was* **shaking** **in** **his** **shoes** *at the thought of flying for the first time.* □ *Two boys who were to be punished were* **shaking** **in** **their** **shoes** *as they waited outside the headmaster's room.*

shake like a jelly/leaf dridhem si purteka në ujë

□ *After she had been told of the accident, the woman began to* **shake** **like** **an** **aspen leaf.** □ *Ma, who had recovered equilibrium, now spoke down the microphone,* **shaking** **like** **a** **jelly.** □ *They even more kindly invited all women passengers into the cockpit; one of them emerged* **shaking** **like** **a** **leaf.** *'They asked me to fly the plane.'*

shake off heq qafe, flak tej

□ *She tried to* **shake** *him* **off** *but he continued to pester her.* □ *I wish I could* **shake** **off** *this confounded cold.* □ *I got a little the better of my uneasiness when I went to school next day, and a good deal the better next day and so* **shook** *it* **off** *by degrees.*

shake one's head tund kokën

□ *'Have a liqueur?' Jon* **shook** **his** **head.** □ *'My poor cousin has passed away. His end was very peaceful.' Dr.*

Bottwink, his hands thrust deep into his pockets **shook his head.** □ *Hugo* **shook his head** *at me and put his finger to his lips and gave his attention to Lefty.*

shake one's sides with laughter/ laughing mbaj ijët (barkun, brinjët) me dorë, shkulem së qeshuri

□ *The audience* **shook their sides,** *listening to the witty cross-talk.* □ *He laughed till* **his sides shook.**

shake sb's faith/confidence lëkund besimin e

□ *Still, sir, I don't want to* **shake his confidence,** *or break his confidence....*

shake up 1. tund

□ *The contents should be well* **shaken up** *until all the sediments disappears.* □ **Shake up** *the salad-dressing before you put it on.*

2. shkund, gjallëroj, nxjerr nga plogështia (mefshtësia, apatia etj.)

□ *We've got to* **shake up** *all these people with old-fashioned ideas.*

3. trondit, trazoj, shqetësoj

□ *When the aircraft finally landed, most of us felt badly* **shaken up.**

shame on you turp të kesh

□ *How could you treat her so badly?* **Shame on you!**

share and share alike ndaj barabar (përgjysmë, në pjesë të barabarta); ndarje e barabartë

□ *'Now,' if you have anything really reasonable to offer I would be glad to hear it.* '**Share and share alike,** *and three-fourths of the remainder,' repeated Cowperwood, grimly.* □ *Don't be so selfish—it's* **share and share alike** *in this house.* □ *The partners agreed that, if they made a profit, they would* **share and share alike.** □ *Nothing to do except go over to Mac's there and drink his beer, and*

he comes here to drink mine. **A share and share alike,** *with no one to worry you, and all the time in the world.*

sharpen one's wits vras mendjen, shtrydh trutë

□ *Steve's a nice chap but far too easygoing. He'll need to* **sharpen his wits** *a bit if he hopes to get on in business.*

shed crocodile tears derdh lotë krokodili

□ *I think that Smith was* **shedding crocodile tears** *when he said how sorry he was to see Jones go. Everyone knows that they hated each other.*

shed light on/upon sth sqaroj, hedh dritë mbi

□ *Considerable* **light** *was* **shed on** *recent events by his statement to the police.* □ *Government sources were refusing to* **shed** *any more* **light** *than appeared yesterday* **on** *the television interview.* □ *Excavations have* **shed** *new* **light on** *the history of the ancient Albanian craftsmanship.*

shed tears over derdh lot, shpreh keqardhjen

□ *'You're not going to* **shed** *any* **tears over** *my Sandy, are you?'* □ *'The famous Templar family is bankrupt.' 'I don't believe it.' 'I'm afraid it's true. The great and mighty Saunders wouldn't* **shed tears over** *anything but lack of money.'*

shell out paguaj, nxjerr nga xhepi

□ *I know that when the collection box comes round I shall be expected to* **shell out** *the most.* □ *I'm tired of* **shelling out** *on repairs to this car.*

shift for oneself eci me këmbët e mia; ia dal mbanë vetë; përballoj jetën (pa kurrëfarë ndihme), siguroj jetesën; bëj si bëj

□ *Poor Tom borrowed enough money to pay for his fare and like other* emigrants set out for the city of Chicago where he hoped to **shift for himself**. □ If you're marooned on an island, I won't be able to help you— you'll have to **shift for yourself**. □ But Jurgis had been round the world enough to know that a man has to **shift for himself** in it. □ There will be no-one in the house tonight to prepare the meal, so we have to **shift for ourselves**. □ When their parents died, the children had to **shift for themselves**.

shift the blame/responsibility onto sb ia hedh fajin dikujt
□ When his plans miscarry, he always looks around for somebody to **shift the blame onto**. □ Much of **the responsibility** for the disaster was **shifted onto** Menzies, and this was quite undeserved. □ Don't try to **shift the blame onto** the others.

shift the ground ndryshoj qëndrim; ndryshoj argument (gjatë diskutimit)
□ A friend, as willing to **shift his ground** as I, gave me an overture which I accepted.

shining example (of sb/sth), a shembull i ndritur i
□ Friends regard Joan and Phillip as **a shining example of** a happily married couple. □ John Bently is **a shining example of** an ordinary man who was not content with his corner in the pub.

shining/guiding light, a yll, fener ndriçues
□ He is also the undisputed expert in the field of medieval and renaissance music, and his Early Music Consort of London is **a shining light** in the vast field of British music and musicians.

shipshape (and Bristol fashion) në rregull të plotë; xham, shumë i pastër
□ We were responsible for constantly

keeping the vessel '**shipshape and Bristol fashion**'. □ The officer inspected our room and found that everything was **shipshape**. □ One of the most curious expressions in common use is '**all shipshape and Bristol fashion**. □ Jim Larkin arrives at a Devonshire hotel to find everything **shipshape and Bristol fashion**—only there's no owner, no staff and no guests.

ships that pass into the night takime të rastit
□ 'You remember, Fleur? The Young Englishman I met at Mount Vernon.' '**Ships that pass into the night**!' said Fleur.

shoot a glance hedh një shikim të shpejtë
□ **The glance** he **shot at** Charles from beneath his straggling white eyebrows was, of all things, a slightly envious one. □ The clerk at the hotel desk **shot an** inquisitive **glance at** the young man near the newspaper kiosk.

shoot a line ekzagjeroj; gënjej
□ She said she was an expert skier but I think she was just **shooting a line**. □ When I was new to England I tried once or twice to explain to people how we lived, and found that they thought I was **shooting the line**.

shoot one's bolt i zbrazi tërë fishekët; i përdori të gjitha mundësitë
□ I think I've **shot my bolt** here. I've done what little I can and I must go and start somewhere else. □ The general said that he would launch one last attack but, if that failed, he would have **shot his bolt**. He would have to surrender.

shoot one's mouth off/shoot off one's mouth flas me mburrje; i jap gojës
□ He is always **shooting his mouth off** about how important his job was.

□ *'We were hoping to keep the party a secret—it was meant to be a surprise for Jane. What made you go and **shoot your mouth off** about it?*

shoot one's way in/into sth/shoot one's way out/out of sth hyj (dal) me ndihmën e zjarrit të armëve

□ *The gangster stole a gun and **shot his way out** of prison.*

shoot sth/sb down rrëzoj

□ *The enemy bomber was **shot down** in flames. □ You'd be lucky to **shoot** a fighter **down** with a light machine gun. □ His last theories have been **shot down** in flames by the experts.*

shoot the breeze flas ngeshëm (shtruar); përgojoj, marr nëpër gojë

□ *We sat about in the bar, **shooting the breeze**. □ They spent all the time sitting around the dock and **shooting the breeze**.*

shoot up 1. rritem, zgjatem

□ *'My word, you have **shot up** since I saw you last.' □ Billy had always been a small boy, but when he was thirteen years old he began to **shoot up**.*

2. ngrihet, rritet

□ *We shall do what we can to stop prices **shooting up** still further. □ My pulse rate would suddenly **shoot up** alarmingly.*

3. terrorizoj (duke qëlluar me armë në ajër)

□ *'Nobody can scare them off; they'll come back and **shoot** the place **up**, just for kicks.' □ The gangsters ran into the bar and started **shooting it up**.*

shop around i bie pazarit rrotull (vërdallë); kërkoj me kujdes

□ *Don't buy the first car you see: **shop around** a bit. □ 'Has Peter decided which universities he's going to apply to?' 'Not yet. He's **shopping***

around for a course with a good choice of options.'

short cut, a rrugë e shkurtër

□ *I know **a short cut** across the field; let's take it. □ He made for the Western Highway by **a short cut** through the suburban roads I did not know. □ There are no **short cuts** to these qualifications.*

short of 1. pa; nëse nuk ndodh

□ *Chaps like you are always **short of** money. If you don't take the cash you'll regret it tomorrow. □ **Short of** a miracle, we're certain to lose now.*

2. më pak se; më poshtë se

□ *At last he struck the wall and followed it, stopping a few feet **short of** the point where he believed St. Sabas to be lying. □ 'How tall is he?' 'Just **short of** six feet, I'd guess.' □ The car's performance was far **short of** what I'd been led to expect.*

shot in the arm nxitje; shtysë; ndihmë; frymëzim; stimulim

□ *The chairman of the company said that the order, worth millions of pounds, was a real **shot in the arm**. □ The improved trade figures are a much-needed **shot in the arm** for the economy. □ We were ready to quit but the coach's talk was **a shot in the arm**.*

shot in the dark hamendje; hamendësim

□ *I didn't know the correct answer, so I just had **a shot in the dark**.*

shot through with mbushur me

□ *His story was **shot through with** lies.*

shoulder a burden (of sth) marr përsipër; marr mbi supe (mbi shpatulla, mbi vete)

□ *He **shouldered a** heavy **burden of** teaching and supervision, now reflected in the growing achievements* *of a brilliant galaxy of pupils.* □ *Who cares whether the doctor wears a frock coat or a boiler suit so long as he is prepared to **shoulder the burden of** our woes?*

shoulder one's way in/through/past hap, çaj rrugën (me bërryla)

□ *The platform swarmed with people and we had to **shoulder our way through** the crowd.*

shoulder to shoulder krah për krah

□ *They fought **shoulder to shoulder** in the last war.* □ *If he were free he would be fighting **shoulder to shoulder** with us to win the strike.*

shout sb down mbyt

□ *The crowd **shouted** the speaker **down**.*

show a clean pair of heels ua mbath (ua jap) këmbëve; i bëj këmbët të lehta

□ *The thief **showed a clean pairs of heels**.* □ *Ian watched him nervously, ready to **show a clean pair of heels** as soon as the fuse was lighted.*

show a leg ngrihem nga krevati (nga gjumi)

□ *'Come on, you lazy so-and-sos', said Brian, lifting the tent flap, '**show a leg**.'* □ *It's often 11 o'clock before he **shows a leg**.'*

show off 1. spikat, nxjerr në pah, evidencon

□ *The room, very plain, formal and grey was intended primarily to **show off** the drawings that were hung there.* □ *The cut of her dress **shows off** her figure to perfection.*

2. dukem, bie në sy, dal në pah, tërheq vëmendjen

□ *'Do stop **showing off**, Andrew. Nobody's impressed.'* □ *He **shows off** tremendously.*

show one's hand/cards hap letrat; zbuloj synimet (planet)

□ *I suspect they are they're planning*

something but they haven't **shown their hands** yet. □ *He and his daughter know the use of and power of money, and they know how to wait and watch and to be silent and not to **show their hand**.*

show one's face/nose dukem, dal, shfaqem

□ *'And if you lose me a customer, don't **show your face** here again.'* □ *My aunt had so frightened him, that he never once **showed his nose** in the place all the time we lived there.* □ *He won't dare **show his face** again at the club after the way he behaved there last time.*

show one's teeth i tregoj dhëmbët

□ *The guarantors determined, one cold Wednesday morning, to **show their teeth**. They exercized their contractual right to replace Polanski and Bransberg as producers.* □ *Matron looked a comfortable, motherly soul but she soon **showed her teeth** if any of the inmates gave signs of having minds of their own.*

show/reveal one's (true) colors tregoi fytyrën e vërtetë

□ *Another election. Could he stand a second time without **showing his true colors**?* □ *We all thought that our new neighbour was a charming man: it was only later that he **showed his true colors**.* □ *We thought Tony was timid, but he **showed his colors** when he rescued the ponies from the burning bars.*

show promise premton, jep (ngjall) shpresa

□ *It is 69 years since an anonymous critic wrote in 'The Era', 'Master Charles Chaplin as a newsboy known as Sam **showed promise**.'*

show signs of tregon shenja të

□ *Sarah retains much of her energy,*

*but **shows signs of** her age and her troubles.* □ *He waited for Froulish to ask what that was, but the novelist was rolling herself a cigarette and **showed** no **signs of** hearing, so he went on.*

show sb the cold shoulder i kthej krahët, i sillem (i rri) ftohtë, nuk e përfill

□ *She got to dislike me at last and to **show me the cold shoulder**.*

show sb the door i tregoj derën dikujt

□ *Well, he had **shown** the insolent baggage **the door**.* □ *He behaved so badly to my other guests that I **showed him the door**.* □ *Ruth was so upsetting to other children, so I **showed her the door**.*

show sb the ropes i tregoj kleçkat, hollësitë (e një pune etj)

□ *At first I did not know what to do: then one of the other workers **showed me the ropes**.* □ *He is a past master; He'll **show** you all **the ropes**.* □ *'You can move into the main office', said his father. 'There's a small room free next to Bannister. He'll **show** you all the ropes.'*

show sb the way 1. i tregoj udhën (rrugën) dikujt

□ *He **showed me the way** to the station.*

2. bëhet shembull për

□ *Let's hope her bravery will **show the way** for other young people.*

show the white feather frikësohem, më zë frika

□ *He did not intend to **show the white feather**...* □ *It was reported he has certainly **shown the white feather** in his regiment.*

show up 1. shfaqem, vij, dukem

□ *Her place was laid for lunch and again for dinner. But she didn't **show up**.* □ *'We've been waiting for hours*

*for you to **show up**.'*

2. duket qartë

□ *At times like these the true character of the man **shows up**.*

show willing tregohem i gatshëm

□ *I think he has plenty of helpers as it is, but I'd better go along and **show willing**.* □ *I wish now that I hadn't half-heartedly concurred that early August day. But I wanted to **show willing** to Ike.*

shrink (away, back) from sth/sb prapsem, zmbrapsem; tërhiqem

□ *Nicky **shrank back**, he couldn't bear sharp voices.* □ *Always he **shrank back from** actual commitment; he would rather be unvolved.*

shrug one's shoulders ngre supet

□ *Asked if he wanted to spend a night in the cells, he merely **shrugged his shoulders**.* □ *Felix stared at Virginia unhappily. Chris looked at Felix, **shrugged his** fleshy **shoulders** and took his sherry over to the fire.* □ *He shrinks, looks at them for a sort of forgiveness, and then **shrugging his shoulders**, turns and goes.*

shudder to think dridhem (rrënqethem) kur mendoj

□ *Imagine having to live in such conditions and sleep five or six to a room! I **shudder to think** of it.*

shut down mbyll; ndërpres punën

□ *The commission has ordered two mines to **shut down**.* □ *The workshop has **shut down** and the workers are unemployed.*

shut in mbyllem

□ *She **shuts** herself **in** her study for hours.* □ *For four months in the year the snow virtually isolates them and they are **shut in** upon themselves.*

shut off mbyll, ndaloj

□ *'I haven't had a bath for days—they've **shut off** the hot water supply.'*

□ *You must **shut** the gas supply **off** if there's a leak.*

shut oneself into one's shell mbyllem në guaskën time, mbyllem në vetvete
□ *Writers never **shut** themselves **up in their shells**.* □ *'The secrecy is to safeguard the organization from the enemy, not to hide behind a screen and **shut** ourselves **up in our own shell**.'*

shut/close one's eyes to sth mbyll sytë para
□ *Unfortunately, it is fatally easy for anyone who gets a comfortable living to **shut his eyes to** the injustices of the system; but a journalist has less excuse than most people because he has more chance to see both sides of an issue.* □ *'I can't help remembering how much I had to **shut my eyes to** the lipstick on Godfrey's handkerchiefs.'*
□ *The company has to **shut its eyes to** petty pilfering, if only because it would be too expensive to prevent.*
□ *The government **shuts its eyes to** poverty.*

shut one's mouth/face mbylle, qepe (gojën)
□ ***Shut your mouth**, nobody asked you!* □ *Letouzel: Use your brains, you silly little fellow, or else **shut your mouth** while the rest of us use ours.*

shut sb/sth away mbyll, kyç; izoloj
□ *Jeremy **shut** himself **away** for a month to catch up on his academic work.* □ *'What made him **shut** himself **away** in the heart of the country?'*

shut/slam the door in sb's face ia përplasi derën në fytyrë, ia mbylli derën përpara hundës
□ *'This is my house', he said: 'I manage my own affairs. I've told you once—I tell you again: 'We are not at home'. And in young Jolyon's face he **slammed the door**.*

shut/lock the stable door/stable-door after/when the horse/the steed is stolen si kofini pas të vjelit, kur erdhën mendtë, tretën dhentë
□ *To take measures now is like **shutting the stable door after the horse is stolen**.*

shut up 1. mbyll (dyert e dritaret)
□ *I **shut** the room **up** and left the key with the porter.* □ *We **shut up** the house before going on vacation.*
2. mbyll gojën
□ *'For Heaven's sake, **shut** him **up**; he said quite enough already.'*
3. mbyll, kyç
□ *We **shut** him **up** in his room.* □ *The vital documents are kept **shut up** in a safe.*

shy away from sth/doing sth ngurroj, druhem
□ *I have always **shied away from** close friendships.* □ *Modern English writers tend to **shy away from** using the stage for direct autobiographical expression.*

sick at heart me zemër të vrarë
□ *He himself had come out of the First World War so old with killing and so **sick at heart** that he had only one clear instinct and that was to get away from the scene as quickly as possible.* □ *I left the Near East **sick at heart**, ferociously determined to make any new institute in London first and foremost an effective medium for the enlargement of technical understanding.*

sick and tired of e kam në majë të hundës, jam shumë i inatosur, nuk e duroj dot më, më është neveritur
□ *'There are times,' said Luke, 'when I get **sick and tired of** you wise old men.'* □ *I get **sick and tired of** you in that baggy cardigan and no collar on.*
□ *I'm **sick and tired of** students coming late to class.*

sick to death of sb/sth i mërzitur tej mase (sa s'ka), s'duroj dot më, më vjen në majë të hundës
□ *I read of Paris fashion till I'm* **sick to death** *of it.* □ *Can't we change the subject? I'm sure that, after a school day, James is* **sick to death of** *kids and conversations about kids.* □ *I'm* **sick and tired of** *your constant complaints.*

side by side (with sb/sth) krah për krah
□ *We must stand* **side by side** *and help each other.*

side with marr anën e
□ *He will always* **side with** *a minority against the official or established line.* □ *She* **sided with** *her brother against the others in the class.*

sift the wheat from the chaff ndaj shapin nga sheqeri
□ *It's high time we* **sift the wheat from the chaff.**

sign sth away tjetërsoj; shes
□ *Read the document carefully, so that you know what you are* **signing away.** □ *With one stroke of the pen he had* **signed away** *his country's independence.*

sign for firmos
□ *The postman asked me to* **sign for** *the parcel.*

sign off 1. lë (ndërpres) punën
□ *June* **signed off** *early to go to the dentist.*

2. mbyll letrën
□ *She* **signed off** *with 'Yours ever, Janet'.*

3. mbyll transmetimin (televiziv, radiofonik)
□ *This is your resident DJ* **signing off** *for another week with our signature tune.*

sign over tjetërsoj, e bëj pronë të dikujt
□ *She has* **signed** *her house* **over** *to her daughter.*

sign up marr, pajtoj (me marrëveshje të nënshkruar)
□ *Arsenal has* **signed up** *a number of promising youngsters this season.*

silence gives consent heshtja është miratim
□ *When Mr. Green's name was proposed for chairman, the secretary asked if anyone disagreed: when no one spoke, the secretary said, '***Silence gives consent.***' and Mr. Green became the new chairman.*

silence is golden heshtja është flori
□ *I'm thinking of putting up a '***Silence is golden***' placard in the office. Nobody can hear themselves think.*

simmer down qetësohet
□ *'Give him a minute to* **simmer down**—*he's always like this when we discuss politics.* □ *When things have* **simmered down** *a bit more, talks can be started.* □ ***Simmer down*** *now, and stop shouting.*

sing a different song/tune ndryshoj qëndrim, i bie tjetër avazi, flas ndryshe
□ *'Anna says she wants to have a large family.' 'Maybe by the time she's had one or two she'll be* **singing a different tune.'** □ *My father's bankers thought he had gone completely mad. Today they* **sing a** *very* **different song** *as they watch the figures rise month by month.* □ *Charles said that all smokers should be expelled from the team, but he* **sang a different tune** *after the coach caught him smoking.*

sing sb's praises/sing the praises of sb ngre në qiell, lavdëroj pa masë, mburr sa s'ka ku të shkojë më
□ *The conversation had been swung in that direction by Mrs. Morse, who had been insidiously* **singing the praises of** *Mr. Smith.* □ *It was one of the most exasperating attributes of*

Bounderby that he not only **sang his own praises** but stimulated other men to sing them. □ Jack's team won and, when he came home, he **sang the praises of** the players who scored the winning goal. □ If he adopts the same position he will be accused by those who now **sing his praises** not only of illogicality but of jettisoning principle for the sake of expediency. □ You won't endear yourself to the doctor by continually **singing the praises of** his predecessor.

sink one's differences lë mënjanë (harroj) mosmarrëveshjet (armiqësitë etj.)

□ We must **sink our differences** and save our firm. □ Let us **sink our differences** and work together.

sink or swim fundoset apo del mbi ujë; dështon apo ka sukses; vdes apo mbijeton

□ Milly: Personally I think we should let the younger generation **sink or swim** without any further comment from us. □ I have helped him many times and he has never thanked me; now he can **sink or swim**, I don't care. □ The refugees had lost their homes and their possessions and it was now a case of **sink or swim.**

sit about/around rri (qëndroj) ulur

□ School discipline is very largely relaxed, and you have time to **sit about** and gossip. □ The foreign correspondents seemed to spend most of the time **sitting around** in bars.

sit back çlodhem, prehem; shtendosem, relaksohem

□ After a long walk, it's pleasant to **sit back** with a drink and look at the view. □ Now it was all over, we could **sit back** with our feet up. □ 'When we needed your help, all you did was **sit back** and twiddle your thumbs.'

sit down ulem

□ When I came in, the others were already **sitting down**. □ 'Sit your guests **down** and give them a drink.'

sit down under duroj, vuaj (pa protestuar, pa u ankuar)

□ He is a patient man, but not even he could **sit down under** that kind of provocation. □ He should not **sit down under** these accusations.

sit for jap (provim)

□ A number of sixth-formers came up that week to **sit for** university entrance.

sit in okupoj një fabrikë (institucion) duke u ulur në tokë (në shenjë proteste); bëj grevë ulur

□ The workers are **sitting in** against the factory closures. □ A company admitted this week that it had passed information on to the Special Branch on certain workers **sitting in** at its factory.

sit on thorns/pins/pins and needles rri si mbi gjemba

□ Mr. Symposon seemed to **sit on pins and needles**. He was for ever looking out of the window, and listening for chariot wheels.

sit on the fence rri (qëndron) në dy karrige

□ No one knows which side Jim supports; he just **sits on the fence** and refuses to vote. □ It is my view that he always **sat on the fence**, never committed himself, and never gave a decision. □ Colonel: I think you may take after me a little, my dear. You like to **sit on the fence** because it's more comfortable and more peaceful.

sit tight (and wait) rri në vend, mbaj vendin, rri pa lëvizur, rri e pres

□ Don't go out; just **sit tight** until the storm is over. □ Jean: I've been driven crazy, here all night—listening *to her. What could I do? We'll have to* **sit tight and wait.** □ *All the others run away, but I* **sat tight.**

sit up 1. rri (ngrihem) ndenjur

□ *I think the patient is well enough now to* **sit up** *in bed.* □ *We* **sat** *the baby* **up** *to feed her.*

2. rri natën vonë, rri zgjuar

□ *They* **sat up** *till the small hours, exchanging gossip.* □ *He had insisted on Nurse Ellen* **sitting up** *with her, although the need for a night nurse was past.* □ *'I'll get back very late, so don't* **sit up** *for me.'*

3. habitem

□ *Janice really* **sat up** *when I told her the gossip about Tom.*

sit up and take notice (of) tregoj vëmendje; tregohem i vëmendshëm

□ *He was not well known until his recent, successful play; but since then people have begun to* **sit up and take notice.** □ *'Just you wait. In the new year we'll spring our new sports model on them. That'll make them* **sit up and take notice.***

six of one and half-a-dozen of the other njësoj, një okë e dhjetë, një okë pa dhjetë; një okë e pesë, një okë pa pesë

□ *'Your father is bound to think of this as it affects your name and family's.* **'Six of one and half-a-dozen of the other,** *so far as that goes.'* □ *On this route, there is no difference in time or money between travelling by rail and travelling by bus: it's* **six of one and half-a-dozen of the other.** □ *His brother is known to be no better than himself in inclination. In the old phrase it is* **six of one and half a dozen of the other.***

size sb/sth up gjykoj, vlerësoj, krijoj një mendim për

□ *I was trying to* **size** *you* **up,** *and*

failing because you didn't fit into any type I knew. □ *He attempted to* **size up** *the reaction of the audience: how were they being received?*

skate on thin ice rrezikoj, shkoj në majë të briskut, eci në buzë të greminës, eci në dërrasë të kalbur

□ *The managing director explained as carefully as he could that with the decline in demand we might be forced to lay people off, but of course he's used to* **skating on thin ice** *and managed the situation as well as he could be hoped.* □ *'If I were you, I shouldn't come in here telling experienced staff their business; you're* **skating on very thin ice.***

skeleton in the closet/cupboard, a sekret familjar, e fshehtë e familjes

□ *And it is from these that we shall arrive at some particulars regarding the Newcome family, which will show us that they have* **a skeleton** *or two* **in their closets,** *as well as their neighbours.* □ *Mr. Settelewhite smiled again. 'That entirely depends on how many* **skeletons** *you have* **in your cupboard.'** □ *Reticence and taste for privacy seem to have been Thomas Hardy's motives rather than any grisly* **skeleton in the cupboard.** □ *Lew Archer moves through the flashy corrupt world of Southern California, opening* **the cupboards** *and watching* **the skeleton** *fall out.* □ *The police inspector says that some of the witnesses may have been lying because they have some* **skeletons in the cupboards** *which they don't want to make public.*

sketch sth out skicoj, përvijoj

□ *'Give me a pad and a pencil and I'll* **sketch out** *what I have in mind.'* □ *He* **sketched** *out his proposals for a new road.*

skin sb alive ia ndreq (ia rregulloj) samarin, ndëshkoj rëndë, e rrjep të gjallë, ia marr shpirtin

□ *If I ever find out who broke into our house, I'll **skin him alive**.* □ *Your father'll **skin** you **alive** when he sees this!*

skin and bone(s) kockë e lëkurë

□ *He could see nothing attractive in women that were all **skin and bone**.* □ *She's gone to **skin and bone** now, poor girl, stomach ulcers.* □ *When the family who had been lost in the jungle were finally rescued, they were only **skin and bones**.* □ *I don't know why you carry saccharin to put in your tea and coffee. You're nothing but **skin and bone** as it is.*

skirt around/round shmang, i kaloj anash

□ *'Let's not **skirt round** the awkward questions—let's try and answer them.'* □ *'The question of who is to pay has been **skirted around**. I suppose that's because you assume I will foot the bill.* □ *She **skirted round** the problem of high cost.*

slam the door in sb's face ia mbyll derën në fytyrë

□ *In my name, we'd gate-crash everywhere—cocktails, weekends, even a couple of house parties. I used to hope that one day, somebody would have the guts to **slam the door in our faces**, but they didn't. They were too well-bred.* □ *He was a door-to-door salesman for a bit, but he soon got tired of having **the door slammed in his face**.*

slap in the face, a një shuplakë e fortë; një goditje e rëndë, një fyerje e rëndë (poshtëruese)

□ *It was a bit of **a slap in the face** when she refused to see me.*

sleep like a log/top fle si i vdekur, fle top

□ *'I'm afraid you didn't have a very good night.' 'Oh, yes, I did. I **slept like a top**.'* □ *I've got rather a headache. I **slept like a log**, and now I feel lousy.* □ *'I was fair exhausted last night, says Les. 'Slept **like a log**— woke up in the fireplace. Terrible joke that.'* □ *Mademoiselle Dupont said she hoped the children had not been frightened by the storm? '**Slept like tops**,' Pa said.* □ *She snuggled into bed and **slept like a** comfy old **top**.*

sleep rough fle jashtë, fle ku të mundem (në natyrë)

□ *But the boy would constantly 'go missing' at nights from his foster home because his mother had taken to **sleeping rough** in the park.* □ *But you never get used to the travel. For months at a stretch, it can be like **sleeping rough** in luxury hotels.*

sleep sth off heq (largoj) me gjumë

□ *'I know he's in an evil mood, but let's give him a night to **sleep it off**, shall we?'*

sleep the clock round fle gjithë ditën

□ *I feel as if I could **sleep the clock round**, and probably I would only sleep a wink.*

sleep tight gjumë të ëmbël

□ *Good night, **sleep tight**!*

sling one's hook iki fshehurazi, vidhem; çaj ferrën

□ *I've plenty to feel guilty about, but not her, really. She saw to that. Anyhow she's gone, walked out, **slung her hook**.* □ *And I'll lose that race and I'll let him know it when I'm about to get out—if I don't **sling my hook** even before the race.*

slip through sb's fingers më rrëshqet (më ikën, më shpëton) nga duart

□ *That opportunity will **slip through our fingers** if we do not take advantage of it soon.* □ *The police are* *furious because he **slipped through their fingers**. □ Just because of one silly mistake, a fortune has **slipped through our fingers**.*

slip of the pen shkarje e penës, lapsus calami

□ *It was by **a slip of the pen** that Petrit's letter was directed to Ziçisht instead of Hoçisht. □ Could you let me have that check back I've just given you: I think I made a **slip of the pen** and wrote $50,000 instead of $500. □ Yet, one cannot doubt the depth and power of the love that brought them together—Wells, as an interesting **slip of the pen** reveals, considered their relationship a marriage. □ That was a **slip of the pen**, I meant to write September, not November.*

slip of the tongue shkarje e gojës, lapsus linguae

□ *By a **slip of the tongue** Arta said that the meeting would be held on Sunday instead of Monday. □ I hope that Doctor Green was not offended when I introduced him as Mister Green; it was a **slip of the tongue**. □ The nervous strain of addressing a large conference can sometimes cause speakers to make silly **slips of the tongue**; like Harold Wilson calling Harold Macmillan 'Harold Wilson' for example. □ He turned red in the face and went stamping and bumbling away. A **slip of the tongue**, you see: but what it did signify? □ No one would have known our plans if Kay hadn't made a **slip of the tongue**.*

slip/from/sb's mind/memory më del nga mendja

□ *It **slipped** Wormold's **memory** that his nephew was now long past seventeen and had probably given up his*

*stamp collection long ago. □ He's my child, too—a fact which sometimes seems to **slip your memory**! □ What Stocker actually did think of Celia, I never found out. Or if I did, it's **slipped my mind**. □ The main purpose of my visit had **slipped from** his failing **memory**. □ The name has **slipped from my mind**. □ Do excuse me. It had **slipped my memory** that you have good reasons to be indisposed for joining in my chatter.*

slip up on (sth) bëj gabim

□ *Somebody must have **slipped up** badly in your report. They seem to have left out her stage name. □ There is a slightly uncomfortable feeling of somebody having **slipped up**. □ Could you check these figures, and see where I have **slipped up**?*

slog away (at) punoj pa pushim, punoj me ngulm

□ *Nick's been **slogging away at** his multiplication tables all morning. □ 'Keep **slogging away**! You've nearly broken the back of the problem.'*

slowly but surely ngadalë (avash) por me siguri

□ ***Slowly but surely** and relentlessly, the lost ground was recovered and we began to pass from the defensive to the offensive. □ The first ingredient acts on weeds through the leaf and **slowly but surely** kills them. □ **Slowly but surely** the great ship glided into the water.*

slow down 1. ul (ngadalësoj) shpejtësinë

□ *At first he drove rather fast and then **slowed down** to a silent crawl. □ 'The motor's overheating. Can't you **slow it down**?'*

2. punoj më shtruar, jo me rrëmbim

□ *'You really ought to **slow down**— all these late nights are doing you no* good.' □ 'If I could find some way of **slowing** my father **down** I would; he's taking on far too much work.'

slow up punoj avash (me më pak vrull, efektivitet)

□ I think he's beginning to **slow up**— his latest book is much weaker than the previous one. □ He's over sixty, but he shows no signs of **slowing up**.

small beer gjë pa shumë rëndësi; njeri pa shumë rëndësi

□ The actual demands set out in the document are **small beer** indeed.

□ Old Jolyon, in whom a desperate honesty welled up at times, would allude to his ancestors as: 'Yeomen— I suppose very **small beer**.' □ That grant was pretty **small beer**; we shall need a lot more money.

small fortune, a një thes me para, një shumë e madhe (parash)

□ The car cost me **a small fortune**.

small fry 1. kalamajtë, fëmijët e vegjël

□ It was decided to have a staff dinner-and-dance on December 18 and an afternoon party for the **small fry** on a date to be decided later. □ In the park, a sandbox is provided for the **small fry**. □ **Small fry**, nephews, nieces would consider the following super: ball-point pen, visit to a zoo, home-made ice-lolly set.

2. gjë pa shumë rëndësi; njeri pa rëndësi, peshk i vogël

□ The forest giants among the trees do not kill the **small fry** under them. □ The group that got the most money had the most power and was able to eliminate the **smaller fry** from the increasingly grueling race.

small potatoes gjë pa rëndësi; njeri pa rëndësi

□ Against these increases, the cuts in spending looked like very **small potatoes**. □ This boy was big for his years

and thought he was no **small potatoes**. He dressed in a flamboyant manner, and affected white golf shoes. □ But these achievements, impressive enough in themselves, were **small potatoes** compared with his real aspirations.

small talk fjalë (llafe) kote

□ I met him at coffee time and we had a chat, but it was just **small talk**, nothing worth repeating. □ He made some **small talk**, staring down Whitehall, so that I could see his knave of diamonds profile. Then he turned full on me. □ Andre Previn and Oscar Peterson pulled off another impossible trick, exchanging riveting **small talk** while a thousand people in the audience sat there eavesdropping.

smarten up 1. spitullohem, pispillosem

□ You'll have to **smarten up** a bit before the visitors arrive. □ 'You'll spend the rest of your life in the ice-cream factory if don't **smarten** yourself **up** a bit.'

2. rregulloj

□ The shop will have to be **smartened up** a bit if you want to cater for the top end of the market.

smash sb's face in ia thyej turinjtë

□ 'If you mess my girl about, I'll **smash your face in!**' □ Anyone trying to muscle in on the gang's territory would get **his face smashed in**.

smell a rat nuhas diçka që s'shkon, diçka të dyshimtë; bie në erë (gjurmë)

□ Ah, you begin to **smell a rat**, do you? You thought yourself pretty safe. □ A milkman had several times seen a dark-green Mercedes passing slowly in front of the Tunisian Embassy. **Smelling a rat**, he had jotted down the license number. □ He **smelt a rat**, but he kept mum. □ The police inspector said, 'There's something about his story that makes me *smell a rat*. I am going to investigate it further.

smell out zbuloj, diktoj me huhatje
□ *Specially trained dogs smell out drugs.* □ *'Lead the way with the tracker-dog; he'll soon smell the fellow out.'*

smell to high heaven qelbet erë
□ *'When was the last time you cleaned out the parrot's cage? It smells to high heaven.'* □ *'Of course there's been dirty dealing over the allocation of building permits. The whole thing smells to high heaven.*

smile on sb/sth miraton, inkurajon; buzëqesh
□ *The council did not smile on our plan.* □ *Fortune smiled on us.*

smoke like a chimney e pi duhanin me hundë, tymos si oxhak
□ *Miss Greece had a cigarette though and the papers said, 'Miss Greece— never seen without a cigarette in her hand smoked like a chimney.'* □ *'How many cigarettes do you smoke, do you think?' '20 a day— unless I'm worried or upset. Then I smoke like a chimney.'*

smoke out/out of 1. nxjerr jashtë me tym
□ *We used a piece of pipe connected to a car exhaust to smoke the rats out.* □ *He was determined to smoke out the leaders of the gang.*
2. tymos, mbush me tym
□ *Turn off that pan—you're smoking the place out!*

smoke screen, a perde tymi
□ *The 'Daily Mirror' calls Thorne- croft's plan a smoke screen.* □ *... an apparent insensitivity which added as much to the smoke screen of shy- ness that cut the children off from*

their parents as did Bernard's inept artificiality.

smooth sb's path lehtësoj, hap (shtroj) udhën për, e ndihmoj të kapërcejë më lehtë (një gjendje të vështirë), ia pakësoj vështirësitë
□ *Good behavior in the international sphere, like good manners in society, may smooth the path of international intercourse.* □ *Trade unionists pay only lip service to the need for re- search. Certainly they could do a lot more than they are doing to smooth the way for its application within the industry.*

smooth sth away heq, zhduk, eliminoj
□ *We'll smooth away any difficulties when we reach them.* □ *Money helps to smooth away most difficulties.*

smooth over zbus, qetësoj, sheshoj
□ *It'll be difficult for you to smooth over your differences after so many years.* □ *This was a genuine attempt to placate him and smooth this thing over.* □ *They were now arguing furiously with James standing by and trying to smooth the quarrel over.*

snake in the grass, a gjarpër i mbuluar
□ *I am really angry at how that snake in the grass has treated me, after all the kindness I have shown him.* □ *That snake in the grass reported me to the boss.*

snake (its way) across, past, through etc. gjarpëron përmes, tej
□ *The river snaked away in the dis- tance.* □ *The road snaked its way through the mountains.*

snap one's fingers at sb/sth/snap one's fingers in sb's face 1. trajtoj me përbuzje (përçmim)
□ *No petty official was going to stop Philip from getting into the enclo- sure. He would just snap his fingers*

at them. □ *At his elbow was Cowper-wood* **snapping his fingers in the face of** *his enemies.* □ *In a fortnight now she could* **snap her fingers** *at it all.* □ *Don't* **snap your fingers** *at his proposal, it merits careful consideration.*
2. kërcas gishtat (për të tërhequr vëmendjen etj.)
□ *He* **snapped his fingers** *to attract the waiter.*

snap sb's head off i flas ashpër dikujt, reagoj ashpër ndaj dikujt
□ *... she has never got out of the habit of nagging Higgins, that was established on the fatal night when she won his bet for him. She* **snaps his head off** *on the faintest provocation, or on none.* □ *She whispered 'try to find out what's bothering her. She just* **snaps my head off.** *'* □ *'Don't ask why he's come in late again—you'll only get* **your head snapped off.** *'* □ *If they spoke out of their turn they would get their* **heads snapped off.**

snap up marr, pranoj, ble me dëshirë
□ *The cheapest articles at the sale were quickly* **snapped up.** □ *Mr. Jones told Tom he would take him skiing and Tom* **snapped up** *the offer.*

snatch at kap, mbërthej
□ *A man darted from a doorway and* **snatched at** *his briefcase.* □ *He* **snatched at** *the rope ladder, but it eluded his grasp.* □ *There are a few vacancies on the production side every year, but they come and go quickly. You have to* **snatch at** *them.*

snow sb in/up bllokoj, mbyll brenda (në shtëpi)
□ *We were* **snowed in** *for three days last winter by the blizzards.*

snow sb under (with sth) mbys me punë etj.
□ *'Don't give me any extra jobs; I'm*

snowed under already.' □ *Don't be a clock watcher, be willing to work late if he's* **snowed under** *with work.* □ *At that time we were being* **snowed under** *with requests for medical aid.*

so as to me qëllim që
□ *I left a message* **so as to** *be sure of contacting her.* □ *He disconnected the phone* **so as** *not to be disturbed.*

so be it ashtu qoftë
□ *If he doesn't want to be involved, then* **so be it.**

so far deri tani; deri këtu
□ *Goodness knows what size he is, but he's the biggest albatross I've seen* **so far.** □ *Everything is in order* **so far.** □ *Now that we have come* **so far** *we may as well go all the way.*

so far, so good deri tani çdo gjë ka shkuar për mrekulli
□ *The pile was going up, the first installment of heavy water had arrived;* **so far, so good.** □ *'Let's have it. What happened?' Don Vincente asked. 'So far, so good,' Mark said.* □ *So far, so good; I hope we keep on with such good luck.*

so far as me sa
□ *There are no mistakes* **so far as** *I can see.*

so long mirupafshim
□ *So long, I'll be back tomorrow.*

so much the better/worse for aq më mirë/keq për
□ *'I seem to have made my curry hotter than usual.' 'So much the better.'* □ *'If Ned could find some means of integrating his contribution in the general framework, all right; if not, so much the worse for the general framework.'* □ *In old days I was always trying to beat other fellows. Now, I concentrate simply on improving my own play. If I happen to win, so much the better.*

so-so njëfarësoj; as mirë, as keq
□ *I'm just feeling **so-so** at the moment: not as ill as I was, but not completely well either.* □ *'How is the patient tonight, sir?' asked Giles. '**So-so**,' returned the doctor.*

so to speak/say si të thuash
□ *From London one can travel direct to all the main cities in Europe: London is, **so to speak**, the gateway to Europe.* □ *She went away, treading, **so to speak**, on Cork Street.* □ *This fact is reflected in practical problems met with in color printing. For magneto does not, **so to speak**, respond well to being used subtractively.*

so what? edhe pastaj?
□ *'Professor Black is very angry at your behavior in class yesterday.' '**So what?** I'm dropping his subject anyway.'* □ *You're twenty-one and you're married to me. **So what?** If your mother doesn't like it, she can do the other thing.*

soak sth off/out heq me të lagur
□ *Rather than paint over the paper you'd better **soak** it **off**.* □ *They can **soak** them **off** with pieces of wet cotton wool*

soak to the skin lag deri në palcë
□ *A storm burst over them as they slept in a field and they were **soaked to the skin**.* □ *A passing bus swept through a large puddle by the side of the road and **soaked** us **to the skin**.*

soak sb through bëhet qull (ujë)
□ *'Don't stand out there; you'll be **soaked through**.'*

soak up 1. pi, thith
□ *If you spill ink on the carpet, **soak** it **up** straight away.* □ *This sandy soil **soaks up** moisture very quickly.*
2. thith, përvetëson, asimilon
□ *'There's no holding the boy; he **soaks up** new information like a sponge.'*

sober as a judge 1. esëll, i kthjellët
□ *I did not take any drink at all last night, and so I went to bed **as sober as a judge**.*
2. i rëndë, hijerëndë, serioz
□ *Everyone else was relaxed and happy, but he was **as sober as a judge**.*

sob one's heart out qaj me ngashërim (me dënesë)
□ *When she heard her husband was leaving, Mary just **sobbed her heart out**.*

sober down qetësohem, bie në fashë
□ *'Now just **sober down**, everybody. I've important news for you.'*

sober up esëllohem, bëhem esëll
□ *'Put his head under the cold tap—that'll **sober** him **up**.'* □ *When he finally **sobered up**, he found that his wallet had been taken.* □ *I stopped grinning; not out of politeness but because what he said really did **sober** me **up**.*

soft in the head kokëtul, kokëmish, kokëkungull, i papjekur nga mendja
□ *Anyone who has such stupid ideas must be **soft in the head**.*

soft job, a punë e lehtë (e rehatshme)
□ *We'll check and sign these later. It's a nice **soft job** here.* □ *Anybody who thinks teaching in a nursery school is a **soft job** should try it.*

soft option rruga më e lehtë, gjëja më e lehtë
□ *I won't be able to rely on Jack to support me if things become difficult; he always goes for the **soft option**.*

soil one's hands ndyj duart
□ *He refused to **soil his hands**.*

some day një ditë
□ ***Some day** I shall go there.* □ *You will show repentance for it **some day**.*

somehow or other në një mënyrë a në
një tjetër
  □ *Well, I must act **somehow or other**,*
  but it's bore—a great bore.
something else diçka tepër e veçantë
  □ *His paintings really are **something***
  ***else**: I haven't seen anything so good*
  from any living artist.
something else again diçka e
ndryshme, diçka tjetër
  □ *I don't mind if the children play qui-*
  etly in this room, but I'm afraid that
  *playing with a ball is **something else***
  ***again**. They could break a window.*
  □ *I don't care if you borrow my dictio-*
  nary sometimes, but taking it without
  *asking and keeping it is **something***
  ***else again**.*
something like 1. pikërisht ajo që dua
(pëlqej, shpresoj etj.)
  □ *'Now, this is **something like it**!' the*
  tutor said, giving Polly's exercise full
  marks. □ *You say he's put the price*
  *up to $1,000? Now that's **something***
  ***like it**!*
2. afërsisht, përafërsisht, në mënyrë
të përafërt
  □ *There must have been **something***
  ***like** a dozen pills left in the bottle.*
  □ *The outline road program is on*
  ***something like** the scale required.*
3. thuajse si, njëlloj si
  □ *He is **something like** his brother.*
  □ *A thesaurus is **something like** a*
  dictionary.
something/somewhat of a në një farë
shkalle (mase), thuajse një
  □ *He was a simple man—and **some-***
  ***what of a** worried one.* □ *It was*
  *certainly **something of a** problem to*
  know where to go next. □ *Some few*
  times, however, at long intervals, I was
  allowed to go there, and then found out
  *that Mr. Barkis was **something of a***
  miser. □ *I'm **something of a** carpenter.*

something or other diç, diçka
  □ *I'm sure I've lost **something or***
  ***other**.*
sometime or other ndonjë ditë
  □ *I'd like to read it **sometime or***
  other**.* □ *I'd like to see Saranda **some-
  ***time or other**.*
son of a bitch, a bir kurve (bushtre)
  □ *Finally, **the son of a bitch** walked*
  out of one of the buildings near the
  runaway there. □ *Still the outboard*
  motor wouldn't start. 'Come on, fire,
  ***you son of a bitch**!' Tom swore,*
  yanking at the cord.
sooner or later herët a vonë
  □ ***Sooner or later** in British football*
  there will have to be a reorientation
  of thinking. □ *She has to know about*
  *it **sooner or later**.*
sooner the better, the sa më shpejt aq
më mirë
  □ *'When should I ask him?' **The***
  ***sooner the better**.'*
soothe the savage breast zbus inatin
(zemërimin), qetësoj shpirtin e trazuar
  □ *Music has charms to **soothe a***
  ***savage breast**.* □ *I discovered also*
  that the appropriate look or word
  *could '**soothe the savage breast**' and*
  bring him to heel.
sore spot/point pikë e dobët (delikate)
  □ *Then there is **the sore point** of the*
  income tax—not the national per-
  sonal income tax, which everybody
  pays, but the additional tax that has
  nothing to do with the rates that many
  states now impose. □ *The secrecy*
  *with which they got married is still **a***
  ***sore point** with Tina's parents.* □ *I*
  wouldn't ask him about his job inter-
  *view; it's rather **a sore point** with him*
  at the moment
sore subject temë delikate
  □ *Don't mention football in his pres-*
  *ence. It has been **a sore subject** with*

him since his team was knocked out in the first round of the cup.

so/and/that's/was/that ja kështu është puna, ja kjo është e gjitha

□ *'Tell Fleur that's no good, please, I must do as my father wished before he died.' 'So that's that,' he thought and passed out of the front door.* □ *I've told you before and I'm repeating it again now, I won't go, and that's that! Please understand me!*

sorry state, a gjendje e pakënaqshme (e mjerueshme, tragjike etj.)

□ *The facts quoted would reveal a sorry state of affairs in any community.* □ *Kean and Scott, the tiny house furnisher and textile wholesaling group, were in a sorry state when Wilson bought a controlling stake.*

sort of, a një lloj

□ *I had a sort of feeling he wouldn't come.*

sort of në një farë mase (mënyre)

□ *I sort of thought this might happen.*

sort oneself out sistemohem, rregullohem

□ *I need to sort myself out a bit, before I start looking for a new job.* □ *You can sleep here till you get yourself fixed up ... get yourself sorted out.*

sort out 1. zgjedh, ndaj në (grupe, klasa, kategori etj.)

□ *She spent a happy afternoon sorting out her coins and stamps.* □ *Members of the armed forces have been sorted out by trades and occupations.*

2. zgjidh, rregulloj, vë në rregull

□ *You'd better send somebody over to sort the situation out.* □ *It's his job to sort out real grievances.*

sound as a bell/roach, as shëndoshë e mirë, shëndoshë si molla

□ *Don Pedro. ...He hath a heart as*

sound as a bell, and his heart thinks, his tongue speaks. □ *'Nessie doesn't take after you, Mr. Brondie,' remarked the first speaker. 'She doesn't look too strong!' Brodie glowered at him exclaiming angrily: 'She's as sound as a bell....'* □ *Her constitution was sound as a bell—illness never came near her....* □ *Walpole. ...Look at me! I've no symptoms. I'm as sound as a bell.*

sound off 1. flas me zë të lartë e me pompozitet (mburrje)

□ *He's always sounding off about how he would manage the firm.* □ *I wonder when he will stop sounding off about this fabulous house he's building.* □ *'Please don't raise that topic: you'll start George sounding off on his pet theory.'*

2. sondoj, kërkoj të di

□ *'Have you sounded out your wife on the move to Australia yet?'* □ *'Where does he stand on this issue?' 'I don't know; I must sound him out.'*

sound the (death) knell of sb/sth paralajmëroj fundin e

□ *The safety regulations have sounded the convertible's death-knell.* □ *One tourist had recently been killed by a stray bullet and the death sounded the knell of the all-in-tour.*

sour grapes rrush i pabërë (**fig.**)

□ *But because we cannot satisfy the desires of our hearts—why should we cry 'sour grapes' at them?* □ *He says he didn't want to marry her anyway, but that's just sour grapes.*

sow one's wild oats bëj jetë të shthurur

□ *He sowed all his wild oats before he married.* □ *If he were really and truly courting her, it would be a very good thing, I believe—and the children would respond. But as it is, they are merely used to seeing a young man*

*sowing what young men like to call
their wild oats.* □ *I don't think that we
should criticize him now for what he
did when he was young; he was probably just sowing his wild oats.* □ *If
they keep on dancing they may not
marry so soon. Why shouldn't girls
sow their wild oats too?* □ *Myra:
Tony, before you settle down to being
an honest electrician, I wish you'd
take that money and—Tony: What?
Sow a few wild oats?*

sow the seeds of sth mbjell (hedh)
farën e
□ *Clearly there was much fertile
ground in which evil persons could
sow the seeds of discontent and
trouble.*

sow the wind and reap the whirlwind
mbjell erën e korr furtunën
□ *But the calf of Samaria shall be
broken in pieces. For they have sown
the wind and they shall reap the
whirlwind.*

spare no efforts bëj të gjitha përpjekjet, bëj çmos
□ *We'll spare no efforts to turn into
reality the decisions of the meeting.*
□ *He submitted himself to this procedure no fewer than 163 times, and no
effort was spared standardizing the
experimental conditions.*

spare no pains s'lë kusur, bëj gjithçka
të mundur, i luaj të gjithë gurët
□ *The hotel staff spared no pains to
ensure that our stay was as enjoyable
as possible.* □ *You did what you could
with no pains spared. There may be
much to regret, but you have nothing
to blame yourself for.*

spare sb's blushes nuk turpëroj dikë,
nuk i skuq faqen dikujt, nuk bëj me
turp
□ *Funny, he told me he was going to
tell you about the gift of money, but I*

*expect he was too bashful. He wanted
to spare your blushes.* □ *'If I'm not
driving myself, I'd rather have my
wife at the wheel than anyone else.'
'Spare my blushes, will you, Jack,
and give the windscreen a wipe.'*

spare sb's feelings shmang prekjen në
ndjenja të
□ *He spared her feelings by not criticizing her husband in front of her.*

spare the rod and spoil the child druri
ka dalë nga xheneti
□ *The very phrase 'spoiled child' has
an old fashioned ring. To spare the rod
was, traditionally, to spoil the child.*

spark off ndez, nxit
□ *His comment sparked off a quarrel
between them.* □ *The incident sparked
off a whole chain of disasters.*

speak ill of sb flas keq për
□ *You should not speak ill of him.*
□ *Don't speak ill of the dead.* □ *I've
never spoken ill of him in my life.*

speak for itself flet vetë
□ *But I need not detain them—the fact
speaks for itself.* □ *He was a war hero,
great writer and famous politician;
his achievements speak for themselves.* □ *The events of that evening
speak for themselves.* □ *There is little
need to comment on this record; it is
true to say that it speaks for itself.*

speak for oneself flas vetë
□ *I'm quite capable of speaking for
myself, thank you!'*

speak for sb 1. flas në emër të
□ *We believe that in putting forward
our policies we are speaking for the
majority of the people.* □ *'I know I am
speaking for all of us when I say how
grateful we are to our hosts.'*
2. flas në mbështetje (favor) të
□ *At the meeting John spoke for the
change in the rules.* □ *Certain Members would be prepared to speak for*

the introduction of the death penalty for violent crime involving the use of explosives.

speak for yourself fol për veten tënde
□ 'We all played very badly.' '**Speak for yourself**, I think I played quite well.' □ 'I think we've done enough drinking for one evening.' '**Speak for yourself**, John!' □ 'Perhaps it's time we were leaving.' '**Speak for yourselves**, darlings.'

speak of sth flet (tregon) për
□ Her behavior **speaks of** suffering bravely borne.

speak of the devil and he appears kujto (zër në gojë) qenin, rrëmbe (bëj gati) shkopin
□ I am surprised that Jones has not come—well, **speak of the devil and he appears**. □ We were just talking about Bill when he came in the door. **Speak of the devil and he appears**.

speak one's mind shfaq (shpreh) hapur mendimin tim, them troç atë që mendoj
□ He impressed most of the senior officers who had to deal with him as a man who learned quickly, thought hard, and **spoke his mind**. □ There was nowhere I could retreat to, no need to be pleasant to anyone. I could afford the luxury of **speaking my mind**. □ I hope that what I am going to say will not offend anyone, but I feel that I must **speak my mind**. □ When we asked the students about their opinion of the new teaching programs, they **spoke their minds** freely.

speak/say the truth them të vërtetën
□ She brought her family up in her own way; she taught us to **speak the truth**, come what may. □ 'You know Captain Segura?' 'He is a friend of my

daughter.' 'How can I tell that you are **speaking the truth**?' □ Whatever lies her tongue might still be impelled to tell, her face at last **spoke the truth**. □ Timson... I must **speak the truth** and shame the devil! □ Mr. Abel made no answer, and, to **say the truth**, kept a long way from the bed and very near the door.

speak to 1. flas, bisedoj me
□ 'Have a word with grandmother—she doesn't often get a chance of **speaking to** young people.'
2. flas, hyj në bisedë me
□ 'There's something wrong with the plumbing. I'll have to **speak to** the landlord about it.'
3. qortoj
□ 'You must **speak to** the children, Henry; they never listen to a word I say.'

speak to the wind i flas murit
□ Speaking to Aileen is like **speaking to the wind**.

speak up 1. flas me zë të lartë e të qartë
□ '**Speak up**; we can't hear you at the back!' □ I do wish he'd stop mumbling and learn to **speak up**.
2. flas pro (kundër) dikujt; flas në mbështetje të
□ Never be frightened to **speak up** for your beliefs. □ Willie **spoke up** for Dan as club president.

speak volumes for sb/sth provon (dëshmon) më së miri, përbën një dëshmi të qartë, flet qartë
□ These facts **speak volumes of** her honesty. □ At the end of his talk, his wife did not say anything, but the expression on her face **spoke volumes**. □ His readiness to accomplish any arduous task **speaks volumes of** his high sense of discipline. □ He was twenty minutes behind time, and to me who knew so well his gluttonous

despatch of business... the fact *spoke volumes.*

speak well for sb flet mirë për, flet (dëshmon) në favor (në të mirë) të

□ *Her reputation as a good mother* **speaks well for her.** □ *Her behavior* **speaks well for her.**

speak with one's tongue in one's cheek flas me të tallur (me ironi)

□ *There was no* **speaking with his tongue in his cheek.** *He spoke straight from the heart.*

speed up shpejtoj, rris shpejtësinë

□ *There is now a system designed to* **speed up** *the work of factory inspection departments.* □ *The train soon* **speeded up.**

spell out shkoqis, sqaroj qartë, shpjegoj me hollësi

□ *His speech will* **spell out** *in some detail a short-term and a long-term strategy for growth.* □ *The possible economic benefits of the treaty were* **spelt out** *in his recent book.*

spend money like water i derdh paratë lumë

□ *Helen: It's a wedding present from that young man of mine. He* **spends** *his* **money like water,** *you know.* □ *Ford money is being* **spent like water**—*nearly $10 million so far for this year. The television screens are stiff with Ford advertising.*

spick and span i pastër akull, xham, i rregullt

□ *She always keeps her kitchen* **spick and span.** □ *She looks after the house very well; it is always* **spick and span.** □ *The bed had been made, fresh towels were in the bathroom and everything was* **spick and span.**

spike sb's guns prish planet e

□ *Jephson, sensing the import of what he was doing—how most likely he was, as he would have phrased it*

'spiking' one of Mr. Manson's best guns, continued with: 'How old were you then, Clyde, did you say?' □ *Listen, we'll get married tomorrow. That will* **spike** *the old lady's* **guns.** *God, I would like to see her face!*

□ *They will do anything to* **spike the guns** *of the opposition, even at the risk of underpricing themselves out of business.* □ *He smiled with satisfaction—he had made a confession of an action that troubled his conscience and* **spiked John's guns** *at the same time.* □ *We knew they intended to use the main square for their meeting, so we* **spiked their guns** *by getting there first and using it for our own.*

spill the beans nxjerr një të fshehtë (sekretin) me ose pa qëllim

□ *I stop because I am just about to* **spill the beans** *about Conroy's being married and I promised not to tell.* □ *Listen, I'll go to jail if I let bastards like Stacey* **spill the beans** *on me and get away with it.* □ *The police have arrested four men suspected of committing the robbery; they are trying to get one of them to* **spill the beans.** □ *Harold did not always* **spill the beans** *at once; he would bide his time and adopt a sphinx-like air.* □ *Many diplomatic wives find it easier not even to know* **the beans** *they must not* **spill**—*but there are other ways of being indiscreet.* □ *You can't keep a secret; you see no reason why you shouldn't* **spill the beans.** □ *He didn't know what he was going to do with her, not now that she'd* **spilled the beans** *all over the place.*

spin sb a yarn i rrëfej (i kallëzoj) dikujt një histori (për ta zbavitur, mashtruar apo hequr qafe)

□ *Jason: Just get rid of that young*

man. *Alex: How? JASON: Spin him a
yarn, a tall story.* □ *Geof: Do people
ever tell the truth about themselves?
Jo: Why should she want to spin me a
yarn like that? Geof: She likes to
make an effect.* □ *The old sailor loves
to spin yarns about his life at sea.*
□ *Somerset Maugham is a great sto-
ryteller; he can spin a good yarn.* □ *I
don't believe what he says; I think
he's just spinning yarns.*

spit and image/spitting image of sb
gjallë, njësoj si, gjithë, tërë; kopje e
□ *I'm sorry, I confused you with
someone else I knew some years
ago; you're his spitting image.* □ *She
was trying to make Alice feel thoroughly uncomfortable by references
to the good looks of her lover, the
spit-and-image of Jean Marais, darling.* □ *He was a grand man. He died
in his 70s lifting weights. A great way
to go. And Leon is the spitting image
of him.* □ *I've seen any number of
seals bobbing up out of the water
all round us and all of them looking
the spitting image of my butcher in
Nottingam.*

spit it out qis, nxjerr nga goja
□ *'What are you trying to say? Come
on, spit it out, man.'*

split away/off ndahet, shkëputet,
shqitet
□ *The wood is cracking in the heat,
and pieces are splitting away.* □ *The
group have split off from the official
union.*

split hairs ndan qimen katërsh (dysh),
kapet pas gjërave të vogla, hyn në
hollësira të panevojshme, merret me
vogëlima (cingërima)
□ *Pray don't let us be splitting hairs ...,
or there'll never be an end of the
cause or the cost.* □ *The Colonel
shrugged his shoulders. 'I can't split*

hairs,' he said. □ *He could split hairs,
talk about how little time he had,
and that this work was not at all in
his line—but this kind of game was
tiring Yasha's candor, he decided.*
□ *You say you were five minutes
late and I say you were ten minutes
late; but lets not split hairs—the
point is that you did not arrive on
time.* □ *A kidnapping is a kidnapping
whether the child be hidden by a vin-
dictive parent or by a stranger. To
split hairs over these cases being
civil or criminal offences is unworthy
of us all.*

**split one's sides laughing/with
laughter** gajasem së qeshuri, mbaj
barkun (brinjët, ijet) me dorë,
këputem së qeshuri
□ *The children in the audience were
splitting their sides at the funny
antics of the clowns.* □ *I'll tell you a
good story about that, that will make
you split your sides with laughing.*
□ *Mr. Jonas was infinitely amused,
protesting that he had seldom seen
better company in all his life and that
he was enough to make a man split
his sides with laughing.*

split up 1. ndahem, prish (fejesën,
martesën etj.)
□ *'Who told you that Mary and I had
split up?'* □ *There's is nothing in the
rumor that they're splitting up.*
2. ndaj
□ *For art and craft lessons the class
is split up into small groups*

spoiling for a fight kërkon (hap) sherr,
i ha dora, mezi pret të zihet (grindet,
ndeshet etj.), lëshon brezin
□ *We have well-trained troops, who
are spoiling for a fight.* □ *Yes, sir, I'm
very worried. She's absolutely
spoiling for a fight—won't hear of an
apology.* □ *Don't say anything likely*

*to annoy Jack tonight; he's **spoiling for a fight**.*

spoil the ship for ha' porth/ha'penny worth of tar për një plesht djeg jorganin

□ *If you were willing to pay $90 for a coat why **spoil the ship for a ha' porth of tar**? Get yourself a smart hat, too.* □ *It would only have needed a kilo or two of weed killer every spring to keep the garden right. **Spoiling the ship for a ha'penny worth of tar** I call it.*

spread like wildfire merr dhenë, përhapet si era, përhapet me të shpejtë

□ *The news of the great disaster was **spreading like wildfire**.* □ *This business would **spread like wildfire** if it once got out, even without the help of newspapers or radio.* □ *A genuine response is only possible if the document is immediately released, otherwise misunderstandings about it could **spread like fire**.*

spread oneself 1. shtrihem sa gjerë gjatë

□ *Since there was no one else in the compartment I was able to **spread myself**.*

2. mundohem, përpiqem shumë

□ *He had promised to **spread himself** in the preparation of this meal.*

spread one's net shtrij rrjetin

□ *In fact contacting Rohauer is not easy; having **spread his net**, he waits quietly for someone to stumble in.* □ *When the police had gathered fresh men and **spread the net** systematically over the area, a suspect would be picked up even if it were pitch dark.*

spread one's wings merr krahë (fletë), hapet (shtrihet) me guxim

□ *Oh, but they must **spread their***

wings a little. They must make friends in many places.

spread out 1. hap

□ *Mr. Micawber **spread** it **out** on a table....* □ *He **spread out** the map.*

2. hapem, përhapem

□ *The search party **spread out** all over the moor.* □ *Don't all sit together, **spread** yourself **out**.*

spring a leak 1. hapet, çahet (tubi etj.)

□ *One of our pipes **sprung a leak** and flooded the floor.*

2. nxjerr të dhëna

□ *'Would it be possible for Kingsley to **spring a leak** if we put him under sudden arrest?'*

spring to life gjallërohem, veproj aktivisht (me gjallëri)

□ *On hearing his name called the sleeping dog **sprang to life**.* □ *Many dormant branches of our organization are now **springing to** active **life**.*

spring to one's feet brof në këmbë

□ *As the headmaster entered the classroom, 4B **sprang** noisily **to its feet**.* □ *Henry **sprang to his feet** to help his mother with the heavy dish.*

spring to sb's defence hidhem në mbrojtje të

□ *Till now he had ignored the lady to whose **defence** Mason had so gallantly **sprung**.* □ *The stockbroker's wife **sprung to her** husband's **defense**.*

spruce up nisem e stolisem, lahem e rregullohem

□ *I decided to go home and **spruce** myself **up**, to let everyone know that life had not got me down.* □ *The girls were all **spruced up** for the great occasion.* □ *'Tell the children to get **spruced up** for the guests.'*

square meal, a një vakt i bollshëm, i shijshëm etj.

□ *We have been living on biscuits and*

water; we haven't had *a square meal* for ages. □ He looks as though he hasn't had *a square meal* for months.

square peg (in a round hole), a njeri jo në vendin e vet, njeri i papërshtatshëm në punën (pozitën) e vet

□ Poor little snipe—*square peg in round hole* wherever he might be, and all other pegs—thousands upon thousands, that would never fit in. □ I like working outside and they have given me an office job: I am just *a square peg in a round hole.* □ 'Poor Miss Gretry!' he observed. 'Always the square peg in round hole.'

square one's accounts/accounts with shlyej (laj) llogarinë me

□ I should manage to *square accounts with* the bank before the end of the quarter. □ I have no further quarrel with him; *my account with him is squared.*

square one's shoulders ngre supet

□ John *squared his shoulders* as he walked into the interview.

square up (with sb) paguaj llogarinë (në hotel, restorant etj.); rregulloj llogarinë me

□ 'Can I leave you to *square up with* the waiter?' □ 'It's high time I *squared up with* you.'

square the circle orvatem të bëj diçka të pamundur, të zgjidh një problem të pazgjidhshëm

□ There are always new ways of *squaring the circle* just around the next technological corner. □ Tolstoy knew very well from past experience that the gulf between master and peasant could not be bridged. The way to *square the circle* was to get hold of the peasant and educate them.

squeeze one's way in çaj rrugën, futem me zor, rrasem

□ We entered the office in company...

with as many spectators as could *squeeze their way in.*

squeeze out/out of 1. shtrydh (nxjerr) duke shtrydhur

□ 'The lemon looks dry to me, but you may be able to *squeeze out* a few drops. □ We have reached the point where cheese and meat paste can be *squeezed out of* tubes.

2. marr (nxjerr) me dhunë

□ This government will *squeeze* every penny it can *out of* the unfortunate tax-payers. □ If you give in to the blackmailer, he will return to *squeeze out* another hundred later.

squeeze up ngjeshem

□ 'Squeeze up a bit more and let the others sit down.' □ There'll be enough room if we all *squeeze up* a bit.

stab in the back i ngul thikën prapa kurrizit, godas prapa shpine

□ Do not trust anyone in business: they will *stab you in the back* if it suits them. □ While the country was engaged in the north with the enemy, it was *stabbed in the back* by another.

stamp one's foot përplas këmbët

□ 'Don't keep saying that!' Helen *stamped her feet* lightly. 'I've never asked you to pay me back.' □ The audience signified their disapproval with that slow *stamping of feet* that's apt to put the wind up performers of any kind.

stamp out eleminoj, zhduk

□ The police and the medical profession were trying to *stamp out* the increasing wave of drug addiction in young people. □ All the resistance to the regime had been ruthlessly *stamped out.*

stand/have a chance ka mundësi, ka ngjasa

□ I have voted for him, but I don't really think he *stands a chance* of being elected. □ *With his thorough preparations and his skill he* **stands a** *good* **chance** *of winning the contest.* □ *I'm afraid Lisa's family do not* **stand a chance.** *I doubt if their advisers will let them take it to court.* □ *Great numbers of people were smuggled into the country and hidden in remote and distant settlements where they* **stood** *less* **chance** *of being detected.*

stand aside 1. mënjanem, hiqem (bëj) mënjanë

□ *People on the pavement were asked to* **stand aside** *to let the procession through.*

2. rri mënjanë

□ *He* **stands aside** *and lets the current of events sweep past him.* □ *Don't* **stand aside** *and let the others decide the important issues.*

stand back (from) 1. është (qëndron) larg

□ *The school* **stands** *well* **back from** *a busy thoroughfare.* □ *The house* **stands back from** *the road.*

2. qëndroj larg (në distancë)

□ *Sometimes the administrator must* **stand back from** *day-to-day business to grasp the wider patterns of events.*

3. tërhiqem

□ *These were vital discussions* **from** *which he couldn't afford to* **stand back.**

stand by 1. qëndroj përkrah, mbështes, ndihmoj

□ *He was very honorable, Traddles was, and held it as a solemn duty to* **stand by** *one another.* □ *'I'll* **stand by** *you. I'll help you till you get some work.'*

2. rri e shikoj

□ *How can you* **stand by** *and let him treat his dog like that?* □ *We cannot*

stand *idly* **by** *while children go hungry.*

3. i përmbahem, i qëndroj besnik

□ *'I* **stand by** *every word of what I wrote,' I said aloud.* □ *He is a boy who always* **stands by** *his promises.*

stand down 1. largohem nga banka e dëshmitarit

□ *'Unless you have any further questions for him, I think this witness may* **stand down.**

2. tërhiqem, tërheq kërkesën (kandidaturën etj.)

□ *The secretary is proposing to* **stand down** *in favor of a younger man.*

3. çmobilizohet

□ *Certain regiments have chosen to* **stand down** *rather than be amalgamated with other units.*

stand firm/fast qëndroj i paepur (i patundur)

□ *In spite of repeated attempts to storm or fire the gates, the citadel itself still* **stood firm.** □ *If I had not* **stood firm** *and insisted that my plan would be carried through, we would not have won.* □ *The general ordered his soldiers to* **stand fast** *when the enemy advanced.*

stand for 1. përfaqëson

□ *I condemn fascism and all it* **stands for.** □ *I dislike the man and all he* **stands for.**

2. jam për

□ *I* **stand for** *racial tolerance.* □ *The new president* **stood for** *honest government.*

3. duroj

□ *They had been wearing pyjamas until afternoon. Fiorella wouldn't* **stand for** *it.* □ *I won't* **stand for** *this insolence.*

stand guard over sb/sth qëndroj në roje të

□ *Four soldiers* **stood guard over**

the coffin. □ *The Albanian people* **stand** *firm* **guard over** *the independence and sovereignty of their country.*

stand in awe of kam respekt të madh për

□ *The students* **stood in awe of** *their professor because of his fame as a scientist.* □ *The soldier always* **stood in awe of** *his officers.*

stand in (for sb) zëvendëson, zë vendin e

□ *My assistant will* **stand in for** *me while I'm away.* □ *Another man* **stands in for** *the big star in the dangerous scenes.*

stand in one's own light pengoj veten, dëmtoj, i bëj dëm vetes, pengoj realizimin e qëllimeve të veta

□ *Anyhow, if we could see Stener first the latter would not be such a fool as to* **stand in his own light** *in a crisis like that.* □ *Even from the first, you* **stood in your own light** *and darkened mine.*

stand in sb's light pengoj, bëhem pengesë për

□ *I really ought to apologize to you for having* **stood in your light** *so long.* □ *Higgins: You're going to take her away, double quick. (He crosses to the hearth and rings the bell). Doolittle (rising): Now governor. Don't say that. I'm not the man to* **stand in my girl's light.**

stand in sb's way/in the way of sb pengoj, bëhem pengesë për

□ *June's marriage might depend on it. Irene could not decently* **stand in the way of** *Irene's marriage.* □ *If you want to study medicine, we won't* **stand in your way.** □ *'If you want to go overseas to teach, I certainly shan't* **stand in your way.'** □ *No difficulty under heaven could* **stand in the**

way of *that moment which he and Sonia so valued.*

stand on/upon ceremony sillem me ceremoni, bëj ceremonira

□ *One can't* **stand on ceremony** *with fellows like that.* □ *'Come in!' said Dick. 'Don't* **stand upon ceremony.'** □ *... I have no wish to force my conversation on any man who does not desire it. Perhaps you would like to take a nap. If so, pray do not* **stand on ceremony.** □ *I don't like too much* **standing on ceremony** *at a simple party like that.* □ *'Now I'm going to kiss you too, just to show we don't* **stand on ceremony** *here.'* □ *Our distinguished host told us not to* **stand on ceremony,** *just be relaxed and feel at home.*

stand on its head përmbys, kthej përmbys (me kokë poshtë)

□ *She* **stood** *our argument* **on its head.** □ *John* **stood** *the curator's argument* **on its head,** *saying that charging admission to museums would attract more, not fewer, people to them.* □ *In this, as in so many other ways, telepathy and clairvoyance seem to be intent on* **standing** *the ordinary, accepted and understandable course of nature* **on its head.**

stand one's ground ruaj pozicion (luftarak); qëndroj në timen, mbroj pikëpamjet e mia

□ *When Jurgis started slowly across the street toward him, he gave a quick glance about, meditating retreat but then he decided to* **stand his ground.** □ *He was prepared whatever Roberta might think or say to* **stand his ground.** □ *Like a gallant soldier when his musket misses fire, he* **stood his ground,** *and charged with a bayonet.*

stand on one's own (two) feet/legs
qëndron me këmbët e veta

□ *The situation had now become desperate. Some of the family lost their jobs, and Jurgis, had to work in the hell of a fertilizer factory. Then came another accident, of a different type. Ona, his wife was treated vilely by the foreman and Jurgis thrashed the foreman and then he was sent to jail. Now the family could not **stand on its feet** for both Jurgis and Ona lost their jobs.* □ *I'm not giving my son any more help with his business:. He'll have to learn to **stand on his own feet**.* □ *If he doesn't **stand on his own feet** at his age, he'll lose his self-respect.* □ *I **stood** squarely **on my own feet**—I became to a large extent financially independent of my father.*

stand out 1. shquhet, spikat, theks, duket qartë

□ *The black smoke **stood out** in sharp contrast to the white fountains sent up by the enemy shells.* □ *Against a pale blue evening sky, the vapor trails **stood out** clearly.*

2. është shumë më e mirë se, dallon (shquan) shumë nga

□ *Her work **stands out** from the rest as easily as the best.* □ *In this list two names **stand out** particularly.*

3. qëndroj i patundur (i paepur), vazhdoj kundërshtimin (rezistencën)

□ *The troops **stood out** against the enemy until their ammunition were exhausted.* □ *We managed to **stand out** against all attempts to close the company down.*

stand out to sea dal në det të hapur

□ *A destroyer, doubtless part of the local navy, was **standing out to sea**.* □ *They were ordered to **stand** well **out to sea**, out of the range of shore batteries.*

stand pat kundërshtoj (jam kundër) ndryshimeve; nuk ndryshoj (këmbej) mendim; qëndroj i paepur

□ *We tried to get him to change his mind, but he just **stood pat**.* □ *Bill had made up his mind on the question and when his friends tried to change his mind, he **stood pat**.*

stand sb in good stead shërben, hyn në punë, ka vlerë (dobi); është i dobishëm

□ *The picks and shovels they had lent us **stood us in good stead**.* □ *He had a pictorial imagination, which **stood** him **in good stead** in the first hasty shaping of the new museum.* □ *My anorak has **stood** me **in good stead** this winter.* □ *Your university education will **stand you in good stead** when you have to find a job.*

stand still rri në vend-numëro, qëndron pa lëvizur, nuk bën asnjë përparim, ngec në vend

□ *Seeing time apparently **stand still** for three years while the rest of the world surges ahead in the race of life, the Oxford student cannot help wondering what are these intangible values he is supposed to be acquiring.* □ *Police departments have not **stood still**. More men have been sent to cities in the north, and over 85 arrests were made last year.*

stand the strain (of sth) mbaj peshën e

□ *It's a very lucrative job if you can **stand the strain of** almost constant travel.* □ *It's doubtful if his heart would **stand the strain of** another major operation.*

stand the test of time i qëndron sprovave të kohës

□ *Perhaps there is the germ of a novel there based on a theme that has already **stood the test of time**.* □ *His pictures sell for quite large sums now* *but who is to say whether they will* **stand the test of time**.

stand treat paguaj, qeras, gostit
  □ *We had very merry party at Vauxhall. Gus insisting on* **standing treat**.
  □ *We offered to* **stand treat** *to all of us*.

stand up (for) 1. ngrihem në këmbë
  □ *When the Headmaster entered the room, the class would* **stand up** *as a mark of respect*.
2. mbështes, marr anën e
  □ *Despite his dislike of Robin, he had always* **stood up** *for him if some other boy at school attacked him*.

stand up to 1. duron, qëndron gjatë në gjendje (kushte) të mira
  □ *Structurally the desks are sound, and will obviously* **stand up to** *a good deal of wear and tear*. □ *Will this car* **stand up to** *winter conditions here?*
2. rezistoj, i bëj ballë dikujt
  □ *How will Sarah* **stand up to** *her partner's antagonism?* □ *It was brave of her to* **stand up to** *those bullies*.

stand well with sb kam marrëdhënie të mira me
  □ *To proceed with the next phase of their program, they would need more capital. And whether they got the support they needed would depend on how* **well** *they* **stood with** *their overseas backers*.

stare sb in the face 1. e sheh në sy
  □ *Death* **stared** *him* **in the face** *more than once*.
2. është para sysh, ia bën me sy
  □ *The book I was looking for was* **staring** *me* **in the face**. □ *'No wonder you woke up, with that piece of gold plate* **staring** *you* **in the face.'**
3. është i pashmangshëm, i paevitueshëm
  □ *Ruin and bankruptcy were* **staring** *them* **in the face**.

start back 1. kthehem
  □ *Isn't it time we* **started back**? *It's getting dark*.
2. hidhem përpjetë (nga frika etj.)
  □ *I might cause her to* **start back** *in revulsion and terror*. □ *The next moment she* **started back** *and I heard her catch her breath sharply*.

start from scratch nis (filloj) nga hiçi
  □ *The company lost all its plant through enemy bombing, so that in 1945 they* **started** *absolutely* **from scratch**. □ *Jimmy: I'll close that damned sweet stall, and we'll* **start** *everything* **from scratch**. *What do you say? We'll get away from this place*. □ *His business was* **started from scratch** *with $2,000 he'd managed to borrow from a relative*. □ *He lost all his money and had to* **start from scratch**.

start in on sb filloj të qortoj (kritikoj) dikë; filloj t'i bërtas dikujt
  □ *The team were hardly settled in the dressing room before the manager* **started in on** *them for slovenly, unaggressive play*. □ *He* **started in on** *us for poor work*.

start in to do sth/on sth/on doing sth filloj (të bëj diçka)
  □ *Bob, one of the guides, was reading the mail. He put it aside when I came in, brought me a beer, and we* **started in on** *analyzing the climb*. □ *We went back into the living room and* **started in on** *breakfast*.

start off (on) 1. nis, filloj
  □ *He* **started off** *by pointing out the dangers involved in rock climbing*.
2. vë të punojnë
  □ *It's a bright class. I can* **start** *them* **off on** *German in the second year*.

start off on the right/wrong foot (with) filloj mirë/keq me, filloj mbarë/mbrapsht

□ *The new student started off on the wrong foot with the teacher by answering back rudely.* □ *I want the girl to start off on the right foot with my mother.* □ *'Don't light a cigarette when you meet the boss; you'll start off on the wrong foot.'*

start out 1. nisem për udhë (udhëtim)
□ *The small party of explorers started out with high hopes.* □ *What time did you start out?*
2. synoj të bëj
□ *You've done what you started out to do.*

start the ball rolling filloj (nis) bisedën etj.
□ *We've met today to discuss the political situation; perhaps it would be best if I started the ball rolling by asking a few questions.* □ *It was Jane who started the ball rolling.*

start up 1. nis, ndez
□ *The engine started up suddenly.*
□ *The driver started up the motor of the car.*
2. nis karrierën në
□ *Twice he had raised the money and started up in engineering.*
3. ngrihem menjëherë
□ *When he heard the bell, he started up from the chair.*
4. nis ekzekutimin e muzikës
□ *The conductor waved his baton, and the band started up.*

stay away (from sb/sth) qëndroj larg nga
□ *Tell him to stay away from my sister!* □ *Stay away from my children!*

stay behind rri mbas
□ *Several students stayed behind after the lecture to ask question.*
□ *They stayed behind after the party to help clear up.*

stay in rri brenda në shtëpi
□ *The doctor advised me to stay in for*

a few days. □ *We stayed in all that week, while the rain poured down outside.*

stay on qëndron në vend
□ *My hat won't stay on properly.*
□ *You can't load any very large parcels onto the roof rack. They won't stay on in a strong wind, or if you're driving fast.*

stay out (of) 1. rri jashtë
□ *I don't like you staying out so long?*
2. qëndroj larg
□ *Father hoped we'd stay out of trouble in that big city.*

stay put rri në vend, qëndron pa lëvizur
□ *'Ronald, sit down here and stay put,' Tempest said to her husband.*
□ *If there is a serious accident, just stay put until the police arrive.*
□ *Harry's father told him to stay put until he came.* □ *The little child is so full of energy that refuses to stay put for any length of time.* □ *Although I knot my tie carefully, it never seems to stay put.*

stay the course çoj deri në fund (garën, luftën etj.)
□ *I don't think he's sufficiently dedicated to stay the course.*

stay up 1. rri zgjuar
□ *'Will you let us stay up till he comes?* *'Yes, if it's not too late.'*
2. qëndron në vend (varur, ngritur etj.)
□ *The poster only stayed up a few hours, before it was stolen*

stay with 1. qëndroj në shtëpinë e
□ *At half-term we had planned to stay with my sister at her house near London.*
2. vazhdoj të dëgjoj dikë me vëmendje
□ *Please stay with me a moment longer—I'm getting to the point of the story.* □ *'Just stay with me a minute longer. I'm sure I can convince you that we have a reasonable case.*

steady on kujdes, më avash, më shtruar

◻ *Steady on, you two, you'll be hurting each other in a minute.* ◻ *I say, steady on! You can't say things like that about someone you've never met.*

steal a glance/look at sb/sth shoh vjedhurazi

◻ *From time to time she stole a glance from under her long eyelashes.* ◻ *The man's wife chattered on, stealing occasional glances at Peter.* ◻ *He stole a look at her while she sat waiting.* ◻ *Stealing a look round, she saw him stroll....*

steal a march on fitoj terren, dal para të tjerëve (duke vepruar fshehurazi ose tinëzisht), fitoj përparësi (avantazh) ndaj

◻ *When it came to promotion, Jack stole a march on the others in the office by quietly doing favors for the manager.* ◻ *Neither of you wants to look as if the other one had stolen a march on him.* ◻ *And while you're not employing them, other people are stealing a march on you in some other trade.* ◻ *The army stole a march on the enemy by marching at night and attacking them in the morning.*

steal sb's thunder i marr lavdinë (meritat) dikujt

◻ *I know that a later speaker is going to tell you some interesting facts about our trip to Europe, so I am not going to steal his thunder by mentioning them now.* ◻ *Damn them! They will not let me play run, but they steal my thunder!* ◻ *By then Mr. Powell had stolen everyone's thunder with his extraordinary speech at Stockport.* ◻ *Bill intended to nominate Fred for president, but John got up first and stole Fred's thunder.*

steal the show/scene tërheq vëmendjen kryesore, korr duartrokitje të fuqishme të publikut, fitoj admirimin e publikut

◻ *It was a little girl singer that no one had ever heard of before who stole the show.* ◻ *Mary was in only one scene of the play, but she stole the show from the stars.*

steer a middle course gjej një rrugë të mesme

◻ *The judge will have to steer a middle course between being too severe with the accused men and being too easy on them.* ◻ *The reporter, whose business is to present relevant facts in an acceptable form, could and should steer a middle course.* ◻ *Working hard at school had a very definite negative rating. But my mother had taught me to love books and feel the fascination of learning. So I steered a middle course.*

steer clear of evitoj, qëndroj larg prej

◻ *Try to steer clear of political topics at the dinner party tonight: some of our guests have very strong opinions on politics.* ◻ *'What the hell's going on here?' said Robert. People were beginning to steer clear of me and Cartridge, and he must have wanted to investigate.*

stem the flow (of sth) ndaloj rrjedhën e

◻ *I took out a packet of cigarettes and offered him one, hoping to stem the flow a bit, but he accepted it and lit it without breaking the conversational rhythm.* ◻ *There is a need for a great many local industries to be set up to stem the flow of young people to the cities.*

stem the tide (of sth) ndaloj (pengoj) shpërthimin e

□ *The second argument looks to the home rather than the school for methods of breaking the cycle of deprivation and* **stemming the** *rising tide of illiteracy.*

step by step hap pas hapi
□ *The development of the uprising was a whole process which began with anti-fascist demonstrations and small fighting actions and was raised* **step by step** *to the general uprising of the people.* □ **Step by step** *the work was brought to a close.*

step down 1. heq dorë; jap dorëheqjen
□ *If they disagreed seriously while I was chairman, I would at once* **step down.** □ *If the people want him to form a new party he will do so, or even* **step down** *if they say so.*
2. ul shpejtësinë
□ *The train was approaching the station, so the engineer* **stepped** *it* **down.**

step in ndërhyj
□ *If the police had not* **stepped in** *when they did, there would have been serious violence.* □ *Seeing that I was lost for an answer, John* **stepped in** *to save the situation.* □ *The union leadership* **stepped in** *and made the strike official.*

step into sb's shoes zë vendin e
□ *When the chairman retires, the vice-chairman will* **step into his shoes.** □ *The father handed over control, and Geoffrey* **stepped into** *the director's shoes with the confidence of someone who had been measuring himself carefully for the responsibility involved.* □ *There were a half dozen available candidates, anyone of whom would have rejoiced to* **step into his shoes.**

step on it/step on the gas 1. shpejtoj, rris shpejtësinë, shkel gazin
□ *'Tell the driver to* **step on it**—*we*

don't want to be late!' □ **Step on it** *if you don't want to be behind everybody!*
2. nxitoj, luaj këmbët, i jap këmbëve,
□ *Don't be so slow,* **step on it.**

step on sb's toes/corns e shkel (e prek) në kallo (në lyth) dikë, lëndoj, prek ndjenjat e
□ *'As a new boy here, I'm anxious not to* **step on** *anyone's* **toes,** *but it seems to me that something ought to be done about the tremendous losses through pilfering.* □ *He walks into every new situation with the sensitivity of an ox,* **stepping on** *people's* **corns** *right and left.*

step up 1. ngrihem (hipi) në pozitë
□ *This year Mary is secretary of the club, but I am sure she will* **step up** *to president next year.*
2. shtoj, rris; përmirësoj
□ *Resources allotted to these operations should be* **stepped up.**

stew in one's own juice tiganiset (cingariset, skuqet, fërgohet) me dhjamin e vet
□ *'Johnson's been trying to stir up trouble between the two of us for months and now his scheming has bounced back on him.' 'Well, don't feel obliged to make things comfortable for him. He can* **stew in his own juice** *for a bit.'* □ *He was very nasty to everyone and now no one will speak to him; let him* **stew in his own juice.** □ *John lied to Tom, but Tom found out. Now Tom is making John* **stew in his own juice.** □ *They were compelled... to* **stew in their own juice....**

stick about/around rri (pres) diku afër
□ *'Stick around for a while—the boss will soon be back.'* □ *John's father told him to* **stick around** *and they would go fishing.*

451

stick at sth këmbëngul; punoj me këmbëngulje, nuk i ndahem (punës); jepem (qepem) pas

□ *I stick at my painting five or six hours a day.* □ *'You can get the report written inside a week, but you'll need to stick at it.'*

stick at nothing nuk ndalet para asgjëje

□ *'Like you? Of course he doesn't like you. He'll stick at nothing to get you out of the way!'*

stick by sb qëndron në krah të dikujt

□ *Her husband stuck by her in good times and bad.* □ *The older staff would stick by the firm through thick and thin.*

stick down 1. ngjit

□ *'Don't forget to put the postal order in before you stick down the envelope.'* □ *The corner of the page has been stuck down; I can't read what's written there.*

2. lë, lëshoj

□ *'You can stick the table down in a corner for the time being.'* □ *'Where does the mail go?' 'Oh, stick it down over here.'*

3. shkruaj

□ *'Stick down your names at the top of the form.'*

stick in one's mind mbetet gjallë në mendje, mbetet i pashlyer në mendje

□ *There are passages in that play which still stick in my mind twenty years after the first performance.* □ *It is the unheroic sacrifices of ordinary people that chiefly stick in the mind.* □ *His words on that day must have stuck in the minds of many people.*

stick in one's throat/gullet/craw s'e përtyp dot, s'e kapërdij dot, më ngec në fyt

□ *He offered me a lot of money if I helped; but I could not accept his*

plan: *it stuck in my throat.* □ *When I thought of about marrying Myrtle— yes, there were many, many moments when I did think of marrying her— this angry hurt recurred. I could not get over it. It stuck, as they say, in my craw.* □ *It sticks in my throat to have to accept charity from them.* □ *She knows that her name sticks in my throat.*

stick one's neck/chin out vë veten në rrezik, bëhem (tregohem) trim, nxjerr gjoksin, marr guximin

□ *'I'm not sure of the answer myself, but I'll stick my neck out and say that John's solution is correct.'* □ *'You can support the campaign if you want to, but I'm not sticking my neck out for anybody.'* □ *When I was in trouble, Paul was the only one who would stick his neck out to help me.* □ *I may be sticking my neck out, but I think he's going to win.* □ *It is risky to forecast the results of elections, but I'm going to stick my neck out and say that our party will win the next election with a large majority.*

stick/stand out (a mile) duket qartë (një kilometër larg)

□ *He tried to disguise the purpose of his visit, but his real intentions stuck out a mile.* □ *'It sticks out a mile that he's hoping to take over your job.'* □ *You must be able to see the solution to the problem now; it sticks out a mile!*

stick together qëndroj (jam) i bashkuar

□ *'We've been in worse situations than this before. If we keep calm and stick together, we shall be all right.'* □ *New arrivals in a community are sometimes accused of sticking together. This may be because they are given little encouragement to feel at one with their neighbours.*

stick to 1. i përmbahem
□ *I find his lectures very confusing; he never **sticks to** the point.* □ *'This is getting us nowhere. Let us **stick to** the facts.'*
2. i qëndroj besnik
□ *'Once we've sorted out a program of events, let's for Heaven's sake try to **stick to** it.'*
3. vazhdoj, nuk i ndahem
□ *He **stuck to** the task until it was finished.*

stick to one's colors qëndroj në timen, mbroj bindjet (pikëpamjet) e mia
□ *But I called to mind that I was speaking for his good and **stuck to my colors**.*

stick/stand to one's guns qëndroj në timen, mbroj pikëpamjet e mia, ruaj pozicionin tim
□ *So far he has **stuck to his guns**, regardless of the pressure put on him.* □ *Anthony... It has been said that I am not the man I was ... However that may be, I am man enough to **stand to my guns**.* □ *I **stuck to my guns** and refused to be overruled by my political masters.* □ *'If you think you have a reasonable case, don't give way. **Stick to your guns**.'*

stick to sb like a bur/burr/like a limpet/ like a leech iu bë rrodhe (rriqër), iu ngjit si balta (si bajga) pas këpucës
□ *He got rid of his travelling companions, who at first **stuck as fast as burs**.*

stick up 1. vendos, fiksoj, ngjis
□ *Supporters of the government **stuck up** pictures of the Prime Minister in their front windows.*
2. kërcënoj me armë (për të grabitur)
□ *Masked bandits **stuck up** a bullion train yesterday.*

still waters run deep thëngjilli i mbuluar djeg i përvëluar
□ *Jane is a very quiet girl, but she may surprise us all one day. **Still waters run deep**, you know.* □ *'She's never shown any sign of having a mind of her own before.' 'Perhaps she's never needed to. **Still waters run deep**.'*

sting sb to the quick lëndon, prek thellë
□ *The insult to her **stung him to the quick**.*

stir one's/the blood ia ndez gjakun (shpirtin), ngre peshë, bëj të gjallërohet (të marrë hov)
□ *The music really **stirred my blood**.* □ *Speak for yourself. The sound of bagpipes doesn't **stir my blood**.*

stir up ndez, nxis, provokoj, shkaktoj
□ *He is blamed for **stirring up** hatred between nations.* □ *The men are being **stirred up** by the outsiders.*

stir up a hornet's nest trazoj folenë e grenxave
□ *The principal **stirred up a hornets's nest** by changing the rules at school.*

stone's throw (away) from, a dy hapa larg, shumë afër
□ *Not **a stone's throw from** Whitehall, there stands, amidst all the hum and bustle of the great metropolis, an old decaying pile.* □ *Police and demonstrators have fought viciously in Red Lion Square, only **a stone's throw from** this office.*

stone-broke/stony-broke trokë, pa një dysh në xhep
□ *The man gambled and was soon **stone-broke**.* □ *Could you buy me a cup of tea; I'm **stony-broke**.*

stoop so low (as to do sth) e ul veten kaq poshtë sa të
□ *He tried to make me accept a bribe— I hope I would never **stoop so low**.*

stop at nothing s'ndalet para asgjëje

☐ *He is a dangerous man, who will* ***stop at nothing*** *to get what he wants.*

stop dead (in one's track) ndaloj befas (në vend), ngrij në vend, ndaloj menjëherë

☐ *As I did so, a figure appeared round the corner of the corridor. All three of us* ***stopped dead.*** ☐ *'Perhaps you need a new battery?' 'I'd have had some warning if it was that. The transmission just* ***stopped dead.'*** ☐ *She went to Adrian's office after leaving him, and was rather disconcerted to find her Uncle Lionel there. They* ***stopped dead*** *in their discussion.*

stop off/over (at/in) ndalem, qëndroj diku rrugës për pak kohë

☐ *'We'll* ***stop off*** *for a few days in Paris to visit your cousins.'* ☐ *We* ***stopped off*** *after school at the soda fountain before going home.* ☐ *These are pictures of the Jumbo-jet passengers when they* ***stopped over*** *in Rome.*

stop short ndalem, qëndroj në vend

☐ *He had just recollection sufficient to* ***stop short*** *in the midst of the dangerous sentence.* ☐ *He ran down the main road,* ***stopped short*** *when he saw the police car and doubled back up the alley.* ☐ *He* ***stopped short*** *in the middle of the story.*

stop short of sth/doing sth nuk shkon aq larg sa të, nuk arrin deri në

☐ *He can be ruthless in getting what he wants, but I believe he would* ***stop short of*** *blackmail.* ☐ *... I had but just* ***stopped short of*** *insulting the beautiful being by whom it was proffered.*

stop up rri natën vonë, rri ngritur (çuar)

☐ *We* ***stopped up*** *late to hear the midnight news.* ☐ *'I shall be in late, but don't bother to* ***stop up*** *for me.'*

storm in the tea-cup shumë zhurmë për asgjë, furtunë në një gotë uji

☐ *All the argument about the elections to the village council is just* ***a storm in a teacup.*** ☐ *And really it was all such* ***a storm in a teacup***, *to make this fuss about somebody coming back unexpectedly to spend a Sunday!* ☐ *Let us suppose that the whole matter comes to nothing, that it turns out to be* ***a storm in a tea-cup***, *a chimera.*

straight from the horse's mouth nga burim i drejtpërdrejtë, nga burim i besueshëm

☐ *I swear that this information is genuine: I got it* ***straight from the horse's mouth.*** ☐ *They are going to be married. I got the news* ***straight from the horse's mouth.***

straight from the shoulder drejtpërdrejt, hapur, sinqerisht, sy ndër sy

☐ *Johnson always says what he thinks you'd like to hear. I prefer a man who speaks* ***straight from the shoulder***. ☐ *This was a rebuff* ***straight from the shoulder*** *and there was no way to conceal his embarrassment.* ☐ *What's really the matter with me, doctor? I'm not a child, you know—you needn't be afraid to give it to me* ***straight from the shoulder***.

straight out pa ngurrim; sy ndër sy

☐ *I told him* ***straight out*** *that I thought he was lying.*

straighten out zgjidh, sqaroj; heq dyshimin nga mendja

☐ *We have inherited a very confused situation, which we are now trying to* ***straighten out.*** ☐ *The disagreement between them will not be* ***straightened out*** *overnight.* ☐ *He seriously misunderstands certain aspects of our plan; I'd like to* ***straighten him out*** *on these.*

strain every nerve tendos nervat, vë të gjitha forcat, bëj të gjitha përpjekjet
□ *They* **strained every nerve** *to make the action a success.*

strain one's ears i bëj veshët katër
□ *He* **strained his ears** *to catch any possible movement.*

strain one's eyes lodh (sforcoj) sytë; i bëj sytë katër
□ *The sentry thought he had seen something moving in the dark and* **strained his eyes** *to make out what it was.* □ *... You should* **strain your eyes** *and don't overlook such a fact.*

strange to say çuditërisht, për çudi
□ *He was supposed to have died during the war but,* **strange to say,** *many people reported seeing him alive many years afterwards.* □ **Strange to say,** *he won!*

straw in the wind, a shenjë paralajmëruese
□ *I had to set myself to wait, picking up any rumor from Barford, any* **straw in the wind.** □ *It's something more than mere hooliganism. There have been one or two other* **straws in the wind.** □ *Both countries have increased the size of their armies; many people are taking this as* **a straw in the wind** *that they may soon be at war with each other.* □ *The doctor's worried face was* **a straw in the wind.**

straw that breaks the camel's back pika që mbush kupën
□ *If they add another fifty pence to the price of this article it will be the* **straw that breaks the camel's back.** *People will stop buying it.*

streets ahead (of sb/sth) qëndron larg, s'mund të krahasohet, është si nata me ditën, ku e ku më i mirë (më i aftë, më i mençur etj.)
□ *We're* **Streets Ahead Of** *The Rest!*

In linen hire and garments it's the care we take that makes us great.

strengthen sb's hand i jep dorë
□ *The power stations, which have so far coped remarkably well with the problems thrown up by the miners' strike, will be disturbed by an overtime ban and work-to-rule. This will both* **strengthen** *the miners'* **hand** *and produce a drastic worsening of the problems of keeping the country adequately supplied with fuel.*

stretch/strain a point 1. bëj një përjashtim (një lëshim)
□ *You really should have your ticket with you to be admitted, but since you are a regular customer, we'll* **stretch a point.** □ *She doesn't have all the qualifications but I think we should* **stretch a point** *in her favor.*
2. kaloj kufijtë e arsyeshëm
□ *We've not quite so much proof as I could wish. It would be* **straining a point** *to arrest him, as it stands.* □ *It would be* **stretching a point** *to say that he is a brilliant pianist, although he is certainly very good.*

stretch one's legs shpij këmbët
□ *One of the advantages of travelling long distances by train is that you can always get up and* **stretch** *your* **legs** *by walking along the train.*

stretch out zgjat, shtrij
□ *The child* **stretched out** *its hands to seize the toy.*

stretch (oneself) out shtrihem sa gjerë gjatë
□ *He* **stretched (himself) out** *in front of the fire and fell asleep.* □ *A few holiday makers were* **stretched out** *in the sun outside the window.*

strictly speaking në kuptimin e ngushtë (e përpiktë)
□ **Strictly speakin,** *a whale is not a fish.* □ *Social psychology,* **strictly**

speaking deals with the behavior of the people.

strike an attitude/pose marr një pozë
□ *Hylda Baker came out from behind the bar, **struck an attitude** and began to declaim.* □ *He **struck an attitude** of defiance with a typically hard-hitting speech.*

strike a balance (between ... and ...) gjej një rrugë të mesme, mbaj drejtpeshimin mes, vendos një përpjesëtim të drejtë mes
□ *You have to **strike a balance** between working too hard **and** working hard enough.* □ *It was difficult to **strike** the right **balance** between justice **and** expediency.*

strike a bargain with sb arrij në marrëveshje, bie në ujdi, arrij një pazar
□ *We could not agree on a price for some time, but finally we **struck a bargain**.* □ *Let's **strike a bargain**. If you let me read your books, I'll let you read mine.*

strike a blow for ndihmoj, i vij në ndihmë, veproj në mbështetje të
□ *By publishing such an article criticizing the government, the newspaper has **struck a blow for** the freedom of press.* □ *By their action, they **struck a blow for** democracy.*

strike/sound a false note stonon
□ *He **struck a false note** when he arrived for the wedding in old clothes.*

strike at the root of shkatërroj që në rrënjë; zbuloj burimin e
□ *By building these factories, the government hopes to **strike at the root of** poverty in this country.*

strike down rrëzon, këput, e vë poshtë (sëmundja etj.)
□ *Many active professional men at the peak of their careers have been **struck down** by heart disease.*

strike fear/terror into sb's heart i kall frikën (tmerrin, datën)
□ *The news of the epidemic **struck terror** into the population.*

strike gold gjej Amerikën
□ *With one van, he opened up a small delivery business, somewhat tentatively, but soon found that he'd **struck gold**.*

strike (it) lucky kam fat
□ *We certainly **struck it lucky** with the weather.* □ *It was the Americans who first drilled for oil here and **struck lucky**.*

strike it rich bëhem i pasur
□ *Sonia: Everyone who made a terrible fortune has been out of their mind. There was a man with motor cars in America and that man who **struck it rich** with frying oil.* □ *Everyone wanted to buy one of the new gadgets, and their inventor **struck it rich**.*

strike off 1. këpus, pres
□ *He **struck off** the head of the dandelion with a swish of his cane.* □ *He **struck off** the rotten branches with an axe.*
2. heq emrin
□ ***Strike** her name **off** the list.* □ *The Law Society ordered that their names be **struck off** the roll of solicitors.*

strike out 1. i heq vizë (kryq)
□ *The editor **struck out** the whole paragraph.* □ *The offending parts of the article have been **struck out**.*
2. godas, qëlloj me forcë
□ *He lost his temper and **struck out** wildly.*

strike/take root lëshon (zë, hedh, shtie) rrënjë, zë vend të qëndrueshëm, rrënjoset fort
□ *The cause has **taken** deep **root**, and has spread its branches far and wide.*

strike sb dumb/speechless lë pa gojë, lë gojëhapur

□ *When he heard that, he was **struck dumb** with amazement.*

strike up zë, nis

□ *He'd **strike up** conversations with people to hear them speak in the local accent. □ In some way we **struck up** quite a friendship... He seemed to take a fancy to me from the first and within two days of our meeting he came to see me at Lee.*

strike while the iron is hot hekuri rrihet sa është i nxehtë

□ *I have just been chosen the salesman of the year, so I have decided to ask for a raise in salary now; I might as well **strike while the iron is hot**. □ His aunt was in a good mood and, thinking to **strike while the iron was hot**, he put Tina's proposal to her then. □ **Striking the iron while it was hot**, Daniel said they might as well stroll along to look at it now. He would first telephone the dealer to say they were coming.*

string along 1. mashtroj, tërheq për hunde

□ *'I've a feeling that the young man is just **stringing us along**. Check his credentials.' □ Mary was **stringing John along** for years but she didn't mean to marry him.*

2. rri me, shoqëroj dikë, shkoj pas

□ *Take my advice—**string along** with me, I know this business inside out.*

string sb up var në litar

□ *If the crowd catches him, they'll **string** him **up** on the nearest tree. □ Two of the rebel leaders were **strung up** as a warning to the others.*

string together lidh, kombinoj

□ *It was as much as he could do to **string together** a few words of French. □ His sentences were so*

badly **strung together** *that it was difficult to grasp their meaning.*

stuff and nonsense gjepura, dokrra

□ *Don't believe about what you read about him in the newspapers; it's **stuff and nonsense**. □ **Stuff and nonsense**! You don't know what you're talking about. □ And how could anything be after her? What sort of thing? Oh, **stuff and nonsense**, it was time she got over her childish fears.*

stumbling block, a pengesë

□ *The failure to agree on manning levels is **a** major **stumbling block** to progress in the talks.*

such as si, të tilla si

□ *Wild flowers **such as** orchids and primroses are becoming rare.*

suck sb's blood pi (thith) gjakun e

□ *The wealth he had acquired by **sucking the blood** of his miserable victims, had but swelled him like a bloated spider.*

suit/fit sb's book përputhet me dëshirat (planet, synimet etj.), i vjen për shtat

□ *Dawson wouldn't have taken Mark into partnership if it hadn't **suited his book**. □ It **suits my book**, if I never have to go there again. □ Yes, bring the parcel on Thursday, that will **suit my book** quite well.*

suit sb down to the ground i përshtatet për mrekulli, i shkon shumë për shtat

□ *Joe had got himself a job as one of the gardeners. Literally and metaphorically it **suited** him **down to the ground**.*

suit the action to the word/suit one's actions to one's words përputh fjalën me veprimin, përputh fjalët me veprat

□ *'Politicians should learn to **suit their actions to their words**. Of*

*course, I say this more in hope than
expectation.* □ *'There's nothing we can
do except give you a drink.' He suited
the action to the word.* □ *On this occasion the action was suited to the word.
A check arrived by the next post.*

sum up përmbledh, bëj një përm-
bledhje

□ *I find it hard to sum up after such a
wide-ranging debate.*

summon up 1. ngjall, sjell, evokon

□ *The odor summoned up memories
of my childhood.*

2. mbledh

□ *Summoning up his last ounce of
strength, he flung himself over the
finishing line.*

sure enough në të vërtetë, ç'është e
vërteta

□ *We didn't really expect our team to
win and, sure enough, they were
beaten 3-0.* □ *I said it would happen,
and sure enough it did.*

swallow one's pride ul hundën, ul
kokën, heq dorë nga mëndjemadhësia
(krenaria)

□ *Where money was concerned she
had little pride. What little she had
she swallowed and wrote to Elvira.*
□ *He had more practical matters to
deal with. Having swallowed the
pride, he did not intend to prostrate
himself for nothing.* □ *After Bill lost
the race, he swallowed his pride and
shook hands with the winner.*

swallow one's words gëlltit (ha) fjalët

□ *He told me I wouldn't pass the test
but I'm determined to make him
swallow his words.*

swarm with gëlon, mizëron, zien nga

□ *The beach was swarming with
bathers.*

swear by 1. betohem

□ *A witness swears by the Bible that
he will tell the truth.*

2. kam besim te, i zë besë

□ *When John has to go somewhere fast,
he swears by his bike to get there.*

swear sb to secrecy përbetoj dikë të
mos nxjerrë sekretin

□ *I swore her to secrecy about what I
told her.* □ *Everyone connected with
the project was sworn to secrecy.*

swear in vë (shtie) në be; bën betimin

□ *Let the witness be sworn in.* □ *The
full committee has to attend when a
new member is sworn in.*

sweat blood 1. punoj shumë, më kullon
djersa, derdh djersë, më del shpirti

□ *You're not used to sweating blood
for your money. But that's not the
way to get it. Just lie on your back
and whistle and it'll come.* □ *He
must have sweated blood dragging
himself out of there with a broken
leg.*

2. jam i shqetësuar, nuk e ndiej veten
të qetë, rri si mbi gjemba

□ *The students sweated blood as they
waited for the results of their exams.*
□ *The engine of the airplane stopped,
and the pilot sweated blood as he
glided to a safe landing.*

sweat one's guts out rraskapitem;
punoj si kalë

□ *'Why should I sweat my guts out
for twelve pounds a week?'* □ *Normally, I sweated my guts out on a
milling-machine with the rest.*

sweat out 1. shëroj (nxjerr, heq) me
djersë

□ *When you feel a flu coming on, get
into the bed and sweat it out.*

2. pres me ankth

□ *John was sweating out the results
of the college exams.*

sweep sb off his feet entuziazmoj pa
masë, mbush me emocion (entuziazëm, admirim, dashuri etj.); impre-
sionoj; ngre më këmbë

□ *His speeches were calculated to sweep uncommitted people off their feet.* □ *The handsome young man swept her off her feet.*

sweep sth under the carpet/rug fsheh, mbuloj, mbaj të fshehur

□ *Unpleasant episodes in his early career were swept under the carpet.*

□ *'There's enough hard evidence swept under the carpet to start a couple of major scandals.'* □ *In many places, drug abuse by school children is swept under the rug.*

swim against the current/stream/tide shkoj kundër rrymës

□ *He is trying to persuade people to use up less fuel, but I'm afraid he's swimming against the tide.*

switch off mbyll (dritën etj.)

□ *Television sets have the great advantage that they can be switched off.* □ *Switch off the gas at the main.*

switch on hap (dritën etj.)

□ *She had come to switch on the lights and light the fires.* □ *Don't switch the radio on yet.*

T

take aback habis, i ngjall habi; shastis, lë pa mend, lë me gojë hapur

□ *The reply **took** him so much **aback** that for a moment he was lost for words.* □ *He caught sight of my appearance for the first time and was **taken aback** at how different I looked.* □ *He was somewhat **taken aback** by the news that the police intended to prosecute him.*

take a back seat kaloj në plan të dytë, zë një vend të parëndësishëm, luaj një rol të

□ *He used to be the most important man in the team, but since his illness he has had to **take a back seat**.* □ *She does not have to **take a back seat** to any singer alive.* □ *It is highly unlikely that Slater intends to move out of the scene or even **take a back seat** for long.* □ *After forty years in the business it's time for me to **take a back seat** and make room for younger men and new ideas.*

take a bad turn merr për keq; keqësohet nga shëndeti

□ *His affairs **took a bad turn**.* □ *He was just walking to work when suddenly he **took a bad turn** and had to be taken to the hospital.*

take a bow pranoj falënderimet (duartrokitjet etj.) duke u përkulur me nderim

□ *It was a delicious meal, Sheila. You must come and **take a bow**.*

take a chance/chances on sth rrezikoj, riskoj, ndërmarr një veprim të rrezikshëm, veproj me rrezik (me risk)

□ *He said people should be ready to **take chances**. He said people shouldn't be afraid.* □ *John's a wonderful driver. He'd have been prepared to **take chances** that no other driver would take.* □ *Johnie thinks he's smart, but he's **taking** a lot of **chances**. He'll end up in court yet.* □ *The thieves **took a chance** on the owner of the house staying away all day—a chance that paid off handsomely.*

take account of marr (kam) parasysh, i jap rëndësinë e duhur

□ *I cannot promise that the parcel will arrive in time; we have to **take account of** the fact that the postmen may be going on strike soon.* □ *When judging his performance, don't **take** his age **into account**.* □ *In judging the progress he has made in his studies, we must **take account of** the fact that he has been working hard all the year round.* □ *The time comes for a country to **take account of** its situation.*

take action marr masa

□ *Immediate **action** must be **taken** to stop the fire spreading.* □ *They **took** prompt **action** to finish it in time.* □ *We have **taken action** to eliminate insect pests.*

take a decision marr vendim

□ *They had **taken the decision** without consulting me—which they had no right to do.* □ ***Decisions** to depart from the rules should not be **taken** lightly, nor should they be taken by individual police officers.*

take a dim view of 1. shoh me dyshim, ndjehem i pasigurt (i shqetësuar) për
□ *Tom took a dim view of his chances of passing the exam.*
2. jam kundër, nuk miratoj (pëlqej)
□ *I cannot phone you; my boss takes a dim view of employees using the phone.* □ *John's father took a dim view of his wanting to borrow the car.*

take a dislike to sb/sth s'më pëlqen, s'e honeps dot, kam antipati
□ *Mrs. Shaw took as vehement a dislike as it was possible for one of gentle nature to do against Milton.* □ *I don't know why, but I took a strong dislike to him as soon as I saw him.*

take advantage of sb/sth 1. përdor, shfrytëzoj mirë
□ *They took full advantage of the hotel's facilities.*
2. shfrytëzoj, përfitoj, nxjerr përfitime
□ *She took advantage of my generosity.* □ *He has mastered papa's weakness and taken advantage of them.* □ *He was himself conscious of the awkward situation yet he was determined in his own interests to take advantage of it to the full.* □ *To increase our working efficiency it is necessary to take advantage of every moment we have.*

take a fancy to pëlqej, më hyn në qejf, më hyn në zemër, shtie sevda
□ *I've suddenly taken a fancy to detective stories.* □ *What would his father be advising now... what would he say to this menace against her to whom he had taken such a fancy in the last weeks of his life?* □ *'He seemed to take rather a fancy to me...'* □ *I imagine he did not think I was a beggar, but an eccentric sort of lady, who had taken a fancy to his brown loaf.*

take a firm/strong line mbaj (ndjek) një qëndrim të vendosur
□ *School regulations still included the wearing of a uniform and the headmaster took a very firm line on this.* □ *'I've no use for that kind of woman,' Harold said. 'If he had to have her around, he should have taken a strong line with her from the first.*

take after sb i ngjaj
□ *Helen: You're not fond of work, are you? Jo: No, I take after you.* □ *Your daughter does not take after you in any way.* □ *The son seems to take much after his mother than his father.*

take a hand (in) ndërhyn, angazhohet, vë dorë
□ *A salesman who is doing the rounds in Newtown seems to be too clever for the law, that is until Sgt Watt takes a hand in events*

take a hint kuptoj aluzionin
□ *'I don't know what you're talking about,' he muttered, in a tone that was clearly intended to put an end to the discussion. But Dr. Bottwink seemed incapable of taking a hint.*
□ *She yawned and stretched her arms. 'Time for me to go,' said Peter. 'I can take a hint.'* □ *I think he'll move out. I'm sure the hint has been taken.* □ *It was around midnight when my host remarked that he would have to get up very early the next day. I took the hint and left.*

take a jaundiced view of shikoj me dyshim (cmirë, xhelozi, zemërim etj.)
□ *I must say that I take a jaundiced view of Bill's promises; he has broken his promises so many times in the past.*

take a joke pranoj shaka
□ *He danced and rode well; and was*

courteous to ladies; he could take a joke, and make one.

take a leaf out of sb's book kopjoj, imitoj dikë; veproj (sillem) njëlloj si

□ *I am going to take a leaf out of your book, and stop smoking, just as you have done.*

take a liking to pëlqej, më hyn në zemër

□ *I saw a good deal of Mrs. Strong, both because she had taken a liking to me, on the morning of my introduction to the Doctor, and was always afterwards kind to me.* □ *He had taken an immediate liking to Battersea Park.*

take a look (at) shikoj, shqyrtoj, kontrolloj; hedh një sy

□ *'Those drawings, did you examine them?' 'I sent them straight on.' 'Well, take a good look at them now!'* □ *He took a quick look at his notes.*

take a load/weight off sb's mind çliroj nga një barrë e rëndë, i heq merakun (shqetësimin)

□ *It would take a load from all their minds.*

take an interest in interesohem, tregoj interes për

□ *It was declared by the nurse and by some women in the neighbourhood who had taken a lively interest in me...* □ *It was wonderful, when one came to think of it that these men should have taken an interest in the work they did.* □ *You never took an interest in what he did.* □ *Rock-climbing is an activity in which more and more young people are taking an interest.*

take/swear an oath betohem

□ *He took an oath that he would never return to England until he had found his missing son.* □ *Before giving evidence the witness had to*

take an oath. □ *Government employees swear an oath not to reveal official secrets.*

take apart 1. zbërthej, çmontoj

□ *Nick had taken the fuel gauge apart and spread the bits all over the carpet.* 2. mund, shpartalloj

□ *Becker took Connors apart in the third set.* 3. kritikoj ashpër

□ *Her second novel was taken apart by the critics.*

take (a) pride in sb/sth krenohem me

□ *She takes great pride in her children's success.* □ *He takes a great pride in his work.*

take a rise out of sb ngacmoj, nxeh

□ *My intention was just to take a rise out of you.* □ *Don't pay any attention to what they say; they're taking a rise out of you.*

take a risk/risks rrezikoj, riskoj

□ *'But she'd take the risk of losing me,' he thought. 'Sooner than lose her child!...'* □ *The Eskimos take risks with their lives, of course, just because they live in such a difficult and hostile environment, but the whole concept of going out to look for an adventure is totally alien to them.* □ *You mean you've never seen this house you've bought? Aren't you taking rather a risk?* □ *You can't get rich without taking risks.* □ *That's a risk I'm prepared to take.*

take a shine to sb/sth filloj të pëlqej, të më hyjë në zemër

□ *Our little girl doesn't usually like visitors, but she's taken quite a shine to you.* □ *I think that dog has taken a shine to me; it follows me everywhere.* □ *He took a shine to his new teacher the very first day.*

take a short cut i bie shkurt, pres shkurt

□ We **took a short cut** to the faculty avoiding the main road. □ I **took a short cut** across the field to get to school.

take a sight marr shenjë, marr nishan

□ You should **take a** careful **sight** before firing.

take a stand marr (mbaj) qëndrim, shpreh mendimin (pikëpamjen) time

□ She **took a** firm **stand** on nuclear disarmament.

take a turn bëj një shëtitje të shkurtër

□ 'Half an hour to breakfast,' he thought, 'I'll **take a turn** in the Garden.' □ We wanted to **take a turn** on a bicycle.

take a turn for the better merr për mirë, përmirësohet

□ When he parted from Bramwell he ventured the hope that the case might quickly **take a turn for the better.**

□ Business was poor until last Sunday, but things have **taken a turn for the better** since then.

take a turn for the worse merr për keq, keqësohet

□ His illness **took a turn for the worse.**

take away/out 1. marr me vete

□ 'They do a very good curry here, and you can **take** food **out** if you like.

□ Two chicken curries and rice to **take away,** please.

2. heq, largoj

□ The doctor has given her some tablets to **take away** her pain. □ This queer worry and apprehension had **taken away** all her pleasure in her regained mobility.

3. heq, zbres

□ '**Take away** this number from that, and tell me how much you have left.'

take back 1. tërheq (fjalët etj.), marr mbrapsht (fjalët etj.)

□ He would have given anything to be

a small boy, who by saying '**Take back** what I said,' could erase a whole conversation. □ After he saw his mistake he **took back** what he said. □ Unless you **take it back** and apologize within two minutes, I'll sue you for damages for defamation of character.

2. pranoj kthimin e

□ We only **take** goods **back** if customers can produce the receipt.

3. i rikujton, i sjell ndër mend; e kthen prapa

□ The smell of seaweed **took** him **back** to his childhood.

take by kap për (në)

□ He **took** Mary gently **by** the wrist, and drew her aside. □ Don't **take** the knife **by** the blade.

take by storm 1. marr me sulm

□ We waited until it was dark and then **took** the fort **by storm.** □ Our troops **took** the village **by storm.**

2. pushton, fiton zemrën, bën për vete

□ His new play **took** London **by storm;** everyone was talking about it.

□ Even during the morning she received a congratulatory message. 'You seem to have **taken** the town **by storm,**' he wrote. □ 'You have **taken** my confidence **by storm,**' he continued. □ The comic **took** the audience **by storm.**

take care ki (bëj) kujdes

□ Always **take care** when you are crossing a busy road. □ Goodbye, and **take care!** □ He wouldn't suffer half as much as he does with his stomach if he **took care** to eat properly.

take care of kujdesem, përkujdesem për

□ '**Take care of** him, officer,' said the old gentlemen, raising his hands instinctively; 'he'll fall down.'

□ *Blodwen'll* **take care of** *you.*
□ *Little Katrina had to* **take care of** *her little brother who was a cripple.*
□ *You must go: we'll* **take care of** *the house until you come back.*
2. merrem, përgjigjem për
□ *Smith* **takes care of** *marketing and publicity.*

take charge of marr drejtimin (kontrollin) e, marr përsipër (një detyrë), marr në ngarkim
□ *But I am afraid I had a supreme satisfaction in* **taking charge of** *Mr. Barkis' will.* □ *They have* **taken charge of** *the press and the radio and the state legislatures, through their lobby system.* □ *The Baronet promised to* **take charge of** *the lad at school.* □ *You will be* **taking charge of** *this department as from Monday.*

take cognizance of sth vërej; njoh zyrtarisht
□ *We have to* **take cognizance of** *new evidence.*

take counsel with sb këshillohem (konsultohem) me
□ *He* **took counsel with** *him before he started upon the trip.*

take courage marr zemër, marr guxim, marr kurajo
□ *Looking into the room, she saw him lying calmly on his bed, and soon* **took courage** *to enter.*

take credit (to oneself) for sth i atribuoj vetes meritat
□ *'He will also* **take the credit** *for getting rid of a dangerous agent.'* □ *'Of course the exhibition was a tremendous success, and for this you must* **take full credit.'** □ *I can't* **take** *any* **credit**; *the others did all the work.* □ *He never* **took credit** *to himself for making technical innovations.* □ *I know no sort of lying which is more frequent in Vanity Fair than this; and*

it may be remarked how people who practice it **take credit** *to themselves for their hypocrisy...*

take delight in sth/doing sth kënaqem, gjej kënaqësi
□ *The boy* **takes** *great* **delight in** *playing basketball.* □ *He* **takes** *great* **delight in** *proving others wrong.*

take down 1. ul, heq, marr
□ *An old tradition has it that Christmas decorations must be* **taken down** *before Twelfth Night.* □ *He* **took down** *a book from the top shelf.* □ *She* **took down** *the pictures from the wall.*
2. shkruaj, marr (mbaj) shënim
□ *Anything you say will be* **taken down**, *and may be used in evidence.*
□ *His speech was* **taken down** *in shorthand.*
3. zbërthej, çmontoj
□ *They have* **taken down** *the iron railings on this side of the park.* □ *They* **took down** *the crane.*

take effect 1. vepron, bën efekt
□ *I'm going to give you a pain-killing injection. In a minute or two, when it* **takes effect**, *you'll feel more comfortable.* □ *But the mixture of whisky and beer, coming as it did on an empty stomach, was beginning to* **take effect**, *and he sat with half-closed eyes, oblivious to their angry gestures and comments.* □ *'It has* **taken effect** *at last,' murmured the girl.* □ *I could see that the medicine was* **taking effect** *and that her pain was lessening.* □ *The sleeping-pills should begin to* **take effect** *in a few minutes.*
2. hyn në fuqi
□ *The new regulations* **take effect** *from midnight on Sunday.* □ *The new tax law will not* **take effect** *until January.* □ *It's definitely been decided that the Upton branch will close*

down but I don't know yet when this is due to **take effect**.

take exception to 1. kundërshtoj, jam kundër

□ *It seems that Mr. Muskham took exception.*

2. fyhem, ofendohem

□ *He took exception to what I said.*
□ *I must say I take exception to the nasty remarks he made about doctors. I think that doctors do a fine job.*

3. kritikoj

□ *There was nothing in the speech you could take exception to.*

take fire 1. ndizet, merr flakë, merr zjarr

□ *Dry wood soon takes fire.*

2. jepem me mish e me shpirt, jepem i tëri pas

□ *'I'll study algebra,' he concluded.... He took fire with unexampled rapidity.*

take flight/take to fight iki me të katra, ua mbath këmbëve

□ *Mrs. Donner, overwhelmed, took flight with a nervous laugh.* □ *The gang took (to) flight when they heard the police car.*

take (it) for granted e quaj (e marr) si të vërtetë (si të qënë, si të natyrshme); afërmendsh

□ *Cyril Robertson was a stimulating, provocative man who took nothing for granted.* □ *If he is not ready, my doors are shut against him henceforth, and yours, I take it for granted, are open to him.* □ *He took it for granted that she was doing very well and he was relieved of further worry.*
□ *Things went on there in the packing house all the time, and were taken for granted by everybody...*

take French leave iki pa lejë (pa rënë në sy, pa njoftuar, tinëz)

□ *But as I was certain I should not be allowed to leave the enclosure, my only plan was to take French leave and slip out when nobody was watching.... □ Other times they would simply take French leave—firmly locking the headmaster in as they went.*

take fright/alarm frikësohem, alarmohem

□ *They shot another of our agents in the street and he's taken fright. A third's gone underground.* □ *Over seven hundred animals quietly queued up to drink and took alarm only when flocks of Quelea finches and sandgrouse gave warning of the approach of predators, man or lion.*

take heart marr zemër, marr guxim

□ *It was impossible not to take heart in the company of such a man as this.* □ *I took heart to tell him that I had nothing all night.* □ *Take heart,— you're a brave fellow. I wish in my heart you were safe through.* □ *'You're perfect. Couldn't be nicer. Splendid!' She took heart. 'I wish your friends would think so.'* □ *Whenever I spoke of the Bushman a look of wonder would come into their eyes, and I took heart from that.* □ *We took heart from our leader's words.*

take heed (of) tregoj kujdes, i vë veshin

□ *When your parents give you advice, you should always take heed.* □ *Take heed of your doctor's advice.* □ *Of the strangers he took no heed whatever.* □ *Mr. Murdstone took no heed of me when I went into the parlour.*

take hold of kap, zë, mbërthej

□ *'And who's this shaver?' said one of the gentlemen, taking hold of me.* □ *He knelt down, took hold of Memo's arms and threw them over his shoulder.*

take in 1. marr, pranoj, strehoj

□ *Many households in the neighbour-hood of the University add to their income by **taking in** students.*

2. marr (pranoj) punë (në shtëpi)

□ *Mrs. Peters, who is a widow with young children, **takes in** washing to supplement her pension.*

3. shkurtoj, zvogëloj, ngushtoj

□ *The dress is not a bad fit, but it needs **taking in** a little.* □ *'I'll have the waistbands **taken in** for you a couple of inches.'* □ *This dress needs to be **taken in** at the waist.*

4. përfshin, mbulon

□ *Forensic science **takes in** crimi-nology, which covers the causes of crime.* □ *Soon we are going to have a bus tour that **takes in** some cities in South Albania.*

5. kuptoj, bluaj në mendje, përpij

□ *I really couldn't help thinking, as I sat **taking in** all this, that the misfor-tunes extended to some other mem-bers of the family besides Mrs. Gummidge.* □ *Isabel wondered how much Irma was **taking in** of what was said.*

6. vërej, shoh

□ *He **took in** the scene at a glance.* □ *Her eyes were **taking in** nothing but the telephone.*

7. mashtroj

□ *Don't be **taken in** by his charming manner; he's completely ruthless.* □ *I'm sorry you're all so easy to **take in**. You ought to know better with all your experience of the trade.*

8. shkoj të shikoj një film, të vizitoj një muzeum etj.

□ *I generally try to **take in** a show when I'm in New York on business.*

take in hand 1. marr në dorë, vë nën kontroll

□ *The garden is growing a bit wild: I think I shall have to **take** it **in hand** this summer.* □ *Mr. Dobbin, having **taken** the matter **in hand**, was most extraordinarily eager in the conduct of it.* □ *Dr. Riccardo is **taking** the case seriously **in hand**. Perhaps he will be able to make a permanent improvement.*

2. ndërmarr, nis

□ *We are just now **taking in hand** a massive program for the redevelop-ment of the city center.* □ *The plans which have been laid before you will be **taken in hand** by the autumn.*

take into account marr parasysh

□ *One has to **take** all the facts **into account**.* □ *The results are good, especially when we **take into account** the fact that they have studied the lan-guage for a short time.* □ *When judging his performance, don't **take** his age **into account**.* □ *When we are making up the bill, we shall have to **take into account** all the extra work that was done at the end.* □ *The third reason why Birkhoff went wrong lies in his failure to **take into account** some additional complexities.* □ *In this case there are special features to be **taken into account**.*

take into consideration marr parasysh, marr në konsideratë

□ *In your proposals you haven't **taken into consideration** the special needs of the people.* □ *I always **take** fuel consumption **into consideration** when buying a car.* □ *Before we came to a decision we must make sure we have **taken into consideration** all the relevant facts.*

take into one's confidence i besoj dikujt një të fshehtë, i jap besë, ia them në mirëbesim

□ *He had contemplated **taking** Mr. Mackay **into his confidence**, and*

asking his advice about his difficult
position. □ Much of the success of the
project is due to the fact that the
unions were **taken into** the employers'
confidence from the outset.

take issue with hahem, grindem,
debatoj, kapem me fjalë
□ I want to **take issue with** you on the
last point that you raised.

take it (that) 1. besoj, kujtoj, ma merr
mendja
□ Can I **take it that** you will be staying
for dinner? □ You'll be joining us later,
I **take it**?
2. duroj, përballoj
□ I hope you saw how quickly he gave
in; he can dish it out but he can't **take
it**. □ To go on living for me is to go on
learning about life, and everything
that makes life. Wanting to go on
learning makes one vulnerable, of
course; you are always exposing
yourself to risk. I hope I can **take it**.
□ 'Well, there's no need to provoke her,
is there?' she said. 'Why, it's only a bit
of fun—she can't **take it**, that's all.'

take it easy e marr shtruar, e marr
avash
□ 'If you leave at 10 you should get
there by midday all right.' 'I'd rather
leave earlier and **take it easy**.'
□ 'Take it easy,' one of the men said.
'You are all right now, boy.' □ **Take it
easy**; we've got plenty of time. □ You
look tired. Why don't you just **take it
easy** for a while?

take it into one's head më shkrep në
kokë, më hipën në kokë; më thotë
(mbushet) mendja
□ Somehow he'd **taken into his head**
that his wife was trying to poison him.
□ If I should **take it into my head** to
tell what I heard, tremendous mischief could result. □ But Mr. Mills,
who was always doing something or

other to annoy me had brought his
conduct to a climax, by **taking it into
his head** that he would go to India.
□ That if Irene were to **take it into
her head** to—he could hardly frame
the thought,—to leave Soames? □ I
didn't tell him my thoughts. If he **took
it into his head** that I was coming
here for such or such a purpose, why,
that's his look. I don't stand committed by that.

take its course ndjek rrjedhën (proçe-
durën) e vet
□ The decision cannot be reversed;
the law must **take its course**.

take its toll shkakton humbje (dëm);
merr jetë (njerëzish)
□ Every year at Christmas drunken
driving **takes its toll**. □ The bombs
had **taken their tolls** on the little
town.

take kindly to pëlqen; vlerëson
□ Remember to say only good things
about his new book; he doesn't **take
kindly to** criticism. □ He doesn't **take
kindly to** any suggestions about running his business.

take one's leave (of sb) ndahem nga
(me); iki, shkoj
□ I'll **take my leave** now, if you don't
mind. I have another appointment
somewhere else. □ It was going to
be very difficult, after such a close
working partnership, to **take our
leave of** each other. □ So we were left
to **take leave of** one another.... □ 'I'm
so glad you don't like mills.' said
Fanny as she rose to accompany her
mother, who was **taking leave of**
Mrs. Hale with rustling dignity.
□ He muttered, 'We'll soon have
her right. Come to the surgery in
half an hour I'll give you a bottle of
medicine.' He **took his leave of** them
and with his head down, thinking

desperately he trudged back to the surgery.

take leave of one senses luan mendsh (nga mendtë, nga fiqiri), i iku mendja (e kokës), shkalloi nga mendtë

□ *Judging by the strange way he is behaving, I think he must have* **taken leave of his senses.** □ *Come down from the roof, Harry! Have you* **taken leave of your senses?** □ *'Copperfield,' he said at length in a breathless voice, 'have you* **taken leave of your senses?'** *'I have taken leave of you,' said I wresting my hand away.* □ *'They'll think I've* **taken leave of my senses,'** *was his way of putting it.* □ *For a second, Andrew wondered if Denny had* **taken leave of his senses.**

take liberties (with) sillem lirshëm me, veproj lirisht me, kam dorë të lirë (liri veprimi) me

□ *She told him to stop* **taking liberties.** □ *Just because I was nice to him, he started to* **take liberties.**

take matters into one's own hands i marr vetë punët në dorë, veproj vetë

□ *The headmaster was plainly going to do nothing to ensure my allowance was paid, so I* **took matters into my hands** *and went to see someone at the Education Office.* □ *'Don't* **take matters into your own hands;** *make your application through the usual channels.'*

take no account of s'marr parasysh

□ *But his mind would* **take no account of** *these familiar features.*

take no notice (of sb/sth) s'i kushtoj vëmendje, nuk i vë veshin

□ *Oxborrow and Medle* **took no notice of** *Andrew's success.* □ *'Take* **no notice of** *him, Nan. To hell with him and what he said to you.'*

take note of dëgjoj me vëmendje, i

kushtoj vëmendje, i vë vesh (veshin); marr në konsideratë

□ *Your remarks have been* **taken careful note of,** *and I hope soon to give a detailed reply to each of them.* □ *The Authority will* **take note of** *teacher's stated preference for one posting rather than another, though it cannot undertake to send every teacher to the school of his first choice.* □ *Please* **take note of** *this announcement.* □ *He* **took** *silent* **note of** *Tom's availability.*

take notice of vërej, vështroj me kujdes, i kushtoj vëmendje, i vë veshin

□ *Don't* **take** *any* **notice of** *your friend's criticism or advice.* □ *It seemed to me a bold thing even to* **take notice of** *that passage...* □ *Then little Antanas would open his eyes— he was beginning to* **take notice of** *things now; and he would smile....* □ *He flapped away, chuckling to his place at the head of the table. None of the colleagues who were already seated* **took** *any* **notice of** *him.*

take occasion përfitoj nga rasti, shfrytëzoj rastin

□ *He* **took occasion** *to say a few words about the matter.* □ *... and Jurgis* **took occasion** *to broach a weighty subject.*

take off 1. heq, zhvesh

□ *'Take* **your shoes** *off* **and dry your feet.'** □ *Accordingly, I* **took** *the jacket* **off,** *that I might learn to do without it.* □ *... until he actually got down into the pit and* **took off** *his coat.* □ *Take* **your things** *off.* **I want to examine you.**

2. ngrihet, shkëputet nga toka (aeroplani etj.)

□ *A helicopter is able to* **take off** *and land straight up or down.* □ *The plane* **took off** *easily.* □ *The plane* **took off** *from the Rinas airport.*

3. imitoj, përqesh

□ *Bill* ***took off*** *the Prime Minister to perfection.* □ *Did you not see that he was only* ***taking*** *you* ***off***?

4. heq, çmontoj

□ *The intense heat* ***took*** *most of the paint* ***off*** *the doors.* □ *Before the body of the car can be properly repaired, all the external fittings must be* ***taken off***.

5. heq nga shërbimi

□ *They've had to* ***take*** *two of the evening buses* ***off*** *this route because of a shortage of crews.*

6. pres

□ *Gangrene was far advanced, and the leg had to be* ***taken off*** *above the knee.*

7. heq nga menuja

□ *'We're running low on steak. You'll have to* ***take*** *it* ***off*** *the menu.'* □ *My favorite dish has usually been* ***taken off*** *just before I get to the restaurant.*

8. marr (bëj) pushim

□ *'You need a break. Why not* ***take*** *a fortnight* ***off*** *from work?'*

9. iki, largohem me të shpejtë

□ *I grabbed my hat and* ***took off*** *for the Town Hall.* □ *The moment he saw a police car turn the corner, Bloggs* ***took off*** *in the opposite direction.*

take offense (at sth) prekem, fyhem, zemërohem

□ *Val looked at the fellow with renewed suspicion but the good humor in his eyes was such that he really could not* ***take offense***. □ *If she was going to* ***take offense at*** *everything he said, she had got to be put right straight away.* □ *I couldn't* ***take offense at*** *his tone, but I resolved to be more careful in front of him in future.* □ *'Well,' he said,* ***taking offense at*** *her manner, 'you needn't get mad about it. I'm just*

asking you.' □ *She's quick to* ***take offense***.

take off one's hat to sb i heq kapelën

□ *When her husband died, she raised a family of five children all on her own. I* ***take off*** *my hat to her.* □ *That's a real idea you have, Cowperwood. I* ***take off*** *my hat to you.* □ *I* ***take my hat off*** *to anyone who is prepared to work underground for long hours.* □ *He was doing important work for very little money, and I* ***took my hat off*** *to him.*

take on 1. marr, pranoj në punë

□ *They no longer have to* ***take on*** *large numbers of temporary staff to do the checking.* □ *The packers* ***took on*** *more hands.*

2. ndërmarr, marr përsipër

□ *He blamed his own weakness for letting her* ***take on*** *too much work.* □ *I'm beginning to regret that I* ***took*** *the job* ***on***; *I'm working overtime every evening.*

3. merr, përfton

□ *Now her hair has* ***taken on*** *a healthy shine.* □ *In this context the words of Socrates in the Phaedo,* ***take on*** *a new significance.*

4. merr (pasagjerë, ngarkesë etj.)

□ *The bus stopped to* ***take on*** *more passengers.* □ *The ship* ***took on*** *more fuel at Freetown.*

take one's courage in both hands marr zemër, marr kurajë, bëhem burrë, tregohem trim

□ *Feeling that he was wasting time and strength and money all for nothing, he* ***took the courage*** *of a Forsyte* ***in both hands***... □ *Evan's daughter had a solitary friend, a woman who knew that the girl was desperately ill and who,* ***taking her courage in her hands*** *had at the last moment resolved to act and put a call through.*

take one's departure iki, largohem, nisem

□ *And about the same time, a carriage driving up to the inn, he **took his departure**.* □ *He **took his departure** at two o'clock pm.*

take one's ease rehatohem, relaksohem

□ *She sat down and **took her ease** by the fire.* □ *Not more than a dozen guests stood around, **taking their ease** and watching the latest arrivals.* □ *It's your dog, Elsie. Why should your father have to be walking it out on a cold night while you **take your ease** by the fire?*

take oneself in hand e mbledh (zotëroj) veten

□ *I **took myself in hand** in time.* □ *In the effort of **taking** himself **in hand**, he....*

take one's life in one's hand rrezikoj veten, vë kokën në rrezik

□ *At such times Jurgis would dodge under the gates and run across the tracks and between the cars, **taking his life into his hands**.* □ *You **take your life in your hands** simply crossing the road these days!* □ *Anyone who takes his car out in these conditions is **taking his life in his hands**.*

take one's medicine pranoj ndëshkimin (dënimin) pa u shfajësuar

□ *You have broken the rules, and you have been caught: I'm afraid you will just have to **take your medicine**.* □ *The boy said he was sorry he broke the window and was ready to **take his medicine**.*

take one's own life vras veten

□ *And it seems to have been this idealism, coupled with ill-health and depression that finally brought him to **take his own life**.*

take one's revenge on sb shpaguhem,

hakmerrem, ia marr hakun

□ *They swore to **take their revenge on** the kidnappers.*

take one's time nuk ngutem, nuk nxitoj, e marr shtruar

□ ***Take your time** over the job and do it well.* □ *'Now **take your time**, and tell me plainly what you want.'* □ *He likes to **take his time** over breakfast.* □ *It's an important decision for you, my dear, so **take your time** to think it over.* □ *He can write as neatly and legibly as the next person if he **takes his time over it**.*

take one's way iki, shkoj, nisem

□ *He subjected himself to necessity and **took the way** to Europe by sea.*

take on trust besoj, i zë besë

□ *'Sarah **takes everyone on trust**, just like you do. Nicky is more like me.'* □ *You don't have to **take** everything he says **on trust**. Do a little checking up occasionally.*

take orders from marr urdhëra nga

□ *She said she wouldn't **take orders from** a junior clerk.*

take out 1. nxjerr jashtë

□ *At last. He almost sobbed with relief. He slipped a pad of gauze on the blooded stump. Stumbling to his knees he said: '**Take** him **out**.'* □ *He **took** his wife **out** to dinner.*

2. heq

□ *How can I **take out** these ink stains from my blouse?* □ *I had my tooth **taken out** yesterday.*

3. shkatërroj, neutralizoj, nxjerr jashtë luftimit

□ *Enemy missiles **took out** two of our fighters.*

4. tërheq

□ *How much do you need to **take out** of the bank?*

5. ul, zbres, heq

□ *Monthly contributions to the pension scheme will be **taken out** of your salary.*

take out of sb's hands heq nga duart e

□ *'I shall have to make a report to my office. Then if you don't cooperate, it will be **taken out of my hands**.'*

take over 1. marr në dorëzim (detyrën etj); marr drejtimin (kontrollin) e

□ *He expects to **take over** the business when his father retires.* □ *When will you be ready to **take over** the task?* □ *The airplane pilot fainted and his co-pilot had to **take over**.*

2. çoj, shpie

□ *I was thinking of **taking** the children **over** to my mother's this weekend.* □ *The fishermen **took** me **over** to the bank in their boat.*

3. marr

□ *The Japanese have **taken over** many European ways of life.*

take pains mundohem, marr mundimin të, përpiqem, bëj çmos

□ *Her garden is her great passion—she **takes** more **pains** over it than she does over bringing up her children.* □ *The lawyer **took** great **pains** to explain to me all the difficult points of the case.* □ *Both in his sister's presence, and after she had left the room, the whelp **took** no **pains** to hide his contempt for Mr. Bonnderby.* □ *He found that he was spending a long time over this case, **taking** special **pains**, detaining the young man earnestly.* □ *I am grateful to you for **taking pains** to show me how to do the work.*

take part in marr pjesë në

□ *Jurgis wanted to know what was going on at the meetings, and to be able to **take part in** them....* □ *They say that he **took part in** last week's big bank robbery.* □ *How many*

countries will be **taking part in** the World Cup?* □ *They were asked to **take a part in** organizing the emergency preparations that were gaining momentum.*

take pity on sb ndiej keqardhje për

□ *Everybody **took pity on** Mr. Wickfield.* □ *The little boy looks so disappointed that I **took pity on** him and gave him some money.* □ *She was so vexed with curiosity, that Virginia **took pity on** her and restored her peace of mind.* □ *She would bring into the house stray animals **on** whom she had **taken pity**.*

take place ndodh, ngjet, zhvillohet

□ *The accident **took place** only a block from his home.* □ *All this **took place** in London many years ago.* □ *But even if a similar creation of life did **take place** on any other planet, Pringle thinks it would not have developed beyond the earliest, simple forms.* □ *When does the ceremony **take place**?* □ *We have never discovered what **took place** between them that night.* □ *From this I rightly conjectured that no improvement had **taken place** since my last visit in the state of Mr. Gummidge's spirits.*

take pleasure in sth ndiej (gjej) kënaqësi në

□ *'I should be sorry to suppose, Charles, that you **took a pleasure in** aggravating me.'* □ *He had been feeling so well **taking pleasure in** what he ate...* □ *They **take** great **pleasure in** reminding us of our poverty.* □ *She **took** no **pleasure in** her work.*

take possession of sth zotëroj, bëhem zot a pronar i, marr në zotërim

□ *Jos' face grew paler and paler. Alarm began to **take** entire **possession of** the stout civilian.* □ *Mr. Bounderby had **taken possession of** a* *house and grounds about fifteen miles from the town.* □ *I fell to work, in my silent way, on a new fancy, which* **took** *strong* **possession of** *me.*

take precedence over ka (merr) përparësi mbi

□ *This question must* **take precedence over** *all other at the meeting.* □ *The needs of the community must* **take precedence over** *individual requirements.*

take pride in krehohem, ndiej krenari, e ndiej veten krenar

□ *Nurse Ellen sewed beautifully and* **took** *great* **pride in** *her work.* □ *He seems to* **take** *a* **pride in** *being offensive to everyone he meets.* □ *I can assure you, I* **take** *no* **pride in** *the way some of our employees have behaved.* □ *These craftsmen* **take pride in** *the things that they make.*

take refuge in strehohem, gjej strehim (strehë, mbrojtje); përdor si maskë (mbulesë)

□ *Bill, feeling at a disadvantage,* **took refuge in** *words.* □ *Mrs Curry* **took refuge** *for a moment in licking her little lips.* □ *Well, one couldn't ask a question so personal, and Holly* **took refuge in** *a general remark.*

take revenge on sb for sth hakmerrem, marr hak

□ *He felt at once there were many things he could do to make her life miserable, and* **take revenge on** *Lynde, but he decided that he would not.*

take root rrënjoset, zë (hedh, shtie) rrënjë

□ *You seem to have given them good advice. I only hope your words of wisdom will* **take root.** □ *And experience proves that such an institution will die. It is choked by its own perfection. It cannot* **take root** *for lack of soil.*

□ *The cause has* **taken** *a deep* **root,** *and has spread its branches far and wide.* □ *His affection for her has* **taken root.**

take shape merr formë

□ *The plans for the ceremony are beginning to* **take shape.** □ *Suspicion of a frame-up began to* **take shape** *in many minds.* □ *Then, out of the haze which had covered them, the face of the men in the crowd* **took shape** *again.* □ *The new building is beginning to* **take shape.**

take sides (with) marr (mbaj) anën e

□ *It is clear that she would* **take sides with** *us.* □ *Why did our labor leaders* **take sides with** *the owners in every strike that took place?* □ *The referee in a football match is not supposed to* **take sides.** □ *If she* **took sides** *in their disputes, as she sometimes did, they both resented it.* □ *'I don't like the implication of some of your questions—I thought you were on my side.' 'It's not a question of* **taking sides** *with anyone but of establishing the facts.*

take sb/sth as one finds him/it; take sb/sth as he/it is pranoj dikë/diçka ashtu siç është

□ *Well, I'm sorry. I have to say what I think. You must* **take me as you find me.** □ *He thought what a nice wife he had, and that she would be perfect if she would only* **take** *him* **as she found him.** □ *'Well, she's never shown that side of her character to me.' 'I'm sorry—I don't mean to turn you against her.' 'You haven't. It's always best to* **take** *people* **as you find them,** *don't you think?'*

take sb at his word/take sb's word for it/that besoj, i zë besë fjalës të

□ *Mrs. Bessie and Ted told him to make himself at home, come and go* *as he pleased. He **took them at their word**, and spent most of the time camped on the veranda, or in a room.* □ *I **take your word for it** that you never said such a thing.* □ *'They can do without you, **take my word for it**. But without them, you're lost— nothing.'* □ *'Oh, don't worry to explain, Gerrie, I'll **take your word for it**—that it's important.'* □ ***Take my word for it**; this work could be completed in a much shorter time.*

take sb by surprise 1. zë (kap) në befasi
□ *'Margaret,' said he 'is **taking her by surprise**.'* □ *She opened the drawing room softly, meaning to **take him by surprise**.* □ *The gang **took us by surprise**: we were not expecting them.*
2. vjen si surprizë, si diçka e papritur
□ *Our home team's winning the cup **took** everyone **by surprise**; nobody thought they could do it.*

take/hold sb captive/prisoner zë (mbaj) dikë rob
□ *They were **held captive** by masked gunmen.*

take/bring sb down a peg/notch (or two) ia ul hundën, i tregoj vendin
□ *You've put on considerably many frills since I've been away. I'll **take you down a peg** before I get done with you.* □ *Now, Jim Cargedee, with the sailor's love for a sailor's joke, had determined when he pulled into the cabin, to **bring** its inmate **down a peg** or so.* □ *I'm glad that the new manager is being strict with Jane, that should **take her down a notch**.* □ *I've never heard such pretentious rubbish; he needs to be **taken down a peg or two**.*

take sb for a ride mashtroj, ia hedh
□ *'If you paid more than $500 for that car, you've been **taken for a ride**!'*

□ *Vin was the sharp, clever boy who wasn't to be **taken for a ride** by anybody, the boy who knew all the answers.*

take sb's breath away habis, mahnis, mrekulloj, befasoj, lë pa gojë
□ *'Going to leave the Dragon!' cried Mr. Pinch, looking at him with great astonishment. 'Why, Mark, you **take my breath away**.'* □ *The appetite with which he consumed during these next few days, really **took my breath away**.* □ *It **takes one's breath away** to see how much the place has changed in a few years.* □ *Every letter that I see in Mr. Grandgrin's hand **takes my breath away**.*

take sb's life vras, marr jetën e
□ *For your own sake, for my sake, flee, they'll **take your life**!*

take/get sb's drift/meaning kuptoj nëntekstin (domethënien), kuptoj ku do me dalë
□ *Oh, I **took her drift** all right, though I pretended not to. She's hoping her mother can come to us from hospital to convalesce, but I didn't want to commit myself to anything till I'd discussed it with you.*

take/get sb's measure vlerësoj, mas me sy, peshoj
□ *Mrs. Kno bows gravely looking keenly at Dora and **taking her measure** without prejudice.* □ *Before the contest began, he watched his opponent carefully, trying to **take his measure**.* □ *He detested Aneurin Bevan, largely because Bevan had **got his measure** and once remarked that he was not a man with whom one should go shooting tigers.*

take sb'd mind off sth ia heq (largon) mendjen nga
□ *Hard work always **takes your mind off** domestic problems.*

take sb's part marr (mbaj) anën e
□ *His mother always **takes his part**.*
□ *Why do you **take the part of** your brothers?*

take sb's place zëvendësoj, zë vendin e
□ *She couldn't attend the meeting so her assistant **took her place**.*

take sb's side marr anën e
□ *'I heard what you said to George, and I think you should be ashamed.' 'Eh? What?—demanded Mr. Early in a tone of stupefaction. 'Are you **taking his side**?'* □ *I decided to **take his side** against the others.*

take sb to task (about/for/over sth) qortoj, kritikoj
□ *We were sure that the gate had been left unlocked. We would **take** the night-watchman **to task over** it.* □ *Mrs. Sedley **took** her husband **to task for** his cruel conduct to poor Joe.* □ *It's wrong of you to **take** the child **to task for** such trifling things.* □ *They **took** him **to task for** his idleness.*

take/catch sb unawares kap, zë në befasi (gafil)
□ ***Taken unawares** by the sudden storm we got very wet.* □ *You **caught** us **unawares** by coming so early.*

take sth amiss/ill e marr ters, e marr për të keq
□ *Don't **take** it **amiss** if I point out your errors.* □ *I hope you will not **take** my criticisms of your article **amiss**, they are merely intended to suggest ways in which you might improve it.* □ *'When are you two going to get married? I'm glad you didn't **take** it **amiss** when I said that.' He wagged his globe-shaped head with satisfaction.* □ *She's so touchy about being able to look after herself that your offers of help may easily be **taken amiss**.* □ *Please don't **take** it **amiss** if*

I say I'd rather you didn't come to the station to see me off.

take sth in good part e marr pa të keq
□ *People made funny remarks about Jack's brightly colored tie, but he **took** it all **in good part**.* □ *I had no sooner made the remark than I regretted it, fortunately he **took** it **in good part**.* □ *He **took** the teasing **in good part**.*

take sth in one's stride kryej, pranoj me lehtësi (pa ngurrim, pa vështirësi)
□ *Some people find retiring difficult, but he has **taken** it all **in his stride**.*

take sth to heart 1. marr (mendoj) seriozisht
□ *Poor little Sylvia! She **took** things awfully **to heart**.*
2. prekem thellë në zemër (shpirt), e marr për zemër
□ *Peggotty seemed to **take** this aspersion very much **to heart**, I thought.* □ *I **took** your criticism very much **to heart**.* □ *'Come now, we have been through much together. Do not **take** a little incident so much **to heart**.*

take sth with a grain/pinch of salt marr me rezervë
□ *Cowperwood, as was natural, heard much of her stage life. At first he **took** all this palaver **with a grain of salt**... □ Many of them **took** my budding local pretensions to being somebody **with a** very large **grain of salt**.*

take steps (to do sth) marr masa
□ *The authorities are very worried about the accident, and they are **taking steps to** see that nothing like that happens again.* □ *Nor was Dr. Gruber, who would have **taken steps to** prevent the onset of such affliction.* □ *The city is **taking steps to** replace its cars with buses.*

take stock of 1. analizoj, vlerësoj, bëj vlerësimin

□ *But he did not permit himself to realize just what that meant to* take careful **stock** *of his emotions.* □ *Andrew* **took stock** *of the long fawn carpeted room.* □ *Let's* **take stock** *of the situation, and then make our decision.* □ *Before deciding to buy a house, Jane* **took stock** *of her financial situation.*
2. inventarizoj, bëj inventarin e
□ *The shop is closed on the last Friday of every month, when we* **take stock**. □ *The grocery store* **took stock** *every week on Monday mornings.*

take the air 1. dal jashtë të marr ajër të pastër
□ *Cuckoos were still calling across the fields in their late bubbling voices and a few people were wandering among Ma's flower beds,* **taking the air**. □ *'Where are you going now, for goodness' sake?' 'Nowhere—just to* **take the air** *on the lawn before I go to bed.* □ *On such a nice day, one should get out and* **take the air.**
2. fillon transmetimin (radiofonik)
□ *The new radio station will* **take the air** *next week.*

take the biscuit/cake është gjëja më idiote (më zbavitëse, më e habitshme, më e mërzitshme, më e tmerrshme)
□ *He's done stupid things before, but this really* **takes the biscuit**. □ *I think that his rude behavior at the party really* **took the biscuit.**

take the bit in/between one's teeth ka dalë nga kapistalli (freri), vepron me kokë të vet, s'pranon kontroll (drejtim)
□ *The way he had of* **taking the bit in his teeth** *offended his employer.* □ *You will find it difficult to stop your daughter becoming an actress now; she's* **got the bit between her teeth.**

take the bloom off sth venit, i heq hijeshinë (bukurinë, freskinë, përsosmërinë etj.)
□ *Their frequent rows* **took the bloom off** *their marriage.*

take the bread out of sb's mouth i heq bukën e gojës
□ *He was advised to go back home, where he belonged, not come there* **taking** *honest men's* **bread out of their mouths.**

take the bull by the horns e kap demin për brirësh (nga brirët)
□ *'See here,' he exclaimed, suddenly, looking sharply at the musician and deciding to* **take the bull by the horns**, *'you are in quite as delicate a situation as I am, if you only stop to think.'* □ *He decided to* **take the bull by the horns** *and demand a raise in salary even though it might cost him his job.* □ *My boss has ignored my hints about increasing my pay, so I'm just going to* **take the bull by the horns** *and ask him directly.* □ *Determined to* **take the bull by the horns** ... *I stepped forward.* □ *'You won't get the financial support you need by staying here.* **Take the bull by the horns**. *Go and speak to your bank manager.'*

take the chair 1. drejtoj mbledhjen
□ *The vice-president* **took the chair** *when the president was ill.* □ *He will also* **take the chair** *at a lecture tomorrow on the scientific work of the British-North Greenland expedition.*
2. hap mbledhjen
□ *When the hour fixed for the meeting to begin arrives, the presiding officer* **takes the chair** *and directs the secretary to read the minutes of the last meeting.*

take the chill off ngroh paksa, thyej (heq) të ftohtin

□ *This little fire does not fully heat the room, but it does take the chill off it.*

take the consequences of sth pranoj pasojat e

□ *I'm warning you that if you come in late again, you will have to take the consequences.* □ *I have to come out in the open and print my information. And take the consequences if I make a mistake.* □ *Let him take the consequences of his undutifulness and folly.*

take the edge off sth çmpreh, topis, ul, prish, zvogëloj, zbut, thyej

□ *'If you keep using that chisel as a screwdriver you'll take the edge right off it.'* □ *Stocker was halfway through his lunch, and had taken the edge off his appetite sufficiently to talk.* □ *She had no money, no clothes other than those she had on. She was in a strange country and not so very used to travelling alone. It took the edge off her determination to resist, but she was not conquered by any means.* □ *I need a sandwich to take the edge off my appetite.* □ *His brother's failure took the edge off his own success.* □ *He made many serious complaints, but at the end he told quite a funny joke, which helped to take the edge off his previous remarks.* □ *I ate some biscuits before dinner, and they took the edge off my appetite.*

take the floor 1. marr fjalën

□ *There was some dispute with the antisemitic doctors on the staff, as a result of which Schnitzler's chief adversary took the floor at a meeting and proposed a vote of no-confidence in him.* □ *Teuta was the first to take the floor at the meeting.* □ *The young man took the floor and spoke very well.*

2. nis vallëzimin, ngrihem për vallëzim

□ *The band struck up and several couples took the floor.* □ *She took the floor with her husband.*

take the gilt off the gingerbread prish gjithë lezetin (bukurinë)

□ *The company has given me a gift of £5,000 for my service, but the fact that I shall have to pay tax on it rather takes the gilt off the gingerbread.*

take the heart out of sb demoralizoj, ligështoj, ia thyej zemrën

□ *Even so they might have managed it but for cruel accidents which have almost taken the heart out of them.*

take the initiative marr iniciativën

□ *It's up to this country to take the initiative in banning nuclear weapons.*

take the law into one's own hands bën ligjin, bëhet zot i ligjit, shpërfill ligjin; vetë zot, vetë shkop

□ *He has taken the law into his own hands, by mast-heading me for eight hours...* □ *In the old days, ordinary people would sometimes take the law in their own hands by breaking into prisons and killing the prisoners.* □ *Where troops and police have to operate against urban guerillas, it may be hard to prevent sections of the public taking the law into their own hands.*

take the lead udhëheq, prij, vihem në krye (në ballë), jap shembullin

□ *He was the oldest boarder also and ... took the lead in the house, as Mrs. Todgers had already said.* □ *The shepherd, as the man who knew the country best, took the lead and guided them round....*

take the liberty of/to marr guximin të

□ *But I know what I am about, my love, and will take the liberty of expressing myself accordingly.* □ *I took the liberty of reading your newspapers while you were away. I hope you don't mind.* □ *I took the liberty of borrowing your lawnmower while you were away.*

take the occasion to shfrytëzoj rastin, përfitoj nga rasti
□ *Since I am here, perhaps I can take the occasion to thank you for the help you have given me.*

take the offensive kaloj në sulm
□ *In meetings she always takes the offensive before she can be criticized.*

take the opportunity shfrytëzoj rastin, përfitoj nga rasti
□ *Finding his nephew Val at dinner there the first night, he took the opportunity of asking him.* □ *Let me take this opportunity to say a few words.* □ *We took the opportunity of visiting the place.* □ *They looked so settled—in that he took the opportunity to slip out for a moment.*

take/sign the pledge jap fjalën (të mos pi pije alkolike)
□ *He used to drink a lot, but now he has taken the pledge.*

take the plunge marr (bëj) një hap vendimtar, marr një vendim të prerë
□ *One day he took the plunge and spent all that he had in his pockets....* □ *They have finally decided to take the plunge and get married.*

take the road nisem, shkoj
□ *I do not know whether he continued to pursue his idea, for I myself took the road next morning.*

take the shine out of/of/off of eklipsoj, ia kaloj
□ *I think this picture here takes the shine out of all the pictures.* □ *I am only sorry I didn't bring Seth Sprague along with me, with his pitch pipe, just to take the shine off of them there singers.*

take the trouble to do sth mundohem, përpiqem, bëj çmos, marr mundimin të
□ *I thanked him with all my heart, for it was friendly in him to offer to take the trouble.* □ *I need not withdraw if I can prove my statement. I have taken the trouble to collect my evidence.* □ *Some of those who live in these earthquake-prone areas have taken a great deal of trouble to construct houses that shall resist damage by earthquake waves.* □ *Decent journalists should take the trouble to check their facts.*

take the wind out of sb's sail i pres krahët, lë si peshku pa ujë, vë në gjendje të vështirë
□ *The answer was so cool, so rich in bravado, that somehow it took the wind out of his sail.* □ *What strengthened my hands and completely took the wind out of his sails was a most opportune letter from my uncle.* □ *Say what one will, to have the love of a man like Cowperwood away from a woman like Aileen was to leave her high and dry on land, as a fish out of its native element, to take all the wind out of her sails, almost to kill her.*

take the words out of one's mouth ia marr fjalët nga goja
□ *You've taken the words out of my mouth: I was about to say the same thing.* □ *'Let's go to the beach tomorrow.' 'You took the words right out of my mouth.'*

take thought mendoj mirë (me kujdes)
□ *You should take thought before you spend too much money.*

take time do kohë
□ *It was merely a matter of shock to the nerve centers. Such a thing sometimes took time to mend. The important thing was not to worry.* □ *The safest procedure would be to get*

written authority from the London office but that **takes time** *coming— during which this fellow may find another buyer.*

take time by the forelock gjej rastin e volitshëm; paraprij rastin; veproj pa vonesë; planifikoj paraprakisht

□ *Mrs. Rouncewell foresees that the family may shortly be expected and hence the stately old dame,* **taking time by the forelock,** *leads him up and down the stair case, to witness that every thing is ready.* □ *We must* **take time by the forelock;** *for when it is once past, there is no recalling it.*

take to sb/sth 1. pëlqej, më hyn në zemër

□ *We* **took to** *the boy as soon as we saw him.* □ *She* **took** *so kindly* **to** *me, that in the course of a few weeks she shortened my adopted name of Trotwood into Trot.*

2. jepem pas

□ *Some men would go off their heads. Others'd* **take to** *drink.* □ *He* **took to** *gardening in his retirement.*

3. shkoj diku (për të shpëtuar)

□ *As the enemy advance continued, whole families would* **take to** *the forests carrying all their belongings.*

take to one's bed zë krevatin (shtratin)

□ *Half the boys in the form had* **taken their beds** *with streaming cold.* □ *If everybody with a disordered metabolism* **took to bed** *it would never do.* □ *He* **took to his bed** *for three weeks.*

take to one's bossom përqafoj

□ *His Italian listeners were* **taken to his bossom,** *and their hearts beat with his.*

take to one's heels ua mbathi këmbëve, ia dha vrapit

□ *If I had seen a moderately large wave that came tumbling in, I should have* **taken to my heels** *with an awful*

recollection of her drowned relations. □ *I told them to clear off, and they* **took to their heels.** □ *Then, he darted through the door and* **took to his heels.** □ *When the boys saw the police coming, they* **took to their heels.**

take to pieces/bits çmontoj, zbërthej

□ *The gas-fitter* **took** *the stove* **to pieces** *before Virginia had a chance to cook supper.* □ *He's has* **taken** *the record-payer* **to bits.** *The question is, can he put it together again?*

take turns bëj me radhë

□ *Mary and Diana* **took turns** *at sitting up with their sick mother.* □ *We* **take** *it in* **turns,** *once a fortnight, my brother and me, to give the place a thorough going over.* □ *If you can't agree, you'll have to* **take turns** *to sleep in the top bunk. Now, no more argument.*

take umbrage (at sth) fyhem, ofendohem, ndjehem i ofenduar (i pakënaqur)

□ *'He's like the rest of you, forever* **taking umbrage** *about something.'* □ *Although Steve was given to lying, he never* **took umbrage at** *being accused of it.* □ *Are you surprised that she* **took umbrage?** *Didn't you realise that it was her husband you'd described as a cross between a shark and a limpet?* □ *Len, who was also starting to look a little flushed,* **took umbrage at** *this.* □ *It's impossible to have a normal conversation with him—he* **takes umbrage at** *every third thing you say to him.*

take up 1. ngre

□ *She* **took up** *her pen and began to write.* □ *He* **took up** *his book from the floor.*

2. marr (pasagjerë)

□ *We found the coach very near at hand and got upon the roof; but I was so dead sleepy that when he stopped on the road to* **take up** *somebody else, they put me inside where there were no passengers and where I slept profoundly.*

3. thith, pi

□ *The cloth is saturated: it can't* **take up** *anymore of the liquid.* □ *Blotting paper* **takes up** *ink.* □ *He* **took up** *the ink from the notebook with the blotting paper.*

4. merrem, i hyj, filloj të merrem

□ *Why not* **take up** *some outdoor sport as a relaxation from office work?*

5. nis, filloj

□ *Charley threw up his job to* **take up** *more respectable, more sensible employment.* □ *She has* **taken up** *a job as a teacher.*

6. marr në mbrojtje

□ *A young actor will find hard to make his way on the London stage unless he is exceptionally talented or has someone established to* **take** *him* **up.**

7. vazhdoj

□ *She* **took up** *the narrative where John had left off.*

8. zë (vend, kohë)

□ *This table* **takes up** *too much space.* □ *'How can you move about in here? The bed* **takes up** *half the room.'* □ *My time is fully* **taken up** *with writing.*

9. ndërpres (për ta kontradiktuar, kritikuar)

□ *'I wonder if you'll find them likeable?' 'What's the difference?' he* **took** *me* **up** *sharply.*

10. mbledh, koleksionoj

□ *We are* **taking up** *a collection to buy flowers for John, because he is in the hospital.*

11. heq, marr

□ *John had his driver's license* **taken up** *for speeding.*

12. fus, ngushtoj, shkurtoj

□ *The tailor* **took up** *the legs of the trousers.*

13. pranoj

□ *She* **took up** *his offer of a drink.*

14. ngre, rimarr

□ *I'd like to* **take up** *the point you raised earlier.*

take up a position zë pozicion

□ *The evening before the battle, Wellington* **took up** *a defensive position along, and to the rear of, a long ridge.* □ *'Now, while the fieldmen are* **taking up** *their positions for the left-hander, I'll bring you up to date on the score-card.'*

take up arms rrëmbej, rrok armët

□ *The country would certainly* **take up arms** *in its own defence.* □ *His people and the Emperor Charles would* **take up arms** *against him if he killed either the woman or her daughter.* □ *The peasants up in the mountains have* **taken up arms** *against the government.*

take up one's residence banon, jeton, ngulet, vendoset, zë vend

□ *For part of the year, the Queen* **takes up residence** *at Sandringham.* □ *Snakes sometimes* **take up residence** *in the disused portions of the nest.*

take up the cudgels for përkrah, mbroj fuqishëm

□ *His wife had* **taken up the cudgels** *for her friend.*

take vengeance hakmerrem, marr hak

□ *They were determined to* **take vengeance** *on the enemy.*

take wing fluturon, ngrihet në fluturim; merr krahë

□ *The huge bird ran along the ground and then at last* **took flight.** □ *Flocks of guira cuckoos would wait until the lumbering car was within six feet of them, and then they would* **take wing** *and stream off like a flock of brown-paper darts.* □ *'You get a good wage—what on earth do you do with your money?' 'I don't know, it just seems to take wing.'* □ *After the publication of his first book, his career as an author has taken wings.*

talk about 1. flas për (rreth)

□ *He brought out a bottle of whisky, and began to talk about old times.*

□ *She smiled, 'What do you want to talk about?'* □ *Grandmother, Majauszkiene had lived in the midst of misfortunes so long that it had come to be her element and she talked about starvation, sickness, and death as other people might about weddings and holidays.*

2. flitet, përflitet, merret nëpër gojë

□ *'Why must she go about with that dreadful man? She's beginning to get herself talked about.'*

talk back replikoj, ia kthej fjalën (me shpërfillje, vrazhdësi, arrogancë, harbutëri)

□ *When the teacher told the boy to sit down, he talked back to her and said she couldn't make him.*

talk big mburrem, lavdërohem, flas me mburrje

□ *Rex likes to talk big as though he were a very important person.* □ *He talks big about his pitching, but he hasn't won a match.* □ *He talks big but doesn't actually do anything.*

talk business flas (diskutoj) për çështje pune

'I've got to dine with a man in Downhaven.' 'Nasty wretch, why didn't he ask me?' said Isabel. 'We shall only be talking business. You wouldn't be interested.'

talk down 1. bëj dikë të heshtë (duke ngritur zërin etj.)

□ *I objected to the proposal, but they*

talked me down. □ *He made another weak protest and was talked down by Jenny.*

2. flas me një ndjenjë superioriteti

□ *'Credit the child with some intelligence; try to avoid talking down.'*

talk nineteen to the dozen llomotis, flas pa pushim, flas si çatalle mulliri

□ *At tea time he came down to the drawing room, and found them talking, as he expressed it, nineteen to the dozen.*

talk of the devil (and he appears) përmend qenin, bëj gati shkopin

□ *'Dr. Hasselbacher!' Wormold called to him. 'Oh, it is you, Mr. Wormold. I was just thinking of you. Talk of the devil,' he said, making a joke of it, but Wormold could have sworn that the devil had scared him.* □ *'Well, well,' said Alice, welcoming him in, 'talk of the devil and he's sure to appear. I was just wondering if you'd be up here for Easter.'*

talk sense flas në mënyrë të arsyeshme, flas me mend; flas me vend

□ *It was, he felt, too much to expect that she would talk sense about him as an author, since he did not write for idiot minds like hers.* □ *'Well, if you want an exciting holiday, instead of lying on a beach for a fortnight in the sun, why don't you go to Greenland?' 'Ah! Now you're taking sense!'*

talk shop flas (diskutoj) për çështje pune

□ *They never discuss plays or books or films, or anything outside their jobs:. They just talk shop all the time.* □ *Also, a tea break with the nurses is immensely valuable. We always talk shop. It's the only real chance we get to chat about our patients.* □ *Two chemists were talking shop, and I hardly understood a word they said.*

talk one's/sb's head off dërdëllit, flas pa pushim (pa hesap); i çaj veshët, i lodh kokën (duke folur)

□ *Lady Britomart: Andrew, you can* **talk my head off**, *but you can't change wrong into right.* □ *'Don't expect me to sit here like a good boy while Smithers is up there* **taking his** *fat* **head off!** *'* □ *'When me and Jeremy are by ourselves, he talks, he talks, he* **talks my head off**. *'*

talk over 1. bisedoj, diskutoj (një çështje etj.)

□ *We* **talked** *the matter* **over**. □ *When they had gotten him to sleep, however, they sat by the kitchen fire and* **talked** *it* **over** *in... whispers.* □ *Come now, Nurse Lloyd, don't misunderstand me. Suppose we* **talk** *this* **over** *together in the front room.*

2. bind, i kthej mendjen

□ *Fred is trying to* **talk** *Bill* **over** *to our side.*

talk round sth flas larg e larg

□ *'Don't try to put me off this time. I don't want to* **talk round** *the subject, I want to talk about it.'* □ *'With him, you never get a direct discussion of the point that's bothering you. He'll always* **talk round** *it.'*

talk sb into/out of doing sth kandis (bind, i mbush mendjen dikujt) për të (mos) bërë diçka

□ *'I know you've got a smooth tongue, so don't even start to* **talk** *me* **into** *buying.'* □ *He* **talked** *his father* **into** *lending him the car.*

talk sb over/round bëj të kthejë (ndërrojë) mendje (mendim)

□ *He was against our proposal at first but eventually we* **talked** *him* **over**. □ *He thought he could* **talk** *me* **round** *like last time, when he had me voting*

for some candidate who refused to stand.

talk through (a hole in) one's hat flas budallallëqe (gjepura, mbroçkulla, dokrra), flas kodra pas bregut

□ *If he says he saw me in the town last night, he's* **talking through a hole in** *his hat:* I *was at home all evening.* □ *John said that the earth is near the sun in summer, but the teacher said he was* **talking through his hat**.

talk to sb qortoj, heq vërejtjen

□ *'That child needs to be* **talked** *to, and you are the person to do it.'*

talk to sb like a Dutch uncle qortoj butë (me të butë), i flas ashpër pa të keq, i flas dikujt si një plak i moçëm

□ *Stop* **talking to** *me* **like a Dutch uncle** *about my duty to my family, my school and my country.* □ *I don't like* **talking to** *young people* **like a Dutch uncle**, *but sometimes it is useful.* □ *He says he's had to* **talk to** *them* **like a Dutch uncle**, *but it's no use this time.* □ *Tomorrow I'll* **talk to** *them* **like a Dutch uncle**... *I could count the real sailors amongst them on the fingers of one hand.*

talk the hind leg off a donkey/mule prashis, flas shumë, flas pa pushim

□ *She would* **talk the hind leg off** *a donkey*, *she goes on and on.* □ *He would obviously do very well in politics—he could* **talk the hind legs off a donkey**. □ *I dried her tears and exercized an old man's privilege of* **talking the hind leg off a donkey**.

talk turkey flas seriozisht

□ *If you are interested in the job, I don't say we couldn't* **talk turkey** *over a drink of beer.* □ *'I don't think I'll come. Fancy-dress parties aren't really my scene.' 'Not even if I tell you Sue will be there?' 'Ah, now you're* *taking turkey!'* □ *Let's talk turkey and get this matter settled.*

talk up 1. flas në favor (mbështetje) të, mbështes

□ *Let's talk up the game and get a big crowd.*

2. flas më qartë

□ *The teacher asked the student to talk up.*

tall order, a gjë e vështirë (të bëhet, arrihet etj.)

□ *The group leader expects each member of the group to sell £20 worth of tickets: I think that's a tall order.*

tall story/tale, a përrallë me mbret

□ *Do you believe that yarn, Bertie? It sounds to me a pretty tall story.* □ *He tells some tall stories about his war experiences; personally, I don't believe them.*

tan sb's hide rrah, zhdëp në dru, ia bëj kurrizin më të butë se barkun

□ *... I'll have to quit or Grandma will sure tan my hide.* □ *Bob's father tanned his hide for staying out too late.*

tarred with the same brush të një kallëpi, të një brumi, miell i një thesi, bukë e një mielli

□ *I would not trust anyone from that group; they are all tarred with the same brush.* □ *They are all tarred with one brush—all stuffed with a heap of lies.*

teach one's grandmother to suck eggs i tregon (i rrëfen) babit arat, hajde baba të të tregoj arat (vreshtin)

□ *Would the house accord him its 'customary indulgence', or would it say: 'Young fellow, teaching your grandmother to suck eggs, shut up!'* □ *Tom could never resist the satisfaction of teaching his grandmother to suck eggs. 'One can be jealous without being in love,' he went on, but*

one can't be in love without being jealous.' □ *Once we started playing our game of tennis I discovered that the man I had been giving advice to was actually a better player than I was. I had been teaching my grandmother to suck eggs.*

teach sb a lesson i jap dikujt një mësim të mirë

□ *He was almost run down by a car because he ran across the road without looking first; I hope that his narrow escape will teach him a lesson.*

teach sb to do sth ia rregulloj (ia tregoj, ia ujdis) qejfin

□ *Wait till I get hold of him! I'll teach him to tell lies about me!*

tear down 1. rrëzoj për tokë

□ *Streets of terrace houses have been torn down to make way for blocks of council apartments.* □ *The workmen tore down the old house and built a new one in its place.*

2. zbërthej, çmontoj

□ *The mechanics had to tear down the engine, and fix it, and put it together again.*

tear oneself away from ndahem, shkëputem, shqitem

□ *She could scarcely tear herself away from the book.* □ *Do tear yourself away from the television and come out for a walk.* □ *I found the program absolutely fascinating. I couldn't tear myself away even to finish an urgent letter.*

tear one's hair shkul flokët (nga hidhërimi, etj.)

□ *Uncle Daniel tore his hair with rage when he learned that Emily had gone away.* □ *She stamped and raged and tore her hair, and swore she'd never been so insulted.*

tear sb off a strip/tear a strip/strips off sb qortoj ashpër

□ *Why did she feel frightened of Anna, as if the other was going to start **tearing a strip off** Jenny's family.* □ *'You've been a long time with the boss. Hasn't been **tearing you off a strip**, has he?'*

tear to pieces/shreds 1. copëtoj, bëj copa -copa

□ *Material passed through this machine is **torn to shreds** by a set of powerful blades.* □ *Slowly and deliberately he **tore** her letter **to pieces**.*

2. rrëzoj, hedh poshtë, bëj fërtele

□ *She had reached the point where she couldn't face having another piece of work **torn to pieces** by her tutor.* □ *'Your case would never stand up in court; a good criminal lawyer would **tear** it **to shreds**.*

tear up 1. gris, copëtoj, bëj copa-copa

□ *'Did you mean me to keep the receipt? I'm afraid I've **torn** it **up**.'* □ *'Daddy hasn't got your letter at all. I have. I took it and **tore** it **up**.'*

2. braktis, hedh poshtë

□ *The other side clearly doesn't regard such agreements as binding; they can be **torn up** at will.*

tell its own tale flet vetë

□ *No one had to tell me that my precious vase had been broken. The broken pieces on the floor **told their own tale**.*

tell it/that to the marines! shiti gjetkë, shitja tjetërkujt këto!

□ *The climate's all right when it isn't too dry or too wet—it suits my wife fine, but when they talk about making your fortune all I can say is **tell it to the marines**.* □ *You say that you have been studying hard; after such poor results, you can **tell that to the Marines!***

tell me another! mos më përrallis! tregoja tjetërkujt ato!

□ *Pygmalion ... ! So come to the point, I have succeeded in making artificial human beings. Real live ones, I mean. Incredulous voices. Oh, come! **Tell us another.***

tell off qortoj

□ *I was ten minutes late and she **told me off** in front of everyone.* □ *He didn't like being **told off** for something he hadn't done.* □ *He **told** the boy **off** for making so many careless mistakes.*

tell on kallëzoj

□ *'I won't ever do it again. I swear. Please don't **tell on** me!'* □ *Andy hit a little girl and John **told** the teacher **on** him.*

tell sb apart dalloj, shquaj, ndaj

□ *Every day is identical with the one before. I literally can't **tell** them **apart**.* □ *Even when magnified, the two organisms are difficult to **tell apart**.* □ *The two brothers were so similar in appearance that it was almost impossible to **tell** them **apart**.*

tell/see sth a mile off dalloj, shikoj një kilometër larg

□ *He's lying: you can **see that a mile off**.* □ *Now that everybody in our yard hadn't been a struggler—and still was—one way or another. But you could **tell a mile off** that she was a struggler, and that was what nobody liked.* □ *'Do you think these two are in love?' 'Do I think? Anyone can **see that a mile off**.*

tell tales (about sb) 1. trilloj, nxjerr e përhap lart e poshtë të fshehtat (prapësitë, gabimet etj.) e dikujt; përhap thashetheme për

□ *All the boys were fond of him, and was he, Ernest, to **tell tales** about him?* □ *Dead men **tell no tales**.*

2. gënjej, mashtroj, tregoj rrena

□ *He was punished for **telling** so many **tales**.*

tell tales out of school nxjerr fjalë jashtë, nxjerr një fshehtë jashtë

□ *A very handsome supper, at which, to **tell tales out of school** ... the guests used to behave abominably.*

tell the truth them të vërtetën

□ *'Daddy hasn't got your letter at all. I took it and tore it up.' Prissie's face grew still. She sank into a chair. 'Nicky! Are you **telling the truth**?'* □ *Jo: I had to drag it out of her. She didn't want to tell me.* □ *Bob: That doesn't mean to say it's the truth. Do people ever **tell the truth** about themselves?* □ *The sergeant said slowly, 'There is something wrong here. I can smell it. You are not **telling the truth**.'*

tell the world shpall botërisht, njoftoj (bëj të njohur) publikisht

□ *We all know you've done a good job, but do you have to **tell the world**?* □ *Granny Barnacle gave notice to the doctor that she refused further treatment, was discharging herself next day, and that she would **tell the world** why.*

tell (the) time njoh orën

□ *Can Mary **tell the time** yet?* □ *She's only five, she can't **tell the time** yet.*

tempest in the teapot furtunë në një gotë ujë

□ *The debate over the naming of the new town park was **a tempest in a teapot**.*

temp fate/fortune/Providence veproj me rrezik; provoj fatin

□ *When he attempted to break the land speed record last year his car blew up; now he is trying it again. He seems to be **tempting fate**.* □ *I had no doubt that Martin did not know of the letter; it would have seemed to hint **tempting fate**. For myself, I felt the same kind of superstition.* □ *'He paid the £150 deposit so readily I might*

*have asked for more.' 'And then he might have backed out of the deal altogether. £150 is all you need to go ahead and there's no sense in **tempting Providence**.*

ten to one me ngjasë, ka shumë të ngjarë; me sa duket

□ *There was a considerable dust-storm in progress. '**Ten to one** they can't come down here.'* □ *'No', he thought, at last, '**ten to one** he isn't in...'* □ *Here's a man.... in such rotten shape that if I sent a good horse after him now it's **ten to one** he couldn't get on him.*

thank one's lucky stars jam fatlum, jam me fat

□ *You can **thank your lucky stars** that you don't have to go to this dreary reception.* □ *You should **thank your lucky stars** that you didn't have to see her at the last. Your memory is pure, you will always remember her as she used to be.*

thank you faleminderit, ju faleminderit

□ ***Thank you** for giving me a lift.*

thanks to falë, në sajë të, për hir të

□ *Five years ago I could have been made into a boring, heartless climber whom everyone ran a mile from. But, **thanks to** you, I have grasped that a certain fundamental decency to others is necessary if one is to get anywhere.* □ *The play succeeded **thanks to** fine acting by all the cast.* □ ***Thanks to** the bad weather, the match had been cancelled.* □ ***Thanks to** your help we were successful.*

that's all kjo është e gjitha

□ *'You're not going to tell on me, Mr. Lampton?' 'No, you fool. Just don't do it again, **that's all**.'* □ *You don't have to wait for an answer. Just put the note in the mailbox, **that's all**.*

that's is for certain/sure kjo është e sigurt, si një e një që bëjnë dy

□ *'Nice for them to have a friend in the building trade.' 'Oh, Bill won't do the job for nothing, **that's for sure.***

that's life kjo është jeta, kështu e ka jeta

□ *I've always liked black-haired and dark-eyed men, but I fell in love with a blond, blue-eyed boy. Oh well, **that's life**, I suppose.* □ *At first the decision to close was accepted as just another one of those cruel surprises that often emerge when a big business gobbles up a little business. The women were sad, regretful, but, well what can you do? **That's life.***

that is (to say) domethënë; pra, si për-fundim

□ *The next step after preparing the maps is for the engineer to decide on the 'grade line,' **that is**, the height of the center of the road along the whole route.* □ *He's a local government administrator, **that is to say**, a civil worker.*

that's that kjo është e gjitha; kaq!

□ *As he finished off painting his house, Jack said: 'Well, **that's that** for another few years.'* □ *I take it **that's that**—we've heard your final offer?*

then and there/there and then aty për aty, sakaq, menjëherë

□ *He was not in the office and I even-tually tracked him down in the dining room. So we discussed the problem **then and there**.* □ *I decided to do it **then and there**.* □ *I made my choice **then and there**.*

there and back vajtje e ardhje, vajtje e kthim

□ *Can I go **there and back** in a day?* □ *He lived a long way out of the city and thought nothing of making the daily journey, **there and back**, throughout the three terms.*

there's many a slip 'twixt (the) cup and (the) lip me të thënë e me të bërë shkon në mes një lumë i tërë

□ *'They are bound to win now.' 'Unless one of them breaks an oar or something. **There's many a slip 'twixt the cup and the lip.'*** □ *Of course advertising works, and so does public relations: but as Party Political Broadcasts show, **there's many a slip 'twixt the cup and the curling lip**.*

there's no place like home s'ka si shtëpia; bukë e hi e në shtëpi

□ *She drew the curtains and sat down by Harold's side, and took his hand, and when he said, '**There's no place like home**, is there?' her thoughts did not wince at this too obvious remark.* □ *I adore seeing the world. But, let's face it, **there** really **is no place** quite **like** your own **home**.*

thick and fast lumë, si lumë

□ *Offers of help are coming in **thick and fast**.* □ *The cars came **thick and fast** during the rush hour.*

thick with plot me, mbushur me

□ *The air is **thick with** dust.* □ *The building was **thick with** reporters.*

think about sb/sth mendoj për

□ *Please **think about** the proposal and let me have your views tomorrow.* □ *'What are you **thinking about**?' 'Oh, nothing in particular.'* □ *I'm interested in buying your house, but I'd like more time to **think about** it before making a decision.*

think better of sb krijoj mendim më të mirë për

□ *We **think better of** him since we've learnt the facts.* □ *I **think better of** you than to believe you refused to help him.*

think better of sth ndërroj mendje (qëndrim), rimendoj diçka, kthej mendje

□ *I was going to go out for a walk this evening, but, when I saw the rain, I* **thought better of** *it.* □ *In the morning you will* **think better of** *your decision to go on such a long hike.* □ *'He said plainly that he was not going to do it!' 'Yes, I know he did, but I fancied he might have* **thought better of** *it.'* □ *He shook hands with him and was about to tell him about the matter when he* **thought better of** *it.* □ *I was going to buy a pair of shoes, but I* **thought better of** *it.*

think fit to do sth e shoh me vend, e shoh të arsyeshme, e shoh të udhës

□ *He did not* **think fit** *to do what I suggested.* □ *Do as you* **think fit.**

think highly of vlerësoj shumë (lart), kam mendim shumë të mirë për

□ *He is a great admirer of yours; he* **thinks** *very* **highly of** *your work.*

think little of vlerësoj pak, konsideroj të parëndësishëm (të pavlerë)

□ *John* **thought little of** *Ted's plan for the party.* □ *He must* **think** *very* **little of** *his wife if he treats her so badly.*

think nothing of 1. s'e ka për gjë, e ka kollaj, e ka gjë të zakonshme, s'e ka problem të

□ *Some would have thought these large transfers of money highly suspicious, but at least his colleagues* **thought nothing of** *it.* □ *He* **thinks nothing of** *walking 10 miles a day.* □ *He trains very hard; he* **thinks nothing of** *running 12 miles every day.*

2. s'ka gjë

□ *'I am very grateful to you for helping me.' 'Oh,* **think nothing of** *it.'* □ *'I'm sorry if I interrupted your meal.' 'Oh, that's all right.* **Think nothing of** *it.'*

think of sth/doing sth 1. marr parasysh, shqyrtoj, mendoj

□ *I have a hundred and one things to* **think of** *before I can go there.* □ *He's a wonderful organizer; he* **thinks of** *everything!*

2. kujtoj, sjell ndër mend

□ *'I can't* **think of** *his name at the moment, but he was a tall chap with glasses.'*

3. përfytyroj, imagjinoj, më shkon nëpër mend

□ *I couldn't* **think of** *such a thing.*

4. parashtroj; sugjeroj, propozoj

□ *Can anybody* **think of** *a way to raise money?*

think sth out mendoj, peshoj mirë

□ *There is little opportunity to* **think out** *what the long-term solution may be.* □ **Think out** *your answer before you start writing.*

think sth over mendohem mirë (thellë); rrah mirë me mend; persiatem; e peshoj mirë; bluaj në mendje

□ *She had* **thought** *the plan* **over;** *it was important that he would think it had been his idea.* □ *Please* **think over** *what I've said.* □ *She was left alone to* **think over** *the sudden and wonderful events of the day.* □ *Jurgis went out and walked down the street to* **think** *it* **over.**

think sth up ideoj, mendoj, nxjerr nga mendja; trilloj, sajoj, shpik nga mendja

□ *Here's no knowing what he will* **think up** *next.* □ *There were one or two fellows who* **thought up** *ideas of their own.* □ *He would have to* **think up** *some more catchy names for those designs.*

think twice mendoj mirë

□ *You should* **think twice** *before buying such an expensive house. It*

will take you a long time to pay for it.
□ *Do not* **think twice** *about it, but say 'No'; that's all.* □ *The teacher advised John to* **think twice** *before deciding to quit school.*

thirst for sth kam etje për, jam i etur për

□ *He* **thirsted for** *knowledge.* □ *He was surrounded by savages* **thirsting for** *his blood.* □ *These advertisements are calculated to appeal to young men* **thirsting for** *adventure.*

thorn in one's flesh/side, a halë në sy, ferrë (gjemb) në këmbë, bezdi e madhe

□ *The Cranstons and the Finchleys were in the main* **a thorn in the flesh** *of the remainder of the elite of Lycurgus— too showy and too aggressive.* □ *Julia was his eldest step-brother's wife, and* **a thorn in his side.** □ *He's been* **a thorn in my side** *since he joined this department.* □ *He's a relative of course, but* **a thorn in the flesh.** *I wish he could emigrate or something.*

thrash sth out rrah, shoshit (një çështje); shkoq një punë hollë-hollë

□ *We decided to* **thrash out** *all our problems.* □ *He was worried enough to call a meeting at the Windsor Hotel to* **thrash** *the problem* **out.** □ *We can leave the second part to them, and lastly we can* **thrash out** *our conclusions.*

thrash sb within an inch of his life rrah për vdekje

□ *... I should like to* **thrash you within an inch of your life.**

thread one's way through hyj (futem, kaloj, eci) me zor mes

□ *He* **threaded his way** *swiftly among the piled furniture.* □ *He* **threaded his way through** *the crowded streets of the town.* □ *I* **threaded my way through** *the crowd with the dog at my heels.*

through and through krejtësisht, plotësisht, fund e krye

□ *He had been caught in the rain and is wet* **through and through.** □ *He is not just a crook. He's mean and rotten* **through and through.**

□ *Mrs. Warren... I know you* **through and through** *by your likeness to your father....* □ *And she had only been with him once for a weekend; but her thoughts had been so constantly with him that she felt she knew him* **through and through.** □ *He read the book* **through and through.** □ *Have nothing to with him; he is a villain* **through and through.**

through thick and thin në të mirë e në të keq, në ditë të mirë e në ditë të keqe

□ *She has been very loyal to her husband; she stood by him* **through thick and thin.** □ *Yet Stilwell was an almost impossible man to work with, and even the small group of American officers who stuck loyally by him* **through thick and thin** *were frightened of him.* □ *A real friend is one who will stand by you* **through thick and thin.**

throw a party jap një pritje

□ *Jack is* **throwing a party** *next week to celebrate his twenty-first birthday.* □ **Throw a** *small* **party** *and make that an excuse for contacting him.* □ *'Could I come up for a weekend and bring my fiance with me?' 'You do that, and we'll* **throw a party for** *you.'*

throw a monkey wrench/throw a wrench in the works hedh gurë në rrota, vë (fut) shkopinj në rrota, nxjerr pengesa

□ *The game was going smoothly until you* **threw a monkey wrench into the works** *by fussing about the rules.*

throw a spanner in the works hedh gurë në rrota, vë (fut) shkopinj në rrota, nxjerr pengesa; pengoj (sabotoj) planet e

□ *We were going to have a meeting tonight but Jim **threw a spanner in the works** by saying that he couldn't come.*

throw away 1. hedh, flak

□ *Beer is now often sold in cans that can be **thrown away**. □ Don't **throw** your bus ticket **away**, the inspector may want to see it.*

2. humb, nuk e shfrytëzoj, lë të shkojë

□ *The visiting team built up an impressive lead in the first half, then **threw** it **away** by loose defensive play in the second.*

3. shkapërdredh, harxhoj kot, bë rrush e kumbulla

□ *You may be **throwing** your savings **away** on shares that will be worthless in a few years.*

throw a wet blanket on/upon shkurajoj, i pres hovin (vrullin etj.)

□ *The latter came and at once **threw a blanket over** me; he was so utterly dull and commonplace.*

throw caution/discretion to the winds lë mënjanë qëndrimin e kujdesshëm, lë mënjanë përkujdesjen

□ *The general decided to **throw caution to the winds** and attack boldly during the daylight. □ After the guests had a few drinks, **discretion** was **thrown to the winds** and a good deal of malicious gossip flew about.*

throw cold water on pres ftohtë, mbaj qëndrim të ftohtë (shkurajues) ndaj, tregohem i ftohtë ndaj

□ *She immediately **threw cold water on** the proposition. □ Father **threw cold water on** our plan to camp in the mountains because he thought it was dangerous. □ Bill **threw cold water on** the new plan. He said that it would never work.*

throw doubt upon dyshoj, vë në dyshim

□ *You have no right to **throw doubt on** his veracity.*

throw down one's arms dorëzon (hedh) armët

□ *The enemy soldiers **threw down their arms**.*

throw down the gaunlet hedh dorezën, sfidoj

□ *The champion will soon have to defend his title again—a young American contender has **thrown down the gaunlet**. □ Another candidate for the presidency has **thrown down the gaunlet**.*

throw dust in sb's eyes i hedh hi syve

□ *Dave said it to **throw dust in your eyes**. □ It required a long discourse to **throw dust in the eyes of** common sense.*

throw in shtoj, përfshij diçka (pa rritur çmimin)

□ *'If you're set on buying the house, we'll **throw in** the carpets and curtains at no extra cost.' □ You can have the piano for $200, and I'll **throw in** the stool as well.*

throw in one's lot with sb lidh fatin me

□ *After the rebels' great victory against the government forces, many people **threw in their lot with** the rebel army. □ After years in the political wilderness, Stephens has **thrown in his lot with** the new party leadership. □ He was hoping to convey the impression that he had been encouraged to **throw in his lot with** Bunder, and was hesitating.*

throw in the sponge/the towel hedh peshqirin, dorëzohem, pranoj humbjen

□ *'They ain't nothin' but scrap. No **throwin' up the sponge**. This is a grudge fight an' it's to a finish.'*

□ *... he felt a kind of professional pride in the girl for carrying the thing off so splendidly despite Yates's line-up of tricks. 'Yates', he said, 'don't you think you'd better* **throw in the towel**?' □ *After being knocked down four times in one round, he decided to* **throw in the towel**. □ *After his man had been knocked to the floor twice for a count of eight, the second decided he'd had enough and* **threw in the towel**. □ *'I know you've been going through a tough time, but it's a bit early to* **throw in the towel**.

throw into confusion pështjelloj, shkaktoj pështjellim

□ *Her unexpected arrival* **threw us into** *total* **confusion**. □ *This unexpected change of plans* **threw everyone into confusion**.

throw into relief spikat, bie në sy, del në pah

□ *The roofs of the city are* **thrown into** *sharp* **relief** *against the evening sky.* □ *Skilfully placed lights* **throw** *the marble figures* **into** *clear* **relief**.

throw light on/upon sth hedh dritë mbi

□ *Hugo's inquiries rarely failed to* **throw** *an extraordinary amount of* **light on** *whatever he concerned himself with.* □ *As his statement was read a very clear* **light was thrown upon** *the situation.* □ *What she said* **threw** *new* **light on** *the matter.*

throw mud at hedh baltë mbi

□ *A woman in my position must expect to have more* **mud thrown at** *her than a less important people.*

throw off 1. heq shpejt e shpejt

□ *He* **threw off** *his shirt and trousers and plunged into the cool water.*

2. flak tej

□ *If only he would* **throw off** *that carefully cultivated manner!*

3. heq qafe

□ *'I can't manage the meeting tonight. I'm still trying to* **throw off** *this wretched cold.'*

4. krijoj, kompozoj aty për aty

□ *The two men sat down over a bottle of wine and* **threw off** *a few songs and sketches for the evening's concert.*

throw oneself into sth i futem me mish e me shpirt, nis me vrull (entusiazëm)

□ *She tried again to* **throw herself** *with a will* **into** *life.* □ *The Bafutians had obviously* **thrown themselves** *wholeheartedly* **into** *the task.* □ *He* **threw himself** *passionately* **into** *the completion of the circle.*

throw oneself on/upon sb's mercy lë veten në mëshirën e

□ *John was clearly guilty and could only* **throw himself on the mercy of** *the court.* □ *The accused man was clearly guilty; all he could do now was to* **throw himself upon the mercy of** *the court.*

throw one's weight about/around i jep rëndësi vetes, mbahet rëndë, mbahet me të madh, tundet e shkundet

□ *She was in here the other day,* **throwing her weight about** *as if she was Hedy Lamarr and Katharine Hepburn rolled into one.* □ *John was the star of the class play and was* **throwing his weight around** *telling the director how the scene should be played.* □ *I don't like the way that the boss's son comes into office and* **throws his weight around**.

throw on the defensive kaloj në mbrojtje

□ *The team was* **thrown on the defensive** *as their opponents rallied.*

throw open to sb hap

□ *The Art Gallery is* **thrown open to** *the public every day.*

throw out 1. hedh, flak

□ *There are some bundles of old*

*magazines here that I want to **throw out**.*

2. kundërshtoj, hedh poshtë

□ *The idea was put up to the Faculty Board, but they **threw** it **out**.*

3. hedh, them, shqiptoj tërthorazi (në mënyrë spontane)

□ *I wasn't offering a positive answer. All I was doing was **throwing out** a few suggestions as to how we might proceed.*

4. nxjerr, flak jashtë

□ *'Now that you know why I'm here, am I to be allowed to stay or are you going to **throw** me **out**?'*

5. ngatërroj, hutoj, i heq (i largoj) vëmendjen

□ *Keep quiet for a while or you'll **throw** me **out** in my calculations.*

□ *His calculations were **thrown out** by his mistaking a badly formed eight for three.*

throw out of gear stakoj

□ *The manager has changed the time of our lunch hour and it has **thrown** the whole office **out of gear**.*

throw overboard braktis; heq qafe; flak tej

□ *After heavily losing the election, the party **threw** their leader **overboard**.*

□ *The turncoats **threw overboard** all their former beliefs and abjectly joined the enemy's cause.* □ *We were **throwing overboard** the principle of concentration of effort.*

throw sb over lë, braktis

□ *It's very kind of you Tom not to **throw** Sid **over**.* □ *When he became rich he **threw over** all his old friends.*

throw sth in sb's face/teeth ia tha (ia përplasi) në fytyrë, ia tha ndër sy

□ *'The last thing I want to do is to **throw** a man's past **in his face** unless he's a double-dyed villain.'* □ *The crowd **threw in the** politician's **teeth** the*

promises that he had made to them before the election. □ *'My education, which you **throw in my face**, was an education along humane lines that didn't leave me with any illusions about the division of human beings into classes.*

throw sth up 1. nxjerr, vjell (ushqimin)

□ *He **threw** what he had eaten **up**.*

□ *'How horribly servile and ingratiating that man is. He makes me want to **throw up**!'*

2. lë, braktis, tërhiqem, heq dorë

□ *Charley had enough sense to **throw up** his job at the tax inspector's office.*

□ *You have **thrown up** a very promising career.*

3. nxjerr në pah

□ *Her research has **thrown up** some interesting facts.*

throw (cast) stones at sulmoj, akuzoj

□ *My dear, I have my doubts whether our duty does not stop at seeing to ourselves, without **throwing stones at** others.*

throw straw against the wind rrah ujë në havan

□ *You'll be **throwing straw against the wind** if you go on like this.*

throw the baby out with the bath-water flak të mirën bashkë me të keqen, hedh grurin bashkë me bykun, djeg të njomin bashkë me të thatin

□ *We must be careful not to **throw the baby out with the bath-water**. Our task now is to control technology, not to turn away from it.* □ *There are weaknesses in the program, but if they act too hastily they may cause **the baby** to be **thrown out with the bath water**.*

thumb a lift/ride udhëtoj me makina të rastit (duke u ngritur dorën, gishtin e madh)

□ *It didn't cost me anything to reach here; I **thumbed a ride**.*

thumb one's nose at ngërdheshem, përqesh, i nxjerr gjuhën dikujt
□ *The boy was punished for thumbing his nose at a teacher.*

tickle sb's ribs gudulis; zbavit
□ *It's British Comedy Time again. Norman Wisdom, Margaret Rutherford and Jerry Desmonde conspire to tickle your ribs and give you the occasional choke.*

tickle pink/to death kënaq (zbavit) pa masë, shkrij fare
□ *Nancy was tickled pink with her new dress.* □ *It tickled me to death to hear how his wife had locked him out all night to cool off, but it can't have pleased him.* □ *First he's in despair because she comes back, and now he's miserable because she's gone away. He should be tickled to death and yet he isn't.*

tick off 1. spuntoj
□ *'Why did you tick these stores off in the inventory when you haven't checked that they're actually in stock? □ Those two jobs can be ticked off. I've already done them.*
2. qortoj
□ *If I went too fast again, I was quite prepared to be sent for and ticked off.*

tide sb over ndihmoj dikë të kapërcejë një periudhë të vështirë, e nxjerr (e qit) dikë në breg, nxjerr mbanë, hedh lumin
□ *It should be sufficient to tide you over your difficulties, Sid.* □ *'Give me something, just to tide me over till a can get a decent, steady job,' said Robert.* □ *Sarah could have found work other than nursing, to tide them over the years till the children could support themselves.*

tidy away heq, vë në vend
□ *'Do tidy your papers away; your desk looks in a terrible mess.'* □ *It was difficult to tell that anyone had stayed at the cottage. Plates, cups, knives and forks had been carefully tied away.*

tidy out pastroj, rregulloj
□ *The boys spent part of the last day of terms tidying out their desks and handling in their books.*

tidy up rregulloj, rregullohem
□ *I say, do try to tidy up your study, all your books are in a muddle.* □ *We need to tidy up the place a bit before the guests start arriving.*

tie down (to) lidh, kufizoj, mbaj të lidhur
□ *I'd like to take a job overseas, but there are too many things tying me down here.* □ *Children do tie you down, don't they?*

tie in with lidh, përputh, përshtat me
□ *This evidence ties in very well with the picture which detectives have already built up.* □ *Doesn't this tie in with what we were told last week?* □ *We managed to tie in our holiday arrangements with my work program for the early summer.*

tied to one's mother's apron strings lidhur pas fustanit të s'ëmës
□ *She will never leave home; she is too tied to her mother's apron strings.* □ *Even after he grew up, he was still tied to his mother's apron strings.*

tie sb's hands i lidh duart dikujt, s'lë dikë të veprojë
□ *These rules of procedure, designed to protect the private from undue interference, do however tie the hands of the police in dealing with somebody whom they have very good reason to suspect of carrying a weapon or illicit or stolen goods.*

tie up 1. lidh
□ *Tie the paintbrushes up into bundles and put them away carefully.*

2. mbyll, përfundoj, kopsit

□ *I like to get all the arrangements for a holiday **tied up** a month in advance.*

□ *'I'm glad I got that all **tied up**, Sarah. I never did like to see any ends sticking out, I always liked to finish things.'*

3. zë (merr) kohën, mban të lidhur (të zënë)

□ *'As far as I can tell, this editing will tie me **up** for the next fortnight.'*

4. lidh, ngatërron, bën lëmsh

□ *The crash of the two trucks **tied up** all traffic in the center of the town.*

5. ndalon, pengon

□ *The strike **tied up** production for a week.*

tighten one's belt shtrëngoj rripin

□ *My salary is going to be cut as from next month, so I shall just have to **tighten my belt**.* □ *In Emily's own family, uncomfortable things are not said, financial problems are real but cloudy, **belts are tightened** and chins kept up.*

tighten the screws i shtrëngoi burgjitë, ia mblodhi mirë

□ *When many students still missed class after he began giving daily quizzes, the teacher **tightened the screws** by failing anyone absent four times.*

tilt at windmills luftoj me mullinjtë e erës

□ *'So let us stop bickering within our ranks. Stop **tilting at the windmills**. Stop talking of victories over our colleagues and concentrate instead on winning victories over the Tories.'*

tilt/tip/turn the scales/the balance përmbys ekuilibrin, ndryshoj gjendjen (situatën)

□ *One of the visiting team's best player was injured and this **tilted the scales** in favor of the home team.*

□ *'We don't need to go to a place like this.' 'What's wrong with it?' he demanded. I might just have managed to **tip the balance**, but unfortunately at that moment Ned spoke up.*

time after time kohë pas kohe

□ *His father was a runaway baker's apprentice from Norfolk, a violent animal who reckoned to be drunk every evening and who **time after time** gambled away his money but somehow lasted the course.*

time and (time) again shpeshherë, shpesh, vazhdimisht

□ *Children are forgetful and must be told **time and time again** how to behave.* □ ***Time and again** I've told you not to read lying in bed.* □ ***Time and again** movements broke down through passes going astray, and much of the play was scrambling in the extreme.*

time and tide wait for no man koha s'pret

□ *We must make the best use of our time because we know that **time and tide wait for no man**.* □ *'The camera is at the bottom of my rucksack and the light will be better in the morning.' But **time and tide wait for no man** and when he went back in the morning the greyland geese had gone.*

time flies koha fluturon

□ *But meanwhile it flies, irretrievable **time flies**.* □ *Peter: Twelve years? But I only left a few months ago. Jason: That's the way **time flies**.*

time hangs/lies heavy on one's hands s'di si të vrasë (kalojë) kohën

□ *He had a rich abundance of idle time, but it never **hung heavy on his hands**, for he interested himself in every new things that was born into the universe of ideas...* □ *While these acts and deeds were in progress in*

and out of the office of Sampson
Brass, Richard Swiveller, being often
left alone therein, began to find that
time hang heavy on his hands. □ Did
he think Irma was lonely? Well, he
couldn't answer that one; she hadn't
time to be lonely in the bar. Loneliness was a matter of feeling time
hanging heavy on your hands,
wasn't it?

time has come (for sb) to do sth, the
ka ardhur koha që
□ Ned had been leaning against the
wall, listening, with his arms folded;
but now he straightened up and came
forward, as if the time had come for
him to take control of the situation.

time is on the side of sb koha është në
anën e
□ But Princess Anne knows that time
isn't on her side. In a recent interview
she was asked when a showjumper
should quit competitive riding. 'When
you lose your nerve, probably,' she
replied. 'It shouldn't take too long.'
□ We may comfort ourselves by
saying that, if we wait, time is on our
side. I have never believed that. Time
is neutral. □ Although she failed the
exam she has time on her side; she'll
still be young enough to take it in her
next year.

time is ripe for sth/sb to do sth, (the)
është pikërisht koha që
□ The sea was now choppy and one
slightly seasick voice suggested that
the time was ripe to return to the
warm comfort of the hotel.

time of one's life çastet më të mira (më
të lumtura) të jetës
□ Your son seems to enjoy staying
with us; he's been having the time of
his life.

time (alone) will tell/show/reveal
koha do ta tregojë

□ Time will show which of us is right.
□ Time will alone reveal whether
they were wise decisions—but good
or bad I made them, and the full
responsibility is mine.

times out of (without) number një
mijë herë, sa e sa herë
□ I have read that novel times
without number.

tip of the iceberg, the maja e ajsbergut
□ Theirs was one of the biggest tax
evasion cases ever prosecuted,
although the million dollars involved
was described by a Government
lawyer as 'only the tip of the iceberg'. □ Having seen the mass of documents (you see only the tip of the
iceberg in the book), there's no question in my mind that ...

tip sb a wink ia bëj me sy, i shkel
syrin, i luaj syrin
□ If he tipped Elsie a wink, she'd drop
in that day, all casual-like, he was
sure she would.

tip sb the wink informoj, sinjalizoj,
paralajmëroj fshehurazi
□ 'That's right, slow and steady wins
the race. You stay in for a while, but
when you're ready, tip us the wink.'
□ A friend of his tipped him the wink
that the police were searching for
him, so he went into hiding.

tit for tat me të njëjtën monedhë, majë
për majë, flakë për flakë
□ Tom pushed Polly off her chair.
Then she got up and gave him tit for
tat by pushing him off his. □ I told him
if he did me any harm I would return
tit for tat.

to a degree/extent 1. deri diku, në një
farë shkallë
□ 'I find myself in a situation which to
a certain extent disqualifies me for
going into society.' □ I took Clarence
into my confidence, to a certain

degree, and we went to work. □ *I agree with you to a certain extent.*
2. shumë, tepër, jashtëzakonisht, jashtë mase
□ *She's rather an interfering type, but kindhearted and generous to a degree.* □ *Parsimonious to a degree, Ibsen invested every penny he could in guilt-edged securities.* □ *Dick is vain to a high degree.*

to advantage më mirë, më së miri; me efekt (rezultat pozitiv), në mënyrë të favorshme
□ *The garden is seen to advantage in summer when all the flowers are in bloom.* □ *The picture may be seen to advantage against a plain wall.* □ *For short distance measurement the surveyor's tachymeter is now widely used to advantage.* □ *She gave her pearls to her grand-daughter, round whose young throat she felt they would be displayed to greater advantage.* □ *On that route are the ports, and on that route we can use our sea power to the best advantage.*

to a fault së tepërmi, pa masë
□ *He is hard-working to a fault. I think it would be better if he were more relaxed.* □ *She is generous to a fault.*

to a hair 1. tamam, për mrekulli, në mënyrë të përsosur
□ *Three or four single men, who suit my temper to a hair.* □ *'The vocation will fit you to a hair,' I thought...* □ *The little girl's boot fitted to a hair.*
2. pikë për pikë, fije për fije, fije e për fe, me imtësi
□ *You've described him to a hair.*

to all appearances si duket, me sa duket, në dukje, në pamjen e jashtme
□ *'Did you suspect anything of this yourself?' 'No. To all appearances, they were a happily married couple.'*

□ *To all appearances, he is as healthy as ever, but I still think that a doctor should examine him.* □ *He did not answer and was to all appearance asleep.* □ *... a world featureless, colorless, and, to all appearance, boundless.*

to all intents and purposes thuajse në të gjitha drejtimet kryesore; gati; praktikisht; në të vërtetë, në fakt
□ *'Is this your first novel?' 'Well, to all intents and purposes, yes...'* □ *The house is ours to all intents and purposes, although we still have a few legal documents to sign.* □ *He was, in fact at fifty-eight, to all intents the same Paul Wagget who had decided thirteen years ago to abandon chartered accountancy in London for the life of a Highland sportsman.*

to a man/to the last man të gjithë pa përjashtim, nga i pari tek i fundit; si një trup i vetëm
□ *But some of the best poker players in the country live in Vengas. Almost to a man, they are Southernes.* □ *To a man, the crew said that they would follow their captain.* □ *They answered 'yes' to a man.* □ *They were killed, to the last man, in a futile attack.* □ *To a man, John's friends stood by him in his trouble.*

to and fro lart e poshtë, poshtë e përpjetë, tutje-tëhu, andej e këndej
□ *The huge floor was crowded with people walking to and fro, and every one of the chairs round the walls was occupied.* □ *Money and titles may be tossed to and fro, but not hearts.* □ *As she rocked to and fro she fell....* □ *The train was full. The guard went to and fro opening, closing, locking, unlocking the doors.*

to a nicety saktësisht, me saktësi (përpikëri)

The manner in which she received him was calculated to a nicety to seem cool without being uncivil. □ *He had calculated to a nicety how much material he would need to finish the job.* □ *He figured out his program for the day to a nicety.* □ *He judged the distance to a nicety.*

to a T/tee/turn tamam, për mrekulli, për bukuri

□ *My new job suits me to a T; it's just what I wanted.* □ *The roast was done to a turn.*

to begin with 1. pikësëpari, së pari, para së gjithash

□ *I'm not going. To begin with I haven't a ticket, and secondly I don't like the play.* □ *To begin with I don't like its color.*

2. si fillim

□ *To begin with he had no money, but later he became quite rich.* □ *What have you to say about that, to begin with?*

to be sure natyrisht, sigurisht, në të vërtetë

□ *He is clever, to be sure, but not very hard working.* □ *He is not, to be sure, as young as he used to be.*

to date deri më sot, deri tani

□ *To date, Pan Am has carried more than a million and a quarter jet passengers—far more than any other airline.* □ *They've been advertising in all the local papers for a nurse-companion, but with no result to date.* □ *We haven't heard from him to date.* □ *To date, we have not received any replies.* □ *This is the biggest donation we've had to date.* □ *Here is a record of all the money I have spent to date.*

toe the line/the mark zbatoj rregullat (urdhërat, detyrat, direktivat etj.) ndjek vijën (direktivat e)

□ *The new teacher will make Joe toe the line.* □ *Bill's father is strict with him and he has to toe the line.* □ *A middle-aged scientist said apologetically, 'You must understand; I have a family to support, so what else I can do but toe the line?'*

together with tok me, së bashku me, si dhe

□ *These new facts, together with the other evidence, prove the prisoner's innocence.* □ *John, together with his brother, has gone to the party.*

to little purpose pa dobi

□ *All the doctor's efforts were to little purpose. The child died.*

to my way of thinking sipas mendimit tim

□ *He is, to my way of thinking, the best player.*

tone down ul, zbut; bie, qetësohet

□ *Their enthusiasm has toned down since they discovered the cost.* □ *You'd better tone down the more offensive remarks in your article.* □ *His excitement toned down.* □ *The apology toned down his anger.*

tone in (with) shkon me, harmonizohet me

□ *These curtains tone in well with your rug.*

to my mind sipas mendimit tim

□ *To my mind, Bach is unsurpassed as a composer.* □ *The important paragraphs, to my mind, were the first four, which ran as follows...*

tone up forcon, gjallëron

□ *More exercise and a change of diet —that's what you need to tone you up.* □ *After a quick dip and a brisk rubdown his whole system felt toned up.* □ *Exercise tones up the muscles.*

to no purpose/avail pa dobi, pa sukses, më kot, pa rezultat

□ *He walked the floor of his little office, and later that of his room, putting one thing and another together to no avail.* □ *I have tried hard for you, but all to no purpose.* □ *For over a quarter of an hour he pottered about the barn, going stall to stall, rummaging the harness room and feed room, all to no purpose.* □ *I tried to save him from drowning, but my efforts were to no avail.*

too many cooks spoil the broth shumë dado e mbysin fëmijën

□ *Mrs Butcher: Work together? You mad? Peter: Many hands make light— how does it go? Alex: Too many cooks spoil the broth? Peter: Oh shut up, Judas. You must pool resources—pull together—work in harmony—share the labor, share the treasure.* □ *If everybody was allowed to have his say the things would never get built. Too many cooks spoil the broth, you know.*

to one's cost mbi kurriz, në kurriz të

□ *Derek's a sponger, as two or three of us here know to our cost, but I'm sure he's not a thief.*

to one's face para syve të, në sy të, në prani të

□ *The patrons and experts of those days were usually identifiable and could therefore be praised or abused almost to their faces.* □ *I told him to his face what I thought of him.* □ *I'm not saying anything against him, but why didn't he come and tell me to my face?* □ *He had in his service a pious, soft-spoken, middle-aged Irishman for whom Guy felt much affection, and whom he called Tony to his face.*

to one's feet më këmbë

□ *His speech brought the audience to his feet, shouting and cheering.*

to one's finger-tips kokë e këmbë, deri në thonj, nga maja e flokut te thonjtë

e këmbëve

□ *She's an artist to the finger-tips. You can see that in her clothes and her house, never mind the paintings that have made her name.*

to one's heart's content sa t'i dojë qejfi, sa të dojë

□ *He has been very happy since he retired because he can play golf to one's heart's content.* □ *The monastery is in use but you can wander round to your heart's content. It's quiet, there aren't many visitors.* □ *Peter: Playing chess? I'll give you a game. Alex: Not on your Nelly— I only play against myself. This way I can cheat to my heart's content and I never lose.* □ *She told them they could eat cake to their heart's content.*

to one's knowledge me sa di, me sa kam dijeni

□ *To my knowledge, she has never been late before.* □ *It's wrong of Annie to say her family never visits her. John and his wife have been up there, to my knowledge, at least three times in the last month.*

to one's liking si ç'më pëlqen, pas midesë

□ *I don't intend to get carried away by auction excitement. If I don't see anything to my liking I'll leave before the bidding starts.* □ *As Chris Kingsley says, man'll have to come to terms with his environment. And I guess the terms won't be altogether to his liking.*

to one's name në emër të, në pronësi të

□ *David did not have a book to his name.* □ *Ed had only a suit to his name.*

to one's taste sipas shijes së

□ *The silence went on and on, broken only by the munching of horses, who*

had found something **to their taste.**
□ *'Well,'* she said looking around her, *'there are color schemes more* **to my taste** *than purple and green, but the place is clean enough.'*

to perfection në përfeksion
□ *It was a dish cooked* **to perfection.**

to say the least pa e tepruar
□ *It wasn't a very good composition,* **to say the least** *of it.* □ *I was surprise at what he said,* **to say the least.**

to say/tell the truth me thënë të vërtetën, të them (themi) të vërtetën
□ *Mr. Abel made no answer, and,* **to say the truth,** *kept a long way from the bed and very near the door.* □ ***To tell** you **the truth,** I don't like this book.* □ ***To tell** you **the truth,** I forgot all about your request.*

toss off 1. pi, kthej menjëherë, pi me fund, rrëkëllej
□ *I never met a man who could* **toss off** *so many drinks in so short a time.*
□ *He* **tossed off** *a glass of water.*
2. bëj, krijoj shpejt e shpejt, pa mund (pa sforco)
□ *I can* **toss off** *my article for the local newspaper in half an hour.*

to the backbone deri në palcë, sa s'ka ku të vejë më, deri në kockë, në kulm, plotësisht, tërësisht
□ *He is a nice fellow* **to the backbone.**

to the bad/good me humbje (fitim)
□ *He is three hundred pounds* **to the bad.** □ *He had passed completely out of their lives, leaving them £150 per annum* **to the good.**

to the best advantage sa më mirë, më së miri, më mirë
□ *He now drew a little table to his bedside, and arranging the light and a small oblong music-book* **to the best advantage,** *took his flute from its box, and began to play most mournfully.*

□ *The painting is seen* **to the best advantage** *from that distance.* □ *Ruth checked Tom before the window of a large Upholstery and furniture Warehouse to call his attention to something very magnificent and ingenious, displayed there* **to the best advantage,** *for the admiration and temptation of the public.*

to the best of one's knowledge/belief me sa di unë
□ ***To the best of my knowledge,** she is still living there.* □ *I last saw him in London and,* **to the best of my belief,** *he is still living there.*

to the best of one's recollection me sa më kujtohet
□ *'He wasn't paid by T. Dan. At least not so far as I'm aware.' 'Not* **to the best of your recollection?'** □ *'Not* **to the best of my recollection.'**

to the bitter end deri në fund, deri në pikën e fundit të gjakut
□ *They fought against the invaders* **to the bitter end.**

to the contrary në të kundërtën, ndryshe
□ *You can assume that I shall be in the United States, unless you hear from me* **to the contrary.** □ *I will come on Monday unless you write me* **to the contrary.** □ *I shall continue to believe it until I get proof* **to the contrary.**

to the core deri në palcë
□ *'... then the motive must be that the detectives were trying to destroy the accused for the sake of promotion. If this were the case,' His Honor observed gravely, 'then the police system was rotten* **to the core.'** □ *He loves his country more than anything: he is a nationalist* **to the core.**

to the effect that me kuptimin se, për të thënë se, duke thënë se
□ *He left a note* **to the effect that** *he*

497

would not be returning. □ *I can't remember what he said exactly, but it was to the effect that he would be back soon.* □ *He made a speech to the effect that we would all keep our jobs even if the factory was sold.*

to the eye për syrin; në dukje, në të parë
□ *The display of flowers was very pleasing to the eye.* □ *That girl looks to the eye like a nice girl to know, but she is rather mean*

to the fore në krye, në plan të parë; në pah, në dukje
□ *He is doing well in the competition; he is well in the fore.* □ *After a year's hard work he has come to the fore in the study of English.* □ *The hidden skill of the lawyer came to the fore during the trial.*

to the full plotësisht; pa masë
□ *They were to come on the morrow, and he would have the papers all drawn up. This matter of papers was one in which Jurgis understood to the full the need of caution.* □ *We have enjoyed ourselves to the full at the party. The campers enjoyed their trip to the full.* □ *He was ill a short while ago, but now he is well again, enjoying life to the full.*

to the last deri në fund, deri në vdekje
□ *He died in prison sixteen years later, protesting his innocence to the last.* □ *We'll remain faithful to our country to the last.*

to the letter pikë për pikë, me për-pikëri, deri më një
□ *I followed your instructions to the letter.* □ *Mrs. Horsfall had one virtue, orders received from Mac-Turk she obeyed to the letter.* □ *I followed your instructions to the letter.* □ *When writing a test you should follow the instructions to the letter.*

to the life si i gjallë, si i vërtetë, besnikërisht, me vërtetësi (besnikëri)
□ *He portrayed him to the life.* □ *'That's an excellent portrait of your father.' 'Yes, it's him to the life, isn't it?'* □ *Hodgin... She says you got my Soonday expression to the life.* □ *He can imitate a stag bellowing to the life and has often brought one within gunshot that way.*

to the marrow deri në palcë, i tëri
□ *I felt frozen to the marrow.* □ *She was shocked to the marrow by his actions.*

to the nth degree në kulm, në mak-simum, në shkallën më të lartë, sa më shumë që të jetë e mundur
□ *Scales must be accurate to the nth degree.* □ *The rule that everyone coming into the building must be searched has to be followed to the nth degree.*

to the point brenda temës, lidhur me temën (thelbin e çështjes)
□ *Stocker mechanically put in a few words that weren't strictly to the point but Ned ignored him and ploughed on.* □ *It was a flabby piece anybody could have written. Usually he writes well and to the point.* □ *I must speak to the point or not at all.* □ *His speech was short and to the point.*

to the point of deri në
□ *His manner was abrupt to the point of rudeness.*

to the purpose në temë, lidhur me temën, brenda temës
□ *The reply was so little to the purpose that it was not worth our consideration.* □ *All you have said has been to the purpose and I'll take notice of it.*

to the tune of në shumën (sasinë, vlerën e)
□ *The accountant stole money from*

his company *to the tune of* one million pounds.

to the utmost në kulm

□ *They made a hearty meal and enjoyed it to the utmost.*

touch and go i dyshimtë, i pasigurt; i rrezikshëm

□ *The doctors don't know whether he will live or not; it's touch and go.* □ *It was touch and go whether we would get to the airport in time.*

touch at futet, hyn, ndalon në port

□ *Our ship touched at Naples.*

touch bottom 1. prek fundin

□ *The ship has touched bottom—the estuary must be shallower than we thought.*

2. arrij në pikën e fundit

□ *When he was forced to beg from his friends he felt he had touched bottom and could sink no longer.*

touch down zbret, ulet në tokë (aeroplani)

□ *We touched down at Galena. We made as good a landing as could be expected.* □ *The plane touched down.*

touch off 1. plas, shpërthen

□ *This explosive needs to be handled very carefully; the slightest jolt will touch it off.*

2. nxit, shkaton

□ *Fresh violence was touched off when police moved in to disperse the crowd.* □ *Arguments continued as to what exactly touched off the disturbances.*

touch on/upon përmend, cek, trajtoj shkurtimisht

□ *Your correspondent had only touched upon the fringe of the matter.* □ *Let me now deal more fully with the important question that was touched on earlier.* □ *In his lecture on geology he touched on the subject of climate.*

touch sb on the raw prek në kallo, prek në tela, prek aty ku dhemb

□ *He was teasing me out of kindness, but touched me so accurately on the raw that I barely held back any retort.* □ *I had touched him on the raw somewhere, so I got up and said I was sorry to have taken up his time.* □ *Touched on the raw, Winton said icily. 'Indeed you will be good enough to comply with my wish, all the same.'*

touch up ndreq, rregulloj, vë dorë; retushoj

□ *There! If ever any scapegrace was trimmed and touched up to perfection, you are Steerforth.* □ *He has two short articles almost ready for publication; they just need to be touched up.*

tower above/over qëndron, ngrihet, lartësohet mbi

□ *Shakespeare towers above all other Elizabethan dramatists.* □ *Above the Victorian houses and shops tower the monster office blocks of the redeveloped center.*

toy with sth 1. luaj; trajtoj me mospër-fillje, qesëndis, tallem me

□ *He sat well back in his chair, his feet on the desk, toying with a glass paperweight.* □ *'He makes a great show of being fond of her in front of other people—just to show he's not altogether heartless—but he's only toying with her really.'*

2. luaj, marr me të qeshur (me shaka)

□ *He toyed with the idea of going back to his university town and getting a contract from his college.*

track sb/sth down gjej (duke kërkuar, gjurmuar), gjurmoj

□ *I finally tracked down the reference in a dictionary of quotations.* □ *The workers at length succeeded in tracking down the fault to a defect in the cable.*

travel light udhëtoj me pak bagazh
□ *I always **travel light** on short trips.*

tread on air ngazëllehem, fluturoj nga
gëzimi
□ *So the young man really was interested after all. He was calling for her that evening. All afternoon Margaret trod on air.* □ *We seemed to **tread on air**—work was over for a month.* □ *His experiment came out with flying colors. He felt as if he were **treading on air**.*

tread on sb's corns/toes lëndoj, fyej,
shkel në kallo dikë
□ *He is very proud of the modern paintings in his house, so don't **tread on his toes** by making funny remarks about them.* □ *Robert, of course, hated Baxter from the first. But Ned arranged it so that they didn't **tread on each other's toes**.* □ *In dealing with people we must be careful not to **tread on** anyone's toes.*

tread on sb's heels shkoj pas gjurmëve
të, ndjek këmba-këmbës
□ *They **trod on the heels** of Mr. Brownbee.*

treat sb like dirt/a dog trajtoj dikë si
leckë (si qen), trajtoj pa respekt
□ *Maybe they are overworked at the Job Center, but they should still **treat you like a human being instead of like dirt**.* □ *Oh, she'd been quick enough when apologizing, but the damage was done. She'd been **treated like dirt**.*

tricks of the trade, the të fshehtat
(kleçkat) e zanatit
□ *One's apprenticeship is so important. I've been learning my craft for 27 years, like a carpenter, taught by masters to pick up **the tricks of the trade**.* □ *On my first day as a salesman, I learnt some of **the tricks of the trade** that the other salesmen used in order to get people to buy.*

trip sb up 1. pengoj, i vë stërkëmbësh
□ *I **tripped** him **up** and he nearly fell.*
□ *The wrestler **tripped up** the opponent.*
2. ngatërroj, ngec
□ *'Be careful—there may be questions in the paper designed to **trip** you **up**.'* □ *The witness **tripped up** rather badly under close cross-examination.*

Trojan horse, a kali i Trojës
□ *In very gradual, complex ways, Britain may prove to be, not **the Trojan horse** of American influence.*

trouble one's head about sth vras
mendjen për
□ *He does not **trouble** his **head** about such matters.*

trump up sajoj, shpik
□ *He **trumped up** an excuse for his late arrival.* □ *The case against the prisoner was clearly **trumped up**; the authorities had evidently decided that an example should be made of a leading opposition figure.*

trust in sb i besoj, kam besim te
□ *I **trust in** him. He has never gone back on his word.* □ *'I told you it didn't pay to **trust in** him—he's let us down again.'* □ *We felt that we could **trust in** his wide experience of the property market.*

trust to sth besoj, var shpresat te
□ *There's not much room for cold analysis in judging human character; you have to **trust to** intuition.* □ *You **trust** your memory too much.* □ *You must have the whole project carefully planned in advance—don't just **trust to luck**.*

try on provoj (rrobat, këpucët, etj.)
□ *They are always sending for her to come and **try** something **on**.* □ *She **tried on** ten pairs of shoes before she found any that suited her.* □ *'Would you like to **try** this jacket **on** for size,*

sir?' □ The tailor asked the girl to try on the dress.

try one's hand at provoj dorën në

□ *He is trying his hand at prose writing.* □ *My dear old Traddles has tried his hand at the same pursuit, but it is not in Traddles way.* □ *Mr. Bounderby sighed like some large sea-animal. 'I cannot bear to see you so,' said Mrs. Sparsit. 'Try a hand at backgammon, sir...' □ I'm old enough to play poker and do something with it. I'll try my hand tonight.* □ *I have never played golf before but I'd like to try my hand at it.*

try one's luck provoj fatin

□ *At the suggestion of my uncle Steve I decided to try my luck as a window cleaner.* □ *Soon Ellington was hiring out four or five bands a night; he owned a car and a house and operated a sign-and-poster-printing business. All before he went to try his luck in New York.*

try out vë në provë, provoj

□ *The truck needs to be tried out.* □ *Having constructed the motorboat, they decided to try it out in the sea.* □ *'I wonder if you can solve this problem.' 'I shan't know until you try me out.*

try sb's patience provoj durimin e

□ *He then started to circle the barn, keeping close to the far wall. The circling of the barn tried his patience hard.* □ *Someone will sorely try your patience, but you won't want to answer back.*

tuck into sth i hyj, i futem me oreks, me qejf të madh

□ *He tucked into the delicious meal.*

tumble to sth kap, kuptoj

□ *At last he tumbled to what I was hinting at.* □ *He tries to keep his intentions well hidden, but it doesn't take too long to tumble to him.*

tune in (to sth) sintonizoj (radion) etj.

□ *'Don't forget to tune in next Sunday at the same time, when we present another program of old favorites.'* □ *You cannot expect the reception to be clear unless the set is properly tuned in.*

tune up akordoj (instrumentin)

□ *Several members of the orchestra were tuning up their instruments.* □ *The instruments should be tuned up before each performance.*

turn a blind eye to sth bëj një sy qorr

□ *The corrupt police chief turned a blind eye to the open gambling in the town.* □ *We should never turn a blind eye to such irregularities.* □ *Bob turned a blind eye to the 'No Fishing' sign.* □ *By turning a blind eye to the small faults of juniors, your popularity and prestige should grow.* □ *These are petty infringements, to which the officials usually turn a blind eye.* □ *Near the exam time, some students miss my lectures and go to the library to study, but I just turn a blind eye to that.*

turn a deaf ear to bëj veshin e shurdhër

□ *'Do you think, I don't know,' said my aunt turning a deaf ear to the sister, and continuing to address her brother.* □ *But to these remonstrances Mr. Quilp turned a deaf ear.* □ *Several of the customers were angry, but he simply turned a deaf ear to their complaints.* □ *Affairs should move extremely well, provided that you turn a deaf ear to the chatter of a frustrated female.* □ *To all these accusations of foul play, the referee turned a resolutely deaf ear.*

turn back kthehem prapa

□ *One of the party **turned back** to help a friend who had sprained an ankle.* □ *The sight of the Castle was the end of her walk, and meant she must **turn back**.* □ *It's getting dark—we'd better **turn back**.*

turn color ndryshon ngjyrë

□ *In the fall the leaves **turn color**.* □ *When the dye was added, the solution **turned color**.*

turn down refuzoj, hedh poshtë

□ *'I'm always proposing to you and you always **turn me down**.'* □ *The proposal was **turned down**.*

turn in 1. bie të fle

□ *And you don't ought to watch and work both. That won't do. You go home and **turn in**.* □ *I want to **turn in** early tonight.*

2. kthej

□ *'I'll give the machine one more week to behave itself. And if it doesn't then I'll **turn in** for another.'* □ *'Don't forget to **turn in** all your camping gear before you leave.'*

3. dorëzoj

□ *'I know you think I probably deserve it, but please don't **turn me in**, please!'*

4. lë, braktis, heq dorë

□ *The job was damaging his health so he had to **turn it in**.*

turn in upon oneself shkëputem nga njerëzit e merrem me punët e mia

□ *She's really **turned in on herself** since Peter left her.*

turn inside out kthej së prapthi

□ *'Are you sure you haven't got the key on you? **Turn** your pockets **inside out**.'* □ *The wind **turned** my umbrella **inside out**.* □ *He **turned** his pockets **inside out** in search of his keys.*

turn night into day e bëj natën ditë

□ *The scientist went on with his experiment **turning night into a day**.*

turn of events ndryshim i papritur i ngjarjeve

□ *This remarkable **turn of events** amazed everyone.*

turn of the century kapërcyell i shekullit

□ *This was the kind of house people lived in at the **turn of the century**.*

turn off 1. mbyll (dritën, rubinetin, etj.)

□ *Don't forget to **turn** the lights **off** before you come to bed.* □ ***Turn** the water **off**, don't waste it.* □ *The electricity supply must be **turned off** at the mains before you alter the lighting circuit.*

2. kthehem, marr kthesën

□ ***Turn off** about a mile further on.*

3. largon, zverëtit, zvjerdh

□ *Bad breath is guaranteed to **turn** a woman **off**!*

turn on 1. hap

□ ***Turn on** the gas and light the oven.* □ *He **turned on** the radio.*

2. varet nga

□ *The success of a picnic usually **turns on** the weather.*

3. sulmoj

□ *Don't tease the dog, it may **turn on** you.* □ *'There's no need to **turn on** me just because rain spoiled the picnic.'*

4. nxit, eksitoj, stimuloj

□ *'I think she's a marvellous girl, she really **turns** me **on**!'*

turn one's back iki, largohem, kthej krahët

□ *It seems I can't **turn my back** without one of you hurting yourself or doing something silly.* □ *Yes, and as soon as **my back's turned** you'll be off with this sailor boy and ruin* *yourself for good.* □ *It's very badly done. I'll have to put another coat of paint on myself, but I'll wait till his back's turned. He'll never notice, if nothing is said.*

turn one's back on sb i kthej krahët dikujt

□ *Yet I lingered about and could not tear myself away; thinking of all possible harm that might happen to the child and feeling as if evil must ensue if I turned my back upon the place.* □ *Since he has become wealthy, he has turned his back on all his friends.* □ *He turned his back on his family when they needed help.*

turn one's coat kthej (ndërroj) pllakën (fletën), ndryshoj mendim (qëndrim); kaloj në anën e kundërshtarit

□ *Sir John Urrie had already changed sides twice during the Civil War, and was destined to turn his coat a third time before it ended.* □ *James had been dead a quarter of a century and the doctors had turned their coats several times since.*

turn one's attention/mind/thoughts to sth drejtoj vëmendjen te

□ *Please turn your attention to something more important.*

turn one's hand to sth mirrem, provoj, zë me dorë

□ *He can turn his hand to most jobs about the house.* □ *He is successful at everything he turns his hand to.* □ *I'm not an interior decorator, but I could always turn my hand to most things.* □ *I know you've always thought that you could do anything you turned your hand to, and mostly you could.*

turn one's stomach të përzien stomakun, të çon të pështjellët, të vjen për të vjellë

□ *The conditions inside the prison were so horrible that they turned my stomach.* □ *The rolling of the boat turned his stomach.* □ *Ward is more obsequious than ever to your mamma. It turns my stomach, it does, to hear him flatter.*

turn sb's head i prish mendjen dikujt

□ *I had never been spontaneously approached by a publisher before and such condescension rather turned my head.* □ *'I'm glad,' Mavis said later, 'these things, like that letter, happened now, and not when I was 25. I think my head would have been turned then.* □ *So much incense and nonsense, and all the rest of it, is enough to turn a stronger head than mine.* □ *It turned my head, not just a little, but a good deal.*

turn on/upon one's heel (s) kthehem menjëherë

□ *Shame, compunction, sense of futility flooded his whole being, he turned on his heel and went straight out.* □ *He turned on his heel and went out, angrily slamming the door behind him.* □ *When John saw Fred approaching him, he turned on his heel.*

turn out 1. prodhon, nxjerr

□ *Our new factory is turning out large quantities of goods.* □ *Our school has turned out well prepared pupils.*

2. del, rezulton

□ *Whether I shall turn out to be the hero of my own life, or whether that station will be held by anybody else, these pages must show.* □ *It turned out he was born in the Caledonian Road.* □ *It turned out to be a sunny day.*

3. fik, shuaj, mbyll

□ *'Make sure all the lights are **turned out** before you come up to bed. 'The lights were turned out....* □ *Please **turn out** the lights.*

4. dëboj, përzë, nxjerr jashtë

□ *Mr. Murdstone comes out, takes the book, throws it at me or boxes my ears, and **turns** me **out** of the room by the shoulders.* □ *His father **turned him out** of the house.*

5. dal

□ *Tens of thousands of people **turned out** for the rally.* □ *The weather prevented people from **turning out** in large numbers to watch the athletics meeting.*

6. zbras

□ *'But you must have the tickets on you somewhere. **Turn out** your pockets again.'*

turn over 1. kthej, kthehem

□ *Jurgis **turned over** in his bed, and was snoring again before the two had closed the door.* □ *The nurse **turned** the old man **over** and gave him an injection in the left buttock.*

2. kaloj

□ *The day-to-day management of the firm has been **turned over** to someone appointed from outside the company.*

3. dorëzoj

□ *'How do you know he isn't wanted by the police.' 'Why should he be?' 'If he is, we ought to **turn** him **over**.'*

turn over a new leaf hap një fletë të re, nis një jetë të re

□ *'Forgive me inquiring,' said the chaplain... 'but what will you do now? I hope you are going to'—'How could he put it?' '**Turn over a new leaf**?'* □ *I want to settle down, **turn over a new leaf**.* □ *It is due to his protection and advice that I remained at Sanhurst, **turned over a new leaf**, and survived to make good.* □ *He*

used to get up to all sorts of mischief, but now he seems to have **turned over a new leaf**.

turn over in one's mind/head/ thought bluaj në mendje (në kokë), sjell e përsjell nëpër mend, e vërtit nëpër mendje

□ *He had the air of a man who is **turning over** a number of things **in his mind**.* □ *He had plenty of time before him to **turn** the idea **over in his mind**.* □ *But, **in his mind** nothing was settled; everything **turned over** and over again...* □ *I remained in the study, **turning** the whole matter **over and over in my head**.* □ *I will **turn** the matter **over in my mind** and give you an answer tomorrow.*

turn tail mbledh bishtin dhe iki me vrap (me të katra), ua mbath këmbëve

□ *... As soon as his back was turned the new boy snatched a stone, threw it, and hit between the shoulders, and then **turned tail** and ran like an antelope.* □ *Then, suddenly, the dogs' courage failed them, and they all **turned tail** and fled up the hill again, leaving the mongoose on its hind legs in the field of battle.* □ *As they walked through a stone archway Mrs Shaw went chalk white and started trembling. After a few seconds, she **turned tail** and ran out of the castle.* □ *As soon as they saw the police, they **turned tail** and ran.*

turn the cold shoulder upon sb trajtoj (sillem) ftohtë me, i kthej krahët

□ *'Here in the boarding house, if one would have friends and be popular instead of having the **cold shoulder turned upon him**, he must be prosperous.'*

turn the corner hedh (kaloj) lumin (hendekun), kaloj (kapërcej) një vështirësi; kaloj gjendjen kritike

□ *His temperature is still going down, and he's breathing more easily. I think we can safely say he's **turned the corner**.* □ *The corner was **turned**, this time it seemed for ever, and The Albert Hall, freshly cleaned, trimmed and refurbished, had started a new career.* □ *There's no doubt in my mind, this England team under Ron Greewood has **turned the corner**, and is on course again to be a real force in world football. The solicitude of people had a healing influence....* □ *Hilary began sending funny little notes the moment she had **turned the corner**.* □ *According to the doctor, the patient has definitely **turned the corner** and now it is just a matter of recuperation.*

turn the other cheek kthej faqen tjetër
□ *When he treats her badly, she simply **turns the other cheek**.* □ *'What did you go hitting him on the nose for?' 'He has given me a thick ear first. I know it was an excellent opportunity for **turning the other cheek**, but I didn't think of it in time.'*

turn the tables on përmbys situatën në favor të
□ *Without doubt she had **the tables turned upon** her, she who had been cold so many years to every mark of tenderness, it was her part now to be neglected....* □ *'Essex had to act quickly and drastically,' Asquith said. 'Don't get mad with him. He had to **turn the tables on** you to save himself.'* □ *We have talked of Joseph Sedly being as vain as a girl. Heaven help us! The girls have only to **turn the tables**, and say of one of their own sex. 'She's as vain as a man,' and they will have perfect reason.*

turn the tide ndryshoj gjendjen
□ *We were losing the battle, but the arrival of some extra reinforcements **turned the tide** in our favor.* □ *A touchdown in the final minute play **turned the tide** against us.* □ *This seemed to have **turned the tide** in favor of the official Labor candidate.*

turn to 1. i drejtohem
□ *The child felt there was no one he could **turn to** with his problems.* □ *It would have taken hours to work the sum out, so I **turned to** my pocket calculator.*
2. i hyj, i futem punës me vrull
□ *We **turned to** and got the whole house cleaned in an afternoon.* □ *Well, I must **turn to** it now and try to get this piece of work done by six o'clock.*

turn to account përdor, shfrytëzoj
□ *He had some terrible experience during his childhood, but he **turned** them **to** good **account** in writing his novels.* □ *The quarrel gave the elder lady numberless advantages which she did not fail to **turn to account**....* □ *He at once saw how this might be **turned to** excellent **account**.*

turn turtle përmbyset
□ *The canoe **turned turtle**.* □ *Tossed to and fro by the waves, the little craft finally **turned turtle**.*

turn up 1. vij, dukem, shfaqem
□ *He promised to come, but hasn't **turned up** yet.* □ *She hasn't **turned up** this morning. I hope she isn't ill.*
2. ngrihet, rritet, përmirësohet
□ *Investment is **turning up** sharply.*
3. ndodh, ngjan
□ *Like Mr. Micawber, he is still waiting for something to **turn up**.* □ *At present, and until something **turns up**, I have nothing to bestow but advice.*
4. ngre
□ *He **turned up** his coat collar against the chill wind.*

5. shkurtoj, përthyej, kthej

□ *These trousers are too long; they will need to be **turned up**.*

6. gjej, zbuloj

□ *The police searched the house hoping to **turn up** more clues.*

turn up like a bad penny shfaqet si parja e kuqe

□ *We have tried to discourage him from coming to our meetings, but he keeps **turning up like a bad penny**.*

□ *If the whole thing was not disposed of within the next few months the fellow would **turn up** again **like a bad penny**.*

turn up one's toes kthej këmbët nga dielli, vdes

□ *When my mother **turns up her toes**, you shall take the five pounds off....*

□ *Then there are the funeral expenses. It must be done nicely. I have much to save. And Barry may **turn up his toes** any day.*

turn up one's nose at rrudh hundët (buzët, turinjtë), përbuz, përçmoj

□ *Mrs. H.... This Hornblower hates us; he thinks we **turn up our noses at** him.*

□ *No matter how carefully I prepare the food, he **turns up his nose at** it.* □ *I know it's only sausages and mash again, but there's no need to **turn your nose at** it.* □ *Some people **turn up their noses** if you say your father was a miner or a docker.*

twiddle one's thumbs tund (dredh) zinxhirin, rri kot, e kalon kohën kot, vret miza

□ *I've got to be busy. I can't sit down and **twiddle my thumbs**.* □ *I'd rather work than stand around here **twiddling my thumbs**.* □ *The plane will not be taking off for another four hours, so, in the meantime, we have to sit here **twiddling our thumbs**.*

□ *Seeing vast fields where the sheep seemed to be grazing in their thousands, I imagined the owner **twiddling his thumbs** or fishing for trout. But these farmers are both hard-working and anxious.*

twist one's arm i përdredh krahun dikujt, detyroj (bind) dikë të bëjë diçka

□ *I don't want to go on the committee but some friends have been **twisting my arm**.* □ *She'll let you borrow the car if you **twist her arm**.*

twist sb round one's little finger e sjell vërdallë, e heq për hunde

□ *He thought he could **twist** Dick **round his finger** but he grossly miscalculated.*

two heads are better than one dy mendje janë më mirë se një

□ *'What about Edwards? Do I tell him?' 'That I must leave to you. **Two heads are** often **better than one**.'*

two and two make four si dy e dy që bëjnë katër, si buka që hamë, me siguri, pa asnjë dyshim

□ *Anybody with brains enough to know that **two and two make four** could have guessed the outcome of that situation.*

U

under a cloud 1. në zymti; në siklet; në humor të keq, në ditë të keqe

□ *I was not feeling bright that morning. Indeed my powers seemed a bit **under a cloud**.* □ *We'll not live **under a cloud** always.*

2. (shihet) me sy të keq, me dyshim

□ *I want my brother back in his regiment... He is **under a cloud** owing to that Bolivian expedition with professor Hallorsen.*

under age nën moshë, jashtë moshe

□ *The government is trying to stop **under age** drinking.*

under an obligation i detyruar

□ *I ask you to depart from this place tonight, **under an obligation** never to return to it.*

under arrest nën arrest

□ *The man believed to have robbed the bank was placed **under arrest**.*

under consideration në shqyrtim

□ *The question is now **under consideration**.* □ *The proposals they submitted to the committee are still **under consideration**.*

under control nën kontroll

□ *I noticed that his legs are not well **under control**.*

under cover/under cover of 1. i fshehur (mbuluar, maskuar) nga, nën maskën (mbulesën) e

□ *Some policemen are here **under cover**.* □ *The prisoners escaped **under cover of** darkness.* □ *He leaned forward to pat the horse's neck and **under cover of** the movement extracted the Mauser.*

2. nën pretekstin e

□ *I heard reports of big military installations under construction, stories of widespread forest clearance **under cover of** forest fire.*

under discussion në diskutim, në shqyrtim

□ *The question is still **under discussion**.* □ *The plans have been **under discussion** for a year now, but no decision has been reached.*

under fire nën goditjen (zjarrin) e

□ *The soldiers stood firm **under fire** of the enemy.* □ *We have been **under fire** for twenty minutes.*

under foot nën këmbë

□ *Here the grass ended and there was a loose sandy soil **under foot**.*

under one's breath nën zë, me zë të ulët

□ *We should speak **under** our **breath** when a performance is on.* □ *Then he turned round and walked away and we heard him muttering **under** his **breath**.* □ *The teacher heard the boy say something **under** his **breath** and asked him to repeat it aloud.*

under one's own steam me forcat e veta, pa ndihmën e

□ *I didn't get help from anyone in building up my business: I did it all **under my own steam**.* □ *Philip: Where is Rosemary? She said she'd get here **under her own steam**.* □ *Oh, he's got the hang of the job now. I leave him to carry on **under his own steam** for a bit.* □ *'Have you made up your mind if you want Myrtle to go with you to America or not?' 'If she likes to go **under her own steam**.'*

under one's wing nën mbrojtje
□ *Jack has taken the new student under his wing and is helping him.*

under pain/penalty of me rrezik të, nën kërcënimin e
□ *Prisoners were forbidden to approach the fence under pain of death.*

under sb's colors nën flamurin e
□ *Years after Northmour was killed fighting under the colors of Garibaldi for the liberation of Toryl.*

under sb's eyes para syve të
□ *He stole the stuff from under my very eyes.*

under sb's nose nën hundën e, para syve të
□ *'Have you a match to light the gas with?' 'There's a box of matches right under your nose.'* □ *In every tense situation that takes of place in public there are always one or two people about who don't see what is happening under their noses.* □ *I've been looking everywhere for this pen and here it is, right under my nose.* □ *The thief walked out of the museum with the painting, right under the nose of the guards.* □ *I looked everywhere for the book. Although it was under my nose, I didn't see it.*

under sb's thumb nën pushtetin e, nën diktatin e, nën thundrën e
□ *You're going to be able to write. If I could just keep you under my thumb for four or five weeks I think I could make something out of you.* □ *If anyone else had been in my place during that last few years by this time he would have had Mr. Wickfield under his thumb.* □ *The Jones family is under the thumb of the mother.* □ *Jack is a bully. He keeps all the younger children under his thumb.*

under the auspices of nën patronazhin e; me ndihmën (mbështetjen) e
□ *The school fair was held under the auspices of the Parents' Association.*

under the circumstances në kushte të tilla
□ *It's raining and very few people have turned up so, under the circumstances, I think the best thing is to cancel the concert.* □ *Under the circumstances, the stage coach passengers had to give the robbers their money.*

under the counter nën dorë, nën banak
□ *These goods are not really for sale, but quite a few are being sold under the counter.* □ *That book has been banned, but there's one place you can get it under the counter.*

under the hammer në ankand
□ *The contents of the house will soon be under the hammer.* □ *The picture I wanted to bid came under the hammer soon after I arrived.*

under the sun në botë
□ *Nowhere under the sun have I seen such a beautiful painting!* □ *The president's assassination shocked everyone under the sun.*

under the weather pa qejf
□ *I thought he looked frail tonight, a trifle under the weather.* □ *You must not fancy I am sick, only overdriven and under the weather.*

under way në proces, në zhvillim e sipër
□ *Enormous irrigation projects are under way in all parts of our country.* □ *The project is under way but it will take five years to finish it.*

up and about/up and doing më këmbë
□ *The patient is up and about today for the first time.*

up and down poshtë e lart, poshtë e përpjetë
□ *She opened the door of the sitting-room. Wilfrid was pacing up and*

down. □ *He thrust his hands into his pockets and walked* **up and down** *the office with measured steps.* □ *She continued to pace* **up and down**... □ *The launching of the lifeboat was the perfect complement to the program, reminding us of the great debt we owe to that fine body of men* **up and down** *the country.*

up a tree në pozitë (situatë, gjendje) të vështirë

□ *John's father has him* **up a tree** *in the checker game.* □ *I'm* **up a gum tree** *financially; I owe $5,000 and I have no money left at all.*

up in arms i armatosur, i ngritur me armë

□ *Some areas in the south of the country are already* **up in arms.** □ *The whole village is* **up in arms** *about the proposal to build an airport nearby.*

up in the air në hava

□ *Our holiday plans are* **up in the air** *for the time being; nothing has been decided.*

upon my word për fjalë të nderit

□ *'Are you serious?'* **'Upon my word** *I am,' exclaimed his new acquaintance.* □ **Upon my word** *and honor, Captain Gills, it would be a charity to give me the pleasure of your acquaintance.*

ups and downs uljet dhe ngritjet, kulmet e rëniet, gëzimet e hidhërimet, zigzaget

□ *If you analyze the movement of market prices for longer periods... you will find that the fluctuations of market prices, their deviations from* values, their **ups and downs**, paralyze and compensate each other. □ *There were* **ups and downs** *at the business...* □ *You have to learn to accept the* **ups and downs** *of life.* □ *People, we assume, are much the same everywhere: personality will even out, and the* **ups and downs** *of life are much the same everywhere too.*

upset the/sb's apple-cart prish planet e, i prish punë dikujt

□ *Setting the tray down, she gave a squeal. 'I say, you do look a sight! Something* **upset your apple-cart?'** □ *'She was in, of course, I knew that.' 'No, she wasn't, she went out, that was what* **upset the apple-cart.'** □ *You have* **upset** *the Persian* **apple-cart,** *my boy, clumsily but dangerously.* □ *We are planning a surprise party for Bill, so don't let Mary* **upset the apple-cart** *by telling him before the party.*

use one's head/loaf vras mendjen

□ *'I can't remember who told me.' 'Then* **use your head** *and do remember.'* □ *He can put things right if he will only* **use his head** *and be unselfish.* □ *That box will hold all the empty bottles if you stack the top layer upside down. It's just a case of* **using your head,** *you see.* □ *'Oh,* **use your loaf,** *for Christ's sake!' I shouted. His incomprehension was beginning to get me down.*

use up 1. mbaroj

□ *He* **used up** *his reserves in fruitless counterattacks during the spring.* □ *'There isn't any more coal; it's all been* **used up.'**

V

vanish into thin air avullon, bëhet erë, zhduket pa lënë gjurmë

□ *I couldn't find him anywhere. He seemed to have vanished into the thin air.*

venture on/upon ndërmarr

□ *The hope of making further discoveries led them to venture upon a second trip.*

vicious circle, a rreth vicioz

□ *Debtors were caught in a vicious circle: they could not be freed until they had paid their debt, and were not able to pay their debt as long as they were in prison.* □ *It vexed her to feel as she did, and vexation turned to guilt, and guilt increased her unrest. It was a vicious circle.*

vote in/into zgjidhet, fitoj në votim

□ *The Democrats were voted into power on a program of wide-ranging social reform.*

vote sb/sth down hedh poshtë me shumicë votash

□ *Someone proposed that the proceedings of the meeting should be recorded on tape, but the suggestion was voted down.* □ *The bill was voted down by the parliament.*

W

wade in/into sulmoj energjikisht
- □ *He just* **waded into** *the bigger boy with both fists flying.* □ *She* **waded** *straight into her critics with her opening remarks.*

wage war bëj luftë
- □ *No country wants to* **wage** *a nuclear war.*

wait a bit/a jiffy/a minute/a moment/ second etc. pres pak (një çast, një minutë, një sekondë)
- □ *Please* **wait a minute.**

wait and see prit të shohim, prit të presim
- □ *It is probably one of those things that are too complicated for direct calculation. We shall have to* **wait and see.** *I'm afraid.* □ *Kate says as far as her future goes, we'll have to* **wait and see.**

wait at table(s)/wait on table i shërbej tavolinës, i bëj shërbim tavolinës, shërbej në tavolinë
- □ *I got holiday jobs in guest houses, washing dishes and* **waiting on the tables.** □ *This week the hotel manager is giving the staff some training on how to* **wait at table.** □ **Waiting at table** *is a skilled job, requiring careful training.*

wait for the cat to jump shoh nga fryn era
- □ *There is nothing for it but to* **wait for the cat to jump.**

wait one's turn pres radhën
- □ *To see the waiter taking our order and making them* **waiting their turn** *was too much for a formidable matron among them.* □ *I had hoped the game would finish in time for me to catch the 4:15 but at 4:15 I was still* **waiting my turn** *to bat.*

wait on sb hand and foot i shërbej me të gjitha mënyrat, bëj gjithçka për
- □ *Ever since her husband became ill, she has* **waited on him hand and foot.** □ *Sally is spoiled because her mother* **waits on her hand and foot.** □ *At home the boys never lifted a finger. We girls had to* **wait on them hand and foot.**

wake up to sth kuptoj, ndërgjegjë- sohem, bëhem i vetëdijshëm
- □ *They should* **wake up** *and see the problems they've got on their hands.* □ *He hasn't yet* **woken up to** *the seriousness of the situation.* □ *It's time you* **woke up to** *the fact that you're not very popular.*

walk all over sb 1. mund thellësisht
- □ *The visiting team was too strong— they* **walked all over us.**

2. trajtoj keq; shpërfill, shkel me këmbë; trajtoj si skllav
- □ *We wanted the man's business, so we let him* **walk all over us.**

walk away from sb mund me lehtësi
- □ *He* **walked away from** *all his competitors.*

walk away/off with sth 1. fitoj me lehtësi
- □ *'It's no good; they have lost. They should have* **walked away with** *the game.* □ *He* **walked away with** *two first prizes.*

2. marr, vjedh
- □ *Somebody has* **walked away with** *my pen.* □ *How can a thief* **walk off with** *a safe in broad daylight?* □ *'Don't leave your suitcases unguarded. Somebody may* **walk off with** *them.'*

walk into 1. bie (në kurth, pritë etj)
□ *'He loves to set traps for the unwary. You wouldn't be the first to walk into one.'* □ *The enemy soldiers walked into our ambush.*
2. ndeshem, përplasem
□ *She wasn't looking where she was going and walked straight into me.*

walk on air fluturoj nga gëzimi, galdoj
□ *His father's compliment left John walking on air.* □ *He was walking on air after Sally said she would marry him.* □ *The execution of this arrangement so thrilled Tollifer that he felt as though he were walking on air.*

walk out 1. bëj grevë, dal në grevë
□ *Construction workers walked out during the morning in protest at the sacking of a bricklayer.*
2. iki, largohem nga mbledhja
□ *At various times, both teams of negotiators had walked out of the peace talks.*

walk out on sb lë, braktis
□ *He had a fight with his wife and just walked out on her.* □ *'You have got his baby; you can't just walk out on him because he doesn't get on with your family.'*

walk sb off his feet këput nga këmbët
□ *'Let me sit down for a moment; the children have been walking me off my feet.'* □ *'If you want a leisurely stroll through the museum, don't take that guide—she'll walk all of you off your feet.'*

walk the floor lëviz poshtë e lartë nëpër shtëpi, vjen rrotull nëpër shtëpi
□ *Mr. Black walked the floor trying to reach a decision.* □ *His toothache hurt so much that he got up and walked the floor*

walls have ears muri ka veshë; fusha ka sy e muri ka veshë
□ *'Shall I come to your hotel?' 'Better*

if we meet in the Park. Walls have ears.' □ *You don't know what it is to live in a police state where walls have ears and your child may be encouraged to inform against you.*

waltz off with sth 1. marr, vjedh
□ *He's just waltzed off with my cigarette lighter!*
2. fitoj lehtësisht
□ *Later in the week, the Kenyans waltzed off with gold medals in the 5000 meters and the steeplechase.*

war/battle of nerves, a luftë nervash
□ *As the two fleets sailed towards each other, each side waited for the other to give in first; it was a war of nerves.*

war of words, a luftë fjalësh
□ *As the election approaches the war of words between the main political parties becomes increasingly intense.*

warm the cockles of one's heart i ngroh zemrën (shpirtin); i kënaq zemrën (shpirtin)
□ *The sight of my daughter playing with her children, my grandchildren, really warmed the cockles of my heart.* □ *This tea is very comforting, Briggs. It warms the cockles.*

warm up 1. ngroh
□ *'Just a minute while I warm up some milk on the gas.'* □ *Mr. Jones was so late that his dinner got cold; his wife had to warm it up.*
2. ngrohet
□ *In cold weather pull the choke out half-way, and let the engine warm up, before you move off.*
3. ngroh, gjallëroj
□ *We agreed about the port and whisky. It would warm them all up.* □ *The comedian told a few quick jokes to get his audience warmed up.*
4. nxehem, shpihem, bëj nxemje
□ *The German manager has one of*

*his substitutes **warming up** on the touch-line now.*

wash and wear laj e thaj, laj e vesh

□ *Dick bought three **wash and wear** shirts to take on his trip.*

wash away zhvendos, lëviz nga vendi, largoj

□ *The river flooded its banks **washing away** part of the main railway line.*

wash down (with) 1. laj me çurg uji

□ *On Sundays, he **washes** his car **down** with the garden hose.*

2. shtyj, shoqëroj

□ *We ate sausages and **washed it down** with a whisky.*

wash off laj, heq me larje

□ *I tried to remove the grease spots from the wall but they wouldn't **wash off**.* □ *Go and **wash** the mud **off** your face at once.*

wash one's dirty linen in public nxjerr të palarat në shesh

□ *In telling the story of his life, he mentioned a lot of things which should have been kept private; one shouldn't **wash one's dirty linen in public**.* □ *It was a timely spur to Soames's intense and rooted distaste for the **washing of dirty linen in public**.*

wash one's hands of i laj duart nga, s'kam punë me, heq dorë nga

□ *After my mother's death, I **wash my hands of** you.* □ *'Have what you please. I **wash my hands of it**.'* □ *I think that this is a stupid and dangerous plan. I **wash my hands of it**.*

wash out laj, heq me larje

□ *Don't trouble about those coffee stains, we can soon **wash** them **out**.*

wash up laj enët

□ *After supper we'd **wash up** and she'd sit by the fire.*

waste away thahet, tretet, dobësohet, i kanë dalë kockat, u bë kockë e lëkurë

□ *Matthew was looking dreadful the last time I saw him—he's **wasting away** to skin and bone*

waste one's breath harxhoj frymën kot

□ *Don't give him any more advice; you're **wasting your breath**, he won't listen.* □ *The teacher saw she was **wasting her breath**; the children refused to believe her.* □ *I know what I want. You're **wasting your breath**.* □ *Don't **waste your breath** trying to persuade me.*

waste one's time e kaloj (harxhoj) kohën kot

□ *It's you who are a fool standing there **wasting time** talking when we should be arranging to get away.* □ *Don't **waste your time**.*

waste words harxhoi fjalët kot

□ *Don't **waste words** on John. He is very stubborn.*

watch every penny shikoj (kujdesem, llogarit) çdo qindarkë

□ *Also, he **watches every penny** he spends, which gives him a reputation for meanness.*

watch it kujdes, ki kujdes, hap sytë

□ ***Watch it** when you are putting that light bulb in; the electricity may still be switched on.* □ *But recent information indicates that Ponia is working his cops round the clock to spell out a simple lesson. I am in control here, he is saying: so **watch it**.*

watch one's step kam kujdes, hap sytë, mbaj sytë hapur

□ *Wiggam after Clyde had gone, whispered to Kemerer as well as to several others, that Clyde might readily prove to be someone who was a protege of the chief—and therefore they determined to '**watch their step**' at least until they knew what his standing here was to be.*

□ *'I'm the chucker-out,' said Charles, 'so watch your step.'* □ *Watch your step with this fellow. He's been around a bit; he maybe knows just as much as you do.*

watch/mind one's language/tongue mbaj gojën, kafshoj gjuhën

□ *Watch your tongue, my lad, and wipe that grin off your face unless you want me to do it for you.* □ *It would pay him to watch his language and improve himself.*

watch sb/sth like a hawk ndjek me sy, vështroj me vëmendje, përgjoj si macja miun

□ *You know how unreasonable girls are and she'll be watching her sister and me all the time like a hawk.*

watch sb out of the corner of one's eye shikoj me bisht të syrit

□ *Now, as Carrie watched him out of the corner of her eye, certain sound thoughts came into her head.*

watch out rri në bef, bëj bef; kam kujdes, hap sytë

□ *I said I should be sick, and that I must watch out for symptoms.* □ *'You need to watch out here. The ground's a bit boggy on either side of the path.'* □ *'You'll be in direct trouble if you don't watch out.'*

watch the clock sheh orën kohë e pa kohë (për të pushuar, për të lënë punën etj.)

□ *I wouldn't have him on the premises. Chatting up the typists and watching the clock is all he's good for.*

water down holloj me ujë; zbut

□ *There was no more whisky left, not even a drop to water down.* □ *I have considerably watered down Blaize's criticisms of the guilty men.*

ways and means rrugë, mënyra, forma

□ *He has been devising ways and means all the way there of explaining*

himself, and has been satisfied with none. □ *There are ways and means of making a living even in this country.* □ *All the feeling she had started out with had perished in the search for ways and means to express it.* □ *'How did you get the dollar to come through America?' I grinned. 'There are ways and means.'*

weak at the knees me gjunjë të prerë (të këputur)

□ *'How do you feel?' 'Fine, really. A bit weak at the knees but that will pass.*

wear and tear konsumim, dëmtim, vjetërim, amortizim

□ *The luxurious interior sprung mattress is guaranteed by the manufacturers for 5 years against fair wear and tear.* □ *A pair of shoes may have lasted her for five years, for the wear and tear that she took out of them.*

wear down 1. ha, konsumon

□ *Running water wears down rocks with the help of particles of sand and gravel.* □ *Get the cobbler to fit metal studs to your boots—they won't wear down so quickly.* □ *'Your back tires are badly worn down. You should fit new ones.* □ *The heels of these shoes are wearing down.*

2. mund, mposht

□ *The young Quaker strove to wear down malice by his patient and forgiving mood.* □ *Through perseverance, they wore down the enemy's resistance.*

3. lodh

□ *Worn down by loneliness, finally smashed by grief, the scholar's mind resolves all these things in a confusion.*

wear off/away 1. prish, fshij, zhduk

□ *Time and weather have worn off the name on the gravestone.* □ *The*

inscription has **worn away**. □ *Wind and rain have* **worn away** *the sharp ridges of these mountains.*
2. del, ikën, kalon
□ *'Don't polish those badges; the gilt will* **wear off** *in time if you do.* □ *The drink inside them had* **worn off**, *leaving only a sour feeling in the stomach.* □ *Lunch succeeded to our sightseeing and the short winter day* **wore away**.

wear on kalon ngadalë (mërzitshëm)
□ *The gloomy afternoon* **wore on**.
□ *The fields were covered with ice and, as September* **wore on**, *the noisy rivers were gradually silenced.*

wear one's heart on one's sleeve shfaq hapur ndjenjat (emocionet)
□ *Jack doesn't say much but he feels his father's death very deeply. He never was one to* **wear his heart on his sleeve**. □ *We do not specially respect him who* **wears his heart upon his sleeve** *for daws to peck at.*
□ *Summerhay did not* **wear his heart on his sleeve** *and when he left his chambers to walk to that last meeting, his face was much as usual.*

wear out 1. prish, konsumoj, gris
□ *Children's clothes* **wear out** *very quickly—they get so much rough treatment.*
2. lodh, dërrmoj, stërmundoj, rraskapit
□ *Anne,* **worn out** *with anxiety and strain, followed from one house to the next.* □ *I've seen plenty of girls* **wear** *themselves* **out** *trying to run a home and a job.*

wear the pants/the trousers bëhem gjel, sundoj mbi burrin
□ *People say of that couple that she* **wears the trousers**. □ *It would be quite false to call Tom a hen-pecked husband; nevertheless one does gather the impression that she* **wears**

the trousers. □ *I choose his clothes for him. Not that he doesn't* **wear the trousers** *in our house. He does what he wants.*

wear well mbahet mirë
□ *Mr. Tomas's* **wearing well**. □ *This suit has* **worn well**. *I've had it for three years now and it still looks new.*

weather/ride the storm çaj (kaloj) furtunat; dal në breg, ia dal mbanë; kaloj (kapërcej) me sukses një vështirësi
□ *For a long time he was in political disgrace, but he* **weathered the storm** *successfully and now he runs an important ministry.* □ *How beautiful is the love that has* **weathered the storms** *of life!* □ *... decidedly she could not be expected to* **weather** *the* **storm** *alone.* □ *Still England has been some weeks in the dismal straits of having no pilot ... to* **weather the storm**; *and the marvellous part of the matter is that England has not appeared to care very much about it....*

weigh anchor ngre spirancën
□ *The ship will* **weigh anchor** *at dawn, and should be well down the river by noon.* □ *He looked over to the landing craft; she was* **weighing anchor** *to get away before the falling tide left her stranded.*

weigh a ton peshon shumë, peshon një ton
□ *That damn suitcase* **weighs a ton** *before you start putting anything in it.* □ *There was also an eighteenth-century Indian elephant, made of wood though* **weighing a ton**.

weigh down mposht, mundoj (vras) shpirtërisht, vë poshtë, ligështoj nga ana morale
□ *He doesn't let the cares of parenthood* **weigh him down**. □ *John seems*

altogether **weighed down** by all the extra work they're pushing on him.

weigh in (with) ndërhyj me forcë me
□ *At that point, the chairman **weighed in with** a strong defence of company policy.*

weigh one's words peshoj fjalët
□ *I must **weigh my** words to avoid any misunderstanding.* □ *It was obviously an important question, because the Prime Minister seemed to **weigh her words** before she spoke.* □ *He was as deliberate in his speech as he was in his work, **weighing** his **words** momentously.*

weigh on/upon sb's mind/heart e mundon, i rëndon në shpirt (në zemër)
□ *This trouble **weighed** heavily **upon his mind.*** □ *It **weighs upon my heart** to see Nancy suffer.*

weigh on sb i rëndon, ka mbi kurriz
□ *'Don't disturb your father; he has so many things **weighing on** his mind.'*

weigh out peshoj
□ *The ingredients for the cake were all carefully **weighed out.***

weigh the consequences vlerësoj pasojat
□ *A footballer's mind has to work fast, as well as his feet. He can't stop, like a chess-player, to **weigh the consequences** of every move.*

weigh the evidence vlerësoj të dhënat
□ *Some believe that a person's political opinions are consciously arrived at after a thorough **weighing of the evidence** and are modifiable.* □ *Lawyers are used to **weighing the evidence** of witnesses and getting through a lot of it.*

well and good mirë e bukur, në rregull, bukur fort
□ *If she comes here tonight, **well***

and good; if she doesn't, I'll see her tomorrow.* □ *The job is done—that's all **well and good**—but what about the bonus we were promised?*

well done (!) të lumtë, bravo
□ *At the final whistle he marches to the dressing room. '**Well done**, lads,' he tells them as they come.*

wend one's way shkoj (marr rrugën) drejt
□ *'If I ever do come back, and mix myself up with these people again,' thought Mr. Winkle, as he **wended his way** to the Peacock, 'I shall deserve to be horse-whipped myself—that's all.' ... all **wending** their **way** in the same direction.*

wet behind the ears i ka buzët me qumësht, i papjekur, s'ka përvojë
□ *I have been doing this job for ten years. I object to being given instructions by people who are still **wet behind the ears**.* □ *The new student is still **wet behind the ears**; he has not yet learned the tricks that the boys play on each other.*

wet blanket, a dikush (diçka) që të prish qejfin (humorin); gazprishës, lezetprishës
□ *Don't invite Jack to the party; he's a bit of **a wet blanket**.* □ *I don't drink, smoke or dance and I haven't much light conversation either. I'd just be **a wet blanket** at your party.* □ *It was an unlucky toast.... It was **a wet blanket** to the evening.*

wet one's whistle lag gurmazin, njom fytin
□ *'Now, I'll tell you what, young Copperfield,' said he: 'the wine shall be kept to **wet your whistle** when you are story telling.'* □ *Let's go into this bar for a drink; I haven't **wet my whistle** today.* □ *Are you coming out to **wet***

your whistle, Dad, or do you want to watch the rest of the programme?

what are we waiting for? ç'presim?

□ *'Why not come over to our place instead? We have cold salmon in the fridge and a roast in the oven, and wine to go with both.' 'What are we waiting for?' said John, rising at once.*

what for përse

□ *What is this tool for?* □ *'I have to go back to town.' 'What for?'*

what good wind brings you here?/what wind blows you here? ç'e mirë ju solli?

□ *'Well, Miss Trotwood,' said Mr. Wickfield... 'what wind blows you here?'* □ *'Good evening, Dance,' says the doctor, with a nod. And good evening to you, friend Jim. What good wind brings you here?'*

what if? po sikur?

□ *What if it rains when we can't get under shelter?* □ *You make it all sound very easy, but what if the idea doesn't come off?* □ *What if the rumor is true?* □ *'If I'm not back by the time you arrive, get a key from the people next door.' 'And what if they are not in?'*

(and) what not e të tjera

□ *I described a queerly arranged group of different colored lights in the distance—yellow, red, green and what not.* □ *He hurried her on, however, past lingering lawyers' clerks, witnesses and what not.*

what's in the wind? ç'të reja kemi? ç'flitet? ç'thuhet?

□ *'Why,' said Laura, as she sat dawn at her place, 'why Pagie, what is in the wind today?'* □ *Uncle, do tell me exactly what's in the wind.*

wheels within wheels punë (çështje) të ngatërruara

□ *The ordinary citizen often feels that, with a little good will, some matters of international politics could be easily settled, but there are always wheels within wheels.*

when in Rome do as the Romans do sipas vendit dhe kuvendi

□ *When I go abroad, I try to avoid international restaurants, and eat only local food: when in Rome do as the Romans do.* □ *'Just tell your friends you can't eat three enormous meals a day.' 'I wouldn't like to offend them. In Rome, better do as the Romans do especially as it's only for a week.'*

when/while the cat's away, the mice will play kur ikën macja, luajnë minjtë; kur s'është macja në shtëpi, minjtë bëjnë gjurulldi

□ *'The hotel is run by Miss Dupont. But it seems she's away in Brest for the day.' 'When the cat's away,' Ma said.*

while away kaloj (kohën)

□ *He had a volume of Pascal open on his desk to while away the time.* □ *I was glad of his company to while away an hour until the train came.* □ *It's foolish to while away one's time in idle talk.*

white lie, a gënjeshtër pa të keq

□ *My husband was so exhausted when he came home that I told our guests a white lie. I said he was ill and would have to go straight to bed.* □ *'Have you ever told a white lie?' Certainly, to have to admit to having told lies is to put oneself in a poor light, yet very few people could truthfully answer 'No'.* □ *I said there was no more drink in the house—a white lie amply justified by the need to get him sobered up.*

whys and (the) therefores, the arsyet, shkaqet, psetë

517

□ *If you say that you are going to break your agreement with him, he'll want to know* **the whys and therefores.** □ *I learned not only secrets of reviving flagging flowers, drying leaves and blooms without loss of color but* **the whys and therefores** *as well.* □ *I found when I was 16 years old, that I didn't sleep and I was able to do without it. I've never looked into* **the whys and therefores** *of it. It's just a simple fact.*

wide awake syhapët, vigjilent
□ *Instantly, realizing what had happened, she was* **wide awake.**

widow's mite, the kontribut i vogël
□ *Don't feel ashamed—we don't despise* **the widow's mite,** *and as they say, every penny helps.*

wild goose chase kërkim i kotë (i pashpresë)
□ *We went on* **a wild goose chase** *all over town looking for a particular book that he wanted to buy. Of course we didn't find it.*

wind up 1. kurdis
□ *She* **wound up** *the toy mouse and set it running across the carpet.*
2. mbyll, mbaroj, përfundoj
□ *As I walked along, Blaize* **wound up** *his story.*
3. ngacmoj, nervozoj, eksitoj
□ *Are you deliberately* **winding** *me* **up?**

wind up one's affairs mbyll (mbaroj) punët
□ *In the last month I was* **winding up** *my affairs in England and saying goodbye to all my friends.*

wine and dine ha e pi
□ *So we* **wined and dined** *and walked and talked, and when I stopped to think, as occasionally I did, I thought, 'Well, it won't last.'*

win hands down fitoj pa vështirësi, me lehtësi të madhe

□ *The local team* **won** *the match* **hands down.** □ *If you will, we can* **win hands down.**

win the hand (and heart) of sb fitoj dorën e (zemrën) e
□ *Anyone who hopes to* **win the hand** *of the fair Gillian would need to have a lot of more money than Ian.*

win the heart of sb fitoj zemrën e
□ *The child has quite* **won** *the old man's* **heart.** □ *Both my parents who, as I have indicated elsewhere, led nomadic lives, used to* **win the hearts** *of their servants.*

window on the world, a një dritare në botë, për të njohur botën
□ *International new broadcasts provide* **a window on the world.**

wipe off the face of the earth/off the map fshij nga faqja e dheut
□ *Whole villages were* **wiped off the map** *as a reprisal for alleged atrocities.* □ *'We* **wiped** *that company* **off the face of the earth.'** *She spoke with cruel satisfaction.*

wipe out 1. pastroj, fshij
□ *This vase wasn't* **wiped out** *properly before it was put away.* □ *'Make sure the inside of the coffee pot is thoroughly* **wiped out.'**
2. zhduk
□ *A summer fire can* **wipe out** *all the pasture feed.* □ *The earthquake* **wiped out** *the town.*

wise after the event i erdhën mendtë kur ikën dhëntë, pas të vjelash, pas pilafit, me shumë vonesë
□ *Mr. Paradock: I could see it coming. Mrs. Paradock: You mean you could see it coming. You're being* **wise after the event** *again.*

wish sb well i uroj gjithë të mirat
□ *Show-business agents come and go in his London hotel room, talking of Dustin Hoffman and* **wishing** *each*

other well. □ *I wish him well in his new job.*

with (a) good grace njerëzisht, me kënaqësi; me dëshirë, me hir

□ *He obeyed the order with good grace.* □ *Waldegaard's team seemed prepared to accept the decision with good grace.*

with (a) bad grace panjerëzisht, me vrazhdësi; me pahir, me zor

□ *The apology was made with bad grace.* □ *The tennis player took his defeat with a bad grace, even refusing to shake hands with his opponents.*

with all one's heart/soul me gjithë zemër (shpirt)

□ *'At the same time I am bound to say, and I do say with all my heart,'* observed the hostess earnestly, *'that her looks and manner almost disarm suspicion.'* □ *I hope with all my heart that you succeed.* □ *'I pledge you, with all my soul,'* said I, filling my glass to the brim.

with all one's might me gjithë fuqinë

□ *He looked and saw Bullivant on his feet thumping the boy at the desk in front with all his might.* □ *Don't blame me. I tried with all my might to make her change her mind.*

with all one's wits about one me mendjen në vend (në kokë), me mendje të mbledhur; me mendjen okë

□ *Throughout all this my lord was like a cold, kind spectator with his wits about him.* □ *Sir Howard. ... When Miles died, he left an estate in one of the West Indian Islands. It was in charge of an agent who was a sharpish fellow, with all his wits about him. He quite simply took the estate for himself and kept it.*

with a view to me synim që; me shpresë që; me syrin që

He is decorating the house with a view to selling it. □ *Attempts are being made to organize a conference with a view to setting up an international convention on adoption law.*

with a will me qejf, me dëshirë; me ngulm

□ *He started digging the garden with a will.* □ *Having been promised £1 each if they made a good job of it, the boys set to it with a will.*

with both hands me të gjitha forcat (fuqitë); me të dyja duart

□ *You couldn't deny that, if you tried with both hands.* □ *John spent his money with both hands.*

with ease kollaj, me lehtësi, pa vështirësi

□ *Provided we encounter no unforeseen difficulties, we should be able to complete the work with ease by the end of the month.* □ *He passed the test with ease.*

with fire and sword me zjarr e hekur

□ *They held on to their markets as an eagle holds on to its prey, and throwing their apostolic masks, defended their annexations with fire and sword.*

with half a heart me gjysmë zemre, pa qejf, pa dëshirë

□ *He took it up with half a heart.*

withing an ace of/an inch of gati për, për pak, për një qime

□ *Our horse was within an ace of winning the race, but he stumbled at the last fence.*

within an inch of one's life gati për vdekje

□ *The men who attacked him beat him within an inch of his life.*

within a stone's throw një vrap pele, fare afër, pranë

□ *'And who is the Mr. Heddegan they*

*used to call David?' 'An old man who lives **within a stone's throw** from father's.'*

withing/in living memory me sa mbahet mend (nga njerëzit që janë gjallë)

□ *The villagers say that no one has climbed that mountain **within living memory**.*

with might and main me të gjitha forcat (fuqitë)

□ *The two combatants fought **with might and main**. □ I'm sure I've striven **with might and main** to bring these children up properly, but sometimes I think I haven't made a very good job of it. □ He ran home **with all his might and main**. □ I used to set, at a little distance, with my notebook on my knee, fagging after him **with all my might and main**.*

with one accord njëzëri, unanimisht

□ ***With one accord** they all stood up and cheered.*

with one foot in the grave me një këmbë në varr

□ *An old fellow **with one foot** in the House of Lords and one **in the grave**, and no difference between them, to speak of.*

with one voice unanimisht, njëzëri

□ *They said **with one voice** that they have been hoping and waiting for such an approach for a long time.*

with open arms krahëhapur

□ *The heroes were welcomed **with open arms** by the people of Vlora. □ He welcomed us **with open arms**.*

without a bean pa një grosh

□ *After I had paid for my meal, I was left **without a bean**.*

without avail më kot, pa rezultat, pa dobi

□ *All the attempts made by doctors to*

*save the patient proved to be **without avail**.*

without a/one word pa thënë asnjë fjalë

□ *I recognized it as the parcel containing my manuscripts. I reached out for it and she passed it over **without a word**. □ Who was this dark-haired dark-eyed girl? Why had Fegus decided to bring her here **without one word** to her first.*

without doubt pa dyshim

□ *Don't be anxious, he'll come **without doubt**.*

without fail pa një pa dy, patjetër, me siguri

□ *Don't worry, I shall be there **without fail**. □ 'I'll bring them tonight **without fail**,' Alan said. □ I shall be at the concert at seven **without fail**.*

without further/more ado pa vonesë; pa shumë zhurmë; pa mëdyshje

□ *She was working at an oil painting on an easel, and she went back to this **without more ado**.*

without question pa dyshim

□ *He is **without question**, the best football player in Europe.*

without turning a hair pa iu dridhur qerpiku i syrit

□ *He is completely fearless. He entered the burning building **without turning a hair**.*

with reference/regard to lidhur me, për sa i takon

□ *I am writing **with reference to** your letter of the 25th of May 1998. □ They made some comments **with regard to** your proposals.*

with respect to lidhur me

□ *This is true **with respect to** English, but not to French. □ **With respect to** your enquiry, I enclose an explanatory leaflet.*

wolf in sheep's clothing, a ujk me lëkurë qengji

□ *Beware of false prophets, which come to you* **in sheep's clothing,** *but inwardly they are ravening* **wolves.** □ *Stevenson hadn't been an innocent dupe of anyone; he too was* **a wolf in sheep's clothing.** □ *Don't trust that man; he may seem friendly and harmless, but he's* **a wolf in sheep's clothing.**

word for word fjalë për fjalë

□ *I suppose you'll be wondering how it is that I'm able to tell you* **word for word** *what Jim's man said to him.* □ *He copied the document* **word for word.** □ *If you translate from a foreign language into English* **word for word,** *the resulting English version will usually be wrong.*

word in season, a një këshillë në kohën e duhur

□ *But you will admit that I tried, however obliquely, to give you* **a word in season.** □ *A* **word in season** *if properly heeded, can save one a good deal of trouble.* □ *Sometimes it is only sensible to interfere.* **A word in season** *might have saved Paterson from his own folly.*

work it/things (so) that e rregulloj, i rregulloj punët

□ *We'll try to* **work it that** *we travel down to London together*

worked off one's feet këput nga këmbët, rraskapit, stërmundoj

□ *This has been a terribly busy day for us; we have been* **worked off our feet.**

work like a charm vepron si me magji

□ *'There,' he said. 'Drink that, it'll help you to pull yourself together.' I don't know what was in it but it* **worked like a charm.**

work like a horse/like slaves punon si kalë (si skllav)

□ *To do the battery full justice, both officers and men appreciated the situation and* **worked like slaves.** □ *The 14th is too soon. Even if we all* **worked like horses** *from now till then the exhibition couldn't be got ready.*

work miracles/wonders bëj mrekulli

□ *'It's no use, Sister. I can't* **work miracles.'** □ *This tonic will* **work miracles** *for your depression.* □ *She had thought that being happy would* **work a miracle** *in him and turn him into a normal confident person.* □ *'A good night's rest will* **work wonders** *for Mrs. Sholto...'*

work off çlirohem; likujdoj; heq qafe

□ *'It will take months to* **work off** *this bank loan. In the meantime how can we possibly afford to take a holiday?*

work one's fingers to the bone bie copë, robtohem sa s'ka ku të shkojë më

□ *She* **worked her fingers to the bone** *so that her children could have a good education.*

work out 1. hartoj, krijoj, bëj

□ *A sub-committee has been appointed to* **work out** *a new constitution for the club.* □ *The general* **worked out** *a new plan of attack.*

2. llogarit

□ *We have computers to* **work out** *our salaries these days.* □ *I've* **worked out** *your share of the expenses at $100.*

3. zgjidh

□ *You seem to have the problem nicely* **worked out.** *All the details are in place.* □ *See if you can* **work** *this puzzle* **out.**

4. kuptoj natyrën e

□ *'You are funny, I shall never* **work** *you* **out.'**

□ *For as long as I've known him, I've never been able to* **work Martin out.**

5. zhvillohet, ndodh, ngjan, shkon

□ *I'm glad that things are* **working out** *so well for them in Australia.*
□ *How will things* **work out***?*
6. stërvitem, ushtrohem
□ *Mohammed Ali spoke to reporters after* **working out** *at the gym this morning.*

work sb to death mundoj për vdekje
□ *Don't* **work** *your poor wife* **to death.**

work things out zgjidh punët (problemet) e veta
□ *'I wish their parents would leave them to* **work things out** *for themselves. You know how young people hate interference from their elders.'*

work up 1. krijoj, zgjeroj, përmirësoj
□ *It took Smith some years to* **work up** *a market for his products.* □ *The retail side of the business was* **worked out** *by his father.*
2. rrit, shtoj
□ *Local organizations are trying to* **work up** *more support for the party before the election.*
3. nxit, stimuloj
□ *He doesn't seem to be able to* **work up** *any enthusiasm for his studies.*

worth it ia vlen
□ *I've cut smoking to a pack a week in order to pay the bill, but it is* **worth it.**

wring one's neck ia përdredh kokën
□ *If we find the person who did this, I'll* **wring his neck***!* □ *'Of course he has to come in to our office.' 'To see you, no doubt. If he ever makes a pass at you, I'll* **wring his neck.'**

Y

year after year vit pas viti, çdo vit
□ *Winter fades into spring **year after year**.* □ *The child was growing up **year after year**.*
year by year nga viti në vit, me kalimin e viteve
□ ***Year by year** their affection for each other grew stronger. Their hostilities were growing **year by year**.*

year in, (and) year out vit pas viti, çdo vit; vazhdimisht
□ *You see other girls having splendid times and enjoying life, while you grind **year in and year out**.*
yield one's breath jap shpirt
□ *He **yielded his** last **breath** as Gower Woodseer was lowering him to his pillow.*

Z

zero hour ora e fillimit të sulmit
□ *The soldiers waited nervously for* **zero hour**, *which had been fixed for 9 a.m.*

Other Albanian Interest Titles by Hippocrene Books

ALBANIAN-ENGLISH/ENGLISH-ALBANIAN PRACTICAL DICTIONARY
18,000 entries • 400 pages • 4⅜ x 7 • ISBN 0-7818-0419-1
• $14.95 paperback • (483)

ALBANIAN DICTIONARY AND PHRASEBOOK
2,000 entries • 200 pages • 3¾ x 7 • ISBN 0-7818-0793-X
• $11.95 paperback • (498)

ALBANIAN PHRASEBOOK
299 pages • 3½ x 6½ • ISBN 0-7818-0791-3
• $9.95 paperback • (106)

ENGLISH-ALBANIAN COMPREHENSIVE DICTIONARY
60,000 entries • 1,000 pages • 6 x 9½ • ISBN 0-7818-0510-4
• $60.00 hardcover • (615)

ENGLISH-ALBANIAN COMPREHENSIVE DICTIONARY
60,000 entries • 1,000 pages • 6 x 9½ • ISBN 0-7818-0792-1
• $35.00 paperback • (305)

BEST OF ALBANIAN COOKING: FAVORITE FAMILY RECIPES
168 pages • 5½ x 8½ • ISBN 0-7818-0609-7
• $22.50 hardcover • (721)

Other Hippocrene East European Language Titles

BOSNIAN-ENGLISH/ENGLISH-BOSNIAN COMPACT DICTIONARY
8,500 entries • 332 pages • 3½ x 4¾ • ISBN 0-7818-0499-X
• $8.95 paperback • (204)

BOSNIAN-ENGLISH/ENGLISH-BOSNIAN DICTIONARY AND PHRASEBOOK
1,500 entries • 175 pages • 3¾ x 7 • ISBN 0-7818-0596-1
• $11.95 paperback • (691)

BULGARIAN-ENGLISH COMPREHENSIVE DICTIONARY
47,000 entries • 1,050 pages • 6¾ x 9¾ • ISBN 0-7818-0507-4
• $90.00 2-vol set • (613)

BULGARIAN-ENGLISH/ENGLISH-BULGARIAN COMPACT DICTIONARY
6,500 entries • 323 pages • ISBN 0-7818-0535-X
• $8.95 paperback • (623)

BULGARIAN-ENGLISH/ENGLISH-BULGARIAN PRACTICAL DICTIONARY
6,500 entries • 323 pages • 4⅜ x 7 • ISBN 0-87052-145-4
• $14.95 paperback • (331)

BEGINNER'S BULGARIAN
207 pages • 5½ x 8½ • ISBN 0-7818-0300-4
• $9.95 paperback • (76)

BYELORUSSIAN-ENGLISH/ENGLISH-BYELORUSSIAN CONCISE DICTIONARY
6,500 entries • 290 pages • ISBN 0-87052-114-4
• $9.95 paperback • (395)

CZECH-ENGLISH/ENGLISH-CZECH STANDARD DICTIONARY
10TH Revised Edition
40,000 entries • 1,072 pages • ISBN 0-7818-0653-4
• $39.50 hardcover • (740)

AMERICAN ENGLISH-CZECH COMPREHENSIVE DICTIONARY
40,000 entries • 1,183 pages • ISBN 80-238-0456-1
• $55.00 hardcover • (654)

CZECH-ENGLISH/ENGLISH-CZECH CONCISE DICTIONARY
7,500 entries • 594 pages • ISBN 0-87052-981-1 • $11.95 paperback • (276)

CZECH HANDY EXTRA DICTIONARY
2,600 entries • 186 pages • ISBN 0-7818-0138-9 • $8.95 paperback • (63) ·

HIPPOCRENE CHILDREN'S ILLUSTRATED CZECH DICTIONARY
Ages 5-10
English-Czech/Czech-English
96 pages • 500 words with full-color illustrations • 8½ x 11 • ISBN 0-7818-0732-8 • $14.95 hardcover • (188)

BEGINNER'S LITHUANIAN
471 pages • 6 x 9 • ISBN 0-7818-0678-X • $19.95 paperback • (764)

LITHUANIAN-ENGLISH/ENGLISH-LITHUANIAN CONCISE DICTIONARY
10,000 entries • 382 pages • 6 x 9 • ISBN 0-7818-0151-6 • $14.95 paperback • (489)

LITHUANIAN-ENGLISH/ENGLISH-LITHUANIAN COMPACT DICTIONARY
10,000 entries • 382 pages • 3½ x 4¾ • ISBN 0-7818-0536-8 • $8.95 paperback • (624)

LATVIAN-ENGLISH/ENGLISH-LATVIAN PRACTICAL DICTIONARY
16,000 entries • 474 pages • 4⅜ x 7 • ISBN 0-7818-0059-5 • $16.95 paperback • (194)

MACEDONIAN-ENGLISH/ENGLISH-MACEDONIAN CONCISE DICTIONARY
14,000 entries • 400 pages • 4 x 6 • ISBN 0-7818-0516-3 • $14.95 paperback • (619)

POLISH-ENGLISH UNABRIDGED DICTIONARY
250,000 entries 3-volume set • 3,800 pages
• ISBN 0-7818-0441-8 • $200.00 hardcover • (526)
CD-ROM (requires Windows 95): ISBN 0-7818-0728-X
• $55.00 • (951)

POLISH HANDY EXTRA DICTIONARY
2,800 entries • 125 pages • 4 x 6 • ISBN 0-7818-0504-X
• $11.95 paperback • (607)

HIGHLANDER
POLISH-ENGLISH/ENGLISH-HIGHLANDER
POLISH DICTIONARY
2,000 entries • 111 pages • 4 x 6 • ISBN 0-7818-0303-9
• $9.95 paperback • (297)

POLISH-ENGLISH/ENGLISH-POLISH
CONCISE DICTIONARY,
With Complete Phonetics
8,000 entries • 408 pages • 3⅝ x 7 • ISBN 0-7818-0133-8
• $9.95 paperback • (268)

POLISH-ENGLISH/ENGLISH-POLISH
COMPACT DICTIONARY
9,000 entries • 240 pages • 4 x 6 • ISBN 0-7818-0496-5
• $8.95 paperback • (609)

POLISH-ENGLISH/ENGLISH-POLISH PRACTICAL
DICTIONARY
31,000 entries • 703 pages • 5¼ x 8½ • ISBN 0-7818-0085-4
• $11.95 paperback • (450)

POLISH-ENGLISH/ENGLISH-POLISH
STANDARD DICTIONARY,
Revised Edition With Business Terms
32,000 entries • 780 pages • 5½ x 8½ •ISBN 0-7818-0282-2
• $19.95 paperback • (298)

POLISH PHRASEBOOK AND DICTIONARY
252 pages • 5½ x 8½ • ISBN 0-7818-0134-6
• $11.95 paperback • (192)

MASTERING POLISH
288 pages • 5½ x 8½ • ISBN 0-7818-0015-3
• $14.95 paperback • (381)
2 Cassettes: • ISBN 0-7818-0016-1 • W • $12.95 • (389)

THE POLISH-ENGLISH DICTIONARY OF SLANG AND COLLOQUIALISM
5,000 entries • 361 pages • 6 x 9 • ISBN 0-7818-0570-8
• $19.95 paperback • (692)

BEGINNER'S ROMANIAN
200 pages • 5½ x 8½ • ISBN 0-7818-0208-3
• $7.95 paperback • (79)

ROMANIAN CONVERSATION GUIDE
200 pages • 5½ x 8½ • ISBN 0-87052-803-3
• $9.95 paperback • (153)

ROMANIAN GRAMMAR
100 pages • 5½ x 8½ • ISBN 0-87052-892-0
• $8.95 paperback • (232)

SERBIAN-ENGLISH/ENGLISH-SERBIAN CONCISE DICTIONARY
14,000 entries • 400 pages • 4 x 6 • ISBN 0-7818-0556-2
• $14.95 paperback • (326)

SLOVAK-ENGLISH/ENGLISH-SLOVAK CONCISE DICTIONARY
7,500 entries • 360 pages • 4 x 6 • ISBN 0-87052-115-2
• $11.95 paperback • (390)

SLOVAK HANDY EXTRA DICTIONARY
3,000 entries • 200 pages • 5 x 7¾ • ISBN 0-7818-0101-X
• $12.95 paperback • (359)

SLOVAK-ENGLISH/ENGLISH-SLOVAK COMPACT DICTIONARY

7,500 entries • 360 pages • 3½ x 4¾ • ISBN 0-7818-0501-5
• $8.95 paperback • (107)

SLOVAK-ENGLISH/ENGLISH-SLOVAK DICTIONARY AND PHRASEBOOK

1,300 entries • 180 pages • 3¾ x 7 • ISBN 0-7818-0663-1
• $13.95 paperback • (754)

SLOVENE-ENGLISH/ENGLISH-SLOVENE MODERN DICTIONARY

36,000 entries • 935 pages • 5½ x 3½ • ISBN 0-7818-0252-0
• $24.95 paperback • (19)

UKRAINIAN-ENGLISH/ENGLISH-UKRAINIAN PRACTICAL DICTIONARY

Revised Edition with Menu Terms
16,000 entries • 406 pages • ISBN 0-7818-0306-3
• $14.95 paperback • (343)

Prices subject to change without notice.

To order **Hippocrene Books**, contact your local bookstore, call (718) 454-2366, or write to: **Hippocrene Books**, 171 Madison Avenue, New York, NY 10016. Please enclose check or money order adding $5.00 shipping (UPS) for the first book and $.50 for each additional title.